Lecture Notes in Economics and Mathematical Systems

Operations Research, Computer Science, Social Science

Edited by M. Beckmann, Providence, G. Goos, Karlsruhe, and H. P. Künzi, Zürich

78

GI

Gesellschaft für Informatik e. V.

2. Jahrestagung

Karlsruhe, 2.–4. Oktober 1972

Herausgegeben im Auftrag der Gesellschaft für Informatik von Peter Deussen

Springer-Verlag
Berlin · Heidelberg · New York 1973

Prof. Dr. Peter Deussen
(Herausgeber)
Prof. Dr. Gerhard Goos
(Vorsitzender des Programmkomitees)

Institut für Informatik
der Universität Karlsruhe

AMS Subject Classifications (1970): 68 A 00, 68 A 02, 68 A 05, 68 A 10, 68 A 15, 68 A 20, 68 A 25, 68 A 30, 68 A 50, 68 A 55

ISBN-13:978-3-540-06127-4 e-ISBN-13:978-3-642-80732-9
DOI: 10.1007/978-3-642-80732-9

N A C H R U F

Mitten in den letzten Vorbereitungen erreichte uns die traurige Nachricht, daß Herr E. Heimbach, Mitglied des Programmkomitees, in den Bergen am 24.8.72 tödlich verunglückte.

Wir bewahren ihm ein ehrendes und dankbares Angedenken.

Gerhard Goos
im Namen aller Teilnehmer an der
Jahresversammlung

VORWORT

Über die Bedeutung, welche der Informatik in Wissenschaft, Industrie und im öffentlichen Leben heute zukommt, braucht an dieser Stelle nichts mehr gesagt werden. Sie spiegelt sich schon in dem Anwachsen der Mitgliederzahl der Gesellschaft für Informatik, in der Zunahme der Beteiligten an den Fach- und Jahrestagungen der GI und nicht zuletzt in der erfreulichen Vielfalt von Vortragsmeldungen für diese Jahrestagung wider.
So hatte das Programmkomitee bestehend aus den Herren P. Deussen (Uni Karlsruhe), A. Endres (IBM Böblingen), G. Goos (Uni Karlsruhe), E. Heimbach (Siemens AG München), G. Krüger (Gesellschaft für Kernforschung Karlsruhe, Institut für Datenverarbeitung in der Technik) die schwierige Aufgabe, aus den vielen Vortragsmeldungen einen Querschnitt auszuwählen, der sich in den vorgesehenen zeitlichen Rahmen der Jahrestagung einpassen ließ.

Das Spektrum der Vortäge reicht von der Theorie bis zu Anwendungsfällen, von Übersichten bis hin zu Themen, die für den Spezialisten bestimmt sind. Den derzeitigen Fragestellungen und Bedürfnissen der Informatik entsprechend behandeln die meisten Vorträge den Themenkreis Betriebssysteme, ihm folgen Fragen der Rechnerstruktur, der Programmiersysteme und der Informationssysteme, um nur einige zu nennen. Die vorliegende Zusammenstellung der Vorträge orientiert sich an der Reihenfolge, in der sie gehalten wurden.

Zusätzlich zu den Vorträgen sollte den Teilnehmern an der Jahrestagung genügend Gelegenheit gegeben werden, aktuelle Probleme öffentlich zu diskutieren, wozu vier Podiumsdiskussionen

Methodik der Software-Entwicklung
(Leitung: H.J.Hoffmann, TH Darmstadt)

Informationssysteme - Utopie und Praxis
(Leitung: H.-J.Schneider, Universität Stuttgart)

Prozeßrechnersprachen
(Leitung: R.Baumann, TU München)

Das Berufsbild des Informatikers
(Leitung: G.Seegmüller, Universität München)

abgehalten wurden. Aus organisatorischen, zeitlichen und finanziellen Gründen, war es nicht möglich, die Podiumsdiskussionen in den Bericht aufzunehmen.

Allen, die zum Gelingen der 2.Jahrestagung der Gesellschaft für Informatik beitrugen, sei an dieser Stelle herzlichst gedankt: den Vortragenden für die Anregungen und Erkenntnisse, die sie vermittelten; den Teilnehmern für ihr gezeigtes Interesse und ihre Diskussionsbeiträge; den Mitarbeitern des Organisationskomitees für ihren selbstlosen Einsatz vor, während und nach der Tagung, ohne den sie niemals hätte gelingen können.

Karlsruhe im Oktober 1972 Der Herausgeber

INHALTSVERZEICHNIS

HAUPTVORTRÄGE 1

Computer System Architecture - A Philosophy of Design
R.S.Barton 2

Informationssysteme
E.J.Neuhold 8

Hardware-Architecture and Computer Organisation
F.H.Sumner 22

Methoden der syntaktischen Analyse bei formalen Sprachen
J.Eickel 37

AUTOMATEN- UND GRAPHENTHEORIE, FORMALE SPRACHEN 55

Das Transitionsmonoid bei der Parallelkomposition von endlichen Automaten
K.Ecker 56

Klassifizierung von primitiv-rekursiven Transformationen und Automatentransduktionen
F.W.v.Henke, K.Weihrauch 63

Untersuchungen über haltende Programme für Turing-Maschinen mit 2 Zeichen und bis zu 5 Befehlen
B.Weimann, K.Casper, W. Fenzl 72

An Algorithm for Coloring the Vertices of an Arbitrary Finite Graph
K.Dürre 82

A Necessary and Sufficient Condition for Chomsky-Productions over Partially Ordered Symbol Sets
H.J.Schneider 90

Die Größe des minimalen Analysators einer kontextfreien Grammatik
R.Kemp 99

Programmschemata mit booleschen Unterprogrammen
K.Indermark..107

PROGRAMMIERSYSTEME..117

A Hierarchy of Control Structures
E.Wegner..118

Mehrdeutige Entscheidungstabellen
G.Dathe..125

Design of a Generalized Audit Command Language (ACL)
H.J.Will..133

Ein Programmiersystem zur problemnahen Erstellung adaptierter Software
W.Sonnenberg..143

DIALIS - Ein einfaches Dialogsystem für eine Listensprache
H.Rohlfing..150

Messung der Effizienz eines einfachen " Incremental Compiler "
H.A.Schmid, B.Nienaber..159

The Structures of the NCC SIMULA COMPILERS and Bench Mark Comparisons with Other Major Languages
S.Kubosch..169

Error Reporting, Error Treatment, and Error Correction in ALGOL Translation
Part 1
C.H.A.Koster..179
Part 2
B.Eggers..188

BETRIEBSSYSTEME..197

Verallgemeinerung und Implementierung von Synchronisationsoperationen
R.Göller..198

Aufruf von Systemleistungen in einem schichtenweise gegliederten Betriebssystem
K.Lagally..208

Übersetzung von Kommandosprachen
Th.Weller et al. 214

Modularity of Non-Sequential Programs
K.-P.Löhr..223

Classes of Optimal Schedules for Multiprocessor Systems
S.Schindler..233

Durchsatzoptimale Rechnerkern- und Transportkanalvergabe für ein Rechnermodell mit 2 Arbeitsspeicherplätzen
H.-J.Küspert 243

Simulation von Betriebssoftware auf einer virtuellen PL/1-Maschine
G.Fleck, J.Nehmer 253

Einplanung eines leistungsfähigen Software-Meßsystemes bei der Entwicklung eines Betriebssystemes
E.F.Pantele 263

Analysis of Demand Paging Algorithms
A.Palmboom 274

Einige Methoden zur Vorhersage des Verhaltens kleiner Systeme mit virtuellem Speicher
K.M.Schulz 284

Funktionsklassen und dynamische Speicherverwaltung in Realzeit-Datenverarbeitungssystemen
C.Kuck 292

Modell eines Auftragssystems für die Zeitdienstverwaltung eines Prozeßrechners
D.Hilse 302

Auftragsverkehr über einen generellen Auftragspuffer bei Prozeßrechnersystemen
J.Bautz 312

GRAPHISCHE SYSTEME 321

Sprach- und Datenstruktur des Systems GRAPHIC
R.Schuster, G.Enderle, K.Leinemann, E.G.Schlechtendahl
H.Schnauder, U.Schumann 322

Die Graphik-Software des TR 440
H.Kääb 332

FICHE-Software und COM-Programmierung
M.Schwarzhuber 341

ZENTRALEINHEITEN UND ENTWICKLUNGSAUTOMATISIERUNG 349

Das Problem der Assoziativspeicherdurchlaufzeit bei Paging-Verfahren im Zehn-Nanosekundenbereich
H.Schecher 350

Einige Untersuchungen zur Hardware-Realisierung von Software - Operatoren
D.Schmid 360

Performance Evaluation of Processor Design
L.J.Zeckendorf.. 370

Zur Optimierung von Zuverlässigkeit und Nutzungsgrad von Systemen mit Selbstdiagnose
W.Schneeweiss... 378

Realisierung des Streaming-Konzepts
W.J.Paul.. 387

Durchsatzsteigerung in Rechenanlagen bei Verwendung von kleinen Pufferspeichern
A.Bächle.. 395

Experimentiersystem für ein technisches Informatikpraktikum
R.Hartenstein... 406

Plazieren und Pseudoleitungsfinden bei Schaltkreiskarten
K.Grotz... 414

Interaktiver Einsatz von Sichtgeräten beim rechnerunterstützten Entwurf von Großrechner-Leiterplatten mit Hilfe des Programmsystems ZEISIG
K.Horn.. 424

Die Grundlagen des Programms ATEDIS
K.Pfeuffer.. 432

INFORMATIONSSYSTEME.................................... 441

NEOS - Ein Ansatz zur Lösung einiger offener Probleme bei der Kozeption von Datenbanksystemen
E.Falkenberg et al. 442

Verfahren zur Sicherung und Wiederherstellung von Datenbeständen
D.F.Jung.. 452

Juristisches Informationssystem: Eine Fallstudie für ein Informationssystem großen Umfangs
F.Gebhard, P.C.Lockemann.............................. 464

Das "Pflegeproblem" bei Information-Retrieval-Systemen
J.Martin, P.Schnupp................................... 473

Formalisieren von Inhalt natürlicher Sprachen durch Deutervalenzen und Deuterkriterien
P.Kümmel.. 480

Wortstamm-Retrieval in TELDOK 440
D.L.Holmberg, B.S.Müller.............................. 490

Dynamische Dokumentenräume
E.Konrad.. 499

BIBLIS - Ein Bibliotheks-, Informations- und Verwaltungssystem
H.-J.Schneider, G.Siewert et al. 503

PROZESSINFORMATIK.................................... 513

Aufbau betriebssicherer und bedienungsfreundlicher Mehrrechnersysteme zur Prozeßüberwachung
H.Wildpaner.. 514

KOSE - Eine Dialogsprache für Prozeßrechner
M.Abel... 524

Informationsdarstellung auf Sichtgeräten
C.Benz... 533

Der Großrechner als Hilfsmittel beim Erstellen und Testen lauffähiger Programme für Prozeßrechner
B.Krüger...543

Die Prozeßprogrammiersprache PEARL - Systembeschreibung und E/A-Konzept
B.Eichenauer... 552

Das Task- und Timing-Konzept von PEARL
P.Rieder... 561

Adressen der Autoren.................................571

HAUPTVORTRÄGE

COMPUTER SYSTEM ARCHITECTURE
- A PHILOSOPHY OF DESIGN -

R.S.BARTON

Introduction

Designs based upon once valid assumptions may lose their integrity when a technology or range of application changes. Unfortunately, designers usually accept such changes reluctantly.

This has been the case in the computer industry. The first computers were designed and constructed to mechanize computations, now however, "computation" only describes what computers do if its original meaning is extended. Most computers do little computing; their main activities are information storage and retrieval and management of their own resources. Moreover, the larger the computer system the more time must be devoted to these latter tasks.

Each major advance in computers over the past twenty years has begun in system architecture and subsequently forced a revision of system programs and programming techniques. Each advance has necessitated extensive redesign and reimplementation, but seldom have the improvements been more than superficial. Fundamental structural innovations have been rare, however the superficial changes have often been difficult to implement.

We have been misled by the claims of generality advanced in favor of the concept of shared program computers. The actual achievement of generality depends upon programmers who often fail to ask why the accomplishment of their tasks should be so difficult.

In what follows, the author examines the consequences of his skepticism about the appropriateness of orthodox computer structure. The author has long pursued some intuitions about form in information machines. Various realizations of these ideas exist as products manufactured by the Burroughs Corporation: the B-5000 and its successors, the B-6700 and most recently the B-1700. The ideal machine has not been implemented; the actual machines have been deformed by pressures to conform to de facto standards. Still the concepts are represented quite effectively and may be fairly evaluated. Here we have a case of technology preceding science. The theories of machine structure have tended to follow the introduction of the machines themselves.

The B-5000

It is astonishing that several significant new ideas, imperfectly articulated, were successfully incorporated into this machine which was hastily designed in 1960. It was the product of amateurs, too inexperienced to be timid. They have now had the satisfaction of much delayed recognition.

The key concept was the integration of machine architecture and system programs. Algol 60 was the primary influence. It provided a model for a software implementation language, a guide for designing certain machine functions and an edifying example of the power of recursive definition and hierarchial structure.

While it is easy to state these design concepts, the notions of stacks, Polish operator machine language and descriptors were arrived at concurrently. It is not novel to base a machine on a language since, after all, an interpretive program in its host computer _is_ such a machine; the challenge is to model the machine on the essential structure of a language while dealing with the external representation and syntax through a translator. The B-5000 used Algol 60 in this capacity, but it was _not_ strictly an Algol machine.

Of course there were other bases: Algol 60 defined no input-output or formatting functions, so extensions were required. These were not always in the spirit of Algol, though, in 1960 Algol was not too well understood nor, if we are to interpret the phrase as meaning recursively defined in every possible way, was the language itself entirely satisfactory.

While a language model can be very useful, it is insufficient by itself. Higher level languages serve to conceal hardware, relegating matters of resource allocation and storage mapping to operating systems, compilers and interpretors. Part of the deficiency can be remedied by choosing a language designed for simulation and control rather than the usual procedural language. By 1966 when the B-6700 (originally B-6500) program had begun, this was well understood and at least two Algol-style simulation languages had been invented. But in 1960, on the other hand, the programming system staff actually overlooked the use of the stack for handling of interrupts, and there was much apology for the supposed inefficiency incurred in accessing data and program via descriptors.

In creative work, intuition must play a key role: succinct formualizations and felicitous descriptions must come later, which is just to say that we can only talk well about that which has become familiar. The experience which led to the B-5000 was rather different from that obtainable in the mainstream of the American computer industry. The overriding consideration was that the hard structure of a computer could be based on the principle of economy of representation of those data and program constructs that arise naturally in the description of an information handling process.

Looking back, it is clear that what was accomplished was to first take a step towards freeing oneself from the fixed size word and fixed size blocks of words by using syllable strings modeled on Polish notation rather than instruction words and by providing for addressing segments of variable, though restricted, length.

The program syllable used to encode operators, names and literals permitted representation of arithmetic, relational and Boolean expressions as defined in Algol, while the descriptor denoted an array or procedure and provided a length, base address and certain codes for typing and protection. This natural representation of program objects should be contrasted with fixed instruction formats having one or more addresses and the commonly used paging techniques.[1]

Marked compaction of program representation and improved integration of two level storage were worthwhile consequences of the overall design concepts followed. A more complete exploitation of the notion of addressable program objects would have resulted if registers had been replaced by a vector operator mechanism as the designers had intended early in the project. This innovation was later rejected. An early exposure to Iverson's ideas on programming languages inspired this consideration; thus it can be considered another example of language-influenced computer architecture.

---

[1] First embodied in the Manchester University Computer ATLAS

The B-6700

The eventual success of the B-5000 in the improved version marketed as the B-5500 led to substantial upgrading and redesign in 1967. Address range restrictions were largely removed through redesign of the descriptor formats and introduction of several syllable lengths. Data types were added and protection extended. Context addressing following Algol block structure and process environments were added. In most respects, the original ideas were generalized and representational restrictions were, for practical purposes eliminated.

Still much effort and some ingenuity went into fitting fields into words in an attempt to find choices that allowed for both generality and economy of representation. Just outside the range of the Algol model lay other challenges: processors for lists and strings, simulation models and vector calculators. For each of these at least one interesting language specimen was available for study: The Bell Laboratories L-6, TRAC, Strachey's Macrogenerator, Simula and Iverson's APL. It was easy enough to see how the essentials of these systems could be expressed in the recursively-defined style of Algol, but fitting everything into an already functionally rich machine seemed a hopeless task.

By late 1963, the author had become convinced that an indispensable requirement for an elegantly structured machine, i.e. one which would utilize storage efficiently and execute programs expressed in a diverse collection of languages, was the elimination of the fixed character, word and block sizes on the machine language level. This meant that field sizes had to be programmatically definable. As simple and obvious as this idea appears now, it was quite difficult at that time to imagine its consequences. Twelve years of experience argued against it even when such benefits as nested relative addressing and generalized bounds registers were taken into account.

The B-1700

By 1967 such conviction had developed that a design was attempted which led eventually to the B-1700, a new and revolutionary machine announced in the Spring of 1972. Two principles dominated its design: first, storage fields were to be programmatically definable and secondly, the object code produced from a programming language was to be run with programmed interpretors usually with associated translators. The second of these principles had its origin in the mid-fifties. It seemed then that the rapid decline of interpretive programs in favor of compiling techniques need not be inevitable if computers were designed to facilitate interpretation. In particular, if the decomposition of what were then called pseudo-instructions and entry to subroutines were made efficient by hardware innovations, interpretation could be made more efficient.

What was undertaken was a computer system architecture with virtual storage, program definable data structures and program format, and, in fact, program defined virtual machines (interpretors). Even after a decade of experience with the virtual (segmented, not paged) storage of the B-5000 and its successors, the gradually introduced freeing of formats and the versatile hardware subroutine mechanism were ambitious undertakings.

On the favorable side, the availability of semiconductor stores in small sizes invited definable registers and promised adequate speed.

Substantial experience has been accumulated and some mild surprises noted with the world's first defined field, interpretive computer. Programs were compressed resulting in improvements in execution speed, in addition to the expected space savings. At one level such a result must be expected, but experience misled most programmers in thinking that the more compact representations would require excessive time to decode. In fact, however, Huffman codes provide a suggestive model for programs.

Wilner[2] has reported on the striking performance improvements with standard, rather mundane languages such as COBOL, RPG, and FORTRAN. It is also clear that the B-1700 has superior characteristics for the so-called emulation of other computers - the B-5700 and B-6700 are candidates. Most interesting to the author however, is the potential for application in computer science research, especially in the areas of programming languages, data structures, and computer organization. As a laboratory tool it should be unexcelled for university use. Many of us have learned that rigid representational choices and restricted machine languages inhibit much design and impede large program development. These difficulties have now been largely overcome and on a low-cost machine.

---

[2] Wilner, Wayne T. "Design of the B-1700" FJCC (to appear)

Conclusion

A single guiding theme has pervaded the design of a number of Burroughs computer systems. From some critical thinking about the actual use of machines, as distinquished from images promulgated in the marketplace, there has resulted a revision of machine structure that goes deeper than may be realized. There has been great improvement in representational efficiency along with enhancement of programmability and operational characteristics.

We have more to learn about applying these ideas in machines over a wide range of computational power. Much of what is found implemented in hardware in the B-6700 can be provided interpretively at much lower speeds in the B-1700.

Definable field operation is fundamental. It must henceforth be considered essential to storage economy and eventually only definable field machines will merit the description "general-purpose". For the present, word-organized stores are still valid especially for scientific computations, though the writer believes that in time alternatives to all parallel, as distinguished from concurrent, operation will be available. Another revision of thinking will be required to bring this about. In the meantime, the defined field, interpretive system will help to extend our horizons and further the creation of a scientific basis for computer application and organization.

INFORMATIONSSYSTEME

E.J.NEUHOLD

Abstract:

Der grundsätzliche Aufbau eines Systems zur Informationsverwaltung ist in großem Maße abhängig von

a) der Art, in der Aufgaben im System erledigt werden
   - batch oder online - und

b) den Hilfsmitteln, die zur Benutzung des Systems zur Verfügung gestellt werden - self-contained oder host-language.

Zukünftige generelle Informationssysteme müssen in ihrer Gesamtstruktur genügend Flexibilität enthalten, um die während der langen Lebensdauer solcher Systeme notwendigen Anpassungen und Weiterentwicklungen zu ermöglichen. Eine solche Flexibilität ist durch Trennung der Anforderungen der Benutzer von den logischen Systemaufgaben und dieser wiederum vom physikalischen Aufbau des Systems erreichbar.

1. Übersicht über generelle Informationssysteme

Der Vortrag setzt sich mit Informationssystemen im weiteren Sinn (generellen Informationssystemen, generalized data base systems) auseinander. Die in großer Anzahl für spezielle Anwendungsgebiete entworfenen Informationssysteme, z.B. Textsysteme oder Flugplatzreservierungssysteme, werden nicht besprochen. Ihre Eigenschaften stellen sehr oft Spezialisierungen der in generellen Informationssystemen bereitgestellten Mechanismen dar.

Schon vor der Zeit der mechanischen und elektronischen Datenverarbeitung wurden Daten in Karteien abgespeichert. Die Benutzer der Daten arbeiteten direkt mit den Karteikarten, um die entsprechenden Informationen zu erhalten (Abb. 1). Nach der Einführung der elektronischen Datenverarbeitung ging diese unmittelbare Arbeitsweise verloren. Zwischen dem Benutzer und der Datenverarbeitungsanlage wird ein Anwendungsprogrammierer eingeschaltet, der die Daten des Benutzers und seine Verarbeitungsprobleme in computergerechte Form bringt und alle notwendigen ausführenden Aktionen veranlaßt. Der Benutzer dieses <u>batch</u>

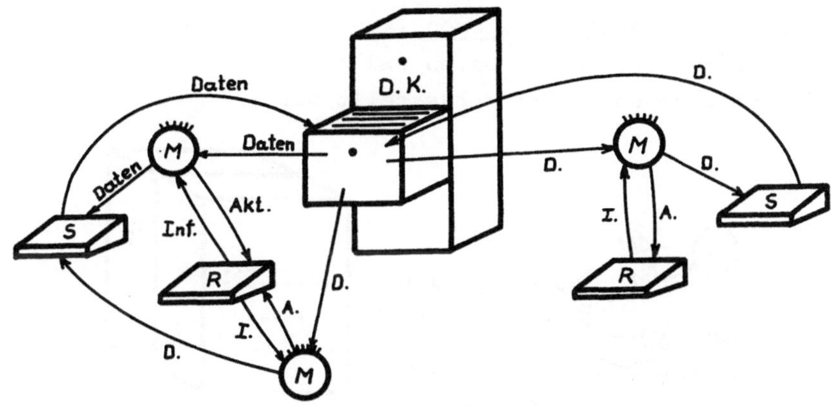

INFORMATIONSSYSTEM 1

Abb. 1

<u>Systems</u> erhält erst die von ihm gewünschten endgültigen Resultate zurück. (Abb.2) Neben den unmittelbar einleuchtenden Vorteilen birgt dieses Verfahren sehr schwere Nachteile. Die Reaktionsgeschwindigkeit

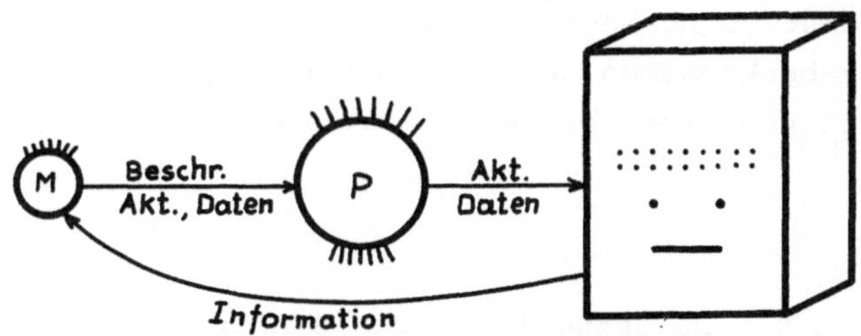

INFORMATIONSSYSTEM 2

Abb. 2

des Gesamtsystems wird erheblich verringert. Dieser Verlust kann besonders bei kleineren Aufgaben durch die größere Verarbeitungsgeschwindigkeit der Computer nicht wettgemacht werden. Ein noch wichtigerer Aspekt ist jedoch, daß ein Benutzer oftmals nur geringes Verständnis für seine Aufgaben und deren Lösungen erzielt. Damit wird seine Motivierung herabgesetzt, und es kann zu großen Abneigungen gegenüber der Benutzung von Informationssystemen kommen. /1/

Diese Nachteile der batch-orientierten Informationssysteme führten zur Entwicklung von online Systemen (Abb. 3), wo die Unmittelbarkeit zwischen dem Benutzer, seinen Daten und den zur Lösung seiner Aufgabe notwendigen Handlungen wieder hergestellt wird.

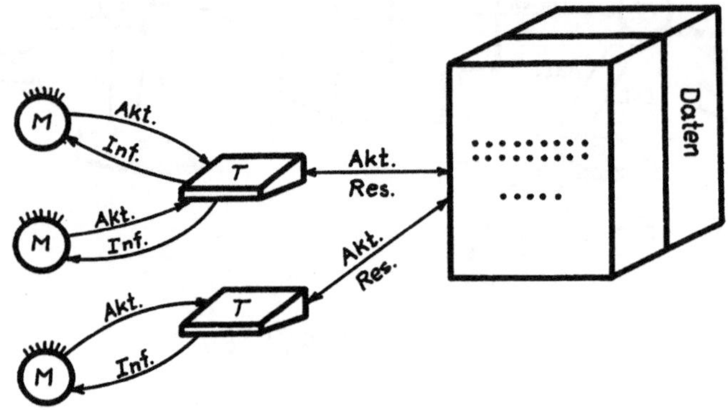

INFORMATIONSSYSTEM 3

Abb. 3

Es ist interessant zu beobachten, daß viele der Probleme eines modernen online Datenbanksystems schon beim Karteisystem auftraten, daß jedoch bei jenen noch sehr oft eine unmittelbare Lösung möglich war.

Die Koordination des Datenzugriffes zur Sicherung der Integrität des Systems wird im Karteisystem entweder durch automatisches Anstellen der verschiedenen Benutzer am Karteischrank (Warteschlange) oder durch Entfernen der zu bearbeitenden Karteikarte erzielt. Diese Aktionen müssen im online System künstlich nachgebildet werden. Durch die im online System fehlende unmittelbare Kommunikation zwischen den einzelnen Benutzern entstehen jedoch weitere Probleme, z.B. dead locking, deren Lösung einen großen Teil der Aufmerksamkeit beim Entwurf von

Datenbanksystemen verlangt.

Die Redundanz der gespeicherten Daten wurde im Karteisystem schon aus Platzgründen niedrig gehalten. So war es für einen Benutzer auch ohne Schwierigkeiten möglich, seine Informationen aus mehreren Karteikästen zusammenzutragen. In dem dateiorientierten Aufbau der meisten batch Systeme ist diese Flexibilität verloren gegangen. Schon leichte Unterschiede in der Problemstellung führen zur Konstruktion neuer Dateien, in denen große Teile der ursprünglichen Daten nochmals gespeichert werden. In online Systemen muß,wegen der großen gleichzeitig zur Verfügung stehenden Datenmenge, kleine Datenredundanz erzielt werden. Durch die immer noch starken Orientierung dieser Systeme auf die Datenorganisationen der batch Systeme, i.e. file-record-field, stellt diese Anforderung oft ein schwer zu lösendes Problem dar /2/.

Die Datensicherheit wird im Karteisystem durch lokale Zugriffskontrollen, wie zum Beispiel menschliche Beobachtung oder Kontrolle beim Betreten der Räumlichkeiten, gewährleistet. Im batch System ist Datensicherheit praktisch nicht realisierbar und muß durch externe Methoden erzielt werden. Für die Datensicherheit im online System kann jedoch wieder die Identität des Benutzers herangezogen werden, da der Benutzer wieder unmittelbar an dem System arbeitet.

Neben den batch/online Eigenschaften eines generellen Informationssystems ist auch die Art, in der ein Benutzer des Systems seine Aktionen spezifiziert, von großer Bedeutung.

Im host-language System wird eine der existierenden Programmiersprachen, wie zum Beispiel PL/I, COBOL, ALGOL, durch Mechanismen zum Bearbeiten einer Datenbank ergänzt. Im self-contained-language System wird eine eigene, meist benutzerorientierte, Sprache zur Verfügung gestellt, die Mechanismen sowohl zur Datenmanipulation als auch zur Durchführung der notwendigen Kalkulationen und Ausführungskontrollen enthält.

Zur Illustration der besprochenen Typen von Informationssystemen wird ein einfaches Beispiel (Abb. 4) herangezogen. Eine Datei, die Personalinformation enthält, ist aus Sätzen bestehend, aus Personalnummer, Adresse und Gehalt, aufgebaut. Update Funktionen zur Einfügung neuer Adressen und Gehälter sollen zur Verfügung gestellt werden.

PROBLEM:

DATEI:

MANNO	ADDRESS	SALARY
4523	MÜNCHEN	3000

Neuer Gehalt
Neue Adresse
sollen eingefügt werden

BEISPIEL I: Batch-Host Language System

BEISPIEL II: Online-Self Contained System

Abb. 4

Abb. 5 zeigt das Beispiel als ein auf PL/I basierendes batch/host-language System, Abb. 6 als online/self-contained-language System.

BEISPIEL I:

AKTION 1:

```
DATENBANKDEFINITION:
  1 PERSONNEL,
      2 MANNO,
      2 ADDRESS CHAR (40)
      2 SALARY FIXED;
```

AKTION 2:

```
NEW SALARY: PROCEDURE;
   DCL 1 NSAL, 2 MNO, 2 SAL FIXED;
   % INCLUDE DATENBANK;
   L: GET LIST (NSAL);
   CALL UPDATE (PERSONNEL, NSAL);
   GOTO L;
   END;
NEW ADDRESS: PROCEDURE;...
```

AKTION 3:

Sammeln & Sortieren der Daten
Ablochen
Gehalt-update
Adresse-update

Abb. 5

BEISPIEL II:

AKTION 1:

```
DATENBANKDEFINITION:
   SET PERSONNEL OF MANNO,
                    ADDRESS STRING (40),
                    SALARY.
```

AKTION 2:

```
SCHEMADEFINITION:
   DEFINE CHANGE NAME(X) OF
         VALUE(Y) TO VALUE(Z).   AS
         UPDATE PERSONNEL.X TO Z WHERE
         MANNO=Y.
```

AKTION 3:

```
CHANGE SALARY OF 4523 TO 3200.
CHANGE ADDRESS OF 2512 TO NEW YORK.
```

Abb. 6

In beiden Systemen muß die Datenorganisation zuerst durch die Datenbankverwaltung festgelegt werden. Im batch/host-language System werden die zur Aufgabenlösung benötigten Programme durch den Anwendungsprogrammierer erstellt, der auch die Ausführung der Programme im Rahmen der Betriebssysteme veranlaßt. In den Programmen werden die zur Verfügung gestellten Datenmanipulationsmechanismen, z.B. UPDATE, verwendet.

Im online/self-contained language System werden zusätzlich zu den Datenmanipulationsmechanismen, z.B. UPDATE, noch Hilfsmittel zur Verfügung gestellt, die es erlauben, die Manipulationssprache an spezielle Anforderung bestimmter Benutzerklassen (Ingenieur, Hilfskraft, etc.) anzupassen. Diese Anpassungen werden nicht mehr von einem Anwendungsprogrammierer sondern von einem Fachspezialisten ausgeführt, der über konventionelle Programmiersysteme nicht Bescheid zu wissen braucht, jedoch das Arbeitsgebiet seiner Benutzerklasse genauestens kennt.

Die wichtigsten existierenden oder in Entwicklung befindlichen generellen Informationssysteme sind in Tabelle 1 angeführt und entsprechend ihrer batch/online und host-language/self-contained-language Eigenschaften klassifiziert. Zusätzlich wird angegeben, ob als Benutzer hauptsächlich

ÜBERSICHT:

		H/S	B/O	AP/NP
GIS	IBM	S	O, B	NP
MARK IV	Informatics	S	B	NP
NIPS/FFS	(IBM)	S	B, O	NP,AP
TDMS	SDC	S	O	NP
UL/I	RCA	S	B	NP
IDS	Honeywell	H	B	AP
IMS	IBM	H	B	AP
SC/I	WEL, Auerb.	H,S	B	AP
DBTG	CODASYL	H	B	AP
(DBR)	Share/Guide	S, H	B, O	AP/NP
Rel. Mod.	E.F. Codd	S, H	O(B)	NP

Tabelle 1

Programmierer (AP) oder Nichtprogrammierer (NP) vorgesehen sind.

GIS /3/ baut auf IBM's OS/360 Datenorganisationen auf und akzeptiert daher, bei nötiger Vorsicht, auch Dateien, die durch andere OS/360 Programmiersysteme erstellt wurden.

MARK IV /4/ verwendet zur besseren Unterstützung der Benutzer vorgedruckte Formulare zur Beschreibung aller Datenmanipulationen.

NIPS-FFS /5/ kann für große Aufgaben als batch System verwendet werden, während es für kleinere Anfragen und Aktionen als online System eingerichtet ist.

TDMS /6/ wurde durch fortschrittliche Datenorganisationen auf eine hohe Verarbeitungsgeschwindigkeit ausgerichtet.

UL-I /7/ ist speziell für Nichtprogrammierer vorgesehen.

IDS /8/ ist ein host-language System, dessen Verwendung für die host-language COBOL geplant wurde.

IMS /9/ verwendet Datenorganisationen, die nicht IBM OS/360 kompatibel sind.

SC-1 /10/ kann sowohl als host- als auch als self-contained language System verwendet werden.

DBTG /11/ stellt Funktionen zur Datendefinition und Datenmanipulation zur Verfügung. An Implementierungen wird zur Zeit gearbeitet. Als host-language ist im CODASYL Bericht COBOL vorgesehen. Die Sprache kann jedoch auch auf andere host-languages ausgerichtet werden. (Eine ausführliche Diskussion der bis jetzt angeführten Systeme kann in /23/ gefunden werden.)

DBR GUIDE/SHARE /12/ versucht die allgemeinen Anforderungen an ein generelles Informationssystem zu beschreiben. Der Bericht stellt daher eigentlich kein zur Implementierung vorgesehenes System dar. In einer Veröffentlichung von P.Y. Tani /13/ werden die DBR Anforderungen mit den in DBTG zur Verfügung gestellten Funktionen verglichen.

Das <u>Relational Model</u> von E.F. Codd /14/ basiert auf der Überlegung, daß die Beziehungen zwischen Daten in Datenbanken immer als Relationen dargestellt werden können und daher Beschreibungen basierend auf dem mathematischen Relationsbegriff viel eher den Gegebenheiten eines generellen Informationssystems entsprechen als die immer noch übliche Abstützung auf das physikalisch orientierte Konzept der Files-Records-Fields. Das Relationsmodell hat große Beachtung gefunden, und es gibt eine Reihe von weiteren Untersuchungen über das Modell /15-21/. Es erlaubt einfachere mathematische Behandlung von Datenbankproblemen und kann dennoch mit den konventionellen Datenorganisationen in Beziehung gebracht werden /2,22/.

2. Aufbau eines generellen Informationssystems

Aus einer Analyse der im vorhergehenden Abschnitt beschriebenen Informationssysteme lassen sich eine Reihe von Anforderungen an den Aufbau eines generellen Informationssystems ableiten:

Leichte Verwendbarkeit für die verschiedenen Benutzerkategorien
geringe Redundanz der Daten
batch und online Eigenschaften
Erweiterbarkeit
schnelle Verarbeitung
Integrität
Sicherheit

Diese Anforderungen können am besten durch eine dreistufige Organisation des Systems befriedigt werden (Abb.7).

STRUKTUR DER INFORMATIONSSYSTEME

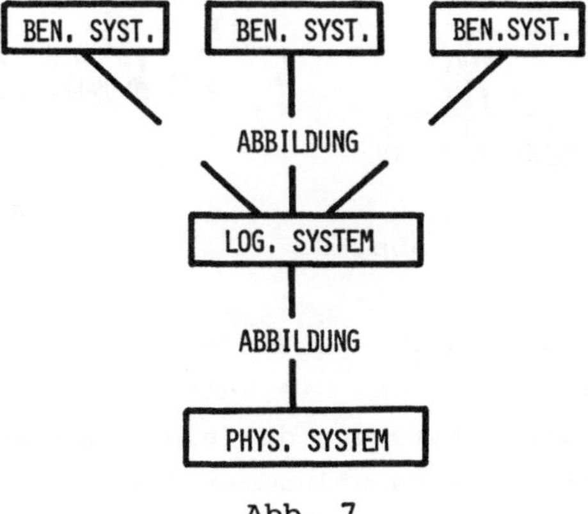

Abb. 7

Die oberste Ebene stellt die verschiedenen Benutzerstandpunkte dar. Verschiedene Benutzerklassen werden oft auch gleiche Daten in verschiedenen Zusammenhängen sehen. Für jede Benutzerklasse wird ein eigenes Benutzersystem zur Verfügung gestellt, in dem ein Benutzer sowohl die für ihn am besten geeignete Datenorganisation als auch die an seinen Bedarf angepaßten Datenmanipulationsmechanismen (Abb. 6) vorfindet. Um die vom System vorzunehmenden Kontrollen durchführen zu können, müssen die verschiedenartigen Benutzersysteme auf eine gemeinsame Basis - das logische System - zurückgeführt werden. Das logische System ist auf einfache Anwendung der Autorisierungs- und Integritätskontrollen ausgerichtet. Es kann nicht mit dem physikalischen System identisch sein, da die verfügbare Gerätekombination zusammen mit dem Ziel schneller Verarbeitung die physikalische Struktur des Systems nach anderen Gesichtspunkten festlegt.

Ein wichtiger Bestandteil jeder der drei Ebenen ist die Definition der erlaubten Datenorganisationen. In den Benutzersystemen werden die Organisationen weitgehend von den Anforderungen der Benutzer festgelegt. Drei häufige Datenorganisationsformen sind in Abb. 8 dargestellt,

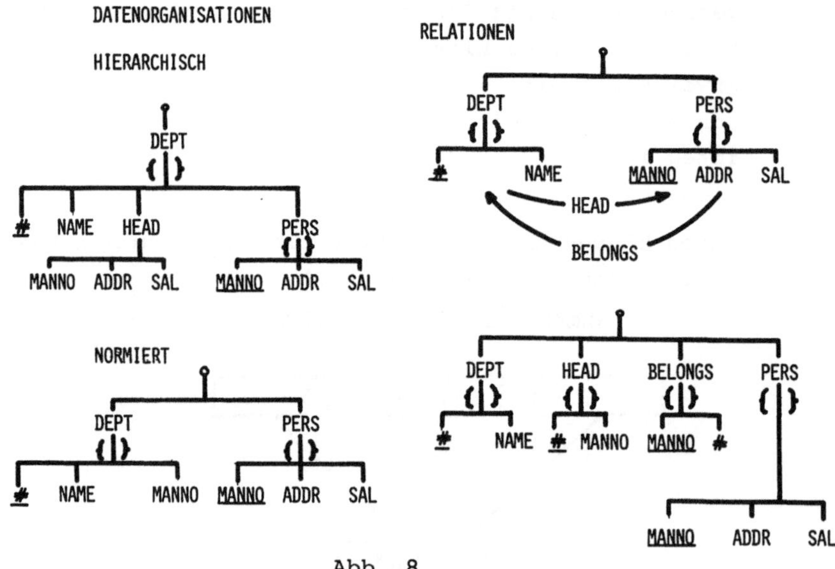

Abb. 8

wobei die geschwungenen Klammern { } Wiederholungen der entsprechenden Teilorganisationen symbolisieren. Die unterstrichenen Komponenten dienen zur eindeutigen Identifizierung der einzelnen Wiederholungen. Zum Beispiel identifiziert die Personalnummer (gekennzeichnet durch MANNO) eindeutig einen Mitarbeiter einer Abteilung.

Mit Hilfe dreier Grundbausteine (Abb. 9) lassen sich alle gezeigten

Datenorganisationen beschreiben. Die Basiselemente stellen die eigent-

DATEN ELEMENTE

BASISELEMENT
NEW YORK,2520

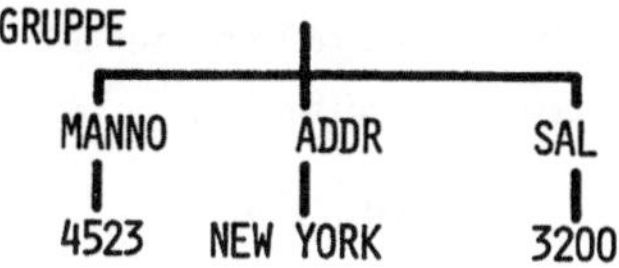

KOLLEKTION

DEPT $\{E_1, E_2, E_3\}$

Abb. 9

lichen Datenwerte der Datenbank dar. Eine Gruppe ist als eine ungeordnete Menge von Datenelementen definiert, in der jedes Element durch einen eindeutigen Namen gekennzeichnet ist. In Abb. 9, zum Beispiel, kennzeichnet der Name MANNO das Basiselement 4523, ADDR das Basiselement NEW YORK etc. Eine bestimmte Reihenfolge für die Elemente einer Gruppe ist nicht festgelegt. Kollektionen repräsentieren eine ungeordnete Menge von Datenelementen, wobei jedoch das gleiche Element mehrmals in einer Kollektion auftreten kann. Eine Definition dieser Datenelementformen mittels formaler Methoden ist in /2/ angegeben.

Die in Abb. 8 gezeigte hierarchische Struktur besteht aus einer Kollektion (DEPT) von Gruppen, die jeweils vier unmittelbare Komponenten besitzen (#, NAME, HEAD, PERS). HEAD beschreibt wieder eine Gruppe, während PERS eine Kollektion darstellt. In der normierten Struktur kann eine Datenbank nur aus Kollektionen von Gruppen bestehen, die selbst nur mehr Basiselemente enthalten dürfen. In der Datenstruktur mit Relationen (im DBTG Sinn) kann man beobachten, daß sich die Kollektionen DEPT und PERS funktionell nicht von den Relationen HEAD und BELONGS unterscheiden, und daher der logische Aufbau durch Umschreiben nicht verändert wird. Die neue Struktur stellt eine normierte Datenorganisation dar, kann aber natürlich immer noch im logischen Sinne als Gruppe von vier Relationen bezeichnet werden. Wenn man Kollektionen als Relationen denkt, dann stellt jede in der Kollektion enthaltene Gruppe eine der durch die Relation bestimmten Wertetupel dar. Eine solche Definition entspricht genau der von E. F. Codd /14/ gegebenen Definition des normierten Relational Models.

Die normierte Datenorganisationsform hat eine einfache Struktur und bietet sich als Organisationsform für das logische System an /22/. Betrachtungen über das physikalische System verlassen den Rahmen dieses Vortrags, da dafür auch physikalische Eigenschaften der Hardwarekonfiguration untersucht werden müssen.

DATENMANIPULATION

AKTION	BEREICH	PRÄMISSE
PRINT ({MANNO(X)})	X ∈ PERS	SAL(X)<3500
UPDATE(ADDR(X),N.Y.)	X ∈ PERS	MANNO(X)=2512

OPERATIONEN

ARITHMETIK: +,-,<,=
PRÄD.KALKOL: &, V, ∀, ∃
GRUPPENOP: BUILT, SELECT,=,≠
KOLL.OP: MENGENLEHRE
AKTIONEN: ERZEUGEN - ÄNDERN - LESEN

Abb. 10

In Abb. 10 wird der prinzipielle Aufbau zweier Anweisungen an das Informationssystem

FINDE MANNO ALLER PERS MIT SAL < 3500.
ÄNDERE ADDR DER PERS MIT MANNO = 2512 ZU NEW YORK.

gezeigt. Jede Anweisung enthält einen Aktionsteil, einen bereichseinschränkenden Teil und eine Prämisse, die erfüllt sein muß, damit die entsprechende Aktion durchgeführt werden kann. Die in Abb. 10 gezeigten zusätzlichen Operationen können ebenfalls in Anweisungen an das Informationssystem auftreten.

Anweisungen an ein Benutzersystem müssen zur Ausführung in Anweisungen an das physikalische System umgeformt werden. Die notwendigen Schritte sind in Abb. 11 illustriert.

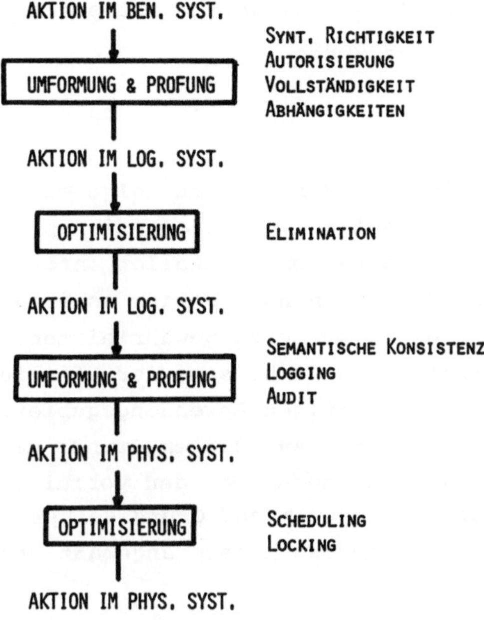

Abb. 11

Die Abbildungen zwischen den verschiedenen Systemebenen werden zur Durchführung der notwendigen Kontrollen benutzt. Nach der synthetischen Analyse wird die Autorisierung des Benutzers überprüft. Zusätzlich wird geprüft, ob alle notwendigen Daten bei der Anweisung angegeben wurden und ob zusätzliche Abhängigkeiten in der Datenorganisation existieren, so daß eine Ausführung der verlangten Aktion auch noch andere davon abhängige Aktionen nach sich zieht. Wenn zum Beispiel die Information "Anzahl der Personen in New York" im System existiert, dann bedingt eine Adressänderung eine Veränderung dieser Information.

Nach der Umformung einer Anweisung ist notwendig, die durch den indirekten Weg verursachten ungünstigen Anfrageformen durch Optimisierung zu verbessern, um unnötige Ausführungsschritte zu eliminieren /2/.

Eine ähnliche Vorgangsweise bildet die logische Form der Anweisung auf das physikalische System ab. Dabei werden wieder Überwachungsfunktionen ausgeführt und zusätzlich die notwendigen Steuermechanis-

zur endgültigen Ausführung bereitgestellt, z.B. scheduling und locking Strategien. Falls nötig, werden entsprechende Aktionen in die umgeformte Anweisung eingebaut.

3. Zusammenfassung

Eine Untersuchung existierender Systeme zeigt eine oft unnötige Vielfalt in Philosophie und Aufbau von Informationssystemen. Vor der Entwicklung der nächsten Generation genereller Informationssysteme sollten die allgemeinen Prinzipien noch weiter untersucht werden, um eine gemeinsame Basis für die Systeme zu gewährleisten. Besonders unzureichend sind die Mittel zur Vorhersage der Effizienz von Informationssystemen, da auch die zukünftigen Anwendungsgebiete der Systeme noch nicht voll verstanden werden. Aus diesem Grunde hat der in Abschnitt 2 beschriebene Systemaufbau auch noch den Vorteil, daß bei fehlerhaften Entscheidungen das System auf Grund seiner Flexibilität später immer noch an die Gegebenheiten besser angepaßt werden kann.

Literatur

/1/ E. J. Neuhold, G. Rabe: Cooperative Use-Development of Interactive Systems. - Proc. of ONLINE 72, Uxbridge, Sept. 1972.

/2/ E. J. Neuhold: The use of formal description techniques in large data banks. - Proc. of Internat. Computing Symposium, Venice, April 1972.

/3/ J. Bryant and P. Semple: GIS and File Management. - Proc. of ACM 21st National Conference, 1966.

/4/ J. A. Postley: The MARK IV System. - Datamation January 1968.

/5/ National Military Command System Information Processing System 360 Formated File System (NIPS 360 FFS), Users Manual. - Computer System Manual CSM UM 15A-68.

/6/ The Time-Shared Data Management System (TDMS), Language Specifications. - SDC TM-3370.

/7/ T. W. Olle: UL/I: A Non-Procedural Language for Retrieving Information from Data Bases. - Proc. IFIP Congress 1968, Edinbourgh, Scotland.

/8/ C. W. Bachman, S. B. Williams: A General Purpose Programming System for Random Access Memories. - Proc. FJCC 1964.

/9/ Information Management System/360, Application Description Manual (Version 2) GH 20-0892, IBM, 1970.

/10/ System Control-1, Users Guide. - Information Systems Engineering, Western Elektric, January 1970.

/11/ CODASYL Data Base Task Group Report. - April 1971.

/12/ GUIDE/SHARE Data Base Report, Nov. 1970.

/13/ P. Y. Tani: Comparison of Data Base Management Systems Reports. - IBM TR 00.2244, October 1971.

/14/ E. F. Codd: A Relational Model of Data for Large Shared Data Banks. - Comm. of ACM, June 1970.

/15/ E. F. Codd: Further Normalization of the Data Base Relational Model. - Courant Computer Science Symposia 6, "Data Base Systems", to be published Prentice Hall, 1971.

/16/ E. F. Codd: Relational Completeness of Data Base Sublanguages. - Courant Computer Sciences Symposia 6, "Data Base Systems", to be published Prentice Hall, 1971.

/17/ E. F. Codd: A Data Base Sublanguage Founded on the Relational Calculus. - ACM SIGFIDET Workshop on Data Description, Access & Control, San Diego, Nov. 1971.

/18/ I. J. Heath: Unacceptable File Operations in a Relational Data Base. - ACM SIGFIDET Workshop on Data Description, Access & Control, San Diego, Nov. 1971.

/19/ C. J. Date, P. Hopewell: File Definition and Logical Data Independence. - ACM SIGFIDET Workshop on Data Description, Access & Control, San Diego, Nov. 1971.

/20/ C. J. Date, P. Hopewell: Storage Structure and Physical Data Independence. - ACM SIGFIDET Workshop on Data Description, Access & Control, San Diego, Nov. 1971.

/21/ A. L. Strnad: The Relational Approach to the Management of Data Bases. - IFIP Congress, Ljubljana 1971.

/22/ E. J. Neuhold: Data Mapping: A Formal Hierarchical and Relational View. - Courant Computer Science Symposia 6, "Data Base Systems", to be published Prentice Hall, 1971.

/23/ CODASYL: Feature Analysis of Generalized Data Base Management Systems, May 1971.

HARDWARE-ARCHITECTURE AND COMPUTER ORGANISATION

F.H.SUMNER

I. INTRODUCTION

My general theme is the development of computer design at the University of Manchester with particular reference to our present system the MU5. As its name implies this is the fifth system designed at Manchester, the first coming into operation in 1951.

Three of the systems Mark I (1951) Mercury (1956) and Atlas (1962) were produced commercially and provided the whole of the University computing service from 1951 to 1971. The management of this computing service was the responsibility of the Computer Science Department. As designers we were therefore in a fortunate, if sometimes embarrassing position, having designed the complete hardware and software of each system we had to run it as a service machine. The users were never slow to tell us of the deficiencies of the system and we could observe in detail the system performance. The integration of the hardware and software design and the detailed association with the users has been of immense value in the design of all our systems.

2. MARK I to MERCURY

Our first machine which came into operation in 1951 gave the user very few facilities. There were 512 words of store, fixed point arithmetic, A "Store resident executive" of some 16 words and all programmes were written directly in machine code using an unwieldy set of 32 symbols. The user had a raw empty machine to himself and its efficient use was entirely his responsibility.

Whilst having some nostalgia for the freedom of these early days the effort involved was enormous and the memory of this effort provides some consolation when fighting the idiosyncrasies of today's high level languages and complex operating systems.

The principal outcome of the users experience with this system was a plea for some form of higher level programming language and the provision of automatic floating point facilities. These were introduced in our next system the Mercury in 1956 which had engineered floating point and a high level language Mercury autocode which was roughly equivalent to the early versions of Fortran.

3. MERCURY to ATLAS

As a designer one has great difficulty in getting programmers to make constructive comments on the features he would like in the next machine. This is understandable as he is being asked for what he would like in two to three years time, when he is fighting to make the best or even second best use of the machine he has got from the designers previous efforts. An example of the difficulties and dangers of extrapolation occurred in the design of the Atlas. The forerunner of the Atlas was the Mercury and as stated above this had a high level language Mercury autocode. This language used single letters to identify integers and reals, with integers restricted to some 12 letters. With the 6 modifier registers available on the Mercury it was decided to keep integers in the store and to transfer to modifier registers as required. Atlas was designed with 128 registers in the hope that all integers could be kept in fast registers even in a multi-programming environment, however, by the early 60's when Atlas came into general use high level languages permitted the definition of a large number of integers and the decision was again made to keep the integers in the store and load the modifiers as required!

The two most significant design requirements which emerged from discussions with the users of the Mercury was that they did not like explicitly addressed registers and that they would like an infinitely large directly addressable high speed store!

It was this slightly unrealistic request plus the obvious need for multi-programming which led to the development of virtual addressing and paging which were introduced in the Atlas.

4. ATLAS to MU5

When we started to design the MU5 in 1966 our overall aim was to produce a computer with a power of some 20 times Atlas which would be efficient at compiling and executing programs written in high level languages.

In Atlas some of the speed was obtained by overlapping instruction execution. The average rate of completing instructions being one every 3 μ sec compared with an average instruction length of 7 μ sec. In order to obtain the desired performance on MU5 far more overlapping or pipelining would be required with a corresponding increase in the problems presented by branch instructions. In Atlas the fixed point add time was 280 n sec compared with a store access time of 1600 n sec. The MU5 technology should give 40 n sec and 600 n sec for the corresponding operations showing a far greater descrepancy between logic speeds and store access times.

The major difficulty in achieving our design aim is therefore to solve the problems of getting instructions and operands from the store at a sufficient rate.

4.1 OPERAND ACCESSING

In computers such as the CDC 6600 and CDC 7600 the technique for solving the operand problem is to have a small number of explicitly addressed central registers which contain the operands and which therefore reduce the number of accesses to the store. The attainment of the maximum possible speeds in such register systems is very dependent upon putting the right operands in the registers at the right time. This can be accomplished by careful hand coding but is far more difficult for a high level language compiler. The compiler writer would prefer his operands to be in a single store of effectively infinite length. This in turn implies a large core store which is expensive and not very fast. All the operands would be brought from this store as required, and the effect of access times would be disasterous. This situation of conflicting designs - on the one hand the high speed engineer's machine which is difficult to program, and on the other hand the compiler writer's machine which is difficult to make fast - has been getting more acute as computers have become more complex and more use has been made of high level languages. In the design of the MU5 we have attempted to bring the two approaches together. We began this process by studying the behaviour of the Atlas system when obeying programs written in high level languages. In these languages there are basically two classes of operand - named operands, which can be reals integers or descriptors of arrays, in the one class, and array elements in the other class. One of the major languages in use on the Atlas is Atlas Autocode. This is an Algol-like language written by members of the Department, and we modified the compiler for this language so that it would produce statistics on the run-time usage of the different types of operand. By monitoring the accesses to the operands in some hundred different programs we found that 80 per cent of the accesses were for named operands and 20 per cent of the accesses were for array elements. If this is rather difficult to believe, consider the very simple expression A = B(i). this is taking the value of an element of a one-dimensional array and putting it into a named real quantity. To obey this expression we would require three accesses to names for A, i and the array name of B and only one array access for the actual element of the array. Having established the two classes of operand which are to be brought from the store, and having determined the relative number of accesses for the different types, the next problem is to determine how many different names are in use in a program. Again by a study of the programs submitted to the Atlas Computing Service the number of names used and the number of names declared in a program was, generally speaking, under a hundred, and the number of names declared in any routine was nearly always less than 64. This is the number of names declared statically at the beginning of the routine and the number of names in dynamic use in any area of the routine will be less than this. There is therefore the possibility of keeping these named operands in a small store close to the central processor and therefore of obtaining very fast access to such operands.

Some of the basic design features of the MU5 are summarised on Page 4. It is expected that there will be more than 16 processes in the system at any time, but that not more than 16 of these will be active. The organisation of the segmented store permits a process to have private, shared or common segments, and these have access control for read, write and obey. The three classes of object which need to be brought from the addressable memory are instructions, named quantities and array elements. These can therefore be placed in distinct segments and the mode of access and the management of the different segments can reflect the type of object that they contain. For example, the instructions are in pure procedures and are held in obey only segments.

SOME BASIC FEATURES OF MU5

1. Character length 8 bits.
   Basic instruction 16 bits.
   Floating point number 64 bits.

2. Minimum number of central registers.

3. Instruction format:

F	k	n
7	3	6
Function	Type of operand	Operand address relative to a base address

4. Large virtual address space arranged in a segmented manner.
   Address format:

P	S	B	L	B_y
Process	Segment	Page	Line	Byte
4	14	16		2

The store is paged over 3 levels, A 250 ns plated wire store, A 2·5 μsec core and a drum. The page size is variable in powers of 2 from 16 to 64K lines.

The named operands can generally be kept in one segment (maximum size 64K) and the organisation of this segment is shown in Fig. 1. There are three central registers associated with the accessing of operands in this segment: these are the stack front register (SF) which contains the address of the stack front, the name base register (NB) which contains the address of the first named variable of the current routine and the extra named base register (XNB) which can be set to point to the first named variable of any routine. The directory is accessed by using names relative to a dummy name base of zero.

The address development of named and stacked quantities is shown in Fig. 2. In general terms there are two groups of named operands - integers and array descriptors on the one hand, which are required to evaluate the addresses of array elements, and reals which go directly to the main arithmetic unit (floating point, fixed point or decimal). A small 32-line associative store is provided to trap the frequently used integer and array names. The performance of the final system will depend critically on the hit rate achieved in this store. In order to gain some idea as to the correctness of the design four Atlas Autocode and two Fortran programs were taken from the University computing service, programs using a large number of names were chosen, and the complete pattern of name accesses for these programs was determined and stored on a set of magnetic tapes.

These operand access patterns were then used to investigate the performance of buffers of different size and design. The variation of hit rate with number of lines for one program is shown in Fig. 3, which also lists the hit rates for a 32-line buffer for the six programs considered. All the Atlas Autocode programs had hit rates in access of 99 per cent for a store as small as 24 lines. Experiments on replacement algorithms suggested that a simple cyclic system was sufficient and that any money or space spent on more elaborate algorithms would have been better used in increasing the length of the store. These operands, which the system almost completely traps in the store, are defined quite naturally by the compiler in the production of the object code. This is due to the close similarity between the structure of the high level language program and the structure of the hardware.

A second associative buffer for the real name operands is provided near to the arithmetic unit. This buffer is 24 lines long and gives a hit-rate of over 99% for three of the sample programs and about 80% for the others which used a very large number of distinct names. Lower hit-rates in this buffer are not critical as the consequence store access can be overlapped with the relatively slow floating point arithmetic operations.

So far only the accessing of named operands has been considered. The development of an address of an array quantity is illustrated in Fig. 4. Consider the accessing of an element of a one-dimensional array a(i + j + 3), 3 B orders are required using the named intergers i and j and the literal 3 to compute the value of i + j + 3 in the B register. Then an order is obeyed in which the N field defines the 64 bit descriptor of the array a and the k field indicates the action to be taken, the F field defines the function to be performed on the array element when it has been accessed. The 64 bit descriptor contains the origin of the array, the type of element and the bound of the array. The descriptor arithmetic unit checks that the displacement i + j + 3 in register B is within range then forms the address by adding B to the origin and accesses the store for the operand. On obtaining the value of the array element this is sent together with the function to the appropriate arithmetic unit.

In the initial design only a small array element buffer was provided. This buffer is 8 lines long and two floating point words wide. When an operand not in the buffer is required that operand together with the other half of the double word is brought from the store and placed in the buffer. This buffer is two words wide as the main store is also two words wide and it is economical to bring two words if there is a reasonable chance of the second being used. This is quite likely for array quantities which tend to be scanned sequentially. Traces of the array operand accesses for the six programs referred to above indicate, that even this very small buffer has a hit rate of approximately 60 per cent.

The overall pipeline structure and buffer organisation is shown in Fig. 5. For the Atlas Autocode programs the operands trapped in the buffers are over 99% of the names and 60% of the array elements, that is 92% of all operand accesses. This is quite a good hit-rate as the total buffer size is only 576 bytes. Furthermore, those operands which must be accessed quickly to maintain a good overlap in the pipeline are virtually all trapped in the buffers. For the Fortran programs the overall figure is 80%, but again nearly all of the essential operands are trapped in the BD buffer.

The restriction of array elements to a particular buffer should permit the using of a buffer which makes considerable use of the sequential mode of addressing of most arrays. A range of such buffers was studied with the traces of the six programs, and whilst it was not possible to include any of these designs in the current version of the MU5 it is of interest to note that hit-rates in excess of 90% were obtained, on a 16 line two word wide buffer in which a system of predictive loading was employed. This is a further proof of the value of permitting the structure of the hardware to match the structure of the data of the programs being obeyed.

4.2 INSTRUCTION FETCHING

Before going on to consider solutions to the instruction problem it is interesting to go back to the design of the Atlas. As stated above there was a considerable amount of overlap of the various stages of instruction execution in order to achieve a high speed. However, it was decided that all test codes and other orders which may or may not transfer control would be taken to completion, taking 7 μ sec before the request for the next instruction was made to the store. This simplified the design and at the time it was not felt that the effect would be significant. The hoped for speed was approximately 2 μsec per order and after the machine was completed various tests of its speed were made using long sequences of instructions which confirmed this performance. However, observations of the number of orders obeyed in a day gave an average time of 3 μ sec. The descrepancy was originally put down to store clashes but when a later version of the system with a much larger store gave the same results, it was concluded that the overlap in practice was not as good as had been expected, but no particular reasons were put forward.

At the time when we were beginning to think about our next computer project, modifications were made to our Atlas to permit the collection of statistics on the number of orders of the different types which were obeyed. These showed that over a very large sample of programs, the proportion of orders which may transfer control was about 20%. This clearly explains the discrepancy.

$$0.8 \times 2 + 0.2 \times 7 = 3\,\mu\text{sec.}$$

The first reaction to this figure of 20% was one of disbelief but it has since been confirmed on several different computer systems.

Other statistics provided by the Atlas monitoring are summarised below.

ATLAS CONTROL TRANSFER STATISTICS

Percentage of obeyed orders which may transfer control 20%

Percentage of these which actually cause a transfer 70%

14% or 1 in 7 orders transfer control

Distribution of transfer orders

	Obeyed	Jump
Unconditional transfers	5.5%	5.5%
Test and count	5.0%	3.9%
Arithmetic tests	9.5%	4.6%

Distance of jumps 34% < 4
6% 4-16
60% > 16

For MU5 if we assume that only tests which jump affect the pipeline and if we compare the instructions, which are shorter and less powerful than those on Atlas, then we can expect one jump every 15 orders. For the MU5 the maximum rate at which the central processor can execute instructions is one 16 bit instruction every 40 n sec. The store can supply instructions at the required rate but in order to cope with the long access time, instructions will have to be requested very far in advance of being obeyed.

A simple early call approach is all right for long sequences of instructions but the incidence of a transfer completely wrecks the system. Assuming one jump in 15 orders, a store access time of 500 n sec and 6 orders in the pipeline, gives an average instruction time of

$$(1/15)\ (14 \times 40 + 1 \times 740) = 87\ \text{n sec.}$$

i.e. less than half the maximum speed.

The distances jumped make it clear that a simple instruction buffer of reasonable size will not be much use. The first system that we considered is summarised in Fig. 6. All instructions proceed as if there are no transfers and when a transfer occurs and the new address has been computed this is presented to a small associative store to get the first few orders at the jumped to address, this permits an early call to the main store to get subsequent orders without any additional delay. The loss here is a pipeline of instructions, 240n sec. plus the access time to the small store, 80 n sec., total 320 sec. (The 240n sec. could be slightly reduced for unconditional transfers).

If the jumped to address was always in the store this would give a maximum rate of:

$$(1/15)\ (14 \times 40 + 320) = 55\ \text{n sec.}$$

In order to test the efficiency of this type of approach detailed traces of several programs were made and a typical result for various numbers of lines of associative stores is:

lines	% in buffer	limit (n sec.)
4	45	74
8	80	64
16	81	64

However, each line has to be very wide to give the early call chance to catch up after a transfer, probably about 200 bits, and it was felt that this was too expensive and that the performance was not good enough.

The system that we propose to implement is summarised in Fig.7. In order to make an early call system work it is necessary that the requests to the store should be for the correct instructions even if these instructions are not in sequential addresses. The system starts with the associative store empty and a stream of instructions from sequential addresses is brought from the store and presented to the central processor. When a control transfer occurs, it is easy for the central processor to detect that the next order in the pipeline, which should of course be out of sequence is, in fact, in sequence, because each instruction is accompanied by a single bit indicating that it is an "in sequence" instruction. A request is therefore made to the store for the instruction at the jumped to address and subsequent requests to the store are for the instructions following this address At the same time an entry is made in the associative store which consists of the jumped from address on the associative side and the jumped to address on the value side. As can be seen from the diagram, all instruction addresses are presented to the associative store before being allowed to go to the main store. If, therefore, at some later time, a request is about to be made to the store for the instruction in the jumped from address, it is easy for the system to detect this and substitute a request for the instruction in the jumped to address, and to continue the stream of instructions from this address. When the instruction from the jumped to address is presented to the central processor, the extra bit is set to say "not in sequence". Therefore, if the transfer again occurs the next instruction in the pipeline will be the correct one and there will be no break in the overlapped operation of the pipeline. This means that whenever a jump occurs which has not been anticipated, there will be a gap of 740 nsec. (500 + 6 x 40) but for an anticipated transfer there will be no gap. These arguments only apply to jump orders with literal addresses, jumps such as return links which go to a variety of places are not included and always cause a gap in the pipeline.

This model has been tested with the same program traces as the previous system with the following results:

lines	% correct	limit (n sec.)
4	43	66
8	74	52
16	76	51

The reason for the fall in the percentage of correct accesses relative to the same number of lines of the previous system is that the new system will occasionally predict a transfer which does not occur.

The lines of the associative store in the new system are only 48 bits wide and the limit on the computing speed for the same number of lines is considerably less than in the previous system.

A system with 8 lines of associative store has been implemented in MU5.

5. MU5 to MU6

MU5 will be operational by early 1973. There has already been a considerable amount of system simulation. The maximum rate at which instructions would be processed from the pipeline is one every 40 sec. however, disruptions occur for many reasons, branch orders not guessed by the early call system, operands not in fast buffers, slow floating point arithmetic functions and tests which have to wait for arithmetic results. The net effect of all this is for the pipeline to only be used at about 33% of its maximum efficiency.

There is no necessity in a pipeline system for instructions in adjacent stages of the pipeline to belong to the same instruction stream or process. This offers a chance for a considerable increase in performance, ifseveral processes can share the pipeline then when one stream is held up others can proceed. We have done a few experiments with systems with similar structures to MU5, i.e. with name and array element buffers but with simple instruction fetching systems. In such systems the load on the store is not great so that any increase in store activity caused by more efficient use of the pipeline is unlikely to result in the bottleneck being transferred to the store access channel. Fig. 8 shows the increase in efficiency in the use of the pipeline if multiple streams are used. There is clearly a possibility of dramatic improvement in system performance if this type of system can be implemented.

The University computing service is now provided on a CDC 7600 and an ICL 1906A computer, so that we will not be guaranteed the same interaction with users on MU5 as we were with previous systems. There will be, however, a limited (six hours per day) service offered on MU5, and it is hoped that this will provide sufficient interaction with users.

As MU5 is a research machine it has several design features and a considerable amount of extra equipment to permit the detailed monitoring of all aspects of its operation. The monitor will permit the counting of events at up to once every 40 n sec. These counters can be read by the system so that the results may be accumulated inside the file store.

On the Atlas it was virtually impossible to judge the effect of variation of page size. This is an important area of design and the MU5 is made so that page sizes can be varied, in powers of two between 16 words and 64K words. Each segment of virtual space may have its own page size and this can be chosen to reflect the contents of the segment and the mode and pattern of use.

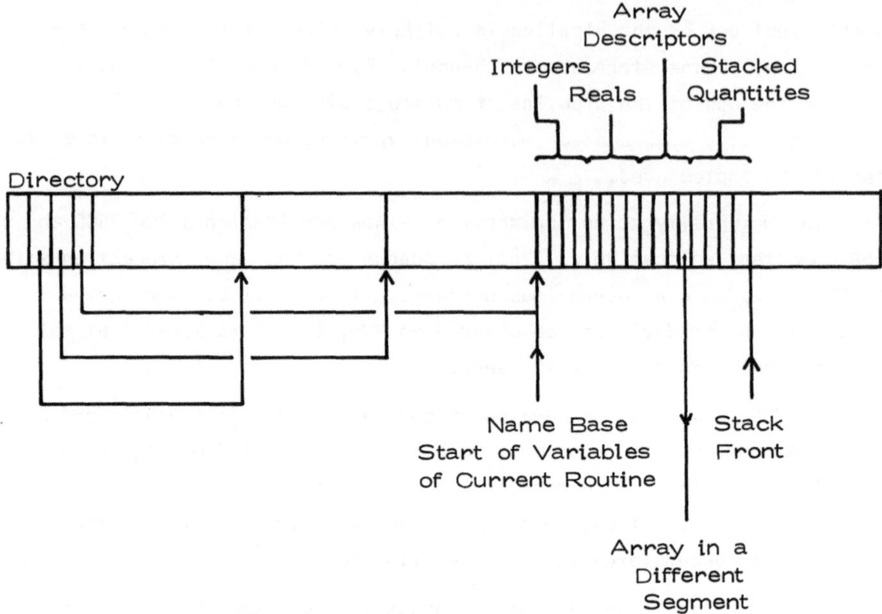

Fig. 1. NAME SEGMENT ORGANISATION

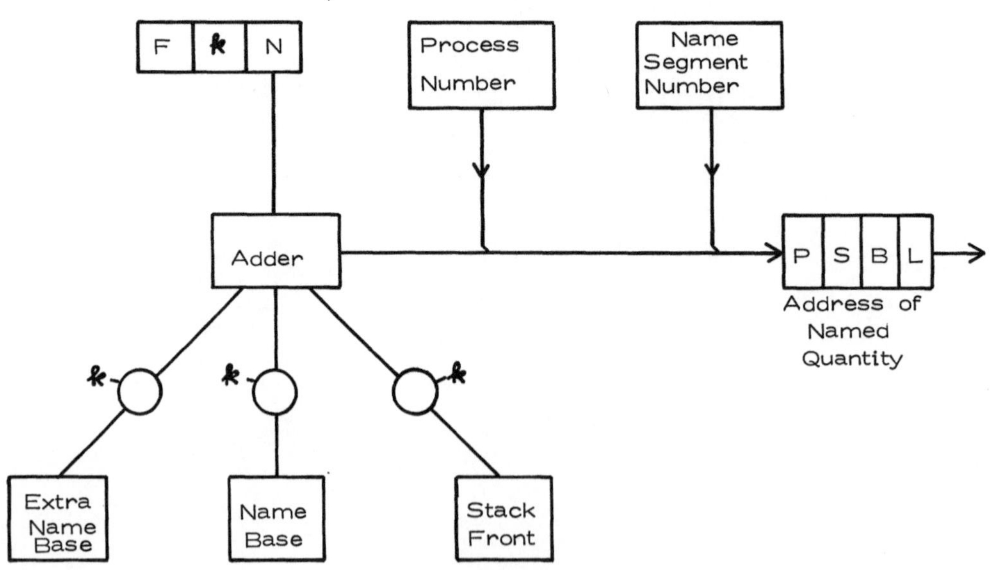

Fig. 2. ADDRESS DEVELOPMENT (NAMES)

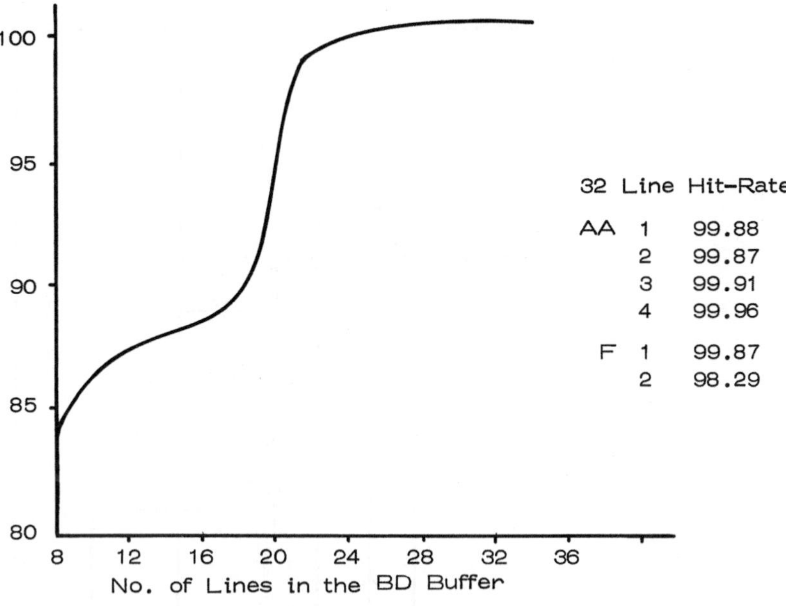

Fig. 3. NAME STORE HIT-RATES

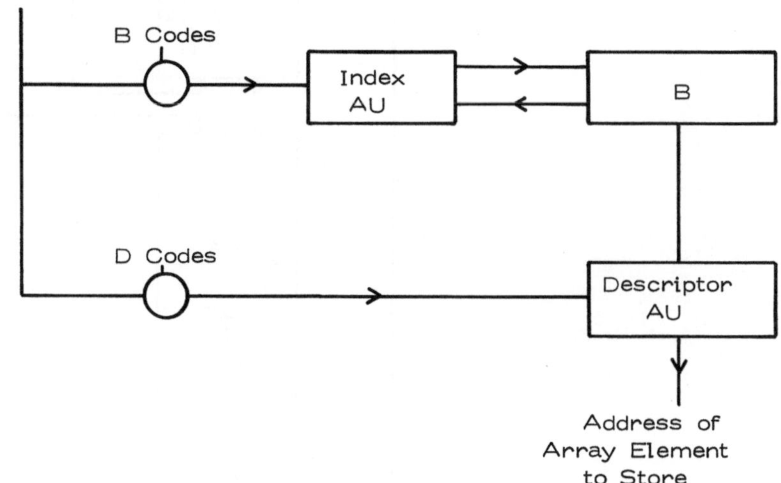

Fig. 4. ADDRESS DEVELOPMENT (ARRAY ELEMENTS)

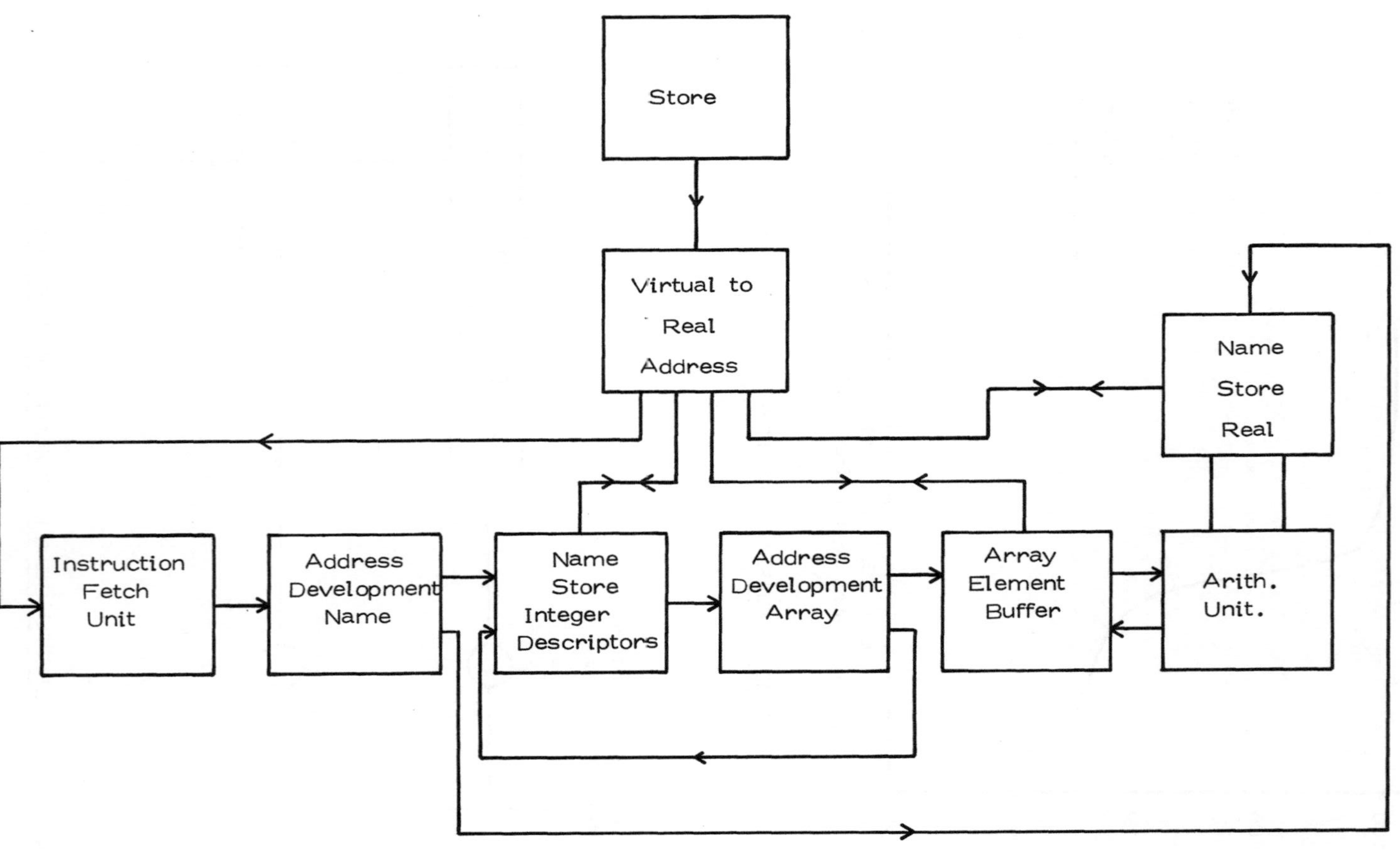

Fig. 5. BLOCK DIAGRAM OF MU5 CENTRAL PROCESSOR

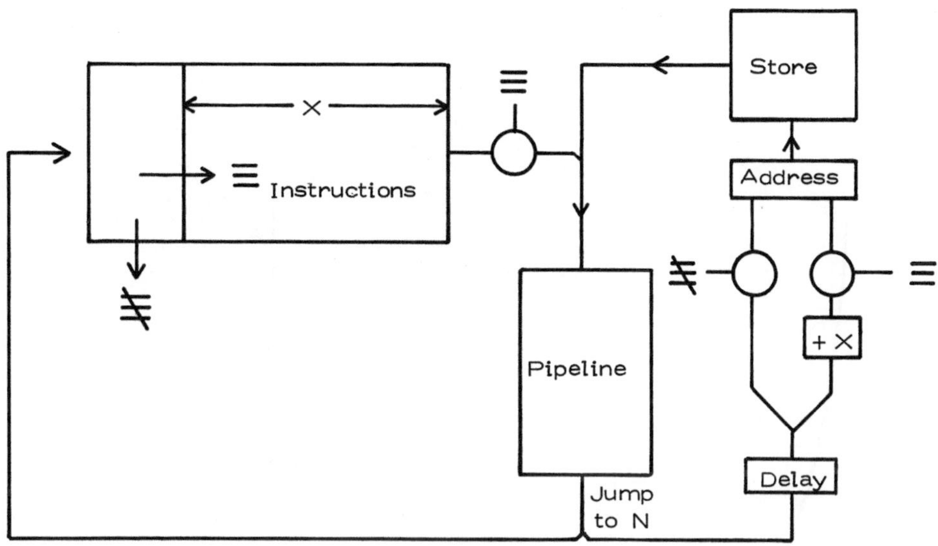

Fig. 6. SYSTEM 1 - ASSOCIATIVELY ADDRESSED BUFFER

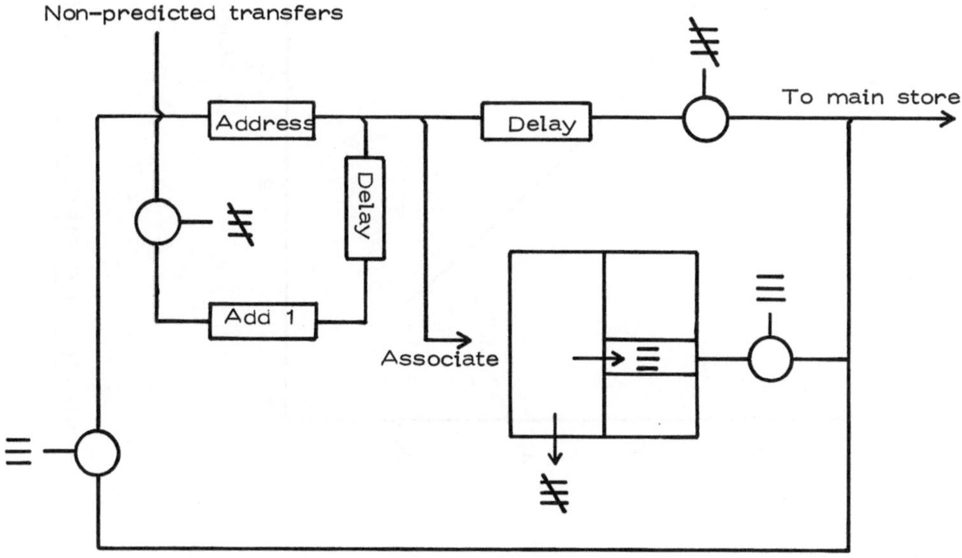

Fig. 7. PROPOSED EARLY CALL SYSTEM

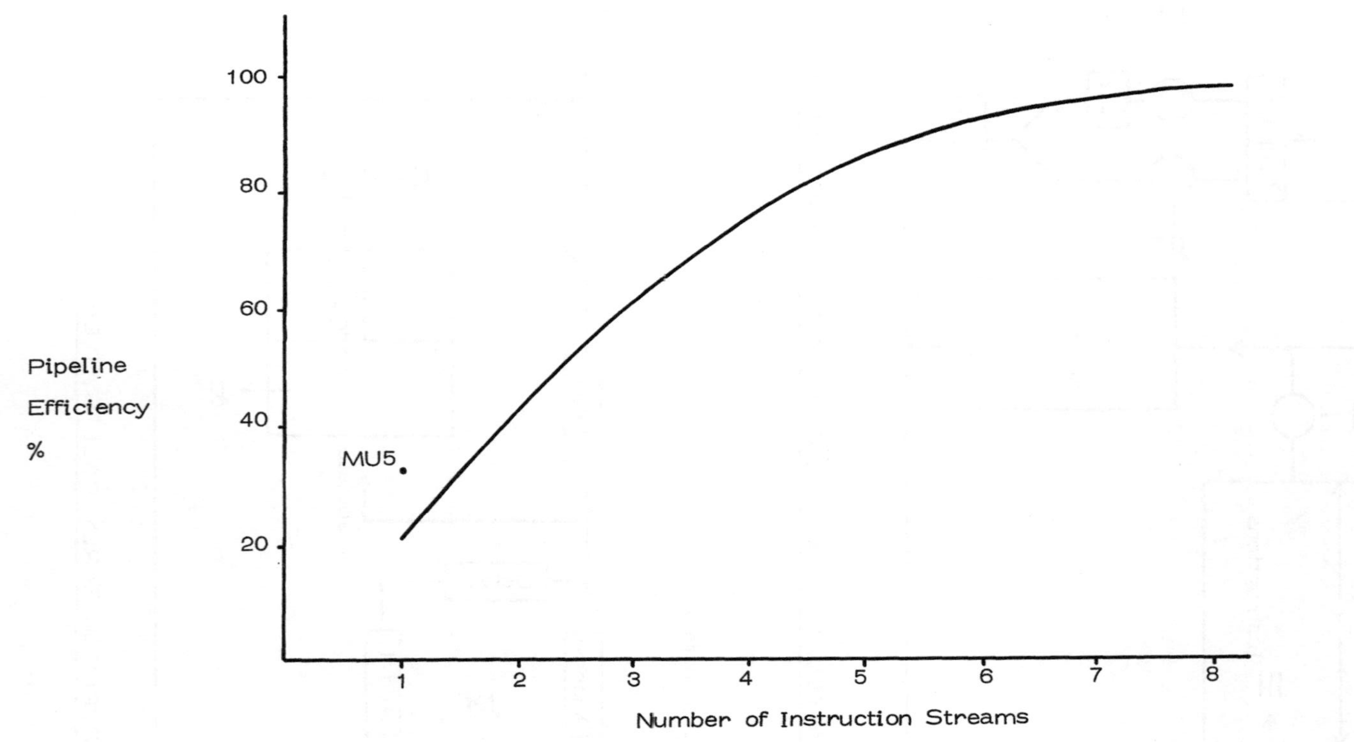

Fig. 8. VARIATION OF PIPELINE EFFICIENCY

METHODEN DER SYNTAKTISCHEN ANALYSE BEI FORMALEN SPRACHEN

J.EICKEL

Das Interesse an Algorithmen zur syntaktischen Analyse bei formalen Sprachen stammt von der Konstruktion von Übersetzern für Programmiersprachen und dem Bemühen, diese Konstruktion wenigstens teilweise zu automatisieren. Inzwischen gibt es eine Fülle von sich mehr oder weniger unterscheidenden Analysemethoden, während nur wenige davon in syntaxgesteuerten (d.h. anhand der formalen Beschreibung der Syntax analysierenden) Compilern oder in (teilweise) automatisch erzeugten Compilern Verwendung gefunden haben. Dieses liegt zum größten Teil daran, daß man bei dem Auffinden von Methoden zur effizienten syntaktischen Analyse weitgehend die Erfassung einer möglichst großen Teilklasse der Klasse kontextfreier Sprachen erstrebte. Bei dem tatsächlichen Bau von Compilern zieht man es jedoch im allgemeinen vor, die syntaktische Beschreibung der Programmiersprache gegebenenfalls soweit zu ändern, daß es dafür ein zwar nur auf eine eng eingeschränkte Klasse anwendbares, aber einfaches Analyseverfahren gibt. Ferner ist die Theorie der Analysealgorithmen sehr stark auf den Fall kontextfreier Sprachen beschränkt, während man neuerdings zur syntaktischen Beschreibung von höheren Programmiersprachen wie etwa bei ALGOL 68 auch komplexere Systeme benutzt.

Ziel dieses Vortrages ist es, soweit es zeitlich möglich ist, den wesentlichen, gemeinsamen Teil, welcher hinter fast allen Analysemethoden für kontextfreie Sprachen steckt, in möglichst einfacher und auch einführender Weise aufzudecken. Damit hat man nicht nur die Möglichkeit, spezielle Algorithmen einzuordnen, sondern auch Ansätze, wie sich die Methoden auf komplexere Sprachklassen übertragen lassen. Vielleicht vermag auch der hier eingenommene Blickpunkt erkennen zu lassen, in welche Richtung weitere Bemühungen sich bewegen sollten. Tatsächlich braucht man weniger immer neuere Analysealgorithmen. Es interessiert mehr die Frage, wie man zu einer vorgegebenen formalen Sprache automatisch die ihr angepaßte und vielleicht sogar von ihr abhängige Analysemethode erkennen und dann den entsprechenden Algorithmus erzeugen kann.

Bezüglich Literatur in Zusammenhang mit Compiler-erzeugenden Systemen sei auf /FG 68/ verwiesen.

1. Grundbegriffe

Eine CHOMSKY-Grammatik ist ein Quadrupel $\Gamma = (\mathfrak{V}, \mathcal{T}, \Pi, Z)$. Hierbei sei $\mathfrak{V}$ eine endliche Menge, der "Zeichenvorrat"; $\mathcal{T} \subset \mathfrak{V}$, der "terminale Zeichenvorrat"; $\Pi \subset \mathfrak{V}^* \times \mathfrak{V}^*$ eine endliche Menge von "Produktionen" und $Z \in \mathfrak{V} \setminus \mathcal{T}$ das sogenannte Axiom. [$\mathfrak{V}^*$ bezeichne die Menge aller Zeichenreihen über $\mathfrak{V}$]

Gilt $\Pi \subset \mathfrak{V} \setminus \mathcal{T} \times \mathfrak{V}^*$, so heißt die Grammatik kontextfrei. Im folgenden betrachten wir der Einfachheit wegen nur diesen Fall.

Eine Produktion (A,b) $\quad A \in \mathfrak{V} \setminus \mathcal{T}, \quad b \in \mathfrak{V}^*$
werde wie üblich in der Form A ::= b geschrieben. b heißt die rechte und A die linke Seite der Produktion. Das endliche Produktionensystem Π erzeugt in folgenderweise eine Relation $\rightarrow \subset \mathfrak{V}^* \times \mathfrak{V}^*$:

Für $u,v \in \mathfrak{V}^*$ gilt:

$$u \rightarrow v \quad \Leftrightarrow \quad \exists\ l,r \in \mathfrak{V}^* \quad \exists\ (A::=b) \in \Pi : \quad u = l\,A\,r \quad v = l\,b\,r$$

Man sagt "v ist direkt aus u ableitbar" und " A::=b kommt in der Ableitung von u nach v vor".

$\Rightarrow$ und $\stackrel{*}{\Rightarrow}$ bezeichnen die transitive bzw. die reflexive und transitive Hülle von $\rightarrow$. Gilt also $u \Rightarrow v$ [$u \stackrel{*}{\Rightarrow} v$], so gibt es eine sogenannte Ableitung von u nach v:

$u_o, u_1, \ldots u_n; \qquad n > o \quad$ [bzw $n \geq o$]
wobei $u_o=u$, $u_n=v$ und $u_{\nu-1} \rightarrow u_\nu$ für $\nu = 1,\ldots,n$.

Man sagt A::=b kommt in der Ableitung vor, wenn die Produktion in einem Ableitungsschritt von einem $u_{\nu-1}$ nach u_ν vorkommt. Im allgemeinen hat man verschiedene Vorkommnisse ein und derselben Produktion in einer Ableitung.

Eine kontextfreie Grammatik erzeugt einen Sprachschatz $\gamma \subset \mathcal{T}^*$ in der folgenden Weise:

$$\gamma = \{ a \mid a \in \mathcal{T}^* \wedge Z \Rightarrow a \}$$

Die Elemente $a \in \gamma$ heissen Sätze, und unter einer Ableitung eines Satzes versteht man eine Ableitung von Z nach a. Das Paar (Γ, γ) einer kontextfreien Grammatik Γ mit ihrem erzeugten Sprachschatz γ heißt kontextfreie Sprache.

Neben $\longrightarrow$ betrachtet man auch die Relationen $\xrightarrow[L]{}$ bzw $\xrightarrow[R]{}$ und deren transitiven [und reflexiven] Hüllen $\overset{+}{\underset{L}{\Longrightarrow}}$, $\overset{*}{\underset{L}{\Longrightarrow}}$, $\overset{+}{\underset{R}{\Longrightarrow}}$, $\overset{*}{\underset{R}{\Longrightarrow}}$, die genau so definiert sind wie $\longrightarrow$, nur daß bei $\xrightarrow[L]{}$ $l \in \mathcal{T}^*$ und bei $\xrightarrow[R]{}$ $r \in \mathcal{T}^*$ verlangt wird. Eine Ableitung $u_o, \ldots, u_n$ mit $u_{\nu-1} \xrightarrow[L]{} u_\nu$ für $\nu = 1, \ldots, n$ heißt <u>linkskanonische Ableitung</u>, und analog wird für $\xrightarrow[R]{}$ die <u>rechtskanonische Ableitung</u> definiert. Ableitungen werden als äquivalent angesehen, wenn sie sich nur "in der Reihenfolge der Anwendung von Produktionen" unterscheiden. Ohne die bekannte exakte Definition dieses Äquivalenzbegriffes hier zu bringen, sei erwähnt, daß bei kontextfreien Sprachen in jeder Äquivalenzklasse von Ableitungen genau eine links- und eine rechtskanonische Ableitung vorkommt.

Eine Äquivalenzklasse von Ableitungen von u nach v heißt auch <u>syntaktische Struktur</u> von u nach v [bzw. von v schlechthin, wenn u = Z das Axiom ist]. Das Auffinden einer syntaktischen Struktur eines Satzes nennt man <u>syntaktische Analyse.</u> Zur Angabe der Struktur genügt es, einen kanonischen Repräsentanten anzugeben. Hat ein Satz mehrere Strukturen, so heißt er <u>mehrdeutig.</u>

Falls es nur eine Struktur von u nach v gibt oder festliegt, welche gemeint ist, so schreiben wir auch $u \underset{u}{\Longrightarrow} v$, wenn zusätzlich diese Äquivalenzklasse nur aus einem Element besteht, und reden von der <u>unitären</u> Ableitung von u nach v.

<u>2. Kontext und Zerlegung in Teilstrukturen</u>

Zu jedem Vorkommen einer Produktion A ::= b in einer Ableitung $Z = u_o, u_1, \ldots, u_n = a$ eines Satzes $a \in \mathcal{S}$ gibt es einen Linkskontext l und einen Rechtskontext r sowie eine Zerlegung von a in l_t, b_t, r_t. Dabei sind diese Größen bei vorgegebener Ableitung und vorgegebenen Vorkommen von A::= b (etwa beim Übergang von u_i zu u_{i+1} ; $i \in \{o, \ldots, n-1\}$) eindeutig festgelegt durch

$$Z \overset{*}{\Longrightarrow} l\,A\,r = u_i \longrightarrow l\,b\,r = u_{i+1} \overset{*}{\Longrightarrow} a$$

und $l \overset{*}{\Longrightarrow} l_t$, $b \overset{*}{\Longrightarrow} b_t$, $r \overset{*}{\Longrightarrow} r_t$, $a = l_t\, b_t\, r_t$.

Als Spezialfälle interessieren hierbei:

1. (reduzierter Kontext)

   $Z = u_o, \ldots, u_i = l\,A\,r,\ u_{i+1} = l\,b\,r$ ist eine unitäre Ableitung; die so eindeutig bestimmten l und r heißen der reduzierte Links- bzw. Rechtskontext (in Zeichen : l_r , r_r).

2. (terminaler Kontext)

$l = l_t \in \mathcal{T}^*$ bzw. $r = r_t \in \mathcal{T}^*$; l_t und r_t heißen der terminale Links - bzw. Rechtskontext.

In jeder zur obigen Ableitung $Z = u_o , u_1, \ldots, u_n = a$ äquivalenten Ableitung entspricht nun dem Vorkommen von A ::= b in der ursprünglichen Ableitung ein Vorkommen der gleichen Produktion mit gleicher Zerlegung von a in l_t , b_t , r_t aber i.a. verschiedenem Kontext l', r'.
l und l' stehen in der Beziehung $l_r \Rightarrow l \Rightarrow l' \Rightarrow l_t$

oder $l_r \Rightarrow l' \Rightarrow l \Rightarrow l_t$.

Analoges gilt für r_r , r, r' und r_t.

Im Zusammenahng mit dem Begriff der Struktur (d.h. einer Äquivalenzklasse von Ableitungen) von a kann man also zu dem Vorkommen der Produktion A ::= b zwar von der zugehörigen Zerlegung von a in l_t ,b_t,r_t (durch diese Zerlegung ist das "Vorkommen" definiert) und von dem zugehörigen <u>reduzierten</u> Links- und Rechtskontext, nicht aber mehr von dem zugehörigen Links- bzw. Rechtskontext reden wie bei einer einzelnen Ableitung. Stattdessen hat man die zugehörigen Äquivalenzklassen von Ableitungen von l_r nach l_t (im folgenden zugehörige Linkskontextstruktur genannt), von r_r nach r_t (Rechtskontextstruktur) und b nach b_t (Phrasenstruktur). Die zugehörige (unitäre) Ableitung von Z nach l_r A r_r (zugehöriger Sockel genannt) ist eindeutig festgelegt.

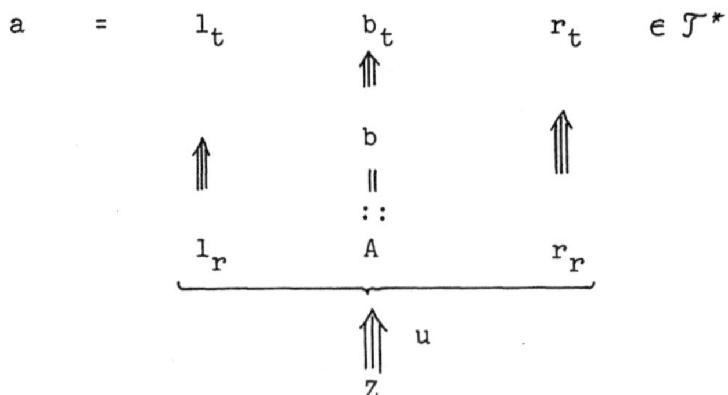

3. Analysestrategien

Das Auffinden der Struktur, die syntaktische Analyse, würde nun daraus bestehen, alle Vorkommnisse von Produktionen zusammen mit den zugehörigen Teilstrukturen (Links-, Rechts-, Phrasen-Struktur und Sockel) anzugeben. Eine solche Information ist jedoch stark redundant; genau so, wie man sich anstelle der Angabe einer vollen Äquivalenzklasse auf die Angabe eines (ausgezeichneten) Repräsentanten beschränken kann, genügt es, wenn man sich bei der syntaktischen Analyse vorher auf eine feste Analysestrategie festlegt. Diese besteht in einer Vorschrift, die die Reihenfolge, in der die einzelnen Vorkommnisse von Produktionen bei der Strukturauffindung eines Satzes bestimmt werden sollen, vollständig determiniert. Dadurch ist dann auch jeweils bei dem Auffinden eines Vorkommens einer Produktion bekannt, wie weit bis dahin die einzelnen der vier zugehörigen Teilstrukturen aufgefunden wurden.
In natürlicher Weise bieten sich als Spezialfälle für Analysestrategien die an, bei denen jeweils zu dem Vorkommen einer Produktion gewisse der Teilstrukturen bereits vollständig und die anderen noch gar nicht aufgefunden wurden. Die Links-Rechts-Analyse ist durch das jeweilige Bekanntsein der Linkskontextstruktur bei noch unbekannter Rechtskontextstruktur gekennzeichnet. Da hierdurch jedoch die Reihenfolge des Auffindens der Struktur noch nicht vollständig festgelegt ist, handelt es sich bei der Links-Rechts-Analyse noch nicht um eine Analysestrategie im obigen Sinne. Dieses ist erst der Fall, wenn auch über den Stand des Aufbaus der Phrasenstruktur und des Sockels bei dem Feststellen einer Produktionsanwendung Festsetzungen getroffen sind.
Als Grenzfälle bieten sich hierbei an:

1) bottom-up Analyse: Der Sockel ist jeweils unbekannt, während die Phrasenstruktur vollständig erkannt ist.

2) top-down (bzw. zielorientierte) Analyse: Der Sockel ist bereits aufgefunden, die Phrasenstruktur unbekannt.

Als interessante Sonderfälle von Analysestrategien haben wir also die Links- Rechts-, bottom-up-Strategie und die Links-Rechts-, top-down-Strategie. Natürlich erhält man zwei weitere, wenn man analog die entsprechenden Rechts-Links-Strategien einführt.

links-rechts bottom-up

l_t b_t

l_r b r_t

A

r_r

u

Z

links-rechts top-down

b_t r_t

b

A r_r

l_t

l_r

u

Z

Die genannten Analysestrategien fallen nicht nur als Grenzfälle in natürlicher Weise an, sondern sie ermöglichen auch eine ökonomische Buchführung gemäß dem BAUER-SAMELSON'schen Kellerprinzip über die bereits aufgefundenen Teile der Struktur. Zu Beginn des Auffindens eines Vorkommens der Produktion A::= b hat man im bottom-up-Fall die Linkskontext- und Phrasenstruktur vollständig erkannt und braucht als Information hierüber nur die Zeichenreihe l_r b bzw. nach Auffinden der Produktion $l_r A$. Zur weiteren Verarbeitung benötigt man ferner den noch nicht verarbeiteten Teil r_t der Eingabe $a = l_t\ b_t\ r_t$ (sowie Z).

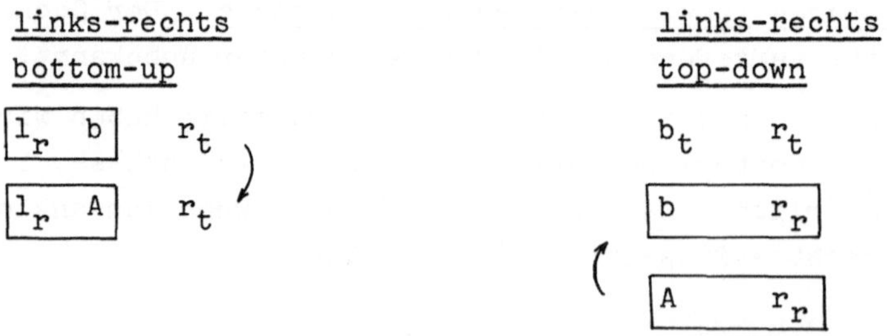

Ganz ähnlich benötigt man beim Auffinden einer Produktionsanwendung im top-down-Fall nicht die volle Information über die gefundenen Teilstrukturen, sondern nur die zugehörigen Zeichenreihen A r_r und danach br_r und als noch nicht verarbeitete Eingabe b_t r_t .

Die syntaktische Analyse läßt sich bei diesen Strategien mit sogenannten Kellerautomaten bewerkstelligen: Die in der obigen Figur eingerahmten Teile werden in einem Kellerspeicher (last in - first out) reserviert. Sie stellen im bottom-up-Fall die noch benötigte Information über den bereits verarbeiteten Teil l_t b_t der Eingabe dar (l_r b $\Rightarrow$ l_t b_t) und im top-down-Fall über den noch zu verarbeitenden Teil b_t r_t der Eingabe (A r_r $\Rightarrow$ b_t r_t). Dem Anwenden der Produktion A ::= b entspricht beim bottom-up-Kellerautomaten die Ersetzung einer(evtl.leeren) Zeichenreihe b am "oberen" Ende des Kellers durch ein Zeichen A und beim top-down-Kellerautomaten die Ersetzung eines Zeichens A am "oberen" Kellerende durch eine Zeichenreihe b.
Neben der Verwendung von Kellerautomaten sind auch andere verwandte Techniken insbesondere für den top-down Fall und zur Bewerkstelligung von noch zu erwähnenden back-up-Verfahren üblich:
Bei FLOYD - EVANS - production language / F E/ ähnlichen Verfahren wird das Produktionensystem mit einer Verweisstruktur versehen, wodurch eine ökonomische Übersicht über den bereits analysierten Teil erzielt wird. Bei der Technik, den Produktionen Prozeduren und dem Vorkommen von Produktionen in einer Struktur Prozeduraufrufe zuzuordnen, steckt eine keller-artige Analyse verkappt in der Verarbeitung der rekursiven Prozeduraufrufe.
Außer den hier betrachteten Grenzfällen von Analysestrategien sind noch beliebige andere denkbar. In der Literatur findet sich beispielsweise als Variante die left-corner-Strategie /R L/ , welche automatentheoretisch gesehen zu einem Mischfall zwischen top-down- und bottom-up Automaten führt. Sie ist dadurch gekennzeichnet, daß beim Auffinden des Vorkommens einer Prozedur A ::= b (mit b = B b') die Linkskontextstruktur und genau der Teil der Phrasenstruktur, der zu dem ersten Element B (left corner) der rechten Seite b gehört, bereits bekannt sind. Zusätzlich ist der Sockel soweit gefunden, wie das mit den beiden anderen Forderungen verträglich ist.

4. Sprachabhängige Analysestrategien

Bei den bisher angeführten Analysestrategien wird die Reihenfolge des Auffindens von Produktionsanwendungen nach deren Lage in der Struktur des Satzes festgelegt. Daneben besteht aber auch noch die Möglichkeit der sprachabhängigen Strategie und Mischfällen wie links-rechts-orientierter, sprachabhängiger Strategie. Die Sprachabhängigkeit kann darin bestehen, daß das Produktionensystem eine Ordnungsstruktur trägt, welche in die Analysestrategie eingeht (MARKOV-Algorithmen, FLOYD-EVANS production language /FE/). Verwandt damit ist die Möglichkeit, daß man verschiedene Arten von Produktionen (etwa kritische und unkritische) unterscheidet und diese Arten in die Analysestrategie eingehen läßt. So werden in /EP/ die Produktionen als unkritisch angesehen, die bei der bottom-up Analyse bei Auffindung nie in Sackgassen führen können, und die Analysestrategie wird so festgelegt, daß sowohl der Linkskontext als auch der Rechtskontext bei einer Produktionsanwendung soweit reduziert ist, wie das mit Hilfe von unkritischen Produktionen möglich ist. Während die zuletzt erwähnten Analysestrategien i.a. komplexere automatentheoretische Hilfsmittel zur Durchführung der syntaktischen Analyse bedingen, haben sie den großen Vorteil, Sprachen effizient analysieren zu können, die mit bottom-up- oder top-down-Kellerautomaten nur sehr uneffizient oder aber mit zu großer Übergangsmatrix analysierbar sind. Allerdings ist das Problem, zu einer beliebigen formalen Sprache einer bestimmten Klasse eine optimale evtl. sprachabhängige Analysestrategie zu finden, nach der die Sprache sich effizient analysieren läßt, nahezu unerforscht.

5. Sackgassenfreie syntaktische Analyse

Im folgenden soll auf die im letzten Abschnitt angesprochene Effizienz von Analyseverfahren eingegangen werden. Grob gesprochen besteht die syntaktische Analyse in der Aufgabe, zu einem Satz aus den Produktionen als den lokalen Bausteinen die Struktur des Satzes zusammenzufügen. Bei diesem Zusammenfügen kann man dadurch in Sackgassen geraten, daß man durch zu kurzsichtiges Arbeiten Pseudo-Strukturteile zusammenfügt, die gar nicht zur Lösung beitragen.

Ein Analyseverfahren kann dann so angelegt sein, daß bei der syntaktischen Analyse jeweils mehr oder weniger spät das Aufbauen von Pseudostrukturen erkannt und wieder rückgängig gemacht wird (back-up). Solche Verfahren sind zu verwerfen, da sie zu zeitraubend sind. Man versucht stattdessen, den Aufbau von Pseudostrukturen (auch häufig "das Eindringen in Sackgassen" genannt) durch Betrachten der zugehörigen Teilstrukturen bei der Anwendung einer Produktion vollständig zu vermeiden.

Bei dieser sackgassenfreien Analysemethode (no back-up) hat man zunächst zu jeder Produktion Bedingungen zu generieren, deren Beachtung dann bei der Anwendung von Produktionen während der syntaktischen Analyse das Eindringen in Sackgassen verhindert. Solche Bedingungen bestehen in der Angabe charakteristischer Teile der zugehörigen, umgebenden Teilstrukturen (in der Regel sind das nur Zeichenreihen, "Kontexte" genannt) und/oder in der Angabe der Reihenfolge, in der Produktionen anzuwenden sind. Dabei läßt sich der letzte Fall begrifflich unter den ersten subsumieren.
Bei der sackgassenfreien Analyse hat man also zwei Phasen:

1. Die generative Phase, in der die Bedingungen zu den einzelnen Produktionen erzeugt werden. Diese Phase kann als Transformation der ursprünglichen syntaktischen Beschreibung in eine sackgassenfreie Beschreibung interpretiert werden.
2. Die eigentliche syntaktische (nun sackgassenfreie) Analyse von Sätzen anhand der in der generativen Phase erzeugten syntaktischen Beschreibung.

Die wesentliche Aufgabe bei sackgassenfreien Analyseverfahren besteht darin, einen Algorithmus zur Durchführung der 1. Phase zu finden. Solche Algorithmen funktionieren in der Regel nur für eine Teilklasse der kontextfreien Sprachen. In der Praxis könnte man diesen Nachteil der sackgassenfreien Analyse dadurch beheben, daß man kontextfreie Sprachen, für die man in der ersten Phase noch keine vollständig sackgassenfreie, syntaktische Beschreibung gefunden hat, nur in den noch nicht geklärten Situationen back-up-mäßig analysiert. Dabei könnte ein erneutes back-up bei der gleichen Situation vermieden werden, indem man vorübergehend die 1. Phase in geeigneter Weise wieder anstößt, bis die syntaktische Beschreibung auch für diesen Fall sackgassenfrei ist.

Zwischen back-up und sackgassenfreien Analyseverfahren finden noch sogenannte "partielle back-up Verfahren" Verwendung. Diese bestehen darin, daß man einfache Bedingungen für das Produktionensystem findet, bei deren Erfülltsein man alle Sätze der Sprache mit einem vereinfachten back-up Verfahren analysieren kann. (siehe auch /Kn 71/).

6. Konstruktion von Kontextbedingungen-Abhängigkeit von der Analysestrategie

Ein Transformationsalgorithmus als 1. Phase eines sackgassenfreien Analysealgorithmus hängt von der Analysestrategie ab. Eine Links-Rechts-bottom-up Strategie erzeugt zu einem Satz a eine rechtskanonische

Ableitung

$u_o = Z,\ u_1,\ \ldots,\ u_n = a \qquad (u_{\nu-1} \underset{R}{\rightarrow} u_\nu)$

und zwar in der umgekehrten Reihenfolge $u_n, \ldots, u_o$.

Man kann genau dann in Sackgassen geraten, wenn es eine "rechtskanonische Satzform" u (d.h. es gilt $Z \underset{R}{\Rrightarrow} u \underset{R}{\Rrightarrow} a \in \mathcal{T}^*$) und eine nicht-rechtskanonische Satzform v mit $v \underset{R}{\rightarrow} u$ gibt (es gilt also nicht $Z \underset{R}{\Rrightarrow} v$). Kommt in einer Satzform u die rechte Seite b einer Produktion $A::= b$ vor ($u=l_r\, b\, r_t,\ r_t \in \mathcal{T}^*$; vgl. Abschnitt 3), so darf man nur dann zu $v=l_r A\, r_t$ übergehen, wenn es ein $r_r \in \mathcal{V}^*$ gibt mit $r_r \Rrightarrow r_t$ und $Z \underset{u}{\Rrightarrow} l_r\, A\, r_r$. (Äquivalent hierzu ist die Bedingung $Z \underset{R}{\Rrightarrow} l_r\, A\, r_t$). Andernfalls hat man mit dem Anwenden von $A::=b$ begonnen, eine Pseudostruktion aufzubauen.

Somit ist bei Links-Rechts-bottom-up Verfahren zur Entscheidung, wann eine Produktion $A::=b$ sackgassenfrei anwendbar ist, die <u>"Kontextklasse"</u>

$$\mathfrak{K}_{A::=b} := \{(l_r\, b,\, r_t) \mid l_r b \in \mathcal{V}^*,\ r_t \in \mathcal{T}^*,\ Z \underset{R}{\Rrightarrow} l_r A r_t\}$$

von Interesse. Bei einem zugehörigen Kellerautomaten darf das Ende b des Kellerinhaltes lb durch A ersetzt werden, falls bei noch nicht verarbeitetem Eingabeteil r $(lb, r) \in \mathfrak{K}_{A::=b}$ gilt.

In Abschnitt 3. war noch nicht der shift-Fall beim Kellerautomaten erwähnt worden, bei dem im Gegensatz zum Reduktionsfall nicht eine Zeichenreihe b durch ein Zeichen A ersetzt wird, sondern bei dem das nächste Eingabezeichen B oben in den Keller eingetragen wird. Die zugehörige Kontextklasse $\mathfrak{K}_{shift}$ ist aus der folgenden Figur ersichtlich:

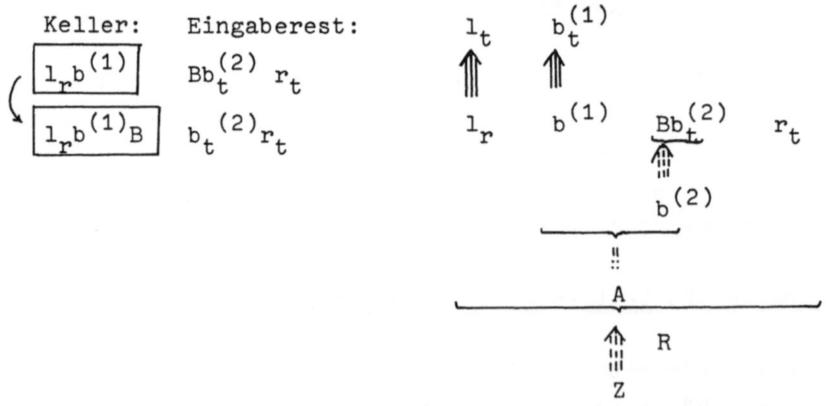

Keller:	Eingaberest:
$l_r b^{(1)}$	$Bb_t^{(2)}\ r_t$
$l_r b^{(1)} B$	$b_t^{(2)} r_t$

$l_t \quad b_t^{(1)}$

$\Uparrow \quad \Uparrow$

$l_r \quad b^{(1)} \quad Bb_t^{(2)} \quad r_t$

$b^{(2)}$

A

R

Z

$$\mathcal{K}_{shift} := \{(l_r b^{(1)}, Bb_t^{(2)} r_t) \mid l_r b^{(1)} \in \mathcal{V}^*, B \in \mathcal{T}, b_t^{(2)} r_t \in \mathcal{T}^*, \exists (A::=b) \in \Pi : b = b^{(1)} b^{(2)}, b^{(2)} \Rightarrow Bb_t^{(2)}, Z \underset{R}{\Rightarrow} l_r A r_t\}$$

Sind die zu den einzelnen Produktionen gehörenden Kontextklassen $\mathcal{K}_{A::=b}$, $(A::=b) \in \Pi$, und die Kontextklasse $\mathcal{K}_{shift}$ paarweise disjunkt, so ist die Grammatik eindeutig, d.h. jeder Satz hat nur eine Struktur. Ferner wäre die syntaktische Analyse anhand der Kontextklassen sackgassenfrei durchführbar. Aus praktischen Gründen ist jedoch die Angabe der Kontextklassen i.a. keine Lösung der Aufgabe, die syntaktische Beschreibung in eine sackgassenfreie Form zu transformieren; nämlich dann nicht, wenn die Kontextklassen nicht in einfacher Weise angebbar sind und wenn sich die Frage nach leerem Durchschnitt nicht effektiv lösen läßt. In der Tat ist ja das allgemeine Mehrdeutigkeitsproblem unlösbar und somit auch das Problem, einen Algorithmus anzugeben, der für beliebige kontextfreie Sprachen feststellt, ob ihre Kontextklassen paarweise disjunkt sind.

Bei der Konstruktion sackgassenfreier Analysealgorithmen versucht man nun Obermengen

$$\mathcal{O}_{shift}, \mathcal{O}_{A::=b} \qquad (A::=b) \in \Pi$$

zu den Kontextklassen

$$\mathcal{K}_{shift}, \mathcal{K}_{A::=b} \qquad (A::=b) \in \Pi$$

zu finden, derart daß die Obermengen einfach angebbar sind und sich in effektiv durchführbarer Weise als leer erweisen. Hier liegt der Grund dafür, daß ein derartiger Analysealgorithmus nur für eine Teilklasse von kontextfreien Sprachen funktioniert.

KNUTH erkannte, daß die Mengen

$$\mathcal{K}_{A::=b,r} := \{ l \mid \exists r' \in \mathcal{T}^* (l, rr') \in \mathcal{K}_{A::=b}\} \text{ für festes } (A::=b) \in \Pi$$

und $r \in \mathcal{T}^*$ und die analogen Mengen für den shift-Fall regulär und damit im obigen Sinne brauchbar sind. Falls sich ein System von paarweise disjunkten Obermengen

$$\mathcal{O}_{A::=b} := \bigcup_{r \in \mathcal{R}} (\mathcal{K}_{A::=b,r} \times \{r\} \mathcal{T}^*) \supset \mathcal{K}_{A::=b}$$

(und ein analoges $\mathcal{O}_{shift}$) angeben lassen, wobei $\mathcal{R}$ jeweils eine endliche Menge von Zeichenreihen der maximalen Länge k ist, so haben wir den Fall der <u>LR(k)Grammatik</u> vorliegen /Kn 65/. Hierbei ist jeweils aus den maximal k nächsten Zeichen der noch zu verarbeitenden Zeichenreihe anhand der regulären

Mengen $\mathcal{O}_{A::=b}$ eine sackgassenfreie Analyse ermöglicht.

In speziellen Fällen lassen sich auch noch die Mengen $\mathcal{K}_{A::=b,r} \times \{r\}\mathcal{T}^*$ (analog $\mathcal{K}_{shift} \times \{r\}\mathcal{T}^*$) in paarweise disjunkte Obermengen der Form

$$\mathcal{O}_{A::=b,r} = \bigcup_{l \in \mathcal{L}} (\mathcal{V}^*\{l\} \times \{r\}\mathcal{T}^*)$$

mit endlichem $\mathcal{L}$ einbetten. Damit kann man durch Betrachten der maximal k nächsten Eingabezeichen und der oberen Kellerzeichen bis zu einer maximalen Länge sackgassenfrei analysieren. Dieses ist der bekannte Fall der bounded-context Grammatiken /Fl 64/, welche zwar einfacher handhabbar sind, dafür aber eine eingeschränktere Klasse darstellen. So wie die bounded-context Grammatiken historisch älter als die LR(k)-Grammatiken sind, kannte man vor ihnen Spezialfälle als besser handhabbare Verfahren, die jedoch einer zu engen Sprachklasse entsprachen.

Für die Links-Rechts-top-down Analysestrategie hat man eine andere Art von Sackgassenfreiheit: Wenn $Ar_r \underset{L}{\Rightarrow} b_t\ r_t$ gilt, darf man A nur durch b ersetzen, falls $(A::=b) \in \Pi$ und auch noch $br_r \underset{L}{\Rightarrow} b_t\ r_t$ gilt. Im übrigen lassen sich analoge Betrachtungen zu denen im bottom-up Fall anstellen. Als Analogen zu den LR(k) Grammatiken hat man die LL(k) Grammatiken /Kn 71/. Hier geht es jedoch weniger um einen Vergleich dieser Methoden; es sollen vielmehr die wesentlichen Schritte bei dem Generatorteil (1.Phase) eines sackgassenfreien Analyseverfahrens angegeben werden:

1. In Abhängigkeit von der Analysestrategie werden Kontextklassen definiert.
2. Anstelle der entsprechenden Kontextklassen werden einfacher handhabbare Obermengen effektiv konstruiert.
3. Während der Konstruktion werden Prüfungen auf leeren Durchschnitt durchgeführt. Als sehr interessantes Nebenergebnis des Generator-Laufs ergeben sich dabei Aufdeckungen von Mehrdeutigkeiten der Grammatik, die in speziellen Fällen zu einer vollständigen Übersicht über die Mehrdeutigkeiten einer Grammatik führen können.

Bei der Konstruktion der Obermengen tastet man sich iterativ über immer kleinere Obermengen an die Kontextklassen heran, soweit das notwendig ist. Der Generatorteil wird damit zu einem iterativen Verfahren, das eine immer sackgassenfreiere, aber umfangreichere Beschreibung der Syntax liefert.

Zur technischen Durchführung dieser Schritte sei etwa auf /L 70/, /Kn 71/, /EP/,/Ea/, /Re/, /Ba/, /Kor/ verwiesen.
Ziel des Generatorteils ist es, nicht nur Bedingungen etwa in Form von Obermengen von Kontextklassen zu finden, welche eine sackgassenfreie Analyse ermöglichen. Auch die Anzahl dieser Bedingungen soll möglichst gering und sie selbst in einer regelartigen Schreibweise und automatentheoretisch einfach handhabbaren Weise abgefaßt sein. Da nun diese Anzahl wesentlich von der gewählten Analysestrategie abhängt, ist der übliche Weg, erst die Analysestrategie festzulegen und dann den zugehörigen Generatorteil zu konstruieren, bequem, aber eigentlich falsch. In Wirklichkeit hat man das Problem, zu einer vorgegebenen Sprache eine solche Analysestrategie zu finden, daß man zu dieser Strategie eine möglichst geringe Anzahl einfacher, sackgassenfrei-machender Bedingungen findet. Dabei muß es erlaubt sein, Obervoraussetzungen an die Analysestrategien zu machen, wie sie sich etwa aus der Art der Verknüpfung der Semantik- an die Syntaxbeschreibung oder aus rein automatentheoretischen Gründen ergeben.

7. Nachbarschaft und Präzedenzen

In den Algorithmen zur Konstruktion von einfachen Obermengen für Kontextklassen steckt in irgendeiner Form das Problem, die Nachbarschaftsrelationen $\sim$ zu konstruieren:

$N \sim M \Leftrightarrow_{Df}$ NM kann als Zeichenreihe in einer Satzform vorkommen

Hierzu definiert man die Relationen α, ω sowie deren transitiven Hüllen α^+, ω^+ und transitiven und reflexiven Hüllen α^*, ω^* sowie die Relation $\doteq$.

$$N \,\alpha\, M \Leftrightarrow_{Df} \exists\, v \in \mathfrak{V}^* \quad (M::=Nv) \in \Pi$$

$$N \,\omega\, M \Leftrightarrow_{Df} \exists\, u \in \mathfrak{V}^* \quad (M::=uN) \in \Pi$$

$$N \doteq M \Leftrightarrow_{Df} \exists\, O \in \mathfrak{V}\setminus\mathfrak{T} \quad \exists v_1, v_2 \in \mathfrak{V}^* : \quad (O::= v_1 NM\, v_2) \in \Pi$$

Mit Hilfe des Relationenprodukts und der Inversen $(\quad)^{-1}$ einer Relation läßt sich dann $\sim$ bei reduzierten Grammatiken folgendermaßen angeben:

$$\begin{aligned} \sim \; &= \omega^* \doteq (\alpha^*)^{-1} \\ &= \doteq \;\cup\; (\omega^+ \doteq) \;\cup\; (\doteq(\alpha^+)^{-1}) \\ &\qquad\qquad\qquad\;\cup\; (\omega^+ \doteq (\alpha^+)^{-1}) \end{aligned}$$

Häufig benutzt man die in der zweiten Gleichung gegebene Überdeckung in Form von Präzedenzrelationen, etwa $\gtrdot \; := \; \omega^{+} \doteq \; \cup \; \omega^{+} \; \doteq (\alpha^{+})^{-1}$

$\lessdot \; := \; \doteq (\alpha^{+})^{-1}$

und $\doteq$

Mit dieser feineren Differenzierung läßt sich neben der möglichen Nachbarschaft auch noch die Art, in der die Teilstrukturen zueinanderstehen können, erkennen. In der Literatur gibt es viele Varianten zu den Präzedenzmethoden (siehe etwa /WW/, /IM/, /ADU/,/Zi/), die alle mit dem bisher Gesagten in Verbindung gebracht werden können.

8. Syntaktische Analyse anhand spezieller Zeichen

Zum Abschluß soll hier nur noch eine wichtige Verallgemeinerung der Relation $\sim$ angegeben werden. Schon bei den Operator-Präzedenz-Grammatiken von FLOYD /Fl 63/ wird darauf verzichtet, alle Zeichen zur syntaktischen Analyse heranzuziehen. Sei $\mathcal{J}$ die Teilmenge von Zeichen, die allein als wesentlich für die syntaktische Analyse erkannt seien. Dann interessiert anstelle von $\sim$ die Relation $\sim[\mathcal{J}]$: $N \sim[\mathcal{J}] M \Leftrightarrow_{Df} N,M \in \mathcal{J}$ und $\exists u \in (\mathcal{V} \setminus \mathcal{J})^*$:
NuM kann als Zeichenreihe in einer Satzform vorkommen.

Die Relation $\sim[\mathcal{J}]$ bekommt man genauso wie $\sim$, nur muß man jetzt α, ω und $\doteq$ durch die folgenden Relationen $\alpha[\mathcal{J}]$, $\omega[\mathcal{J}]$ und $\doteq[\mathcal{J}]$ ersetzen:
Für $N,M \in \mathcal{V}$ gelte:

$$N \; \alpha[\mathcal{J}] \; M \Leftrightarrow_{Df} \exists u \in (\mathcal{V} \setminus \mathcal{J})^* \quad \exists v \in \mathcal{V}^* : (M ::= u\, Nv) \in \Pi$$

$$N \; \omega[\mathcal{J}] \; M \Leftrightarrow_{Df} \exists u \in \mathcal{V}^* \quad \exists v \in (\mathcal{V} \setminus \mathcal{J})^* : (M ::= uNv) \in \Pi$$

$$N \doteq[\mathcal{J}] \; M \Leftrightarrow_{Df} \exists u \in (\mathcal{V} \setminus \mathcal{J})^* \quad \exists v_1, v_2 \in \mathcal{V}^* \quad \exists O \in \mathcal{V} \setminus \mathcal{T} : \quad (O ::= v_1 NuMv_2) \in \Pi$$

Für reduzierte Grammatiken gilt:

$$\sim[\mathcal{J}] = (\omega[\mathcal{J}] \;)^* \doteq[\mathcal{J}] \quad (\alpha[\mathcal{J}]^* \;)^{-1} \cap \quad (\mathcal{J} \times \mathcal{J})$$

Durch Verwendung von einer Teilmenge $\mathcal{J}$ von Zeichen zur syntaktischen Analyse kommt man häufig mit weniger und einfacheren Kontextbedingungen aus. Beispielsweise braucht man bei der syntaktischen Analyse arithmetischer Ausdrücke in ALGOL60 nur die Operatoren +, $\times$, -, / und Klammern (,), nicht dagegen die Begriffe <Variable> sowie die höheren syntaktischen Begriffe <Primary> , <Factor>, <Term> und <arithmetischer Ausdruck> . Allerdings erhält man nur eine Grobanalyse: Semantisch ohnehin irrelevante Teilstrukturen wie

<Variable> $\rightarrow$ <Primary> $\rightarrow$ <Factor>

fallen bei der Analyse nicht an.

Es dürfte allgemein von Interesse sein, einer Grammatik die richtige Teilmenge $\mathcal{J} \subset \mathcal{V}$ ansehen zu können, mit der man die syntaktische Analyse durchführen oder in einfach zu lösende oder nicht weiter interessierende Teilaufgaben zerlegen kann. Die Konstruktion von Kontextklassen bzw. einfacher Obermengen davon führt zu Bedingungen, die sich formal ähnlich wie Produktionen der Random Context Languages von VAN DER WALT /Wa/ schreiben lassen. Bei geeigneter Wahl von $\mathcal{J}$ erhält man i.a. sehr wenig umfangreiche, sackgassenfreie Syntaxbeschreibungen.

9. Syntaxalgorithmen für komplexere Grammatiken

Eine Übertragung der hier angestellten Betrachtungen und auch die Konstruktion von Algorithmen, welche eine syntaktische Beschreibung in eine sackgassenfreie transformieren, ist für den Fall von uneingeschränkten CHOMSKY-Grammatiken leicht möglich. (Siehe /EP/, /L 69/). Die CHOMSKY-0 Grammatiken sind allerdings zur Beschreibung der Syntax von Programmiersprachen weniger geeignet als WIJNGAARDEN-Grammatiken, Affix-Grammatiken /Kos/ oder indizierte CHOMSKY-Grammatiken.
Man kann heute noch nicht absehen, welche Arten von komplexeren Systemen zur Syntax-bzw. Syntax-Semantik-Beschreibung von Interesse sein werden.

Um nicht für jeden neuen Typ eigene Analysealgorithmen erfinden zu müssen (wie etwa in /Cr/ für Affix-Grammatiken), wäre es nützlich, eine allgemeine Theorie der Konstruktion von Analysealgorithmen zu haben, so daß bei Einführung neuer Systeme die Hauptteile direkt übertragen werden und nur technische Details echt neu geklärt werden müssen.
Anders ausgedrückt sollte man in einem vorhandenen Programm zur Konstruktion von Analysealgorithmen bzw. von kontextuellen Bedingungen nur Unterprogramme ändern müssen. Einen Ansatz hierzu sollte dieser Vortrag liefern.

Literatur

/ADU/ AHO, A.V. DENNING, P.J. ULMAN, J.D.: Weak and mixed strategy precedence parsing. Journal ACM 19.2. (April 1972), 225-243

/Ba/ BACKES, S.: Top-down syntax analysis and FLOYD-EVANS produkction language. Proc. IFIP Congress 1971 North Holland Pub.Co., 504-508

/Cr/ CROWE, D.: Generating parsers for affix grammars.
Comm. ACM 15.8. (August 1972) 728-734

/Ea/ EARLEY, J.: An efficient context-free parsing algorithm
Comm. ACM 13.2. (Feb. 1970) 94-102

/EP/ EICKEL, J. PAUL, M.: The parsing and ambiguity problem for COMSKY languages
in: formal language description languages for computer programming (STEEL ed.) North Holland Pub.Co., Amsterdam (1966) 52-75

/FE/ FLOYD, R.W.: A descriptive language for symbol manipulation.
Journal ACM 8 (Okt. 1961), 579-584
EVANS, A.: An ALGOL 60 compiler
Ann. R. 4 (1964), 87-124
EVANS, A.: Syntax analysis by a production language
Carnegie Mellon U., Pittsburgh 1965

/FG 68/ FELDMAN, J. GRIES, D.: Translator writing systems
Comm. ACM 11.2. (Febr. 68), 77-113
GRIES, D.: Compiler construction for digital computers
John Wiley & Sons, New York 1971

/Fl 63/ FLOYD, R.W.: Syntactic analysis and operator precedence
Journal ACM 10.3 (July 1963), 316-333

/FL 64/ FLOYD, R.W.: Bounded context syntactic analysis
Comm. ACM 7 (1964) 62-67

/IM/ ICHBIAH, J.D., MORSE S.P.: A technique for generating almost optimal FLOYD-EVANS productions for precedence grammars.
Comm. ACM 13.8. (Aug. 1970) 501-508

/Kn 65/ KNUTH, D.E.: On the translation from left to right
Information & Control 8 (1965) 607-639

/Kn 71/ KNUTH, D.E.: Top-down syntax analysis
Acta Informatica 1. (1971) 79-110

/Kor/ KORENJAK, A.J.: A practical method for constructing
LR (k) processors.
Comm. ACM 12.11 (Nov.1969) 613-623

/Kos/ KOSTER, C.H.A.: Affix grammars. In ALGOL 68 implementation
North-Holland Pub.Co., Amsterdam (1971),p.95

/L 69/ LOECKX, J.: Mechanical construction of bounded-context
parsers for CHOMSKY 0-type languages
(Doct. th.) Philips Res.Rep. 24,Suppl.No.3(1969)

/L 70/ LOECKX, J.: An algorithm for the construction of bounded-
context parsers.
Comm. ACM 13.5. (May 1970) 297-307

/Re/ DE REMER, F.L.: Simple LR (k) grammars
Comm. ACM 14.7. (July 1971)

/RL/ ROSENKRANTZ, D.J., LEWIS II P.M.: Deterministic left
corner parsing. Proc. IEEE Symp.
Switching and Automata Theory 11 (1970)139-152

/Wa/ VAN DER WALT, A.P.J.: Random context languages
IFIP Congress 1971,North Holland Pub.Co.,66-68

/WW/ WIRTH, N., WEBER, H.: EULER- A generalization of ALGOL and
its formal definition. Part I.
Comm. ACM 9 (Jan. 1966) 13-25

/Zi/ ZIMMER, R.: Soft precedence
Inf. Proc. Letters 1 (1972) 108-110

AUTOMATEN- UND GRAPHENTHEORIE, FORMALE SPRACHEN

DAS TRANSITIONSMONOID BEI DER PARALLELKOMPOSITION VON ENDLICHEN AUTOMATEN

K.ECKER

1. EINLEITUNG

Von grundlegender Bedeutung für die algebraische Automatentheorie ist die Realisierung von Automaten durch Kaskadenprodukte. KROHN und RHODES ([4]) haben in diesem Zusammenhang sich ausführlich mit Zerlegungseigenschaften von Monoiden beschäftigt. Aussagen, die sich daraus für den spezielleren Fall der Parallelkomposition ergeben, sind allerdings von sehr allgemeinem Charakter. In der vorliegenden Arbeit werden Parallelkompositionen von Automaten betrachtet und Eigenschaften des Transitionsmonoides angegeben.

2. BEZEICHNUNGEN UND VORBEMERKUNGEN

Da wir uns hier nur mit der Eingabeseite von Automaten beschäftigen, also Ausgaben überhaupt nicht berücksichtigen, genügt es, Halbautomaten etwa im Sinne der "semiautomata" von GINZBURG ([3]) zu betrachten. Ein Halbautomat ist ein Tripel (S,X,δ) mit der Zustandsmenge S, dem Eingabealphabet X und der Zustandüberführungsfunktion $\delta\colon S\times X \to S$, die sequentiell angenommen wird: $(s,ax)\delta = ((s,a)\delta,x)\delta$ $(s\in S,\ x\in X,\ a\in X^*)$. [Abbildungen werden stets von rechts angewendet.] X^* ist das freie Monoid über X mit dem leeren Wort Λ als Einselement und der Hintereinanderschreibung als Verknüpfung. Statt Halbautomat schreiben wir abkürzend Automat.

Jedem Wort $x\in X^*$ wird eine Abbildung δ_x auf S durch $s\delta_x = (s,x)\delta$ für $x \neq \Lambda$ und $s\delta_\Lambda = s$ $(s\in S)$ zugeordnet. Die Menge $T^M = \{\delta_x : x\in X^*\}$ mit der Verknüpfung $\delta_x\delta_y = \delta_{xy}$ ist das Transitionsmonoid von M. Das Transitionsmonoid T^M ist als homomorphes Bild des freien Monoides X^* darstellbar. Ist $\mathfrak{r} \subset X^*\times X^*$ die Relation

(2.1) $(x,y)\in \mathfrak{r} \Leftrightarrow \delta_x = \delta_y$,

so ist $\mathfrak{r}$ Kongruenzrelation, und T^M ist isomorph zu $X^*/\mathfrak{r}$, in

Zeichen: $T^M \cong X^*/\kappa$, man vgl. [3].

Sei $I = \{1,\dots,n\}$. Ist $\{M_i = (S_i, X, \delta_i) : i \in I\}$ eine Menge von Automaten mit gleichem Eingabealphabet, so ist die Parallelkomposition (Parallelprodukt) $\textcircled{||}_{i\in I} M_i$ der Automat $(\times_{i\in I} S_i, X, \delta)$ mit
$((s_1,\dots,s_n),x)\delta = ((s_1,x)\delta_1,\dots,(s_n,x)\delta_n)$ für $(s_1,\dots,s_n) \in \times_{i\in I} S_i$ und $x \in X^*$ $\left[\times_{i\in I} S_i\right.$ ist das direkte Produkt von $\left.S_1,\dots,S_n\right]$.

In der vorliegenden Arbeit wird $I = \{1,2\}$ gesetzt, es werden also nur Parallelkompositionen von zwei Automaten M_1 und M_1 betrachtet. Sämtliche Ergebnisse lassen sich jedoch auf n-fache Parallelkompositionen verallgemeinern. Der Index i bedeutet von nun an stets 1 oder 2.

Zur Bezeichnung sei noch bemerkt, daß eine Funktion $f : A \longrightarrow B$ (A, B Mengen) auch als Teilmenge von $A \times B$ aufgefasst wird. Der Kern von f, $\ker f = f \circ f^{-1}$. Ist η eine Äquivalenzrelation über A und $a \in A$, dann sei a^{η} die das Element a enthaltende Äquivalenzklasse von η. Für die Äquivalenzrelation, deren Äquivalenzklassen alle einelementig sind, schreiben wir Δ_A (Diagonale von A).

3. EIGENSCHAFTEN DES TRANSITIONSMONOIDES EINES PARALLELPRODUKTES

Seien im folgenden $M_i = (S_i, X, \delta_i)$ Automaten mit gleichem Eingabealphabet X, und sei $M = M_1 \textcircled{||} M_2$ das Parallelprodukt. Für die Transitionsmonoide schreiben wir zur Vereinfachung der Notation T_i und T anstelle von T^{M_i} und T^M. Die zu M_i und M gehörigen, durch (2.1) definierten Kongruenzen auf X^* seien κ_i und κ.

In diesem Abschnitt werden einige Eigenschaften von T bzw. von κ angegeben. Das Ziel ist, mit Hilfe von T_1 und T_2 das Monoid T möglichst genau zu beschreiben. Dabei leistet die Tatsache $T \cong X^*/\kappa$ und $T_i \cong X^*/\kappa_i$ wertvolle Hilfe.

Aus der Definition der Parallelkomposition folgt sofort Lemma 3.1.

3.1 LEMMA. Sind M_1 und M_2 Automaten mit gleichem Eingabealphabet X, und ist $M = M_1 \textcircled{\shortparallel} M_2$ die Parallelkomposition, und sind $\mathfrak{r}_i$ und $\mathfrak{r}$ die durch (2.1) definierten, zu M_i und M gehörigen Kongruenzen auf X^*, so gilt: $\mathfrak{r} = \mathfrak{r}_1 \cap \mathfrak{r}_2$.

Als Folge dieses Lemmas erhält man:

3.2 KOROLLAR. Ist M_1 ein Automat mit dem Transitionsmonoid T_1, so ist das Transitionsmonoid T der Parallelkomposition $M = M_1 \textcircled{\shortparallel} M_1$ isomorph zu T_1.

Vermöge Lemma 3.1 ist T durch die Kongruenzen $\mathfrak{r}_i$ bis auf Isomorphie eindeutig festgelegt. Die dadurch gegebene Beschreibung von T hat jedoch den Nachteil einer gewissen Unanschaulichkeit, da man es doch mit der unendlichen Menge X^* und mit Kongruenzen darauf zu tun hat.

In Satz 3.3 werden wir eine durchsichtigere Beschreibung von T angeben. Von einem auf sehr einfache Weise konstruierbaren Monoid H, das subdirektes Produkt von T_1 und T_2 ist, wird die Isomorphie zu T gezeigt. Dazu betrachten wir die Teilmenge $H = \{(\delta_{1x}, \delta_{2x}) : x \in X^*\}$ von $T_1 \times T_2$. Definiert man das Produkt zweier Elemente von H so, wie in $T_1 \times T_2$ üblich, also durch $(\delta_{1x}, \delta_{2x})(\delta_{1y}, \delta_{2y}) = (\delta_{1x}\delta_{1y}, \delta_{2x}\delta_{2y})$, dann ist H ein Monoid. Außerdem ist H subdirektes Produkt von T_1 und T_2 (man vergleiche die Definition des subdirekten Produktes z.B. in [1]), denn die Abbildungen $\bar{p}_1 : (\delta_{1x}, \delta_{2y}) \longmapsto \delta_{1x}$ und $\bar{p}_2 : (\delta_{1x}, \delta_{2y}) \longmapsto \delta_{2y}$ von $T_1 \times T_2$ auf T_i sind Projektionen, und die Restriktionen p_i von $\bar{p}_i$ auf H sind surjektiv.

3.3 SATZ. Seien $M_i = (S_i, X, \delta_i)$ Automaten mit den Transitionsmonoiden T_i $(i = 1,2)$, und sei $M = M_1 \textcircled{\shortparallel} M_2$. Dann ist das Transitionsmonoid T von M isomorph zum subdirekten Produkt $H = \{(\delta_{1x}, \delta_{2x}) : x \in X^*\}$ der Monoide T_i.

Wir deuten den Beweis an: Die Abbildung $\ell : (\delta_{1x}, \delta_{2x}) \longmapsto \delta_x$ ist bijektiv und ein Epimorphismus von H auf T.

Die in Lemma 3.1 und in Satz 3.3 formulierten Beschreibungen von T haben den Nachteil, daß das Eingabealphabet X bzw. die freie Halbgruppe X^* explizite benötigt wird. Andererseits wäre es aber denkbar, daß T aus T_1 und T_2 unabhängig von der Menge X bestimmt werden kann. Aus Satz 3.3 wissen wir, daß T isomorph zu einem subdirekten Produkt von T_1 und T_2 ist. Im allgemeinen sind jedoch subdirekte Produkte nicht eindeutig. Es tritt daher die Frage auf, ob jedes subdirekte Produkt von T_1 und T_2 isomorph zum Transitionsmonoid einer Parallelkomposition geeigneter Automaten M_1 und M_2 mit $T^{M_i} \cong T_i$ ist. Ohne Schwierigkeiten lassen sich Beispiele angeben, die zeigen, daß eine eindeutige Beschreibung von T durch T_1 und T_2, die nur die abstrakte Monoid-Struktur von T_1 und T_2 benützt, nicht möglich ist. Für Automaten bedeutet das: Seien M_i und M_i' Automaten mit Eingabemengen X und X' und mit den Transitionsmonoiden T_i und T_i' $(i = 1,2)$. Die Parallelkompositionen $M = M_1 \circledR M_2$ und $M' = M_1' \circledR M_2'$ sollen die Transitionsmonoide T und T' besitzen. Ist dann $T_1 \cong T_1'$ und $T_2 \cong T_2'$, so kann daraus nicht auf $T \cong T'$ geschlossen werden.

Es kann nun gezeigt werden, daß eine genauere Charakterisierung von T durch T_1 und T_2 ohne Berücksichtigung weiterer Informationen, etwa, daß T, T_1, T_2 homomorphe Bilder des freien Monoides X^* über einem fest vorgegebenen Alphabet X sind, nicht möglich ist. Um dies deutlicher zu machen, gehen wir von endlichen abstrakten Monoiden L_1 und L_2 aus; sei L ein subdirektes Produkt von L_1 und L_2. Zu jedem derartigen L können, wenn wir ein geeignetes Alphabet X wählen, sodaß L, L_1 und L_2 homomorphe Bilder von X^* sind, Automaten M, M_1 und M_2 konstruiert werden, für die $M = M_1 \circledR M_2$ gilt, und deren Transitionsmonoide isomorph zu L, L_1 und L_2 sind. Dies wird in Satz 3.5 durchgeführt.

Bekanntlich kann zu einem Monoid stets ein Automat konstruiert werden, dessen Transitionsmonoid isomorph zum gegebenen Monoid ist. In 3.4 wird eine Konstruktion durchgeführt, die in Satz 3.5 Anwendung findet.

<u>3.4 BEMERKUNG.</u> Ist L ein Monoid, so besitzt der im folgenden konstruierte Automat ein zu L isomorphes Transitionsmonoid. Es sei

$E \subset L$ eine Erzeugendenmenge für L. Weiters sei X eine Menge, deren Kardinalzahl nicht kleiner als die Kardinalzahl von E ist. $\theta' : X \to E$ sei surjektiv. Dann ist die Abbildung

$$\theta : \Lambda \mapsto e \quad (e \text{ sei die Einheit von } L),$$

$$\theta : x_{\alpha_1} \dots x_{\alpha_n} \mapsto \theta'(x_{\alpha_1}) \dots \theta'(x_{\alpha_n}) \quad (x_{\alpha_1}, \dots, x_{\alpha_n} \in X)$$

ein Homomorphismus vom freien Monoid X^* auf L. Der zum Kern $\vartheta = \ker \theta$ korrespondierende Automat mit den Kongruenzklassen von ϑ als Zuständen und X als Eingabemenge (man vgl. [3]) hat die gewünschte Eigenschaft: Das Transitionsmonoid ist isomorph zu X^*/ϑ, und damit zu L.

<u>3.5 SATZ.</u> <u>Seien</u> L_1, L_2 <u>Monoide, und sei</u> L <u>subdirektes Produkt von</u> L_1 <u>und</u> L_2. <u>Dann gibt es Automaten</u> M_1, M_2 <u>und</u> $M = M_1 \circledR M_2$ <u>mit Transitionsmonoiden</u> T_1, T_2 <u>und</u> T, <u>für die gilt</u>: $T_1 \cong L_1$, $T_2 \cong L_2$ und $T \cong L$.

<u>Beweis.</u> L ist subdirektes Produkt von L_1 und L_2, daher gibt es Epimorphismen $q_i : L \to L_i$.

Grundlage ist das in 3.4 erwähnte Konstruktionsverfahren, das zu einem gegebenen Monoid einen Automaten mit dazu isomorphem Transitionsmonoid liefert. Sei demnach X ein Alphabet und ν eine Kongruenz auf X^* mit der Eigenschaft $L \cong X^*/\nu$. Sei $k : X^*/\nu \to L$ ein Isomorphismus. Dann ist L_i homomorphes Bild von X^*/ν; seien $g_i : X^*/\nu \to L_i$ die durch $g_i = k \circ q_i$ gegebenen Epimorphismen. Sei außerdem $\nu_i = \ker(\mathrm{nat}\,\nu \circ g_i)$ $(i = 1,2)$. Aufgrund des 1. Isomorphietheorems gibt es Isomorphismen $k_i : X^*/\nu_i \to L_i$ mit $\mathrm{nat}\,\nu_i \circ k_i = \mathrm{nat}\,\nu \circ g_i$.

Wir wählen nun Automaten M_1 und M_2 und zeigen, daß diese die gewünschten Eigenschaften besitzen. Sei $M_i = (S_i, X, \delta_i)$ der zu ν_i korrespondierende Automat, d.h.,

$$S_i = \{x^{\nu_i} : x \in X^*\} \quad \text{und} \quad (x^{\nu_i}, z)\delta_i = (xz)^{\nu_i} \quad \text{für} \quad z \in X^*.$$

Das Transitionsmonoid T_i von M_i ist isomorph zu L_i $(\cong X^*/\nu_i)$.

Zu zeigen ist: das Transitionsmonoid T von $M_1 \textcircled{||} M_2$ ist isomorph zu L. Wegen $T \cong X^*/\mathscr{V}_1 \cap \mathscr{V}_2$ (Lemma 3.1) und $L \cong X^*/\mathscr{V}$ ist $\mathscr{V} = \mathscr{V}_1 \cap \mathscr{V}_2$ zu zeigen. Ohne Schwierigkeit folgt zunächst $\mathscr{V}_i \supset \mathscr{V}$ (i = 1,2), also $\mathscr{V} \subset \mathscr{V}_1 \cap \mathscr{V}_2$:

$$\mathscr{V}_i = \ker(\mathrm{nat}\,\mathscr{V} \circ g_i) = \mathrm{nat}\,\mathscr{V} \circ g_i \circ g_i^{-1} \circ (\mathrm{nat}\,\mathscr{V})^{-1} \supset \mathrm{nat}\,\mathscr{V} \circ (\mathrm{nat}\,\mathscr{V})^{-1} = \mathscr{V}.$$

Mit $\mathrm{nat}\,\mathscr{V}_i \circ k_i = \mathrm{nat}\,\mathscr{V} \circ g_i$ sind wir nun in der Lage, $\mathscr{V} = \mathscr{V}_1 \cap \mathscr{V}_2$ zu beweisen: Wegen $\mathscr{V} \subset \mathscr{V}_i$ ist $x^{\mathscr{V}} \subset x^{\mathscr{V}_i}$. Sei $y \in x^{\mathscr{V}_1} \cap x^{\mathscr{V}_2}$; dann folgt

$$x^{\mathscr{V}} g_i = x^{\mathscr{V}_i} k_i = y^{\mathscr{V}_i} k_i = y^{\mathscr{V}} g_i \qquad (i = 1,2).$$

Aus $g_i = k \circ q_i$ und L subdirektes Produkt von L_1 und L_2 (d.h., der Durchschnitt der Kerne von q_1 und q_2 ist die Diagonale von L) erhält man $x^{\mathscr{V}} = y^{\mathscr{V}}$. Also ist $x^{\mathscr{V}_1} \cap x^{\mathscr{V}_2} \subset x^{\mathscr{V}}$, und daher ist $\mathscr{V} = \mathscr{V}_1 \cap \mathscr{V}_2$. Q.e.d.

4. ABSCHLIESSENDE BEMERKUNGEN

Bisher wurden Parallelkompositionen von Automaten und Eigenschaften des zugehörigen Transitionsmonoides betrachtet. Auf die Frage, unter welchen vernünftigen hinreichenden Bedingungen ein Automat nichttrivial parallelzerlegbar ist, wurde hier keine Antwort gegeben. Von großem praktischen Interesse sind Parallelzerlegungen von Automaten in Gruppenautomaten und kombinatorische Automaten (das sind solche, deren Transitionsmonoide kombinatorisch sind, d.h., jede Untergruppe ist einelementig).

In diesem Zusammenhang betrachten wir abschließend die Möglichkeit der isomorphen Darstellung eines Automaten M als Parallelkomposition eines Gruppenautomaten und eines kombinatorischen Automaten. Wegen Satz 3.3 ist es für die Existenz einer derartigen Darstellung notwendig, daß T^M als subdirektes Produkt einer Gruppe und eines kombinatorischen Monoides isomorph dargestellt werden kann. Wir führen zwei Klassen von Halbgruppen an, die in dieser Weise zerlegbar sind. Dazu vergleiche man [2]. Ist H eine Halbgruppe, so bezeichnen wir mit $\mathscr{E}$ die Menge der idempotenten Elemente von H und mit G_k $(k \in \mathscr{E})$

die größte Untergruppe von H, die k als Einselement besitzt.

3.6 SATZ. Ist H eine Halbgruppe und $H = \bigcup_{k \in \mathfrak{k}} G_k$, so gilt: H ist subdirekt zerlegbar in eine Gruppe und eine kombinatorische Halbgruppe genau dann, wenn es Kongruenzen $\mathfrak{a}$ und $\mathfrak{b}$ auf H gibt mit

(a) $\forall k \in \mathfrak{k} : k^{\mathfrak{a}} = \mathfrak{k}$

(b) $\forall k \in \mathfrak{k} : k^{\mathfrak{b}} = G_k$.

3.7 SATZ. Sei H Monoid mit dem Einselement e, und es gelte $k k' = k$ für alle $k, k' \in \mathfrak{k}$, $k \neq e$. Sei außerdem $G_e = \{e\}$. Dann gilt: H ist subdirekt zerlegbar in eine Gruppe und eine kombinatorische Halbgruppe.

Satz 3.7 ist speziell auf die Transitionsmonoide linearer Automaten anwendbar; ergänzend sei angemerkt, daß lineare Automaten (wieder im Sinne von Halbautomaten) stets isomorph zu Parallelprodukten nichtsingulärer und nilpotenter Automaten sind.

LITERATUR

[1] Cohn, P.M., Universal algebra. Harper & Row, LTD, London 1965.

[2] Ecker, K., Über die subdirekte Zerlegbarkeit von Halbgruppen. In Vorbereitung.

[3] Ginzburg, A., Algebraic theory of automata. Academic Press, New York 1968.

[4] Krohn, K.B. and J.L. Rhodes, Algebraic theory of machines. I. Prime decomposition theorem for finite semigroups and machines. Trans Amer. Math. Soc 116, 450 - 464 (1965).

KLASSIFIZIERUNG VON PRIMITIV-REKURSIVEN TRANSFORMATIONEN UND AUTOMATENTRANSDUKTIONEN

F.W. V.HENKE, K.WEIHRAUCH

1. Einleitung

Das Studium von subrekursiven Funktionenklassen als Teil der Theorie der berechenbaren Funktionen wird gewöhnlich in zwei Richtungen betrieben: einerseits werden subrekursive Klassen dadurch konstruiert, daß gewisse Operationen wie Komposition, Rekursion und Iteration auf eine Menge von „erzeugenden" oder Basisfunktionen wiederholt angewendet werden; Beispiele sind die Klasse der primitiv-rekursiven Funktionen und deren Teilklassen. Andererseits definiert auch jeder Automatentyp (z.B. Keller-, Stack-, endlicher Automat) eine Funktionenklasse. Mehrfach wurden bereits Funktionenklassen miteinander verglichen, die auf solche unterschiedliche Weise definiert sind (s.z.B. [KRR, RI1, MÜL]). Da aber auf die erste Weise in der Regel nur Klassen von arithmetischen Funktionen definiert werden, während Automaten auf Worten, d.h. Zeichenketten, arbeiten, können solche Vergleiche nur mit Hilfe von „Kodierungen" der natürlichen Zahlen in Worte angestellt werden. Um diese Kodierungen zu vermeiden und einen natürlichen Vergleich der Funktionenklassen zu ermöglichen, liegt es nahe, von primitiv-rekursiven Wortfunktionen, wie sie von Asser [ASS] und Eilenberg - Elgot [EIE] definiert wurden, auszugehen. Nicht zuletzt motivieren auch die verschiedensten Richtungen innerhalb der theoretischen Informatik, statt der natürlichen Zahlen Zeichenketten als Grundelemente anzusehen.

In dem vorliegenden Beitrag werden zunächst in Verallgemeinerung der entsprechenden Begriffe für arithmetische Funktionen drei Hierarchien von primitiv-rekursiven Wortfunktionen definiert: die Grzegorczyk-, die Rekursionszahl- und die Loop- Hierarchie. Ihre mengentheoretischen Beziehungen zueinander werden unter Benutzung eines Satzes über die Beschreibung von Turingmaschinen durch primitiv-rekursive Wortfunktionen angegeben. Dieser Satz führt ebenfalls zu Zusammenhängen zwischen Hierarchieklassen und Komplexitätsklassen, wodurch eine einfache Einordnung verschiedener Klassen von Automatentransduktionen ermöglicht wird. Der Rest des Beitrags ist dem Studium von Transformationen gewidmet: der Begriff „primitiv-rekursiv" wird auf Funktionen zwischen Wortmengen über verschiedenen Alphabeten verallgemeinert; analog zu den Wortfunktionen wird eine Hierarchie von Teilklassen abgeleitet. Verschiedene Beziehungen zwischen den Wortfunktionen- und Transformationenklassen werden aufgezeigt, und es wird untersucht, wieweit Kodierungen für die Einordnung von Automatentransduktionen relevant sind.

Im folgenden werden Sätze im allgemeinen ohne Beweise angegeben. Diese sowie weitere Einzelheiten finden sich in [HEN, HIW, WEI].

In diesem Beitrag bezeichnet Σ^* das freie Monoid, das von dem Alphabet $\Sigma = \{a_1,\dots,a_r\}$ erzeugt wird, und e das leere Wort. Für $w \in \Sigma^*$ bezeichnet $|w|$ die Länge von w . Für ein Tupel $(w_1,\dots,w_k)$ wird oft kurz $\tilde{w}$ geschrieben, analog $|\tilde{w}|$ für $(|w_1|,\dots,|w_k|)$. $F^{(k)}(\Sigma)$ steht für die Menge alle Funktionen $f : (\Sigma^*)^k \longrightarrow \Sigma^*$ und $F(\Sigma)$ für $\bigcup_{k \in \mathbb{N}} F^{(k)}(\Sigma)$; falls $|\Sigma| = 1$, wird Σ fortgelassen.

Ist $M \subseteq F(\Sigma)$, so ist $M^{(k)} := M \cap F^{(k)}(\Sigma)$.

2. Hierarchien primitiv-rekursiver Wortfunktionen

Die Klasse der primitiv-rekursiven Wortfunktionen wird aus Grundfunktionen durch die Operationen „Einsetzung" und „primitive Rekursion" erzeugt. Als Grundfunktionen werden bezeichnet:

(a) die k-stelligen Projektionen $\pi_j^{(k)}$ mit
$\pi_j^{(k)}(w_1,\dots,w_k) := w_j \qquad (1 \le j \le k)$.

(b) die Nullfunktionen $\omega^{(o)}$ und $\omega^{(1)}$, die definiert sind durch
$\omega^{(o)} = e$ und $\omega^{(1)}(w) = e$.

(c) für $i = 1,\dots,r$ die i-te Links- Nachfolgerfunktion
λ_i mit $\lambda_i(w) = a_i w$.

Statt der Links- Nachfolgerfunktionen könnten auch die Rechts- Nachfolgerfunktionen als Grundfunktionen genommen werden, ohne daß die Ergebnisse beeinflußt würden.

Eine Funktion $g \varepsilon F^{(m)}(\Sigma)$ entsteht durch <u>Einsetzung</u> aus $f \varepsilon F^{(k)}(\Sigma)$ und $h_1,\dots,h_k \varepsilon F^{(m)}(\Sigma)$ (Schreibweise: $g = f \circ (h_1,\dots,h_k)$) , wenn $g(\tilde{x}) = f(h_1(\tilde{x}),\dots,h_k(\tilde{x}))$. $g \varepsilon F^{(k+1)}(\Sigma)$ wird durch <u>primitive Rekursion</u> mit $f \varepsilon F^{(k)}(\Sigma)$ und $h_1,\dots,h_r \varepsilon F^{(k+2)}(\Sigma)$ gebildet $(g = \mathcal{P}(f_i(h_i)))$, wenn gilt

$$g(\tilde{x},e) = f(\tilde{x}) \quad \text{und} \quad g(\tilde{x},a_i w) = h_i(\tilde{x},w,g(\tilde{x},w)) \quad \text{für} \quad i = 1,\dots,r .$$

Gibt es zusätzlich ein $d \varepsilon F^{(k+1)}(\Sigma)$, so daß $|g(\tilde{z})| \leq |d(\tilde{z})|$ für alle $\tilde{z} \varepsilon (\Sigma^*)^{k+1}$, so ist g durch <u>beschränkte Rekursion</u> gebildet. In analoger Weise werden <u>simultane</u> und <u>beschränkte simultane Rekursion</u> definiert.

<u>DEFINITION 1</u>: Die Klasse $Pr(\Sigma)$ der primitiv-rekursiven Wortfunktionen über Σ^* ist die kleinste Teilklasse von $F(\Sigma)$, die die Grundfunktionen enthält und unter Einsetzung und primitiver Rekursion abgeschlossen ist.

<u>DEFINITION 2</u>: (a) Die Rekursionszahlklassen $R_n(\Sigma)$ sind als Teilklassen von $Pr(\Sigma)$ induktiv definiert durch:

(i) $R_o(\Sigma)$ ist die kleinste Teilklasse, die die Grundfunktionen enthält und unter Einsetzung abgeschlossen ist.

(ii) $R_{n+1}(\Sigma)$ ist die kleinste Klasse, die $R_n(\Sigma)$ enthält und unter Einsetzung und primitiver Rekursion mit Funktionen aus $R_n(\Sigma)$ abgeschlossen ist (d.h. mit $g,(h_i) \varepsilon R_n(\Sigma)$ ist auch $f = \mathcal{P}(g,(h_i)) \varepsilon R_{n+1}(\Sigma)$) .

(b) Die Loop- Klassen $L_n(\Sigma)$ sind wie die Klassen $R_n(\Sigma)$ definiert, wobei „primitive Rekursion" durch „simultane Rekursion" zu ersetzen ist.

Zur Definition der hier besonders interessierenden Teilklassen werden verallgemeinerte <u>Ackermannfunktionen</u> benötigt: Für $n \varepsilon \mathbb{N}$ sind die Funktionen $A_n \varepsilon Pr^{(2)}(\Sigma)$ definiert durch $A_o(x,y) = a_1 y$, $A_1(x,e) = x$, $A_2(x,e) = e$, $A_m(x,e) = a_1$, falls $m \geq 3$ und $A_{n+1}(x,a_i y) = A_n(x,A_{n+1}(x,y))$.

<u>DEFINITION 3</u>: $E_n(\Sigma)$ ist die kleinste Teilklasse von $Pr(\Sigma)$, die die Grundfunktionen und A_n enthält und unter Einsetzung und beschränkter Rekursion abgeschlossen ist.

Alle hier gegebenen Definitionen geben Verallgemeinerungen der entsprechenden Begriffe für arithmetische Funktionen aus [AXT, HEI, MER, RI2, SCH] .

Die bisher bekannten mengentheoretischen Beziehungen zwischen den oben definierten Klassen werden in dem folgenden Satz zusammengefaßt:

SATZ 1:

(i) Die Familien $(E_n(\Sigma))$, $(R_n(\Sigma))$ und $(L_n(\Sigma))$, bilden Hierarchien innerhalb $Pr(\Sigma)$, d.h. es gilt für alle $n \in \mathbb{N}$ $E_n(\Sigma) \neq E_{n+1}(\Sigma)$ usw.

(ii) $\bigcup_{n\in\mathbb{N}} E_n(\Sigma) = \bigcup_{n\in\mathbb{N}} R_n(\Sigma) = \bigcup_{n\in\mathbb{N}} L_n(\Sigma) = Pr(\Sigma)$.

(iii) Zwischen den Hierarchien bestehen Zusammenhänge, die in folgendem Diagramm dargestellt sind:

(*)

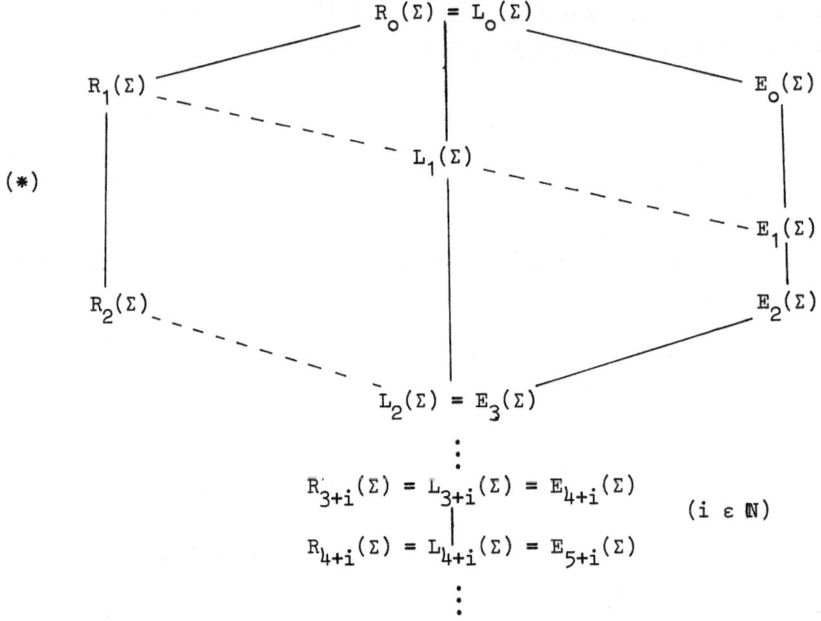

$$R_{3+i}(\Sigma) = L_{3+i}(\Sigma) = E_{4+i}(\Sigma) \qquad (i \in \mathbb{N})$$
$$R_{4+i}(\Sigma) = L_{4+i}(\Sigma) = E_{5+i}(\Sigma)$$

Hierbei bedeuten fallende Linien echte Inklusionen; für die gestrichelten Linien konnte die Echtheit der Inklusion noch nicht gezeigt werden.

Die Aussagen des Satzes 1 lassen sich zum Teil direkt beweisen (z.B. die Hierarchieeigenschaft der Familie $(E_n(\Sigma))_{n\in\mathbb{N}}$ $(E_n(\Sigma) \neq E_{n+1}(\Sigma))$ durch ein Diagonalisierungsargument), zum Teil wird ein Satz benötigt, der die Simulation der Aktion einer Turingmaschine durch primitiv-rekursive Funktionen beschreibt; auf ihn werden wir weiter unten eingehen.

Die im Diagramm (*) dargestellten Inklusionen stimmen genau mit den für Klassen arithmetischer Funktionen bekannten überein (s. [SCH, MER]). Ähnlich lassen sich viele andere Eigenschaften für Klassen primitiv-rekursiver Wortfunktionen verallgemeinern, ohne daß sich Unterschiede zu den arithmetischen Klassen ergeben. Hier seien jedoch zwei für etliche Beweise wichtige Eigenschaften erwähnt, bei denen Unterschiede festgestellt werden können:

Für $r = |\Sigma| > 1$ gibt es eine Paarungsfunktion in $E_1(\Sigma)$ (sogar in $R_1(\Sigma)$), für $r = 1$ erst in $E_2(\Sigma) \cap R_2(\Sigma)$.

Mit Hilfe dieser Eigenschaft kann simultane Rekursion auf einfache primitive Rekursion zurückgeführt werden:

SATZ 2: Für $r = 1$ ist $E_n(\Sigma)$ unter simultaner beschränkter Rekursion abgeschlossen, falls $n \geq 2$, für $r > 1$ auch, falls $n = 1$.

Da die Hierarchien bis auf die kurzen Anfangsteile sowieso übereinstimmen und die Grzegorczyk-Klassen die interessantesten zu sein scheinen, werden wir uns im folgenden wesentlich auf sie beschränken.

3. Turingmaschinen-Simulation und Automatentransduktionen

Die bereits oben erwähnte Simulation von Turingmaschinen bezieht sich auf Maschinen des folgenden Typs: Die Maschinen haben n Eingabe- , m Arbeits- und ein Einwegausgabeband und arbeiten deterministisch; stopt eine Maschine, so wird das Wort auf dem Ausgabeband als Ausgabe angesehen. Ist zu einer Maschine M dieser Art O die Funktion, die zu einem Eingabentupel x und einem Wort $y \in \Sigma^*$ die Inschrift des Ausgabebands nach $|y|$ Rechenschritten angibt, so gilt

LEMMA 1: Für $|\Sigma| = 1$ ist $O \in E_2(\Sigma) \cap L_2(\Sigma)$, für $|\Sigma| > 1$ gilt $O \in E_1(\Sigma) \cap L_2(\Sigma) \cap R_3(\Sigma)$.

Mit diesem Lemma folgt

SATZ 3: Wird die Funktion f_M von der Turingmaschine M berechnet und wird die zugehörige Schrittzahlfunktion T_M durch die Funktion t beschränkt, so gilt für $|\Sigma| > 1$

$$t \in E_n \Longrightarrow f_M \in E_n(\Sigma) \qquad \text{falls } n \geq 1$$

analog für L_n, $n \geq 2$ bzw. R_n, $n \geq 3$.

Satz 3 gibt ein gutes Hilfsmittel zur Einordnung von Automatentransduktionen in die Hierarchien ab, wenn für den betreffenden Automatentyp die Turingmaschinen- Zeitkomplexität bekannt ist. Für die genaue Einordnung der Klassen sind jedoch meist noch spezielle Betrachtungen notwendig. Im folgenden werden für einige bekannte Klassen die wichtigsten Resultate zusammengefaßt; „eine Klasse von Wortmengen ist in $E_n(\Sigma)$ erkennbar" soll dabei bedeuten, daß die entsprechenden charakteristischen Funktionen in $E_n(\Sigma)$ liegen.

SATZ 4: (i) Die regulären Mengen sind in $E_o(\Sigma)$ erkennbar.

(ii) Die endlichen Automaten und die deterministischen Kellerautomaten definieren Funktionen aus $E_1(\Sigma)$; beide Klassen enthalten nicht $E_o(\Sigma)$.

(iii) Die deterministischen kontextfreien Sprachen sind in $E_1(\Sigma)$ erkennbar, die nichtdeterministischen in $E_2(\Sigma)$.

(iv) Die „linear bounded"- und (Einweg- und Zweiweg-) Stack-Transduktionen sind Teilklassen von $E_3(\Sigma)$.

4. Primitiv-rekursive Transformationen

Der Begriff „primitiv-rekursiv" läßt sich auf Funktionen zwischen verschiedenen Monoiden nicht in ähnlicher Weise verallgemeinern wie von den arithmetischen auf die Wortfunktionen. Hier werden zwei Möglichkeiten angegeben, die sich als äquivalent erweisen.

Sei π neben Σ ein weiteres Alphabet. $K(\Sigma,\pi)$ sei diejenige Klasse von Funktionen $c : \Sigma^* \longrightarrow \pi^*$, für die gilt: Zu jedem $f \in Pr(\Sigma)$ gibt es ein $f' \in Pr(\pi)$, so daß gilt $c \circ f = f' \circ c$. $c \in K(\Sigma,\pi)$ heißt Kodierung.

DEFINITION 4: Die Klasse

$$Pr(\Sigma,\pi) := \{c \circ f \mid c \in K(\Sigma,\pi) \wedge f \in Pr(\Sigma)\}$$

heißt Klasse der primitiv-rekursiven Transformationen von Σ^* nach π^*.

Transformationen können auch als Einschränkungen von primitiv-rekursiven Funktionen über einem größeren Monoid aufgefaßt werden: Sind $\iota : \Sigma^* \longrightarrow (\Sigma \cup \pi)^*$ und $v : (\Sigma \cup \pi)^* \longrightarrow \pi^*$ Einbettung bzw. Projektion, so sei $T(\Sigma,\pi) := \{v \circ f \circ \iota \mid f \in Pr(\Sigma \cup \pi)\}$. Für diese Klasse gilt nun

SATZ 5: $Pr(\Sigma,\pi) = T(\Sigma,\pi)$.

Dieser Satz führt zu einer einfachen Hierarchiedefinition für Transformationen und Kodierungen: es wird einfach gesetzt

$$E_n(\Sigma,\pi) = \{v \circ f \circ \iota \mid f \in E_n(\Sigma \cup \pi)\}$$

usw.. Auf diese Weise lassen sich für Transformationenklassen Inklusionsbeziehungen wie die in Satz 1 ebenfalls zeigen.

Es stellt sich nun die Frage, wie sich Transformationen aus bestimmten Klassen auf die Hierarchie der üblichen p.r. Funktionen auswirken, insbesondere wieweit Kodierungen einen Einfluß haben. Hier zeigen sich entscheidene Unterschiede, je nachdem, ob in $\mathbb{N}$ oder ein „größeres" Monoid kodiert wird.

SATZ 6: Für $n \geq 1$, falls $|\pi| > 1$, und $n \geq 3$, falls $|\pi| = 1$, gilt:

(i) Ist c eine Bijektion, so daß $c \in E_n(\Sigma,\pi)$, $c^{-1} \in E_n(\pi,\Sigma)$ und c und c^{-1} Kodierungen, so ist für alle $m \geq n$

$$E_m(\Sigma) = \{c^{-1} \circ f \circ c \mid f \in E_m(\pi)\} \text{ und } E_m(\pi) = \{c \circ g \circ c^{-1} \mid g \in E_m(\Sigma)\} .$$

(ii) Es gibt jeweils solche Kodierungen c .

Satz 6 gilt sogar allgemeiner für beliebige Kodierungen, wenn statt c^{-1} eine Art „Dekodierung" $d : \pi^* \longrightarrow \Sigma^*$ den Voraussetzungen genügt. Dies führt nun - unter Berücksichtigung der im Satz 4 angegebenen Abschätzungen - mit weiteren Detailüberlegungen zu folgenden Schlüssen:

(1) Die Alphabetvergrößerung oder -verkleinerung wirkt sich praktisch gar nicht aus, vorallem nicht auf die gegebenen Einordnungen von Automatentransduktionen, sofern jeweils mindestens zwei Elemente vorhanden sind und man eine genügend einfache Kodierung wählt; dieses Ergebnis wird auch zum Beweis zu Lemma 1 / Satz 3 benutzt.

(2) Wird in die natürlichen Zahlen kodiert, so ist dies erst ab E_3 bzw. $E_3(\Sigma)$ ohne Wirkung; für die Klassen darunter gibt es Verschiebungen. Nun ist dies gerade der Bereich, in den alle bekannten Klassen von (gegenüber der Turingmaschine) eingeschränkten Automatentransduktionen eingeordnet werden, so daß es für die Abschätzung der „Kompliziertheit" solcher Transduktionen von Bedeutung ist, ob sie als Funktionen über natürlichen Zahlen oder Worten definiert sind.

In der Tat sind sich daraus ergebende Unterschiede für endliche Automaten seit längerem bekannt [COB]; für andere Automatentypen wurden sie freilich bisher nie in Betracht gezogen.

Literatur

ASS ASSER, G.:
Rekursive Wortfunktionen.
Zeitschr. math. Logik Grdl. Math. 6 (1960), S. 258-278.

AXT AXT, P.:
Iteration of primitive recursion.
Zeitschr. math. Logik Grdl. Math. 11 (1965), S. 253-255.

COB COBHAM, A.:
On the base-dependence of sets of numbers recognizable by finite automata.
Math. Syst. Th. 3 (1969), S. 186-192.

EIE EILENBERG, S., ELGOT, C.C.:
Recursiveness .
Academic Press, New York - London 1970.

HEI HEINERMANN, W.:
Untersuchungen über die Rekursionszahlen rekursiver Funktionen.
Diss. Univ. Münster (1961).

HEN v.HENKE, F.W.:
Primitiv-rekursive Transformationen.
(in Vorbereitung)

HIW v.HENKE, F.W., INDERMARK, K., WEIHRAUCH, K.:
Hierarchies of primitive recursive wordfunctions and transductions defined by automata.
Proc. of Symp. on Automata, Languages and Programming, IRIA, Paris 1972.

KRR KREIDER, D.L., RITCHIE, R.W.:
A universal two-way automaton.
Archiv math. Logik Grdl. 9 (1966), S. 43-58.

MER MEYER, A.R., RITCHIE, D.M.:
Computational complexity and program structure.
IBM Research Report CR 1817 (1967).

MÜL MÜLLER, H.:
Über die mit Stackautomaten berechenbaren Funktionen.
Archiv math. Logik Grdl. 13 (1970), S. 60-73.

RI1 RITCHIE, R.W.:
Classes of predictably computable functions.
Trans. AMS 106 (1963), S. 139-173.

RI2 RITCHIE, R.W.:
Classes of recursive functions based on Ackermann's function.
Pacific J. Math. 15 (1965), S. 1027-1044.

SCH SCHWICHTENBERG, H.:
Rekursionszahlen und die Grzegorczyk-Hierarchie.
Archiv math. Logik Grdl. 12 (1969), S. 85-97.

WEI WEIHRAUCH, K.:
Teilklassen primitiv-rekursiver Wortfunktionen.
(in Vorbereitung)

UNTERSUCHUNGEN ÜBER HALTENDE PROGRAMME FÜR TURING-MASCHINEN MIT 2 ZEICHEN UND BIS ZU 5 BEFEHLEN

B.WEIMANN, K.CASPER, W.FENZL

Zunächst sollen Definitionen von Begriffen gegeben werden, die in Richtung auf das Ziel dieser Arbeit hin sehr spezieller Natur sind und sich nicht mit den sonst üblichen Definitionen zu decken brauchen.

Def.1: Eine Turing-Maschine besteht im wesentlichen aus einer Zentraleinheit (ZE), einem Band, das nach beiden Seiten unbegrenzt ist und einem Lese- und Schreibkopf (LS). Das Band ist in Felder eingeteilt, die durchnummeriert sind, und zwar vom Feld 0 ausgehend nach rechts die Felder 1,2,3,... und nach links die Felder -1,-2,-3,... Der LS steht über einem Feld des Bandes, dem Arbeitsfeld (AF). Die ZE kann von einem Turingprogramm (TP) gesteuert das Zeichen auf dem AF lesen und in Abhängigkeit davon und dem TP ein Zeichen auf das AF schreiben. Zwei Zeichen stehen zur Verfügung: B und I, wobei B für Leerzeichen steht. Grundsätzlich wird beim Schreibvorgang das AF überschrieben. Mit B überschreiben heißt, das AF löschen. Weiter kann die ZE wieder in Abhängigkeit vom gelesenen Zeichen und vom TP den LS um ein Feld nach rechts oder links verschieben.

Def.2: Ein Turingprogramm besteht aus einer endlichen Anzahl (N) von Befehlen. Jeder Befehl besteht aus zwei Teilbefehlen und hat folgende Form:

$$\begin{array}{l} i\ B\ Z_1\ V_1\ n_1 \\ i\ I\ Z_2\ V_2\ n_2 \end{array}$$

Dabei bedeuten: i ist die Nummer des Befehls; B und I regeln in Abhängigkeit vom Inhalt der AF's, welcher Teilbefehl durchgeführt wird, d.h. steht auf dem AF ein I, wird der 2. Teilbefehl durchgeführt; $Z_1, Z_2 \in \{B,I\}$ sind die Zeichen, die auf das AF geschrieben werden; $V_1, V_2 \in \{R,L\}$ sind die auszuführenden Verschiebeoperationen, d.h. $V_i = R$, so wird der LS ein Feld nach rechts verschoben; $n_i \in \{1,...,N\}$ ist die Nummer desjenigen Befehls, die die ZE als nächsten ausführt. Ist ein Teilbefehl von der Form iBZ bzw. iIZ, d.h. sind V und n nicht definiert, so handelt es sich um einen Stopbefehl. Dabei wird das Zeichen Z noch auf das AF geschrieben, bevor die ZE die Turingmaschine anhält.

Generalvoraussetzung: TP-e werden nur daraufhin untersucht, was sie bewirken, wenn sie mit dem 1. Befehl gestartet werden und beim Start ein leeres Band und als AF das Feld mit Nummer 0 vorfinden. Wird also ausgesagt, daß ein TP stopt, so gilt dies nur unter obiger Voraussetzung.

Will man alle möglichen TP-e mit n Befehlen unter Berücksichtigung obiger Generalvoraussetzung untersuchen, so wird dieser Versuch bei $(4\cdot(n+1))^{2n}$ möglichen Programmen sehr schnell zum Scheitern verurteilt sein. Es muß der Versuch gemacht werden, die große Zahl der TP-e durch sinnvolle Identifizierungen in möglichst wenige Äquivalenzklassen einzuteilen. So konnten S. Lin und T. Rado [1] durch Identifizierungen die bei 3 Befehlen möglichen 16 777 216 TP-e auf 82944 Äquivalenzklassen aufteilen. Ihr Verfahren auf TP-e mit 4 Befehlen angewandt, würde zu 100 663 296 Äquivalenzklassen führen. Durch die im folgenden definierten Identifizierungen von TP-en gelang es, die Anzahl der Äquivalenzklassen (bei 4 Befehlen) auf 1 198 690 zu reduzieren.

Folgende TP-e werden miteinander identifiziert:

1. Numeriert man die 2n Teilbefehle bei TP-en mit n Befehlen in kanonischer Reihenfolge durch und wird der Ablauf eines TP-s durch eine Folge der Nummern der nacheinander von der ZE ausgeführten Teilbefehle beschrieben, so werden zwei TP-e mit den Folgen $i_1, i_2, i_3, \ldots$ bzw. $j_1, j_2, j_3, \ldots$ für die Beschreibung des Ablaufs miteinander identifiziert, wenn gilt:

   a) $i_k = i_j \quad k = 1,2,3,\ldots,s$ für TP-e, die nach Ausführung von genau s Teilbefehlen anhalten.

   $k \in \mathbb{N}$ für nicht-haltende TP-e

   b) Der Teilbefehl mit Nummer i_k ist bei beiden TP-en identisch.

   Die nicht benutzten Teilbefehle können als Stopbefehle aufgefaßt werden.

   Notation: Ein Teilbefehl, der beim Ablauf eines TP-s nicht benutzt wird, soll durch die Form iB* bzw. iI* gekennzeichnet werden.

2. Zwei TP-e, die sich nur durch eine Permutation der Reihenfolge der Befehle bei entsprechender Permutation der Nummern der aufzurufenden Befehle unterscheiden.

3. Zwei TP-e, die sich nur dadurch unterscheiden, daß sie alle Verschiebeoperationen spiegelbildlich zueinander ausführen, d.h. wo ein R im ersten TP steht, steht im zweiten ein L und umgekehrt.

Mit Hilfe dieser Identifizierungen bleiben für den ersten Teilbefehl des ersten Befehls (dies ist immer der Startbefehl) nur zwei Möglichkeiten (bei TP-en mit mehr als einem Befehl):

a) 1BIR2 b) 1BBR2

Wird im folgenden von einer Menge von TP-en gesprochen, so ist eine Teilmenge derjenigen Menge gemeint, die aus je einem Vertreter jeder der durch obige Identifizierungen entstehenden Äquivalenzklassen besteht.

Die Gesamtheit aller TP-e wird nun in folgende disjunkte Teilmengen aufgespalten:

TP $\in$ S(n,m) $\Longleftrightarrow$ 1. TP stopt
2. TP besitzt n Befehle
3. m Teilbefehle von TP werden nach dem Start benutzt
4. Von jedem Befehl wird mindestens 1 Teilbefehl benutzt (n = m)

TP $\in$ U(n,m) $\Longleftrightarrow$ 1. TP stopt nicht
2., 3. und 4. wie bei S(n,m)

Wie man sich leicht überlegt, erhält man für n=1 folgende Teilmengen:

$$S(1,1) = \left\{\begin{pmatrix}1BI\\1I*\end{pmatrix}, \begin{pmatrix}1BB\\1I*\end{pmatrix}\right\} \qquad U(1,1) = \left\{\begin{pmatrix}1BIR1\\1I*\end{pmatrix}, \begin{pmatrix}1BBR1\\1I*\end{pmatrix}\right\}$$

$$S(1,2) = \emptyset \qquad U(1,2) = \emptyset$$

Man kann nun, nacheinander von S(1,1) anfangend, alle Teilmengen S(n,m) und U(n,m) aufbauen. Um S(n,m) zu ermitteln, benötigt man alle TP-e, die stoppen und m-1 verschiedene Teilbefehle bis zum Stop benutzen. Dies sind

$$S_{n,m} = S(n,m-1) \cup S(n-1,m-1) \quad \text{für } m > n$$
$$S_{n,m} = S(n-1,m-1) \quad \text{für } m = n$$

Zu allen TP-en aus S(n-1,m-1) wird zunächst ein n-ter Befehl hinzugenommen, der von der Form $\begin{matrix}nB*\\nI*\end{matrix}$ ist, so daß alle TP-e aus $S_{n,m}$ n Befehle aufweisen. Folgender Prozeß wird für jedes TP aus $S_{n,m}$ durchgeführt. Sei TP1 $\in S_{n,m}$ und TP1 stoppe auf dem Teilbefehl iB...(iI...). Dieser Teilbefehl wird dann nacheinander ersetzt durch alle Teilbefehle der Form iBZVn$_1$(iIZVn$_2$) mit $Z \in \{B,I\}$, $V \in \{R,L\}$, $n_1 \in \{1,\ldots,n\}$ ($n_2 \in \{1,\ldots,n\}$). Jedes der so entstandenen TP-e wird daraufhin geprüft, ob es anhält oder nicht. Hält es an, kommt es zur Menge S(n,m). Hält es nicht an, so werden genau wie bei TP1 m-1 Teilbefehle benutzt. (Jeder nicht benutzte Teilbefehl bei TP1 ist von der Form iB* bzw. iI* und damit Stopbefehl). Dieses Programm kommt dann zur Menge U(n-1,m-1) bzw. U(n,m-1), je nachdem, ob TP1 $\in$ S(n-1,m-1) oder TP1 $\in$ S(n,m-1). Der Aufbauprozeß ist in Abb. 1 schematisch wiedergegeben.

Es muß untersucht werden, ob bei diesem Aufbau aus jeder Äquivalenzklasse genau ein Vertreter konstruiert wird. Bei diesen Überlegungen macht nur die Frage Schwierigkeiten, ob zwei TP-e konstruiert werden können, die wegen Identifizierung 2 derselben Äquivalenzklasse angehören. Für ein TP mit n Befehlen sei $i_1, i_2, i_3, ..$ die Folge der Nummern der nach dem Start nacheinander auszuführenden Befehle (<u>nicht</u> Teilbefehle), also $i_k \in \{1,\ldots,n\}$, k=1,2,3,..., so gibt es unter der Voraussetzung, daß in der Folge $i_1, i_2, ..$ alle Zahlen von 1 bis n vorkommen (diese Voraussetzung ist durch die Definition von S(n,m) und U(n,m) erfüllt), genau eine Permutation π auf $\{1,..,n\}$, die folgendes leistet:

$$\pi(i_{j+1}) \leq \max\{\pi(i_k) \mid k = 1,\dots,j\}+1$$
$$\pi(i_1) = 1$$
$$\pi(i_{j+1}) = \max\{\pi(i_k) \mid k = 1,\dots,j\}+1, \text{ wenn } i_{j+1} \text{ mit keiner der Zahlen } i_1,\dots,i_j \text{ übereinstimmt.}$$

Wie man leicht sieht, werden beim geschilderten Aufbau nur TP-e zugelassen, die Folgen (wie oben beschrieben) besitzen, bei denen die Identität die eindeutig bestimmte Permutation ist, die dies leistet.

Um die Hauptergebnisse dieser Arbeit formulieren zu können, müssen einige Funktionen definiert werden.

Def. 3: Die Funktionen σ, φ, β: $S(n,m) \longrightarrow \mathbb{N}$ für alle $n,m \in \mathbb{N}$ $n \leq m \leq 2n$ und k,s,f,b: $\mathbb{N}^2 \longrightarrow \mathbb{N}$ werden definiert durch:

$\sigma(TP)$ = Anzahl der Teilbefehle, die bis zum Stopbefehl einschließlich durchgeführt werden.

$\varphi(TP)$ = Anzahl der verschiedenen Felder, die als Arbeitsfelder auftreten (Feldweite von TP).

$\beta(TP)$ = Anzahl der I's, die nach dem Stop auf dem Band stehen.

$k(n,m) = |S(n,m)|$ = Anzahl der TP-e in $S(n,m)$

$s(n,m) = \max\{\sigma(TP) \mid TP \in S(n,m)\}$

$f(n,m) = \max\{\varphi(TP) \mid TP \in S(n,m)\}$

$b(n,m) = \max\{\beta(TP) \mid TP \in S(n,m)\}$ (Busy-Beaver-Spiel)

Um einen noch genaueren Überblick zu bekommen, wurden die Teilmengen $S(n,m)$ und $U(n,m)$ in disjunkte Teilmengen zerlegt:

$$S(n,m) = S_{BR}(n,m) \cup S_{IR}(n,m) \cup S_{BB}(n,m) \cup S_{IB}(n,m)$$
$$U(n,m) = U_{BR}(n,m) \cup U_{IR}(n,m) \cup U_{BB}(n,m) \cup U_{IB}(n,m)$$

Die einzelnen Teilmengen werden definiert durch:

$TP \in S_{BR}(n,m) \Longleftrightarrow$ 1. TP $S(n,m)$
2. Der erste Befehl lautet 1BBR2
3. Alle benötigten AF's haben eine Nummer ≥ 0 (Nur die "rechte Seite" des Bandes wird benutzt)

$TP \in S_{IR}(n,m) \Longleftrightarrow$ 1. und 3. wie bei $S_{BR}(n,m)$
2. Der erste Befehl lautet 1BIR2

$TP \in S_{BB}(n,m) \Longleftrightarrow$ 1. und 2. wie bei $S_{BR}(n,m)$
3. "Beide Seiten" des Bandes werden benutzt.

$TP \in S_{IB}(n,m) \Longleftrightarrow$ 1. und 3. wie bei $S_{BB}(n,m)$, 2. wie bei $S_{IR}(n,m)$

Entsprechend werden die Teilmengen von $U(n,m)$ definiert. Durch Indizierung der Funktionen k,s,f,b (z.B. $k_{BR}, k_{IR}, \dots$) sollen die Funktionen gekennzeichnet werden, die dadurch entstehen, daß in den Definitionen statt der Menge $S(n,m)$ die der Indizierung entsprechende Teilmenge zugrunde gelegt wird.

n,m	k_{BR}	S_{BR}	f_{BR}	i_{BR}	k_{IR}	S_{IR}	f_{IR}	i_{IR}	k_{BB}	S_{BB}	f_{BB}	i_{BB}	k_{IB}	S_{IB}	f_{IB}	i_{IB}
2,2	2	2	2	1	2	2	2	2	--	--	--	--	--	--	--	--
2,3	2	4	2	1	8	3	2	2	--	--	--	--	--	--	--	--
2,4	2	6	3	2	8	4	2	2	--	--	--	--	12	6	4	4
3,3	8	3	3	2	8	3	3	3	--	--	--	--	--	--	--	--
3,4	38	5	3	2	54	5	3	3	4	5	3	2	36	5	4	4
3,5	138	9	4	4	266	10	4	4	32	9	4	4	282	17	5	5
3,6	378	14	5	4	590	13	5	4	180	17	6	5	1492	21	7	6
4,4	24	4	4	3	24	4	4	4	8	4	3	3	8	4	3	3
4,5	320	7	4	4	424	7	4	4	98	8	4	4	366	8	5	5
4,6	2376	18	5	5	3362	12	5	5	1210	18	6	5	4704	20	6	6
4,7	14148	24	7	6	20446	23	7	5	10864	30	8	7	45548	38	10	9
4,8	45504	43	11	7	59664	58	10	7	56082	71	12	10	230762	107	16	13

Tabelle 1

n,m	k_{BR}	S_{BR}	f_{BR}	i_{BR}	k_{IR}	S_{IR}	f_{IR}	i_{IR}
5,5	96	5	5	4	96	5	5	5
5,6	2036	9	5	5	2320	9	5	5
5,7	27804	19	6	6	36180	19	6	6
5,8	276610	33	9	8	357192	39	9	8
5,9	?	178	16	12	?	84	14	13
5,10	?	237	21	18	?	189	22	19

Tabelle 2

TP	1BBR2 1IBL2 2BBR3 2IIL4 3BIL1 3IIR3 4BBL1 4IB	1BBR2 1IBL4 2BBR3 2IIR2 3BIR4 3IBR4 4BIL1 4II	1BBR2 1IIL3 2BIR3 2IIR2 3BIR4 3IIL1 4BIL1 4II	1BIR2 1IBL3 2BIR3 2IB 3BIR4 3IBR2 4BIL4 4IBL1	1BIR2 1IIL3 2BBR3 2IIR3 3BIL1 3IIR4 4BI 4IBR2	1BIR2 1IBL2 2BBR3 2IIR4 3BIL1 3IBR4 4BIR3 4II	1BBR2 1IIL3 2BIL1 2IIR2 3BIL2 3IBL4 4BI 4IBL1	1BBR2 1IIR2 2BIL3 2IIR3 3BIR1 3IIL4 4BI 4IBL3	1BBR2 1IIL3 2BIR3 2IIR1 3BIL1 3IBL4 4BIR1 4II
*) Index	BR	BR	BR	IR	IR	IR	BB	BB	BB
σ(TP)	43	35	20	58	42	19	71	45	64
φ(TP)	6	11	7	8	10	7	12	12	11
β(TP)	2	5	7	4	7	7	8	9	10

TP	1BIR2 1IIL2 2BIL1 2IBL3 3BI 3IIL4 4BIR4 4IBR1	1BIR2 1IBR3 2BIL1 2IIR1 3BI 3IIR4 4BIL4 4IBL2	1BIR2 1IBR1 2BIL3 2IBR4 3BBL4 3IBL2 4BIR1 4II
*) Index	IB	IB	IB
σ(TP)	107	96	61
φ(TP)	14	14	16
β(TP)	13	13	9

TP	1BBR2 1IBL1 2BBR3 2IBL5 3BIR4 3IBL4 4BIL1 4IIR5 5BIR3 5IB	1BBR2 1IIR5 2BBR3 2II 3BIL4 3IIR2 4BIR1 4IBL4 5BIR3 5IIR2	1BIR2 1IBL1 2BBR3 2IIL2 3BIR4 3IIR3 4BIR5 4IBR5 5BIL1 5II	1BIR2 1IBL1 2BBR3 2IIR5 3BBR4 3II 4BIL1 4IIR3 5BIR4 5IIR3
*) Index	BR	BR	IR	IR
σ(TP)	237	169	189	170
φ(TP)	15	21	19	22
β(TP)	5	18	18	19

Tabelle 3

*) z.B. Index=IB $\Leftrightarrow$ TP $\in S_{IB}(n,m)$

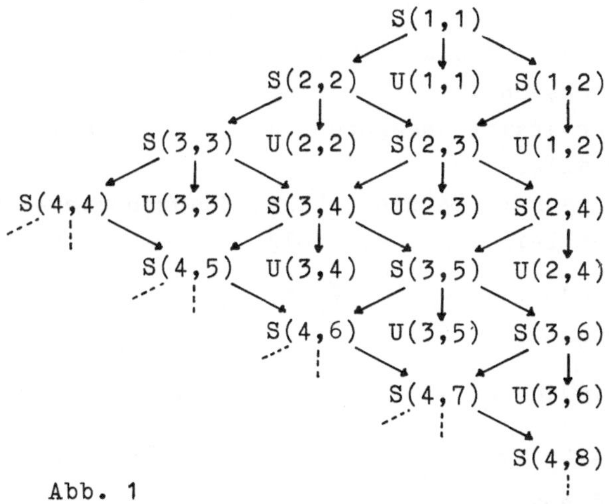

Abb. 1

Die Menge S^n aller haltenden TP-e mit n Befehlen unter Beachtung der Identifikationen 1,2 und 3 ergibt sich zu:

$$S^n = \sum_{i=1}^{n} \sum_{j=1}^{2n} S(i,j)$$

Entsprechend ergibt sich die Menge U^n aller nicht-haltenden TP-e mit n Befehlen zu:

$$U^n = \sum_{i=1}^{n} \sum_{j=1}^{2n} U(i,j)$$

Um die Teilmengen S(n,m) und U(n,m) zu ermitteln, wurde ein Computerprogramm geschrieben, das den in Abbildung 1 schematisch dargestellten Aufbau leistet. Die Entscheidung, ob ein TP bei Variation des Teilbefehls, auf dem es stopt, noch anhält, wurde zunächst danach getroffen, ob es hält, bevor eine vorgegebene Anzahl von Teilbefehlen ausgeführt ist, d.h. ein TP könnte zunächst fälschlicherweise als nicht-haltend gelten, wenn σ(TP) größer als ein vorgegebener Wert ist. Die zunächst als nicht-haltend angenommenen TP-e wurden dann, wie noch geschildert wird, mit Hilfe weiterer Computerprogramme exakt daraufhin untersucht, ob sie halten oder nicht. Alle als nicht-haltend angenommenen TP-e wurden dann auch als solche erkannt,so daß die in Tabelle 1 angegebenen Werte für n=4 als bewiesen anzusehen sind. Damit ist unter anderem das Busy-Beaver-Spiel für n=4 gelöst (Lösung: 13).
In Tabelle 2 sind noch einige Werte angegeben, die erhalten wurden bei dem Versuch, auch die Teilmengen S(5,i), $i \in \{5,\dots,10\}$ und die Werte der entsprechenden Funktionen zu bestimmen.
Auf Grund des enormen Anwachsens der Rechenzeiten der Computerprogramme konnte dies nur teilweise gelöst werden. Die angegebenen Werte gelten unter der Voraussetzung:

$$TP \in S_{BR}(5,10) \cup S_{IR}(5,10) \Longrightarrow \sigma(TP) \leq 500$$

d.h., die zunächst wie bei n=4 als nicht-haltend angenommenen TP-e wurden nicht weiter untersucht.
In der Tabelle 3 sind Programme angegeben, die einige Maximalwerte der Tabellen 1 und 2 realisieren.
Zur Untersuchung der zunächst als nicht-haltend angenommenen TP-e wurden die verschiedenen Teilmengen wie folgt zusammengefaßt:

$U^2_{BR} = U_{BR}(2,2) \cup U_{BR}(1,2)$

$U^3_{BR} = U_{BR}(3,3) \cup U_{BR}(2,3)$

$U^4_{BR} = U_{BR}(4,4) \cup U_{BR}(3,4) \cup U_{BR}(2,4)$

$U^5_{BR} = U_{BR}(4,5) \cup U_{BR}(3,5)$

$U^6_{BR} = U_{BR}(4,6) \cup U_{BR}(3,6)$

$U^7_{BR} = U_{BR}(4,7)$

$U^8_{BR}=U_{BR}(4,8)$ braucht nicht gebildet zu werden, da TP-e aus U^8_{BR} keinen Stopbefehl besitzen und somit trivialerweise nicht halten. Analog zu

U^i_{BR} werden die Mengen U^i_{IR}, U^i_{BB} und U^i_{IB} gebildet.

Vier Algorithmen wurden aufgestellt, mit deren Hilfe bei bestimmten Bedingungen das Nicht-halten eines TP-s exakt nachgewiesen wurde. Sie sollen hier nur kurz skizziert werden.

1. Algorithmus zur Erkennung einfacher Schleifen (SCH)
   Der Algorithmus versucht, einen Teilbefehl zu finden, der beim Ablauf des Programms immer wieder aufgerufen wird und bei dem die Bandbelegungen, von dem AF aus gesehen, das dieser Teilbefehl benutzt, in allen Feldern, die beim weiteren Ablauf noch als AF-er benutzt werden, identisch ist.

2. Der 2. Algorithmus (ST1) sortiert die TP-e aus, die nicht halten können, weil der (die) Stopbefehl(e) bzw. der (die) nicht benutzte(n) Befehl(e) von keinem Teilbefehl aufgerufen wird (werden).

3. Der 3. Algorithmus (ST2) prüft, welche Möglichkeiten es bei entsprechender Bandbelegung gibt, daß das Programm zu einem Stopbefehl (nicht benutzter Befehl) kommt. Dabei wird versucht, vom Stop her rückwärts den Ablauf der letzten 5 Teilbefehle zu konstruieren. Gibt es keine Bandbelegung, die zum Stop führen könnte, wird das Programm als nicht-haltend aussortiert.

4. Algorithmus zur Erkennung von sich vergrößernden Schleifen (VS). Zur Demonstrierung, was dieser Algorithmus leistet, soll ein Beispiel dienen: Der LS ändert beim Ablauf des Programms unter anderem seine Richtung bei den Feldern 2,3,4,5,... (in chronologischer Reihenfolge), und zwar von rechts nach links. Zwischen den aufgeführten "Wendepunkten" ändert der LS seine Richtung von rechts nach links bei den Feldern 7,9,11,13,... Es wird nun untersucht, ob sich der Zyklus 2⟶ 7 ⟶ 3 (Ablauf des Programms vom AF mit Nummer 2 über das AF mit Nummer 7 zum AF mit Nummer 3) im anschließenden Zyklus 3 ⟶ 9 ⟶ 4 in "gewisser Weise" wiederholt. Läßt sich nachweisen, daß sich diese Art von Wiederholung beliebig fortsetzt, wird das Programm als nicht-haltend aussortiert.

In den Tabellen 4a,b,c,d sind die Zahlen der als nicht-haltend angenommenen TP-e sowie die Zahlen der nach Anwendung der einzelnen Algorithmen übrigbleibende Programme aufgeführt. Die nach Anwendung aller 4 Algorithmen noch übrigbleibenden 396 Programme, mußten dann "per Hand" als nicht-haltend aussortiert werden. Bei diesen TP-en handelt es sich um solche, die mit abgewandelten Algorithmen der 4. Art aussortiert werden können.

i	Anzahl	U^i_{BR} Anzahl nach Reduktion durch SCH	ST1	ST2	VS
2	5	-	-	-	-
3	24	-	-	-	-
4	189	2	-	-	-
5	1409	11	7	5	-
6	9922	164	62	47	-
7	60800	1278	1007	466	40
Σ	72340	1455	1076	518	40

Tabelle 4a

i	Anzahl	U^i_{IR} Anzahl nach Reduktion durch SCH	ST1	ST2	VS
2	4	-	-	-	-
3	27	-	-	-	-
4	229	-	-	-	-
5	1890	8	-	-	-
6	13797	96	50	33	-
7	84653	809	372	181	8
Σ	100600	913	422	214	8

Tabelle 4b

i	Anzahl	U^i_{BB} Anzahl nach Reduktion durch SCH	ST1	ST2	VS
2	2	-	-	-	-
3	14	-	-	-	-
4	121	-	-	-	-
5	1223	16	8	5	-
6	10724	373	179	60	-
7	88504	4783	3361	1958	92
Σ	100588	5172	3548	2023	92

Tabelle 4c

i	Anzahl	U^i_{IB} Anzahl nach Reduktion durch SCH	ST1	ST2	VS
2	-	-	-	-	-
3	14	-	-	-	-
4	248	4	-	-	-
5	2940	51	40	27	-
6	34390	1033	391	186	2
7	298086	12044	9822	5334	254
Σ	335678	13132	10253	5547	256

Tabelle 4d

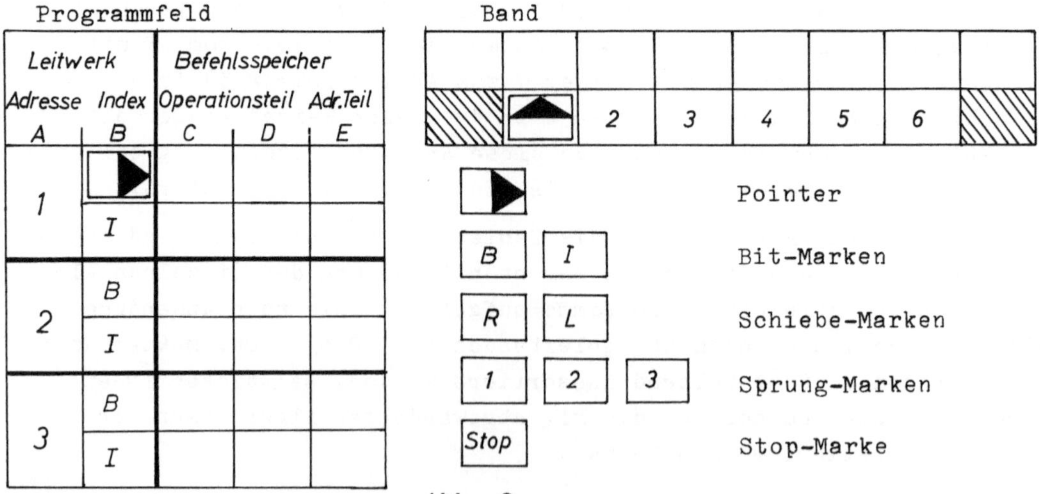

Programmfeld

Leitwerk | Befehlsspeicher
Adresse | Index | Operationsteil | Adr.Teil
A | B | C | D | E
1 | I
2 | B | I
3 | B | I

Band

2 3 4 5 6

Pointer

B I Bit-Marken

R L Schiebe-Marken

1 2 3 Sprung-Marken

Stop Stop-Marke

Abb. 2

Es ist naheliegend, eine leicht modifizierte Turingmaschine als Ausbildungsobjekt im Bereich der Informatik nutzbar zu machen. Die Eignung als Lehrmodell ergibt sich aus der Eigenschaft der Maschine: a) Sie enthält alle grundsätzlichen Funktions- und Strukturelemente, die ein Computer besitzt, b) alle Funktionen und Strukturen sind unmittelbar anschaulich, c) der Gesamtablauf und die Wirkungsweise der Maschine bleiben während des logischen Ablaufs übersichtlich und direkt einsichtig, ohne daß das erzielte Ergebnis trivial ist.
Wir haben als Lehrmodell eine Turingmaschine mit drei Befehlen und einem endlichen Band mit 6 Zellen benutzt. Die Felder werden im Spielablauf durch verschiedene Marken besetzt. Feldabschnitte tragen Namen, die Funktionen im Computer entsprechen. Die Phasen des Spielablaufs werden durch einen "Pointer" im Leitwerk und im unteren Teil des Bandes markiert (s. Abb.2). Die Spielregeln entsprechen denen der Turingmaschine, die Selbsthalteforderung wird aber immer explizit angegeben.

Das Modell kann in verschiedenen Stufen der Ausbildung eingesetzt werden, wir haben es zur Grundausbildung für Programmierer benutzt. Dabei liegt im 1. Teil der Ausbildung, der Spielphase, das Schwergewicht auf der Beschäftigung mit dem Modell. Seine Ausnutzung erfolgt unter 4 Gesichtspunkten:
a) Einsichten in logische Abläufe (durch Nachvollzug gegebener Programme) und Entwicklung konstruktiven Denkens (durch Erstellung von Bandstrukturen), b) Darstellung der Information, die sehr leicht aus den Spielmarken und deren Bedeutung erarbeitet werden kann, c) Veranschaulichung der wichtigsten Computerbegriffe und Verständnis der Rechnerorganisation, d) Grundschemata des Programmierens, wie Sprung, Verzweigung und Schleife. Die Modellaufgaben, der Spielanweisung beigefügt, werden dem Stand der Ausbildung inhaltlich und graduell angepaßt, wobei auch Anregungen zu rein spielerischen Übungen (z.B. maximale Bandbesetzung) eingefügt sind.
Von dieser Spielphase aus aufbauend, erfolgt die Einführung in eine Programmiersprache, wobei jetzt der Hintergrund für den Lernenden wesentlich transparenter ist und viele Begriffs- und Vorstellungsschwierigkeiten bereits überwunden sind. Nach unserer Erfahrung läßt sich der Erfolg in der Spielphase und der Programmierphase korrelieren, so daß sich hieraus ggf. didaktische Möglichkeiten ergeben. Ein systematischer und zahlenmäßiger Zusammenhang wurde jedoch nicht ermittelt, da unsere Bestrebungen mehr auf Nutzung im Unterricht als auf Testeignung gerichtet waren.

---

[1] S. Liu, T. Rado; Journal of the ACM 12 (1965)

AN ALGORITHM FOR COLORING THE VERTICES OF AN ARBITRARY FINITE GRAPH

K.DÜRRE

I. Introductory Remarks and Definitions

Let be $G=(V,E)$ an arbitrary finite graph, where E is the set of edges and $V=\{v_k\}_{k=1}^{n}$ the set of n vertices numbered from 1 to n in an arbitrary order. We write $(v_k,v_l)=e_{kl}\in E$ if the vertices $v_k,v_l\in V$ are connected by an edge, otherwise $e_{kl}\notin E$.

A partition F of the vertex set V into g disjoint subsets (classes) $S_i, 1\leq i\leq g$, (whose union is V) is called a coloration of G, if connected vertices belong to different classes. The partition F defines a function $f: V\rightarrow I_C$, where $I_C=\{i\}_1^g$ and $f(v_k)=f_k=i$ if and only if $v_k\in S_i$. In what follows the elements of I_C are called colors. So F is a coloration of G if $f_k\neq f_l$ for every two vertices $v_k,v_l\in V$ such that $e_{kl}\in E$, i.e. if connected vertices have different colors. Two partitions F and F' of G are said to be equal if they differ from each other only by permutation of their classes (colors).

Let us write a partition F of G as an n-tuple

$$F=(f_1,f_2,\dots,f_n),$$

and let us consider such n-tuples in lexicographic order defined by

$$F\leq F' \Leftrightarrow (f_1<f'_1 \vee \bigvee_{k=2}^{n}(f_k<f'_k \wedge \bigwedge_{i=1}^{k-1} f_i=f'_i)) \vee F=F' .$$

Then the set of equal partitions has a first (smallest) element. In the following we consider only the first n-tuple of any set of equal partitions as a representative of each partition of this set. In any of these n-tuples (or "normalized" partitions) the first vertex v_1 is colored with 1 . If vertex v_k, $2\leq k\leq n$, is colored with i, a vertex with a smaller number must be colored with i-1. Otherwise, we could determine a smaller n-tuple by replacing i by i-1 and vice versa, and with this we would have got a partition which is equal to the normalized partition.

Thus, for all partitions $F=(f_1,f_2,\dots,f_n)$

(1) $f_k \in I_C$ and $f_k \leq k$ where $1 \leq k \leq n$.

Since all these normalized partitions have $f_1 = 1$, according to their lexicographic order the following holds if $F \neq F'$:

(2) $$F < F' \Longleftrightarrow \bigvee_{k=2}^{n} (f_k < f'_k \wedge \bigwedge_{i=1}^{k-1} f_i = f'_i)$$

For the algorithm we need an additional representation of partitions and colorations.

Let be $F = (f_1, f_2, \ldots, f_n)$, $f_k \in \{i\}_1^g$ a partition of V ; we define a partition matrix

(3)
$$C = (c_{ik}),\ 1 \leq i \leq g,\ 1 \leq k \leq n\ ,$$
$$\text{where } c_{ik} \begin{cases} = 1 & \text{if and only if } f_k = i \\ \leq 0 & \text{otherwise} \end{cases}$$

In the algorithm that will be described under II. (where usually not all vertices have a color but only those with an index less than a certain number $<n$), the case $c_{ik} \leq 0$ is specified as follows:

(3a) $c_{ik} = 0$ signifies that vertex v_k is not connected with any vertex v_l, $1 \leq l < k$, which is colored with i, that is $c_{il} = 1$ (and, of course, v_k itself is not colored with i).

(3b) According to (1) a vertex v_k, $1 \leq k < g$, may only have a color $f_k \leq k$. This is initially marked in matrix C by blocking c_{ik} with weight -1 , i.e. we set $c_{ik} = -1$ for all k, $1 \leq k < g$, and for all i, $k < i \leq g$.

(3c) $c_{ik} = -l$, $1 \leq l < k$, signifies that v_k is connected with v_l which is colored with i (that is $c_{il} = 1$), and that there is no vertex with an index less than l which is connected with v_k and colored with i .

(3d) $c_{ik} = -k$ signifies that $c_{ik} = 1$ will cause a total blocking of all colors for a vertex v_l, $k < l \leq n$. Of course, this is only possible if all other colors are blocked for v_l due to vertices with indices less than k.

In the following we consider only graphs without loops, as graphs with a loop are not colorable with any number of colors.

We assume $2 \leq g \leq n$, because only graphs without edges are colorable with one color and because every graph with n vertices is colorable with n colors.

II. The Algorithm

Given a finite graph $G = (V,E)$ without loops, where $V = \{v_k\}_{k=1}^{n}$, and a set $I_C = \{i\}_1^g$, of g colors, $2 \leq g \leq n$. By applying the algorithm it may be determined whether or not G is colorable with g colors.

Step 1. Initially, for all i, $1 \leq i \leq g$, and for all k, $1 \leq k \leq n$,

$$\text{set } c_{ik} = \begin{cases} 0 & \text{if } i \leq k \\ -1 & \text{if } i > k \end{cases}$$

Step 2. Set $k = 1$.

Step 3. If $c_{ik} < 0$ for all $i \in I_C$ go to Step 9; otherwise, look for the smallest number i such that $c_{ik} = 0$, then set $c_{ik} = 1$.

Step 4. If $k = n$, stop:
All vertices have been colored, G is colorable with g colors.

Step 5. For all l, $k < l \leq n$,
set $c_{il} = -k$ if $e_{kl} \in E$ and if $c_{il} = 0$.

Step 6. If, for each l, $k < l \leq n$, there is at least one number i, $1 \leq i \leq g$, such that $c_{il} = 0$, then replace k by $k+1$ and go to Step 3.

Step 7. Look for number i, $1 \leq i \leq g$, such that
$c_{ik} = 1$ and then set $c_{ik} = -k$.

Step 8. For all i, $1 \leq i \leq g$, and for all l, $k < l \leq n$,
set $c_{il} = 0$ if $c_{il} \leq -k$. Then go to Step 3.

Step 9. (from Step 3 only)
If $k > 1$, replace k by $k - 1$ and go to Step 7.
Otherwise, if $k = 1$, stop: G is not colorable with g colors.

If G is colorable we may easily determine the coloration as an n-tuple $F = (f_1, f_2, \ldots, f_n)$ as follows:

For all k, $1 \leq k \leq n$,
look for number i, $1 \leq i \leq g$, such that $c_{ik} = 1$, and then set $f_k = i$.

III. Validity of the Algorithm

In what follows V_k, $1 \leq k \leq n$, stands for the set of the first k vertices of V, $V_k = \{v_l\}_{l=1}^{k}$.

Let us consider a matrix C where (3b) and the following conditions hold:

(A) k is a number so that $2 \leq k \leq n$.
Each vertex $v_l \in V_{k-1}$ has a color $i = h_l$, i.e. $c_{il} = 1$, such that connected vertices have different colors; all colors less than h_l are blocked for v_l (i.e. $c_{jl} < 0$ for all j, $j \in I_C$ and $j < h_l$). All blockings of vertices v_m, $k \leq m \leq n$ caused by vertices $v_l \in V_{k-1}$ are set due to (3c). For each vertex v_m, $k < m \leq n$, there is a number $j \in I_C$, such that $c_{jm} = 0$ (i.e. v_m is not totally blocked) and for all $j \in I_C$ there is $-k < c_{jl} \leq 0$.

For vertex v_k we distinguish between two cases:

(B1) v_k is totally blocked as follows: $-k \leq c_{jk} < 0$ for all $j \in I_C$, and there is at least one number $h \in I_C$ such that $c_{hk} = -k$.

(B2) v_k is not totally blocked: $-k \leq c_{jk} \leq 0$ for all $j \in I_C$, and there is at least one number $h \in I_C$ such that $c_{hk} = 0$.

Due to definition (3) we have the following:

T1. A matrix C where (A) and (B1) hold, has the meaning: There is no coloration $(f_1, f_2, \ldots, f_n)$ of G such that $f_l \leq h_l$ for all l, $1 \leq l < k$.

T2. A matrix C where (A) and (B2) hold, has the meaning: There is no coloration $(f_1, f_2, \ldots, f_n)$ of G so that there is at least one number l, $1 \leq l < k$, such that $f_k < h_l$.

The following will show that by applying the algorithm matrix C will always meet (A) and either (B1) or (B2) at the beginning of Step 3 (except at the very start when C only meets the initial conditions).

a. By applying the algorithm for the first time, the initial conditions are set in C (Step 1) and vertex v_1 gets color 1 (Step 2, Step 3: $c_{11} = 1$). As $n \geq 2$, all blockings are set (Step 4, Step 5); no vertex is totally blocked due to $g \geq 2$ (Step 6), and Step 3 may be applied again with $k = 2$. At that point, matrix C satisfies (A) and (B2) for $k = 2$.

b. We assume that C meets the conditions (A) and either (B1) or (B2) for a certain number k, $2 \leq k \leq n$, and we apply the algorithm beginning with Step 3.

b1. (A) and (B1) hold:
Vertex v_k is totally blocked, i.e. there is no coloration so that each vertex $v_l \in V_{k-1}$ is colored with the same or a smaller color than given in C (due to T1). On the other hand, there may be a coloration which coincides in the first k-2 digits with the coloring of V_{k-1} given in C. Therefore, all we can say so far is that the coloring of vertex v_{k-1} is wrong and the respective color will be blocked for v_{k-1}.

By applying the algorithm matrix C is changed to C' in the following way: Because of (B1), k has to be replaced by $k' = k-1$ (Step 3, Step 9). Then the color $h_{k'} = i$ assigned to $v_{k'}$ has to be blocked for $v_{k'}$ with weight $-k'$ (Step 7: $c'_{ik'} = -k'$) and all blockings caused by $h_{k'}$ will be erased. (Step 8: If $c_{jm} \leq -k'$ then set $c'_{jm} = 0$ for all $j \in I_C$ and for all m, $k' < m \leq n$. Here we may distinguish between blockings that are caused either directly or indirectly by $i = h_{k'}$: all vertices v_m connected with $v_{k'}$ have direct blockings $c_{im} = -k'$. Only vertex v_k, $k = k'+1$, has at least one blocking $c_{jk} = -k < -k'$, $1 \leq j \leq g$ and $j \neq i$. That means that coloring $v_{k'}$ with i and v_k with j will cause a blocking of a vertex with an index greater than k; therefore v_k is "indirectly" blocked for color j by $c_{jk} = -k$. For an implementation of the algorithm it is advisable to take that fact into account.)

All other elements of C and C' are the same. Hence, if $k' \geq 2$, the condition (A) and either (B1) or (B2) hold for C'. The algorithm may be continued at Step 3 with $C = C'$ and $k = k'$.

Otherwise, if $k' = 1$, the first vertex is totally blocked, as this vertex may only be colored with 1 (all other colors are blocked for this vertex due to (A)). That means that there is no coloration of G, the first color of which is 1, i.e. there is no coloration of G, G is not colorable with g colors.

If the algorithm is continued for $k = k' = 1$ in Step 3, it goes immediately to Step 9 and stops there with the result: G is not colorable.

b2. (A) and (B2) hold:
Here vertex v_k is not totally blocked, i.e. there may be a coloration, the first k-1 vertices of which are colored with the same colors assigned to these vertices by matrix C. Therefore we try to color v_k with the smallest possible color $i = h_k$ (Step 3: If i is the smallest number with $c_{ik} = 0$, then set $c'_{ik} = 1$).

If $k = n$, we have a coloration of G and the algorithm stops with the result:

G is colorable (Step 3). If $k < n$, color i will be blocked for vertices v_l, $k < l \leq n$, which are connected with v_k (Step 5).

If none of these vertices v_l is blocked for all colors (Step 6), the conditions (A) and (B2) hold for matrix C' (which has the same elements as C, except those changed by applying the algorithm), with $k' = k+1$. With $C = C'$ and $k = k'$ the algorithm may be applied again beginning with Step 3. On the other hand, if there is at least one vertex v_l which is blocked for all colors, k remains unchanged and color $i = h_k$ has to be blocked (Step 7: $c'_{ik} = -k$) and all blockings caused by h_k will be erased (Step 8). C' satisfies the condition (A) and either (B1) or (B2) for the unchanged k. The algorithm may be applied again from Step 3, with $C = C'$.

Let us summarize:

At the beginning of Step 3 matrix C will always satisfy the conditions (A) and either (B1) or (B2). When running the algorithm from the beginning of Step 3 up to the return to this point, we have the following:

If (B1) holds, k is replaced by $k' = k-1$ and either (B1) or (B2) hold for k'.

If (B2) holds, there are two possibilities:

(B2.1) If it is possible to assign the smallest unblocked color to v_k, k is replaced by $k' = k+1$, and (B2) holds for this k'.

(B2.2) If v_k has to be blocked for the smallest still unblocked color, k remains unchanged and either (B1) or (B2) hold.

Let us consider a partition $P = (p_1, p_2, \ldots, p_n)$ which is not a coloration of G, and let be v_m, $m > g$, the vertex with the smallest index, for which the following holds: there is a set V_P of g vertices such that each $v_l \in V_P$ is connected with v_m and every two vertices v_l, $v_{l'} \in V_P$ have different colors; let k be the greatest index such that $v_k \in V_P$. Now let the first k-1 vertices in C be colored with the first k-1 colors of P; then each vertex with an index greater than k-1 is not totally blocked for all colors. But when color p_k is assigned to v_k, vertex v_m will be totally blocked, and therefore v_k itself will be blocked for color p_k. Before vertex v_k is blocked for color p_k, we can only say: there may be a coloration which coincides with P in the first k digits. Here we have a different case: there may be a coloration which coincides with P in the first k-1 digits; however, each partition that coincides with P in the first k digits, is not a coloration of G. If matrix C is produced by the algorithm, each partition smaller than P - according to the lexicographic order - is not a coloration of G.

If G is not colorable with g colors, no partition of the vertex set is a coloration of G. By applying the algorithm, k will always be smaller than n and finally the algorithm will stop when the first vertex is blocked for color 1.

On the other hand, let be $F = (f_1, f_2, \ldots, f_n)$ a coloration of G and let the first k vertices in C be colored with the first k colors of F. Then, no vertex v_m, $k < m \leq n$, is totally blocked. This holds for all k, $1 \leq k < n$.

If G is colorable, let be F the smallest of all colorations. As all partitions smaller than F are not colorations of G, by using the algorithm vertex v_n will be colored only when all vertices of V_{n-1} have the respective colors of F.

Summarizing the results we can now say:

By using the algorithm described in II, it will be determined whether graph G is colorable or not; if G is colorable, the smallest of the colorations will be given in matrix C.

IV. Final Remarks

IV.1. Chromatic Number.

A number g^* is called the (vertex) coloration number or the chromatic number of a graph G, if G is colorable with g^* colors, and not colorable with g colors, $g < g^*$. This chromatic number may be determined by using the algorithm for different values of g, in which case one should take into account the estimations of g^*, as e.g. described in [3].

IV.2. Implementation.

The algorithm may be shortened by applying Step 5 and Step 6 simultaneously. For it is not necessary to complete Step 5 when a vertex v_l, $k < l < n$, is totally blocked for all colors. A possible shortening of Step 8 is described under III.

The efficiency of the algorithm depends on the order of the vertices of G. It is advisable to number the vertices in such a way that for as many numbers k, $1 \leq k \leq n$, as possible, two subsequent vertices v_k, v_{k+1} are connected with each other.

The algorithm described above was used in a slightly different version in an implementation of a method by H. HEESCH for chromatic reduction; some results of the computation are stated and used in [1].

References:

[1] HEESCH, H., Chromatic Reduction of the Triangulations T_e, $e = e_5 + e_7$, J. of Combinatorial Theory, Vol. 13, No. 1, 8/1972.

[2] HEESCH, H., Untersuchungen zum Vierfarbenproblem, B.I. Hochschulskriptum 810/810a/810b, Mannheim 1969.

[3] ORE, O., The Four-Color Problem, Academic Press, New York, London 1967.

A NECESSARY AND SUFFICIENT CONDITION FOR CHOMSKY-PRODUCTIONS OVER PARTIALLY ORDERED SYMBOL SETS

H.J.SCHNEIDER

Abstract

The concept of Chomsky-grammar is generalized to multi-dimensional arrangement of symbols using multi-graphs the vertices and edges of which are labelled. The question arises in what cases productions preserve partial ordering. We give a necessary and sufficient condition for this. Furthermore, it is shown that context-free string grammars are a special case, but this is not true for context-sensitive grammars. Context-sensitive grammars in our definition are related to scattered context grammars.

o. Introduction

The problem of generalizing the concept of languages over strings is treated by many authors. Two formal concepts are developed to describe structures of higher dimensionality: array grammars [7] and web grammars [8]. (Furthermore, there exist some models not of interest here, describing structures by linear symbol strings [5,11] or by linearized productions [1,3].) Most of the work done in this area, starts from the aspect of pattern recognition. Therefore, the models developed need not be adequate in the area of programming languages where we have two applications: (1) The formal representation of logical program structure uses graphs or trees [2,5,13]; (2) it is possible to write a program immediately in two dimensions using a graphic display. In this case, there is no need to translate symbol strings into graphs [9], but there are two other translation processes involved: (a) rough structure into detailed structure and vice-versa [12]; (b) text structure (two-dimensional arrangement of symbols) into logical program structure. To facilitate these translations, it is suitable to have the same theoretical model to describe the symbol arrangement as well as the logical structure. In 197o, the author has developed a combinatorial system describing generation and transformation of partially ordered, labelled symbol sets called n-diagrams [1o].

We required our model to allow: (1) insertion of a new subdiagram some elements of which are successor (or predecessor) of elements previously generated, but other elements are not; (2) insertion or deletion of relations between elements; (3) insertion or deletion of elements in a branch without changing explicitly other branches. (This last point is not mentioned in [7].)

Further requirements arise from the special aspect of two-dimensional symbol arrangement: (4) concatenation must be possible in at least two directions, i. e. we need two independent successor relations to describe something as "on the right", "on the left", "below" etc. (not mentioned in [8]); (5) because of geometric properties cycles must be excluded.

On the other hand, the aspect of logical program structure requires: (6) the successor relations to be transitive; (7) cycles to be possible, but there are some reasons to recognize them in each case, i.e. it must be impossible to generate implicitly a cycle by changing or inserting subdiagrams.

The following model assumes diagrams to be partially ordered. Cycles may be handled by gathering the backward jumps in a separate relation. Transitivity is not necessary to describe symbol arrangements, but we may consider elements to be immediately adjacent, if they are connected by an edge and there is no path of length ≥ 2 between them.

1. Definitions

We consider a finite set V of symbols:

Definition 1: A representative of an n-diagram over an alphabet V is given by a relational system $(K;\varrho_1,\varrho_2,\dots,\varrho_n;\beta)$ where K is a finite set (the set of vertices), $\varrho_i \subseteq K\times K$ are n sets of edges $(i=1,2,\dots,n)$, and $\beta\colon K \to V$ is a mapping associating a symbol of V with each vertex of K (labelling function). $\mathbb{D}_n(V)$ denotes the set of all such representatives.

A representative may be interpreted as a multi-graph the vertices and edges of which are labelled: symbols of V are attached to vertices and symbols of $\{\varrho_1, \varrho_2,\dots,\varrho_n\}$ to edges. Since we are only interested in the structure and the labelling function, we eliminate the arbitrary choice of K by considering equivalence classes:

Definition 2: Two representatives d_1, d_2 are said to be equivalent: $d_1 \equiv d_2$ if and only if there is a bijective mapping $f\colon K_1 \to K_2$ with [1])

(a) $(x,y)\in\varrho_{i1} \Leftrightarrow (f(x),f(y))\in\varrho_{i2}$ for each $i=1,2,\dots,n$

(b) $\beta_1 = \beta_2 \cdot f$ [2])

An n-diagram over an alphabet V is given by an equivalence class of $\mathbb{D}_n(V)/_{\equiv}$.

Definition 3: An n-diagram D' is called subdiagram of D: $D' \subseteq D$ if and only if there are representatives d' and d such that

(1.1) $K' \subseteq K \;\wedge\; \varrho_i' = \varrho_i \cap (K'\times K') \;\wedge\; \beta' = \beta|K'$ [3])

If $D' \subseteq D$, we define the <u>difference</u> $D'' := D-D'$ by the equivalence class a representative of which is

$$K'' := K-K' \wedge \varrho_i'' := \varrho_i \cap (K''xK'') \wedge \beta'' := \beta | K''.$$

It is easy to see that D" doesn't depend on the choice of d' and d. Replacing a subdiagram by another subdiagram (the principle of combinatorial systems), we have to take into account the <u>embedding</u> of the replaced part, i.e. the edges leaving or entering this subdiagram:

$$E_i^+(d',d) := \varrho_i \cap (K'xK'')$$

$$E_i^-(d',d) := \varrho_i \cap (K''xK')$$

with K', K" as above.

<u>Definition 4</u>: A <u>production rule</u> is given by $p = (d_l, d_r, \pi)$ where d_l, d_r are representatives of two n-diagrams and π is a vector of 2n relations $\pi_i \subseteq K_l x K_r$ $(i=-n,\ldots,-1,1,\ldots,n)$.

Replacing subdiagrams we use the relations π to transform the embedding:

<u>Definition 5</u>: Let $p = (d_l, d_r, \pi)$ be a production and $D \in \mathbb{D}_n/_{\equiv}$ an n-diagram with $[d_l] \subseteq D$. If D is given by a representative with $K_l \subseteq K \wedge (K-K_l) \cap K_r = \emptyset$, then the n-diagram D' a representative of which is

(1.2) $$K' := K_r \cup (K-K_l)$$

(1.3) $$\beta'(k) := \begin{cases} \beta_r(k) & \text{if } k \in K_r \\ \beta(k) & \text{if } k \in K-K_l = K'-K_r =: K'' \end{cases}$$

(1.4) $$\varrho_i' := \varrho_{ir} \cup [\varrho_i \cap (K''xK'')] \cup E_i^+(d_l,d).\pi_i^{-1} \cup \pi_{-i}.E_i^-(d_l,d) \quad (i=1,2,\ldots,n)$$

is called <u>derivable</u> from D by p: $D \xrightarrow[p]{} D'$.

It is easy to show that the following relations hold:

$$[d_r] \subseteq D'$$

$$D - [d_l] = D' - [d_r]$$

$$\left.\begin{array}{l} E_i^+(d_r,d') = E_i^+(d_l,d).\pi_i^{-1} \\ E_i^-(d_r,d') = \pi_{-i}.E_i^-(d_l,d) \end{array}\right\} \; i = 1,2,\ldots,n$$

<u>2. Partially ordered diagrams</u>

As we have mentioned, we restrict our investigations to partially ordered n-diagrams:

<u>Definition 6</u>: An n-diagram D is said to be <u>partially ordered</u> if and only if each (K,ϱ_i) is partially ordered $(i=1,2,\dots,n)$.

If we suppose D and both sides of a production to be partially ordered, the construction of Def. 5 doesn't ensure partial ordering of D'. Therefore, we need some criteria to ensure this:

<u>Lemma 2.1</u>: Let $p = (d_l,d_r,\pi)$ be a production with partially ordered d_l,d_r. If for each partially ordered D with $[d_l]\subseteq D$ and each D' with $D \xrightarrow[p]{} D'$, D' is partially ordered, too, then p satisfies:

(2.1) $\varrho_{ir}\cdot\pi_{-i} \subseteq \pi_{-i}\cdot\varrho_{il}$

(2.2) $\pi_i^{-1}\cdot\varrho_{ir} \subseteq \varrho_{il}\cdot\pi_i^{-1}$

(2.3) $\pi_{-i}\cdot(\varrho_{il}-id_{K_l})\cdot\pi_i^{-1} \subseteq \varrho_{ir}$

(2.4) $\pi_i^{-1}\cdot\pi_{-i} \subseteq \varrho_{il}$

Proof: In each case, we consider an arbitrary p and some vertices satisfying the left-hand side of the implication to prove. Then we construct a partially ordered D such that partial ordering of the corresponding D' implies the right-hand side.

(a) To prove (2.1), i.e.

(2.5) $(k_1,k_2)\in\pi_{-i} \wedge (k_2,k_3)\in\varrho_{ir} \Rightarrow (\exists k'\in K_l)((k_1,k')\in\varrho_{il} \wedge (k',k_3)\in\pi_{-i})$,

we construct $D=[d]$ as follows:

$$K := K_l\cup\{k\} \qquad \text{with } k\notin K_l$$

(2.6) $\varrho_i := \varrho_{il}\cup\{(k,k)\}\cup\{(k,k') : (k_1,k')\in\varrho_{il}\}$

$$\varrho_j := \varrho_{jl}\cup\{(k,k)\} \quad \text{if } j\neq i$$

Because of (2.6) we have

$$(k,k_1)\in E_i^-(d_l,d) \Rightarrow (k,k_2)\in\pi_{-i}\cdot E_i^-(d_l,d)\subseteq\varrho_i'$$

$$\Rightarrow (k,k_3)\in\varrho_i', \text{ especially: } (k,k_3)\in\pi_{-i}\cdot E_i^-(d_l,d)$$

Therefore, there exists a k' with $(k',k_3)\in\pi_{-i}$ and

$$(k,k')\in E_i^-(d_l,d)\subseteq\varrho_i \Rightarrow (k_1,k')\in\varrho_{il}$$

by construction (2.6).

(b) Analogously, we prove (2.2), i.e.

(2.7) $(k_1,k_2)\in\varrho_{ir} \wedge (k_2,k_3)\in\pi_i^{-1} \Rightarrow (\exists k'\in K_l)((k_1,k')\in\pi_i^{-1} \wedge (k',k_3)\in\varrho_{il})$

using an n-diagram with:

$$\varrho_i := \varrho_{il}\cup\{(k,k)\}\cup\{(k',k) : (k',k_3)\in\varrho_{il}\}.$$

(c) To prove (2.3), i.e.

(2.8) $(k_1,k_2)\in\pi_i^{-1} \wedge (k_2,k_3)\in\varrho_{il} \wedge (k_3,k_4)\in\pi_{-i} \wedge k_2\neq k_3 \Rightarrow (k_1,k_4)\in\varrho_{ir}$

we consider the following $[d]$:

$$K := K_1 \cup \{k\} \quad \text{with } k \notin K_1$$

(2.9) $$\varrho_i := \varrho_{i1} \cup \{(k,k)\} \cup \{(k',k) : (k',k_2) \in \varrho_{i1}\} \cup \{(k,k') : (k_3,k') \in \varrho_{i1}\}$$

$$\varrho_j := \varrho_{j1} \cup \{(k,k)\} \quad \text{if } j \neq i$$

Because of (2.9), we have $(k_2,k) \in \varrho_i$ and therefore $(k_2,k) \in E_i^+(d_1,d)$.

$$\Rightarrow (k_1,k) \in E_i^+(d_1,d).\pi_i^{-1} \subseteq \varrho_i^!.$$

Analogously, we prove $(k,k_4) \in \varrho_i^!$. Thus: $(k_1,k_4) \in \varrho_i^!$.

Remark: In the case $k_2 = k_3$, this ϱ_i is not partially ordered.

(d) To show (2.4), i.e.

(2.10) $$(k_1,k_2) \in \pi_{-i} \wedge (k_2,k_3) \in \pi_i^{-1} \Rightarrow (k_1,k_3) \in \varrho_{i1}$$

we need two additional vertices:

$$K := K_1 \cup \{(k,k')\} \quad \text{with } k,k' \notin K_1$$

$$\varrho_i := \varrho_{i1} \cup \{(k,k),(k',k')\} \cup \{(k,k'') : (k_1,k'') \in \varrho_{i1}\} \cup \{(k'',k') : (k'',k_3) \in \varrho_{i1}\} \cup \delta$$

with $$\delta := \begin{cases} \{(k,k')\} & \text{if } (k_1,k_3) \in \varrho_{i1} \\ \emptyset & \text{otherwise} \end{cases}$$

$$\varrho_j := \varrho_{j1} \cup \{(k,k),(k',k')\} \quad \text{if } j \neq i$$

Then we have:

$$(k,k_1) \in E_i^-(d_1,d) \Rightarrow (k,k_2) \in \pi_{-i}.E_i^-(d_1,d) \subseteq \varrho_i^!$$

and analogously : $(k_2,k') \in \varrho_i^!$.

$$\Rightarrow (k,k') \in \varrho_i^! \Rightarrow (k,k') \in \varrho_i.$$

By construction, this is equivalent to $(k_1,k_3) \in \varrho_{i1}$ q.e.d.

<u>Lemma 2.2</u>: Let $p = (d_1,d_r,\pi)$ be a production with partially ordered d_1, d_r satisfying (2.1) - (2.4), and D a partially ordered n-diagram with $[d_1] \subseteq D$, then Def.5 yields a partially ordered D'.

Proof: (a) Trivially, $\varrho_i^!$ is reflexive.

(b) $\varrho_i^! \cap (\varrho_i^!)^{-1} \subseteq id_{K'}$ hold if there are no

(2.11) $$k_1 \in K_r \wedge k_2 \in K' - K_r$$

with $$(k_1,k_2) \in E_i^+(d_1,d).\pi_i^{-1} \wedge (k_2,k_1) \in \pi_{-i}.E_i^-(d_1,d).$$

We assume the contrary. Then there exist $k,k' \in K_1$ with

$$(k_1,k) \in \pi_i^{-1} \wedge (k',k_1) \in \pi_{-i} \Rightarrow (k',k) \in \varrho_{i1}$$

because of (2.4) and

$$(k,k_2)\in E_i^+(d_1,d)\subseteq\varrho_i \wedge (k_2,k')\in E_i^-(d_1,d)\subseteq\varrho_i \Rightarrow (k,k')\in\varrho_{il}$$

Since d_1 is partially ordered, we have $k = k'$; furthermore $k = k_2$ contradicting (2.11).

(c) $\varrho_i'\cdot\varrho_i' = \varrho_i'$ (transitivity):

$$\begin{aligned}\varrho_i'\cdot\varrho_i' = {} & \varrho_{ir}\cdot\varrho_{ir} \cup \varrho_{ir}\cdot\pi_{-i}\cdot E_i^-(d_1,d) \cup \varrho_i''\cdot\varrho_i'' \cup \varrho''_i\cdot E_i^+(d_1,d)\cdot\pi_i^{-1}\\ & \cup E_i^+(d_1,d)\cdot\pi_i^{-1}\cdot\varrho_{ir} \cup E_i^+(d_1,d)\cdot\pi_i^{-1}\cdot\pi_{-i}\cdot E_i^-(d_1,d)\\ & \cup \pi_{-i}\cdot E_i^-(d_1,d)\cdot\varrho_i'' \cup \pi_{-i}\cdot E_i^-(d_1,d)\cdot E_i^+(d_1,d)\cdot\pi_i^{-1}\end{aligned}$$

We simplify this expression using given transitivity:

$$\varrho_{ir}\cdot\varrho_{ir} \subseteq \varrho_{ir}; \quad \varrho_i''\cdot\varrho_i'' \subseteq \varrho_i''$$

$$\varrho_i''\cdot E_i^+(d_1,d) \subseteq E_i^+(d_1,d); \quad E_i^-(d_1,d)\cdot\varrho_i'' \subseteq E_i^-(d_1,d)$$

$$E_i^-(d_1,d)\cdot E_i^+(d_1,d) \subseteq \varrho_{il}-id_{K_1}; \quad E_i^+(d_1,d)\cdot E_i^-(d_1,d) \subseteq \varrho_i''$$

$$E_i^+(d_1,d)\cdot\varrho_{il} \subseteq E_i^+(d_1,d); \quad \varrho_{il}\cdot E_i^-(d_1,d) \subseteq E_i^-(d_1,d)$$

and (2.1) - (2.4).

Then we have:

$$\varrho_i'\cdot\varrho_i' \subseteq \varrho_{ir} \cup \pi_{-i}\cdot E_i^-(d_1,d) \cup \varrho_i'' \cup E_i^+(d_1,d)\cdot\pi_i^{-1} = \varrho_i'.$$

Thus, we obtain:

<u>Theorem 1</u>: Let $p = (d_1,d_r,\pi)$ be a production with partially ordered d_1,d_r. Then <u>each</u> n-diagram derivable by p from a partially ordered one, is partially ordered, too, if and only if p satisfies (2.1) - (2.4).

The context-free grammars are a very important class of string grammars. Here we define:

<u>Definition 7</u>: A production rule is said to be <u>context-free</u> if and only if d_1 contains exactly one vertex.

<u>Theorem 2</u>: Let $p = (d_1,d_r,\pi)$ be a context-free production with partially ordered d_1,d_r. [4]) Then each n-diagram derivable by p from a partially ordered one, is partially ordered, too, if and only if p satisfies:

(2.12) $\quad \varrho_{ir}\cdot\pi_{-i} \subseteq \pi_{-i} \wedge \pi_i^{-1}\cdot\varrho_{ir} \subseteq \pi_i^{-1}$

Proof: If d_1 contains only one vertex, then $\varrho_{il} = id_{K_1}$. Therefore, (2.12) is equivalent to (2.1) and (2.2). (2.3) becomes an empty, (2.4) a trivial relation.

3. String grammars

Of course, we want to have a similar result on string grammars. We may interprete a totally ordered 1-diagram as a string:

Definition 8: An 1-diagram is said to be a string-diagram if and only if ϱ_1 is a total ordering.

Remark: We omit the index 1 in this case and write ϱ, π_-, π_+, E^+, E^- instead of ϱ_1, π_{-1}, π_{+1}, E_1^+, E_1^- resp.

Definition 9: A string-production is given by $p = (d_l, d_r, \pi)$ where d_l, d_r are representatives of string-diagrams.

Lemma 3.1: If p is a string-production satisfying (2.1) - (2.4), then

(3.1) $(\exists k' \in K_l)(k', \min(K_r)) \in \pi_- \iff pr_2(\pi_-) = K_r$ [5])

(3.2) $(\exists k' \in K_l)(k', \max(K_r)) \in \pi_+ \iff pr_2(\pi_+) = K_r$

Proof: $\Leftarrow$ is trivial, $\Rightarrow$ follows from (2.1), (2.2) resp.

Remark: This lemma is true even in the more general case that the right-hand side is partially ordered and possesses a unique minimum (maximum).

Theorem 3: Let $p = (d_l, d_r, \pi)$ be a context-free string-production. Then each 1-diagram derivable by p from a string-diagram, is a string-diagram, too, if and only if p satisfies

(3.3) $pr_2(\pi_-) = pr_2(\pi_+) = K_r$

Proof: Consider a string-diagram $D = [d]$, $D \underset{p}{\longrightarrow} D'$, and a vertex $k \in K - K_l = K' - K_r$. Since (2.12) follows from (3.3), D' is partially ordered. Furthermore: Let be

$$(k, k_l) \in \varrho \Rightarrow (\forall k' \in K_r)((k, k') \in \pi_- . E^-(d_l, d) = E^-(d_r, d'))$$

$$\Rightarrow (\forall k' \in K_r)((k, k') \in \varrho')$$

Analogously, we have:

$$(k_l, k) \in \varrho \Rightarrow (\forall k' \in K_r)((k', k) \in \varrho')$$

Therefore, D' is a string-diagram, and (3.3) is sufficient.

To prove that (3.3) is necessary, we consider a context-free string-production $p = (d_l, d_r, \pi)$ and a suitable, totally ordered D. To ensure partial ordering of D', (2.12) must be satisfied. Furthermore, we need $(k, k') \in \varrho'$ or $(k', k) \in \varrho'$ for all $k \in K' - K_r = K - K_l$ and all $k' \in K_r$:

(a) Consider a k with $(k, \min(K_r)) \in \varrho' \Rightarrow (k_l, \min(K_r)) \in \pi_- \Rightarrow pr_2(\pi_-) = K_r$ because of (3.1).

(b) Analogously, we obtain $pr_2(\pi_+) = K_r$ considering a k with $(\max(K_r), k) \in \varrho'$.

(c) The third case $(\min(K_r), k) \in \varrho' \wedge (k, \max(K_r)) \in \varrho'$ is impossible:

$$\left.\begin{array}{l}(\min(K_r),k)\in\varrho' \Rightarrow (k_1,k)\in\varrho \\ (k,\max(K_r))\in\varrho' \Rightarrow (k,k_1)\in\varrho\end{array}\right\} \Rightarrow k = k_1!$$

As a corollary we have:

Theorem 4: The grammars containing only context-free productions with totally ordered d_r and (3.3), are equivalent to Chomsky's context-free grammars.

Since the vertices of a subdiagram need not be adjacent in the host diagram, a subdiagram of a string-diagram need not be a substring in the usual sense. Therefore, we cannot generalize immediately this theorem to the case of context-sensitive grammars. (In this case, we must suppose 1-diagrams with $(k_1,k_2)\in\varrho$ $(k_2,k_3)\in\varrho \Rightarrow (k_1,k_3)\notin\varrho$. Then all methods of string grammars are applicable without new aspects.)

Combination of some context-free string-productions, satisfying (3.3), yields scattered context productions [4]. For this, we must arrange the left-hand sides and the right-hand sides in the same order by adding suitable elements to ϱ_l and ϱ_r without changing π:

Theorem 5: The grammars containing only productions with

$$K_l := \{k_1,k_2,\dots,k_p\}$$

$$K_r := \{k_1^1,\dots,k_{q_1}^1,k_1^2,\dots,k_{q_2}^2,\dots,k_1^p,\dots,k_{q_p}^p\}$$

$$\varrho_l := \{(k_i,k_j) : 1 \le i \le j \le p\}$$

$$\varrho_r := \{(k_h^i,k_l^j) : i < j \vee i = j \wedge h \le l\}$$

$$\pi_+ := \pi_- := \{(k_i,k_j^i) : 1 \le i \le p \wedge 1 \le j \le q_i\}$$

are equivalent to the scattered context grammars.

Proof: With some minor modifications the proof of Theorem 3 may be used.

4. Acknowledgment

The major part of these investigations was performed during the author's employment at Technical University of Berlin. He wishes to thank Mr. Nagl, Mr. Pecht, and the students of our Erlangen seminar for their helpful comments and suggestions.

Footnotes

[1]) If we want to distinguish some n-diagrams we use the same subscripts or other distinguishing marks in every component without repeating this each time, e.g. $d_j = (K_j;\varrho_{1j},\dots,\varrho_{nj};\beta_j)$ or $d' = (K';\varrho_1',\dots,\varrho_n';\beta')$.

[2]) . denotes the composition of relations:

$$(x,y)\in\varrho_1\cdot\varrho_2 \Leftrightarrow (\exists z)((x,z)\in\varrho_1 \wedge (z,y)\in\varrho_2)$$

and the composition of mappings:

$$y = (g.f)(x) \Leftrightarrow y = g(f(x))$$

[3]) $\beta|K'$ means: β restricted to K'.

[4]) i.e. $\varrho_{i1} = \{(k_1,k_1)\}$ where k_1 is the only element of K_1.

[5]) $pr_2(M) := \{y : (\exists x)((x,y)\in M)\}$

References

[1] S.K. Chang, Picture processing grammar and its applications
Inform. Sciences 3 (1971), p.121-148

[2] K. Culik, Combinatorial problems in the theory of complexity of algorithmic nets without cycles for simple computers
Aplikace Matematiky 16, 3 (1971), p.188-2o2

[3] J. Feder, Plex languages
Inform. Sciences 3 (1971), p.225-241

[4] S. Greibach/J. Hopcroft, Scattered context grammars
J. Comp. Syst. Sciences 3 (1969), p.233-247

[5] P. Lucas/K. Walk, On the formal description of PL/I
Ann. Rev. Aut. Progr. 6, 3 (1969), p.1o5-182

[6] D. Milgram/A. Rosenfeld, A note on scattered context grammars
Information Processing Letters 1 (1971), p.47-5o

[7] D. Milgram/ A. Rosenfeld, Array automata and array grammars
Proc. IFIP Congr. 1971, Booklet TA-2, p.166-173

[8] J.L.Pfaltz/A. Rosenfeld, Web grammars
Proc. Int. Joint Conf. Artif. Intell., Washington, 1969, p.6o9-619

[9] T.W. Pratt, Pair grammars, graph languages and string-to-graph translations
J. Comp. Syst. Sciences 5 (1971), p.56o-595

[1o] H.J. Schneider, Chomsky-Systeme für partielle Ordnungen
Arbeitsber.Inst.Math.Masch.Datenverarb.Universität Erlangen, vol. III, No.3

[11] A.C. Shaw, A formal picture description scheme as a basis for picture processing systems
Inf. Control 14, 1 (1969), p.9-52

[12] N. Wirth, Program development by stepwise refinement
Comm. Assoc. Comp. Mach. 14, 4 (1971), p.221-227

[13] I.I. Yanow, The logical schemes of algorithms
Probl. Cybernetics 1 (196o), p.82-14o

DIE GRÖSSE DES MINIMALEN ANALYSATORS EINER KONTEXTFREIEN GRAMMATIK

R.KEMP

Abstract: Es wird gezeigt, daß die Zustandsmenge des Automaten, der bei der Analyse eines Wortes w jeweils die Stellen im Wort angibt, an denen eine Reduktion vorliegt, durch $C+\sum_{f\in P} l(Z(f))$ abgeschätzt werden kann. Dabei ist P das Produktionssystem der Grammatik, $l(Z(f))$ die Länge der rechten Seite der Regel f und C eine näher zu bestimmende Konstante. Der Automat, für den ein Konstruktionsverfahren angegeben wird, gibt ferner über die an der Reduktionsstelle im Wort w anwendbaren Regeln $f\in P$ Auskunft.

I. Notationen

Zunächst wollen wir einige wichtige und im folgenden oft benutzte Begriffe zusammenstellen.

Definition 1

Eine Chomskygrammatik $G=(I,T,P,S_0)$ heißt »kontextfrei«, wenn jede Regel $f\in P$ von der Gestalt

$$f: Q(f) \longrightarrow Z(f)$$

mit $Q(f)\in I$, $Z(f)\in (I\cup T)^*$ ist. Dabei ist die Menge I das Hilfsalphabet, T das Endalphabet, P das Produktionssystem und S_0 das Axiom. $Q(f)$ ist die »Quelle« und $Z(f)$ das »Ziel« der Regel f.

Definition 2

Ist G eine kontextfreie, chomskyreduzierte Grammatik (KCG), dann verstehen wir unter einem »Regelpaket« (RP) $\{f\}_A$ die Menge

$$\{f\}_A := \{ f\in P \mid Q(f)=A\in I\}$$

Definition 3

Ist G eine KCG, dann verstehen wir unter der »Zielmenge« V_A:

$$V_A := \{ w\in (I\cup T)^+ \mid \exists f\in\{f\}_A \sqcap Z(f)=ww_1, w_1\in (I\cup T)^*\}$$

Definition 4

Die RP $\{f\}_{A_i}$, $1\leq i\leq m\in[1:|I|]$ heißen »präfixfrei«, wenn für die Zielmengen gilt:

$$V_{A_i}\cap V_{A_j}=\emptyset \quad \text{für} \quad i\neq j$$

Definition 5

Die KCG heißt »präfixfrei« ,wenn gilt:

a) $|V_A| = \sum_{f \in \{f\}_A} l(Z(f))$

b) je zwei RP sind präfixfrei

Bemerkung:

Man erkennt leicht,daß für jede präfixfreie KCG gilt: Es existieren keine Regeln in P,deren Ziele den gleichen Anfangsbuchstaben besitzen.

Definition 6

Eine KCG heißt »R-präfixfrei« ,wenn gilt:

Je zwei RP sind präfixfrei

Definition 7

Unter einer »Regelpaketkombination« (RPK) $\{f\}_\sigma$, $\sigma = \{A_1, A_2, \ldots, A_k\}$, verstehen wir:

$$\{f\}_\sigma = \bigsqcup_{i=1}^{k} \{f\}_{A_i}$$

II.Einleitung

In [1] ist mit Hilfe eines Standardereignisses und eines speziellen Homomorphismus eine Möglichkeit zur Konstruktion eines Analysators einer Sprache,welche von einer LR(k)-Grammatik,$k \in \mathbb{N}_0$,erzeugt wird,angegeben worden.In den Arbeiten [2],[3] wurde daraus ein Algorithmus entwickelt,der in einem Schritt sukzessiv die Überführungstafel des minimalen Analysators liefert.Die Minimalität dieses Automaten ist in dem Sinne zu verstehen,daß er folgende Eigenschaften besitzt:

1) Er entscheidet möglichst rasch,ob ein Wort in der von der Grammatik G erzeugten Sprache liegt oder nicht.
2) Falls das Wort zur Sprache gehört,liefert er die Ableitung des Wortes mittels den Produktionsregeln aus P.
3) Er besitzt nur inaequivalente Zustände.

Wenden wir den Analysealgorithmus auf eine LR(0)-Grammatik an,dann ist bei der Analyse eines Wortes aus der von ihr erzeugten Sprache, jeder Schritt determiniert,d.h.in jedem Schritt liefert der Analysator genau eine der Entscheidungen:"Weiterlesen" oder "Reduzieren mittels der Regel f".In [4] ist eine Abschätzung für die Mächtigkeit der Zustandsmenge dieses minimalen Analysators - im Sinne obiger Minimalität - angegeben worden.Es gilt:

$$|\mathfrak{Z}| \leq 2 + \sum_{A \in I} |V_A| + \mu(G) \left[2^{|I|} - 1 - |I|\right]$$

Dabei ist $\mu(G)$ in der Größenordnung der Länge des längsten Anfangswortes der Ziele zweier Regeln,die in verschiedenen RP liegen.Die angegebene Schranke ist sogar scharf,d.h.es gibt Beispiele,für die obige Schranke die genaue Anzahl der Zustände des Analysators liefert. Wir können aber unseren Algorithmus auf jede beliebige KCG G anwenden, insbesondere also auch auf Grammatiken,welche die LR(k)-Bedingung verletzen.In diesem Fall ist bei der Analyse eines Wortes die Determiniertheit einzelner Schritte nicht gesichert,da folgende Situationen in der Überführungstafel des Analysators auftreten können:

1) Es fallen Endzustände in Zwischenzustände
2) Es fallen Endzustände zusammen

Solche Zustände,in denen die Entscheidung "Weiterlesen" oder "Reduzieren" nicht getroffen wird,wollen wir im folgenden als »kritische Zustände« bezeichnen.Genau diese kritischen Zustände sind bei der Analyse dafür verantwortlich,daß man in Sackgassen gerät.In dieser Arbeit wollen wir uns allerdings nicht mit diesem Problemkreis beschäftigen,sondern unser Interesse soll der Größe eines solchen "nichtdeterministischen Analysators" gelten.Der Name Analysator ist trotz der auftretenden kritischen Zustände berechtigt,da man letzten Endes den Ableitungsbaum eines gegebenen Wortes aus der von G erzeugten Sprache mit Hilfe dieses Automaten auffinden kann,indem man z.B.mit seiner Hilfe ein selektives Probierverfahren durchführt.Unsere Aufgabe wird also nicht darin bestehen,zu untersuchen,wie man optimal die Analyse mit diesem Automaten durchführt,sondern wir wollen einige Eigenschaften des Analysators selbst angeben.

III.Das Problem der Minimalität des Analysators

Wir wollen nun den oben eingeführten Begriff der Minimalität abschwächen,indem wir die geforderte Eigenschaft 1) ersetzen durch:

1') Der Automat entscheidet irgendwann bei der Analyse,ob das gegebene Wort nicht in der Sprache liegt.

Der Unterschied zu 1) besteht darin,daß die geforderte Entscheidung nicht "möglichst rasch" erfolgen soll.Falls das Wort in der Sprache liegt,erfolgt die Analyse wie in dem in der Einleitung angegebenen Automaten.Falls das zu analysierende Wort nicht zur Sprache gehört, trifft der Automat,der 1'),2),3) erfüllt,irgendwann die entsprechende

Entscheidung, während der Analysator mit 1),2),3) in dem Augenblick die Entscheidung trifft, in dem er zum ersten Mal während der Analyse auf einen Buchstaben tifft, der an dieser Stelle von keiner Regel $f \in P$ erzeugt worden sein kann. Der Automat 1),2),3) würde an dieser Stelle u.U. weiterreduzieren und erst später die entsprechende Entscheidung treffen. Intuitiv ist klar, daß der letztere Automat weniger Zustände besitzt als der Analysator, welcher in der Einleitung angegeben worden ist. Sein Nachteil besteht darin, daß die Entscheidung, ob das Wort nicht zur Sprache $\mathcal{L}(G)$ - $\mathcal{L}(G)$ ist die von G erzeugte Sprache - gehört, länger auf sich warten läßt. Wir wollen im folgenden den Automaten mit 1),2),3) »A-minimal« und den Analysator, der 1'),2),3) erfüllt, »Z-minimal« nennen. Bevor wir den Z-minimalen Analysator näher untersuchen, wollen wir ein Beispiel zur Verdeutlichung angeben:

Die gegebene KCG sei:

$f_0: S_0 \longrightarrow S\vdash$	$f_4: A \longrightarrow b$
$f_1: S \longrightarrow aA$	$f_5: B \longrightarrow aABd$
$f_2: S \longrightarrow aB$	$f_6: B \longrightarrow d$
$f_3: A \longrightarrow aABc$	

Wenden wir den Analysealgorithmus aus [2],[3] an, dann erhalten wir folgenden A-minimalen Automaten:

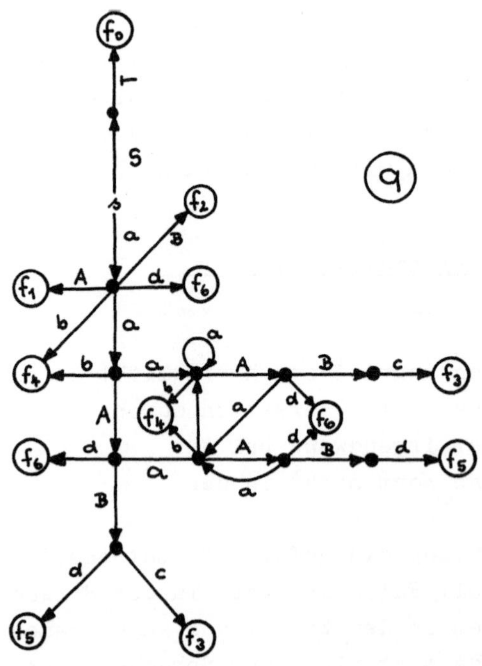

Fig. 1
Der A-minimale Analysator bzgl. obiger LR(o)-Grammatik

Wie man leicht nachprüft, ist der Z-minimale Automat gegeben durch:

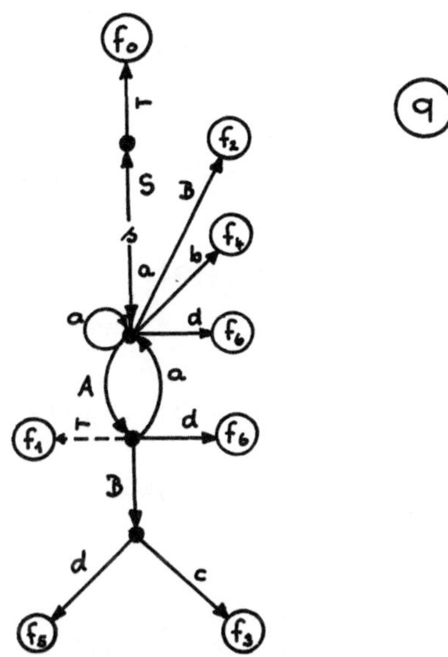

Fig.2
Der Z-minimale Analysator bzgl. obiger LR(o)-Grammatik (In den mit "←--" gekennzeichneten Ästen wird wie LR(1)-analysiert)

Wir erhalten für die Zustandsmengen $\mathfrak{Z}_1, \mathfrak{Z}_2$:

i) A-minimaler Automat: $|\mathfrak{Z}_1| = 19$

ii) Z-minimaler Automat: $|\mathfrak{Z}_2| = 12$

Betrachten wir z.B. das Wort $\mathfrak{L}(G) \ni w = a^4bd^2c\vdash$, dann ist die Reduktionsfolge beim:

i) A-minimalen Analysator: f_4, f_6 mit Analyseabbruch bei der Satzform $a^4ABdc\vdash$

ii) Z-minimalen Analysator: f_4, f_6, f_5, f_2 mit Analyseabbruch bei der Satzform $a^2Sc\vdash$

Wir wollen uns nun im nächsten Kapitel mit folgenden naheliegenden Fragen beschäftigen:

<u>Frage 1:</u> Wie kann der Z-minimale Automat konstruiert werden, u.U. mit Hilfe des A-minimalen Analysators?

<u>Frage 2:</u> Um wieviel vermindert sich die Mächtigkeit der Zustandsmenge des A-minimalen Analysators beim Übergang zum Z-minimalen?

<u>Frage 3:</u> Wann sind der A-minimale und der Z-minimale Analysator identisch?

IV. Der Z-minimale Automat

Wir wollen nun ein Verfahren angeben, welches uns den Z-minimalen Automaten liefert. Hierzu schreiben wir die Grammatik G in eine aequivalente Grammatik $G' = (I', T, P', S_0)$ wie folgt um:

Sei $\Omega := \{ w \in (I \cup T)^+ \mid \exists f, f' \in P \;\overline{m}\; Z(f) = ww', Z(f') = ww'', w' \neq w'' \}$

Wir erweitern nun das Hilfsalphabet I durch die Menge

$$X := \{X_1, X_2, \ldots, X_{|\Omega|}\}$$

Mit $\Omega = \{ w_1, w_2, \ldots, w_r \}$ definieren wir die bijektive Abbildung

$$\varphi : \Omega \longrightarrow X$$
$$\varphi : w_j \longmapsto X_j \qquad 1 \leq j \leq |\Omega| = r$$

In der Grammatik G schreiben wir nun in jedem Ziel, in dem $w \in \Omega$ als Anfangswort auftritt, das Hilfssymbol $\varphi(w)$. Alsdann fügen wir folgende Produktionsregeln dem Produktionssystem P zu: ($j = 1, 2, \ldots, |\Omega|$)

$$g_j : X_j \longrightarrow \begin{cases} w \in \Omega & \text{falls } \neg \exists \tilde{w} \in \Omega \;\overline{m}\; w = \tilde{w}w', w' \in (I \cup T)^+ \\ X_s w' & \text{falls } \exists \tilde{w} \in \Omega \;\overline{m}\; (w = \tilde{w}w', \varphi(\tilde{w}) = X_s, l(\tilde{w}) \\ & \quad \text{maximal}), w' \in (I \cup T)^+ \end{cases}$$

Es gilt nun:

1) $\mathcal{L}(G) = \mathcal{L}(G')$

2) $\bigwedge_{j \in [1:|\Omega|]} |\{f\}_{X_j}| = 1$

3) $|I'| = |I| + |\Omega|$

4) $|P'| = |P| + |\Omega|$

Der Algorithmus liefert uns nun die Überführungsfunktion δ' bzgl. eines Analysators, der $\mathcal{L}(G)$ mittels G' erkennt. Aus dieser Tafel konstruieren wir uns nun die δ-Überführungstafel des Z-minimalen Automaten, indem wir die Zustände, in die man durch das Lesen eines $X_i \in X$ gelangt, wie folgt beseitigen:

Wie jeder LR(o)-Automat hat der eben konstruierte Analysator die Eigenschaft, daß in einem Zustand Z, in dem ein Hilfssymbol A gelesen werden kann, auch alle Anfangsbuchstaben der Ziele des RP $\{f\}_A$ gelesen werden können. Wir nehmen an, daß die Regel g_j die Gestalt "$g_j : X_j \longrightarrow x_1 x_2 \ldots x_\lambda$" mit $j \in [1 : |\Omega|]$ besitzt. In jedem Zustand, in dem X_j gelesen werden kann, muß dann auch das Wort $x_1 x_2 \ldots x_\lambda$ gelesen werden können. Wir betrachten nun in der δ'-Tafel die "X_j-Spalte" — in der X_j-Spalte stehen alle die Zustände, in die man durch das Lesen eines X_j gelangen kann — und finden die Zustände $Z_1, Z_2, \ldots, Z_\xi$, die wir wie folgt verarbeiten:

In der Zeile, in der Z_v, $v \in [1 : \xi]$, steht, ist sicher auch die x_1-Spalte mit dem Zustand R_1 besetzt. In der R_1-Zeile ist sicher die x_2-Spalte mit dem Zustand R_2 besetzt,u.s.f.,in der $R_{\lambda-1}$-Zeile ist sicher die x_λ-Spalte mit dem Zustand $R_\lambda = g_j$ besetzt.Wir suchen also auf die angegebene Art und Weise den Zustand g_j auf— der Vorgehensweise entspricht das Lesen des Wortes $x_1 \ldots x_\lambda$ im Zustand Z_v—und identifizieren g_j mit Z_v,d.h.wir streichen in der δ'-Tafel die Z_v-Zeile,fügen eine g_j-Zeile an,die in allen Spalten,denen kein $X_i \in X$ entspricht,mit der Z_v-Zeile übereinstimmt.Auf diese Art und Weise verfahren wir mit allen Zuständen $Z_i \in \{Z_1,\ldots,Z_\varsigma\}$,so daß wir sukzessiv die neue g_j-Zeile auffüllen.Alsdann verarbeiten wir jeweils alle Zustände in den X_i-Spalten,$1 \leq i \leq |\Omega|$.Falls R_1 ein Endzustand f ist,vereinigen wir den Zustand Z_v mit f zu einem neuen Zustand Z_v,f, welcher die neue Zeile in der δ-Tafel repräsentiert.

Motivation: Bezeichnen wir den Automaten mit der δ'-Tafel mit $\mathfrak{A}'$ und den Z-minimalen Automaten mit $\mathfrak{A}$,dann gilt:
Haben wir im Graphen von $\mathfrak{A}'$ nebenstehende Situation mit $g_i:X_i \longrightarrow w$ und existiert in P eine Regel $f:A \longrightarrow ww'$,dann entspricht dem Anwenden der Regel f während der Analyse eines Wortes mittels G die Anwendung von g_i und dann von f,wenn wir mittels G'reduzieren wollen.Da aber in Z das Wort $Z(g_i)=w$ gelesen werden kann,können wir den Teilast,der auf den Zustand $\delta'(Z,X_i)$ in $\mathfrak{A}'$ folgt,an den Zustand $\delta(Z,w)$ "anhängen",was uns erlaubt,mittels G zu analysieren.

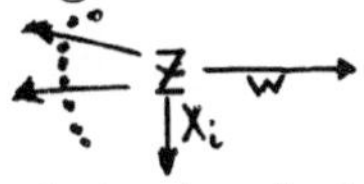

Fig.3

V.Die Größe des Z-minimalen Automaten

In diesem Teil der Arbeit wollen wir untersuchen,wieviel Zustände der Z-minimale Analysator besitzen kann.Es gilt:

Satz: Ist G eine KCG über dem Hilfsalphabet I und dem Endalphabet T, dann gilt für die Mächtigkeit der Zustandsmenge $\mathfrak{Z}$ des Z-minimalen Analysator:

$$|\mathfrak{Z}| \leq \sum_{f \in P} l(Z(f)) \quad + \quad 2 \quad + |\Omega|$$

Beweisskizze:

Beim Analysealgorithmus spielen die RPK eine wichtige Rolle.(vergl.[2] [3].)Die Gesamtheit aller durch die Grammatik definierten Kombinationen bezeichnen wir mit Π.Es gilt: $\sigma \in \Pi \Rightarrow \emptyset \neq V_\sigma = \bigcup_{A \in I} V_A$. Π teilen wir in Klassen $\Pi_i(G)$ ein,wobei jede Kombination aus $\Pi_i(G)$ die Länge i besitzt.In [4] ist bzgl.des Analysealgorithmus gezeigt worden,daß für die Zustands menge i.a.gilt:

$$|\mathfrak{Z}| \leq 2 + \mu(G) \sum_{i=2}^{|I|} \Pi_i(G) + \sum_{\sigma \in \Pi_1(G)} |V_\sigma|$$

falls G eine KCG über dem Hilfsalphabet I ist und $\mu(G)$ die Länge des längsten Anfangswortes der Ziele zweier Regeln, die in verschiedenen RP liegen, darstellt. Mit $\mu(G') = 1$ und $|I \cup \Omega| = |I| + |\Omega|$ gilt nun:

$$|\mathfrak{Z}| \leq 2 + \sum_{i=2}^{|I|+|\Omega|} \Pi_i(G') + \sum_{\sigma \in \Pi_1(G')} |V_\sigma|$$

Beim Übergang von der δ'-Tafel zur δ-Tafel werden mindestens

$$m = \sum_{i=2}^{|I|+|\Omega|} \Pi_i(G')$$

Zustände gestrichen. Damit gilt:

$$|\mathfrak{Z}| \leq 2 + \sum_{\sigma \in \Pi_1(G')} |V_\sigma|$$

Nun beweist man folgende Tatsache: $\sum_{\sigma \in \Pi_1(G)} |V_\sigma| \leq \sum_{f \in P} l(Z(f)) + |\Omega|$

Damit ist die Aussage unseres Satzes bewiesen.

Bemerkung:

Man kann zeigen, daß für die Mächtigkeit der Zustandsmenge des Z-minimalen Analysator gilt:

$$|\mathfrak{Z}| \leq 2 + \sum_{f \in P} l(Z(f))$$

falls $\Pi_1(G') = I'$ ist.

Korollar: Ist G eine R-präfixfreie KCG, dann sind der A-minimale und der Z-minimale Analysator identisch.

Literatur:

[1] Hotz-Claus "Automatentheorie und formale Sprachen", Band III BI Hochschulskripten , 823/823a

[2] K.O.Franz "Untersuchungen über den Aufwand bei der LR(0)-Analyse" , Diplomarbeit, Saarbrücken 1971

[3] R.Kemp "Binäre und unäre Ausdruckssprachengrammatiken im Zusammenhang mit LR(k)-Grammatiken", Diplomarbeit, Saarbrücken 1971

[4] R.Kemp "Größe von LR(0)-Akzeptoren" Tagungsbericht der IRIA, Paris, 3.Juli-7.Juli 1971

PROGRAMMSCHEMATA MIT BOOLESCHEN UNTERPROGRAMMEN

K. INDERMARK

Zusammenfassung

Iterative Programmschemata werden um boolesche Unterprogramme erweitert. Bei der Interpretation durch endliche Automaten bedeutet diese Erweiterung, daß die Ausgabe von einem look-ahead auf dem Eingabeband abhängen kann. Die dadurch bestimmte Klasse von Funktionen liegt schief zu der Klasse der Kellertransduktionen, also der durch die rekursiven Programmschemata bei gleicher Interpretation bestimmten Funktionen.

Einleitung

Ein Programm einer Programmiersprache kann man beschreiben durch ein Programmschema mit Interpretation: das Programmschema gibt den Kontrollfluß bei den Berechnungen des Programms an, während die Interpretation die Bedeutung der in diesem Schema auftretenden Operations- und Testsymbole festlegt. Diese Auffassung gestattet es zwar, Basisoperationen zu neuen Operationen zusammenzusetzen und auch Unterprogramme an ihrer Stelle zu verwenden, jedoch ist bei den theoretischen Untersuchungen bislang kaum berücksichtigt worden, daß Teste mit Hilfe von Operationen erweitert werden können. Programmschemata ermöglichen lediglich aussagenlogische Verknüpfungen der Basisteste.

Aus Programmiersprachen kennt man hingegen durchaus die Möglichkeit, Abfragen durch Operationen zu erweitern, wie das folgende Beispiel zeigt: um den Programmteil <u>IF</u> f(x) = 0 auszuführen, muß der Wert von x das durch f bezeichnete Programm durchlaufen, bevor er auf 0 getestet wird. Man beachte, daß anschließend mit dem ursprünglichen Wert von x weitergerechnet wird. Im Programmschema läßt sich diese Situation folgendermaßen beschreiben:

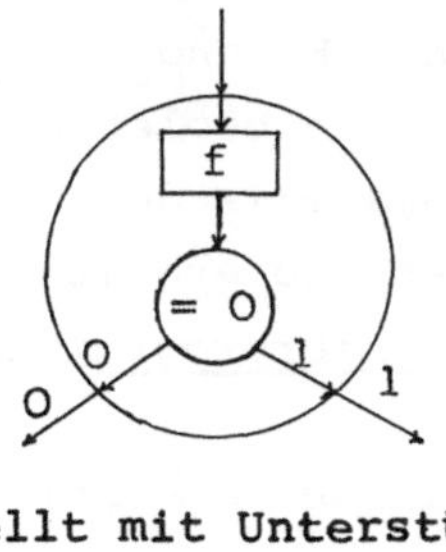

f
= 0
0 1
0 1

Diese Arbeit wurde erstellt mit Unterstützung der Gesellschaft für Mathematik und Datenverarbeitung mbH, Bonn.

Erste Hinweise auf diese um boolesche Unterprogramme erweiterten Programmschemata finden sich bei Ito (68). Hier soll untersucht werden, wie sich die Erweiterung der Abfragemöglichkeit auf die Klasse der durch eine Interpretation bestimmten Funktionen auswirkt. Es stellt sich heraus, daß es Interpretationen gibt, so daß die dadurch bestimmten Funktionenklassen der rekursiven Programmschemata und der Programmschemata mit booleschen Unterprogrammen zueinander schief liegen, d.h. sich gegenseitig nicht enthalten.

Programmschemata

Wir werden Programmschemata als Automaten interpretieren (Scott (67), v. Henke (71)), weil die Hinzunahme von booleschen Unterprogrammen schon vom Standpunkt der Automatentheorie aus von Interesse ist. Dabei werden die Lese- und Arbeitsbänder eines Automaten als Register mit unterschiedlichen Operations- und Testmöglichkeiten aufgefaßt. Dies hat zur Folge, daß die Register noch nicht im Programmschema auftreten können, sondern erst bei der Interpretation berücksichtigt werden. Wir gehen daher von monadischen Programmschemata aus.

Sei $F = \{F_1, F_2, \ldots\}$ ein Alphabet von Operationssymbolen und

$T = \{T_1, T_2, \ldots\}$ ein Alphabet von Testsymbolen.

Ein Befehl (über F und T) ist entweder ein operationeller Befehl, d.h. von der Form $k \cdot F_i;$, oder ein boolescher Befehl, d.h. von der Form $k \cdot T_i\ m,n;$, oder ein Stopbefehl, d.h. von der Form $k \cdot$ STOP; . Dabei sind $k,m,n \in \mathbb{N}$, $F_i \in F$ und $T_i \in T$. k heißt Präfix, m und n Suffixe eines Befehls. Eine nicht-leere, endliche Folge P von Befehlen heißt (monadisches) Programmschema (über F und T) genau dann, wenn (i) der i-te Befehl das Präfix i hat, (ii) jedes Suffix als Präfix vorkommt und (iii) P entweder genau einen oder genau zwei Stopbefehle enthält. Entsprechend der Anzahl der Stopbefehle heißt P operationell oder boolesch. Mit PS sei die Klasse der operationellen monadischen Programmschemata über F und T bezeichnet.
Gestattet man zusätzlich, daß in den booleschen Befehlen eines operationellen Programmschemas anstelle der Testsymbole auch boolesche Programmschemata auftreten können, so erhält man die Klasse BS der Programmschemata mit booleschen Unterprogrammen.

Gestattet man schließlich, daß in den operationellen Befehlen eines operationellen Programmschemas anstelle eines Operationssymbols ein rekursiver Aufruf desselben oder anderer Programmschemata erscheinen kann, so gewinnt man die Klasse RS der monadischen <u>rekursiven Programmschemata.</u> Für eine genaue Definition vergleiche man Strong (71).

Programmschemata lassen sich graphisch durch Flußdiagramme beschreiben.

<u>Beispiele</u> (i) Ein Programmschema aus PS

P_1: 1. F_1;

2. T_1 1,3;

3. STOP;

(ii) Ein boolesches Programmschema

P_2: 1. F_2;

2. T_1 3,4;

3. STOP;

4. STOP;

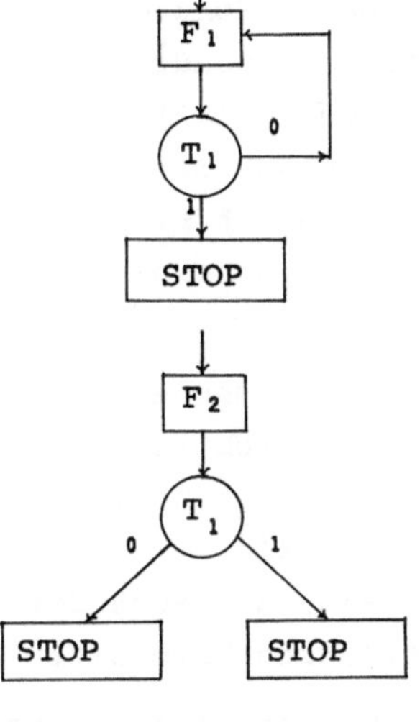

(iii) Ein Programmschema aus BS

P_3: 1. F_1;

2. P_2 1,3;

3. STOP;

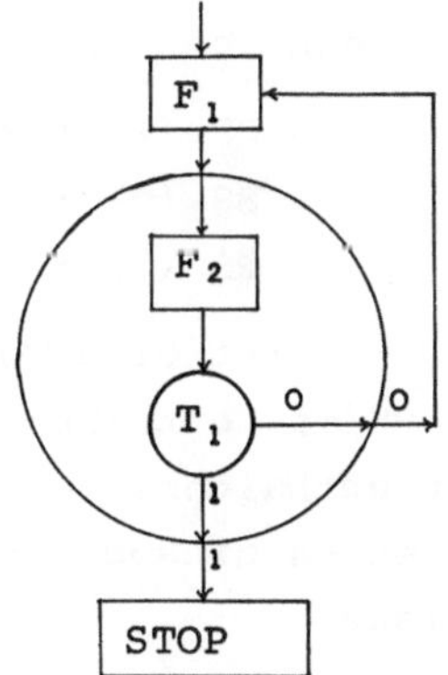

(iv) Ein Programmschema aus RS

P_4: 1. T_1 2,4;

2. F_1;

3. P_4;

4. F_2;

5. STOP;

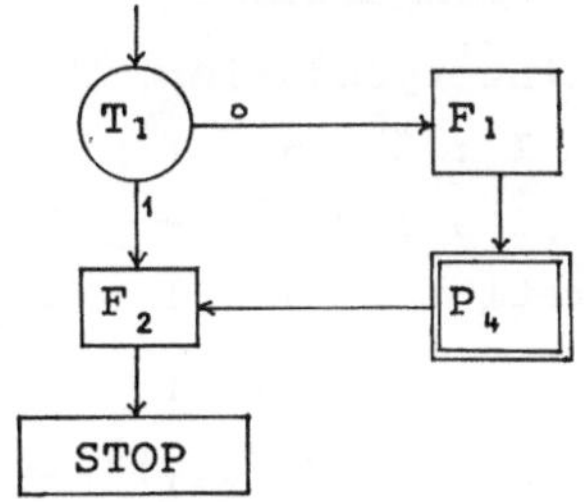

Wortinterpretationen

Um die Verbindung zur Automatentheorie herzustellen, schränken wir den Begriff der Interpretation (von F und T) in geeigneter Weise ein. Sei Σ^* das von $\Sigma = \{a_1,\ldots,a_r\}$ endlich erzeugte, freie Monoid mit dem leeren Wort e. Eine Wortinterpretation Φ von F und T bzgl. Σ ist ein Quadrupel (I, O, φ, n), bestehend aus einer Eingabeabbildung $I : \Sigma^* \to (\Sigma^*)^n$, einer Ausgabeabbildung $O : (\Sigma^*)^n \to \Sigma^*$, einer Vorschrift φ, welche jedem Operationssymbol F_i eine partielle Abbildung $\varphi(F_i) \subseteq : (\Sigma^*)^n \to (\Sigma^*)^n$ und jedem Testsymbol T_i eine partielle Abbildung $\varphi(T_i) \subseteq : (\Sigma^*)^n \to \{0,1\}$ zuordnet, und der Zahl n der Bänder. (Φ wird auch Automat genannt.)

Ein Programmschema P bestimmt bzgl. einer Wortinterpretation Φ eine partielle Abbildung $P(\Phi) \subseteq : \Sigma^* \to \Sigma^*$. Man vergleiche etwa Scott (67) für $P \in PS$ und Strong (71) für $P \in RS$. Damit wird auch der Fall $P \in BS$ klar. Es sei darauf hingewiesen, daß eine präzise Definition von $P(\Phi)$ als auch der Klassen PS, BS und RS mit Hilfe der Scott'schen Fixpunkttheorie gewonnen werden kann. (Scott (70))

Eine Wortinterpretation Φ induziert somit folgende Klassen von Wortfunktionen über Σ :

$$PS(\Phi) := \{ P(\Phi) \mid \Phi \in PS \}$$
$$BS(\Phi) := \{ P(\Phi) \mid \Phi \in BS \}$$
$$RS(\Phi) := \{ P(\Phi) \mid \Phi \in RS \}$$

<u>Satz</u> Es gibt eine Wortinterpretion Φ, so daß $PS(\Phi)$ echt in $BS(\Phi)$ und $RS(\Phi)$ enthalten ist und daß $BS(\Phi)$ und $RS(\Phi)$ sich gegenseitig nicht enthalten.

Wir werden diesen Satz über die Interpretation durch endliche Automaten beweisen.

Die Interpretation E

Die Wortinterpretation $E = (I, O, \varphi, 2)$ sei gegeben durch die

Eingabe $I : \Sigma^* \to \Sigma^* \times \Sigma^*$ mit $I(w) = (w,e)$, die

Ausgabe $O : \Sigma^* \times \Sigma^* \to \Sigma^*$ mit $O(w,w') = w'$,

die Operationen $\varphi(F_i) = sa_i : \Sigma^* \times \Sigma^* \to \Sigma^* \times \Sigma^*$

mit $sa_i(w,w') = (w,w'a_i) \quad (i = 1,\ldots,r)$,

$\varphi(F_{r+1}) = \text{lö} : \Sigma^* \times \Sigma^* \to \Sigma^* \times \Sigma^*$

mit $\text{lö}(a_i w,w') = (w,w')$ und $\text{lö}(e,w') = (e,w')$

und $\varphi(F_i) =$ "leere Funktion" für $i > r + 1$,

und die Teste $\varphi(T_i) = ta_i : \Sigma^* \times \Sigma^* \to \{0, 1\}$ $(i = 1,\ldots,r)$

$$\text{mit } ta_i\ (w,w') = \begin{cases} 0 & \Leftrightarrow w \text{ beginnt mit } a_i \\ 1 & \Leftrightarrow \text{andernfalls} \end{cases}$$

und $\varphi(T_i)$ = "leerer Test" für $i > r$.

Definiert man nun einen E-Automaten A (über Σ) als einen unvollständigen, deterministischen endlichen Automaten mit Σ als Ein- und Ausgabealphabet, einem Anfangszustand, Wortausgabe und der zusätzlichen Eigenschaft, das Ende des Eingabewortes zu erkennen und dadurch evtl. eine zusätzlich Ausgabe zu erzeugen, so beschreibt A eine partielle Abbildung $f(A) \subseteq : \Sigma^* \to \Sigma^*$. Wie man sofort sieht, sind die E-Automaten über Σ und die Programmschemata aus PS mit der Interpretation E in folgendem Sinne äquivalent.

<u>Lemma</u> PS (E) = $\{f(A) \mid A$ E-Automat über $\Sigma\}$

E-Automaten sind bestimmte Normalformen von Programmschemata. Die Programmierung in PS ist flexibler, weil Operationen und Teste nicht in einer bestimmten Reihenfolge ablaufen müssen.

<u>Lemma</u> Für $f \in PS(E)$ gilt:

$$\bigvee_{n \in \mathbb{N}} \ \bigwedge_{w,w' \in \Sigma^*} \ \bigvee_{w'' \in \Sigma^*} \left[w, w\,w' \in \mathrm{Def}\,(f) \Rightarrow f(w\,w') = h_n(f(w))w''\right]$$

Dabei löscht $h_n : \Sigma^* \to \Sigma^*$ die letzten n Buchstaben eines Wortes w, falls w mindestens die Länge n hat, andernfalls $h_n(w) = e$.

Man verifiziert diese Eigenschaft durch die Gleichungsdarstellung endlicher Automaten. Ohne Erkennung des Eingabewortendes gilt dieses Lemma mit $n = 0$. Die entsprechenden Abbildungen heißen dann sequentiell.

<u>Endliche Automaten mit look-ahead</u>

Während die Programmschemata aus PS bei der Interpretation E gerade die endlichen Automaten beschreiben, bedeutet die Erweiterung um boolesche Unterprogramme, daß den endlichen Automaten beim Testen ein Vorlauf auf dem Eingabeband gestattet wird: statt auf $a_i\Sigma^*$ $(i=1,\ldots,r)$ kann auf eine beliebige reguläre Teilmenge von Σ^* getestet werden. Dem Einschub eines booleschen Unterprogramms entspricht der Aufruf eines erkennenden Automaten.

<u>Satz</u> PS (E) $\subsetneq$ (BS (E) $\cap$ RS (E))

<u>Beweis</u> Sei $\Sigma = \{a, b\}$ und $f : \Sigma^* \to \Sigma^*$ definiert durch die Forderung $f(w) = a$, falls a in w vorkommt, und andernfalls $f(w) = w$.
Wie die folgenden Programme zeigen, gilt $f \in BS(E) \cap RS(E)$.

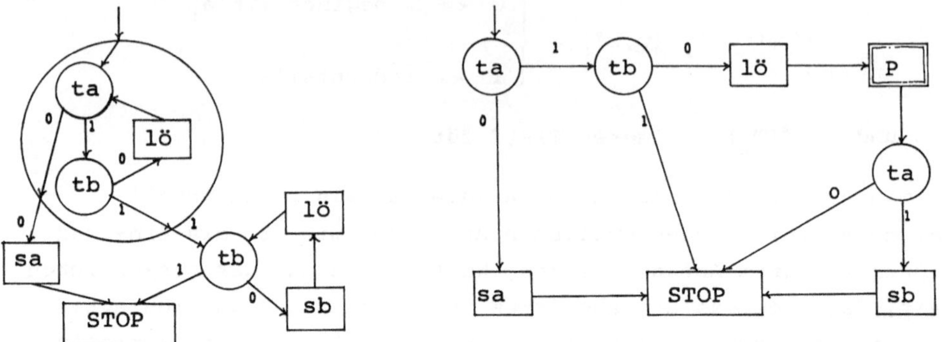

Andererseits erfüllt f wegen $f(b^n a) = a$ und $f(b^n) = b^n$ $(n \in \mathbb{N})$ nicht das obige Lemma für Funktionen aus $PS(E)$: es müßte ein $n_o \in \mathbb{N}$ existieren mit $f(b^n a) = h_{n_o}(f(b^n))w'' = b^{n-n_o} w''$.
Damit gilt: $f \notin PS(E)$.

<u>Satz</u> $BS(E) \not\subseteq RS(E)$
<u>Beweis</u> Sei $\Sigma = \{a, b\}$ und $f : \Sigma^* \to \Sigma^*$ definiert durch die Forderungen $f(e) = e$, $f(w\,a) = a\,w\,a$, $f(w\,b) = b\,w\,b$. Das folgende Programm zeigt, daß $f \in BS(E)$.

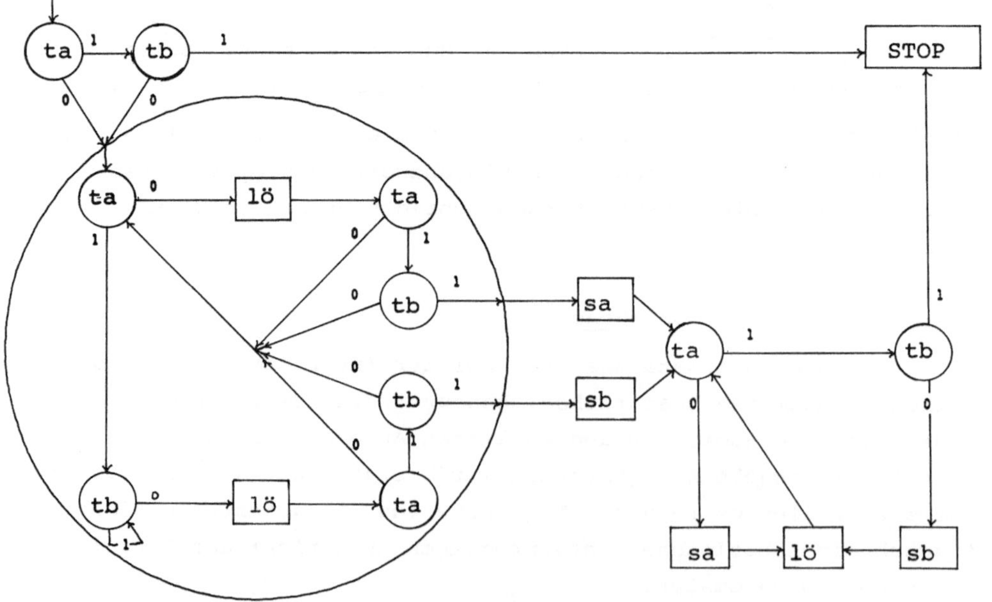

Angenommen, $f \in RS(E)$. Da sich ein rekursives Programmschema durch einen Kellerspeicher simulieren läßt (vgl. z. B. v. Henke (71)), muß es zur Berechnung von f einen Einweg-Kellerautomaten A über Σ geben. Wegen $f(w\ a) = a\ w\ a$ kann A die Ausgabe erst beginnen, wenn das letzte Eingabesymbol gelesen worden ist. Modifiziert man A so, daß während des Lesens der Eingabe diese gleichzeitig ausgegeben wird, so erhält man einen Kellerautomaten A', welcher folgende Funktion berechnet: $f' : \Sigma^* \to \Sigma^*$ mit $f'(e) = e$, $f'(w\ a) = w\ a\ a\ w\ a$ und $f(w\ b) = w\ b\ b\ w\ b$. Nach dem Pumping-Lemma ist Bild(f) nicht kontextfrei. Dies widerspricht aber der Tatsache, daß die Bilder von Kellerfunktionen kontextfreie Sprachen sind (Fischer (66)), also : $f \notin RS(E)$.

Satz $RS(E) \not\subseteq BS(E)$

Da, wie oben schon angedeutet, die Klasse $RS(E)$ übereinstimmt mit der Klasse der durch Einweg-Kellerautomaten über Σ berechenbaren Funktionen, ergibt sich die Behauptung aus dem folgenden Satz.

Satz Für $f \in BS(E)$ gilt: Def (f) ist regulär.

Beweis Die erkennenden endlichen Automaten $A = (S, s_o, F, \sigma)$ und $B = (T, t_o, G, \tau)$ mit dem Eingabealphabet Σ seien folgendermaßen verknüpft: A besitze einen Zustand $s_t \in S$, in welchem der Testautomat B aufgerufen wird. B entscheidet durch look-ahead auf dem Eingabeband, ob s' oder s'' der Folgezustand von s_t in A ist. Zum Beweis der Behauptung genügt es zu zeigen, daß der so konstruierte Automat eine reguläre Menge erkennt.

Während im Ein/Ausgabe-Fall das Hauptprogramm erst weiterarbeiten kann, wenn das Testprogramm die Entscheidung geliefert hat, kann im erkennenden Fall die Entscheidung zurückgestellt und parallel weitergerechnet werden. Jedesmal, wenn A in den Zustand s_t übergeht, ist mit den möglichen Folgezuständen s' und s'' in A als auch mit t_o in B weiterzurechnen. Die Situation läßt sich durch Zustandsbäume beschreiben. Sie sind in ihrer Tiefe durch $|T|$ beschränkt, wenn man vermeidet, daß sich auf einem Pfad ein Zustand von B wiederholt. Dies ist möglich, da bei der Wiederholung eines Zustandes von B durch seinen Platz im Baum die weitere Verzweigung bereits festgelegt ist. Damit wird klar, daß die von dem oben konstruierten Automaten erkannte Wortmenge auch von folgendem Automaten $C = (U, u_o, H, \mu)$ erkannt wird. U ist die Menge der binären Bäume mit folgenden Eigenschaften:

(i) die Verzweigungsknoten sind durch Zustände von B markiert;

(ii) die Endknoten sind durch Zustände von A, nicht aber durch s_t markiert;

(iii) auf einem Pfad tritt ein Zustand höchstens einmal als Marke auf.

Eigenschaft (iii) impliziert, daß $| U | < \infty$.
Anfangszustand u_o ist der triviale Baum s_o .

Der Folgezustand eines Baumes $u \in U$ bei der Eingabe $a \in \Sigma$ wird so konstruiert: man ersetze die Marken der Knoten von u durch die von den Automaten A und B bestimmten Folgezustände. Tritt dabei s_t als Marke auf, so wird der entsprechende Endknoten durch den Teilbaum

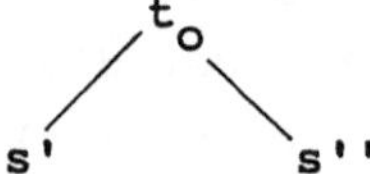

ersetzt. Dann muß der so entstandene Zustandsbaum noch konsistent verkürzt werden: die sich auf einem Pfad wiederholenden Zustände von B werden eliminiert, z.B. geht

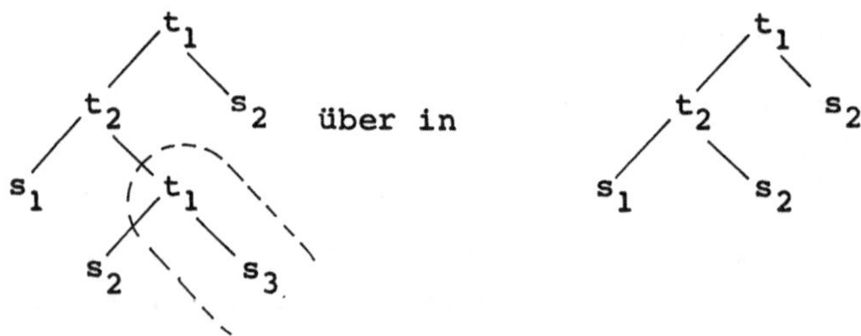

Schließlich ist ein Baum $u \in U$ Endzustand, wenn der durch u selektierte Zustand $s_u \in S$ Endzustand von A ist. Die Selektion eines Baumes u ist dabei durch die Endzustandsmenge von B bestimmt: bei der Marke $t \in T$ geht man nach links, falls $t \in G$, sonst nach rechts. Ausgehend von der Wurzel des Baumes erreicht man so den Endknoten mit der Marke s_u .

Literatur

Fischer, P.C. (66) : Turing machines with restricted memory access. Inf. and Control 9 (1966), 364 - 379

v.Henke, F.W. (71) : Programmschemata und Familien Abstrakter Programme. Mitteilungen der GMD Bonn Nr. 11 (1971)

Ito, R. (68) : Some formal properties of a class of non-deterministic program schemata. IEEE Conf. Rec. IX SWAT (1968), 85 - 98

Luckham, D. , Park, D. and Paterson, M. (70) : On formalised computer programs. Journal of Comp.Syst.Sc. 4 (1970), 220 - 249

Scott, D. (67) : Some definitional suggestions for automata theory. Journal of Comp.Syst.Sc. 1 (1967), 187 - 212

Scott, D. (70) : Outline of a mathematical theory of computation. Oxford University Comp. Lab., Techn. Monograph PRG-2 (1970)

Strong, H. (71) : Translating recursion equations into flow charts. Journal of Comp.Syst.Sc. 5 (1971), 254 - 285

PROGRAMMIERSYSTEME

A HIERARCHY OF CONTROL STRUCTURES

E.WEGNER

Summary: Four classes of control structures for sequential programs are shown to offer increasing expressive power. They allow control to be specified by

(1) four well-chosen structures with one entry and one exit each,

(2) the one-entry loop with escapes,

(3) the distributor-entered loop with escapes, and

(4) the unrestricted jump.

It is shown that a given program scheme can be described by the one-entry loop with escapes if and only if all control paths from the start to a cycle enter that cycle at the same node (irrespective of the number of nodes where the cycle is re-entered).

1. Motivation

Frequently occurring control structures are represented in programming languages by special constructs in order to make programs easy to understand, to prove correct, to modify, to debug, and to optimize globally during compilation. These structures are used for the "deductive" approach to program construction by stepwise refinement (Dijkstra 1970, Wirth 1971). Programs which were originally designed in terms of general flowcharts can be "inductively" structured to fit such language constructs (Ashcroft and Manna 1971) either in order to conform to a programming language not providing the jump or simply to gain the advantages stated above.

2. Programs controlled by the unrestricted jump

Before describing special control structures, let us remember the most general form of control for sequential programs. Let a "program scheme" be a (non-empty and finite) directed graph containing a distinguished node (the "start") from which paths lead to all other nodes. From any node to any other node there leads at most one edge, and there is no reflecting edge. A "program" is a program scheme in which each node is labelled by some executable "action" which has a single entry and any number of exits. Each exit must identify an edge leaving the node. Let us depict each node by a rectangle (labelled or not) and each edge by an arrow connecting two rectangles. Edges that enter the same node are drawn to flow together before entering the node in order to indicate that there is only one entry to its action. The start is marked by an entering edge which leaves no node. A figure representing a part of a program scheme will contain edges entering or leaving that part.

3. The four structures with one entry and one exit each

Dijkstra (1970) and Wirth (1971) use four structures for decomposing actions into subactions: the concatenation, the selection (including two special cases), the pre-checked loop, and the post-checked loop. Each subaction is either a test which cannot be further decomposed or a piece of program with any number of internal paths but only one exit.

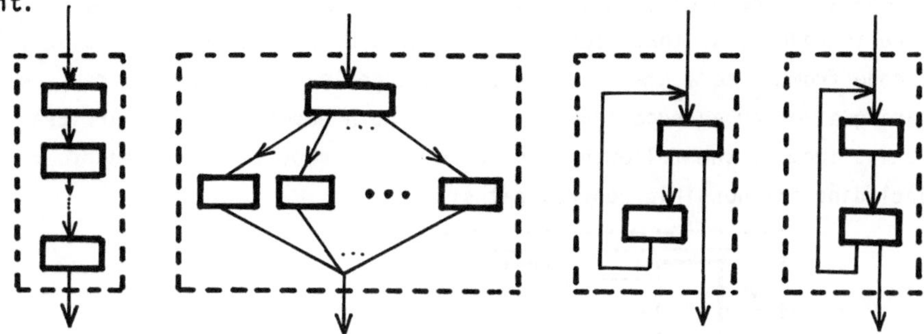

Ashcroft and Manna (1971) give an algorithm to express any flowchart program by some of these control structures (where control variables and branches must be added if and only if the flowchart contains two or more tests and at least one loop that are not contained in inner blocks). These structures meet the objectives in section 1 rather well, but occasionally the programmer is burdened with joining several control paths into the single exit and separating them immediately afterwards. Knuth and Floyd (1971) show that two familiar programs, a table search (a loop with two exits) and a backtracking program (two crossing loops), are more naturally controlled by jumps than expressed in terms of these structures by the addition of some actions.

4. Programs controlled by the one-entry loop with escapes

4.1 The jump to a labelled *end* is frequently used in ALGOL-like languages. Several languages provide special instructions to leave a control construct:

-- ALGOL 68 with its completer (Wijngaarden, Mailloux, Peck, and Koster 1969),

-- BCPL with the break command (Richards 1969), and

-- BLISS with the escape expressions (Wulf, Russell, and Habermann 1971).

Wulf (1971) claims that with the escape "the desirable properties of goto-less graphs are retained", and Clint and Hoare (1972) state that "programs which confine their jumping to genuine returns and exits do not present any great difficulty in the proof of their correctness". Since such an exit jump may terminate the execution of any enclosing control construct, we will not adopt the condition that each control structure has a single exit.

4.2 Definitely the most primitive decomposition of an action A is the decomposition into two subactions A_1 and A_2. The node labelled by A is replaced with two nodes labelled by A_1 and A_2. The definitions in section 2 imply the following rules for the "binary decomposition": The single entry to the action A will transform into the entry to one of the subactions, say A_1. Consequently, all edges entering node A will enter A_1, and if node A is the start, then A_1 will be the start. A "forward" edge from A_1 to A_2 must be introduced so that each node can still be reached from the start. A "backward" edge from A_2 to A_1 may be added. Each edge leaving A must be replaced by an edge leaving A_1 or by an edge leaving A_2 or by both edges. Given an arbitrary number of exits from A, the following figure shows the resulting "one-entry loop with escapes" including all possible control paths:

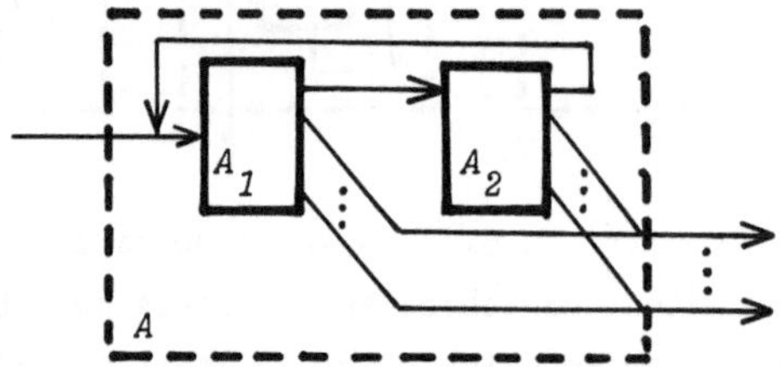

4.3 Conversely, in a given program scheme or program two nodes forming a one-entry loop with escapes may be found and combined into a single node. This "binary composition" is illustrated here for the two programs discussed by Knuth and Floyd:

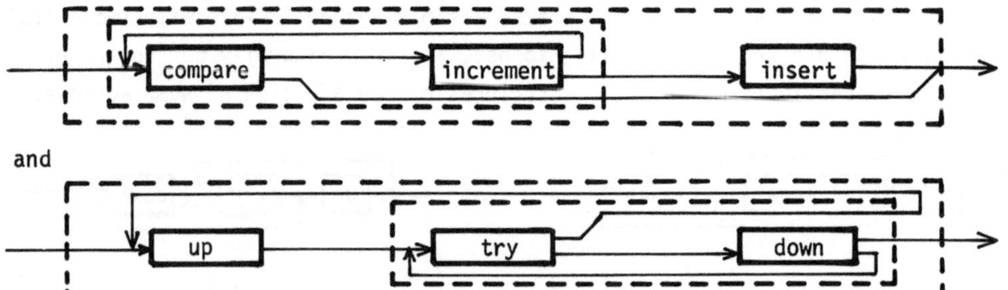

4.4 Theorem: A given program scheme can be reduced to a single node by repeated binary composition if and only if all paths from the start to a cycle enter that cycle at the same node.

Corollary: A given program in linear representation (in which each transfer of control is understood as a jump) can be reduced to a single action by repeated binary composition if there is no forward jump to a point between a backward jump and its target. (The inverse assertion does not hold since there may be e.g. a jump out of a loop and a forward jump back into it.)

4.5 As a preparation for the proof of the theorem, we give an algorithm to check a program scheme for the condition stated and to mark each edge either as forward or as backward. (The edges marked as forward will impose a lattice structure on the set of nodes.) We will use a notation based on ALGOL 68.

```
proc can be reduced = (programscheme p) bool:
begin
   proc mark leaving edges = (node node):
   begin mark node as active;
      for each edge leaving node do
      if the node entered by edge is marked active
      then mark edge as backward;
         if edge is marked forward then goto false fi
      else mark edge as forward;
         if edge is marked backward then goto false fi;
         mark leaving edges (the node entered by edge)
      fi;
      mark node as not active
   end;
   mark all edges as not forward and not backward;
   mark all nodes as not active;
   mark leaving edges (start of p); true exit
   false: false
end
```

4.6 The "only if" assertion of the theorem is obvious. As a proof for the "if" assertion we give an algorithm to accept a program scheme which has been successfully marked by the procedure *can be reduced* in 4.5 and to deliver a "composition tree", that is an ordered tree in which the terminal nodes are the nodes of the given program scheme and in which the terminal nodes of each subtree can be reduced to a single node by repetitive binary composition.

```
proc dependent tree = (node node) tree: co assume a global proc composition = (tree t1,
t2) tree: c the ordered tree having t1 and t2 as its direct subtrees c; assume a global
program scheme p which has been successfully marked; accept as parameter a node node
of p and deliver a subtree of a decomposition tree of p which contains as its terminal
nodes exactly those nodes n of p for which each path from the start to n contains node;
if called with the start of p as parameter, this procedure will deliver a composition
tree of p co
begin node n; tree t:= node;
   while there is a node n such that each forward edge entering n leaves a terminal
   node of t
   do t:= composition (t, if n is entered by a backward edge then dependent tree (n)
   else n fi); t
end
```

4.7 A possible representation of the one-entry loop with escapes is (in semi-precise explanation, related to the definition of ALGOL 68) rep range *r*; s_1; s_2 per where *r* is a "range identifier" defined by the "range declaration" range *r*, the pair rep ...

per encloses the two direct subactions s_1 and s_2 to be executed *rep*eatedly, and each s_i may contain conditional escapes of the form *if* b *then* v *leave* r *fi*; here b is a boolean expression and v yields the value to be delivered by the action if its execution is completed by the conditional escape. (Note how this escape can replace the jumps and the completer in the procedure *can be reduced* above.) For convenience we introduce some contractions:

-- *if true then* v *leave* r *fi* may be replaced by v *leave* r.
-- *skip leave* may be replaced by *leave.*
-- *leave* r, where r identifies the directly containing range, may be replaced by *leave* if simultaneously the declaration of r is removed.

The following contraction allows to represent a one-entry loop with any number of constituents and escapes:

-- *rep rep* ...; *leave per;* ... *per* may be replaced by *rep* ...; ... *per.*

In order to obtain representations of the four one-exit structures, we give some more syntactic sugar:

-- *rep* .... *leave per* may be replaced by *begin* .... *end.*
-- *rep if not* b_1 *then* v_1 *leave fi;* s; *if not* b_2 *then* v_2 *leave fi per* may be replaced by v_1 *while* b_1 *rep* s *per* v_2 *while* b_2.
-- *skip while true* may be omitted.
-- *begin range* r; *begin if* b *then leave fi;* s_2 *leave* r *end;* s_1 *end* may be replaced by *if* b *then* s_1 *else* s_2 *fi.*
-- *else skip fi* may be replaced by *fi.*
-- *if* $i=1$ *then* s_1 *else* s *fi* may be replaced by *case* i *in* s_1 *out* s *esac.*
-- *if* $i=n$ *then* s_n *else case* i *in* $s_1, \ldots, s_{n-1}$ *out* s *esac fi* for $n \geq 2$ may be replaced by *case* i *in* $s_1, \ldots, s_n$ *out* s *esac.*

4.8 The escape from any enclosing control construct is provided in BLISS. The BCPL break command is restricted to escape from the smallest enclosing loop. The ALGOL 68 completer causes completion of the elaboration of the directly surrounding serial-clause but not of a repetitive statement; it can be generalized to complete the elaboration of any containing serial-clause (Wegner 1972). The BLISS escape must and the BCPL break cannot deliver a value, while the ALGOL 68 completer may.

4.9 As Wulf (1971) reports, the escape allows to program conveniently without the jump. The contractions in 4.7 show that the one-entry loop with escapes is at least as powerful as the collection of one-exit structures. Indeed, it is even more powerful since it can describe the two examples of Knuth and Floyd as well as the program that Ashcroft and Manna constructed to demonstrate the need for additional control variables. However, it is less powerful than the unrestricted jump, since the following program cannot be reduced to a single node by binary composition:

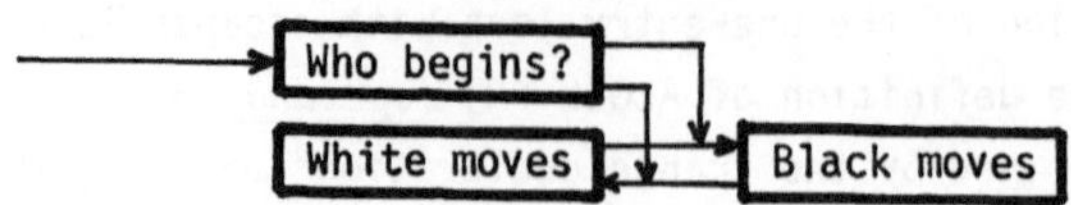

5. The distributor-entered loop with escapes

5.1 The fact that the simple game in 4.9 cannot be described by the one-entry loop with escapes gives rise to an afterthought. Here is a more powerful and complicated control structure, a loop preceded by a distributor to its constituents:

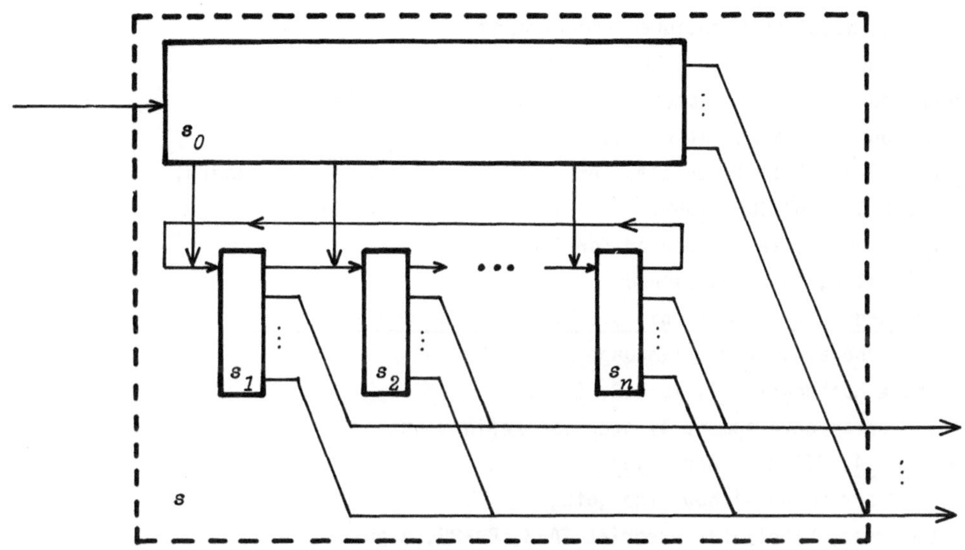

5.2 By a slight extension to the argument in 4.5 and 4.6, a given program scheme can be reduced to a single node by repeatedly combining nodes into such a "distributor-entered loop with escapes" if and only if all paths from the start to a cycle enter that cycle by edges that leave the same node.

5.3 The cases where the distributor s_0 delivers an integer i or a boolean b lend themselves to the representations *at* i *enterloop* $s_1, \ldots, s_n$ *out* s_{n+1} *endloop* (where the *out* s_{n+1} is easily built around the basic construct) and *on* b *enterloop* s_1 *otherwise* s_2 *endloop*. This latter construct effectively allows to transfer control between the *then* and the *else* clauses of an *if* construct. The general construct might read *performing* s_0 *enterloop* $s_1, \ldots, s_n$ *endloop* where s_0 may contain *enter* statements identifying a loop constituent, and each s_i for $i = 0, 1, \ldots, n$ may contain escapes.

5.4 The one-entry loop with escapes is a special case of this structure; let s_0 be *enter 1*. Here is a program which cannot be expressed even by the distributor-entered loop with escapes:

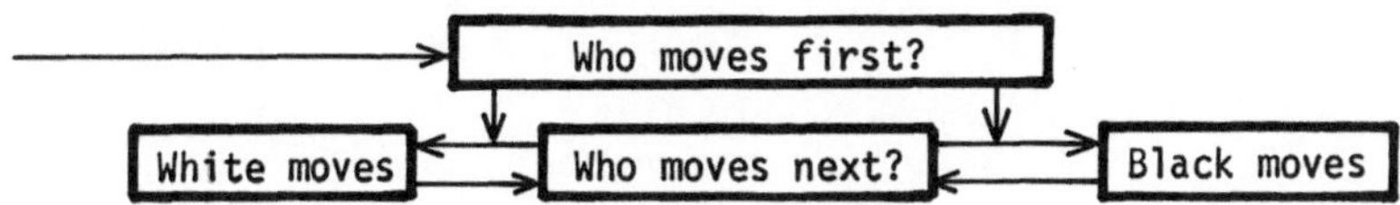

References

E. Ashcroft and Z. Manna, The translation of "go to" programs to "while" programs, IFIP Congress, Ljubljana, preprint TA-2, 147-152, August 1971.

M. Clint and C.A.R. Hoare, Program proving: jumps and functions, Acta informatica 1,214-224, 1972.

E.W. Dijkstra, Notes on structured programming, Report 70-Wsk-03, Technical University Eindhoven, April 1970.

D.E. Knuth and R.W. Floyd, Notes on avoiding "go to" statements, Information processing letters 1, 23-31, February 1971.

M. Richards, BCPL: A tool for compiler writing and systems programming, AFIPS SJCC 34, 557-566, 1969.

E. Wegner, A generalized completer for ALGOL 68, ALGOL Bulletin, to be published.

A.van Wijngaarden, B.J. Mailloux, J.E.L. Peck, and C.H.A. Koster, Report on the algorithmic language ALGOL 68, Numerische Mathematik 14, 79-218, 1969.

N. Wirth, Program development by stepwise refinement, Comm. ACM 14, 221-227, April 1971.

W.A. Wulf, Programming without the goto, IFIP Congress, Ljubljana, preprint TA-3, 84-88, August 1971.

W.A. Wulf, D.B. Russell, and A.N. Habermann, BLISS: A language for systems programming, Comm. ACM 14, 780-790, December 1971.

MEHRDEUTIGE ENTSCHEIDUNGSTABELLEN

G.DATHE

Zusammenfassung

Eindeutigkeit und Mehrdeutigkeit von Entscheidungstabellen werden dadurch definiert, daß die Regeln als Mengen aufgefaßt werden. Die Verarbeitung mehrdeutiger Tabellen wird erläutert. Eine Verbesserung der Matrizenmethode wird erwähnt, die es in gewisser Weise gestattet, die Vorteile von Baum- und Matrizenmethode zu vereinen.

1. Allgemeines

Eine Entscheidungstabelle sei definiert als eine Tabelle aus

- o Aktionen
- o Bedingungen
- o Anzeigern

Bild 1 zeigt eine konkrete Tabelle, die dieser Definition genügt. B_1, B_2 und B_3 stehen darin für Bedingungen, z. B. B_1 für "Steuerklasse = 1?". A_1, A_2, A_3 und A_4 stehen für Aktionen, z. B. A_1 für "Setze Freibetrag auf Null". Die Anzeiger Y, N und - stehen für Bedingung muß erfüllt sein, Bedingung darf nicht erfüllt sein und Bedingung ist irrelevant. Der Anzeiger X steht für Aktion soll ausgeführt werden. Zusammengehörige Anzeiger bilden eine

- o Regel.

b	R_1	R_2	R_3
B_1	Y	-	-
B_2	N	Y	-
B_3	-	-	Y
A_1	X		
A_2	X		X
A_3		X	
A_4	X	X	

Bild 1 Entscheidungstabelle

s	b	F_1	F_2	F_3	F_4	F_5	F_6	F_7	F_8
1	B_1	Y	Y	Y	Y	N	N	N	N
2	B_2	Y	Y	N	N	Y	Y	N	N
4	B_3	Y	N	Y	N	Y	N	Y	N
	K	7	3	5	1	6	2	4	0

Bild 2 Formal mögliche Fälle

Die Tabelle nach Bild 1 besitzt die Regeln R_1, R_2 und R_3.

Bild 1 stellt die übliche Anordnung einer Entscheidungstabelle dar. Manchmal sind jedoch auch Zeilen und Spalten vertauscht.

Sinnvolle Aussagen kann eine Entscheidungstabelle erst liefern, wenn zwischen den Bedingungen logische Operatoren definiert sind. Üblich ist die implizite Definition des logischen

o UND.

Gelegentlich kann man explizit andere logische Operatoren definieren.

Die Aussagen einer Entscheidungstabelle beziehen sich auf bestimmte Fälle. Ein

o Fall

beschreibt eine konkrete Entscheidungssituation, die dadurch gekennzeichnet ist, daß jede Bedingung entweder bejaht oder verneint ist - unbestimmt ist nicht zulässig. Bild 2 zeigt für 3 Bedingungen alle möglichen Fälle. Es liegt nahe, die Fälle als Dualzahlen aufzufassen, indem man z.B. die Bedingungen $B_1 .... B_n$ mit den Stellenwerten $2^o ...... 2^{n-1}$ versieht, N als 0 und Y als L interpretiert. Man erhält damit eine eindeutige Kurzschreibweise K für die durch F_i willkürlich benannten Fälle, z.B.

$K = 5$ für F_3.

Jede Regel kann man als eine Menge auffassen, deren Elemente die Fälle sind, für die sie gilt. Für die Entscheidungstabelle nach Bild 1 gilt

$$R_1 = \{1,5\}; \quad R_2 = \{2,3,6,7\}; \quad R_3 = \{4,5,6,7\}$$

Bei der Analyse von Entscheidungstabellen stehen zwei Begriffe im Vordergrund:

o Vollständigkeit

o Eindeutigkeit/Mehrdeutigkeit

Eine Tabelle heißt vollständig, wenn die Vereinigungsmenge aus den Regeln mit der Menge F, gebildet durch die Fälle, identisch ist.

Eine Tabelle heißt eindeutig, wenn die Schnittmengen

$$R_i \cap R_j \qquad i \neq j$$

für alle möglichen Regelpaare leer sind, sonst mehrdeutig.

Diese Betrachtungen gelten entweder

- o formal - Betrachtung der Menge F_f aus allen formal möglichen Fällen
- o real - Betrachtung nur der Menge F_r aus allen real möglichen Fällen.

Ein Unterschied zwischen F_f und F_r ergibt sich immer, wenn Bedingungen nicht unabhängig voneinander sind, so daß die Aussage WAHR für eine Bedingung mit FALSCH für andere Bedingungen gekoppelt ist. Nehmen wir z.B. für Bild 1 an

B1: Steuerklasse = 1 ?

B2: Steuerklasse = 2 ?

B3: Steuerklasse = 3 ?

so gilt

$$F_f = \{0, 1, 2, 3, 4, 5, 6, 7\}$$
$$F_r = \{0, 1, 2, 4\}$$
$$\overline{F}_r = \{x : x \in F_f, x \notin F_r\} = \{3, 5, 6, 7\}$$

Die Tabelle nach Bild 1 ist

a) formal mehrdeutig:

$$R_1 \cap R_2 = \emptyset \equiv R_{12}$$
$$R_1 \cap R_3 = \{5\} \equiv R_{13}$$
$$R_2 \cap R_3 = \{6,7\} \equiv R_{23}$$

b) real eindeutig:

$$R_{13} \subset \overline{F}_r, \quad R_{23} \subset \overline{F}_r$$

c) formal und real unvollständig:

Der Fall 0 tritt in keiner Regel und damit auch nicht in der Vereinigungsmenge auf, somit

$$R_1 \cup R_2 \cup R_3 \neq F_f$$
$$R_1 \cup R_2 \cup R_3 \neq F_r$$

In Entscheidungstabellenumwandlern lassen sich die formalen Aspekte am besten zur Umwandlungszeit prüfen, d.h. bei der Umwandlung der Tabellen in ein Programm, die realen Aspekte dagegen am besten zur Ausführungszeit, d.h. bei der Ausführung des generierten Programmes. Das liegt daran, daß zur Umwandlungszeit die Kopplung von Bedingungen nicht immer entscheidbar ist, z.B. sind die Bedingungen

B1 : X = A ?

B2: X = B ?

verkoppelt, falls bei dem betreffenden Problem immer

$A \neq B$

gilt.

2. Mehrdeutige Tabellen

Die überwiegende Zahl bisheriger Entscheidungstabellenumwandler benutzt die sogenannte Entscheidungsbaummethode (s. u.); nur zwei käufliche Umwandler benutzen die Matrizenmethode. Da die Entscheidungsbaummethode formal eindeutige Tabellen verlangt, steht die Analyse des Bedingungsteils bisher im Vordergrund. Eine Problemlösung geht also von den Bedingungen aus, betrachtet - zumindest implizit - alle Fälle und bestimmt die zugehörigen Aktionen.

Bei vielen Problemen ist es jedoch angemessener, von den Aktionen auszugehen, zu berücksichtigen, daß die Aktionen nur unter bestimmten Bedingungskonstellationen ausgeführt werden und die Analyse des Bedingungsteils - wenn überhaupt erforderlich - zum Schluß unter dem realen Aspekt, eventuell mit Rechnerunterstützung, durchzuführen. Hierzu ein Beispiel:

Es gebe die Steuerabzüge A, B und C, die jeweils wirksam werden, wenn die zugehörige Steuerart (S-ART) A, B oder C vorliegt. Die Berechnung des Steuerabzugs erfolgt in den Unterprogrammen S-ABA, S-ABB und S-ABC, das Unterprogramm DRUCK drucke Ergebnisse aus. Bild 3 stellt diesen Sachverhalt dar.

	R_1	R_2	R_3
S-ART = A	Y	-	-
S-ART = B	-	Y	-
S-ART = C	-	-	Y
DO S-ABA	X		
DO S-ABB		X	
DO S-ABC			X
DO DRUCK	X	X	X

Bild 3 Steuerabzug - formal mehrdeutig

	R_1	R_2	R_3	R_4	R_5	R_6	R_7
S-ART = A	Y	Y	Y	Y	N	N	N
S-ART = B	Y	Y	N	N	Y	Y	N
S-ART = C	Y	N	Y	N	Y	N	Y
DO S-ABA	X	X	X	X			
DO S-ABB	X	X			X	X	
DO S-ABC	X		X		X		X
DO DRUCK	X	X	X	X	X	X	X

Bild 4 Steuerabzug - formal eindeutig

Es ist besonders zu beachten, daß diese Darstellung unabhängig davon gilt, ob sich die Steuerarten gegenseitig ausschließen (reale Eindeutigkeit) oder nicht (reale Mehrdeutigkeit). Im zweiten Fall muß man lediglich dafür sorgen, daß alle zutreffenden Regeln ausgeführt werden.
Der Zwang zur Formulierung formal eindeutiger Tabellen bedeutet letztlich, daß eine Aktion mit allen Bedingungen verkoppelt wird, obwohl sie vom Problem her nur mit einigen Bedingungen verkoppelt ist:

Bei sich ausschließenden Steuerarten hätte man einen Teil der Irrelevanzanzeiger (-) durch N zu ersetzen. Dadurch leidet die Übersicht, weil nicht vorhandene Abhängigkeiten der Aktionen von Bedingungen vorgetäuscht werden. Die Zergliederung von großen Tabellen in mehrere kleine wird dadurch erschwert. In [1] wird als Hilfsmittel für die Zergliederung formal eindeutiger Tabellen die Aufstellung einer Zergliederungsmatrix vorgeschlagen, die genau die Abhängigkeiten rückgängig macht, die in mehrdeutige Tabellen gar nicht erst eingehen.

Bei sich nicht ausschließenden Steuerarten hat man beim Zwang zu formal eindeutigen Tabellen die Wahl zwischen der Darstellung nach Bild 4 oder in drei getrennten Tabellen.

Die beiden Umwandler, die bisher formal und real mehrdeutige Tabellen zulassen, behandeln die reale Mehrdeutigkeit unterschiedlich:

Der Umwandler DETAB/GT [2] geht zeilenweise vor:
Eine Aktion - als Menge aufgefaßt - repräsentiert die Vereinigungsmenge aller Regeln, in denen die Aktion angekreuzt ist, in Bild 3 z.B.

DO DRUCK = {1, 2, 3, 4, 5, 6, 7}

Ist der Fall Element der jeweiligen Aktion, so wird die Aktion genau einmal ausgeführt.

Der Vorteil zeilenweiser Bearbeitung ist:

- Jede Aktion erscheint statisch nur ein Mal im generierten Programm.

Nachteile sind:

- Der Regelzusammenhang geht verloren.
- Die Reihenfolge der Aktionen muß in allen Regeln gleich sein.
- Jede einzelne Aktion wird relativ aufwendig angesteuert.

Der Umwandler AGENTA [3, 4] geht spalten-, d.h. regelweise vor. Sofern der Fall Element einer

Regel ist, wird die Regel

o akut.

Für den Fall K = 5 werden in Bild 3 die Regeln R_1 und R_3 akut. Die Ausführung akuter Regeln kann durch Paramter gesteuert werden:

o ALL alle akuten Regeln ausführen in der Reihenfolge von links nach rechts

o FIRST die erste akute Regel ausführen.

Daneben existiert als Gegenstück zur ELSE-Regel eine AM-Regel (ambiguity = Mehrdeutigkeit). Sie stellt die Vereinigung der Schnittmengen $R_i \cap R_j$ mit $i \neq j$ für alle möglichen Regelpaarungen dar. Eine AM-Regel in Bild 1 wäre also

$$AM = \{5, 6, 7\} .$$

Wenn die AM-Regel akut ist, wird keine andere akute Regel ausgeführt. Die Parameter ALL und FIRST sowie die AM-Regel schließen sich gegenseitig aus.

Die Vorteile regelweiser Bearbeitung einer Tabelle sind:

o Der Regelzusammenhang bleibt erhalten.

o Die Reihenfolge der Aktionen kann durch Verwendung von Zahlanzeigen statt X für die einzelnen Regeln variieren.

o Sobald eine Regel angesteuert ist, liegen die Aktionen einfach in der Sequenz.

o Optimierung des Zeit- oder/und Speicherbedarfs durch den Programmierer ist möglich.

Der Nachteil ist:

o Jede Aktion erscheint statisch so oft im Programm, wie sie in den einzelnen Regeln auftritt.

Eine Optimierung des Zeitbedarfs ist durch Einsatz des Parameters FIRST möglich, weil dann nur so viele Bedingungen geprüft zu werden brauchen, wie für die Ermittlung der ersten akuten Regel nötig sind. Eine Optimierung des Speicherbedarfs ist u. a. über den Parameter ALL in Verbindung mit unbedingten Regeln ($R_u = F_f$) möglich, in denen alle Aktionen auftreten, die sonst in jeder Regel vorhanden sein müßten.

3. Umwandlung

Es liegt nahe, Methoden der Schaltkreisalgebra auf Entscheidungstabellen zu übertragen. Die Bedingungen entsprechen dabei logischen Variablen, die Regeln logischen Funktionen. Die Irrelevanzanzeiger müssen aufgelöst werden. Obwohl eine zusammenfassende Darstellung dieses Ansatzes noch fehlt, kann man doch erkennen, daß er den Zugang zu der Methode von Veinott [5,6] und zur Entscheidungsbaummethode [z. B. 7] darstellt. Optimierungsmethoden für die Entscheidungsbaummethode werden in letzter Zeit aus Karnaughtafeln entwickelt [8]. Alle diese Methoden setzen formal eindeutige Tabellen voraus.
Im Gegensatz dazu übernimmt die Matrizenmethode [9] den Bedingungsteil der Tabelle in Form einer Matrix aus Binärzeichen ins generierte Programm. Der konkrete Fall wird zur Ausführungszeit in einen Vektor aus Binärzeichen umgewandelt und im Prinzip mit Regelvektoren verglichen, die insgesamt die Matrix bilden. Das Ergebnis der Interpretation ist ein Vektor, bei dem an der Stelle akuter Regeln ein Bit gesetzt ist. Es können also formal und real mehrdeutige Tabellen verarbeitet werden, und die Ausführung akuter Regeln kann über Parameter gesteuert werden.

Im Vergleich zur Entscheidungsbaummethode ist die Matrizenmethode für das generierte Programm

- weniger speicheraufwendig, weil keine Mehrfachgenerierung von Bedingungen erforderlich ist und die Matrizen relativ wenig Platz benötigen,
- zeitaufwendiger, weil alle Bedingungen abgeprüft werden, um den Fallvektor zu bilden.

In einer Weiterentwicklung [10] wird berücksichtigt, daß man die Matrizen im generierten Programm gar nicht benötigt: Anstatt aufgrund einer Bedingungsabfrage ein Bit im Fallvektor zu setzen und zur Interpretation den Umweg über die Matrix zu gehen, kann man doch unmittelbar den Ergebnisvektor bearbeiten. Bei zweckmäßigem Wechsel von vertikaler (regelweiser) und horizontaler (bedingungsweiser) Interpretation kann man erreichen, daß

- alle Bedingungen statisch nur einmal im generierten Programm vorkommen,
- bei Angabe des Parameters FIRST nur soviele Bedingungen geprüft werden, wie zur Ermittlung der ersten zutreffenden Regel erforderlich sind.

Damit ist es möglich, die Vorteile der Entscheidungsbaum- und Matrizenmethode zu kombinieren. Als Nebeneffekt tritt die Einsparung der Matrizen auf. Dadurch entfällt die Notwendigkeit einer bitweisen Verarbeitung, und der Umwandler kann bequem in einer höheren Programmiersprache geschrieben werden (AGENTA z. B. in COBOL).

Schrifttum

[1] Strunz, H.: Eine Methode zur Zergliederung von Entscheidungstabellen. Angew. Informatik 13 (1971) S. 117 - 121

[2] Thurner, R.: Entscheidungstabellen Aufbau-Anwendung-Programmierung. Düsseldorf: VDI-Verlag 1972

[3] -: AGENTA Generator auf der Grundlage von Entscheidungstabellen. Darmstadt: Software AG (Firmenschrift) o.J.

[4] Dathe, G.: Entscheidungstabellen: Wirtschaftlichkeit. Information 26 (1972, H.4) S. 19 - 21

[5] Veinott, C.G.: Programming decision tables in FORTRAN, COBOL or ALGOL. Comm. ACM 9 (1966) S. 31 - 35

[6] Veinott, C.G.: More on programming decision tabels. Comm. ACM 9 (1966) S. 485

[7] Pollack, S.L.: Conversion of limited-entry decision tables to computer programs. Comm.ACM 8 (1965) S. 677 - 682

[8] Rabin, J.: Conversion of limited-entry decision tables into optimal decision trees. ACM SIGPLAN NOTICES 6(1971) S. 68 - 74

[9] Muthukrishnan, C.R., Rajaraman, V.: On the conversion of decision tables to computer programs. Comm. ACM 13 (1970) S. 347 - 351

[10] Dathe, G.: Conversion of decision tables by rule mask method without rule mask. Comm.ACM 15 (1972) (erscheint im Oktoberheft)

DESIGN OF A GENERALIZED AUDIT COMMAND LANGUAGE (ACL)

H.J.WILL

A generalized audit command language (ACL) has been designed in response to recent developments in computer-based auditing and in anticipation of future needs. The syntax of ACL is summarized in this paper with respect to data and model bank audit functions. It is intended to implement ACL in a number of different versions, facilitating explicit and implicit programming by auditors and supporting a variety of audit functions. Various implementation strategies and some of the implications of ACL for teaching and professional practice are discussed as well.

INTRODUCTION

Two recent surveys of specialized programming languages[1,2] do not recognize the important innovations in computer-based auditing,[3] although many of their observations are likewise applicable to auditing as one of the specialized application areas in business and administrative data processing:

> The specialized language help these people [who don't really understand programming] work in their own professional jargon.[4]
>
> There are two advantages here. One is the advantage that accrues to the user in the efficiency of his language in dealing with matters that are directly of his concern. The second is the advantage in the underlying processing algorithms that make use of the underlying implicit assumptions of the domain. These enormous economic advantages that the computer can thereby put at the fingertip of the specialist in his area are the true source of the pressure for special application languages.[5]

The reasons for the design and implementation of generalized computer audit packages (GCAP's), also known as audit data management systems (ADMS), contain merely a few hints about specific audit assumptions that were deliberately built into the various packages:

(i) Facilitate access to data generated by means of a variety of computer systems and stored in computer-readable formats.
(ii) Utilize the speed and accuracy of computer systems for audit purposes in order to reduce the need for clerical analyses.
(iii) Facilitate the execution of the major audit functions in a general and modular fashion by means of computers.
(iv) Improve the range of analytical techniques available to auditors.
(v) Minimize the requirement for computer-technological expertise on the part of the user.
(vi) Provide a workable alternative to 'auditing around the computer' where this technique is not applicable.
(vii) Provide computer-based audit independence.[6]

Audit theory is still a relatively open field;[7] however, the design and implementation of statistical sampling plans for audit purposes and the continuing discussion of their underlying assumptions[8] provide an excellent example of on-going research supporting the further development of a generalized audit command language for professional purposes.

> Indeed it is just such idiosyncratic procedures that become embodied as the interpretive routines of a language which is "natural" to such a specialized area. . . From there on they are no longer conscious considerations in further program writing, or processed internally as axioms. They are now implicit,

pressed down below the level of the explicit considerations of the researcher or manager who is using his own natural language.[9]

Complete uniformity in auditing as a professional activity is currently neither possible nor desirable. It must be remarkable for the non-auditor, however, to notice the considerable variety of implemented computer audit package designs. Currently, more than 25 systems[10] are available, and even an auditor may find it difficult to keep perspective or to evaluate and select the appropriate package for his purposes and circumstances.[11]

In the currently used GCAP's, several language types have been implemented, depending on whether explicit or implicit programming is required of the auditor.[12] Free-form English narrative, keyword form and separator form are used for explicit programming. A fixed position coding form or a questionnaire[13] facilitate implicit programming by guiding the user through his task. It is not surprising to find that these "ideal types" (Weber) are combined in several ways and for different functions. It may surprise, however, that no interactive audit command language has been designed to this date.

While it would lead too far to describe here the current state of affairs in computer-based auditing, it should be evident that the design of a generalized audit command language is advantageous to the auditing profession for a variety of reasons such as:

1. the amount of duplication involved in expanding the about 25-30 existing GCAP's into basically identical packages as far as their scope and applicability are concerned;
2. the costs of such duplication in view of the strong convergence tendencies in international audit practice and technology;
3. the necessity to interface with a growing variety of computerized information systems designs in pursuing internal or external audit objectives;
4. the need for standardization in defining audit problems in "natural" language compatible with modern developments in audit, accounting and information systems theory and practice;
5. the need for documenting the computer-based auditing activities in a common audit language in the auditor's working papers;
6. the professional obligation of and the costs associated with the training of tens of thousands of auditors in the use of GCAP's;
7. the large number of "small practitioners" in auditing who cannot afford to develop their own systems or to become dependent on one or more of the existing systems which were developed by large international audit firms or by specialized software companies;
8. the availability of the required resources for mounting and implementing such a project on an international scale in view of similar demands for a generalized computer audit language in all developed countries and in those developing nations where computers are being used.

This paper is an early phase in the design of ACL as a specialized computer language if one considers the usual phases of language development.[14] On the other hand, since it incorporates the features of most GCAP's it may justifiably be viewed as a generalization, extension, modification or new version of previous audit language designs. The paper summarizes the syntax of ACL and discusses implementation alternatives before concluding with some of its implications for teaching and professional practice.

The syntactical description of ACL modifies the Backus-Naur Form (BNF) slightly in order to indicate flexibilities for implementing ACL in batch and interactive terminal mode. All underlined capital letters of the source language terms are essential for the translation and interpretation of ACL source programs. The ACL terms in the various descriptive statements associated with the ACL commands can be implemented in various ways as batch type commands, as program form headings and as pre-programmed machine requests for interactive auditor responses from terminals. Specific rules for naming, e.g. field names, and for specifying field types have been omitted. The ANSI-COBOL rules for defining PICTURE clauses and arithmetic expressions are assumed to be known to a large number of auditors. The following BNF description of ACL is organized around the various audit functions required for auditing of data and/or model banks.

ACL FOR DATA BANK AUDITS

ACL currently possesses 27 separate commands for data banks audits. They are classified according to the following audit functions: data description and access, testing and validation, reorganization and updating, calculation, selection (interrogation) and analyses, as well as reporting.

Data Description and Access

Since auditors are seldom interested in all data elements of records within files or data banks, it is essential to provide flexible data description (DD) facilities. ACL's DD is centered around the evidential matter contained in individual data fields (elements, items) within records and files. All data structures relevant to audting are assumed to be accessible in this manner. File selection implies DD of a given input file and file extraction assumes the creation of a specially formatted audit data file.

```
<file selection command>:: = SELECT <file name> <test description>
<file extraction command>:: = EXTRACT <file name> FROM <file name> <test description>
```

In both cases, and for output purposes, ACL utilizes the same DD entries:

```
<file description>:: = FILE <file name> <field description>
<file name>:: = <character string>
<field description>:: = FIELD <field name>|<variable>|<constant> <field position>
                        <field type> <field picture> <field header> <field edit picture>
                        <field value clause>|<expression>|<constant>
<variable>:: = <identifier>|<field name>|<table entry>
<identifier>:: = <character string>
<field name>:: = <character string>
<field position>:: = START POSITION <integer>
```

```
<field type>:: = <character string>
<field picture>:: = PICTURE <ANSI-COBOL picture entry>
<field header>:: = HEADER <literal>
<field edit picture>:: = PICTURE <ANSI-COBOL edit picture entry>
<field value>:: = VALUE <constant>
<expression>:: = <well-formed ANSI-COBOL arithmetic or Boolean expression>
<constant>:: = <integer>|<real number>|<literal>|<truth value>
<literal>:: = "<character string>"
<truth value>:: = TRUE|FALSE
```

Testing and Validation

In order to facilitate inclusion or exclusion of records meeting the various test criteria during the access phase or any other audit function, simple or compound TEST statements can be formulated in ACL. Each test condition can be named as well to avoid repeating test formulations for identical conditions. The user therefore has the option to store in a separate file the essential test conditions identifying his information needs.

```
<compound test description>:: = <simple test description> <connector> <simple test
                                 description>
<simple test description>:: = TEST <test name> IF|WHEN <test subject>|<test subject>
                              <connector> <test subject> <relation> <reference value>
<test name>:: = <character string>
<test subject>:: = <field name>|<constant>|<expression>|<variable>
<relation>:: = <|LT|≤|LE|=|EQ|NE|>|GT|≥|GE
<reference value>:: = <field name>|<constant>|<variable>|<validation criterion>
<validation criterion>:: = BLANKS|ZERO|ZEROS|ZEROES|POSITIVE|NEGATIVE|BETWEEN <range
                           clause> |CHARACTER|NUMBER|
<range clause>:: = <constant> AND <constant>
<connector>:: = AND|OR|,|;
```

Reorganization and Updating

While most files to be audited do not require updating, an auditor may want to test the file maintenance procedures. This test might also involve sorting of the original or extracted audit files and merging of files. ACL provides the following statements for these purposes:

```
<sort command>:: = SORT <file name> <sort order> <key field>
<sort order>:: = ASCENDING|DESCENDING
<key field>:: = <field name>
<merge command>:: MERGE <file name> AND <file name> INTO <file name>
<update command>:: = UPDATE <file name> FROM <file name>|<file name>
                 <inter-file change command>|<intra-file change command>
<inter-file change command>:: = INSERT <test description> |DELETE <test description>
                                |SUMMARIZE <test description>
```

<intra-file change command>:: = INCLUDE <field name> |MOVE <field name>|<constant>
TO <field name> <test description>

Calculation

Auditing involves recalculation of data at a large scale and requires extensive calculation facilities. In addition to an assignment statement capability, ACL contains a number of commands for calculations which an auditor performs regularly. Some of these may be implemented as default options during the various audit phases or they can be explicitly specified within an audit program.

<calculation command>:: = CALCULATE <assignment statement>

<assignment statement>:: =<variable> = <arithmetic expression>

<count command>:: = COUNT <file name>|<field name>|<test description> = <variable>

<tally command>:: = TALLY <count statement>

<average command>:: = MEAN|MODE|MEDIAN <field name> = <variable>

<total command>:: = TOTAL <field name> = <variable>

<foot command>:: = FOOT <field name> = <variable>

<percent command>:: = PERCENT <field name>|<arithmetic expression>|<constant>|
<variable> OF <field name>|<variable> = <variable>

<variance command>:: = VARIANCE <field name>|<variable> = <variable>

<stand. deviation command>:: = STANDARD DEVIATION <field name>|<variable> = <variable>

<maximum command>:: = MAXIMUM <field name> = <variable>

<minimum command>:: = MINIMUM <field name> = <variable>

Selection (Interrogation) and Analyses

While analyses can be performed on all data accessed initially as relevant to an audit, a special selection, classification or stratification process is often necessary to establish homogeneous subpopulations. Upon these, different kinds of analyses are often made.

<selection command>:: = SELECT EVERY <integer> RECORD OF <file name> <test description>

<stratify command>:: = STRATIFY <file name> <test description>|<stratum description>

<stratum description>:: = STRATUM <stratum name> <field name> BETWEEN <constant>|
<variable> <connector> <constant>|<variable> <connector>
<constant>|<variable>

<sampling command>:: = SAMPLE <file name> <sample description>

<sample description>:: = <systematic sample description>|<random sample description>|
<attribute sampling description>|
<variable sampling description>|
<special sampling plan description>

<systematic sample description>:: = EVERY <integer> RECORD

<random sample description>:: = EVERY <random number> RECORD| <field name> <test description>

<random number>:: = <variable>|<arithmetic expression>

<attribute sampling description>:: = <field name> PRECISION <variable> % CONFIDENCE LEVEL <variable> % ERROR RATE <variable> %| EXPECTED ERROR RATE <variable> % WITH PROBABILITY <variable> %

<variable sampling description>:: = <field name> PRECISION <variable> % CONFIDENCE LEVEL <variable> % STD. DEVIATION <variable>

<special sampling plan description>:: = <field name> ALPHA RISK <variable> BETA RISK <variable> MATERIAL ERROR <variable>

<evaluate command>:: = EVALUATE <file name> <sample description>

<correlation command>:: = CORRELATE <variable> WITH <variable> BY <variable>

<regression command>:: = REGRESSION <(dependent) variable> WITH <(independent) variable>

Reporting

To facilitate simple listing of file contents and more flexible reporting ACL provides the following commands:

<list command>:: = LIST <file name>

<print command>:: = PRINT <report name>|<confirmation name>|<histogram name>

<write command>:: = WRITE <report name>|<confirmation name>|<histogram name> UPON <storage medium name>

<display command>:: = DISPLAY <report name>|<confirmation name<|<histogram name> UPON <terminal identifier>

<report description>:: = REPORT <report name> <title line description> <header line description> <detail line description> <summary line description> <footing line description> <total line description> <page description>

<report name>:: = <character string>

<title line description>:: = TITLE LINE <literal> START <integer> <space specification>

<header line description>:: = HEADER LINE <literal> START <integer> <space specification>

<detail line description>:: = DETAIL LINE <field description> <space specification>

<summary line description>:: = SUMMARY LINE <field description> <space specification>

<footing line description>:: = FOOTING LINE <field description> <space specification>

<total line description>:: = TOTAL LINE <field description> <space specification>

<page description>:: = PAGE LENGTH <integer>| CONTROL BREAK <field name>

<space specification>:: = SPACE <integer> LINES

<confirmation description>:: = CONFIRMATION <confirmation name> <field description>| <report description>

<confirmation name>:: = <character string>

<histogram description>:: = GRAPH <histogram name> <field name> <test description>| <stratum description> HORIZONTAL|VERTICAL

<histogram name>:: = <character string>
<storage medium name>:: = <character string>
<terminal identifier>:: = <character string>

ACL FOR MODEL BANK AUDITS

The currently identified eight separate commands for the audit of model banks in ACL are subsequently presented for program description and access, test data generation, program tracing, flow charting, program testing (comparisons) and display of the results.

Program Description and Access

In order to access a program the auditor merely specifies the program or routine name and its mode as well as the source language:

<program selection command>:: = SELECT <program name>
<program description>:: = SOURCE <program name>| OBJECT <program name>| LOAD MODULE <program name> IN <language name>
<program name>:: = <character string>
<language name>:: = BAL|BASIC|COBOL|FORTRAN|PL/1|...

Test Data Generation

In order to facilitate test data generation ACL contains the GENERATE command.

<generate command>:: = GENERATE <file name> <test data description>
<test data description>:: = TEST DATA FIELDS <field description> VARYING <field name> FROM <constant> BY <constant> FACTOR| RANDOMIZING <field name> <integer> TIMES

Program Tracing

The auditor can follow a program through its path during execution by means of the ACL TRACE command. It indicates the sequence in which specific instructions or paragraphs are performed and prints out pertinent information such as register contents.

<trace command>:: = TRACE <program name> <trace description>
<trace description>:: = BEGIN <constant> <program step> END <constant> <program step>
<program step>:: = INSTRUCTION|PARAGRAPH|ROUTINE

Flow Charting

Existing source programs in several languages can be graphically documented according to the ANSI Standard by calling the flow charting routine of ACL.

<charting command>:: = CHART <program name> HORIZONTALLY|VERTICALLY

Testing (Comparing)

Program testing is usually accomplished by means of test data (test decks for transactions and dummy companies for master records). In addition, it may be desired to compare different program versions or on-line library programs with vault copies, printing out the variances.

<test command>:: = COMPARE <program name> WITH <program name>

Display

In order to display program structures the auditor can choose between source and object program listings, memory dumps of load modules, and tables indicating transfers in and out of program modules or paragraphs.

<list command>:: = LIST <program name> <constant> <program step>

<dump command>:: = DUMP <program name> <constant> <program step>

<tabulate command>:: = TABULATE <program name> <constant> <program step>

IMPLEMENTATION CONSIDERATIONS

Implementation of ACL is an expensive proposition although it might be possible to develop the language in universities. Full scale implementation should not even be seriously considered unless a comprehensive feasibility study reveals that it is indeed desirable and economical to program ACL in one or more of the mentioned language types. Such a study would ideally be sponsored by the various national institutes which are concerned about the future of computer-based auditing, about the lack of uniformity and standardization in the field, and about the proliferation of GCAP designs. The result might well be that one of the available packages can be developed more economically into a standardized audit language, but it is likewise not improbable that it might prove advantageous to implement ACL in a number of subsets similar to ANSI-COBOL and in stages:

1. Basic ACL could be limited to the simplest functions needed for data bank audits, e.g. access by means of extraction, simple test description, utility sort and merge programs, limited calculation capabilities, systematic sampling and fixed format reporting.
2. Advanced ACL could include all described functions for data bank audits, but it may still be available in various versions, depending on which audit sampling plan and which analysis routines are incorporated.
3. Full ACL would also contain the various model bank audit functions. Again it might be preferable to include utility routines at first and to develop specific ACL logic over time concurrent with the standardization efforts made in the areas of applications programing in general and data management in particular.

The national institutes might want to decide on implementation priorities as far as computer systems and audit functions are concerned. Different consortia and teams might concentrate on alternative design considerations such as precompiler versions and interpretive systems. They may want to accept the sketched ACL modules or decide to develop their own. It might even be possible to utilize existing programs from some of the GCAP's and to pool the considerable design expertise already available for the required professional effort. In addition, special efforts should be made to evaluate the experiences gained with various GCAP designs in the contributing countries in pursuit of internal and external audit objectives.

Another approach worth considering would be the employment of an extensible programming language such as ULANG (user Language)[15] MPL (Meta Programming Language)[16] or REL (Rapidly Extensible Language)[17]. It may be possible in this manner to develop relatively quickly an ACL prototype for the interactive and/or batch job utilization of the language without having to rely on large systems programming teams. The trade-offs between programming and operational efficiency of a prototype ACL are in favour of programming speed although the reverse may be true in case ACL should become the accepted professional command language of auditors.

CONCLUSIONS

Once ACL has been implemented as a special programming language it will become possible to teach it to auditors as well as to students in a variety of contexts. Universities, colleges and the various national institutes can utilize ACL as a powerful didactic tool. It is now possible to interface explicitly with a given or assumed information system. Teachers and students can translate audit considerations immediately into "natural" ACL commands. This extension of audit technology bridges the existing gaps between audit theory and practice and links auditing solidly with modern accounting and information systems designs.

To develop sufficiently extensive and well designed teaching material for courses using ACL is indeed another challenging opportunity for interdisciplinary and international research. It would imply a comparative analysis of current auditing standards and practices in various countries and could lead to greater uniformity internationally.

Should ACL or a similar language be supported by a number of national institutes then it might even be economically feasible to implement it not only on a variety of computer systems but also in several natural languages. Since almost every educational institution now utilizes or has access to a computer, ACL could be taught universally in its current English command language form or in easily translated versions of different languages such as French, German, Russian and Spanish. Seen in this light, the design of ACL might be an early link in a long chain of reactions to the internationally felt need for a generalized audit command language.

Footnotes

1. J.E. Sammet, "An overview of programming languages for specialized application areas", AFIPS Conference Proceedings, Vol. 40, 1972 SJCC, pp. 299-311.

2. F.B. Thompson and B.H. Dostert, "The future of specialized languages", AFIPS Conference Proceedings, Vol. 40, 1972 SJCC, pp. 313-319.

3. H.J. Will, "Computer-Based Auditing - PART I and PART II", Canadian Chartered Accountant, Vol. 100, n. 2 (February 1972), pp. 29-34 and n. 3 (March 1972), pp. 32-35, 38-44 and the mentioned literature.
H.J. Will, "Pruefungssysteme" and "Pruefungsprogramm Systeme", Die Wirtschaftspruefung (in press).

4. Sammet, op.cit., p. 299.

5. Thompson & Dostert, op.cit., p. 315.

6. Will, op.cit., - PART II, p. 33.

7. See, e.g. H.J. Will, "Pruefungssysteme", op.cit. and "Auditing in Systems Perspective", Working Paper No. 148, Faculty of Commerce and Business Administration, The University of British Columbia, Vancouver, B.C., July 1972.

8. See, e.g. Haskins & Sells, Haskins & Sells Auditape System Manual, H & S, 1969, Section 10.
Smith, Kenneth A., "The Relationship of Internal Control Evaluation and Audit Sample Size", The Accounting Review, Vol. XLVII, n. 2 (April 1972), pp. 260-269.
Robert K. Elliott and John R. Rogers, "Relating Statistical Sampling to Audit Objectives", The Journal of Accountancy, Vol. 134, n. 1 (July 1972), pp. 46-55.

9. Thompson & Dostert, op.cit., p. 315.

10. Will, "Pruefungsprogramm Systeme", op.cit.

11. Will, "Evaluation Methods for Audit Data Management Systems", DATA MANAGEMENT (in press).

12. See Will, op.cit., Table 3.

13. For an explication of the various techniques see CODASYL Systems Committee, Feature Analysis of Generalized Data Base Management Systems, New York: Association for Systems Management, May 1971, pp. 41-43.

14. Sammet distinguishes the following phases in the history of a language design:
    1. Initial idea.
    2. First documentation of initial idea.
    3. Preliminary specifications.
    4. "Final" specifications (i.e. those which will be implemented).
    5. "Prototype" running (i.e. as thoroughly debugged as the state of the art will permit, but perhaps not all of the features are included).
    6. "Full Language" compiler (or interpreter) is running.
    7. Usage on real problems by the developers.
    8. Users (on real problems) other than the developers.
    9. Documentation, e.g. manuals and tutorials.
    10. Paper in professional journal or conference. (Sometimes this appears as early as step 3.)
    11. Extension, modification, or new version.

    Jean E. Sammet, "Programming Languages, History and Future", Communications of the ACM, Vol. 15, n. 7 (July 1972), p. 602.

15. Imants F. Freibergs, "ULANG - A Generalized User-Langage", Proceedings of Canadian Computer Conference, Montreal, June 1-3, 1972, pp. 322101-322112.

16. E.N. Ferentzy, "Data Processing Applications of Syntax Driven Translators", ibid., pp. 322301-322207.

17. F. Thompson, P. Lockeman, B. Dostert and R. Deverill, "REL: A rapidly extensible language system", Proceedings of the 24th National Conference of ACM, 1969.

EIN PROGRAMMIERSYSTEM ZUR PROBLEMNAHEN ERSTELLUNG ADAPTIERTER SOFTWARE

W.SONNENBERG

Programme heißen adaptierbar (1), wenn sie an vorhandene Hardware, Kapazitätsschranken und installations- oder benutzerbezogene Kenngrössen angepaßt werden können. Das adaptierte Programm soll immer die optimale Effizienz in Speicher- und Rechnerkernausnutzung aufweisen. Zur Übersetzung adaptierbarer Programme werden flexiblere Systeme benötigt als sie mit den heute benutzten Compilern zur Verfügung stehen.

Hier wird ein flexibles Übersetzungssystem vorgestellt. Seine wesentlichen Komponenten sind:

a. Quellprogrammanalyse
b. Optimierung der Adaptionsparameter
c. Codegenerierung
d. Bibliothek mit verschiedenen Coderealisierungen für Sprachelemente der Benutzersprache

Bei der Adaption werden Steuerparameter benötigt, die bestimmen, welche der Bibliothekselemente bei der Codegenerierung eingesetzt werden. Diese Steuerparameter nehmen direkten Bezug auf die Bibliothekselemente und sind damit für einen Benutzer schwer überschaubar. In diesem System werden daher die Adaptionsparameter aus anderen dem Benutzer vertrauteren Daten berechnet. Im Quellprogramm sind (geschätzte) Kennwerte anzugeben - mit wieviel Elementen die Datenbereiche belegt werden, wie oft Programmschleifen ausgeführt werden oder mit welcher Wahrscheinlichkeit Alternativen bedingter Anweisungen wahr sind. Nach Umrechnung dieser Daten bei der Analyse des Quellprogramms werden die Adaptionsparameter bestimmt. Bei Einhaltung gegebener Kapazitätsschranken wird bei der Adaption die Objektprogrammversion mit kürzester geschätzter Laufzeit generiert.

Wir werden die folgenden Probleme eingehender betrachten:

1. Zerlegung des Quellprogramms in Programmelemente
2. Schätzung der Ausführungszeit eines Programmes
3. Unterschiedliche Realisierungen für Sprachelemente einer Benutzerprogrammsprache
4. Aufbau eines Adaptionsplanes
5. Algorithmus zur Optimierung eines Adaptionsplanes
6. Praktischer Einsatz des Adaptionssystems

1. Zerlegung eines Quellprogramms (2)

Programmiersprachen werden konstruktiv definiert. Die Syntaxdefinition gibt die Menge der möglichen korrekten Programme wieder. Die Semantik wird durch Instruktionen einer abstrakten Maschine definiert. Bei der Übersetzung wird für jede Instruktion ein definierter Code der Objektprogrammaschine abgesetzt.

Bei der Adaption wählen wir zwischen verschiedenen Objektcodes. Zur Bestimmung der optimalen Adaptionsparameter wird für jede der m_i Alternativen zum i-ten Programmelement $(i=1,...,n)$ die Ausführungszeit $r_{i,j}$ $(j=1,...,m_i)$ benötigt. Sie kann aus den vom Benutzer gegebenen Daten zusammen mit Kenninformationen aus der Adaptionsbibliothek bestimmt werden.

2. Schätzung der Ausführungszeit eines Programmes

Das Programm liege in der Form eines Ablaufgraphen vor, zu jeder Kante sei die Ausführungszeit und zu jeder Verzweigung die Wahrscheinlichkeit, mit der sie durchlaufen wird, bekannt; dann läßt sich mit einem von Beizer (3) angegebenen Algorithmus die Laufzeit des Programms schätzen.

Der Ablaufgraph wird bei der Analyse des Quellprogramms extrahiert.

Die benötigten Daten zur Berechnung der Wahrscheinlichkeiten werden vom Benutzer verlangt. Für bedingte Anweisungen sind Schätzungen für die Wahrscheinlichkeit direkt anzuschreiben, für Programmschleifen wird geschätzt, wie oft der Schleifenkörper durchlaufen wird, wenn kein Aussprung von innen erfolgt.

Die Ausführungszeiten K_i der Kanten $(i=1,...,n)$ werden als Variable mitgeführt. Die nach dem Beizeralgorithmus errechnete Funktion

$Z = \sum_{i=1}^{n} a_i \cdot K_i$ wird im Optimierungsalgorithmus als Zielfunktion

minimiert.

3. Unterschiedliche Objektcodes für Sprachelemente eines Benutzerprogramms

Ein Benutzerprogramm arbeite beispielsweise mit Listen. Es enthalte Instruktionen

"anfang i", "weiter i" und "lösche i"

i sei dabei ein Zeiger in eine Liste. Mit "anfang i" werde i auf das erste Element, mit "weiter i" auf das folgende Element gesetzt und mit "lösche i" soll das Listenelement gestrichen werden, auf das i zeigt.

Wird eine Liste aus doppelt verzeigerten Elementen aufgebaut, dann können die Instruktionen wie folgt codiert werden:

```
anfang i    i = Anfang(liste)
weiter i    i = Vorzeiger(Element_i)
lösche i    x = Vorzeiger(Element_i)
            z = Rückzeiger(Element_i)
            Vorzeiger(Element_y) = x
            Rückzeiger(Element_x) = y
```

Wird eine Liste als Vektor aus ihren Elementen gespeichert, so können folgende Codierungen gewählt werden:

```
anfang i    i = 1
weiter i    i = i + 1
lösche i    FOR j = i + 1 STEP 1 UNTIL Elementzahl DO
                Element_j-1 = Element_j
```

Bei einer IBM 360-65 ergäben sich folgende Ausführungszeiten: (in microsec) (4)

	doppelt verzeigert	Vektor
anfang i	1.20	0.90
weiter i	1.20	0.90
lösche i	4.26	9.50+k * 2.32 k=Elementzahl-i-2

Man sieht, daß jede der beiden Implementierungen zeitliche Vorteile besitzt. Hier muß eine Optimierung vorgenommen werden.

4. Der Adaptionsplan

Wir sahen in 3. am Beispiel, daß verschiedene Coderealisierungen nur aufgrund verschiedener Informationsdarstellungen sinnvoll sind. Wir werden in einem Adaptionsplan zu jeder Informationseinheit eines Programms genau eine Informationsdarstellung vorsehen. Dazu ist der Begriff der Informationseinheit noch genauer abzugrenzen:

Jeder Bezeichnung in einem Programm (externes Objekt) ist eine Informationseinheit (internes Objekt) zugeordnet. Das Programm definiert auf den internen Objekten Äquivalenzrelationen (Identität, Referenzen usw.). Jede Äquivalenzklasse der Identitätsrelation kann verschieden implementiert werden. Wir wählen daher diese Klassen als Informationseinheiten.

Ein Adaptionsplan wird dann durch eine Liste beschrieben, beispielsweise bedeute $\langle x_1, y_2, z\rangle$: es gibt drei Informationseinheiten x,y und z ; x soll durch die erste Alternative, y durch die zweite realisiert werden, die Realisierung für z ist nicht definiert. Die Indizes werden Realisierungskennungen genannt. Realisierungskennungen sind verträglich, wenn entweder die Indizes zu gleichen Namen gleich sind, oder wenn eine Kennung nicht definiert ist.

5. Der Optimierungsalgorithmus

5.a) Allgemeine Voraussetzungen

Es liegen n Instruktionen aus der Benutzersprache vor. Die i-te Instruktion A_i hat die s_i Operanden O_{ik} $(k=1,\dots,s_i)$.

Zu A_i sind m_i Codes generierbar. Sei $R_{ij}=1$, wenn die j-te Codealternative gewählt werden soll, sonst $R_{ij}=0$.

5.b) Nebenbedingungen

(i) $\sum_{j=1}^{m_i} R_{kj} = 1 \qquad \text{für } k = 1,\dots,n$

(ii) Die Realisierungskennungen im Adaptionsplan müssen mit den Kennungen für die O_{ik} verträglich sein.

(iii) Es gelten Schranken für die Anzahl der verfügbaren Speicherzellen und Register.

5.c) Die Zielfunktion

$$\sum_{i=1}^{n} a_i \cdot \sum_{j=1}^{m_i} r_{ij} \cdot R_{ij}$$

Soll minimiert werden.

5.d) Allgemeines Verfahren

Zur Optimierung wird ein branch- and bound-Verfahren (5) benutzt. Die Zielfunktion wird stufenweise optimiert. In der i-ten Zwischenstufe wird versucht, die Teilergebnisse aus den Zwischenstufen 1 bis i-1 mit den Alternativen von A_i zu verbinden. Es wird jeweils ein Adaptionsteilplan weitergereicht. Die geschätzten Programmlaufzeiten zu nacheinander weitergereichten Teilplänen wachsen schwach isoton.

5.e) Hilfsdaten

Es werden Wartelisten q_i geführt. Ihre Elemente sind Tripel (z,p,j), mit p = (zp,ap), dabei ist

$$zp = \sum_{k=1}^{i-1} a_k \sum_{h=1}^{m_k} r_{kh} \cdot R_{kh}$$

$$z = zp + r_{ij}$$

ap der Adaptionsplan, nach dem zp berechnet wurde.

Diese Tripel sind nach aufsteigender Zeit z geordnet.

5.g) Ablaufdiagramm des Algorithmus

Start = Stufe (0):

Reiche den Adaptionsplan ohne definierte Realisierungen mit der Zeitangabe 0 an Stufe (1).

Stufe (i):

M1: Übernehme p = (zp,ap) aus Stufe (i-1).
Ordne ($zp + a_i\ r_{i1}$, p, 1) in q_i ein.

M2: Ist q_i leer, dann gib Endemeldung an Stufe (i+1).

Entnehme (z,p,j) mit minimalem z aus q_i (p = (zp,ap)).

Ist $j+1 \leq m_i$ dann ordne $(zp + a_i * r_{i,j+1}, p, j+1)$ in q_i ein.

Ist die Nebenbedingung 5.b(ii) erfüllt, dann gebe den aus p und der j-ten Alternative zu A_i kombinierten Adaptionsteilplan an Stufe (i+1) weiter.

War bei der letzten Entnahme aus q_i j=1 und $i \neq 1$ dann weiter bei M1, sonst bei M2.

Stufe (n+1):

Übernehme solange Teilpläne von Stufe (n) bis die Nebenbedingung 5.b(iii) erfüllt ist.

6. Praktischer Einsatz

Dieses Adaptionssystem steht dem Sprachimplementierer als übersetzererzeugendes System zur Verfügung. Er muß eine Sprache syntaktisch definieren, den syntaktischen Einheiten Semantikfunktionen zuordnen, für jede Semantikfunktion einen Analyseteil zur Analyse des Ablaufgraphen und der Äquivalenzrelationen auf den Datenstrukturen sowie einen Bibliotheksteil mit verschiedenen Codierungen erstellen.

Der Benutzer eines solchen Übersetzers hat dieselben Möglichkeiten wie der Benutzer eines anderen Compilers für die gleiche Programmiersprache. Für die nach 2. notwendigen Daten werden default-Werte angenommen. Ergeben sich Schwierigkeiten mit Kapazitätsbeschränkungen oder mit der Ausführungszeit, so kann der Benutzer durch Angabe ausgewählter Kenndaten eine Anpassung des Programms an seine Problemdaten erreichen.

Benötigt ein Benutzer eine Hilfestellung bei der Ermittlung von Kenndaten, so kann ihm mit Meßrealisierungen aus der Codebibliothek geholfen werden.

Der erfahrene Benutzer kann selbst die Bibliothek erweitern oder schließlich eigene Benutzersprachen definieren.

Quellen

(1) Waite & Poole
Portability and Adaptability
Advanced Course on Software Engineering, München 1972

(2) Gries
Compiler Construction for Digital Computers
Wiley 1971

(3) Beizer
Analytical Techniques for the Statistical Evaluation of Program Running Time
Proc. FJCC 1970, pp. 519-524

(4) IBM Form No. A22-6884
IBM System/360 Model 65
Functional Characteristics

(5) Neumann
Operations Research B
Vorlesung an der Universität Karlsruhe, SS 1970

D I A L I S - EIN EINFACHES DIALOGSYSTEM FÜR EINE LISTENSPRACHE

H.ROHLFING

1. Einleitung

Diese Arbeit diskutiert einige Eigenschaften des Dialogsystems DIALIS, das als Studienobjekt zur Untersuchung einiger Fragestellungen im Zusammenhang mit Dialogsystemen und Dialogsprachen dient. Eine Implementierung des Systems ist auf der Rechenanlage Burroughs B6700 des Informatik-Rechenzentrums der Universität Karlsruhe vorgesehen.

Als Dialogsprache wurde eine algolähnliche Listensprache definiert, die sich, was das Listenkonzept anbetrifft, an die Sprache EULER anlehnt. Auf die sprachlichen Erweiterungen gegenüber EULER wird in dieser Arbeit nicht eingegangen. Die Definition dieser Listensprache erschien deshalb geeignet, da viele Algorithmen, die zur Implementierung der Sprache benötigt werden, auch zur Implementierung vieler Teile des Dialogsystems dienen können, so daß insgesamt der Implementierungsaufwand minimiert wird.

Das Dialogsystem enthält einen Übersetzer und einen Interpreter für die Listensprache. Effizienzfragen, die im Zusammenhang mit der Interpretierung von Programmen auftauchen,wurden vorerst nicht beachtet. Andererseits läßt die Definition der Sprache - mit gewissen Einschränkungen - eine Übersetzung in Maschinensprache zu.

Abschnitt 2 gibt eine kurze Charakterisierung von Dialogsprachen und systemen und enthält einen Katalog von Forderungen an System und Sprache. Abschnitt 3 und 4 diskutieren zwei Systemeigenschaften zur Verwirklichung dieser Forderungen, Abschnitt 5 diskutiert einige Spracheigenschaften.

2. Charakterisierung von Dialogsprachen und -systemen

Unter den Begriffen "Dialogsprache" und "Dialogsystem" soll hier folgendes verstanden werden:

Eine Dialogsprache ist eine Programmiersprache, die den fortlaufenden

Informationsaustausch zwischen den Programmen der Programmiersprache und dem Programmierer über Benutzerstationen (Terminals) erlaubt. Dieser Austausch erfolgt auf der Ebene der Programmiersprache und umfaßt sowohl den Ablauf der Programmentwicklung als auch den Ablauf der Programmausführung. Die Programmiersprache muß insbesondere über Spracheigenschaften verfügen, die sie dialogfähig macht.
Ein Dialogsystem ist ein Programmiersystem für eine Dialogsprache,daß die Implementierung der Übersetzungsphase und der Ablaufphase von Programmen der Dialogsprache übernimmt. Es stellt den ständigen Gesprächspartner des Programmierers dar. Die gemeinsamen Kommunikationsbereiche sind sog. "Arbeitsbereiche", die alle Daten und Programme enthalten, auf die das System und der Programmierer zugreifen können.Als "aktive Daten" werden jene Daten und Programme bezeichnet, auf die der Programmierer während eines Gesprächs zugreifen kann.

Im Gegensatz zu der Art des Informationsaustausches, wie er in Systemen für Stapelverarbeitung gegeben ist, muß im Falle eines Dialogsystems wie DIALIS verlangt werden, daß der Austausch symmetrisch erfolgt in dem Sinne, daß beide, Programmierer und Dialogsystem, Mitteilungen, Fragen und Aufträge aneinander richten können. Im Falle des Systems DIALIS ist die Form des Informationsaustausches ein strenges Wechselgespräch.

Der Inhalt der Information kann ein Übersetzungsauftrag sein, eine Wertzuweisung an eine Variable, das Erzeugen eines Arbeitsbereiches oder die Mitteilung des Systems, daß ein inkonsistenter Zustand des Systems vorliegt.

Der Programmierer verfügt über eine Anzahl Kommandos, mit denen er einen Informationsaustausch ausdrücken kann. Dies sind "Systemkommandos" zur Herstellung und Lösung von Verbindungen zur Rechenanlage und zu den Konsolen, "Bereichskommandos" zur Manipulation von Programmen sowie zur Definition, Erweiterung und Veränderung von Programmierumgebungen und "Sprachkommandos", d.h. Anweisungen und Vereinbarungen der Dialogsprache, die zur Veränderung der Werte einer Programmierumgebung dienen.

Im Vergleich zu Programmiersprachen für den Stapelverarbeitungsbetrieb müssen für Dialogsprachen folgende Unterschiede und Zusatzforderungen gemacht werden:

1. Unterscheidung zwischen "Ausführungsmodus" (immediate mode) und "Definitionsmodus" (stored mode)
2. Langfristige Speicherung von Programmen und Daten in Arbeitsbereichen und Bibliotheken auch über die Dauer eines Gesprächs hinaus.

3. Einbettung (eines Teils) der Kommandosprache des zugrundeliegenden Betriebssystems in die Dialogsprache.
4. Ausführbarkeit von unvollständigen Programmstücken mit offenen Bezugspunkten, deren Bindung dynamisch erfolgt.
5. Einfache Beschreibbarkeit und Wechselbarkeit der Programmierumgebungen.
6. Statische und dynamische Zusammensetzung von Programmstücken zur Übersetzungs- und zur Ausführungszeit.
7. Flexibilität in der Ausführung von Programmen.
8. Flexibilität in der Überwachung der Übersetzungs- und Ausführungsphase von Programmen.
9. Flexibilität in der Korrektur syntaktischer und semantischer Fehler.
10. Verfügbarkeit über ein einfaches und wirkungsvolles Editiersystem.
11. Kompatibilität mit anderen Programmiersystemen.

Das Dialogsystem DIALIS enthält Eigenschaften zur Erfüllung einiger Forderungen, auf die in den folgenden Abschnitten näher eingegangen wird.

3. Arbeitsbereiche

Arbeitsbereiche sind wie im Falle der Programmiersprache APL die Kommunikationsbereiche zwischen Programmierer und Dialogsystem. Sie bilden die Programmierumgebungen für die Ausführung der Kommandos, insbesondere für die Übersetzung und Ausführung von Programmen und Programmstücken der Dialogsprache.

Darüberhinaus enthalten sie für jede Variable, die in dem betreffenden Arbeitsbereich vereinbart ist oder während der Ausführung eines Programms vereinbart wird, einen sog. "Variablenkeller", dessen Inhalt zu jedem Zeitpunkt der Ausführung von Kommandos die Aufrufhierarchie der Programme bezüglich dieser Variablen wiederspiegelt. Das folgende Beispiel deutet für vier Variablen x,y,z und w den Aufbau ihrer Keller mit Mitteln der Listensprache an:

```
a) create workspace abc;          abc & bk = ()

b) real x,y:=2.0; ref real z;     abc & bk = ( ("x", (real, skip) ),
                                               ("y", (real, 2.0 ) ),
                                               ("z", (ref real, nil)))
```

```
c) begin real x:= 3.14; int w;      abc & bk = ( ("x", (real, skip),
        ..........                                 (real, 5.14) )<-┐
        x := x + y;                          ("y", (real, 2.0) ),  │
        z := x;                              ("z", (ref real, ──────┘)),
        ..........                           ("w", ( ),
   end;                                            (int, 2 )) )

d) delete element y;                abc & bk = ( ("x", (real, skip) ),
                                             ("z", (ref real, | )) )
                                                              ↓
                                                   (real, 5.14)
```

Das erste Kommando, ein Systemkommando, führt einen neuen Arbeitsbereich mit der Bezeichnung abc ein, in dem die nachfolgenden Kommandos ausgeführt werden. Das Ergebnis der Vereinbarungen b) für die Variablen x,y und z ist die Errichtung eines Variablenkellers für jede Variable, die zu der Liste abc&bk zusammengefaßt werden. Die Vereinbarung der Variablen x und w in dem Block c) erweitert den Variablenkeller der Variablen x um einen Eintrag, während für die Variable w ein neuer Keller eingerichtet wird, dessen erstes Element undefiniert ist. Die Bindung der in den nachfolgenden Anweisungen auftretenden Variablen erfolgt an das jeweils oberste Kellerelement.

Nach der Ausführung des Bereichskommandos d) gibt die Liste abc&bk den aktuellen Zustand der Variablenkeller der Variablen x und z an. Daraus wird insbesondere ersichtlich, daß im Fall der vorliegenden Listensprache die Lebensdauer einer Variablen solange besteht, wie ein Verweis auf die Variable existiert, d.h. sie kann größer sein als die Lebensdauer des Blocks, der die Vereinbarung enthält.

Während eines Gesprächs existiert zu jedem Zeitpunkt genau ein aktiver Arbeitsbereich. Die Ausführung von System- und Bereichskommandos in dieser Programmierumgebung bewirkt folgende Operationen:

-- Das Löschen des aktiven Arbeitsbereichs und die Bereitstellung eines neuen.
-- Die Speicherung des aktiven Arbeitsbereichs oder einer Kopie in einer öffentlichen oder privaten Programmbibliothek.
-- Das Laden inaktiver Arbeitsbereiche aus Programmbibliotheken oder von Teilen inaktiver Arbeitsbereiche.
-- Den Aufbau eines arbeitsbereichsspezifischen Dialogsystems durch eine Auswahl jener Komponenten des Dialogsystems DIALIS, die für die Ausführung von Kommandos innerhalb dieses Arbeitsbereichs benötigt werden, möglicherweise ergänzt durch Komponenten anderer Programmiersysteme.

4. Moduln

In Abschnitt 2 wurde die Forderung nach der Existenz eines Ausführungsmodus und eines Definitionsmodus erhoben. Der Sinn dieser Forderung liegt darin, daß man auf der einen Seite jedes Kommando unmittelbar nach seinem "Niederschreiben" ausführen möchte, auf der anderen Seite soll es jedoch auch möglich sein, Kommandos zu speichern und zu neuen Einheiten, sog. "Moduln" der Dialogsprache, zusammenfassen zu können, deren Aufruf erst die Ausführung dieser Kommandos bewirkt.

Das folgende Beispiel zeigt die Definition eines Moduls, wobei angenommen wird, daß die Listensprache DIALIS die bedingte Anweisung nicht kennt; somit kann diese Moduldefinition als Definition der bedingten Anweisung dienen:

```
modul  if a then b else c fi [ li]# from 1.0 by 0.1 :
1.0  iff missing b
1.1  take if a then begin end else c fi  off
1.2  iff missing c
1.3  take if a then b else begin end fi  off
1.4  begin list(proc void) li:= (void : b, void : c);
1.5       li[abs[a] + 1] ;
1.6  end;
1.7  endmodul;
```

Das Erkennen des Wortsymbols <u>modul</u> bewirkt einen Übergang vom Ausführungsmodus zum Definitionsmodus, während das Erkennen des Wortsymbols <u>endmodul</u> zum Ausführungsmodus zurückführt.

Der obige Modul besteht aus einem Modulkopf mit der Modulbezeichnung if und den formalen Modulparametern a,b und c, die durch die Modulseparatoren then, else und fi getrennt sind. Die allgemeine Form des Modulkopfs ist der syntaktischen Form der Sprachanweisungen nachempfunden:

<u>modul</u> <Modulbezeichnung> {<formaler Modulparameter> <Modulseparator>}

Der Modulrumpf besteht hier aus drei Rumpfelementen, von denen ein Element in Abhängigkeit von dem jeweiligen Modulaufruf ausgewählt wird. Die Numerierungsangabe

<u>from</u> 1.0 <u>by</u> 0.1

ersetzt die standardmäßige Zeilennumerierung des Moduls. Durch jeden Modulaufruf und der damit verbundenen textuellen Ersetzung der formalen Modulparameter durch aktuelle Parameter, die beliebige Texte sein können, wie in dem Beispiel

```
begin int li;
      ..........;
      if li less 2 then li := li + 2 else li := li - 2 fi;
      ..........
end;
```

wird ein Text erzeugt, der an die Stelle des Aufrufs tritt. Jede Bezeichnung, die in einer "Ersetzungsliste" wie

[li]

auftritt, wird in diesem Text durch eine spezielle Bezeichnung ersetzt, um einen Konflikt zwischen Bezeichnungen aufzulösen, wie das obige Beispiel zeigt.

Die Bestimmung des Modulrumpfs erfolgt, falls die Moduldefinition eine Auswahl ermöglicht, durch die Untersuchung der aktuellen Modulparameter, indem ihr Auftreten oder ihre Gleichheit mit einer Zeichenreihe abgefragt wird:

```
iff missing a or a = "zeichenreihe" take .... off
```

Der rekursive Aufruf von Moduln ist zulässig. Der Inhalt eines Modulrumpfs kann außer einem DIALIS-Programmstück ein beliebiger Text sein, beispielsweise ein ALGOL-Programm.

Die Möglichkeiten zur Verwendung eines Moduls, dessen Rumpf ein DIALIS-Programmstück ist, können folgendermaßen klassifiziert werden:

a) Übersetzung und Ausführung im aktiven Arbeitsbereich, in dem auch die Bindung der freien Variablen erfolgt:

   run >>Modulaufruf<< ;

   Die Angabe des Wortsymbols run ist optional.

b) Übersetzung und Ausführung in einer eigens definierten Programmierumgebung:

   envir >>Vereinbarungen<< ;>> Anweisungen<< ;
   run >>Modulaufruf<< ;

c) Übersetzung im aktiven Arbeitsbereich:

   compile >>Modulaufruf<< ;

   Das Zwischensprachenprogramm als Ergebnis der Übersetzung wird ebenfalls durch die Modulbezeichnung des Moduls identifiziert und kann ausgeführt werden:

   exec >>Modulbezeichnung<< ;   oder
   envir >>Vereinbarungen<< ; >>Anweisungen<< ;
   exec >>Modulbezeichnung<< ;

d) Übersetzung mit Spezifikation der freien Variablen:

```
envir >>Vereinbarungen<< ;
compile >>Modulaufruf<< ;
```

Die Bindung der freien Variablen erfolgt nicht durch die Übersetzung, sondern erst durch die Ausführung.

Im Fall c) bzw. d) ist es möglich, das erzeugte Zwischensprachenprogramm einem weiteren Modul zuzuordnen, der durch die Angabe einer Bezeichnung automatisch bereitgestellt wird:

```
compile >>Modulaufruf<< as >>Bezeichnung<< ;
```

e) Tritt ein Modulaufruf als Anweisung eines Programmstücks auf, so erfolgt eine Einkopierung des Rumpfs zum Zeitpunkt der Übersetzung oder Ausführung des Programmstücks:

```
...; begin ...; >>Modulaufruf<< ; ... end; ...
```

oder

```
...; begin ...; exec >>Modulbezeichnung<< ; ... end; ...
```

Ein weiteres Beispiel soll die Möglichkeit verdeutlichen, Programmstücke aus Moduln zusammensetzen zu können:

```
modul aa :
 >>Modulaufruf<< ; comment Vereinbarungen ;
 >>Modulaufruf<< ; comment Anweisungen ;
endmodul;
```

Die Punkte a) - e) zeigen somit, daß Moduln in hilfreicher Weise zur Entwicklung von Programmen und zur Zusammensetzung von Programmen aus vorgefertigten Teilen dienen können.

Zu jedem Modul gehört ein sog. "Moduldeskriptor", auf dessen Komponenten der Programmierer einen lesenden und/oder schreibenden Zugriff hat. Auszugsweise werden mit Mitteln der Listensprache einige Komponenten vorgestellt:

```
const string modulbezeichnung;
const real anfangszeile, endzeile; real schrittweite;
```

Der Zusatz const vor der jeweiligen Artangabe sagt aus, daß die Variablen dieser Vereinbarung schreibgeschützt sind.

```
const numerierung zeilen;
mit
mode numerierung = ( standard , frei , fest );
list(code) inhalt;
mit
mode code = ( dialiscode , interpretercode , algolcode , ...);
```

Einerseits gibt der Deskriptor den Zustand des Moduls an, andererseits nimmt er Informationen auf, die zur Übersetzungszeit oder zur Ausführungszeit des Moduls benötigt werden. Damit erhält der Programmierer beispielsweise die Gelegenheit, Überwachungsprozeduren dem Deskriptor eines Moduls zuordnen zu können statt sie in den Modulrumpf aufnehmen zu müssen.

5. Einige Spracheigenschaften

Dieser Abschnitt enthält einige Bemerkungen zu Spracheigenschaften der Listensprache, die sie dialogfähig machen.

Ein wesentliches Kontrollmittel des Programmierers während der Übersetzungsphase und Ausführungsphase eines Programms sind sog. "Unterbrechungsanweisungen", die es ihm ermöglichen, die Abarbeitung des Programms an einer bestimmten Stelle zu unterbrechen:

```
hold >>Anweisung<< ;   bzw.   hold
stop >>Anweisung<< ;   bzw.   stop
```

Diese Anweisungen sind programmiert, d.h. sie treten als Anweisungen eines Programms auf, oder sie werden über die Konsole ausgeführt. In jedem Fall erfolgt durch ihre Ausführung eine Unterbrechung der laufenden Übersetzungs- oder Ausführungsphase eines Programms, so daß der Programmierer im Kontext des unterbrochenen Programms ("hold") oder im Kontext des aktiven Arbeitsbereichs ("stop") weitere Kommandos ausführen kann, die nicht notwendigerweise das unterbrochene Programm betreffen müssen.Zu einem späteren Zeitpunkt ist dann die Fortsetzung der Abarbeitung möglich.

Das Dialogsystem als Gesprächspartner des Programmierers verfügt ebenfalls über eigene Unterbrechungsanweisungen, die es ihm erlauben, einen syntaktischen oder semantischen Fehler, einen offenen Bezug oder einen Auftrag dem Programmierer mitzuteilen.

Im Zusammenhang mit Moduln kann der Programmierer einem Modul Überwachungsprozeduren oder sog. "begleitende Prozeduren" zuordnen, die zur Zeit der Ausführung des Moduls ausgewertet werden. Diese Zuordnung kann außerhalb des Modulrumpfs erfolgen:

```
dump >>Modulmarken<< with >>Variablen<< enddump ;
trace >>Modulmarken<< with >>Anweisungen<< endtrace;
check >>Modulmarken<< cond >>Bedingung<<
                      with >>Anweisungen<< endcheck;
```

Das folgende, sehr einfache Beispiel charakterisiert die Verwendung begleitender Prozeduren:

```
modul  abc :
begin real z:=0, u:=x;
      ..........
      do m1: z := z + y; u := u - 1 until m2: u = 0 done;
      ..........
end;
endmodul;
```

Die beiden Anweisungen

```
check abc & m1 cond z + u * y = x * y and u > 0 with stop
                                                  endcheck;
und
check abc & m2 cond z + u * y = x * y and u ≥ 0 with stop
                                                  endcheck;
```

die dem Deskriptor des Moduls abc als begleitende Prozeduren zugeordnet werden, überprüfen die Einhaltung der dem Symbol cond folgenden Bedingung vor der Ausführung der durch die Modulmarken m1 und m2 markierten Anweisungen des Modulrumpfs. Ist die jeweilige Bedingung nicht erfüllt, so erfolgt eine Auswertung der Anweisung, die dem Symbol with folgt.

6. Zusammenfassung

In den Abschnitten 3,4,5 wurde versucht, einige System- und Spracheigenschaften des Dialogsystems DIALIS zu verdeutlichen. Die Flexibilität und die Möglichkeiten ihres Einsatzes konnte in diesem Rahmen nicht erschöpfend behandelt werden. Als wichtigstes Programmiermittel wurden Moduln eingeführt, deren Anwendung es dem Programmierer erlauben soll, in einfacher und übersichtlicher Form die Entwicklung und Ausführung von Programmen in der Form eines Gesprächs mit dem Dialogsystem durchzuführen. Die Untersuchungen in dieser Richtung sind nicht abgeschlossen und werden weitergeführt.

MESSUNG DER EFFIZIENZ EINES EINFACHEN "INCREMENTAL COMPILER"

H.A.SCHMID, B.NIENABER

1. Einleitung

Diese Arbeit beschreibt einen inkrementellen Kompiler, welcher als Diplomarbeit von Bernd Nienaber auf dem System HYDRA II / EL X 8 [1] am Institut für Informatik der Universität Karlsruhe implementiert wurde.

"Inkrementelle" Kompiler gestatten es, im Dialogbetrieb das Erstellen und Austesten eines Programms "stückweise" vorzunehmen. Die Kommunikationseinheit zwischen Benutzer und Kompiler wird Increment genannt. Eine genauere Definition des Begriffs "Incremental Compiler" findet sich in [2] und [3]; hier sei nur kurz erwähnt, daß bei inkrementellen Kompilern die Folge von Programmerstellung, -ausführung und -abänderung beliebig ist. Bei Unterbrechungen der Programmausführung können Variablenwerte inspiziert und abgeändert werden; es ist auch möglich, das Programm abzuändern und danach die Ausführung wiederaufzunehmen.

Die Dialogsprache wird im 2. Abschnitt näher beschrieben. Sie entspricht im wesentlichen einer Untermenge von ALGOL 60 [4], welche zeilenstrukturiert und um Kommandoelemente erweitert ist. Zwei bedeutende Einschränkungen sind gegenüber ALGOL 60 vorgenommen worden: Ein Programm kann nicht in Blöcke gegliedert sein, sondern nur in einen einzigen Block, der aber compound Statements enthalten darf; konsequenterweise sind auch keine Prozeduren zugelassen.

Wegen der ALGOL 60 - Ähnlichkeit der Dialogsprache treten wesentlich mehr Querbezüge zwischen einzelnen Increments auf als bei einfachen Dialogsprachen wie JOSS oder BASIC. Es sind einerseits Querbezüge, welche Datenobjekte betreffen, da Variable deklariert werden müssen; andererseits sind es Querbezüge, welche den Programmkontrollfluß betreffen, da mit Hilfe der IF, FOR, BEGIN und END Increments (siehe Abschnitt 2) komplizierte Kontrollflußstrukturen gebildet werden können.

Die Abarbeitung der Querbezüge zwischen den einzelnen Increments geschieht trotzdem nicht interpretativ; denn dies hat eine nicht sehr effiziente Programmausführung zur Folge. Sie wird entsprechend einigen Prinzipien zur Strukturierung von flexiblen und effizienten Dialogkompilern vorgenommen, welche in [5] geäußert und in [6] formalisiert werden.

Diese Prinzipien besagen, daß Bindungen eines Increments an eine bestimmte Umgebung (diese Bindungen entsprechen den Querbezügen zwischen einzelnen Increments) so spät wie möglich vorgenommen werden, d.h. zu dem Zeitpunkt, unmittelbar bevor ein Increment das erste Mal ausgeführt wird. Diese Bindungen werden dann aber nicht interpretiert, sondern kompiliert. Wenn außerdem Information aufbewahrt wird, welche Bindungen vorgenommen wurden, kann der kompilierte Code solange ausgeführt werden, bis eine Programmabänderung die für dieses Increment relevante Umgebung abändert.

Die Bindungen der Variablen an ihre Deklarationen werden in diesem Kompiler gemäß obigen Prinzipien vorgenommen; die Bindungen der Programmablauf-Kontrollstruktur werden jedoch interpretativ hergestellt. Die gesamte Implementierung wird im 3. Abschnitt beschrieben.

Im 4. Abschnitt wird anhand von Messungen gezeigt, daß der beschriebene Kompiler effizient arbeitet. Einerseits sind die bei Programmabänderungen benötigten Rekompilationszeiten gering, andererseits ist die Ausführungsgeschwindigkeit des generierten Programmes nicht wesentlich langsamer als die von Batch - Code.

2. Benutzersprache des Kompilers

2.1 Allgemeines

Der Ablauf des Dialogs soll für den Benutzer möglichst einfach und übersichtlich gestaltet werden. Daher werden im "User - Interface" des Kompilers keine verschiedenen sprachlichen Ebenen unterschieden; Sprach- und Kommandoelemente der Dialogsprache arbeiten auf derselben Ebene. Mit "Kommandoelemente" seien hier diejenigen Increments bezeichnet, welche den Ablauf von Programmerstellung und -ausführung steuern und sonstige Hilfsdienste leisten. "Sprachelemente" werden diejenigen Increments genannt, welche in ähnlicher Form in Batch - Sprachen vorhanden sind.

2.2 Benutzung und Kommandoelemente

Increments können entweder im direkten oder im indirekten Modus eingegeben werden. Die Eingabe ist völlig unabhängig davon, ob zum Eingabezeitpunkt eine Programmausführung unterbrochen ist oder nicht. Es gibt jedoch Typen von Increments, die nur im direkten oder im indirekten Modus eingegeben werden dürfen.

Bei der indirekten Eingabe wird den Increments eine Incrementnummer vorangestellt. Sie gibt an, an welcher Stelle das Increment logisch in das zu erstellende Programm eingefügt wird. Die logische Folge der Increments im Programm ist damit von der Reihenfolge ihrer Eingabe unabhängig. Die Korrektheit der Aufeinanderfolge von Increments, welche ein Programm bilden (die globale Syntax), wird erst bei der Programmausführung überprüft; die Korrektheit eines Increments (die lokale Syntax) sofort bei der Eingabe. Direkt eingegebene Increments werden sofort ausgeführt.

Damit werden für den Vorgang der Programmerstellung oder -abänderung bis auf eine Ausnahme keine speziellen Kommandos benötigt.
Soll ein Increment nachträglich in ein bereits fertiggestelltes Programm eingefügt werden, so muß es mit der logisch richtigen Incrementnummer versehen indirekt eingegeben werden. Soll ein Increment ein bereits vorhandenes ersetzen, muß es mit derselben Nummer eingegeben werden. Nur zum Entfernen eines Increments aus dem Programm ist das DELETE - Increment notwendig.
Dieses gehört zu einer Gruppe von Kommando-Increments, welche nur direkt eingegeben werden können. Dazu gehört auch das EXECUTE-Increment. Es veranlaßt eine neue Ausführung des Programms. Falls eine alte Ausführung bei seiner Eingabe unterbrochen war, wird sie vorher beendet. Damit sind geschachtelte Ausführungen unmöglich. Das RESUME-Increment dient dazu, eine unterbrochene Ausführung wieder aufzunehmen.
Die weiteren Kommandoelemente sollen hier nicht im einzelnen beschrieben werden.

2.3 Sprachelemente

Zuerst sei eine Gruppe von kontrollstrukturbildenden Increments erwähnt, die nur indirekt eingegeben werden dürfen. Sie besteht aus den BEGIN-, END-, IF- (≙ "<if-clause>") und FOR- (≙ "<for-clause>") Increments. DECLARATION- und BREAKPT- Increments dürfen sinnvollerweise auch nur indirekt eingegeben werden.
Die Increments, welche den Algol- "<basic statements>" ähnlich sind, wie z.B. ASSIGNEMENT-, GOTO-, DUMMY-, READ-, PRINT- und EXTIME-Increment, dürfen direkt und indirekt eingegeben werden.

Mit dem Hinweis, daß die oben erwähnten Increments im großen ganzen eine ähnliche Bedeutung wie die entsprechenden Konstruktionen aus dem Algol-Report [4] haben, sei der informelle Überblick über die Incrementtypen der Dialogsprache abgeschlossen.

Es wird hier auch nicht formell angegben, welche Incrementfolgen ein korrektes Programm bilden; es sei ebenfalls nur informell auf die Ähnlichkeit zu ALGOL 60 verwiesen, mit der Ausnahme, daß ein Programm nur aus einem Block bestehen darf. Dieser darf "Compound Statements" enthalten.

Fehler, welche Querbezüge zwischen Increments betreffen, werden bei der Programmausführung festgestellt. Dazu gehört z.B. der Fehler, daß ein Programm aus mehreren Blöcken besteht, oder daß eine Variable, welche in einem einfachen arithmetischen Ausdruck vorkommt, als Boolsche Variable deklariert ist.

2.4 Anwendungsbeispiel

Das Programmbeispiel Abb. 1 zeigt die Möglichkeiten eines Benutzers bei der Programmerstellung und -abänderung. Der Ausdruck des Kompilers ist in unterstrichenen Großbuchstaben, der Kommentar in Kursivschrift gegeben.

3. Beschreibung der Implementierung

Abb. 3 zeigt die Datenstruktur, welche vom Kompiler beim Dialog erzeugt wird. Ein Teil dieser Datenstruktur wird bei der Eingabe der Increments, ein anderer Teil bei ihrer Ausführung generiert. Die einzelnen Module des Kompilers und ihr Zusammenwirken sind in Abb. 2 dargestellt.

3.1 Eingabe von Increments

Nach der Eingabe eines Increments wird seine lexikalische und syntaktische Analyse durchgeführt. Wird dabei ein Fehler entdeckt, so wird das eingegebene Increment nicht akzeptiert. Die Kontrolle geht dann nach Ausgabe einer Fehlmeldung an den Benutzer zurück.

Sonst wird das eingegebene Increment in Pseudocode umgewandelt. Dieser enthält die Quelltext-Information in kondensierter Form. Wortsymbole, etc. sind verschlüsselt, Bezeichner sind durch Zeiger auf die Variablenliste ersetzt. Ausdrücke werden in Präfixform dargestellt. Denn aus dieser läßt sich sehr einfach Code erzeugen, und der Quelltext kann abgesehen vom Verlust von Lay-Out-Features einfach wiedergewonnen werden.

Bei der indirekten Eingabe eines Increments wird weiterhin ein Eintrag in der Kontrolltafel angelegt, und mit dem vorhandenen Programm verknüpft. Ein solcher Eintrag enthält die Increment_nummer, einen Zeiger auf dem Kontrolltafeleintrag des logisch folgenden Increments, Information über den Typ des Increments, eventuell ein Code-Gültig-Bit, was auf "Nein" gesetzt wird, einen Zeiger auf den Pseudocode, und einen momentan leeren Zeiger auf den Code. Danach geht die Kontrolle an den Benutzer zurück.

Ist das indirekt eingegebene Increment eine Deklaration, oder ist es mit einer Marke versehen, so muß der entsprechende Eintrag in der Variablenliste abgeändert werden. Bei einer einfachen Deklaration wird dort der Variablentyp eingetragen. Bei einer Felddeklaration wird im Sekundärspeicher der Felddeskriptor angelegt und Speicherplatz reserviert; ein Zeiger auf den Deskriptor wird als Wert zusätzlich zum Typ der Variablen in die Variablenliste eingetragen. Bei einer Marke wird ein Zeiger auf den Kontrolltafeleintrag des zugehörigen Increments als Wert zusätzlich zum Typ Marke in die Variablenliste eingetragen.

Der Eintrag einer Deklaration hat außerdem zur Folge, daß alle Code - Gültig - Bits in der Kontrolltafel auf Nein gesetzt werden müssen.

Bei der direkten Eingabe eines Increments wird die dem Incrementtyp entsprechende Routine des Ausführungsmoduls aufgerufen. Der Zeiger auf dem erzeugten Pseudocode wird als Parameter übergeben.
Die Arbeitsweise des Ausführungsmoduls wird im nächsten Abschnitt beschrieben. Nach der Ausführung des Increments geht die Kontrolle an den Benutzer, außer wenn eine Programmausführung veranlaßt wurde.

3.2 Ausführung des Programms

Bei der Ausführung eines abgespeicherten Programmes müssen zwei Aufgaben durchgeführt werden:
Die einzelnen Increments müssen ausgeführt werden; diese Aufgabe wird vom Ausführungsmodul vorgenommen. Andererseits muß die Kontrolle von einem ausgeführten Increment zum nächsten auszuführenden Increment übertragen werden; das geschieht im Kontrollinterpretationsmodul (siehe Abb. 2).

Der Ausführungsmodul enthält für jeden (auszuführenden) Incrementtyp eine spezielle Routine. Diese Ausführungsroutinen werden bei der direkten Eingabe von Increments vom Syntaxanalysemodul als Unterprogramm aufgerufen; bei der indirekten Ausführung eines Programmes werden sie vom Kontrollinterpreter aufgerufen. Gemäß dem Incrementtyp wird ein Teil der Increments von den Ausführungsroutinen interpretiert; bei dem anderen Teil der Increments, welcher Ausdrücke enthält, wird Maschinencode erzeugt und ausgeführt.

Vor jeder Ausführung eines solchen Increments muß das dazugehörige Code-Gültig-Bit in der Kontrolltafel abgefragt werden. Ist es gesetzt, so kann der vorhandene Maschinencode sofort ausgeführt werden. Ist es nicht gesetzt, so wird der Codeerzeugungsmodul aufgerufen, der aus dem Pseudocode mit Hilfe der in die Variablenliste eingetragenen Variablentypen Maschinencode erzeugt. Ein Zeiger auf den erzeugten Code wird in die Kontrolltafel eingetragen, das Code-Gültig-Bit wird gesetzt, und der Code ausgeführt.

Der Kontrollinterpretationsmodul wird durch die Ausführung der direkt eingegebenen Increments EXECUTE, RESUME oder EXECEND aktiviert. Er muß die globale syntaktische Korrektheit des Programms überprüfen und den Programmablaufkontrollfluß steuern, d.h. die Kontrolle von einem zum nächsten auszuführenden Increment weitergeben. Dies geschieht in dieser Kompilerversion völlig interpretativ. Dazu wird bei der Ausführung ein Kontrollkeller benötigt, welcher den globalen syntaktischen Zustand und den Kontrollflußzustand enthält. Der Kontrollkellerzustand und der Typ des logisch folgenden Increments dienen dazu, in einer Übergangsmatrix die durchzuführenden Aktionen zu bestimmen.

3.3 Diskussion der Implementierung

Wie in der Einleitung zitiert wird, werden in [5] und [6] Prinzipien zur Strukturierung von Dialogkompilern angegeben. Betrachtet man diese Implementierung, so stellt man fest, daß diese Prinzipien bezüglich der Datenobjekte verwirklicht werden. Bei Programmabänderungen wird unterschieden, ob sie eine Änderung von Deklarationen zur Folge haben oder nicht. Obwohl im Normalfalle nicht alle Increments eines Programms von einer solchen Deklarationsabänderung betroffen werden, werden alle Code-Gültig-Bits auf "Nein" gesetzt. Damit wird von einer solchen Abänderung ein größerer Rekompilationsaufwand verursacht als es nötig ist; er fällt jedoch trotzdem kaum ins Gewicht, da Codeerzeugung aus der Präfixform für eine Ein-Akkumulator-Maschine und den wenigen vorhandenen Datentypen sehr schnell ist (siehe Abschnitt 4).

Bezüglich der globalen Syntax und des Ablaufkontrollflußes wurden obige Prinzipien nicht befolgt. Ein gewisser Overhead zwischen der Ausführung von zwei Maschinencodestücken läßt sich bei der aus dem Quellprogramm erzeugten Datenstruktur nicht umgehen - er wird hervorgerufen durch die Abfrage des Code-Gültig-Bits, und durch die Fortschaltung von einem Codestück zum nächsten.
In der vorliegenden Implementierung wird jedoch aus gewissen Gründen zusätzlich die globale Syntax interpretativ überprüft und der Ablaufkontrollfluß interpretativ ermittelt. Dadurch wird hier der Overhead bei der Programmausführung größer als es nötig wäre.
Dies ließe sich vermeiden, indem vor einer Programmausführung die Korrektheit der globalen Syntax überprüft wird, und der Ablaufkontrollfluß kompiliert und mit Hilfe von zusätzlichen Zeigern in der Kontrolltafel eingetragen wird.

4. Messung der Effizienz

Die Messungen erfolgen mit Hilfe eines Systemaufrufs, welcher die aufgelaufene Ausführungszeit eines Benutzerprogrammlaufs angibt [1]. Das Auflösungsvermögen der dabei benützten Uhr beträgt 10 msec. Die Ausführungszeiten werden mit denen von Batch-Programmen verglichen, welche vom Hydra 2 Algol-Kompiler [7] übersetzt sind. Günstig ist dabei, daß die Codeerzeugung für Ausdrücke in beiden Kompilern auf dieselbe Weise vorgenommen wird.

Die Messung der Ausführungszeit einer Wertzuweisung (ohne die Fortschaltungszeit zwischen Increments) erfolgt nach Wichmann [8] durch Bildung der Differenz zwischen den Ausführungszeiten der beiden folgenden Programmstücke:

```
for I: = 1 step 1 until 1000 do
;
```

und

```
for I: = 1 step 1 until 1000 do
"Wertzuweisung";
```

Der Vergleich wurde für verschiedene Wertzuweisungen mit den entsprechenden Batch-Werten durchgeführt. Die Abweichungen der entsprechenden Ausführungszeiten voneinander lagen im Rahmen der Meßgenauigkeit, wie es zu erwarten war.

Von größerem Interesse ist jedoch der Vergleich von Gesamtausführungszeiten; diese ergeben sich beim inkrementellen Kompiler aus Ausführungs- und Fortschaltungszeit. Daher hängt das Ergebnis sehr stark von der Programmstruktur des jeweils untersuchten Programmes ab, besonders von der Incrementlänge. Es werden zwei einigermaßen typische Beispiele angegeben.

Bsp.1:

```
B:= 1.57; C:= 4.63; D:= 167.25; E:= 0.3;
for I:= 1 stop 1 until 1000 do
A:= (B + C) / D x E + B / (C + D x E/B);
```

Bsp.2:

```
B:= ....
for I:= 1 stop 1 until 1000 do
begin
A:= (B + C) / D x E + B / (C + D x E / B);
          -  "  -
          -  "  -
          -  "  -
          -  "  -
end
```

Die gemessenen Ausführungszeiten betrugen:

	Batch	Dialog
Bsp.1:	580 msec	1790 msec
Bsp.2:	2390 msec	6420 msec

Das Verhältnis der Ausführungszeiten von Batch-Programmen zu Dialogprogrammen ist damit 1: 3,1 und 1: 2,7.

Weiter von Interesse ist die Rekompilationszeit, welche bei Programmabänderungen erforderlich wird. Sie ist bei allen Abänderungen gleich Null, außer bei der Abänderung von Deklarationen. Denn dann muß der Maschinencode neu generiert werden. Die dafür benötigte Zeit liegt in der Größenordnung von 1 msec für ein Increment, wie z.B. für Increment Nr. 32 aus Bsp.2. Damit ist sie sehr klein und bei der gegebenen Meßgenauigkeit auch für wesentlich längere Programmstücke als Bsp.2 überhaupt nicht meßbar.

5. Folgerungen

Der beschriebene inkrementelle Kompiler ist sehr benutzerfreundlich. Er läßt dem Benutzer größtmögliche Freiheit in den Zyklus von Programmerstellung, -ausführung- und -abänderung. Trotzdem ist seine Programmausführungsgeschwindigkeit beachtlich groß. Bei ihrer Betrachtung darf nicht vernachlässigt werden, daß einerseits der Kontrollfluß interpretiert wird, und daß die Struktur von Ausführungs- und Kontrollinterpreter-Modul sowie die gesamte Implementierung nicht auf das Erzielen höchster Ausführungsgeschwindigkeiten angelegt sind.
Programmabänderungen gehen sehr einfach vor sich und erfordern keinen großen Rekompilationsaufwand.

Damit wurde am Beispiel eines nicht zu komplizierten, überschaubaren und einfachen inkrementellen Kompilers gezeigt, wie die in [5] und [6.3] angegebenen theoretischen Ergebnisse wirkungsvoll angewendet werden können. Die durchgeführten Messungen ergaben, daß inkrementelle Kompiler dieser Art im Vergleich mit interpretativen inkrementellen Kompilern und mit Batch-Kompilern, die dem Dialogbetrieb angepaßt sind, hervorragend abschneiden dürften, wenn man die gesamte (Re-) Kompilations- und Ausführungszeit vergleicht, die zur Fertigstellung eines Programmes bei einer Dialogsitzung benötigt wird.

6. Referenzen

[1] Horst Wettstein, Hydra - Hand - Buch, Institut für Informatik, Universität Karlsruhe, Int. Ber. 69/8

[2] H. Katzan, Batch, Conversational, and Incremental Compilers, SJCC, 1969

[3] W.J. Rishel, Incremental Compilers, Datamation, Jan. 1970

[4] P. Naur, ed., Revised Report on the Algorithmic Language ALGOL 60, CACM, Vol.6, No.1

[5] Hans Albrecht Schmid, The Structure of a Flexible and Efficient Compiler For Algorithmic Conversational Languages, GI-Bericht Fach-

tagg. Programmiersprachen, München 1971

[6] Hans Albrecht Schmid, A User Oriented and Efficient Incremental Compiler, Proc. International Computing Symposium, Venice 1972

[7] M. Brockhaus und P. Schroth, ALGOL-Handbuch, Institut für Informatik, Universität Karlsruhe, Int. Ber. 69/10

[8] B.A. Wichmann, A Comparison of ALGOL 60 Execution Speeds, CCU-Rep. 3, NPL, Teddington

Protokoll der Dialogsitzung	*Kommentar*
10 begin	
20 read (A);	*Programmerstellung*
21 A2:= A×A;	
22 P4:= (35×A2×A2 - 30×A2 + 3)/ 8;	
11 real P4, A2;	*nachträgl. Einfügen*
30 end;	
execute;	*Programmausführung*
EXECUTION SUSPENDED AT INCR.20 AS	*Programmausführung wegen*
VARIABLE NOT DECLARED	*Fehler unterbrochen*
12 integer A;	*Programmabänderung*
26 stop;	
resume;	*Wiederaufnahme d.Ausführung*
A = 1	*Anforderung e. Eingabe*
EXECUTION SUSPENDED AT INCR.26,BREAKPT	*Programmausführung an Haltepunkt unterbrochen*
25 print (A2, P4);	
print (A2, P4);	*direkte Ausgabe*
A2 = 1 P4 = 1	
20 M: read (A);	
27 goto M;	*Programmabänderung*
12 real A;	
resume;	*Wiederaufnahme d.Ausführung*
A = 0.5	*Anforderung einer Eingabe*
A2 = 0.025 P4 = -0.2891	*Ausgabe*

Abb. 1 Programmbeispiel Legendre'sches Polynom

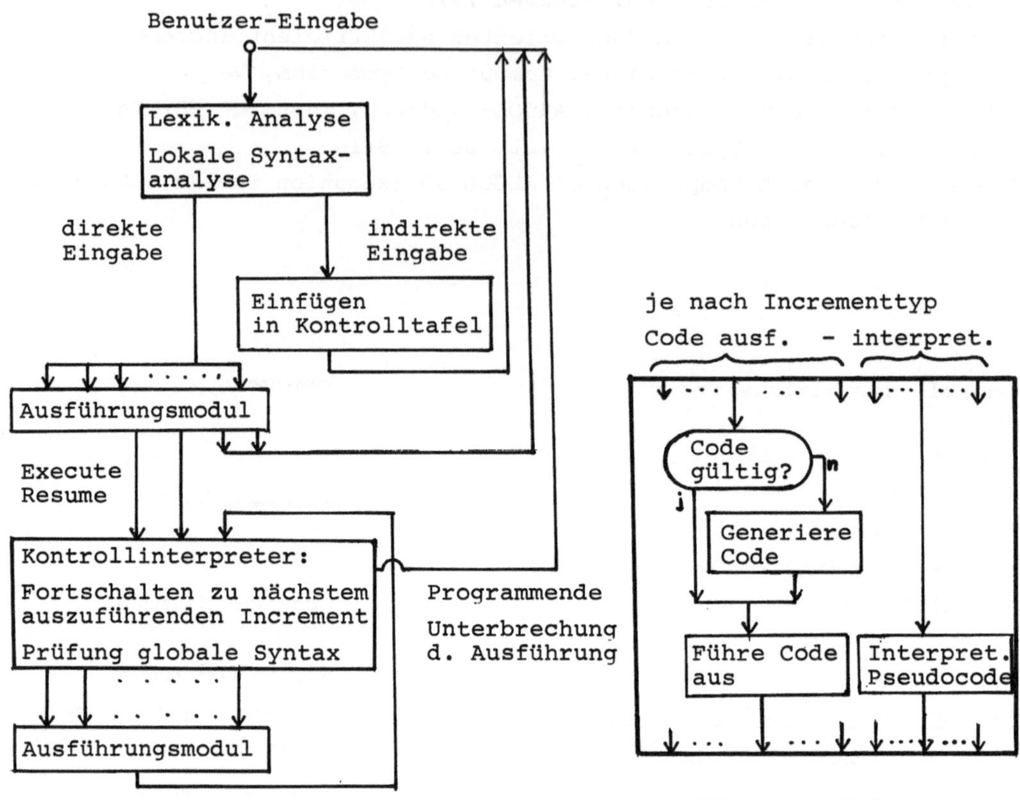

Abb. 2 Module des Kompilers

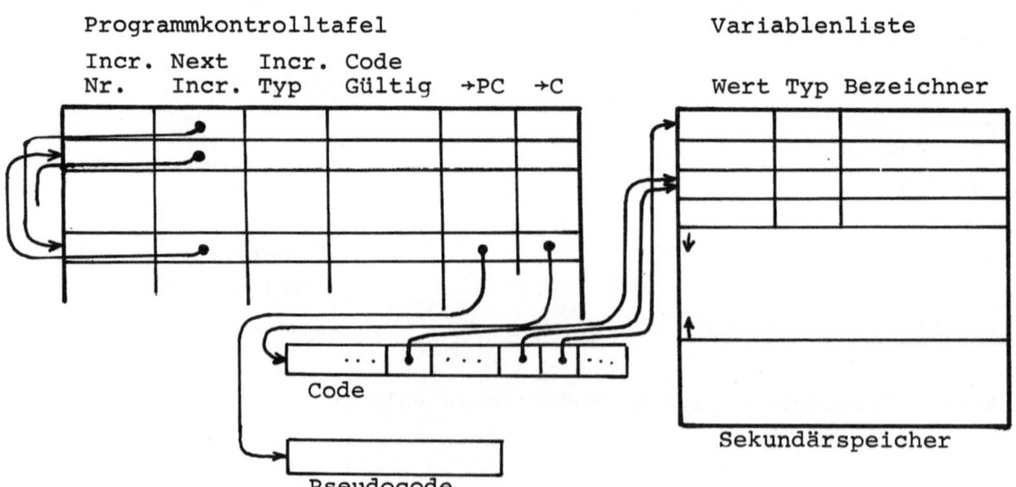

Abb. 3 Aus Quellprogramm erzeugte Datenstruktur

THE STRUCTURES OF THE NCC SIMULA COMPILERS AND BENCH MARK COMPARISONS WITH OTHER MAJOR LANGUAGES

S.KUBOSCH

Introduction

SIMULA is a language for general purpose and for simulation problems, and is defined in "SIMULA Common Base Language" [1].

The objective of this paper is two-fold:

- to describe briefly the structure of SIMULA Systems made by NCC
- to present results of Bench-mark comparisons with other major languages.

For the second part of this paper one should consider that speed of compilation and execution is not the only criterion for the choice of a language. It is, however, outside the scope of this paper to discuss the intricate language-choice problems in general.

Abstract implementation.

During the development for the language definition [1], it was necessary to keep in mind the implementability of the language features, i.e. the ease by which the features may be included in a translator or performed in the users program. For this reason, but also to enable easy communication of the most important aspects to other implementors, a SIMULA implementation guide [2] was developed in parallel to [1]. This guide was subsequently used for five seminars given by NCC for other implementation teams.

It is given in a slightly extended SIMULA language, and covers most of the support routines required during execution of user programs. It contains also some suggestions for the compiler implementation, especially for the processing of the SIMULA data accessing. This abstract definition caused most SIMULA runtime systems to use simular techniques, and simplified both the implementation and the debugging of the different runtime systems. Most debugging problems were indeed encountered where individual implementors "for efficiency reasons" decided to attempt a shortcut of the abstract definition.

NCC implementations

NCC implemented SIMULA for two computer families:
UNIVAC 1108/1106/1110 EXEC8 and IBM 360/370 OS.
Two different project teams worked on these implementations, but a large degree of simularity exists. This is due partly to the implementation guide and partly to the teams being in informal daily contact with each other. Graham Birtwistle is responsible for the IBM system and Sigurd Kubosch for the UNIVAC system.

The UNIVAC system was first released to external users October 1970, the IBM system in April 1972.
Each system consists of a compiler, a runtime system and documentation. The UNIVAC compiler takes about 30K words on the 1108. The 360/370 SIMULA system requires at the moment a minimum region of 124K bytes, but a modification to the subroutine calls in the code generator will result in a reduction of this size in the next release.

The structure of the compilers may be briefly described as follows:
The SIMULA source program is read in and transformed into reloctable form by a series of passes. Each pass (except, of course, the first and the last) accepts as input the output from the previous pass, transforms it one stage further and then outputs the transformed string for the attention of the next pass. Forward references are, of course, resolved by backward passes.
With smaller pgrams, all the transformations can be kept in core. With large programs, however, two utility files are used.

The various transformations are:

LEXICOGRAPHIC SCANNER

This acts as a subroutine to the syntax checker in the EXEC8 SIMULA compiler.
The lexicographic scanner transforms constants, and changes keywords (e.g. <u>begin</u>) annd basic symbols (e.g. ==) into internal representations. Further, each identifier is assigned a serial number.

CROSS REFERENCE LISTING

(not yet available on UNIVAC).
The cross reference listing writes out in an alphabetic order identifiers used in the program together with the line number of each occurrence.

SYNTAX CHECKER

The syntax checkers were written according to the well-known transition table technique [3] and need no special comment.

LOCAL QUANTITY LISTS

This pass is backwards and scans through the output from the syntax checker, gathering up, as it does so, information on all locally declared quantities to the head of the surrounding block.

SEMANTIC CHECKING

The main difference of the two implementations, besides of the different hardware, falls into this section.
The purpose of the semantic checking may be expressed as follows:

The semantic checker replaces all identifiers from their serial form representation into their block level and offset. It sets up a semantic dictionary, matches virtual quantities, treats prefixed classes and blocks, and checks the validity of identifier occurrences in statements and expressions. The semantic checker resolves all qualification checks and converts expressions into reverse polish. Finally fixups are introduced for code branching through IF-statements, FOR-statements etc.

While the whole semantic dictionary is kept in core in the EXEC8 SIMULA system, the 360/370 SIMULA system uses a rather intricate paging system.

CODE GENERATOR

The code generator constructs the object code except that fixups and relocation are left over.

FIXUPS

The output from the code generator is scanned (possibly backwards) to settle all the fixups.

INTERFACE

The last transformation produces relocatable code as required by the operating system.

Three additional points must be mentioned:

SOURCE LISTING

Both compilers have several options to improve the printout of the source program aside/instead of the usual program listing.

ERROR RECOVERY

This has been one of the most difficult and vulnerable tasks of the compiler. As the compilers are built up by several passes, the diagnostics have to be gathered up and to be output at the end of the compilation. The UNIVAC system merges the error messages into the usual source listings.

USER CONVENIENCE

Considerable effort has been made to include, both into the compiler and into the runtime system, features which were found necessary or convenient to achiece better communication between the user, SIMULA and the operating system, or for better exploitation of specific features. The languages implemented are extended versions of [1].

The runtime system consists of:

- initialisation and termination routines
- storage administration routines and garbage collector
- diagnostic routines
- paramter handling routines
- system defined routines
- additional routines for user convenience

The runtime module contains these predefined routines and the relocated object module and card number indications. (Only those runtime routines needed are included).
During program execution, the available storage is divided into a fixed storage area (required for object code, runtime routines and special runtime data) and two dynamic pools for the data created by the user program. Into one pool go data blocks of arbitrary size - blocks, procedures, objects, texts, arrays, and special runtime system objects (e.g. accumulator stacks for saving register values). Into the other pool go special objects all of the same fixed size called drivers and event notices.

The driver technique is fully explained in [2]. It is a means of reducing the size of objects by separating out information which is not needed when the actions of the object are exhausted (it becomes "terminated") and only attributes remain. Event notics are used in the timing tree in simulations. No reference count or simular technique is used to determine when a block of data may no longer be referenced. No storage is hence returned until a garbage collection occurs. This happens automatically when the two pools meet. The garbage collection uses the following mark and compact scheme:

Pass 1 locate and mark all referencable objects, drivers and event notices.

Pass 2 scan the object pool sequentially and compute the addresses to which marked objects will be moved.

Pass 3 move drivers and event notices and update references from drivers to objects.

Pass 4 scan the object pool sequentially and update all object references to where they should point after they have been moved in pass 5.

Pass 5 move objects

Pass 6 update driver-driver and object-driver pointers.

Special attention was paid both to secure data accessing and to debugging facilities to aid the user in the detection of sources of runtime errors.

The documentation

User's Guide [5] [7] which gives the syntax and the semantics of SIMULA with examples in the appropriate hardware representation.

Programmer's Guide/Reference Manual [6] [8] which gives information on the implementation defined parts, error messages, control card options etc.

Technical Documentation whose total number of pages has not been reliably counted. It comes to around 90 cm. The IBM system also has an orange reference card for speesy lookup.

Design decisions

Design decisions to be made when implementing a programming language fall roughly in two categories: decisions directly influencing the users (such as hardware representation, diagnostic facilities, cross-reference facilities, separate compilation, etc.) and those which only indirectly influence users (the language in which the implementation was done, internal representation, capacity limitations, generated code, runtime register usage, etc.). Selecting the minimum configuration on which the system should run was, of course, a major decision. For some of the important decision made, the alternatives and the final choice are given below:

Implementation language: For the UNIVAC system it was natural to use the assembler language, which has a powerful macro (PROC) facility At that time when the decision was made there did not exist any language of the same efficiency either. The choice for the IBM system were assembler or PL/360 [4], and the latter was chosen mainly for the following reasons:

easy to learn,
imcomparably easier to use than assembler without loosing power,
encourages good programming habits, preventing self-modifying programs,
imposes a reasonable sett of rules on the use of base registers,
faster translation.

Hardware representation

The most important questions concerning the hardware representation of SIMULA source programs for the two systems were:

- Should the BCD or EBCDIC character set be used?
- Should the SIMULA basic symbols be represented as enclosed by some special symbol (e.g. "BEGIN") or as reserved words (e.g. BEGIN, END etc. are not legal as identifiers)?

The solutions chosen are not identical for the two systems. The IBM system only accepts EBCDIC using reserved words. The UNIVAC system accepts as standard input the same as the IBM system, but it also has the optional facility that the input may be given in the representation, which was defined by the implementors of SIMULA on the CDC 3300/3600; the CDC 6000 representation is also accepted. The IBM system offers a conversion program instead.

Register usage

Due to different hardware in the two systems, the register usage strategy is quite different. To describe these is outside the scope of this paper, but it is relevant to say that particular attention was paid to the problem of utilizing registers in an efficient manner.

The Bench-mark tests

Benchmarks provide the final judgement as to whether the performance of the compiler and the runtime system is satisfactory.

It is, however, necessary to take into account the complexity of the language. One cannot expect a FORTRAN program to be as efficient as an assembler program, or an ALGOL program to be as efficient as the corresponding FORTRAN program (provided that the same level of software technology is used). The choice of programming language depends (hopefully) also on factors like "time taken to write and debug a program" and "problem area".

The tests which have been performed will only show the quantitative aspects, like source program size, compiler speed and execution speed. These quantities are given in the tables at the end of this paper.

We divided programming languages into two groups:

Conventional languages: FORTRAN, COBOL, ALGOL and PL/1.

Simulation languages: GPSS and SIMSCRIPT.

The programs were chosen from problem areas for which the other languages in each group traditionally are used, thus giving SIMULA a disadvantage.

The test problems for the conventional languages are respectively:

1. Solution of Laplace's equation for temperature distribution in a given square pipe.
2. Gauss-Seidel solution of simultaneous equations.
3. A file-handling problem.
4. Balas-Nghiem algorithm for solving zero-one linear programming problem.
5. N-queen problem.
6. A problem in turbulence.

The test problems for the simulation languages are:

7. Terminals attached to a computer.
8. Cars in a traffic light controlled street crossing.

To conslude, we will just mention some of the figures which the tests indicate:

1. The IBM system compiles roughly twice as fast as PL/1, i.e. SIMULA compiles 2000-3000 cards/cpu-minute on the 370/155. The execution time is the same for the SIMULA and the PL/1 object programs.

2. The EXEC8 SIMULA compiles about 6000 cards/cpu-minute on the 1108, i.e. about the same as NU-ALGOL. The execution time is about the same as NU-ALGOL, i.e. 2-10 times faster than SIMULA 1 (CASE-ALGOL) and twice as fast as SIMSCRIPT, somewhat depending on the output given.

3. I/O is significantly faster in SIMULA than in FORTRAN.

In addition to the quantitative aspects our experience at NCC has been that coding and debugging times have decreased by programming in SIMULA, in comparison with earlier times when FORTRAN, ALGOL, COBOL and assembler were the only used languages. We also have to mention that many of the problems we have been dealing with so far would never have been touched if SIMULA had not been available.

<u>References</u>

1. O.J.Dahl, B.Myhrhaug, K.Nygaard:
"SIMULA Common Base Language"
NCC Publ. S-22, 2nd edition, October 1970.

2. O.J.Dahl, B.Myhrhaug:
"SIMULY Implementation Guide"
NCC Publ. S-9, revised edition, June 1969.

3. D.Gries:
"Use of Transition Matrices in Compiling"
C.A.C.M. vol.11, No.1, January 1968.

4. N.Wirth:
"PL/360 A programming language for 360 computers"
J.A.C.M. vol.15, No.1, January 1968.

5. "SIMULA for IBM-360: User's Guide"
University of Oslo Press, 1971.

6. "SIMULA for IBM-360: Programmer's Guide"
University of Oslo Press, 1971.

7. "EXEC 8 SIMULA User's Guide"
University of Oslo Press, 1971.

8. "EXEC 8 SIMULA Programmer's Reference Manual"
University of Oslo Press, August 1972.

Problem	Language	System	Source size (cards)	Compile time (sec.)	Execution time (sec.)
1	FORTRAN G	370/155	57	1.54	8.58
	SIMULA 67	370/155	45	1.49	2.18
	FORTRAN V	1108	57	0.971	5.524
	SIMULA 67	1108	45	0.839	2.209
2	FORTRAN G	370/155	41	1.08	0.90
	SIMULA 67	370/155	36	1.44	0.76
	FORTRAN V	1108	50	0.737	0.086
	SIMULA 67	1108	32	0.642	0.170
3	COBOL F	370/155	303	5.60	0.31
	SIMULA 67	370/155	286	4.92	0.77
	COBOL	1108	288	4.902	0.188
	SIMULA 67	1108	286	2.598	0.434
4	ALGOL F	370/155	86	1.33	110.15
	SIMULA 67	370/155	74	2.63	66.90
	ALGOL (CASE)	1108	71	1.326	93.544
	SIMULA 67	1108	78	1.431	31.780
	NU ALGOL	1108	70	0.995	44.226
5	PL 1	370/155	167	6.10	1.94
	SIMULA 67	370/155	118	3.17	1.36
	SIMULA 67	1108	118	1.711	0.947
6	FORTRAN G	370/155	356	13.43	2.13
	SIMULA 67	370/155	458	14.03	1.87
	FORTRAN V	1108	345	6.143	1.102
	SIMULA 67	1108	458	6.062	1.031
7	GPSS	370/155	47	0.60	19.80
	SIMULA 67	370/155	223	4.05	9.65
	SIMULA 67	1108	223	2.371	4.113
8	SIMULA 67	370/155	110	2.65	1.53
	SIMULA 67	1108	110	1.571	0.697
	GPSS	370/155	103	1.2	8.4
	SIMSCRIPT I.5	1108	157	11.520*)	1.713

*) SIM-processor & assemblies

ERROR REPORTING, ERROR TREATMENT, AND ERROR CORRECTION IN ALGOL TRANSLATION - PART 1

C.H.A.KOSTER

I. Introduction

A number of tasks of a compiler can be distinguished:

- to check whether the source program is correct
- if it is not correct, to give all useful information for correcting it (treatment of statical errors)
- if it is correct, to translate the program into an equivalent objectcode program
- to cause the object program to be executed
- to report any errors occurring during execution (treatment of dynamical errors)

In this note some pragmatic observations are given concerning the error treatment in, especially, ALGOL compilers.

The art of compilermaking has advanced greatly in the last ten years, and it cannot be denied that much of the development in this field has been spurred on by ALGOL 60. ALGOL 60, at the time it was defined, represented a consensus about the state of the art in programming languages; implementation for it was at the limit of what was well-understood, and slightly beyond.

The first implementation of ALGOL 60, made for the Electrologica X1 by E.W. Dijkstra and J. Zonneveld at the Mathematical Centre, Amsterdam, must be seen more as a proof that the language could be implemented, than as a working tool for production purposes. This is already clear from the incredible amount of work the operator had to do, in order to run one program: Read in the compiler, read in the ALGOL source text (All this on the Creed fast reader, at 50 ch/sec), reread the source text, wait for the tape punch to stop punching the object text, read in the runtime system, read in the <u>last</u> part of the object tape (the so-called cross-reference tape), read in the <u>first</u> part of the object tape, read in the library.

If, by this time, no error or hardware failure had occurred, the operator could choose to start the system, which would then run the program at less than one twentieth of the speed of an equivalent machine-code version.

The error treatment, both at compile-time and at run-time, was of the most primitive kind: occurrence of an error stopped the machine, the contents of the instruction register giving an indication of the nature of the error. Armed with a good knowledge of the machine and the compiler, the operator would spend some time inspecting the contents of the stack, and after twenty minutes he could often give a shrewd guess as to where in the program the error took place.

Still, very shortly after the introduction of this ALGOL 60 system at the MC, virtually all users used ALGOL 60 as their sole programming language, apart from a group of crystallographers that continued to use an existing fast machinecodeprogram, and one man who insisted on inverting large matrices in a 12 K store. Within the small space of the MC, this meant total victory for ALGOL 60: For the advantages of writing in a high level language people gladly accepted a loss of a factor twenty in speed!

Why hasn't the same process taken place in the computing community at large? Why is FORTRAN, although 10 years obsolete, still the de facto standard? Some of the answers to this question can be found in the logbook by R.W. Bemer, entitled: "A politicosocial history of ALGOL". One reason for the lack of widespread use of ALGOL is the bad quality of some large manufacturers ALGOL compilers, especially as regards the treatment of errors.

The pragmatic qualities of a compiler, the feeling it gives to the user, depend among other things on the way his mistakes are presented to him. The naive programmer is only too willing to confuse the properties of a language with those of the compiler, and will say that FORTRAN runs faster, and ALGOL is lousy, just on the strength of the poor choice of compilers offered to him. It now and then seems that compilermakers have gone out of their way to make life hard for the ALGOL programmer.

The purpose of this paper is to bring forward some of the properties a compiler must have with respect to error treatment, and to denounce some malpractices which detract from the usefulness of existing ALGOL 60 compilers, and which have certainly caused many people to turn away from ALGOL.

The worlds largest computermanufacturer, and therefore the worlds largest sinner, will provide some illustrative examples. This does not mean that its ALGOL 60 compiler is notably worse than others, but only that I personally had occasion to struggle with it, and that the documentation was honest and complete enough to show its defects.

Other people will have suffered comparable experiences with other machines, and it is for their solace that this paper is written.

"The poor girl. But that was by no means the end of her sufferings!"
Marquis de Sade, Justine

2. Treatment of statical errors

The compiler has to check correctness of the source program. This check must signal all errors. Therefore the compiler must satisfy certain conditions.

2.1 The compiler must be a total function

Considered as a function from source program to object program, the compiler may not behave like a partial function: all correct programs must be treated as correct, all incorrect programs must be treated as incorrect, and on no account may an incorrect program blow up the compiler or the system.

> *"The true he told as true and the untrue as untrue"*
> Xenophon, Anabasis

2.1.1 A correct sourcecode program must be translated to an equivalent, correct, object code program

Any differences between language standard and the implemented language must not only be documented in the manual, but also whenever a source code program contains a construct which is legal in the language standard but not allowed in the implementation, an errormessage has to go out, saying: *"We humbly apologize, but circumstances forced us to digress from the language standard".* If, e.g., a compiler does not provide integer labels, a refusal of a program using them must be made with many apologies. Mostly the reason for the deviation will be reluctance to cope with all the details of the full language standard, or even impossibility to do so because of some property of the particular machine used.

Deviations from the syntax of the language should in general be unnecessary, because even if some feature of the language is not implemented, the parser should cater for it. If, e.g., an implementation, in deviation from the ALGOL 60 standard, makes specification of parameters compulsory, then it is no great trouble to announce a missing specification with the necessary humility on the implementers behalf, so that programmers should be well aware that the necessity for specification is not a property of ALGOL 60, but a local feature.

A compiler should warn for its own defects.

> *"Warning: The Surgeon General Has Determined That Cigarette Smoking Is Dangerous to Your Health"*
>
> An American package of Cigarettes

2.1.2 No incorrect sourcecode program may be accepted by the compiler without errormessages

Compilermakers of course keep silent about the more shady aspects of their compilers, but now and then some user finds a skeleton in the cupboard.

Thus, the X1 compiler by Dijkstra silently allowed small extensions to ALGOL 60 like

x: = (*y*: = *2*)+ *7*

but, more seriously, it accepted any amount of well chosen gibberish.

This was a consequence of the extremely simple precedence parser on which that compiler was based. A simpleminded use of top-to-bottom methods can lead to much the same result, as is shown by the following example:

statement: **ass statement; cond statement.**
ass statement: **variable, becomes symbol, expression.**
cond statement: **if symbol, expression, then symbol, statement.**

A stupid top-to-bottom parser could, besides

v: = *a* + *b*
if *x* > *0* *then* *y*: = *0*

also accept

v *if* *x* > *0* *then*.*y*: = *0*

without giving a warning message, if it checked for the presence of an **ass state** simply by testing for the presence of a **variable, becomes symbol** and **expression** successively.

The art of parsing has now advanced far enough that there exist numerous techniques which do not have such hidden flaws, but some compilermakers still trust to ad-hoc techniques rather than rigorously sticking to one of the formally adequate techniques, so it may well be that such a compiler, besides the language intended, also accepts Shakespeare sonnets without complaint.

We must aim for the day that at least the parsing component of every compiler is generated directly from the language definition; until that day each individual compiler should be accompanied by a proof that the parser recognizes the language intended, and only that language.

2.1.3 For no input text may the compiler blow up

In the old X1 system, any error found in the sourcetext was sufficient to make further scanning hazardous, since it might leave the working tables of the compiler in an inconsistent state. Thus, the compiler might get in peculiar loops, or start using its own text as name list.

The later X8 ALGOL translator at the Mathematical Centre was used for years without anybody noticing that there was no check on overflow of the name list - until the first victims got highly unintelligible error messages concerning their extremely long and complicated programs.

Many compilers have similar flaws, often in the form of bugs which are noticed only after years of use of the compiler. Often systems programmers know of some diabolical little piece of text, which is certain to wreck the compiler or make it do very odd things.

Any compiler should be accompanied by a proof that it is fool safe: that no input text, however unprobable, can cause it to lose control over the situation.

For a language of the size and complexity of ALGOL 68, where many tables are to be updated in a consistent fashion, this proof may be a noticeable part of the effort of compiler construction.

2.2 Errors should be reported in a helpful fashion

> *"Programmer Response: Probable user error. Make sure the source code is correct and run the job again. If the problem recurs, do the following before calling IBM for programming support: ... "*
>
> IBM System/360 Operating System
> ALGOL Programmer's Guide

Once an error has been found, a message is given which is intended to aid in debugging the program.

In the ground of his heart, the programmer deeply distrusts the machine, its hardware, software, operating system and operating personnel. This makes it necessary that error messages should not just provide a minimum of information concerning an error, but should be of extreme clarity and preciseness, so that even the most hardheaded programmer will be forced to see what he has done wrong. The reporting of errors must be:

2.2.1 specific

An errormessage like "*delimiter* ***then*** *not allowed*" may very well be utterly misleading. It merely tells that the parser did not expect this symbol. The errormessage should tell what the parser expected and did not find, not what it found unexpectedly. It might say for instance "*if clause contains incomplete condition*" but maybe an even more specific message might be generated. There is no point in envisaging all kind of special little errormessages for all the illegal states the parser may get in, it is much better to foresee a number of classes of errors, which are of interest to the programmer, not merely to the parser used.

2.2.2 user-directed

The user must get the errormessage in his own terms, with reference to his own program. It is not sufficient to present him with an errornumber, a line-number, and the symbol at which the parser gave up. Especially in a time-shared environment the programmer will probably not have an up to date listing of his program, so he must be presented with a piece of context for the error, in terms of which he may then and there make a correction using an editing system.

At runtime, errormessages should give at the very least the line number of the context at which the error occurred, but if possible display that context. Certainly it should never be the supervisor (as opposed to the compiler's run time system) which traps dynamic errors, so that the user gets messages which are not in terms of his program or even his programming language, but in terms of systems primitives which are completely alien to him.

2.2.3 complete

The amount of further information to accompany the errormessage should be flexible, adopting itself to the error in hand. The general style of errormessages should not be "*this is wrong*" but "*this is in conflict with what you said there and there*", displaying the there-and-there explicitly.

In case of a redefinition of an identifier, tell in what context it was defined before, with what type. In case of impossible actual-formal correspondence, give the context where the formal parameter was specified, showing how it was specified.

At runtime the system should not say "*index out of bound*", but say which index had what value, and what the bounds were.

2.2.4 of a restrained nature

A naive programmer receiving his brainchild back with page upon page of errormessages may well give in to despair.

Any particular error should be reported once, and once only. An error makes part of a program uninterpretable; if the compiler insits on interpreting that part anyway, then it should be very careful in the errormessages it emits about that part, so that no errors are reported which derive from an error already signaled. It may be much more polite to say "*this part of your program I have not looked at*" than to accuse the programmer of all kinds of errors he never made.

In the same way, an identifier with lacking defining occurrence should, at its first applied occurrence, where the error is reported, get a default-mode **erroneous**, and no further errormessages should be given concerning it. It is very rude to give pages of errormessages when all the programmer did was to forget one declaration.

2.3 The compiler should not impose unnecessary constraints

"Nobody will ever write that"
The unknown Implementer

A compiler has to make the most of a limited machine, and it is clear that the limitations of the machine, especially as regards memory size, must show up in limitations of the compiler. Many compilers,however,impose size restrictions which, by a small effort of the compiler maker, could be loosened.

Sensible compilermakers will choose these restrictions such that no normal user will ever notice them. It turns out, however, that users again and again come up with programs the compiler makers have not foreseen, which violate these restrictions.

2.3.1 no fixed-size lists

Most of the frustrating limitations are there because the compilermaker gave some auxiliary table in the compiler a fixed size.

Thus the IBM 360 ALGOL compiler has some capacity limitations, amongst other:

1) Number of blocks and procedure declarations ≤ 255
2) Number of for statements ≤ 255
3) Length of source program ≤ 255 K
4) Number of semicolons in the whole program ≤ 65535
5) Number of nested blocks, compound statements etc ≤ 999
6) Number of labels declared or additionally generated ≤ 1024
(The compiler generates some labels for certain constructs)

Limitations 3 and 4 look reasonable: an extremely long program cannot be translated.fine. Limitation 5 forbids very deep statical nesting, if I have understood its formulation correctly. So be it.

Limitations 1, 2 and 6 are, however, suspect. There seems to be a table administering all for-statements and another one administering all labels. Obviously, the implementors did not think anyone should write a program containing a thousand labels, or threehundred for-statements. Somebody will - and then the compiler is worthless, because it is a major task to change the size of those tables. Why are these separate tables, instead of being merged in a more general working table? A compiler should not give up because one table is full if there is still room in others. There should be only one size restriction which is dictated by the core allotment for the program.

My programs always consist of hundreds of mutually recursive procedures, where the compiler must generate thousands of implicit labels for conditionals, because my programs are mostly generated by other programs. Therefore the largest IBM computer in the world can not run my programs - its compile-time tables are too small, even though an old and small X8 has no trouble.

2.3.2 identifier identifies

ALGOL 60 does not in any way restrict the length of identifiers. Most compilers have to, because their namelists have a limited size. There are only two implementations that I know of that in no other way restrict identifiers; all others ignore the tail of an identifier of more than so many characters.

One of the pragmatic advantages of ALGOL over so many other languages is the fact that one can use mnemonic identifiers to help in thinking and documentation. This advantage is thrown overboard by many compilers (e.g., the IBM 360 ALGOL compiler recognizes only the first six characters of an identifier), making the compiler unsuitable for teaching.
There is no good reason to limit the recognized length of an identifier: since this limit has to be fairly high, it might just as well be as high as possible, since no advantage can be gained from giving namelist entries a uniform length if that uniform length is excessive.

In the meantime I cannot use the IBM 360 ALGOL implementation, since my identifiers are generated by programs: they may be very long and differ only in their ending.

3 Error correction

The compiler has, in some way, to carry on after an error has been detected. Various methods are being developed to allow the compiler to deal with syntactic errors in the most helpful way possible, by making some assumptions about the kind of error made.

Such errorcorrecting techniques are not only of interest because of the remote chance that they may correct all mistakes the programmer makes. Everybody can think up horrible examples of mistakes which are not uniquely correctable.

The importance of error-correcting lies in the fact that it allows the compiler to react sensibly and flexibly to the errors it finds.

3.1. demarcation of afflicted area

Making use of all the small redundancies in the language, an error correction routine can demarcate boundaries between which the error must have been made, thus helping the programmer in locating it.

3.2 specific reporting

Because of the careful analysis it makes, an error correcting routine can report an error in a specific way and give suggestions as to how to repair it.

3.3 allow continuation

Without error correction, the safest way to continue after a syntactic error has been found, is to ignore some piece of program until the next separator.

This approach can be refined if the effects of an error can be dammed in by error correcting techniques.

In a language like ALGOL 68 it may be of importance to know whether a given construct, which turned out to be erroreous, was intended as a declaration or a statement. Error correcting techniques may provide the answer,

3.4 maybe correction

In a case where correction is sufficiently unique (e.g. a delimiter was misspelt) the error may indeed be corrected, and at least a trial run of the program made.

This is of great usefulness e.g., in a student-batch environment, where programs are likely to be small and contain many bugs, that have to be ironed out by an inexperienced programmer.

4. Conclusion

We are waiting for the day when compiler makers will combine a number of existing techniques to give to the users a satisfactory ALGOL compiler, designed to help at all stages:

It will have incremental compilation and error correction, translating and debugging in dialog with the user.

It will, at run time, provide diagnostics with reference to the source text, allowing tracing and dynamic intervention by the programmer.

It will be totally unlike the relics of the early sixties with which the poor users of large computers have to make do.

R.W. Bemer, "A politico-social History of ALGOL"
in: Annual Review in Automatic Programming 5, 1969.

E.W. Dijkstra, "An ALGOL 60 Translator for the X1"
in: Annual Review in Automatic Programming 3, 1963.

IBM System/360 Operating System ALGOL Programmer's Guide

E. Satterthwaite, "Debugging Tools for High Level Languages", Software-Practice and Experience Vol 2 no 3, July-September 1972

There now exists a version of the IBM ALGOL W compiler, written by Satterthwaite, that at least in its runtime system is striving to provide the facilities wanted.

ERROR REPORTING, ERROR TREATMENT, AND ERROR CORRECTION IN ALGOL TRANSLATION - PART 2

B.EGGERS

Program testing can be used to show the presence of bugs, but never to show their absence!

[2]

I. Introduction

Part II of this paper deals with treatments of statical errors as mentioned in the introduction of Part I. In recent years several attempts have been made to construct parsers for detecting or correcting syntactical errors automatically [3, 6, 7, 9]. We introduce an error correcting algorithm for a part of the ALGOL-60-BNF-Syntax based on techniques for treating regular languages which were developed earlier [3]. Three types of errors are investigated: deletion-(G), mutation-(H) and insertion-(J)-errors. The technique will be demonstrated by choosing two nontrivial examples of the BNF part of the ALGOL-60-syntax, namely the unsigned numbers as a regular event and the arithmetic expressions as a nonregular one.

II. The "regular part"

Consider the BNF-Syntax which generates the set of unsigned numbers [1]. Since the syntactical variables like <unsigned number> , <decimal fraction>, etc. are all non selfimbedding the set of sentences generated by <unsigned number> is regular. There are well known techniques to construct regular expressions from given context-free grammars having no selfimbedding property [8]. Let us for convenience consider the variable <digit> as terminal (that is as syntactical constant). If we adopt the abbreveations $Z := {}_{10}$, D := <digit>, and P for + or - then we have the following regular expression representing the set of unsigned numbers ν :

$$\nu = (\Lambda + < D > .) D < D > + (\Lambda + < D > . D) < D > Z (\Lambda + P) D < D >$$

In this formula + and < > denote union and star operation resp.; Λ denotes the empty word; the parentheses have their usual meaning.

Thus the set of terminals consists of D, Z, P and the decimal point. With the aid of well known algorithms [4] we construct now two finite state machines $\mathfrak{A}$ and $\mathfrak{A}^*$ which accept ν and ν^* resp. (ν^* denotes the set of reversed tapes, e. g. if D Z P D is in ν then D P Z D is in ν^*). To this end we mark all terminals by some indices to distinguish them from each other. Then we have:

$$\nu' = (\Lambda + < D^1 > .^1) D^2 < D^3 > + (\Lambda + < D^4 > .^2 D^5) < D^6 > Z^1 (\Lambda + P^1) D^7 < D^8 >$$

The constructions yield the following transition tables for $\mathfrak{A}$ and $\mathfrak{A}^*$ (the states are denoted by natural numbers; they are represented by sets of marked terminals; 0 is the initial state; final states are underlined; for details cf. [3]):

Table for $\mathfrak{A}$:

	states of $\mathfrak{A}$	D	.	Z	P
0	-	$\underline{1}$	2	3	
$\underline{1}$	$D^1+D^2+D^3+D^4+D^6$	$\underline{1}$	2	3	
2	$.^1+.^2$	$\underline{4}$			
3	Z^1	$\underline{6}$			5
$\underline{4}$	$D^2+D^3+D^5+D^6$	$\underline{4}$		3	
5	P^1	$\underline{6}$			
$\underline{6}$	D^7+D^8	$\underline{6}$			

Table for $\mathfrak{A}^*$:

	states of $\mathfrak{A}^*$	D	.	Z	P
0	-	$\underline{1}$			
$\underline{1}$	$D^2+D^3+D^7+D^8$	$\underline{1}$	$\underline{2}$	$\underline{3}$	5
$\underline{2}$	$.^1+.^2$	$\underline{4}$			
$\underline{3}$	Z^1	$\underline{6}$			
$\underline{4}$	D^1+D^4	$\underline{4}$			
5	P^1			$\underline{3}$	
$\underline{6}$	D^5+D^6	$\underline{6}$			

Let us consider ν' and the transition table of $\mathfrak{A}$. We now substitute in ν' each index k of each terminal T by the sum of all states which contain T^k . For example the states $\underline{1}$ and $\underline{4}$ contain D^2 ; hence 2 in D^2 is replaced by $\underline{1} + \underline{4}$ in ν' , etc.. The same procedure is carried out for ν' with the table of $\mathfrak{A}^*$ except for choosing subnotation. Thus we obtain a new expression $\nu''_{''}$:

$$\nu''_{''} = (\Lambda + < D^1_4 > .^2_2) D^{1+4}_1 < D^{1+4}_1 > +$$

$$(\Lambda + < D^1_4 > .^2_2 D^4_6) < D^{1+4}_6 > Z^3_3 (\Lambda + P^5_5) D^6_1 < D^6_1 >$$

Now we have sufficient structural information for the error correcting algorithm. We define two states k and l of $\mathfrak{A}$ and $\mathfrak{A}^*$ resp. to be

compatible (k C l) iff there is a terminal $T^{\dots+k+\dots}_{\dots+l+\dots}$ in $v''_{''}$,
E.g. 1 C 1 , 4 C 1 , but not 6 C 6 . Let w = D . D Z P D be an unsigned number read by $\mathfrak{A}$ and $\mathfrak{A}^*$ (from left to right and from right to left resp.). Let us imagine that whenever $\mathfrak{A}$ enters the state k when reading the symbol T $\mathfrak{A}$ prints k leaving T^k and that $\mathfrak{A}^*$ acts in the corresponding way leaving, say T_l . Then we obtain a new string $w''_{''}$:

$$w''_{''} = D^1_4 \;.^2_2\; D^4_6 \; Z^3_3 \; P^5_5 \; D^6_1$$

Note that k C l for each symbol in $w''_{''}$.

In general the following theorem holds: Let $\mathfrak{A}$ be a finite state acceptor and $\mathfrak{L}(\mathfrak{A})$ the regular language accepted by $\mathfrak{A}$. Let $\mathfrak{A}^*$ be the corresponding automaton accepting all reversal tapes. Let w be any word and let C be the compatibility relation. Then:

$$w \in \mathfrak{L}(\mathfrak{A}) \quad \text{iff} \quad k \;C\; l \quad \text{for all} \quad T^k_l \quad \text{in} \quad w''_{''}$$

Suppose now $\bar{w}$ is not an unsigned number, say $\bar{w}$ = D Z D D . D .
Then $w''_{''} = D^1 \; Z^3 \; D^6_4 \; D^6_4 \; ._2 \; D_1$ and not 6 C 4 . ($\mathfrak{A}$ and $\mathfrak{A}^*$ each enter a dead state; these are not compatible with any state.) How can we correct $\bar{w}$?

Let r'' be the right context of T^k of length 1 and let $l_{''}$ be the left one of T_l . E.g. (see tables of $\mathfrak{A}$ and $\mathfrak{A}^*$):

$$r''(\, D^4 \,) = Z^3 \quad , \quad r''(\, D^1 \,) = D^1 + .^2 \quad ,$$

$$l_{''}(\, D_1 \,) = D_1 + ._2 + Z_3 + P_5 \quad , \text{etc.}$$

Now we can find all possible G-, H-, and J-corrections in $\bar{w}$. For instance $D^1 \in r''(\, D^1 \,)$, $D_4 \in l_{''}(\, D_4 \,)$, and 1 C 4 . Therefore Z^3 is one possible H-error and the only correction of Z^3 ist D^1_4 .
We add the list of all possible corrections:

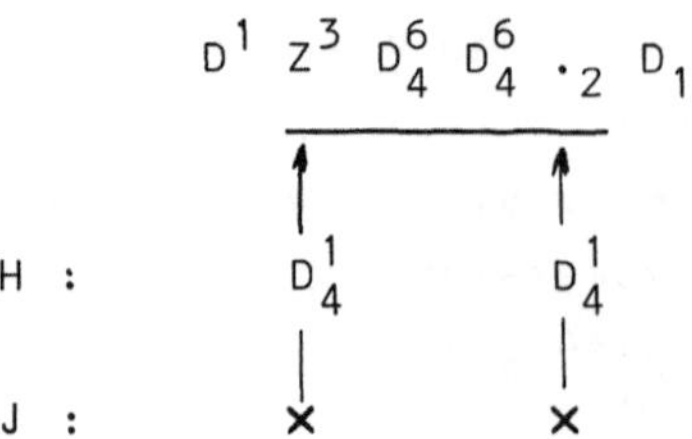

The underlined part is called the *correction part* of $\bar{w}$. Clearly there is no possible correction outside this string.

This error correction algorithm can be generalized for correcting n errors simultaneously. Further details are omitted here (cf. [3])

III. The "non regular part"

We are now going to extend the applicability of the algorithm to context-free grammars. To this end consider the set of arithmetic expressions in ALGOL 60. Applying the same procedures as in the case of a non selfimbedding grammar we obtain a system of two equations
(1) $\alpha = f(\alpha)$, $\beta = g(\beta)$, where α = <arithmetic expression>, β = <Boolean expression>, and $f(\alpha)$, $g(\beta)$ are regular expressions, each containing α and β as the only variables and the constants derivable by α and β .

Again for conveniance of demonstration, but without loss of generality we make the following restrictions: We consider the "smaller" expressions defined by the system (1'):

$$\alpha = \langle\ i\ \beta\ t\ (\Lambda + P)\ (\ U + \underline{(}\alpha\underline{)}\ )\ \langle\ A\ (\Lambda + P)\ (\ U + \underline{(}\alpha\underline{)}\ )\ \rangle\ e\ \rangle$$
$$(\Lambda + P)\ (\ U + \underline{(}\alpha\underline{)}\ )\ \langle\ A\ (\Lambda + P)\ (\ U + \underline{(}\alpha\underline{)}\ )\ \rangle$$
$$\beta = \langle\ i\ \beta\ t\ (\Lambda + \neg)\ (\ L + \underline{(}\beta\underline{)}\ )\ \langle\ B\ (\Lambda + \neg)\ (\ L + \underline{(}\beta\underline{)}\ )\ \rangle\ e\ \rangle$$
$$(\Lambda + \neg)\ (\ L + \underline{(}\beta\underline{)}\ )\ \langle\ B\ (\Lambda + \neg)\ (\ L + \underline{(}\beta\underline{)}\ )\ \rangle$$

where i := <u>if</u>, t := <u>then</u>, e := <u>else</u> and P stands for + or − , A for the arithmetic operators, L for logical values, and B for the binary logical operators such as $\vee$. The underlined brackets are the ALGOL-parentheses. These expressions contain no <variable> and no <function designator>. Again for the sake of clearness we treat U, P, A, L and B as syntactical constants.

If we construct finite state acceptors $\mathfrak{A}$ and $\mathfrak{A}^*$ for α , $\mathfrak{B}$ and $\mathfrak{B}^*$ for β , treating α and β in the regular expressions like the other symbols, carrying then out the same procedure as mentioned in "the regular part", then we obtain the system (1"):

$$\alpha'' =$$
$$\langle\ i^{1}\ \beta^{5}\ t^{8}(\Lambda + P^{10})(\ U^{11} + \underline{(}^{12}\alpha^{15}\underline{)}^{16})\ \langle A^{13}(\Lambda + P^{10})(\ U^{11} + \underline{(}^{12}\alpha^{15}\underline{)}^{16})\ \rangle\ e^{14}\rangle$$
$$(\Lambda + P^{2})(\ U^{3} + \underline{(}^{4}\alpha^{7}\underline{)}^{9})\ \langle\ A^{6}(\Lambda + P^{2})(\ U^{3} + \underline{(}^{4}\alpha^{7}\underline{)}^{9})\ \rangle$$

$$\beta'' =$$
$$\langle\ i^{a}\ \beta^{e}\ t^{h}(\Lambda + \neg^{j})(L^{k} + \underline{(}^{l}\beta^{o}\underline{)}^{p})\ \langle B^{m}(\Lambda + \neg^{j})(L^{k} + \underline{(}^{l}\beta^{o}\underline{)}^{p})\ \rangle e^{n}\ \rangle$$
$$(\Lambda + \neg^{b})(L^{c} + \underline{(}^{d}\beta^{g}\underline{)}^{i})\ \langle B^{f}(\Lambda + \neg^{b})(L^{c} + \underline{(}^{d}\beta^{g}\underline{)}^{i})\ \rangle$$

The indices in α'' and β'' are states of the acceptors $\mathfrak{A}$ and $\mathfrak{B}$ resp.; numbers designate states of $\mathfrak{A}$, small letters those of $\mathfrak{B}$; final states: $\mathfrak{A}$: 3, 9; $\mathfrak{A}^*$: 1,2,3,4; $\mathfrak{B}$: c,i; $\mathfrak{B}^*$: a,b,c,d. There is a one to one mapping between the states of $\mathfrak{A}$ and $\mathfrak{A}^*$ as well as between the states of $\mathfrak{B}$ and $\mathfrak{B}^*$ such that after renaming the states in $\mathfrak{A}^*$ and $\mathfrak{B}^*$ according to this map the Compatability Relations C_α and C_β for α and β become the identity relations. Therefore the subindices in (1") are suppressed. (Not all regular expressions have this property [3]. We choose this example without loss of generality to achieve a clearer demonstration).

How does this system represent arithmetic expressions? Consider the word $w'' = P^2\ U^3\ A^6\ U^3$ represented by α''. Since neither α nor β is in w, w is in α. Now let $w'' = i^1 \beta^5 +^8 \underline{(}^{12} \alpha^{15} \underline{)}^{16} e^{14}\ U^3 A^6 U^3$ which is in α''. Since β^5 and α^{15} are in w'', w is not in α. But we can replace β^5 by some Boolean expression and α^{15} by another arithmetic expression. In this case we have to do some index bookkeeping. We must store the indices of α and β in two stacks as reentry addresses in order to be able to continue correctey with $\underline{)}^{16}$ and $+^8$ for α^{15} and β^5 resp.. Suppose we choose L^c for β^5 and $\underline{(}^4 \alpha^7 \underline{)}^9$ for α^{15} in α''. Then we write $L^{c\ 5}$ for β^5 and $\underline{(}^{4\ 15}\ \alpha^{7\ 15}\ \underline{)}^{9\ 15}$ for α^{15}. If we take U^3 in α'' for $\alpha^{7\ 15}$ then we have a new word

$$v'' = i^1 L^{c\ 5} +^8 \underline{(}^{12} \underline{(}^{4\ 15}\ U^{3\ 7\ 15}\ \underline{)}^{9\ 15}\ \underline{)}^{16}\ e^{14}\ U^3\ A^6\ U^3$$

with the property that v in α. We call each word v'' obtained from left to right as described above an *l-track of* α''. Going from right to left through α'' we can define an *r-track of* α'' similarily.

Notice that v'' is also an r-track of α''. More generally we can assert the following: Let $C := C_\alpha \cup C_\beta$. Let $x = X^1 \ldots X^n$ and $y = Y^1 \ldots Y^n$. Let $x\ C^+ y$ iff $X^i C Y^i$ for all $i = 1,\ldots,n$. Then:

$$\begin{aligned} w \text{ in } \alpha \text{ iff } & \exists \text{ l-track } w'' \text{ of } ''\alpha'' \wedge \\ & \exists \text{ r-track } w_{''} \text{ of } \alpha_{''} \text{ such that} \\ & x\ C^+\ y \text{ for all } T^x_y \text{ in } w''_{''}\ . \end{aligned}$$

Note that in general there might be more than one l- or r-track in an expression γ such that $\exists T^x_y$ in $w''_{''} \wedge \neg x\ C^+ y$ despite of $w \in \gamma$ is possible.

With the aid of r" and l" for α'' and β'' we define two new context functions r^+ and l_+. Call a constant T^k in α'' *begin symbol of* α'' if there is a final state l in $\mathfrak{A}^*$ s.t. k C l. Call each constant T^k in α'' an *end symbol of* α'' if k is a final state in $\mathfrak{A}$; define for β'' correspondingly. E.g. i^1 and U^3 are begin symbols of α'', U^3 is also an end symbol of α''.

Now let $S^l \in r''(T^k)$. Then let $S^{lx} \in r^+(T^{kx})$ if S and T both are constants; let $R^{mlx} \in r^+(T^{kx})$ for each begin symbol R^m in S" if S is a variable and T is a constant; let $S^{lx} \in r^+(R^{mkx})$ for each end symbol R^m in T" if T is a variable and S is a constant; let $Q^{nkx} \in r^+(R^{mlx})$ for all begin symbols Q^m in S" and for all end symbols R^n in T" if S and T both are variables. Finally let $T^k \in r^+(\rightarrow^0)$ for all begin symbols T^k, where $\rightarrow^0$ is a new symbol indexed by the initial state.

Define $l_+(T_l)$ and $l_+(\leftarrow_0)$ correspondingly.

If γ'' and $\gamma_{''}$ are expressions with upper and lower indices then $\gamma''\urcorner$ and $\gamma_{''}\lrcorner$ denote simply the expression without upper or lower indices resp..

Let $w = \ldots R\ S\ T \ldots$ be not in α, e.g. $w = \underline{(}\ U\ A\ \underline{(}\ U\ \underline{)}\ A\ U$. Then there are no l- and r-tracks for w. Call the indexed erroneous words *non-l-track* or *non-r-track* resp.. E.g. the only non-l- non-r-track situation for w is

$$\underline{(}^{4}\ U^{3\ 7}_{3}\ A^{6\ 7}_{6}\ \underline{(}^{4\ 7}_{4}\ U^{3\ 7\ 7}_{3\ 7}\ \underline{)}^{9\ 7}_{9}\ A^{6\ 7}_{6}\ U^{3\ 7}_{3}$$

Assume now between R and S a deletion error, then the following holds for G :

$\underline{G:}$ $\exists\ Q^x_y,\ u,\ v(\ Q \in r^+(R^u)\urcorner \cap l_+(S_v)\lrcorner \wedge x\ C^+ y\ )$

Suppore now S is a mutation error.

Then:

$\underline{H:}$ $\exists\ Q^x_y,\ u,\ v(\ Q \in r^+(R^u)\urcorner \cap l_+(T_v)\lrcorner \wedge x\ C^+ y\ )$

Finally assume that S is an insertion error. Then:

$\underline{J:}$ $\exists\ u,\ v,\ w(\ T^v_w\lrcorner \in r^+(R^u) \wedge v\ C^+ w\ )$.

Let us examine the above example:

	$\rightarrow^0$	$\underline{(}^4$	$U^{3\ 7}_3$		$A^{6\ 7}_6$	$\underline{(}^{4\ 7}_4$	$U^{3\ 7\ 7}_{3\ 7}$	$\underline{)}^{9\ 7}_9$		$A^{6\ 7}_6$	$U^{3\ 7}_3$		$\leftarrow_0$
$\underline{G:}$		↑		↑ $\underline{)}^9_9$		↑			↑ $\underline{)}^9_9$			↑ $\underline{)}^9_9$	
$\underline{H:}$		P^2_2				$P^{2\ 7}_{2\ 7}$							
$\underline{J:}$		×				×							

Thus (U) A (U) A U in α is one of three possible G-corrections, one of the two H-corrections is (U A P U) A U and one of the two J-corrections is (U A U) A U . If we take $w = i\ L\ t\ \underline{(}\ P\ U\ \underline{)}\ A\ U\ A\ U$, then we only have two H-corrections.

$$\rightarrow^{0}\ i^{1}\ L^{c\ 5}\ +^{8}\ \underline{(}^{12}_{4}\ P^{2\ 15}_{2\ 7}\ U^{3\ 15}_{3\ 7}\ \underline{)}^{16}_{9}\ A^{13}_{6}\ U^{11}_{3}\ A^{13}_{6}\ U^{11}_{3}\ \leftarrow_{0}$$

H: (inserted at A^{13}_{6} and at the second A^{13}_{6}): e^{14}_{14}, e^{14}_{14}

We finally mention that this error correction technique allows to correct at most one error between each two "delimiter symbols". We sketch this by giving an example:

$$W'' = i^{1}\ L^{c\ 5}\ +^{8}\ \underline{(}^{12}_{4}\ A_{6\ 7}\ U_{3\ 7}\ \underline{)}_{9}\ A_{6}\ U_{3}\ A_{6}\ U_{3}$$

We test the "delimiter part"

$i^{1}\ +^{8}\ \underline{(}^{12}_{4}\ \underline{)}^{16}_{9}$ and conclude : if a correction in W'' is possible then the upper indexing is correct. We then obtain for H :

$$\rightarrow^{0}\ i^{1}_{1}\ L^{c\ 5}\ +^{8}_{8}\ \underline{(}^{12}_{12}\ A_{6\ 15}\ U_{3\ 15}\ \underline{)}^{16}_{16}\ A^{13}_{6}\ U^{11}_{3}\ A^{13}_{6}\ U^{11}_{3}\ \leftarrow_{0}$$

H: (inserted at A_{6}, A^{13}_{6} and the second A^{13}_{6}): $P^{2\ 15}_{2\ 15}$, e^{14}_{14}, e^{14}_{14}

Hence i L + (P U) e U A U and i L + (P U) A U e U are the only H-corrections.

IV Conclusion

The applicability of the diagnostic- and correction-technique used here can be generalized for detecting and correcting n errors simultaneously if there are algorithms to construct grammars generating sets each member of which can be corrected by deleting, substituting, and inserting at least n Symbols. As far as I know there exist such algorithms (cf [7, 9]).

references:

1. BACKUS et.al. — Rev. Rep. on the Algorithmic Language ALGOL 60
2. DIJKSTRA — Notes on Structured Programming
3. EGGERS — Zur Theorie und Praxis Selbstkorrigierender Regulärer Sprachen
4. GLUSCHKOW — Theorie der abstrakten Automaten
5. HOPCROFT/ ULLMAN — Formal Languages and their Relation to Automata
6. IRONS — An Error-Correcting Parse Algorithm
7. LYON — Least-Errors Recognition of Mutated Context-Free Sentences in Time n^3 log n
8. SALOMAA — Theory of Automata
9. TEITELBAUM — Diagnostics of Syntax Errors

BETRIEBSSYSTEME

VERALLGEMEINERUNG UND IMPLEMENTIERUNG VON SYNCHRONISATIONS-OPERATIONEN

R.GÖLLER

1. Einleitung

Synchronisation ist ein elementares Problem in allen modernen Rechenanlagen, wo mehrere Vorgänge zeitlich parallel oder quasiparallel stattfinden, die im zeitlichen Ablauf an bestimmten Punkten voneinander abhängig sind. In speziellen Fällen übernimmt die hardware die Synchronisation, z.B. mit Unterbrechungs-Möglichkeiten durch die physikalischen Geräte.

Wir haben unser Interesse auf Programmierungsmöglichkeiten für Synchronisationen von Prozessen (tasks) im Sinne logischer Verwaltungseinheiten bei der Abwicklung von Aufgaben (jobs) durch das Betriebssystem gerichtet. Die Überlegungen gelten unabhängig von der Anzahl der beteiligten Prozesse und Prozessoren und der Art der Organisation des Multiprogramming. Die Notwendigkeit der Programmierung von Synchronisationen tritt in erster Linie beim Erstellen von Betriebssystemen auf. Aber auch bei reinen Anwenderprogrammen, die sich auf das Betriebssystem stützen, tritt der Wunsch nach Synchronisation mehrerer Prozesse zur besseren Ausnutzung der Anlage auf.

Da die Implementierung von nur elementaren Synchronisationsoperationen, die den Leistungen der hardware entsprechen, zu unübersichtlichen und fehleranfälligen Programmen führt, sind integrierte Synchronisationsanweisungen in höheren Programmiersprachen erstrebenswert; dies umso mehr, da auch Betriebssysteme oder Teile davon in zunehmendem Maße in höheren Programmiersprachen erstellt werden. Voraussetzung ist eine streng hierarchische und modulare Gliederung des Gesamtsystems (Abb. 1).

Anwenderprogramme
höhere Teile des Betriebssystems
niedere Teile des Betriebssystems Implementierung der Synchronisationen
hardware

Abb. 1: Hierarchischer Aufbau eines Systems

2. Grundlagen des Synchronisationsproblems

Synchronisationen treten in zwei typischen Konstellationen auf:

- Betriebsmittel-Synchronisation
  Mehrere Prozesse benutzen dieselben Betriebsmittel, welche aber jeweils die Benutzung nur durch Prozesse in einer Maximalanzahl N ($N \geq 1$) zulassen. Jeder Prozeß muß also ein Programm der Art

  ... TEST BETRIEBSMITTEL FREI ? nein: WARTEN BIS FREI
  BETRIEBSMITTEL FÜR ANDERE PROZESSE SPERREN
  Betriebsmittel benutzen
  BETRIEBSMITTEL FÜR ANDERE PROZESSE FREIGEBEN ...

  durchlaufen.

- Ereignis-Synchronisation
  Ein Prozeß muß sich vor seinem Fortgang vergewissern, daß ein bestimmtes externes Ereignis eingetreten ist. Es kann sich z.B. um die Bereitstellung von Daten durch einen anderen Prozeß handeln.

  ... TEST EREIGNIS EINGETRETEN ? nein: WARTEN BIS EINGETRETEN...

  Der andere Prozeß muß seinerseits das Eintreten des Ereignises melden:

  ... MELDEN EREIGNIS ...

  Die Unterscheidung folgt aus der verschiedenen Bedeutung der Fälle. Abstrakt lassen sich sowohl Aktionen der Betriebsmittelverwaltung als "Ereignisse" verstehen, als auch umgekehrt benötigte Daten als Betriebsmittel.

  In "WARTEN BIS" sind die Hauptprobleme ausgedrückt:

  Ein blockierter Prozeß muß seine Aktivität aufgeben, um die Anlage nicht unnötig zu belasten. Die Information über wartende (schlafende) Prozesse muß in besonderen Listen geführt werden (Warteschlangen). Die Initiative für den Wiederstart muß von außen, von anderen Prozessen kommen.

3. Synchronisationsoperationen und ihre Implementierung

3.1 Einfache Operationen

Der entscheidendste Beitrag zu dem Problem stammt von DIJKSTRA [1]. Er bewies die Notwendigkeit spezieller Synchronisationsoperationen und Steuervariabler. Die von ihm eingeführten Operationen P und V haben als einfachst mögliche Synchronisationsoperationen genau die notwendigen Funktionen. Als Steuervariable fungieren spezielle

INTEGER-Variable ("Semaphore").

Zum Abfragen und gleichzeitigen Verändern eines Semaphors S dient eine P-Operation. Der Wert von S entscheidet über Fortgang oder Blockieren (Schlafen) des Prozesses.

Das System ordnet jedem Semaphor S eine Warteschlange W_S zu; dort werden alle Prozesse verzeichnet, die auf S warten.

In einer V-Operation wird ein Semaphor verändert mit dem Zweck, einen eventuell darauf wartenden Prozeß wieder anzustoßen (zu wecken).

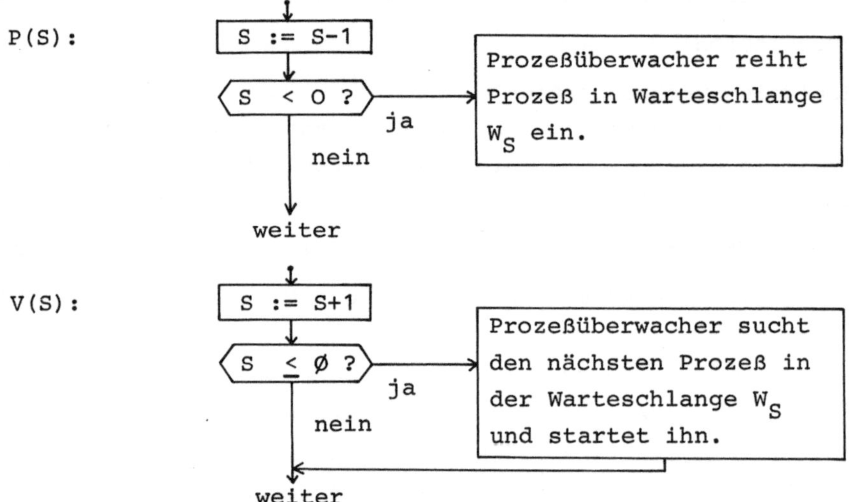

Abb. 2: Einfachste Synchronisationsoperationen nach DIJKSTRA

Die dargestellten Vorgänge sind nicht durch Synchronisationsoperationen anderer Prozesse unterbrechbar. DIJKSTRA hat die unüberwindlichen Schwierigkeiten, die beim Nichtbeachten dieser Forderung entstehen, ausführlich beschrieben.

Zur Synchronisation von Betriebsmitteln werden die einander ausschließenden ("kritischen") Programmabschnitte in P und V eingeklammert:

```
... P(S);
    Benutzung des Betriebsmittels;
    V(S); ...
```

S wird zuvor mit der Maximalanzahl N der gleichzeitig zugreifenden Prozesse initialisiert.

Als Beispiel einer Ereignis-Synchronisation die einfachste Version des bekannten READER-WRITER-Problems:

```
READER: ... P(E);                WRITER: ... P(F);
            read                             write;
            V(F); ... GOTO READER;           V(E); ... GOTO WRITER;
```

Nach der Initialisierung F := 1, E := 0 ergibt sich ein zwangsweise abwechselnder Ablauf der Programmteile "write" und "read". Eventuelle weitere Teile der Programme können beliebig parallel ablaufen.

Diese einfachen Operationen sind bereits zahlreich implementiert. In der Praxis zeigen sich allerdings dadurch entscheidende Nachteile daß eine Operation nur <u>einen</u> Semaphoren als Operanden zuläßt und nur <u>eine</u> definierte Wirkung hat. In Programmen, bei denen infolge komplizierter Abhängigkeiten mehr als eine Semaphorgröße erforderlich ist, sind mehrere Synchronisationsoperationen erforderlich. Sie treten je nach der Problemstruktur hintereinander oder geschachtelt auf. Komplikationen treten nun weniger dadurch auf, daß die Abhängigkeit der Prozesse schwierig zu erfassen ist, als dadurch, daß man vor allem darauf achten muß, daß die Prozesse beim dynamischen Programmablauf keine Verklemmung (deadlock) erleiden können. Schachtelungen sind dann insbesondere dazu nötig, ganze Programmabschnitte die der Synchronisation dienen, nicht unterbrechbar zu machen. Unter dieser Mischung problembezogener und "taktischer" Synchronisationsoperationen leidet die Übersichtlichkeit der Programme stark; die Schwierigkeit, Lösungen zu finden, wird erhöht. Ein Beispiel bietet [5]; hier nur ein einfacher Fall einer Betriebsmittelsynchronisation: Hierbei tritt das Verklemmungsproblem auf, sobald zwei Prozesse mehrere Betriebsmittel aufteilen müssen.

```
Prozeß 1:          ... P(A); x: ...; P(B); ...
Prozeß 2:          ... P(B); x: ...; P(A); ...
```

Befinden sich die Programmabläufe beider Prozesse in dem mit x markierten Bereich, so sind A und B "gesperrt". Die zyklisch voneinander abhängigen blockierten Prozesse können sich selbst nicht aus dieser Verklemmung befreien. Eine Lösung ist z.B. möglich durch ein Verbot der verschiedenen Reihenfolgen des Auftretens von A und B oder durch eine Schachtelung:

```
Prozeß 1:       ... P(M); P(A); x: ...; P(B); V(M); ...
Prozeß 2:       ... P(M); P(B); x: ...; P(A); V(M); ...
```

Das Verklemmungsproblem ist schwerwiegend. Es gibt nach dem heutigen Stand zwei Lösungswege:

Es kann wie in dem Beispiel gelingen, Programme zu schreiben, die mit Sicherheit keine Verklemmung zulassen. Hierzu ist Kenntnis über die Synchronisationen der anderen beteiligten Programme erforderlich. Wo diese Kenntnis fehlt, müssen stark einschränkende Konventionen beachtet werden, wie z.B. die Einhaltung von vorgegebenen Reihenfolgen beim Belegen von Betriebsmitteln.

Der Nachweis für die Korrektheit eines beliebig vorgelegten Programmsystems ist nichttrivial. Bei formalen Methoden steigt der Rechenaufwand hierzu exponentiell mit der Anzahl der Synchronisationspunkte [7]; der Nachweis ist also sehr bald auch maschinell nicht mehr zu erbringen.

Diese erste Art ist oft nicht anwendbar; dann muß das Betriebssystem aktiv an der Verhinderung von Verklemmungen beteiligt werden. Der Nachfrage nach einem Betriebsmittel darf nur stattgegeben werden, wenn dadurch keine Verklemmung droht. Hierfür gibt es Algorithmen [2]; ihre Anwendung führt aber nach den bisherigen Erfahrungen zu ineffektivem Ausnutzen der Betriebsmittel. Wenn man diese Algorithmen schon bei der Implementierung der Synchronisationen einsetzt, laufen sie insbesondere auch dann ab, wenn ein sicheres Programmsystem vorliegt. Es entsteht unnötiger Zeitaufwand.

Aus diesen Ergebnissen leiten wir folgendes ab.

3.2 Verallgemeinerte Synchronisationsoperationen

Synchronisationsoperationen in höheren Programmiersprachen müssen so hoch integriert sein, daß sie

- explizite Programmschachtelungen für die Synchronisation weitestgehend unnötig machen.
- im Interesse einer problemnahen Programmierung beliebig komplizierte Bedingungen als Blockier-Kriterium und beliebige Operationen an den Steuervariablen zulassen.
- sie müssen sowohl explizite Problemlösungen durch den Programmierer erlauben als auch die Anwendung von Prozeduren, die das System z.B. für bestimmte Strategien von Betriebsmittelverwaltungen zur Verfügung stellt. Sie sollen schließlich durch ihre syntaktische Form das Schreiben korrekter Programme begünstigen.

Wichtige Schritte in dieser Richtung sind in einem von HOARE [4] und HANSEN [6] propagierten Konzept enthalten. Dort wird der Tatsache Rechnung getragen, daß komplizierte Synchronisationsoperationen selbst synchronisiert werden müssen. Alle Synchronisationen, die sich gegenseitig ausschließen, werden mit dem Schlüssel REGION und einer Variablen v eingeleitet. Für diese Variablen werden Warteschlangen eingerichtet.

Als Abfrageoperationen sind möglich:

```
REGION v        DO S AWAIT B;
REGION v WHEN B DO S;
```

Eine Meldung von Ereignissen findet in einer Anweisung

```
REGION v        DO S;
```

statt.

Die Prozesse werden in Abhängigkeit von der Bedingung B bei AWAIT bzw. WHEN blockiert und dort wieder aufgenommen. In den Statements S können die Steuergrößen gezählt oder beliebig verändert werden.

Hier soll nun ein darüber hinausgehendes Konzept vorgelegt werden, das neben den obigen Forderungen die folgenden Details berücksichtigt:

- In <u>einer</u> Anweisung müssen Operationen an Semaphoren vor <u>und</u> nach dem Punkt der eventuellen Blockierung möglich sein (Operationen S_I und S_E, s.u.). Ist die Bedingung B zusammengesetzt, so ist das Eintreten einer Teilbedingung nicht hinreichend für den Erfolg der Gesamtabfrage. Also ist die Abfrage der Bedingung eventuell mehrfach erforderlich, jedesmal, wenn eine der beteiligten Größen verändert wurde.

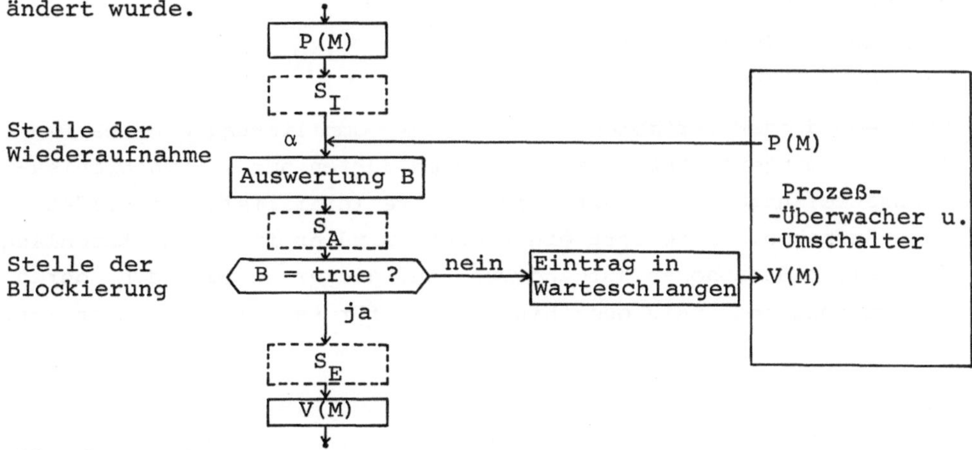

Abb. 3: Implementierung einer TEST-Anweisung

- Daher sind Operationen S_A zweckmäßig, die jedesmal nach einer Auswertung von B, unabhängig vom Ergebnis, stattfinden. Sie können z.B. zum sukzessiven Reservieren von Betriebsmitteln dienen.

Abb. 3 zeigt die Struktur einer solchen verallgemeinerten Abfrage-Synchronisationsanweisung, in die ein Compiler deren einzelne Teile einfügt.

Der Vorschlag für die Syntax dieser Anweisung lautet:

{SAFE M} {IMMEDIATE S_I} TEST B {ALWAYS S_A} ENTER {S_E}

M = BOOLEsche Synchronisationsvariable
B = BOOLEscher Ausdruck } im Sinne von ALGOL 60
S = Statement }

Die eingeklammerten Teile der Anweisung können, unabhängig voneinander, auch fehlen. S_I, S_A und S_E treten dann im Programm nicht auf.

Durch

{SAFE M} NOTICE S_N

wird eine Meldung über Veränderungen an Synchronisationsvariablen programmiert. Die Ausführungen dieser geschlossenen Synchronisationsanweisungen werden selbst synchronisiert, da sie sich gegenseitig ausschließen. Hierzu dient die BOOLEsche Semaphorvariable M innerhalb einfachster Synchronisationsoperationen analog P und V. Fehlt die Angabe SAFE M, wird für M ein Standardwert angenommen.

Als Steuervariablen können alle Größen dienen, die bei ihrer Vereinbarung mit SEMAPHOR gekennzeichnet sind, z.B.

```
SEMAPHOR  BOOLEAN M;
SEMAPHOR  INTEGER RA, WC, WA;
SEMAPHOR  INTEGER ARRAY B [1:N];
```

Für jede dieser Variablen wird bei der Compilierung eine Warteschlange eingerichtet. Die Variablen dürfen nur in Synchronisationsanweisungen verändert werden; ihre Initialisierung bildet eine Ausnahme. Blockiert ein Prozeß, wird er in die Warteschlange derjenigen Semaphoren aufgenommen, auf die er wartet, d.h. deren Veränderung notwendig oder hinreichend für sein Weiterlaufen ist.

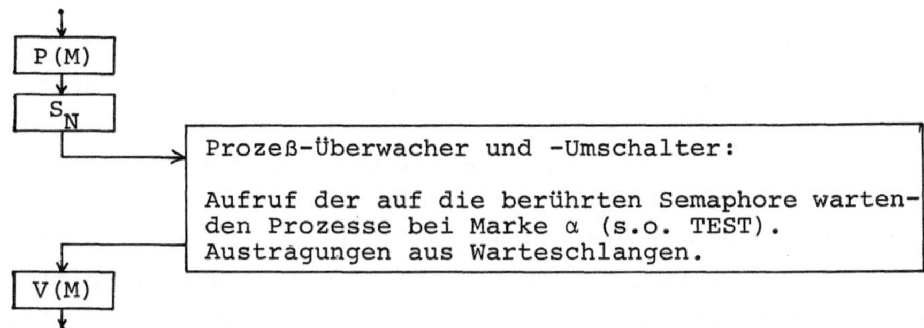

Abb. 4: Implementierung einer NOTICE-Anweisung

Bei der Handhabung der Warteschlangen sind verschiedene Optimierungen denkbar.

Durch die Syntax wird nicht betont, daß es sich bei den Operationen um unterbrechbare Einheiten handelt, dies ist für den Anwender nur von untergeordneter Bedeutung. TEST- und NOTICE-Anweisungen sind vom Compiler gut unterscheidbar.

4. Beispiele

4.1.: Problem READER-WRITER

In dieser Version *) des Problems ist der Ereignis- noch eine Betriebsmittel-Synchronisation überlagert. Im Gegensatz zu der einfachen Version oben wechseln sich READER und WRITER nicht mehr zwangsweise ab, sie schließen sich aber gegenseitig aus. Gemeinsam benutztes Objekt ist ein Datenbereich, den gleichzeitig beliebig viele READER, aber maximal N WRITER benutzen können. Besonders interessant ist eine Priorität von ankommenden WRITER-Prozessen vor ankommenden READER-Prozessen; sie wird durch asymmetrische Operationen nach IMMEDIATE bzw. ENTER in den Programmen erfaßt.

In weiteren Details kommentieren sich die Programme selbst, ein großer Vorteil dieser Programmierungsmöglichkeiten.

```
READER:                    WRITER:
                           IMMEDIATE          WC := WC+1
TEST  WC = Ø               TEST  RA = Ø  AND  WA < N
ENTER  RA := RA+1;         ENTER               WA := WA+1;
read;                      write;
NOTICE  RA := RA-1;        NOTICE BEGIN        WA := WA-1;
                                              WC := WC-1 END;
GOTO READER;               GOTO WRITER;
```

*) Die Problemstellung zusammen mit einer Lösung durch Operationen P und V ist in [5] angegeben.

4.2. Problem Betriebsmittel-Synchronisation

Auch das obige Betriebsmittelproblem soll hier eine Erweiterung erfahren: N gleichartige Prozesse P_I benutzen N Betriebsmittel B_J so, daß ein Prozeß P_I in bestimmten Abschnitten gleichzeitig die zwei Betriebsmittel B_I und $B_{I \bmod N+1}$ benötigt ($1 \leq I, J \leq N$). Die Betriebsmittel lassen nur einen Benutzer gleichzeitig zu. Da jeder Prozeß gleichzeitig mehrere Betriebsmittel belegt und durch die zyklische Symmetrie des Problems ergeben sich bei ungenügenden Lösungen leicht Verklemmungszustände.

Das Beispiel lehnt sich an das von DIJKSTRA [3] sogenannte Philosophenproblem an. Es ist eine formale Gleichheit der Programme für alle Prozesse möglich, die der Symmetrie des Problems gerecht wird.

Jedem Betriebsmittel B_J ist eine Semaphorvariable B[J] aus einem SEMAPHOR INTEGER ARRAY B[1:N] zugeteilt.

$$B[J] = \begin{cases} \emptyset : B_J \text{ ist frei} \\ I : B_J \text{ ist von } P_I \text{ belegt} \end{cases}$$

Möglichkeit a): ohne Reservierung

```
PROZESS I: ...
TEST B[I] = Ø AND B[I mod N + 1] = Ø ENTER B[I]:= B[I mod N+1]:=I;
Benutzung der Betriebsmittel;
NOTICE B[I] := B[I mod N+1] := Ø;  GOTO PROZESS I;
```

Möglichkeit b): mit Reservierung

```
PROZESS I: ...
TEST B[I] = Ø OR B[I] = I AND B [ I mod N+1] = Ø OR B[I mod N+1]= I
ALWAYS BEGIN IF        B[I] = Ø THEN        B[I] := I;
             IF B[I mod  N+1] = Ø THEN B[I mod N+1] := I END;

Benutzung der Betriebsmittel;

NOTICE  B[I] := B[I mod N+1] := Ø; GOTO PROZESS I;
```

Durch die Möglichkeit der zusammengesetzten Abfrage nach TEST, ohne explizite Schachtelungen kann sich keine kreisförmige Verklemmung ausbilden. Durch die Operationen nach ALWAYS werden die Betriebsmittel also reserviert, wenn sie frei sind, oder sofort nachdem sie durch eine NOTICE-Operation freigegeben werden.

Bei den Möglichkeiten a) und b) ist die Lösungsstrategie in den Programmen explizit formuliert. Stehen die entsprechenden, aufeinander abgestimmten Systemprozeduren VERFUEGBAR, RESERVIEREN und FREIGEBEN zur Verfügung, so kann Möglichkeit b) auch ohne Risiko für den Programmierer wie folgt formuliert werden:

c) PROZESS I: ...

```
TEST  VERFUEGBAR (I,B[I], B[I mod N+1])
  ALWAYS RESERVIEREN (I,B[I], B[I mod N+1]) ENTER;
Benutzung der Betriebsmittel;
NOTICE FREIGEBEN (B[I], B[I mod N+1]);  GOTO PROZESS I;
```

Literatur

[1] DIJKSTRA, E.W.: Cooperating Sequential Processes, in Programming Languages, Ed. F. Genuys, Academic Press,London, 1968

[2] HABERMANN, A.N.: Prevention of System Deadlocks, Communications of the ACM, 12,7(July 1969) 373-385

[3] DIJKSTRA, E.W.: Hierarchical Ordering of Sequential Processes, Acta Informatica 1,1971

[4] HOARE, C.A.R.: Towards a Theory of Parallel Programming, International Seminar on Operating System Techniques, Belfast, Northern Ireland, Aug. - Sep. 1971

[5] COURTOIS, P.J., HEYMANS, F., PARNAS, D.L.: Concurrent Control with "Readers" ans "Writers", Communications of the ACM, 14,10 (Okt. 1971) 667-668

[6] HANSEN, P.B.: A Comparison of Two Synchronizing Concepts, Acta Informatica, 1(1972) 190-199

[7] GILBERT, P., CHANDLER, W.J.: Interference Between Communicating Parallel Processes, Communications of the ACM, 15,6 (June 1972) 427-437

AUFRUF VON SYSTEMLEISTUNGEN IN EINEM SCHICHTENWEISE GEGLIEDERTEN BETRIEBSSYSTEM

K. LAGALLY

Zusammenfassung

Rechenanlagen, die für Mehrprogrammbetrieb ausgelegt sind, verfügen im allgemeinen über Hardware-Speicherschutz und mindestens zwei Betriebsmodi ("Prozeßmodus" und "Systemmodus") sowie spezielle Maschinenbefehle "Systemaufruf" (supervisor call) und "Systemrückkehr" zum kontrollierten Übergang zwischen den Modi. Damit läßt sich sicherstellen, daß Benutzerprogramme einander sowie das Betriebssystem nicht zerstören und auch nicht mißbräuchlich aufrufen können.

BSM (Betriebssystem München) erbringt einen Teil der Systemleistungen ebenfalls durch asynchron ablaufende Prozesse, die in eine Folge von Systemschichten eingebettet sind und eine Hierarchie von "Pseudomaschinen" aufbauen. Damit läßt sich der gleiche Schutzmechanismus auch auf die "Systemprozesse" ausdehnen, wobei jedoch der zugängliche Leistungsumfang und seine Realisierung je nach der Stellung des aufrufenden Prozesses unterschiedlich sind.

Der in BSM gewählte Entschlüsselungsmechanismus erfordert auf Seiten des aufrufenden Prozesses keinerlei Information darüber, auf welche Weise die angeforderte Leistung erbracht wird; die Reaktion im Fehlerfalle kann prozeßspezifisch sein.

Interessante Sonderfälle sind etwa:

- Erbringen von Leistungen für einen "Sohn-Prozeß" durch den "Vater-Prozeß",

- dynamische Überwachung der Außenbeziehungen eines Prozesses durch einen Überwacherprozeß,

- Lauf eines Prozesses in einer Test-Umgebung.

1. Einführung

BSM (Betriebssystem München) [1] wird an der TU München für eine Mehrprozessoranlage Telefunken TR440 entwickelt. Im folgenden soll das in BSM verwendete Verfahren zur Entschlüsselung von Systemaufrufen beschrieben und motiviert werden. Dabei wird, soweit möglich, von den speziellen Maschineneigenschaften des TR440 abgesehen.

2. Hardware-Voraussetzungen

Rechenanlagen, die für Mehrprogrammbetrieb verwendet werden sollen, benötigen Hardware-Einrichtungen, welche eine störende wechselseitige Beeinflussung von Benutzerprogrammen zu verhindern gestatten. Insbesondere muß sichergestellt werden können, daß ein Programm nicht Speicherbereiche eines anderen Programmes anspricht (Speicherschutz), und daß keine Kollisionen beim Betrieb der Peripheriegeräte auftreten. Um dies zu erreichen, muß es (mindestens) zwei verschiedene Betriebsmodi geben: einen "Benutzermodus" (Prozeßmodus, user mode, slave mode), in dem die Benutzerprogramme laufen, wobei nur ein Teil des Speichers und ein eingeschränkter Befehlsvorrat zugänglich sind, und einen "Systemmodus" (master mode), in dem alle Befehle und der ganze Speicher angesprochen werden können. Zu jedem im Rechner ablaufenden Benutzerprogramm gehört ein Kontrollblock, der eine Beschreibung des dem Programm zugänglichen Speichers sowie Plätze zur Registerablage für den Fall, daß das Programm gerade nicht von einem Rechnerkern bedient wird, und evtl. weitere prozeßspezifische Daten enthält. Zum kontrollierten Übergang zwischen den beiden Betriebsmodi gibt es im Benutzermodus den Befehl "Systemaufruf" (supervisor call), der eine Programmunterbrechung auslöst, und den privilegierten Befehl "Systemrückkehr", mit dem ein Benutzerprozeß nach einer Unterbrechung fortgesetzt werden kann. Häufig ist der Benutzermodus auch mit relativer Adressierung gekoppelt, so daß ein Benutzerprogramm ohne Abänderung an beliebiger Stelle in den Speicher geladen werden kann. Damit läßt sich die Mehrfachbenutzung desselben Programmkörpers oder auch gemeinsamer Daten einfach organisieren.

Unter den angegebenen Hardware-Voraussetzungen kann man davon sprechen, daß jedem Benutzerprogramm seine eigene "virtuelle Maschine" zur Verfügung steht, die durch den Prozeßkontrollblock beschrieben wird. Sie umfaßt den Adreßraum des Benutzerprogramms sowie einen "Pseudoprozessor". Dessen Befehlsvorrat besteht aus den im Benutzermodus zugänglichen Hardware-Befehlen, ergänzt durch Pseudooperationen, die durch Systemaufruf abgerufen und vom Betriebssystem realisiert werden.

3. Systemprozesse

Ebensowenig wie die reale Hardware braucht die virtuelle Maschine für ein Benutzerprogramm ein sequentieller Automat zu sein; aus Effizienzgründen ist es im Gegenteil vorteilhaft, soweit wie möglich Parallelvorgänge anzustoßen und die Ergebnisse erst bei Bedarf abzurufen. Sieht man einen Mechanismus zur Prozeßkommunikation vor, so läßt sich auch ein Teil des Betriebssystems in Form von im Benutzermodus ablaufenden Prozessen organisieren. Damit läßt sich der mächtige und damit fehleranfällige Systemmodus auf diejenigen Fälle beschränken, wo er wirklich nötig ist: zur Ausführung privilegierter Befehle und zur Realisierung der Prozesse selbst mittels der gegebenen Hardware-Prozessoren. Für die übrigen Teile des Betriebssystems kann man den vollen Schutzmechanismus für Benutzerprozesse ausnützen, ebenso, soweit technisch vorhanden, die Möglichkeiten zur relativen Adressierung. Für jeden Benutzer- oder Systemprozeß läßt sich nun wieder eine virtuelle Maschine definieren, die neben seinem Adreßraum durch die Funktionen beschrieben ist, die der Prozeß in Anspruch nehmen kann. Diese Funktionen werden realisiert durch die Prozesse, die der gegebene Prozeß direkt oder indirekt aufruft, und durch den im Systemmodus ablaufenden Systemkern.

4. Systemschichten

Um Aufträge an Prozesse zu delegieren und die Ergebnisse abzurufen, benötigt man als Operationen zur Prozeßkommunikation mindestens die beiden Operationen "Übersende Auftrag" und "Erwarte Ergebnis". [3] Stellt man keine einschränkenden Forderungen an die möglichen Auftragsbeziehungen zwischen Prozessen, so lassen sich leicht Situationen herstellen, in denen eine Reihe von Prozessen zyklisch aufeinander warten, so daß eine System-Verklemmung eintritt (deadlock, deadly embrace). Solche Verklemmungen können nicht eintreten, wenn die Auftragsbeziehung eine Halbordnungsrelation ist; vergröbert man sie zu einer Totalordnung (was bei gegebener Halbordnung auf mannigfache Weise möglich ist), so sind nicht nur Zyklen ausgeschlossen, sondern es läßt sich auch das ganze System in eine monotone Folge von Schichten zerlegen, derart, daß sich jede Schichtengrenze als eine virtuelle Maschine für die darüberliegenden Prozesse interpretieren läßt. Das wesentliche Charakteristikum einer solchen Schichtung ist nun, daß der Teil des Systems unterhalb einer Schichtengrenze allein durch seine Funktionen beschrieben ist und unter Erhaltung dieser Funktionen durch eine gänzlich andere Implementierung ersetzt werden könnte. Insbesondere ist die Identität der Prozesse unterhalb der Schichtengrenze völlig irrelevant. [2]

5. Funktions-Entschlüsselung

Stellt man an das System die Forderung, daß es so modular aufgebaut ist, daß man jederzeit den Teil unterhalb einer Schichtgrenze durch einen funktionell äquivalenten ersetzen kann, so lassen sich daraus nachfolgende Konsequenzen ableiten:

- man darf sich an einer Schichtgrenze nur auf die dort verfügbaren Funktionen beziehen, nicht auf ihre Implementierung;

- die Abbildung der aufgerufenen Funktion auf ihre Implementierung (als Prozeß oder als Unterprogramm des Systemkerns) muß von der Systemaufrufentschlüsselung des Systemkerns vorgenommen werden in Abhängigkeit von der betroffenen Schichtengrenze.

Die beiden Forderungen sind verträglich, da die Systemaufrufentschlüsselung als Teil des Systemkerns stets zu dem ausgewechselten Teil gehört.
Die Frage, wie die Abbildung (Funktionsnummer, Schichtenkennzeichnung) → (Prozeß oder Systemkern-UP) am zweckmäßigsten zu realisieren ist, hängt stark von der gegebenen Hardware ab. Im BSM, am TR440, wurde folgende Lösung gewählt:
Die Funktionsnummern wurden so festgelegt, daß sie auch ohne Beachtung der Schichtenkennzeichnung im ganzen System eindeutig sind; die Zuordnung (Funktionsnummer → Realisierung) steht in einer systemglobalen Tabelle im Systemkern.
Diese Tabelle wird beim Systemaufbau dynamisch angelegt; damit ist man nicht auf vorgegebene Prozeßnamen festgelegt. Es bleibt noch je Prozeß eine Bit-Tafel übrig, die angibt, ob die betreffende Funktion für diesen Prozeß auf Grund seiner Schichtenhöhe zugänglich ist. Diese Tafel, die bei der Kreation des Prozesses besetzt wird, liegt im Kontrollblock des Prozesses und kann von ihm nicht verändert werden; sie ist von der Implementierung tieferer Schichten unabhängig. Um den speicherresidenten Teil des Betriebssystems nicht zu umfangreich werden zu lassen, wurde das beschriebene Verfahren nicht zu einem universellen Capabilitymechanismus ([4], [5]) ausgebaut. Statt

dessen ist es Aufgabe der durch einen Systemaufruf angesprochenen Auftragnehmer, die Zugriffskontrolle für die von ihnen verwalteten Objekte auszuüben. Dies ist möglich, da bei jedem Auftrag der auftraggebende Prozeß eindeutig identifizierbar ist.
Die angegebene Realisierung gestattet es, über die Kontrolle der durch das Schichtenbild gegebenen Totalordnung hinaus, durch andere Besetzung der Bittabellen der einzelnen Prozesse von der Totalordnung zu einer Halbordnung überzugehen. Allgemeiner läßt sich so für jede System-Funktion ein vorgegebenes Netz von möglichen Auftragsbeziehungen einrichten und überwachen. [6]

6. Fehlerbehandlung und Sonderanwendungen

Versucht ein Prozeß, eine Leistung aufzurufen, die ihm nicht zugänglich sein soll, so wird dieser Fehlerfall erkannt. Die Reaktion darauf läßt sich nun mit Vorteil ebenso behandeln, wie wenn der Prozeß eine legale Funktion "Fehlerbehandlung" aufgerufen hätte; hält man die Implementierung prozeßspezifisch, so lassen sich auf einfache Weise Test- und Meßverfahren damit ins System einbringen.
Neben den Standard-Reaktionen

- Absetzen einer Fehlermeldung ins System-Protokoll
- Alarmieren des Prozesses

lassen sich etwa anschließen:

- Zählung des Aufrufes und Erbringen der Leistung
- Überprüfung der Parameter und Erbringen der Leistung
- Simulation der Leistung (ohne Auswirkung auf den Rest des Systems).

Für die letzteren Möglichkeiten ist es notwendig, daß ein Überwacher-Prozeß sich als Empfänger der Fehlermeldung beim Testobjekt einträgt und die zu testenden Funktionen dort sperrt. Geeignete Hardware-Möglichkeiten vorausgesetzt, läßt sich der gleiche Mechanismus zur dynamischen Überwachung und Ablaufregistrierung eines Prozesses einsetzen.

Literatur

[1] G. Goos, J. Jürgens, K. Lagally:
The Operating System BSM Viewed as a Community of Parallel Processes; Bericht 7208, Mathematisches Institut TU München

[2] E.W. Dijkstra:
The Structure of the THE Multiprogramming System, CACM 11,5 (1968)

[3] P.B. Hansen:
The Nucleus of a Multiprogramming System, CACM 13,4 (1970)

[4] An Undergraduate Course on Operating Systems Principles, COSINE Committee, National Academy of Engineering (U.S.A.), June, 1971

[5] B.W. Lampson:
On Reliable and Extensible Operating Systems, Infotech State of the Art Proceedings, 1970

[6] R.M. Graham:
Protection in an Information Processing Utility, CACM 11,5 (1968)

ÜBERSETZUNG VON KOMMANDOSPRACHEN

TH. WELLER ET AL.

Kommandosprachen, auch job control languages oder command languages genannt, dienen zur Steuerung der Systemsoftware in Rechenanlagen. Sie sind ebenso wie die von ihnen gesteuerten Betriebssysteme in keiner Weise genormt. Während ein Benutzer ein Algol- oder Fortran-Programm manchmal fast ohne Änderungen auf verschiedenen Maschinen rechnen kann, muß er seine Kommandos immer völlig neu schreiben, falls es sich um Maschinen mit unterschiedlichen Betriebssystemen handelt. Wäre es möglich, Kommandosprachen automatisch zu übersetzen, so könnte der Übergang zwischen verschiedenen Betriebssystemen sehr erleichtert werden. Unumgänglich wird ein Übersetzer in einem lastausgleichenden Rechnerverbund mit Rechnern, deren Betriebssysteme unterschiedliche Kommandosprachen besitzen, da hier erst nach Eingabe des Jobs vom zentralen Verteilungsalgorithmus des Rechnerverbunds entschieden wird, auf welchem Rechner - und damit unter welcher Kommandosprache - der Job läuft.

Am Institut für Informatik in Stuttgart beschäftigt sich eine Forschungsgruppe mit dem Problem des Übersetzens von Kommandosprachen. Im folgenden sollen dazu einige grundsätzliche Überlegungen wiedergegeben und anhand eines Beispiels erläutert werden.
Zunächst seien einige prinzipielle Schwierigkeiten beim Übersetzen von Kommandosprachen angedeutet:

- Es gibt Fälle, in denen die Kommandofolge einer gegebenen Kommandosprache sicher nicht in die Kommandofolge einer zweiten Kommandosprache übersetzt werden kann. So kann eine Kommandofolge, die einen bedingten Rückwärtssprung enthält, nicht in die Kommandofolge einer Kommandosprache übersetzt werden, die Rückwärtssprünge nicht zulässt.
- Ein zweites Problem liegt in der uneinheitlichen Abgrenzung zwischen Programmiersprachen und Kommandosprachen. So werden Systemanforderungen, die in einem Betriebssystem mit Hilfe von Kommandos definiert werden, in anderen Systemen mit Hilfe von Anweisungen der betreffenden Programmiersprache definiert, wobei die Parameter der Anweisungen eventuell erst im Programm selbst errechnet werden.
- Zum dritten beziehen sich Kommandosprachen und damit die entsprechen-

den Kommandofolgen in oft unnötigem Maße auf spezielle Eigenschaften des jeweiligen Betriebssystems. Der für ein Betriebssystem vorgegebene Weg der Auftragsbearbeitung wird daher für ein anderes Betriebssystem oft gänzlich ungeeignet oder doch zumindest sehr umständlich sein. Das bedeutet, daß bei der Übersetzung eine für das Ausgangssystem geeignete Bearbeitungsfolge oft mühsam in eine für das Zielsystem geeignete Folge umgeformt werden muß. Wünschenswert wären daher Kommandosprachen, die es erlauben, stärker problem- und weniger rechnerbezogen anzugeben, von welcher Ausgangssituation aus ein vorgegebenes Ziel erreicht werden soll. Der Weg der Auftragsbearbeitung müsste dabei nur grob angegeben werden.

In der hier behandelten Übersetzerversion werden nur Jobs zugelassen, die folgenden Anforderungen genügen:
- Ein Job besteht aus einer Kommandofolge, in die Daten (Quellprogramme, Eingabedaten etc.) eingebettet sind.
- Es handelt sich um Batch-Jobs, die während ihrer Laufzeit auf keinerlei Daten oder Dateien zugreifen, die außerhalb ihrer eigenen Kommandofolge vereinbart wurden ("abgeschlossene Jobs").
- Sämtliche Anweisungen zur Steuerung des Betriebssystems gehören zur Kommandosprache und nicht zur Programmiersprache.

Speziell im Universitätsrechenbetrieb genügen diesen Bedingungen sicher ausreichend viele Jobs, so daß eine gewisse Lastverteilung unter den am Verbund beteiligten Rechnern durchgeführt werden kann.

Die Übersetzung zweier Kommandofolgen wird nur in den seltensten Fällen in Form einer Eins-zu-eins-Übersetzung der Kommandos erfolgen können. Es liegt daher nahe, eine zweistufige Umformung durchzuführen: die Kommandos der Ausgangsfolge werden zunächst in Anweisungen einer Zwischensprache überführt; in einem zweiten Schritt erfolgt dann die Übersetzung in die Kommandofolge der Zielsprache. Als Einheiten der Zwischensprache haben wir sogenannte "Elementarfunktionen des Betriebssystems" [1] oder "Kommandowirkungen" gewählt. Diese Wirkungen sind aus der Sicht des Benutzers definiert und beschreiben die elementaren Funktionen eines gegebenen Kommandos. Eine sinnvolle Definition dieser Wirkungen scheint uns die entscheidende Voraussetzung zur Lösung des Übersetzungsproblems zu sein. Die eleganteste und befriedigendste Lösung wäre, die Wirkungen einer "virtuellen Maschine" zu definieren, die nur mit Datenmengen arbeitet, ohne irgendwelche "Datenbehälter" oder sonstige systemspezifischen Eigenschaften konventioneller Betriebssysteme zu verwenden. Durch das Zerlegen der Kommandos einer Ausgangsfolge in diese Wirkungen könnte

man so eine systemunabhängige Zwischenform erhalten. Diese Methode ist jedoch - bedingt durch die Struktur der gegenwärtigen Kommandosprachen - nicht durchführbar, da selbst bei ausführlicher semantischer Analyse der Kommandofolge im allgemeinen nicht zu erkennen ist, ob der Benutzer eine durch ein spezielles Kommando geforderte Leistung ausdrücklich verlangt, ob er eine ähnliche Leistung auch akzeptieren würde oder ob er überhaupt auf sie verzichten könnte.
Als zweite Möglichkeit bleibt, die Wirkungen von den realen Betriebssystemen ausgehend zu definieren. Dazu betrachtet man in einem gegebenen Betriebssystem jedes einzelne Kommando als Zusammenfassung einiger Wirkungen und zerlegt das Kommando in diese Einheiten. Da der Benutzer in unserer Übersetzerversion nur über das Kommando Zugang zum Betriebssystem hat, erhält man damit nach Zerlegung aller Kommandos einer Kommandosprache die Menge aller für das Betriebssystem benötigten Wirkungen. Führt man diese Zerlegung für alle Betriebssysteme durch, deren Kommandosprachen man ineinander übersetzen will, so erhält man bei n Systemen schließlich n Mengen von Wirkungen. Der Grad der Überlappung zwischen jeweils zwei Mengen ist dabei entscheidend für die Übersetzbarkeit der entsprechenden Kommandosprachen. Die Überlappung hängt im wesentlichen ab von der Ebene, auf der die Wirkungen definiert werden. Sie ist auf der Ebene der Kommandos gering und steigt an, wenn die einzelnen Kommandos weiter unterteilt werden. Bei zu großem Detaillierungsgrad wird die Überlappung wieder geringer, da dann in den Wirkungen in steigendem Maße betriebssystemspezifische Eigenheiten zum Ausdruck kommen. Der optimale Grad der Zerlegung ist von der Gesamtheit der betrachteten Kommandosprachen abhängig und kann nur durch die Analyse der betreffenden Sprachen gefunden werden. Auch bei optimaler Definition der Wirkungen lässt sich eine Wirkungsfolge, die man durch Zerlegung einer Kommandofolge des Ausgangssystems erhält, in der Regel nicht als Zerlegung einer Kommandofolge der Zielsprache interpretieren. In diesen Fällen muß versucht werden, durch Umformungen oder Ersetzungen die Wirkungsfolge so abzuändern, daß eine Abbildung in die Zielsprache möglich ist. So kann z.B. eine Wirkung

"Abändern eines Dateinamens"

gegebenenfalls ersetzt werden durch die Wirkungsfolge

"Kreieren einer Datei"
"Kopieren von einer Datei in eine andere"
"Löschen einer Datei".

Bei einer Ersetzung oder Umformung von Wirkungen oder Wirkungsfolgen darf die Absicht des Benutzers nicht geändert werden. Einen Ausdruck auf dem Schnelldrucker wird man nicht ersetzen können durch einen Ausdruck auf dem Streifenstanzer; dagegen ist es dem Benutzer sicher gleichgültig, ob während des Laufs seines Jobs seine Daten auf einer Trommel oder einer Platte zwischengespeichert werden. Auch hier stört wieder, daß die Absicht des Benutzers oft nicht klar erkennbar ist; im Zweifelsfall sollten aber die Regeln für eine Umformung eher zu streng als zu großzügig formuliert werden.

```
1 | JOB XYZ,:IFI
2 | ALGOL *CR
  | ... Quellprogramm-
  |    zeilen........
  | ////
3 | ASSIGN *TPO,ERGEBNIS
4 | ENTER
5 | LISTFILE ERGEBNIS,*LP
6 | ERASE ERGEBNIS
7 | ENDJOB
  | ****
```

Abb.1: Ausgangsjob (Betriebssystem GEORGE 3)

Im folgenden Beispiel gehen wir von einem Job aus, wie er im Betriebssystem GEORGE 3 auf einem Rechner der ICL-1900-Serie laufen kann. Der Job ist in sich geschlossen und genügt daher unseren Anforderungen. Als Zielsprache dient die Kommandosprache des BS 3 (Betriebssystem des Telefunken-Rechners TR 440). Als Ausgangsfolge sei eine Kommandofolge gegeben (Abb.1), in der ein in die Kommandofolge eingebettetes Quellprogramm kompiliert, gebunden und geladen wird. An das Objektprogramm wird eine Datei "Ergebnis" angeschlossen, in die alle an den Streifenstanzer gerichteten Ausgabedaten des Programms ausgegeben werden. Nach dem Start des Objektprogramms wird die Datei "Ergebnis" auf dem Drucker ausgegeben, "Ergebnis" wird gelöscht und der Job beendet.

Den Eingangsteil des Übersetzers bildet ein zweistufiger Interpreter (Abb.3). Dieser benützt in seinem ersten Teil die vom Compilerbau bekannten Parsing-Techniken zur syntaktischen Zerlegung der einkommenden Kommandofolge. Die in manchen Systemen existierenden "Unterkommandos" werden von ihm als Parameter bestimmter Kommandos oder als eigenständige Kommandos gedeutet. Ferner werden in diesem Teil die Kommando-Parameter mit den betriebssystemspezifischen Voreinstellungen aufgefüllt. Als Ausgabe dieses Interpreterteils erhält man eine in Kommandowörter und Parameter gegliederte Folge. Für jedes Kommandowort ist im Übersetzer eine Kommando-Zerlegungs-Tabelle angelegt, in der das Kommando, abhängig von seinen Parametern, in Folgen von Analyser- und Konverteranweisungen zerlegt wird. Der Interpreter II benützt diese Tabelle, um die ihm übergebene Kommandofolge in eine Reihe von Analyseranweisungen zu zerlegen. Diese Anweisungen steuern den Analyser I. In ihm werden die der Kommandofolge entsprechenden Wirkungen zu einer Wirkungsfolge zusammengestellt;

1	2	3	4	Erläuterung der Wirkungen
1	1	b-ab-a -ifi	(-)s	Eröffnen des Jobs
2	2	t-dl-jd -vr	(dl)s	Daten dl von jd über vr
	3	t-dl-vr -ks	(dl)ls	nach ks
	4	u-dl-d2 -kp-ks-alg	(dl)l;(d2)s	Kompilieren
	5	e-d2-kp -op	(d2)lsb	mit Eigenschaft Codeopti-
	6	e-d2-kp -dp	(d2)lsb	mierung und dumpfähig
	7	t-d2-ks -vr	(d2)ls	Daten d2 von ks über vr
	8	t-d2-vr -ks	(d2)ls	nach ks
	9	u-d2-d3 -bd-ks	(d2)l;(d3)s	Binden; Daten d3 mit Eigen-
	10	e-d3-bd -aa	(d3)lsb	schaft absolut adressiert
	11	t-d3-ks -vr	(d3)ls	wie 7
	12	t-d3-vr -ks	(d3)ls	wie 8
3	13	b-il-a	(il)s	Eröffnen der Datei il
	14	e-il-asa-d3	(il)ls;(d3)ls	Zuordnen von il an d3
4	15	e-d3-s	(d3)l;(-)s	Start von d3
5	16	t-d4-il -vr	(d4)ls;(il)ls	Daten d4 (von d3 erzeugt)
	17	t-d4-vr -dr	(d4)ls	über vr auf den Drucker
7	18	b-ab-b -ifi	(-)l	Beenden des Jobs

Abb.2: Aus dem Ausgangsjob folgende Wirkungsfolge

ferner werden Tabellen angelegt, in denen im Job auftretende Dateien und Daten erfaßt werden. Abb.2 zeigt die beim Übersetzen des Ausgangsjobs entstandene Wirkungsfolge in der Form, wie sie nach Abarbeiten aller Analyseranweisungen vom Analyser I dem Analyser II übergeben wird. Spalte 1 zeigt dabei mit der Nummer i den Beginn der zum Kommando i gehörenden Wirkungen an, während Spalte 2 zur Numerierung der in Spalte 3 enthaltenen Wirkungen dient. Spalte 4 zeigt schließlich die sogenannten Aufbauparameter (s.u.) der Wirkungen. Man unterscheidet 4 Typen von Wirkungen, kenntlich durch den ersten Teil ihres Namens:

- t - Transport von Datenmengen zwischen zwei Aufenthaltsorten
- u - Umformung einer Datenmenge in eine andere (z.B. Kompilation)
- b - Erstellen oder Löschen (bzw. Beenden) von Jobs / Dateien / Datenmengen
- e - Zuweisen von Eigenschaften an Jobs / Dateien / Datenbasen / Datenmengen

Die spezielle Bedeutung einer Wirkung lässt sich aus ihren weiteren Namensteilen erkennen. Die wichtigsten Bezeichnungen dabei sind:

d x.......Datenmenge x   i x.......Datei x

jd.......Job-Beschreibung   ks........Kernspeicher
ab.......Job   s.........Start
vr.......Verfügungsraum (abstrakter Aufenthaltsort, über den jeder Datentransport erfolgt)

Aufgabe des Analysers II ist es, aus der ihm übergebenen Wirkungsfolge einen gerichteten Graphen zu erzeugen, der die zulässigen Umordnungen der Wirkungen angibt (Abb.4 auf S.7). Der Graph entsteht mit Hilfe der Aufbauparameter durch eine Anordnung der Wirkungen nach Abhängigkeitsverhältnissen. Der Aufbauparameter (x)l bedeutet dabei "Bezugnehmen auf den Parameter x", während der Aufbauparameter (x)s bedeutet "Setzen des Parameters x als Bezugspunkt".
Der Graph ist die Eingabe in den nächsten Übersetzerteil, den Konverter I. Dieser versucht in einem ersten Durchgang, eine der zulässigen Wirkungsfolgen in eine Kommandofolge der Zielsprache zu überführen. Eine zulässige Wirkungsfolge erhält man aus dem Graphen, wenn eine bestimmte Wirkung erst dann aus dem Graphen in die Folge übernommen wird, wenn alle Wirkungen längs eines jeden in den Knoten einmündenden Weges schon

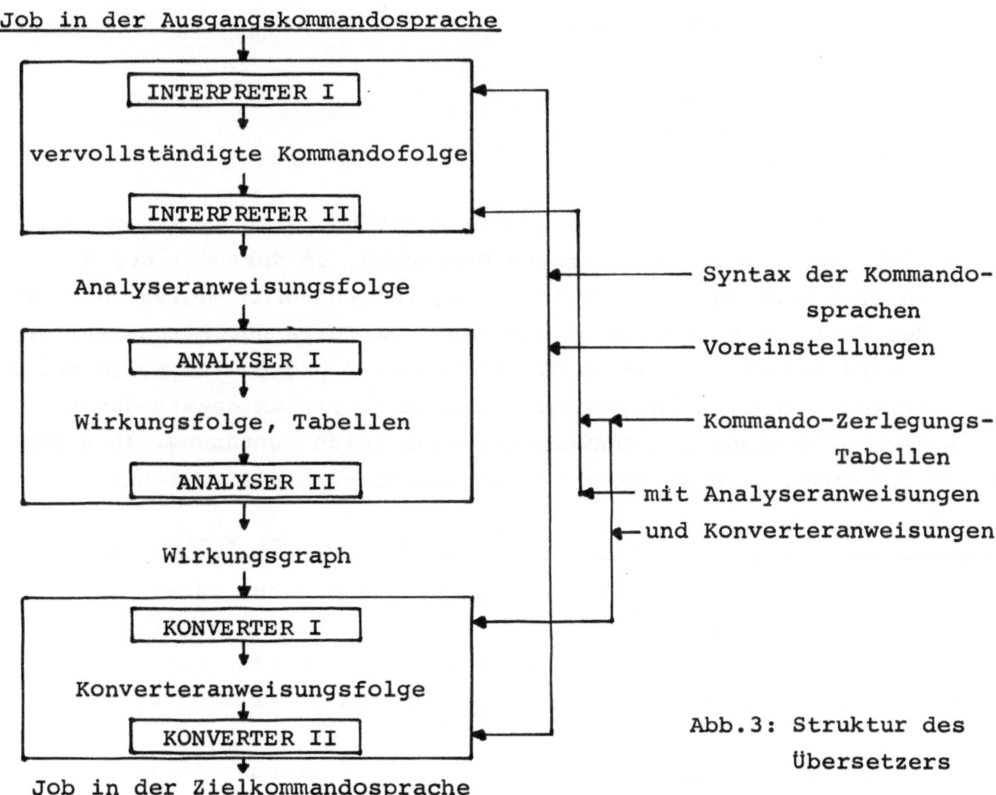

Abb.3: Struktur des Übersetzers

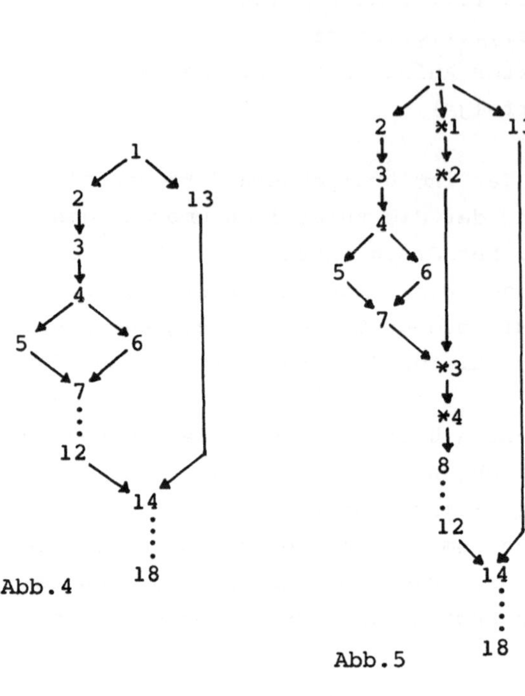

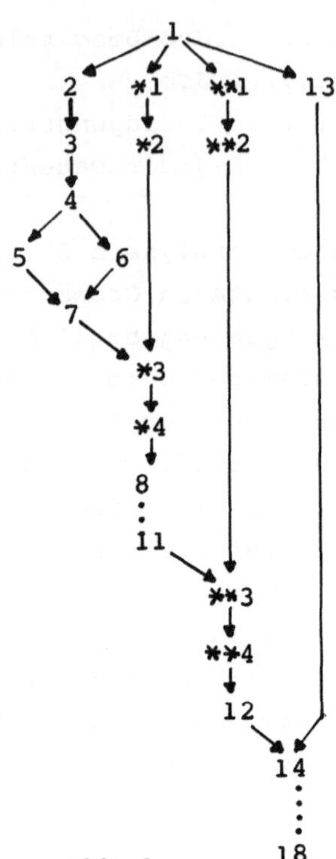

Abb.4: aus der Wirkungsfolge (Abb.2) erzeugter Graph

Abb.5: Graph nach einer Umformung

Abb.6: Graph nach zwei Umformungen

in der Folge enthalten sind. Gelingt die Überführung in eine Kommandofolge der Zielsprache nicht im ersten Durchgang, so versucht der Konverter I, einzelne Wirkungen oder Teilwirkungsfolgen durch äquivalente Wirkungen oder Teilwirkungsfolgen zu ersetzen. Im Falle der Wirkungsfolge der Abb.2 wird zunächst zwischen die Wirkungen 7 und 8 eine Folge von 4 neuen Wirkungen (Abb.7) eingeschoben. Auch mit dem nun entstandenen Graphen (Abb.5) gelingt dem Konverter I noch keine Zuordnung. In einer weiteren Umformung wird dieselbe Wirkungsfolge nochmals zwischen die

2	3	4	Erläuterung der Wirkungen
1	b-i..-a	(i..)s	Eröffnen einer Datei; Eigen-
2	e-i..-bza	(i..)lsb	schaft Bearbeitungszeiger vorn
3	t-d..-vr-i..	(d..)ls;(i..)ls	Daten von vr nach Datei
4	t-d..-i..-vr	(d..)ls;(i..)ls	Daten von Datei nach vr

Abb.7: in den Graphen (Abb.4 bzw. 5) eingefügte Wirkungsfolge

Wirkungs-nummer	Wirkung	Kommandowort der Zielsprache
1	b-ab-a -ifi	XBA
2	t-d1-jd -vr	UEBERSETZE
3	t-d1-vr -ks	
4	u-d1-d2 -kp-ks-alg	
6	e-d2-kp -dp	
5	e-d2-kp -op	
7	t-d2-ks -vr	
*1	b-i2-a	
*2	e-i2-bza	
*3	t-d2-vr -i2	
*4	t-d2-i2 -vr	MONTIERE
8	t-d2-vr -ks	
9	u-d2-d3 -bd-ks	
10	e-d3-bd -aa	
11	t-d3-ks -vr	
**1	b-i3-a	
**2	e-i3-bza	
**3	t-d3-vr -i3	
13	b-i1-a	DATEI
**4	t-d3-i3 -vr	STARTE
12	t-d3-vr -ks	
14	e-i1-asa-d3	
15	e-d3-s	
16	t-d4-i1 -vr	DRUCKE
17	t-d4-vr -dr	
18	b-ab-b -ifi	XEN

Abb.8: zur Übersetzung in die Zielsprache ausgewählte Wirkungsfolge mit zugeordneten Kommandos

Wirkungen 11 und 12 eingeschoben. Mit dem derart erweiterten Graphen (Abb.6; erste Umformung mit * ; zweite Umformung mit **) gelingt dem Konverter I die Zuordnung zu einer Folge von Kommandowörtern der Zielsprache (Abb.8). Abschliessend überführt der Konverter I mit Hilfe der Kommando-Zerlegungs-Tabellen der Zielsprache die von ihm verwendete zulässige Wirkungsfolge in eine Folge von Konverteranweisungen, die den Konverter II steuern. In diesem letzten Teil des Übersetzers werden die Parameter der Kommandos der Zielsprache bestimmt und die vom Ausgangssystem übernommenen Namen auf syntaktische Zulässigkeit geprüft und - wenn notwendig - systematisch abgeändert. Die Ausgabe des Konverters II ist der übersetzte Job (Abb.9)

```
XBA,BEN=IFI
UEBERSETZE,/..Quellprogramm..◊/,ALG60,-STD-,DAT2
MØNTIERE,DAT2,DAT3
DATEI,ERGEBNIS,SEQ,U100,U80Ø,P
STARTE,DAT3,-STD-,,,,1-ERGEBNIS
DRUCKE,DR-DC1,ERGEBNIS
XEN
```

Abb.9: übersetzter Job (Betriebssystem BS 3)

In der hier behandelten Version werden abgeschlossene Jobs in eine vorgegebene Zielkommandosprache übersetzt. Dieses Konzept lässt sich in mehreren Punkten erweitern:

- Der Job kann sich bei seiner Eingabe auf Dateien seines Eingaberechners beziehen. Durch Übernahme der dort enthaltenen Daten in die Jobbeschreibung hat man leicht die Möglichkeit, den Job zu komplettieren, d.h. zu einem abgeschlossenen Job zu erweitern.
- Durch ein Durchmustern des Quellprogramms nach bestimmten Anweisungen kann eine Übersetzung in gewissem Umfang auch bei der Definition von Systemanforderungen durch Anweisungen der Programmiersprache ermöglicht werden.
- Da in einem lastausgleichenden Rechnerverbundsystem für die Bearbeitung eines Jobs zu einem bestimmten Zeitpunkt im allgemeinen verschiedene Rechner in Frage kommen, sollte die Übersetzung der Ausgangsfolge simultan in die in Frage kommenden Kommandosprachen vorgenommen werden können, um während oder nach der Übersetzung den aufgrund der Jobstruktur geeignetsten Rechner auszuwählen.

Literatur:

[1] Final Report to SPARC from Ad-Hoc-Committee on Operating System Control Language; American National Standards Institute, 1971

MODULARITY OF NON-SEQUENTIAL PROGRAMS

K.-P.LÖHR

Abstract: Abstract procedures merely defined by their input/output behaviour are interconnected using buffered communication. Determinacy of such procedures is defined, and conditions for determinacy of composed procedures are given.

1. Introduction

If concurrent programs are exchanging information via shared variables, determinacy is not guaranteed a priori, yet it can be achieved by using the well-known synchronization mechanisms. However, the task of establishing determinacy should not be left to the programmer: testing a program with respect to determinacy is impossible by definition.

There is, however, an elementary tool for ensuring determinacy of interconnected program modules, namely buffered information exchange, which is investigated in this paper.

Certain "procedures" which are defined by their input/output behaviour will serve as program modules. So the functional aspect is stressed and the algorithmic aspect is ignored: an abstract procedure of this kind may be realized by any sequential or non-sequential algorithm with weak properties.

2. Synchronized Input/Output

Assume a process which communicates with its environment by referencing a set of external variables. These variables shall be capable of assuming a special value <u>nil</u> besides the regular values of some type. Let x be such a variable and r a local variable of the process. Two special "input/output operations" for the process are declared as follows:

```
proc receive(r,x);
    region x do begin await x ≠ nil; r:= x; x:= nil end

proc send(r,x);
    region x do begin await x = nil; x:= r end
```

(the language is a free style ALGOL with a form of conditional critical region introduced by Hoare and Brinch Hansen [Bri 72])
With respect to x these operations replace the usual "nondestructive-read" by a "read-out-when-possible" and the usual "overwrite" by a "write-in-when-possible". Disregarding implementation questions, efficiency, and scheduling, the power of such "buffered communication" between processes using common variables is characterized by the following:

1. The elementary producer/consumer problem with arbitrary number of participants is solved directly.
2. Inspection and modification of a common variable need not be programmed as a critical region. If all processes involved are performing actions like x:=f(x) (reading from x performed as "receive" and writing as "send"), these actions cannot overlap.
3. The pure synchronization effect of send and receive includes that of the well-known primitives signal and wait (or V and P) on Boolean semaphores.
4. The conventional read/write is not excluded but shows up as a special case of 2.:

   read(r,x) ≙ receive(r,x); send(r,x)

   write(r,x) ≙ receive(d,x); send(r,x)

   (where d is some dummy variable).

It should be noted, however, that the send/receive feature is not claimed to be a good general purpose synchronization tool for high level languages. It is rather a basic tool for information interchange between concurrent modules of arbitrary internal structure. The idea of interconnecting program modules in such a way first appeared in papers of Morenoff/McLean [MoLe 67] and Constantine [Con 68]. Similar mechanisms of buffered communication in operating systems are mainly known from MULTICS [SpOr 69] and from the RC 4000 Multiprogramming System [Bri 70]. The dynamic aspect of opening and closing conversations is essential to the communication features of an operating system. It will, however, not be dealt with in this paper, the stress is rather on abstract concurrent systems of fixed structure.

3. Procedures

Buffered communication by send/receive is not limited to sequential programs neither to arbitrary programs in any concrete sense whatsoever. This is why programs will be abstracted to their input/output behaviour in the sequel. The interconnection of programs then will be defined so that the buffering is modeled.

The input/output behaviour of an abstract program operating on some external variables can be described by giving a set of possible "runs" of that program, a run being a sequence of "actions", where an action is something like "input/output of value v from/to external variable x". This leads to a formal definition:

Let E and A be disjoint sets their elements being called <u>input variables</u> and <u>output variables</u> respectively. The elements of $X:=E\cup A$ are simply called <u>variables</u> or <u>formal parameters</u>. Let W be a set of <u>values</u>. Elements from $M:=X\times W$ are denoted by (x,w). M^{ω} denotes the set of all sequences of elements from M including the empty sequence ε and all infinite sequences; elements from M^{ω} are simply denoted by strings of elements from M.

<u>Definition 3.1</u>: For given E,A,W let $X:=E\cup A$, $M:=X\times W$. A set $\Pi\subset M^{\omega}$ is called a <u>procedure</u> on W if

(1) $a\in\Pi \wedge b<a \Rightarrow b\in\Pi$ [1])

(2) $a\in\Pi \wedge x\in E \wedge a(x,w)\in\Pi \Rightarrow \bigwedge_{v\in W} a(x,v)\in\Pi$

The elements of M are called <u>actions</u>, the elements of Π are called <u>runs</u>. The maximal elements in the ordered set $(\Pi,<)$ are called <u>complete</u> runs; the set of all complete runs is denoted by Ω.

The <u>history</u> of a run $r\in\Pi$ is the tuple of sequences of values delivered by r for the different variables; it will be denoted by $g(r)$. So e.g. $r=(1,a)(3,d)(1,b)(2,a)(3,c)$ has the history $g(r)=(ab,a,dc)$ (X may be assumed to be totally ordered). The projection $\lceil g(r)\rceil_x$ of some history $g(r)$ of some run r on some variable x is called the history of x during the run r. $\lceil g(r)\rceil_E$ is called <u>input</u> of r, $\lceil g(r)\rceil_A$ is called <u>output</u> of r.

Desirable are procedures having a certain degree of determinacy, in spite of their rather unpredictable behaviour. Complete runs with

[1]) $b<a :\Leftrightarrow$ b is prefix of a. $<$ is an ordering on M^{ω}.

identical inputs should give identical outputs; furthermore, it should not be accepted that two complete runs had compatible [1] but non-identical inputs. This leads us to the following definition:

<u>Definition 3.2</u>: (1) A procedure is called <u>determinate</u> if complete runs with compatible inputs have identical histories.

(2) A procedure is called <u>quasi-determinate</u> if runs with compatible inputs give compatible outputs.

Useful statements on determinate procedures are given in the following lemma. The proof of this lemma as well as of the other lemmas and theorems stated in this paper can be found in [Loe 72].

<u>Lemma 3.1</u>: (1) Determinacy implies quasi-determinacy.

(2) A procedure is determinate iff the following holds: For any two runs a,b with compatible inputs there exist complete runs c,d with $a<c$, $b<d$, $g(c)=g(d)$.

Simple determinate procedures are for instance all sequential programs (with the output uniquely determined by the input). Such procedures will here be called "sequential and definite":

<u>Definition 3.3</u>: A procedure is called <u>sequential</u> if

$$a(x,w)\in\Pi \wedge a(y,v)\in\Pi \Rightarrow x=y \quad ;$$

it is called <u>definite</u> if the additional condition $x\in A$ implies $w=v$.

<u>Lemma 3.2</u>: (1) A procedure Π is sequential and definite iff for arbitrary $a,b\in\Pi$: $\lceil g(a)\rceil_E \mid \lceil g(b)\rceil_E \Rightarrow a|b$ [1]

(2) A sequential and definite procedure is determinate.

Note that no assumptions were made concerning relationships between different runs of a procedure. So e.g. if $a<b$ holds ($a,b\in\Pi$), this does not necessarily mean that the procedure after run a had reached some "state", where it may continue with the rest of b. The concept of "state" is not involved here at all. Further remarks on this topic are made in [Loe 72].

[1]) $x,y\in W^\omega$ are called <u>compatible</u> - denoted by $x|y$ - if either $x<y$ or $y<x$. Two tuples $r=(x^i)_{i\in I}$, $s=(y^i)_{i\in I}$ of sequences $x^i,y^i\in W^\omega$ are called compatible - denoted by $r|s$, too - if $\bigwedge_{i\in I} x^i|y^i$.

Also, until now nothing has been said about the "real nature" of the input/output of those procedures. There is still room for a lot of real I/O mechanisms which are all covered by the model. As definition 3.3 shows, sequential procedures are simply characterized by the property that the variable of the "next action" is always uniquely determined. Non-sequential procedures allow for modeling the I/O behaviour of arbitrary non-sequential computational structures.

4. Interconnection of Procedures

Definition 4.1: A flow schema is a bipartite, finite, directed graph $F=(P,V,K)$ with multiple edges allowed. The nodes from P are called processes, the nodes from V are called variables. K is the set of edges.

A variable possessing only diverging edges is called input variable of F, a variable possessing only converging edges is called output variable; the corresponding sets of variables are denoted by E and A, furthermore we abbreviate $X:=E\cup A$, $C:=V-X$. The elements of X are called external variables, those of C are called internal variables of the flow schema F.

The set of neighbour variables of a process p is denoted by V_p, its elements are called actual parameters of p. The set of edges of a variable v is denoted by K_v.

Examples: (□ = process, ○ = internal variable, ⊗ = external)

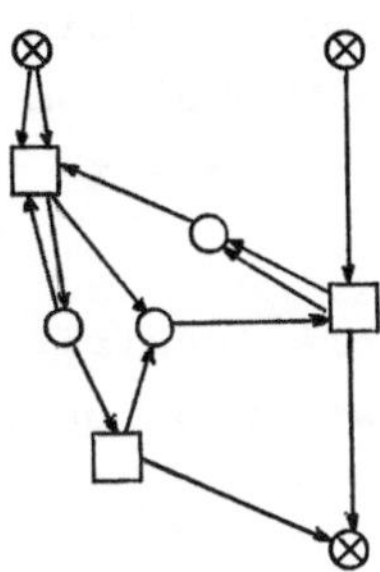

Fig. 1

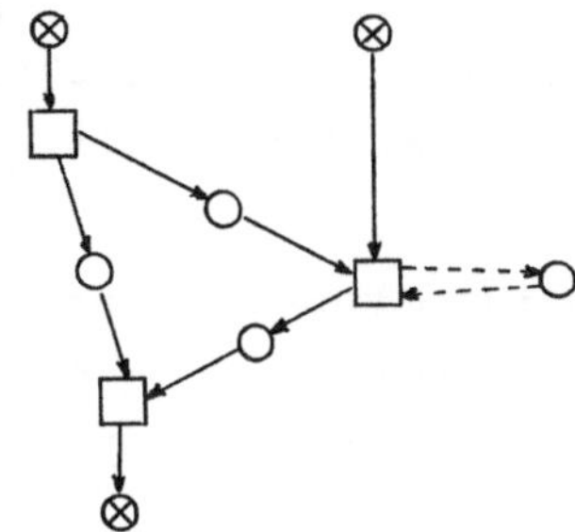

Fig. 2

With the syntactic structure of a flow schema an interpretation can be associated as follows:

1) A set W is given.
2) With each $p\in P$ some procedure Π^p on W is associated.

3) There is a bijection between the edges of a process and the formal parameters of the associated procedure having the property that converging edges belong to input variables of the procedure and diverging edges belong to output variables.

An interpreted flow schema gives rise to a corresponding "composed procedure Π over the flow schema F" which is built up in three steps as follows:

1. Build a set $\tilde{\Pi}$ as follows: actualize the formal parameters of the procedures Π^p by the edges of the flow schema; the variable sets of the procedures Σ^p thus obtained form a partition on K. All mixtures [1]) of complete runs, taken one from each Σ^p, form a set $\tilde{\Omega}$, and $\tilde{\Pi}$ will be the set of all prefixes of elements from $\tilde{\Omega}$. $\tilde{\Pi}$ is a procedure on W with variable set K.

2. Build a set $\overline{\Pi} \subset \tilde{\Pi}$ as follows: $a \in \overline{\Pi}$ iff for any internal variable $c \in C$ the following holds:
   a) If (k,w) with $k \in K_c$ is a read action and (l,v) is the last write action preceding (k,w) and satisfying $l \in K_c$, then w=v (This condition represents the ordinary read/write mechanism).
   b) Read and write actions on c are interchanging after having started with a write action. This condition together with a) represents the send/receive mechanism.

3. Get Π from $\overline{\Pi}$ by replacing each edge by the associated variable and then eliminating all actions on internal variables. Π is a procedure on W with variable set X.

It should be noted that any composed procedure may contain deadlocks or hangups (also with acyclic flow schemata) as known from the various concurrent systems dealt with in literature. This is not pursued here.

We will now introduce flow schemata with a special restricted structure and establish a theorem concerning preservation of quasi-determinacy with this kind of flow schemata.

<u>Definition 4.2</u>: A flow schema is called <u>branched</u> if there exists a variable possessing more than one diverging or more than one

---

[1]) $z \in M^\omega$ is called a <u>mixture</u> of $x^1, x^2, .., x^n \in M^\omega$ if the x^i are non-empty disjoint subsequences of z and there is no proper subsequence of z disjoint to all x^i.

converging edge (see fig. 1). Otherwise it is called unbranched (see fig. 2).

Theorem 4.1: A procedure over an unbranched flow schema is quasi-determinate if all component procedures are.

Quasi-determinacy, however, is only a necessary condition for determinacy (see lemma 3.1(1)). The following example shows that it is not sufficient. Look at fig. 3. All complete runs of Σ^1 are giving variable sequences "axbyuc" or "byuaxc", each history of a run of the first kind also being possible with a run of the second kind, and vice versa. All complete runs of Σ^2 are giving the variable sequence "xyu". Let Σ^1 and Σ^2 be determinate (which is possible, as can readily be seen). Then the complete runs of the composed procedure Π are giving two possible variable sequences:

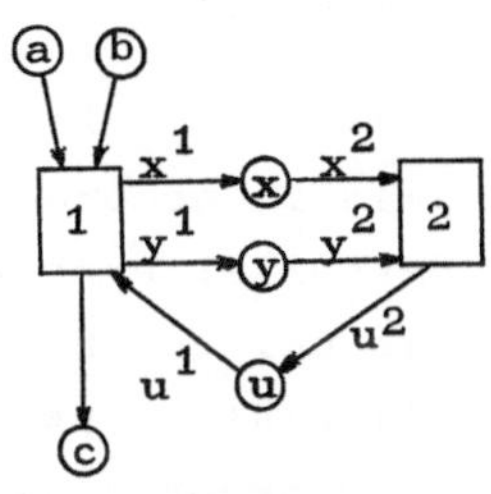

Fig. 3

"b" from by^1 , "abc" from $ax^1by^1x^2y^2u^2u^1c$

$ax^1bx^2y^1y^2u^2u^1c$

$ax^1x^2by^1y^2u^2u^1c$

For an arbitrary run of the first kind there exists a run of the second kind yielding the same b-value, and vice versa. This shows directly that Π is not determinate.

The deadlock produced by "by^1" is a "sporadic" or "non-determinate" one: it will not occur if without changing the b-value a run of type "abc" would be chosen. This non-determinate occurence of sporadic deadlocks obviously has to be avoided. So we have to look for such properties of procedures which make sporadic deadlocks impossible.

5. Preservation of Determinacy

Definition 5.1: A procedure Π is called persistent if the following holds:

$$(1) \quad \left.\begin{array}{l} a(x,w) \in \Pi \\ \wedge\ a(y,v) \in \Pi \\ \wedge\ x \neq y \end{array}\right\} \Rightarrow a(x,w)(y,v) \in \Pi$$

$$(2) \quad \left.\begin{array}{l} a(x,w) \in \Pi \\ \wedge\ ac \in \Omega \end{array}\right\} \Rightarrow c \text{ contains some } (x,v)$$

Definition 5.2: Equivalence of two runs $a,b \in \Pi$:

$$a \sim b \;:\Leftrightarrow\; \{c \mid ac \in \Pi\} = \{d \mid bd \in \Pi\}$$

($\sim$ is an equivalence relation)

Definition 5.3: A procedure Π is called commutative if the following holds:

$$\left.\begin{array}{l} a(x,w)(y,v) \in \Pi \\ \wedge\; a(y,v)(x,w) \in \Pi \\ \wedge\; x \neq y \end{array}\right\} \;\Rightarrow\; a(x,w)(y,v) \sim a(y,v)(x,w)$$

The notions of persistence and commutativity were chosen in accordance with the respective notions from Karp/Miller's "Parallel Program Schemata" [KaMi 69]. The analog to definition 5.1(2) is called "finite delay property" by Karp/Miller yet is not a constituent of persistence in their paper. - Persistent and commutative procedures will be abbreviated "PCP" in the sequel. An important lemma for further investigations on PCP's is the following one:

Lemma 5.1: For arbitrary runs a,b of a PCP the following holds:

(1) $g(a)=g(b) \Leftrightarrow$ there exists a sequence of runs a^k with

$$g(a^k)=g(a), \quad {}_k a^k = {}_k b \qquad (k=0,1,2,..)$$ [1]

(2) $g(a)=g(b) \Rightarrow a \sim b$

Persistence and commutativity will exclude the possibility of sporadic deadlock. Note that our counterexample in section 4 involves a procedure Σ^1 which is not persistent. Similar counterexamples can be given for procedures not being commutative.

First we give a statement which shows the strength of the concepts of persistence and commutativity. Then we will proceed to central theorems on determinacy of composed procedures.

Theorem 5.1: A definite PCP is determinate.

The theorem is proved using lemmas 3.1(2) and 5.1(1). Construction of the sequence of runs a^k is achieved by especially taking into account definition 5.1(2). This theorem is a fortiori also valid for quasi-determinate PCP's since quasi-determinacy implies definiteness.

[1]) ${}_k b$ denotes the prefix of length k of b

Theorem 5.2: A procedure over an unbranched flow schema is a quasi-determinate PCP if all procedures involved are.

Corollary: A procedure over an unbranched flow schema is a determinate PCP if all procedures involved are.

The proof of theorem 5.2 can be given using theorem 4.1 and lemma 5.1.

The theorems stated above make it possible to successively build larger and more complex determinate procedures from smaller and simpler ones, starting with certain "atoms" which are known to be determinate PCP's. Possible atoms are for instance definite sequential procedures which are trivially persistent, commutative, and determinate. These were used in the paper of Morenoff/McLean initially mentioned.

Interpreted unbranched flow schemata may be regarded as generalized "program graphs" [Rod 67] or "graph programs" [Ada 68]. Those graph programs are a priori determinate, this notion being used in a somewhat different sense from how it is used here. The corollary demonstrates the structural affinity of those special composed procedures and the graph programs.

On the other hand, much unlike the graph programs, flow schemata allow for more general composed procedures whose determinacy either is not required or has to be proved for each special case. The situation is then similar to that with "asynchronous computational structures" (Luconi [Luc 68]) or "parallel program schemata". In analogy to theorem 2.6 of Luconi or corollary 2.1 of Karp/Miller the following theorem 5.3 can be proved which is giving a sufficient condition for determinacy of arbitrarily composed procedures.

Theorem 5.3: In the corollary above the unbranchedness can be replaced by the following condition:

$$\left.\begin{array}{l} a(k,w) \in \overline{\Pi} \\ \wedge\ a(l,v) \in \overline{\Pi} \\ \wedge\ k \neq l \end{array}\right\} \Rightarrow \text{ k and l belong to different variables}$$

The results stated in this paper are also related to those of Patil in [Pat 70], who made similar investigations on interconnected Petri-nets. The generalization of our results to multi-item and infinite buffers makes no difficulties. Apart from slight logical differences concerning avoidance of some kind of deadlock, multi-item buffers are mainly giving a practical advantage in real systems, namely that of compensating different speeds of the processes involved. This may be useful not only with the producer/consumer problem but also in certain other cases, for instance updating (say by x:=b*x) a common variable which is "factorized" into several constituents, or taking items of resources from a common pool.

References

[Ada 68] D.A. Adams: A Computation Model with Data Flow Sequencing. Ph.D. thesis, Stanford Univ. 1968

[Con 68] L.L. Constantine: Control of Sequence and Parallelism in Modular Programs. SJCC 1968, AFIPS Conf. Proc. Vol. 32

[Bri 70] P. Brinch Hansen: The Nucleus of a Multiprogramming System. CACM 13,4 (1970)

[Bri 72] P. Brinch Hansen: Structured Multiprogramming. CACM 15,7 (1972)

[KaMi 69] R.M. Karp/R.E. Miller: Parallel Program Schemata. JCSS 3 (1969)

[Loe 72] K.-P. Loehr: Gepufferte Kommunikation in abstrakten Systemen. Bericht BS 2, Fachber. Kybern., Techn. Univ. Berlin 1972

[Luc 68] F.L. Luconi: Asynchronous Computational Structures. Ph.D. thesis, Project MAC, M.I.T. 1968

[MoLe 67] E. Morenoff/J.E. McLean: Interprogram Communications, Program String Structures, and Buffer Files. SJCC 1967, AFIPS Conf. Proc. Vol. 30

[Pat 70] S.S. Patil: Closure Properties of Interconnections of Determinate Systems. Project MAC Conf. on Concurrent Systems and Parallel Computation 1970

[Rod 67] J.E. Rodriguez-Bezos: A Graph Model for Parallel Computations. Sc.D. thesis, Project MAC, M.I.T. 1967

[SpOr 69] M.J. Spier/E.I. Organick: The Multics Interprocess Communication Facility. ACM 2nd Symp. on Operating System Principles, Princeton 1969

CLASSES OF OPTIMAL SCHEDULES FOR MULTIPROCESSOR SYSTEMS

S.SCHINDLER

Summary

Given a multiprocessor system consisting of M identical processors. Given N tasks and precedence rules for the execution of these tasks, represented as a finite, weighted forest G (whose paths are directed from leaves to roots). Given finally an upper bound $T > 0$ for the total processing time of G by the M processors. We assume that preemptions are allowed.

In an elementary way for this model 1) precise lower bounds $T_{min}(G;M)$ and $M_{min}(G;T)$ are developed; 2) and for $T \geq T_{min}(G;M)$ or $M \geq M_{min}(G;T)$ the 'admissible' processor assignments and their maximal running times are derived, and 3) the structure and therefore the set of all schedules is described that lead to complete processing of all tasks of G by M processors within time T.

1. Introduction

The problem of scheduling N tasks - the operational precedence structure of which is represented as a finite, directed, weighted forest G (paths being directed from leaves to roots) - on a multiprocessor system consisting of M identical processors is studied. The weight W_i of node i, $1 \leq i \leq N$, is regarded as the processing time of the task represented by node i. Assuming that preemptions are allowed we are interested in the class $\underline{A}(G;M;T)$ of all schedules for complete processing of G by the M processors within an arbitrary given time T.

The subsequent sections show that all elements of $\underline{A}(G;M;T)$ have a simple description and that $T_{min}(G;M) = \min \{T > 0: \underline{A}(G;M;T) \neq \Phi\}$ and $M_{min}(G;T) = \min \{M \in Z^{+}: \underline{A}(G;M;T) \neq \Phi\}$ can easily be computed. Similar results can be obtained if G is not a forest but an anti-forest or if the processors operate at different speeds. As the complexity of the algorithms grows considerably in both cases these problems are investigated separately (see [6] and [4]).

As the construction of time-optimal schedules is known for forests - namely HUs schedules (nonpreemptive, for equally weighted trees, [1]) and MUNTZ/COFFMANs schedule (preemptive, [2] - a justification of our interest seems to be necessary and is given in [7].

2. Definitions and Notation

G always denotes a directed weighted forest, where the weights belong to the nodes but not to the arrows. We do not draw G in the usual way (see figure 1) but in the way introduced in [3] and shown in figure 2. It should be noticed that the lines in figure 2 (representing the weighted nodes) are placed as low as possible, their lengths representing the weights of the nodes; the dashed lines are used to represent the precedence rules in G unambiguously. The subsequent theorems are derived for the problem represented by G, i.e. no external constraints. But they are valid for the problem shown in figure 3, too, where - due to external reasons - some tasks (T_1 and T_3 for example) cannot be placed lower than indicated by light lines.

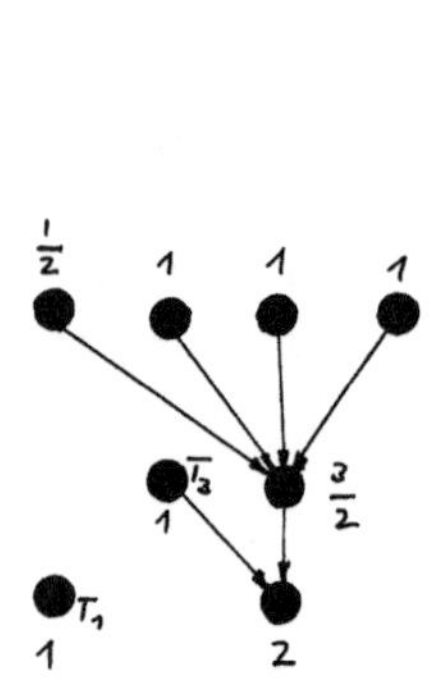

Figure 1
Usual representation of G

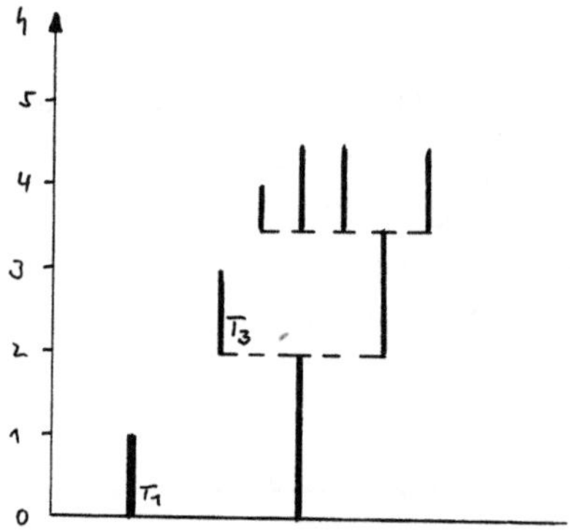

Figure 2
Representation of G used in this paper (without external constraints)

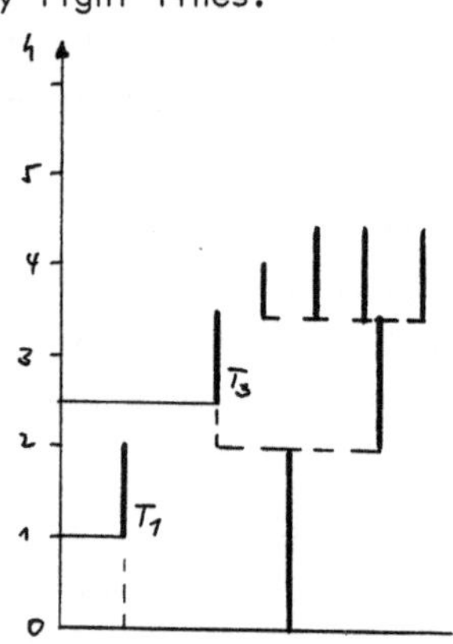

Figure 3
External constraints indicated by light horizontal lines[1)]

The length of a path in G is defined to be the sum of the weights of the nodes on that path. The height of G, denoted H(G), is defined to be the length of the longest path(s) in G. A node without a predecessor is called a free node; a node without a successor is called an end node. We define the height of a node to be the length of the path from this node to an end node in G (both nodes included). Let $\overline{G}$ denote the sum of the weights of all nodes in G. Let U(G;h) denote the part of G below the 'height-line h', $h \in [0,H(G)]$, (see figure 4). Let a piecewise constant integer function w(G;h) be defined as w(G;h) = number of tasks cut by height-line h, $h \in [0,H(G)]$. For example we have in figure 2: w(G;0.5) = 2, w(G;1.5) = 1, w(G;4.2) = 3. BARSKIY [5] interprets w(G;h) as the 'load density function' of G. Obviously

$$\overline{U}(G;h) = \int_0^h w(G;h')\cdot dh', \text{ where } \int\ldots \text{ means the RIEMANN-Integral.}$$

For simplicity we call weighted nodes 'tasks'; the weight of a node we call 'length

---

1) We assume the external constraints to be such that all tasks of G start lower than H(G).

of the task'. We assume that all tasks in G have positive lengths. We can make a processor execute any free task by assigning this free task and the processor to

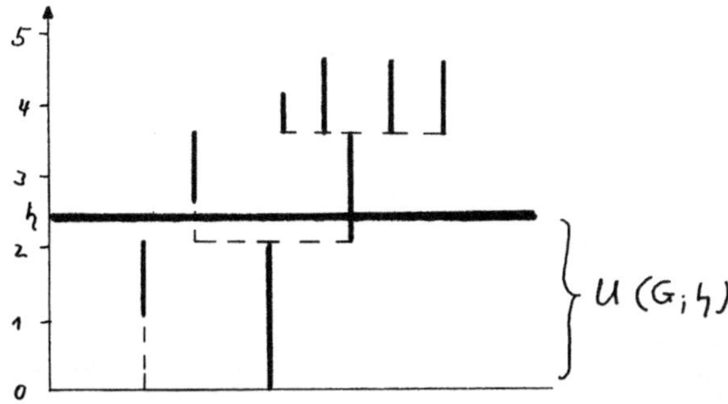

Figure 4

each other. The processor then reduces the length of the task and we say 'the processor processes the task'. The processing of a task by a processor - i.e. the reduction of the length of the task - takes place with a constant, positive and finite speed. The result of such a processor assignment is the original task reduced in length. If the length of a task is reduced to 0, the task, together with its outgoing arrow (if the task is not an end node), is deleted from the graph. The units of length and time are determined such that one processor reduces a task by one unit of length in one time unit; beyond that we do not care about the system of units. If a processor assigned to a task is interrupted before the length of the task has been reduced to 0, we call this a 'preemption' of the processor or of the task. Given a schedule to process G, G_t denotes the portion of the graph that remains to be processed after time $t \geq 0$.

3. A Geometric Representation of the Problem

Figure 5a shows a plot of the function $\overline{U}(G;h)$ versus h. Note that below the horizontal axis G is drawn as explained above but rotated 90°. For a given $h, h \in [0,H(G)]$, let $R(G;h)$ denote the ordered pair $(h,\overline{U}(G;h))$. Let $\underline{R}(G) = \{R(G;h) | h \in [0,H(G)]\}$. $R(G;h)$ is called end corner of $\underline{R}(G)$ iff there is a task ending on height-line h. For a given G let $\underline{E}(G) = \{h' | R(G;h')$ is an end corner of $\underline{R}(G)\} \cup \{H(G)\}$.

We now investigate how $\underline{R}(G_t)$, $0 \leq t \leq \varepsilon, \varepsilon > 0$, changes if one or more processors are assigned to tasks in G_t. Let $E = R(G_t;H(G_t))$.
As long as $M', 0 < M' \leq M$ processors are assigned to free tasks of G, E moves (see figure 5a)

- down vertically if $H(G_t)$ remains unchanged,
- down along a line with slope M' if $H(G_t)$ is reduced.

E cannot move in any other way.
The movement of an endcorner during processing of G_t is still simpler: it moves ver-

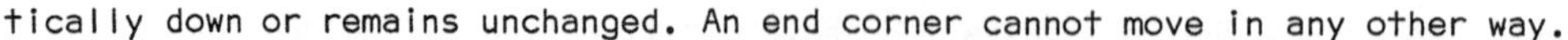

tically down or remains unchanged. An end corner cannot move in any other way.

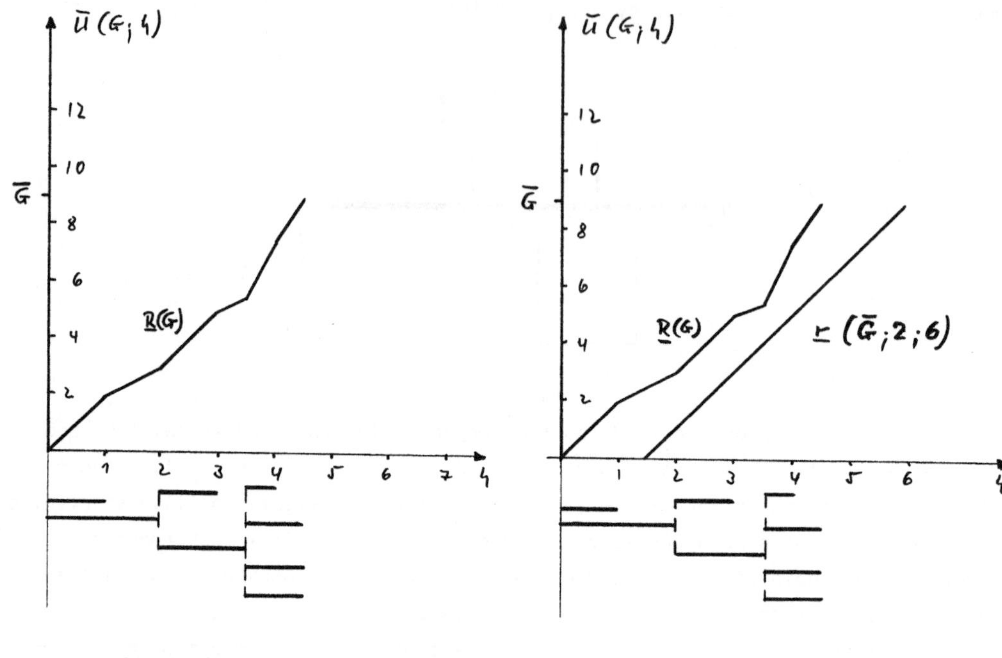

Figure 5a

Figure 5b

Suppose only one processor is assigned to a task of G of height h', where h' < H(G), for a duration $\varepsilon > 0$. Then the height of the task is reduced from h' to h'-ε. We have for $t \in [0,\varepsilon]$:

$$R(G_t;h) = \begin{cases} (h,\overline{U}(G;h)) & \forall h \in [0,h'-t] \\ (h,\overline{U}(G;h) - [t+h-h']) & \forall h \in [h'-t,h'] \\ (h,\overline{U}(G;h) - t) & \forall h \in [h',H(G)]. \end{cases}$$

This knowledge about the changes of $\underline{R}(G)$ during processing tasks of G finally suggests to introduce the line $\underline{r}(\overline{G};M;T)$ that passes through the point $(T,\overline{G})$ and has the slope M, where M is the number of processors in the system and $T > 0$ is an upper bound for the processing time for G. Let $r(\overline{G};M;T;h) = \overline{G} - M\cdot(T-h)$. From figure 5b we immediately see that for given M $\underline{R}(G) \cap \underline{r}(\overline{G};M;T) = \Phi$ if T is chosen large enough and that $\exists h' \in (0,H(G)) : \overline{U}(G;h') < r(\overline{G};M';T';h')$ if M' and T' are chosen small enough (unless we had $w(G;h) = 1 \;\forall h \in [0,H(G)]$). From this second situation a simple consequence can be derived: in this case $\overline{G} - \overline{U}(G;h') > M'\cdot(T'-h')$ and therefore it lasts longer than T' - h' to complete processing of all tasks higher than h'. As U(G;h') has height h', the complete processing of its tasks lasts at least the time h'. It follows that M' processors cannot complete processing of G in the time T'. Thus we obtain

Theorem 1:

Let G be an arbitrary weighted forest of height $H = H(G)$, the paths of which are directed from leaves to roots.
For $M \in Z^+$ let $\overline{T}_{min}(G;M) = \min \{T \geq H: d(G;M;T;h) \geq 0 \ \forall \ h \in [0,H]\}$ and for $T \geq H$ let $\overline{M}_{min}(G;T) = \min \{M \in Z^+ : d(G;M;T;h) \geq 0 \ \forall \ h \in [0,H]\}$.
Let $d(G;M;T;h) = \overline{U}(G;h) - r(\overline{G};M;T;h)$.

A) Given a schedule that causes a complete processing of G by M processors within the time T. Then $d(G_t;M;T-t;h) \geq 0$ for any $t \in [0,T]$ and any $h \in [0,H(G_t)]$.

B) Given M processors. Then $T_{min}(G;M) \geq \overline{T}_{min}(G;M)$.

C) Given an upper bound $T \geq H(G)$ for the total processing time for G. Then $M_{min}(G;T) \geq \overline{M}_{min}(G;T)$.

Remarks:

a) We see now that - if G' is obtained from G by 'shifting nodes up', for example like in figure 3 - we have $\overline{T}_{min}(G';M) \geq \overline{T}_{min}(G;M)$ and $\overline{M}_{min}(G';T) \geq \overline{M}_{min}(G;T)$.

b) Obviously theorem 1 would remain valid if we generalized the definitions for tree-structured graphs used until now for G being a finite, directed, acyclic, weighted graph.

c) Theorem 1 is valid for preemptive and nonpreemptive schedules.

d) Instead of checking all $h \in [0,H]$ it is easily seen (see [7]) that it suffices to check all h from the finite set $\underline{E}(G)$ (for B) and C)) or the finite set $\underline{E}(C_t)$ (for A)).

Several theorems concerning very similar problems are known already ([1,2,3,5,7]), but they all are either less general or more complicated. Moreover it is not clear at all in most cases how to construct the schedules needed from the given G,T and M, whereas for G all suitable schedules can easily be found by applying the above theorem. Before showing that we still simplify our notation: A given <u>triple (G;M;T)</u> is called <u>p-admissible</u> iff G is like in theorem 1, $M \in Z^+$, $T \geq H$ and $M \geq \overline{M}_{min}(G;T)$ or equivalently $T \geq \overline{T}_{min}(G;M)$. For a given p-admissible triple (G;M;T) an assignment X of M' processors to M' free tasks of G, $0 \leq M' \leq M$, is called <u>p-admissible</u> iff there exists a $t > 0$ such that the triple $(G_t;M;T-t)$ is p-admissible, where G_t results from processing G for the time t according assignment X. From these definitions, theorem 1 and the above considerations about the changes of $\underline{R}(G)$ while processing G theorem 2 follows immediately. Theorem 2 shows that- given an arbitrary p-admissible triple (G;M;T) - it is no problem to describe the set of all p-admissible assignments X for this triple.

Theorem 2:

Given an arbitrary p-admissible triple (G;M;T). Let H = H(G).

A) If $d(G;M;T;h) > 0 \ \forall h \in \underline{E}(G)$, then each assignment X of M' processors is p-admissible, $0 \leq M' \leq M$.

B) If $d(G;M;T;h) > 0 \ \forall h \in \underline{E}(G) \cap [0,H)$ and $d(G;M;T;H) = 0$, then an assignment X of M' processors is p-admissible iff the w(H) tasks of height H are assigned, $w(H) \leq M' \leq M$.

C) If $\exists h' \in \underline{E}(G) \cap [0,H) : d(G;M;T;h') = 0$ and $d(G;M;T;h) > 0 \ \forall h \in \underline{E}(G) \cap (h',H]$, then an assignment X is p-admissible iff all M processors are assigned and the heights of the M assigned tasks are greater than h'.

D) If $\exists h' \in \underline{E}(G) \cap [0,H) : d(G;M;T;h') = 0$ and $d(G;M;T;h) > 0 \ \forall h \in \underline{E}(G) \cap (h',H)$ and $d(G;M;T;H) = 0$, then an assignment X is p-admissible iff all M processors are assigned and the heigths of the M assigned tasks are greater than h' and all tasks of height H are assigned.

4. The Algorithm σ and the Set A(G;M;T)

Let (G;M;T) be an arbitrary p-admissible triple and let X be an arbitrary p-admissible assignment of M' processors to free tasks of G, $0 \leq M' \leq M$. The algorithm σ (defined in theorem 3) then computes a $t^X > 0$, i.e. $\sigma : (G;M;T;X) \rightarrow t^X > 0$ such that the triples $(G_t;M;T-t)$ are p-admissible $\forall t \in [0,t^X]$ and are not p-admissible $\forall t > t^X$ if the assignment remains unchanged. t^X is called the time limit (for the assignment period) of assignment X. By means of this algorithm σ it will become obvious how to determine all elements from $\underline{A}(G;M;T)$ (theorem 4).

Let v be the length of the shortest of the tasks assigned by X. Let h_j, $1 \leq j \leq p \leq M'$, be the height-lines on which the processors start, where $H(G) \geq h_p > h_{p-1} > \ldots > h_1 > 0$; let $m_j > 0$ be the number of processors starting on height-line h_j, $1 \leq j \leq p$. Let k_i, $1 \leq i \leq q$, denote those elements in $\underline{E}(G) \cap [h_1-v,H(G)]$ for which - after indexing them such that $H(G) = k_1 > k_2 > \ldots > k_q \geq h_1-v$ - we have $D_1 > D_2 > \ldots > D_q$, where $D_i = \overline{U}(G;k_i) - r(\overline{G};M;T;k_i)$, $1 \leq i \leq q$. For $1 \leq i \leq q$ let f_i be the number of h_j for which $h_j \leq k_i$, $1 \leq j \leq p$. Then

$M_i = \sum_{j=1}^{f_i} m_j$ is the number of processors that are assigned 'below' or 'left of' k_i

(immediately after starting the assignment X), $1 \leq i \leq q$. Together with an assignment X the numbers M',v,q,p,h_j,m_j $(1 \leq j \leq p)$, k_i,f_i and M_i $(1 \leq i \leq q)$ are defined and can easily be computed. During the assignment period of X the numbers M',v,p,q, m_j $(1 \leq j \leq p)$ and k_i $(2 \leq i \leq q)$ are not changed. But as the h_j are reduced during the assignment period of X, the f_i and M_i might be changed, too. This occurs iff there is a $1 \leq j \leq p$, a $1 \leq i \leq q$ and a $t_{ij} \in (0,v)$ such that $h_j - t_{ij} = k_i$. For $1 \leq i \leq q$ and $t \in (0,v)$ let $e_i(t)$ be the number of such $t_{ij} \in (0,t)$. On the interval $(0,v)$ we then define piecewise constant integer functions

$M_i(t) = M_i + \sum_{l=1}^{e_i(t)} m_{f_i+l}$, where the sum vanishes if $e_i(t) = 0$, $1 \leq i \leq q$. Thus $M_i(t)$

is the number of processors that are assigned 'below' or 'left of' k_i at time $t \in (0,v)$ after starting the assignment X.

After the time interval of length dt at the beginning of the assignment period of X the point $(T,\overline{G})$ defining the line $\underline{r}(\overline{G};M;T)$ is to be replaced by $(T-dt,\overline{G}-M'\cdot dt)$. That means that the line $\underline{r}(\overline{G};M;T)$ is shifted to the left for $(1-M'/M)\cdot dt$ during this time interval and therefore that the distances $D_i = \overline{U}(G;k_i) - r(\overline{G};M;T;k_i)$ are reduced by $(1-M'/M)\cdot dt\cdot M$ in this time interval of length dt. On the other hand the point $(k_i,\overline{U}(G;k_i))$ of $\underline{R}(G)$ is shifted vertically down for $M_i\cdot dt$. It follows that during this time interval of length dt the D_i are reduced for $(M-M'+M_i)\cdot dt$, $2 \leq i \leq q$. D_1 is reduced in the same way iff H(G) is not reduced; but D_1 is constant as long as all tasks of G_+ with height $H(G_+)$ are assigned.

Before defining the algorithm σ we still change the indices of the t_{ij} and introduce the abbreviations $\Delta_i(t_s)$ and Δ^s. For a given assignment X let $t' = H(G)-h'$, where h' is the height of a highest unassigned task. Let $t_{s'} = t'$.
Let $\{t_s,\ s = 1,2,\dots,S,\ s \neq s'\} = \bigcup_{i=2}^{q} \{t_{ij}, j = 1,\dots,e_i(v-0)\}$ such that $0 < t_1 < \dots < t_S$

$$s' = \begin{cases} S+2 \text{ if } t' \geq v, \\ 0 \text{ if } t' = 0 \\ \text{between 1 and } S \text{ if } t' \in (0,v). \end{cases}$$

For $1 \leq i \leq q$ and $s = 1,2,\dots,S+1$ let

$$\Delta_i(t_s) = \begin{cases} D_1 \text{ if } i = 1 \text{ and } s \leq s' \\ D_i - (M-M'+M_i(t_{s-1}))\cdot(t_s - t_{s-1}) \text{ otherwise, where } t_{S+1} = v. \end{cases}$$

Let $\Delta^s = \min\{\Delta_i(t_s)/1 \leq i \leq q \wedge i \neq 1 \text{ if } s \leq s'\}$.
These notations and theorem 1 and 2 give us

<u>Theorem 3:</u>

Given an arbitrary p-admissible triple (G;M;T) and an arbitrary p-admissible assignment X of M' processors to M' free tasks of G, $0 \leq M' \leq M$. Then the algorithm σ in figure 6 determines the time limit $t^X \in (0,v]$ of assignment X.

Theorem 4:

Given an arbitrary p-admissible triple (G;M;T). Then

a) $\underline{A}(G;M;T) \neq \Phi$, i.e. $T_{min}(G;M) = \overline{T}_{min}(G;M) \wedge M_{min}(G;T) = \overline{M}_{min}(G;T)$.

b) each schedule of $\underline{A}(G;M;T)$ has the structure described in figure 7.

c) A special schedule of $\underline{A}(G;M;T)$ is characterized by the special choice of X (in 1)) and $\overline{t}$ (in 2)).

d) The total number of preemptions needed for complete processing of G is finite if $\overline{t} = t^X$ is chosen for each (arbitrary but p-admissible) assignment X.

Proof:

Each schedule with the structure described in the diagram (for example: arbitrary choices of $\overline{t}$ and p-admissible X) causes a complete processing of G by M processors within time T, due to the definition of $\underline{r}(\overline{G}_t;M;T-t)$ $\forall t \in [0,T]$ and σ. Therefore such a schedule belongs to $\underline{A}(G;M;T)$.
Now let $A \in \underline{A}(G;M;T)$. Due to theorems 1,2 and 3 A then has the structure described in the diagram. For the proof of d) see [7].

Bounds on the number of preemptions involved by a schedule $A \in \underline{A}(G;M;T)$ are given in [7] for $T = T_{min}(G;M)$. There it is shown, too, that HUs algorithm (in certain cases) and MUNTZ/COFFMANs algorithm belong to $\underline{A}(G;M;T_{min}(G;M))$.

For an arbitrary admissible triple (G;M;T) by theorems 2 and 3 the frame is constituted within which all schedules for complete processing of G with M processors within time T can be found. Note that both theorems do not refer to concrete assignments and their assignment periods but to assignments X and their time limits t^X, where X is to be regarded as a 'noninterpreted assignment function' symbol and t^X as a symbol the value of which is determined (by algorithm σ) after X becomes interpreted. Figure 7 therefore could be regarded as a 'scheduling scheme'.

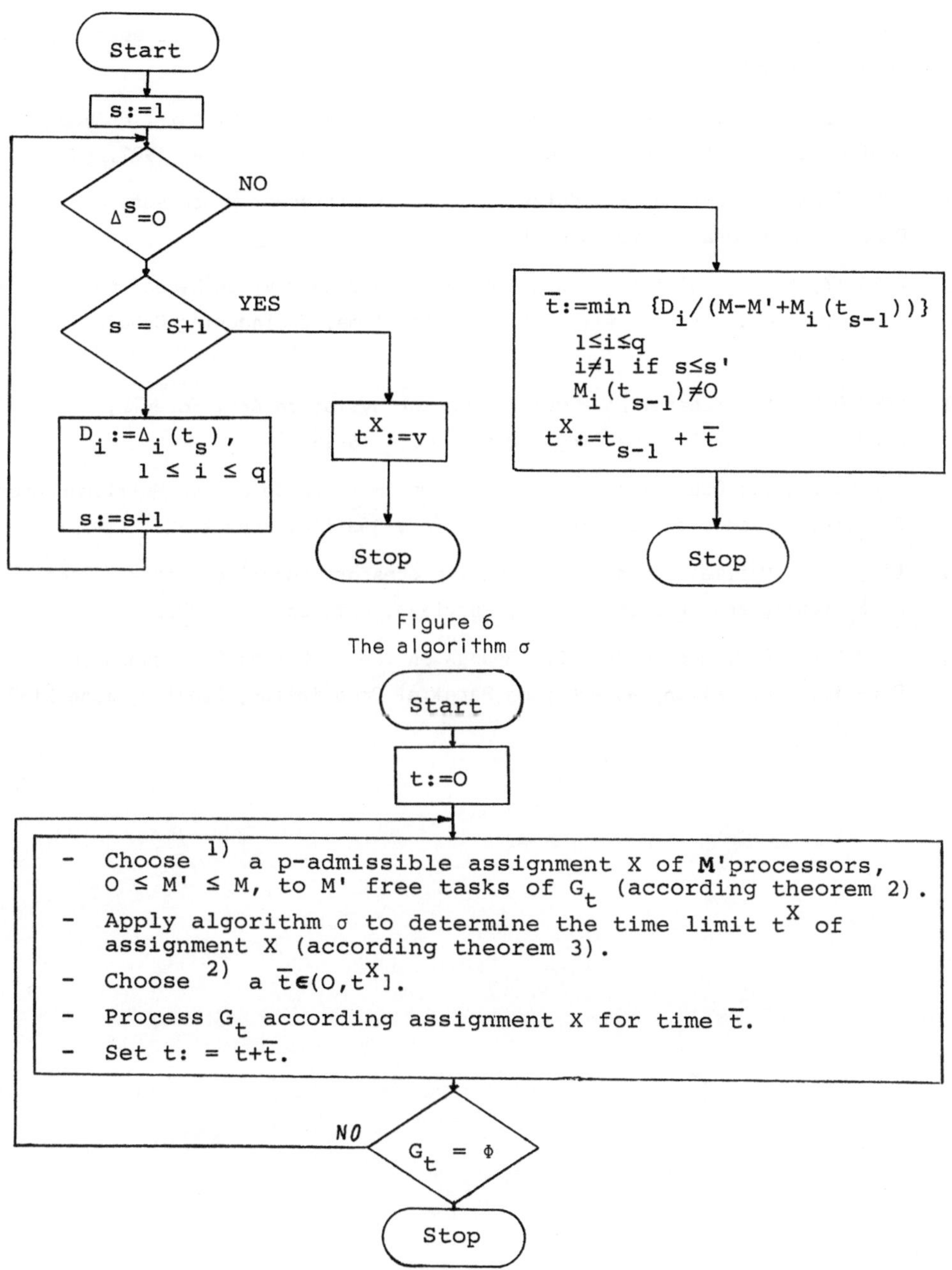

Figure 6
The algorithm σ

Figure 7
Structure of an element of $\underline{A}(G;M;T)$

References

[1] HU, T.C.: Parallel Sequencing and Assembly line Problems, Operations Research 9, No.6 (1961), 841-848.

[2] COFFMAN, E.G. and GRAHAM, R.L.: Optimal Scheduling for Two-Processor Systems, Acta Informatica 2 (1972).

[3] SCHINDLER, S.: On Optimal Schedules for Multiprocessor Systems, Princeton Conference on Information Sciences and Systems, March 23-24, 1972.

[4] SCHINDLER, S.: Optimal Schedules for Several Different Processors on Computational Graphs, to be published.

[5] BARSKIY, A.B.: Minimizing the Number of Computing Devices Needed to Realize a Computational Process within a Specified Time, Engineering Cybernetics, No.6, 1968.

[6] SCHINDLER, S.: Scheduling a Multiprocessor System on Anti-Forests, SIAM-SIGNUM 1972 Fall Meeting, Austin, Oct. 16-18.

[7] SCHINDLER, S.: Quantitative Aspects of Optimal Schedules for Multiprocessor Systems, Workshop on Parallel Computation, Seattle, June 21-23, (1972).

[8] LIU, C.L.: Optimal Scheduling on Multiprocessor Computing Systems, Conference on Switching and Automata Theory, Maryland, Oct. 25-27, (1972).

[9] FERNANDEZ, E.B. and BUSSEL, B.: Bounds on the Number of Processors in Parallel Computation, Workshop on Parallel Computation, Seattle, June 21-23, (1972).

DURCHSATZOPTIMALE RECHNERKERN- UND TRANSPORTKANALVERGABE FÜR EIN RECHNERMODELL MIT ZWEI ARBEITSSPEICHERPLÄTZEN

H.-J.KÜSPERT

1. Einleitung

Ein stapelverarbeitendes System besteht aus einem Rechner und einer Menge von Aufaben, die vom Rechner bearbeitet werden müssen. Nun ist ein Rechner ein derart komplexes Gebilde, daß man stark vereinfachte Modelle betrachten muß, wenn man Aussagen über das Verhalten des Systems gewinnen will. Ebenso bestehen Aufgaben aus so verschiedenartigen Anforderungen an die einzelnen Betriebsmittel, aus denen sich der Rechner zusammensetzt, daß man sich auf stark vereinfachte Modellaufgaben beschränken muß. Als dritte Komponente geht schließlich noch der Zugangsprozeß neuer Aufgaben in das Modell des stapelverarbeitenden Systems ein, der ebenfalls vereinfacht werden muß. So erhält man schließlich das Modell SVS eines stapelverarbeitenden Systems, das sich zusammensetzt aus Rechnermodell R, Zugangsprozeß Z und Aufgabenprofil A :

$$SVS = (R, Z, A) \tag{1.1}$$

Für stapelverarbeitende Systeme ist die Durchsatzmaximierung als Optimierungsziel allgemein anerkannt. Dieses Optimierungsziel wird für das Modell übernommen. Da das Modell jetzt fest gegeben ist, ist der Bereich, auf dem optimiert werden soll, die Menge S aller Möglichkeiten, die Betriebsmittel des Rechners den Aufgaben zur Verfügung zu stellen, die Menge S aller möglichen Betriebsmittelzuteilungsstrategien. Es wird also eine Strategie $s^* \in S$ gesucht mit

$$\text{Durchsatz}(SVS, s^*) = \max_{s \in S} \text{Durchsatz}(SVS, s) \tag{1.2}$$

Diese Strategie s^* wird dadurch ermittelt, daß in jedem möglichen Zustand, den das Modell annehmen kann, untersucht wird, welche der vorhandenen Möglichkeiten, die Betriebsmittel zu vergeben, den Durchsatz maximiert.

2. Modellbeschreibung

Um die gestellte Aufgabe lösen zu können, nämlich die Strategie zu bestimmen, die den Durchsatz maximiert, ist es zunächst erforderlich, das Modell SVS zu beschreiben. Das geschieht durch Beschreibung der drei Komponenten des Modells. Erst im Anschluß daran ist es möglich, Systemzustände, Politiken und Strategien zu definieren.

In Bild 1 ist das Rechnermodell R dargestellt. R besteht aus den passiven Betriebsmitteln Hintergrund- und Arbeitsspeicher und den aktiven Betriebsmitteln

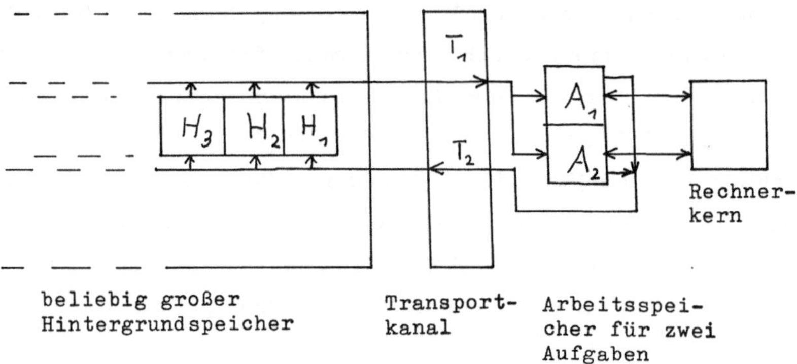

Bild 1: Das Rechnermodell R

Rechnerkern und Transportkanal. Der für Aufgaben verfügbare Teil des Hintergrundspeichers wird so groß angenommen, daß in ihm stets alle zu bearbeitenden Aufgaben gespeichert werden können. Der Arbeitsspeicher dagegen sei so groß, daß in dem verfügbaren Teil stets genau zwei Aufgaben gespeichert werden können. Um die Beschreibung des Systemzustandes zu vereinfachen, wird angenommen, daß der verfügbare Teil des Hintergrundspeichers und des Arbeitsspeichers in Plätze aufgeteilt ist, Diese Plätze werden für jeden Speicher in beliebiger Reihenfolge durchnumeriert.

Der Transportkanal dient zum Transport der Aufgaben zwischen Hintergrund- und Arbeitsspeicher. Transporte dürfen nicht abgebrochen oder unterbrochen werden, und es kann immer nur ein Transport ausgeführt werden. In realen Systemen belegt eine Aufgabe, während sie transportiert wird, Platz sowohl im Hintergrund- als auch im Arbeitsspeicher. Wiederum wegen der einfacheren Beschreibung des Systemzustandes wird diese Tatsache im Modell so dargestellt, daß die Aufgabe, die gerade transportiert wird, den Transportkanal, aber keinen Speicherplatz belegt. Zusätzlich wird aber gefordert, daß jeder Transport von dem Platz (im Arbeits- oder Hintergrundspeicher), den die Aufgabe vor Beginn des Transportes belegte, auf einen nicht von einer Aufgabe belegten Platz erfolgt (im Hintergrund- oder Arbeitsspeicher). Der Transport einer Aufgabe vom Hintergrund- in den Arbeitsspeicher dauert die konstante Zeit T_1, der Transport vom Arbeits- in den Hintergrundspeicher die ebenfalls konstante Zeit T_2.

Der Rechnerkern kann nur eine Aufgabe bearbeiten, die einen Platz im Arbeitsspeicher belegt. Ist der Arbeitsspeicher mit zwei bearbeitbaren Aufgaben belegt, so kann der Rechnerkern ohne Zeitverlust von der Bearbeitung der einen Aufgabe zur Bearbeitung der anderen Aufgabe übergehen.

Der Zugangsprozeß neuer Aufgaben läßt sich folgendermaßen beschreiben: Wenn im System keine Aufgaben mehr auf Bearbeitung warten, treffen M (beliebig) Aufgaben gleichzeitig im Hintergrundspeicher ein. Das Eintreffen im Hintergrundspeicher wurde deshalb angenommen, weil auch in realen Systemen den Aufgaben während der langsamen Ein- und Ausgabe Platz im Hintergrundspeicher zugewiesen wird, damit sie nicht für die ganze Ein- und Ausgabezeit den Arbeitsspeicher blockieren. Ebenso wird angenommen, daß jede Aufgabe Platz im Hintergrundspeicher belegen muß, damit die Ausgabe erfolgen kann. Eine Aufgabe wird als fertig angesehen, sobald sie fertig bearbeitet wieder im Hintergrundspeicher steht. Das Aufgabenprofil A wird folgendermaßen beschrieben: Jede Aufgabe besteht aus der Forderung, vom Rechnerkern für eine bestimmte Zeit T_R bearbeitet zu werden. Diese Zeit T_R ist eine Zufallsvariable, die Rechenzeiten der Aufgaben sind vollständig unabhängige Realisierungen dieser Zufallsvariablen. Die einzelnen Rechenzeiten der Aufgaben sind nicht bekannt, sondern nur die stückweise exponentielle Verteilungsfunktion wird angegeben. Es ist:

$$P(T_R \le t) = P(t) = \begin{cases} 1 - e^{-\mu_1 t} & \text{für } t \le t_g \\ 1 - e^{-(\mu_1 - \mu_2) t_g - \mu_2 t} & \text{für } t > t_g \end{cases} \tag{2.1}$$

Die Rechenzeit einer Aufgabe ist unabhängig davon, wie oft die Bearbeitung der Aufgabe unterbrochen wird. Wird die Bearbeitung einer Aufgabe nach einer Unterbrechung vom Rechnerkern wieder aufgenommen, so braucht die vor der Unterbrechung geleistete Arbeit nicht wiederholt zu werden. Es soll hier darauf hingewiesen werden, daß die Verteilung der restlichen Rechenzeit einer Aufgabe, die schon die Zeit t_o bearbeitet worden aber nicht fertiggestellt ist, wieder eine stückweise exponentielle Verteilung ist, solange $t_o < t_g$ ist. (In (2.1) ist t_g durch $t_g - t_o$ zu ersetzen), und eine exponentielle Verteilung mit dem Parameter μ_2 ist, sobald $t_o > t_g$ ist:

$$P(T_R - t_o \leq t \mid T_R > t_o) = 1 - e^{-\mu_2 t} \qquad (2.2)$$

Diese Arbeit beschränkt sich auf stückweise exponentielle Rechenzeitverteilungen, für die gilt:

$$\mu_1 > \mu_2 \qquad (2.3)$$

Solche Verteilungen eignen sich gut zur Approximation gemessener Rechenzeitverteilungen, sie haben einen größeren Variationskoeffizienten als die Exponentialverteilung (die den Variationskoeffizienten 1 hat). Im übrigen ist für eine stückweise exponentielle Rechenzeitverteilung mit $\mu_1 \leq \mu_2$ die Abarbeitung der Aufgaben in beliebiger Reihenfolge aber ohne Unterbrechungen optimal. Außerdem wird noch gefordert, daß:

$$t_g \leq T_1 \quad \text{und} \quad t_g \leq T_2 \qquad (2.4)$$

ist, das ist bei gemessenen Rechenzeitverteilungen und bei Transportzeiten, wie sie zwischen Kernspeicher und Trommel bzw. Platte auftreten, tatsächlich der Fall. Diese Forderung hat eine erhebliche Vereinfachung der Rechnung zur Folge, und zwar deswegen, weil eine neue Aufgabe, die während eines Transportes bearbeitet wird, solange dies möglich ist, am Ende des Transportes fertiggestellt ist, oder mindestens t_g bearbeitet worden ist und damit exponentielle Restrechenzeitverteilung hat.

Es ist noch zu bemerken, daß Aufgaben zwar grundsätzlich nur aus einer Anforderung des Betriebsmittels Rechnerkern bestehen, da aber der Rechnerkern nur eine Aufgabe bearbeiten kann, die im Arbeitsspeicher ist, fordern die im Hintergrundspeicher wartenden Aufgaben den Transportkanal für einen Transport in den Arbeitsspeicher an. Ebenso fordern vom Rechnerkern fertig bearbeitete Aufgaben im Arbeitsspeicher den Transportkanal für einen Transport in den Hintergrundspeicher an, da sie erst nach diesem Transport fertig bearbeitet sind.

Die Annahme der stückweise exponentiellen Rechenzeitverteilung ist von entscheidender Bedeutung für die Lösbarkeit des gestellten Optimierungsproblems. Die Zahl der Systemzustände, bei denen die optimale Strategie nicht aus der trivialen Anweisung "Augenblickliche Tätigkeit fortsetzen" besteht, ist nämlich endlich, was für Modelle mit anderen Rechenzeitverteilungen, die gemessene Rechenzeitverteilungen ähnlich gut approximieren wie die stückweise exponentielle Verteilung, nicht gilt. Für exponentielle Rechenzeitverteilung ist zwar die Zahl dieser Zustände noch kleiner als bei stückweise exponentieller Verteilung, aber exponentielle Approximationen an gemessene Rechenzeitverteilungen sind so schlecht, daß die sich damit ergebenden Lösungen völlig von der Realität abweichen.

3. Zustände und Politiken I

Eine Strategie s für das Modell SVS ist eine Abbildung von der Menge U der möglichen Zustände, die das Modell annehmen kann, in die Menge der möglichen Anweisungen, welche Aufgaben die aktiven Betriebsmittel bearbeiten sollen. Diese Anweisungen an Rechnerkern und Transportkanal teilen nämlich in eindeutiger Weise alle vier Betriebsmittel den Aufgaben zu. Ein Zweitupel (Anweisung an den Rechnerkern, Anweisung an den Transportkanal) wird Politik genannt.

Der Systemzustand läßt sich durch das $(M+4)$-Tupel

$$u = (u_{K1}, u_{K2}, u_{A1}, u_{A2}, u_{H1}, \dots, u_{HM}) \tag{3.1}$$

beschreiben. Dabei ist:

$$u_{K1}, u_{Ai}, u_{Hi} = \begin{cases} 1 & \text{wenn Platz Nr. } i \text{ leer (d. h. nicht mit einer Aufgabe belegt) ist;} \\ f & \text{wenn Platz Nr. } i \text{ mit einer fertig bearbeiteten Aufgabe belegt ist;} \\ a \in [0, \infty) & \text{wenn Platz Nr. } i \text{ mit einer Aufgabe belegt ist, die vom Rechnerkern die Zeit } a \text{ bearbeitet aber nicht fertiggestellt wurde,} \end{cases}$$

wobei für u_{K1} der Platz im Transportkanal, für u_{Ai} Plätze im Arbeitsspeicher und für u_{Hi} Plätze im Hintergrundspeicher gemeint wird. Außerdem ist:

$$u_{K2} = \begin{cases} 1 & \text{wenn der Transportkanal nicht belegt ist;} \\ t \in (0, T_1) & \text{wenn in den Arbeitsspeicher transportiert wird und der Transport schon die Zeit } t \text{ dauert;} \\ t \in (T_1, T_1+T_2) & \text{wenn in den Hintergrundspeicher transportiert wird und der Transport schon die Zeit } t - T_1 \text{ dauert.} \end{cases}$$

Eine Politik ist ein Zweitupel

$$(Re, T) \text{ mit } Re \in \{RN, R1, R2\} \text{ und } T \in \{TN, TW, V1, V2, L1, \ldots LM\}$$

Dabei bedeuten die einzelnen Anweisungen:

RN: Rechne nicht !

Ri: Rechne an der Aufgabe, die auf Platz Nr. i im Arbeitsspeicher steht ! (i = 1, 2)

TN: Transportiere nicht !

TW: Transportiere die Aufgabe weiter, die gerade transportiert wird !

Vi: Transportiere die Aufgabe in den Hintergrundspeicher (Verdränge), die auf Platz Nr. i im Arbeitsspeicher steht (i = 1, 2)

Li: Transportiere die Aufgabe in den Arbeitsspeicher (Lade), die auf Platz Nr. i im Hintergrundspeicher steht ! (i = 1, 2,... u)

Damit sind jetzt Definitions- und Wertebereich einer Strategie definiert, und man kann daran gehen, die optimale Strategie zu suchen. Das geschieht dadurch, daß man zunächst für bestimmte Zustände die optimale Politik bestimmt, und bei der weiteren Suche nach der optimalen Strategie in allen Zuständen, in denen die optimale Politik bekannt ist, diese anwendet und die Zustandsbeschreibung auf die Zustände beschränkt, in denen die optimale Politik noch nicht bekannt ist, sogenannte Entscheidungszustände.

Es geht über den Rahmen dieser Arbeit hinaus, die schrittweise Verminderung der Anzahl der Entscheidungszustände und der möglicherweise optimalen Politiken nachzuvollziehen. Es sei lediglich erwähnt, daß man mit zwanzig Sätzen die Anzahl der Entscheidungszustände auf $2(M - 1)^2$ reduzieren kann und daß dann in jedem dieser Zustände zwei Politiken möglicherweise optimal sein können. Die zwanzig Sätze sind von zwei Typen:

1. Satz: Politik (Re, T) ist in den Zuständen $u_1, \ldots u_K$ nicht optimal.

2. Satz: Wenn Politik (Re, T) in den Zuständen $u_1, \ldots, u_K$ optimal ist, so

muß sie beibehalten werden, bis entweder ein Ereignis E eintritt oder eine Zeit t verstrichen ist.

Eine weitere Verminderung der Anzahl der Entwicklungszustände ist nicht gelungen.

Es ist an dieser Stelle angebracht, die $2(M-1)^2$ Entwicklungszustände und die noch möglicherweise optimalen Politiken nun zu beschreiben.

4. Zustände und Politiken II

Als erste Folgerung aus den zwanzig Sätzen erhält man folgende Aussage über die optimale Strategie:

Die Anweisung an den Rechnerkern muß in allen Zuständen des Systems lauten: Rechne wenn möglich, bevorzuge dabei Aufgaben, die noch nicht t_g gerechnet sind!

Jetzt kann die die Menge der Entscheidungszustände enthaltende Menge der Grundzustände beschrieben werden. Ein Grundzustand u ist ein Viertupel:

$$u = (v, w, m, n)$$

$$\text{mit } v \text{ bzw. } w = \left\{\begin{array}{l} 1 \\ f \\ t_g \\ o \end{array}\right\} \begin{array}{l} \text{wenn auf Platz} \\ \text{Nr. 1 bzw. 2 im} \\ \text{Arbeitsspeicher} \end{array} \left\{\begin{array}{ll} \text{keine} & \\ \text{eine fertig} & \text{gerechnete} \\ \text{eine mindestens } t_g & \text{"} \\ \text{eine noch nicht} & \text{"} \end{array}\right\} \text{Aufgabe steht.}$$

$$\text{und } \left\{\begin{array}{l} m \\ n \end{array}\right\} = \text{Anzahl der im Hintergrundspeicher wartenden } \left\{\begin{array}{l} \text{noch nicht} \\ \text{mindestens } t_g \end{array}\right\} \text{gerechneten Aufgaben.}$$

Dabei spielt die Anordnung von v und w keine Rolle. Als zweite Folgerung erhält man jetzt die folgende Aussage über die optimale Strategie:

Außer in Grundzuständen muß die optimale Anweisung an den Transportkanal lauten: Fahre fort (zu transportieren bzw. nicht zu transportieren)!

Damit sind jetzt zur Angabe der optimalen Strategie nur noch die Anweisungen an den Transportkanal in Grundzuständen nötig. Möglich sind die folgenden Anweisungen an den Transportkanal:

TN: Transportiere nicht!

LU: Lade unbearbeitete Aufgabe!

LB: Lade mindestens t_g bearbeitete Aufgabe!

VB: Verdränge mindestens t_g bearbeitete Aufgabe!

VF: Verdränge fertige Aufgabe!

Die folgenden Aussagen über Grundzustände lassen sich noch machen:

a) Die Zustände (f, f, m, n) und (o, o, m, n) werden nicht erreicht.

b) In den Zuständen (f, t_g, m, n) und (f, o, m, n) ist die Politik VF optimal.

c) Die Zustände (l, l, m, n) bzw. (l, o, m, n) werden nur für m=M, n=o bzw. m=M-1, n=o erreicht, dann ist in beiden Zuständen die Politik LU optimal.

d) Im Zustand (l, f, o, o) ist die Politik VF optimal.

e) Im Zustand (l, t_g, o, o) ist die Politik TN optimal.

f) In den Zuständen (t_g, t_g, o, n) und (t_g, o, o, n) ist die Politik TN optimal.

g) In den Zuständen (l, f, o, n) und (l, t_g, o, n) (n>o) ist die Politik LB optimal.

h) In den Zuständen (l, f, m, o) und (l, t_g, m, o) (m>o) ist die Politik LU optimal.

i) In den Zuständen (t_g, t_g, m, n) und (t_g, o, m, n) (m>o) können die Politiken TN oder VB optimal sein.

k) In den Zuständen (l, f, m, n) und (l, t_g, m, n) (m>o, n>o) können die Politiken LU oder LB optimal sein.

Die einzigen Entscheidungszustände sind jetzt also noch die hier unter i und k aufgeführten Zustandsklassen. Es ist nicht gelungen, die optimalen Politiken in diesen Zustandsklassen allgemeingültig zu ermitteln. Deshalb wurde ein ALGOL-Programm erstellt, das durch eine Rekursion über m und n die optimalen Politiken in diesen Entscheidungszuständen für spezielle Parameterwerte ermittelt.

5. Optimale Strategien

Für alle untersuchten Rechenzeitverteilungen und Transport-Rechenzeitverhältnisse bekam man dabei die folgenden Ergebnisse:

a) In den Zuständen (t_g, o, m, n) ist die Politik TN optimal.

b) In den Zuständen (l, f, m, n) (m>o, n>o) ist die Politik LB optimal (in gewissen (m, n)-Bereichen ist die Politik in diesen Zuständen ohne Einfluß ohne Einfluß auf den Durchsatz).

c) In den Zuständen (l, t_g, m, n) (m>o, n>o) ist für m = 1 die Politik LB und für m > 1 die Politik LU optimal (in gewissen Bereichen ohne Belang).

Leider lassen die Ergebnisse für die optimale Politik in der Zustandsklasse (t_g, t_g, m, n) nicht so einfach angeben, sie hängen zudem sehr stark von der Rechenzeitverteilung und dem Transport-Rechenzeitverhältnis ab. In Bild 2 sind die optimalen Politiken in dieser Zustandsklasse für eine der untersuchten Rechenzeitverteilungen und verschiedene Transport-Rechenzeitverhältnisse TRZV

dargestellt

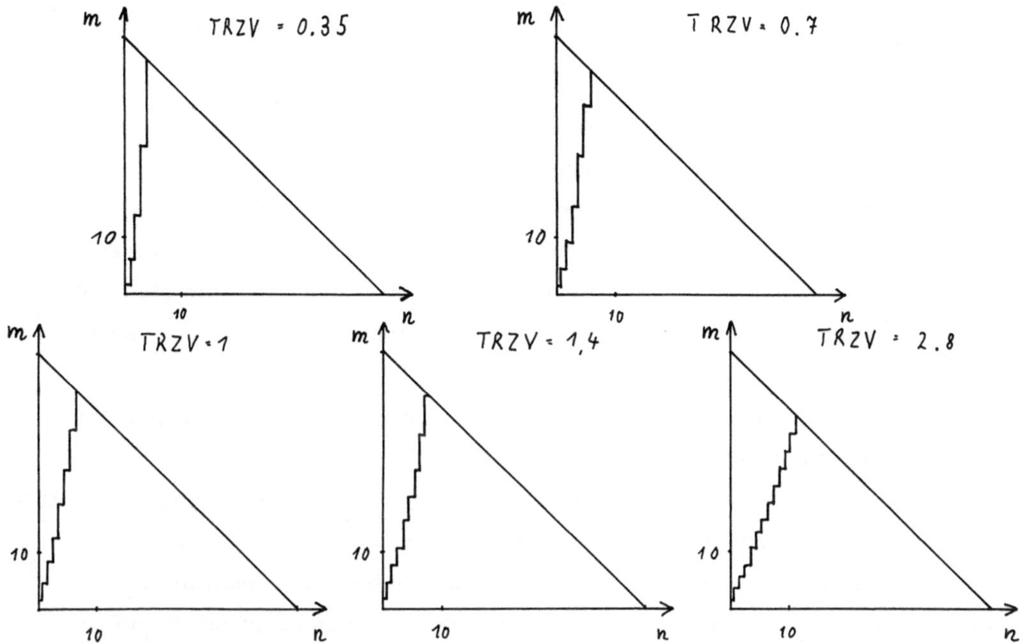

Bild 2: Die optimalen Politiken in den Zuständen (t_g, t_g, m, n) für verschiedenen Transport-Rechenzeitverhältnisse TRZV

Bild 2 zeigt, in welchen (m, n)-Bereichen in den Zuständen (t_g, t_g, m, n) die Politiken VB bzw. TN anzuwenden ist, und zwar für verschiedene Transport-Rechenzeit-Verhältnisse. Diese Rechenzeitverteilung (μ_1 = 315, μ_2 = o. 557, t_g = o, o7) zeichnet sich durch einen kleinen Wert t_g (1/3o* Erwartungswert) und durch einen Variationskoeffizienten von 4 aus. Das ganz herausragende Ergebnis, das auch für andere Rechenzeitverteilungen zutrifft, ist dabei, daß für die Maximierung des Durchsatzes in gewissen Zuständen (t_g, t_g, m, n) nicht fertig bearbeitete Aufgaben aus dem Arbeitsspeicher verdrängt werden müssen. Bisher sind solche verdrängende Strategien nur bei Teilnehmerrechensystemen realisiert, bei denen andere Optimierungskriterien maßgebend sind. Hier ist aber gezeigt, daß auch der Durchsatz eines stapelverarbeitenden Systems durch das Verdrängen von Aufgaben gesteigert werden kann, und zwar läßt sich zeigen, daß durchaus Steigerungen des Durchsatzes um bis zu 25 % möglich sind.

Zum Schluß wird noch einmal eine verbale Beschreibung der optimalen Strategie gegeben.

A. An den Rechnerkern ergeht die Anweisung: Rechne wenn möglich, bevorzuge dabei Aufgaben, die noch nicht t_g bearbeitet sind!

B. Ist nicht gerade ein Grundzustand erreicht worden, so ergeht an den Transportkanal die Anweisung: Fahre fort!

C. Wurde gerade ein Grundzustand, aber kein Entscheidungszustand der Form (t_g, t_g, m, n) $(m>o,\ n\geq o)$ erreicht, so muß der Transportkanal die erste durchführbare der folgenden Anweisungen ausführen:

   1. Lade eine Aufgabe in den Arbeitsspeicher, und zwar eine unbearbeitete, wenn nur solche vorhanden sind oder wenn mehr als eine solche vorhanden ist und der Rechnerkern arbeiten kann, sonst eine schon mindestens t_g bearbeitete!
   2. Verdränge eine fertig bearbeitete Aufgabe aus dem Arbeitsspeicher!
   3. Transportiere nicht!

D. In den Entscheidungszuständen (t_g, t_g, m, n) $(m>o,\ n\geq o)$ verdränge eine Aufgabe, wenn m "groß gegen" n ist, sonst transportiere nicht! Das "groß gegen" wird dabei durch die speziellen Parameterwerte bestimmt.

Zu Punkt D sollte man noch anmerken, daß es für nicht zu große $(T_1+T_2 < E(T_R/T_R > t_g))$ Transport-Rechenzeitverhältnisse nur eine geringfügige (unter $1^o/oo$) Durchsatzminderung bedeutet, wenn man in allen Entscheidungszuständen (t_g, t_g, m, n) $(m>o,\ n\geq o)$ eine Aufgabe verdrängt.

/1/ Küspert, H.-J. und Marte, G.: Optimale Rechenzeitzuteilung bei einem Teilnehmerrechensystem mit jeweils einer Aufgabe im Arbeitsspeicher El. Rechenanl. (12), 1970, Nr. 3, S. 155-162

/2/ Olivier, G.: Optimale Zeitzuteilung für wartende Rechenaufgaben El. Rechenanl. (9), 1967, Nr. 5, S. 218-224

SIMULATION VON BETRIEBS-SOFTWARE AUF EINER VIRTUELLEN PL/1 - MASCHINE

G.FLECK, J.NEHMER

1. Anforderungen an ein Simulationssystem

Problematisch bei der Simulation von Betriebssoftware ist der für eine befriedigende Modelltreue erforderliche hohe Detaillierungsgrad des Modells.

Er verursacht in der Regel beträchtliche Laufzeitkosten, die dem uneingeschränkten Einsatz von Simulationsmethoden in diesem Bereich Schranken setzen.

Die Tauglichkeit eines Simulationssystems soll daher an drei Kriterien gemessen werden.

1. Bequeme Modellbildung mit hohem Dokumentationswert
2. Niedrige Erstellungskosten
3. Hohe Laufzeiteffizienz

Die Kosten sind natürlich immer relativ zu den Gesamtaufwendungen einer Entwicklung zu verstehen / 1 /.

Das von Nehmer / 2 / angegebene Verfahren erfüllt diese Forderungen weitgehend und ist vom ökonomischen Standpunkt wohl nur schwer zu unterbieten. Modellprogramme werden dort in PL/1 formuliert und das zeitliche Verhalten in Echtzeit gemessen.

Nachteilig sind jedoch die relativ hohen Anforderungen an den Zeitservice der Testanlage (Realzeituhr mit hoher Auflösung), die gegenwärtig nur selten von Großrechenanlagen erfüllt werden.

Eine weitere Einschränkung ergibt sich aus der Natur des Verfahrens: Untersuchungen über Auswirkungen von Hardwarestrukturänderungen der simulierten Hardware sind nicht möglich, da gemessene Zeitabläufe Echtzeiten sind und immer die Eigenschaften der Testmaschine widerspiegeln (das ist die Maschine, auf der simuliert wird).

Da das kurzbeschriebene Simulationssystem auch für Untersuchungen dieser Art eingesetzt werden soll, mußte nach anderen Lösungswegen gesucht werden. Dabei wurde an der höheren Programmiersprache PL/1 als Implementierungsbasis für Modellprogramme festgehalten, da sie für die Formulierung von Betriebssoftware ausgezeichnet geeignet ist und eine gute Basis für leicht lesbare, selbstdokumentierende Programme darstellt.

2. Organisation und Arbeitsweise des Simulationssystems

Der vorliegenden Lösung liegt die Idee zugrunde, PL/1-Statements als Maschineninstruktionen einer virtuellen PL/1-Maschine aufzufassen. Sie habe die Fähigkeit, PL/1-Programme auf der Basis von Zeitbewertungen, die einzelnen Statements zugeordnet werden, statementweise kontrolliert auszuführen. PL/1-Statements stellen dabei - äquivalent den Maschineninstruktionen in realen Systemen - unteilbare Aktionen dar.

Die Synchronisation aller Parallelaktivitäten des Systems (wie asynchrone Interrupts, unabhängig arbeitende Kanäle, mehrere Rechnerkerne in einem Mehrprozessorsystem) erfolgt jeweils nach Ausführung eines zeitbewerteten Statements durch eine zentrale Eventsteuerung. Die bei diskreten Simulationstechniken unvermeidlichen systematischen Zeitfehler bleiben durch die statementweise Korrektur wirkungslos.

Abb. 1 zeigt die generelle Struktur des Simulationssystems. Entgegen der sonst üblichen Technik werden Modellprogramme nicht interpretiert, sondern Statement für Statement durchlaufen.

Die PL/1-Maschine führt zu diesem Zweck Unterprogrammsprünge in die Modellprogramme aus und erhält die Regie nach einem bearbeiteten PL/1-Statement zurück. Eine Realisierung dieses Kontrollflusses zwischen PL/1-Maschine und Modellprogrammen erfordert eine entsprechende Aufbereitung des Quellcodes vor der eigentlichen Compilierung durch einen Makroprozessor.

Abb. 2 zeigt an einem einfachen Beispiel die wesentlichen Transformationen, die am Quellcode vorzunehmen sind. Die mit einem führenden Dollarzeichen am Anfang einer Zeile angegebenen Konstanten stellen die bereits erwähnten Bewertungsfaktoren dar, die vom Makroprozessor in gültige PL/1-Statements umgesetzt werden müssen. Alle, durch Zeitbewertungen gekennzeichneten Instruktionen werden für eine spätere Reaktivierung mit Labels versehen, die mit L000, L001, L002 ...... durchnumeriert sind. Das Label des nächsten auszuführenden Statements wird zusammen mit der aufgelaufenen Ausführungszeit in eine dynamische Savearea (DSA) gerettet, die in Form einer BASED-Struktur angelegt ist.

Man erkennt, daß die Ausführung eines Statements in zwei Phasen zerfällt. In der ersten Phase wird eine Zeitkorrektur durch Auswertung der Zeitbewertung durchgeführt, während in der zweiten Phase das Statement tatsächlich abgehandelt wird. Nach Ausführung jedes RETURN-

Statements geht die Kontrolle an die aufrufende PL/1-Maschine zurück, die dann den nächsten Zeitpunkt für die Reaktivierung des Modellprogramms bestimmt. Voraussetzung ist jedoch, daß alle temporären Variablen entweder in einem stationären oder dynamisch kontrollierten Speicherbereich angelegt sind. Die Benutzung automatischer Variablen in PL/1 (Attribut AUTOMATIC), die eine dynamische Einrichtung und Freigabe des zugehörigen Speicherplatzes beim Aufruf oder Verlassen einer Prozedur bewirkt, ist deshalb unzulässig. Zulässig dagegen ist die Ablage der Variablen in Speicherbereichen des Typs CONTROLLED, STATIC oder BASED. Im vorliegenden Modell wurde für alle temporären Variablen der Modellprogramme die Ablage in BASED-Speichern vorgeschrieben. Sie bieten ein einfaches Mittel, um Modellprogramme auf PL/1-Ebene reentrant zu organisieren.

Statements des Quellcodes, die keine Zeitbewertung mitführen, werden vom Makroprozessor unverändert übernommen und tragen deshalb nicht zu Laufzeiten der Programme bei.

Diese Transparenz ist von Vorteil, weil sie auf bequeme Weise gestattet, Kontrollausdrücke oder Zwischenauswertungen einzuschieben, ohne die Eigenschaften des Meßobjektes (= Modellprogramme) zu verändern.

Die Bewertung von Statements innerhalb von Blöcken (Unterprogramme (CALL), BEGIN ... END, DO-Gruppen) ist aufgrund der beschriebenen Kontrollstruktur unzulässig, da der Wiedereintritt in einen Block nur über die zulässige Aktivierungskette aller Blöcke geringerer Schachtelungstiefe erfolgen kann. Dagegen ist es möglich, Blöcken <u>eine</u> Zeitbewertung zuzuordnen und sie im Sinne der PL/1-Maschine wie <u>eine</u> Maschineninstruktion zu behandeln.

Die zeitgerechte Aktivierung aller Funktionen der Maschinensteuerung wird - wie Abb. 1 zeigt - durch die Eventsteuerung kontrolliert, die alle Aktionen des Systems in einer prioritäts- und zeitgeordneten Eventkette verwaltet. Da diese Form der Organisation Standard-Simulationstechnik darstellt, wird hier auf eine weitere Diskussion verzichtet (z.B. / 3,4 /).

Bevor im nächsten Kapitel ein konkretes Beispiel für eine PL/1-Maschine behandelt wird, sollen noch einmal die Vorzüge der geschilderten Simulationsmethode zusammengefaßt werden:

a) Anstelle eines speziellen Übersetzers, der Objektcode für die virtuelle Maschine erzeugt, wird lediglich ein vergleichsweise primitiver Makroprozessor benötigt.

b) Der Aufwand für einen Code-Interpretierer entfällt vollständig.

Zu den damit extrem niedrigen Erstellungskosten gesellen sich hoher Komfort und Dokumentationswert durch Benutzung von PL/1 als Implementierungsbasis sowohl für die PL/1-Maschine als auch für Modellprogramme.

c) Durch die vollständige Vermeidung der Codeinterpretation konnte nach vorsichtigen Schätzungen die Laufzeiteffizienz um mindestens eine 10er-Potenz gegenüber dem herkömmlichen Verfahren gesteigert werden.

3. Struktur einer exemplarischen PL/1-Maschine

Für die Entwicklung der Kernsoftware von symmetrischen Mehrprozessorsystemen, insbesondere der Eingriffsannahme und -bearbeitung, der Rechnerkernvergabe (Dispatching) sowie des Prozessorscheduling wurde auf der Grundlage der vorangegangenen Ausführungen eine PL/1-Maschine mit einer wählbaren Zahl von Rechnerkernen und einem gemeinsamen, keinen Zugriffsbeschränkungen unterworfenen Arbeitsspeicher unbeschränkter Größe implementiert (Abb. 3).

Die Struktur jedes Rechnerkerns spiegelt sich durch eine entsprechende PL/1-Datenstruktur (Abb. 4) wider. Erkennbar sind 4 voneinander trennbare Unterstrukturen, die einerseits den Rechnerkernstatus des aktuellen, d.h. in der Ausführung begriffenen Programmes, des Interruptprogrammes, eines unterbrochenen Programmes und ferner einen Bereich zur Aufnahme von Interrupt-Statusworten enthalten. Anstehende Interrupts werden - stellvertretend durch Interrupt-Statusworte - in einer prioritätsgeordneten Warteschlange bis zu ihrer Aktivierung gepuffert.

Außerdem tragen alle Rechnerkerne eine eindeutige Identifikation in Form einer Nummer, die in der Initialisierungsphase zugeteilt wird.

Abb. 5 verdeutlicht die Funktion der drei Registersätze, die jeweils einen kompletten Rechnerkernstatus enthalten.

Nach Annahme eines Interrupts wird der aktuelle Rechnerkernstatus in den Save-Bereich umgespeichert und anschließend der neue Status des Interruptprogrammes in den aktuellen Bereich geladen. Damit wird das Interruptprogramm zum aktuellen Programm, die Interruptbearbeitung ist initialisiert. Da nur ein Interruptprogramm für die Gesamtheit aller Interrupts existiert, muß die spezifische Reaktion durch programminterne Verzweigungen organisiert werden.

Der Status des unterbrochenen Programmes, der im SAVE-Bereich zur Verfügung steht, kann entweder abgespeichert oder durch eine $RETURN-Maschineninstruktion wieder zum aktuellen Status erklärt werden. Das Programm wird daraufhin fortgesetzt. Bekanntlich bieten doppelte Registersätze dieser Konstruktion die Möglichkeit, kurze Interruptprogramme ohne zeitraubende Registerwechsel über den Arbeitsspeicher in ein laufendes Programm einzublenden.

Der eigentliche Rechnerkernstatus enthält neben dem Programmnamen, dem Hinweis auf einen zugeordneten Arbeitsbereich und der momentanen Priorität den Modus des Rechnerkerns.

Durch die Angabe eines Arbeitsbereiches können alle Programme reentrant organisiert werden. Die Zuweisung und Verwaltung dieses Speichers wird bei der Behandlung der Maschineninstruktionen im folgenden Kapitel näher erläutert.

Eine Besonderheit dieser PL/1-Maschine stellt das Fehlen jeglicher Arbeitsregister dar. Alle Instruktionen wirken daher unmittelbar auf Operanden im Arbeitsspeicher.

Vier unterschiedliche Laufmodi der Rechnerkerne werden unterschieden:

a) RUNNING
   bedeutet, daß ein Rechnerkern Instruktionszyklen ausführt.

b) LOOPING
   bedeutet, daß sich ein Rechnerkern inmitten der Ausführung einer Instruktion befindet.

c) IDLE
   bedeutet, daß ein Rechnerkern keine Instruktionszyklen ausführt. Jeder Interrupt schaltet ihn automatisch in den RUNNING-Modus zurück.

d) PSEUDORUNNING
   bedeutet, daß sich ein Rechnerkern in einem simulierten RUNNING-Modus befindet.

   Dieser, für die effiziente Nutzung der PL/1-Maschine als Simulationsinstrument äußerst wichtige Modus, erlaubt es, in ihren Aktionen unwesentliche Programmstücke eines Modells durch einfache Zeitstrecken nachzubilden. Rechnerkerne werden für diese

Zeitperioden in den Modus PSEUDO-RUNNING versetzt.

Für einen kompletten Simulationslauf entsteht so das Bild von Mikrosimulationsphasen (in denen PL/1-Programme statementweise ausgeführt werden), die beliebig mit Makrophasen in der beschriebenen Form versetzt sind.

Nur die interessierenden Teile der Betriebssoftware werden auf Mikroebene simuliert, während die gesamte Modellumgebung durch Makrophasen nachgebildet wird. Da zur Durchführung der Makrophasen vergleichsweise wenig Rechenzeit benötigt wird, ergibt sich eine beträchtliche Steigerung der Simulationseffizienz.

4. Der Instruktionsvorrat der Maschine

Neben den durch die PL/1-Konventionen festgelegten Grundoperationen setzt sich der Instruktionsvorrat für die im Kapitel 4 definierte PL/1-Maschine aus Systeminstruktionen und Pseudoinstruktionen zusammen.

Systeminstruktionen bilden das notwendige Instrument zur Konfigurations- und Zustandskontrolle der virtuellen Maschine. Achtzehn derartige Instruktionen sind gegenwärtig implementiert, die über standardisierte Prozeduraufrufe von allen Modellprogrammen ansprechbar sind:

$CALL (Programmname)
$RETURN
$JUMP (Programmname)
$RESUME (Statusablageadresse)
$SAVE (Statusablageadresse)
$LOAD-PARMADDR (Ablageadresse)
$STORE-PARMADDR (Ablageadresse)
$INT-STATUS (Ablageadresse)
$ENABLE
$DISABLE
$MASK
$UNMASK
$LOCK (Adresse)
$UNLOCK (Adresse)
$SIGNAL (Rechnerkern-Nr., Priorität)
$IDLE

$SVC (Interrupt-Nr., Priorität)
$CPUTIME

Durch die Instruktionen $CALL, $RETURN, $JUMP, $RESUME sind kontrollierte Übergänge zwischen Modellprozeduren auf der Basis von Unterprogrammaufrufen und Sprüngen ohne Rückkehr möglich. Die dazu erforderlichen Speicherallokationen und -freigaben, Aufräumungsarbeiten und Normierungen in den Arbeitsbereichen der Modellprogramme werden automatisch durchgeführt und sind damit Bestandteil der Hardware der PL/1-Maschine. Der Systemprogrammierer wird dadurch von der Speicherorganisation auf der untersten Ebene der Betriebsorganisation befreit und kann sich in verstärktem Maße den <u>algorithmischen</u> Eigenschaften der zu untersuchenden Modelle widmen.

In ähnlicher Weise werden bei Unterprogrammschachtelungen durch $CALL die Arbeitsbereiche der beteiligten Modellprozeduren automatisch gekettet und die Rücksprungadressen gerettet.

Besondere Bedeutung für Mehrprozessorsysteme haben die Instruktionen $LOCK, $UNLOCK sowie $IDLE und $SIGNAL.

$LOCK/$UNLOCK-Instruktionen stellen ein unentbehrliches Hilfsmittel zur Zugriffssynchronisation von gemeinsam benutzten Daten durch mehrere Rechnerkerne dar / 5 /.

Die Ausführung einer $IDLE-Instruktion versetzt einen Rechnerkern in den IDLE-Modus, in dem keine Instruktionen mehr aus dem Arbeitsspeicher ausgelesen werden. Die daraus resultierende Entlastung des Arbeitsspeichers ist ein wesentlicher Faktor für größere Leistungsfähigkeit bei allen realen Systemen.

Im Simulationsmodell stellt dieser Modus zusätzlich ein einfaches Mittel zur Messung der Rechnerkernauslastung dar.

Die $SIGNAL-Instruktion bietet - neben der Kommunikation über den Arbeitsspeicher - ein zweites Kommunikationshilfsmittel für Rechnerkerne. Das 'Wecken' von IDLE-Rechnerkernen sowie die gezielte Unterbrechung eines Rechnerkerns beim Einsatz von preemptiven Scheduling-Strategien sind zwei typische Anwendungsfälle für diese Instruktion.

Pseudoinstruktionen dienen der Erzeugung von Pseudozuständen der PL/1-Maschine und stellen ausschließlich ein Hilfsmittel für eine effiziente Simulation dar.

Zwei Pseudoinstruktionen sind in der gegenwärtig existierenden Version implementiert:

$RUN (Zeit)
$INTERRUPT (Zeit, Interrupt-Nr., Priorität)

Durch Ausführung der $RUN-Instruktion wird ein Rechnerkern für die Dauer der angegebenen Zeit in den PSEUDORUNNING-Modus versetzt (vgl. Kap. 4).

Mit Hilfe der $INTERRUPT-Instruktion können beliebige Interrupts zu einem definierten Zeitpunkt an dem Rechner generiert werden, der diese Instruktion ausführt.

Beide Instruktionen ermöglichen es auf einfache Weise, Programmlaufzeiten, Ein/Ausgabe-Transferzeiten, Gerätezugriffsverzögerungen und alle Arten von Geräte- und Kanalendeinterrupts zu simulieren und ergänzen somit den Satz der Systeminstruktionen in sinnvoller Weise.

Literaturhinweise

/ 1 / Stephen R. Kimbleton
The Role of Computer System Models in Performance Evaluation
Comm. ACM 15, 7, 1972, pp. 586-590

/ 2 / Jürgen Nehmer
Ein PL/1-Programm zur Simulation von Dispatching-Strategien in einem Mehrprozessorsystem
NTG/GI-Fachtagung in Darmstadt, 12.-14. April 1972,
Nachrichtentechnische Fachberichte, Band 44, 1972

/ 3 / John Smith
Computer Simulation Models
Griffin & Comp. Ltd., 1968

/ 4 / T.H. Naylor et al.
Computer Simulation Techniques
John Wiley & Sons, New York, 1966

/ 5 / Jack B. Dennis and Earl C. Van Horn
Programming Semantics for Multiprogrammed Computations
Comm. ACM 9, 3, 1966, pp. 143-155

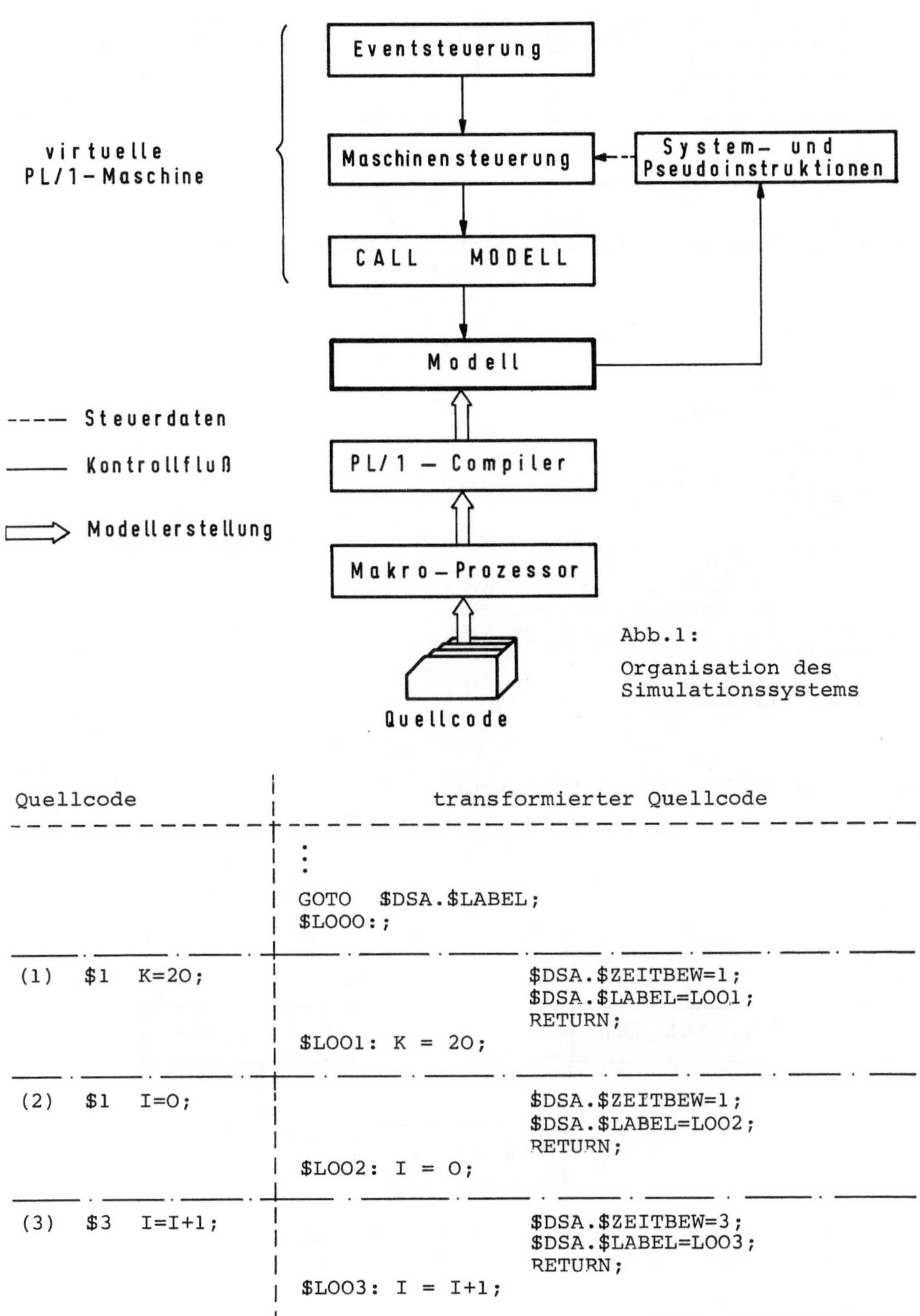

Abb.1:
Organisation des Simulationssystems

Quellcode	transformierter Quellcode
	: GOTO $DSA.$LABEL; $LOOO:;
(1) $1 K=20;	$DSA.$ZEITBEW=1; $DSA.$LABEL=LOO1; RETURN; $LOO1: K = 20;
(2) $1 I=0;	$DSA.$ZEITBEW=1; $DSA.$LABEL=LOO2; RETURN; $LOO2: I = 0;
(3) $3 I=I+1;	$DSA.$ZEITBEW=3; $DSA.$LABEL=LOO3; RETURN; $LOO3: I = I+1;
	:

Abb.2: Transformation des Quellcodes durch den Makroprozessor

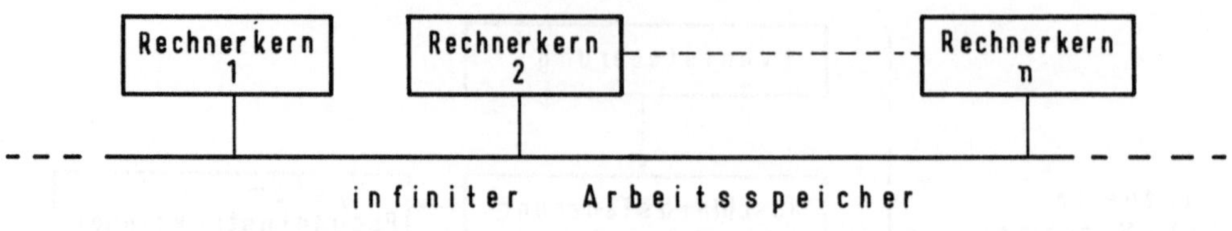

Abb.3: Konfiguration der exemplarischen PL/1-Maschine

```
1 RECHNERKERN,
  2 IDENTIFIKATION,
  2 STATUS_ACT,
    3 PROGRAMMNAME,
    3 ARBEITSBEREICH,
    3 PRIORITÄT,
    3 MODUS,
      4 LAUFMODUS,  /+ RUNNING, LOOPING, IDLE, PSEUDORUNNING +/
      4 INT_MASKE,  /+ MASKED, UNMASKED +/
      4 INT_SPERRE, /+ ENABLED, DISABLED +/
  2 STATUS_INT LIKE STATUS_ACT,
  2 STATUS_SAVE LIKE STATUS_ACT,
  2 INTERRUPT,
    3 INT_STATUSWORT,
    3 INT_PUFFER;
```

Abb.4: Struktur eines Rechnerkerns

—— Registertransporte nach Annahme eines Interrupts
---- Programmwechsel nach Ausführung einer SRETURN-Instruktion

Abb.5: Funktion der drei Registersätze für den Rechnerkernstatus

EINPLANUNG EINES LEISTUNGSFÄHIGEN SOFTWARE-MESSYSTEMES BEI DER ENTWICKLUNG EINES BETRIEBSSYSTEMES

E.F.PANTELE

Vorwort:

Die Erläuterung der Einplanung eines Software-Meßsystemes ist ein umfangreiches Vorhaben. Es beginnt mit der Motivation von Messungen; in diesem Aufsatz sind immer Messungen gemeint, deren Ergebnisse aus dem System herausgebracht werden um der Systementwicklungsgruppe für die weiteren Arbeiten Anhaltspunkte zu geben.
Es gehört dann dazu, was gemessen werden soll, welche Ereignisse, welche Zusammenhänge usw. Dazu hat Mersmann (Lit. [3]) umfangreiche Aussagen geliefert.
Die Beschreibung der Informationsgewinnung und Abspeicherung nach Eintreten von bestimmten Ereignissen ist ein weiterer wichtiger Bestandteil der Erläuterung.
Als letztes gehören dann Auswertung, Darstellung und Interpretation der Meßergebnisse dazu. Dieser Punkt ist bisher in der Fachliteratur am intensivsten behandelt worden.
Der vorliegende Aufsatz konzentriert sich auf die Beschreibung von Techniken zur Informationsgewinnung und -abspeicherung, wobei Meßpunkte und Informationsabspeicherungsverfahren integrierte Bestandteile des Betriebssystemes sind.

Die Einplanung solcher Grundsysteme für Messungen während der Systementwicklung soll am Beispiel BSM (Betriebs-System-München) gezeigt werden.

1. Einführung

Für Tests und Messungen in Betriebssystemen werden immer wieder folgende Forderungen gestellt:

1. - bequeme Möglichkeit zur Durchführung dieser Arbeiten und flexible Verwendbarkeit evtl. vorhandener Test- und Meßeinrichtungen.

2. - <u>keine</u> bzw. <u>geringe</u> Beeinflussung der Betriebssicherheit und des Betriebsverhaltens durch Test- und Meßarbeiten.

3. - die Arbeiten sollen im <u>laufenden</u> Betrieb ohne wesentliche Beeinträchtigung begonnen, durchgeführt oder abgeschlossen werden können.

Aus diesen Gründen muß eine Systementwicklungsgruppe, die die Ergebnisse dieser Tests und der Messungen für die Weiterentwicklung des Systems braucht, im Betriebssystem schon gewisse Grundfunktionen einplanen und einbauen. Diese Grundfunktionen sollen später die Durchführung von Test- und Meßarbeiten erleichtern.

In einem frühen Stadium der Systementwicklung kann man diese Grundfunktion einplanen unter Beachtung von:

1. - Erfahrungen von anderen Leuten mit Projekten auf diesem Gebiet,

2. - den speziellen Charakteristiken bei dem aktuellen System,

3. - den Wünschen bzw. möglichen Wünschen für Test- und Meßarbeiten bei und nach dieser Systementwicklung.

Die <u>Leistungsfähigkeit</u> eines Test- und Meßsystems ist primär in qualitativer Hinsicht zu verstehen, d.h.

1. - das Meßsystem soll mehrere verschiedene Informationsgewinnungsverfahren enthalten, mit denen möglichst alle Test- und Meßprobleme bequem behandelt werden können.

2. - aus Gründen der Sicherheit und Flexibilität sollen einige verschiedene Möglichkeiten der Informationszwischenspeicherung und Informationsausgabe auswählbar sein.

3. - es muß ein bequemes Auswertungsverfahren in Form eines Programmsatzes für
   die Darstellung von Ergebnissen
   die Aufbereitung und Zusammenfassung von Meßreihen
   und die Durchführung von Langzeitmessungen
   eingerichtet sein, um dem Mitarbeiter diese für seine Meß-

interessen meist nebensächlichen jedoch lästigen Arbeiten zu erleichtern.

2. Die Einplanung der Grundfunktionen für ein leistungsfähiges Test- und Meßsystem im Betriebssystem BSM

2.1. Die Erfahrungen beim Einrichten von Test- und Meßverfahren für Betriebssysteme zeigen, daß eine gute modulare Aufteilung des Systems in Systemteile und eine durchdachte Parametrisierung der Systemteile den Einbau von Test-Code und Test-Routinen in den Systemteilen stark vereinfacht. Ein besonderer Vorteil ist ein dynamisch ein- und ausschaltbarer Testmodus für einen Programmablauf.
Post-Mortem-Dumps, ereignis- oder zeitgesteuerte Momentaufnahmen von Register- oder Hauptspeicherinhalten sowie dynamische Ablaufregistrierung (Trace) sind heute die meist verbreiteten Test- und Meßtechniken.

2.2. Die speziellen Systemcharakteristiken von BSM werden im folgenden kurz erläutert.

BSM wird ein Betriebssystem für gemischten Stapel/Dialog-Betrieb, für einen Telefunken Rechner TR440 mit 2 CPUs. Benutzeraufträge und Systemfunktionen können als unabhängige Prozesse ablaufen. Die Gesamtmenge der Prozesse (BSM-Begriff: "Bearbeiter") ist in einer hierarchischen Schichtenstruktur geordnet.
Zur Kommunikation zwischen Bearbeitern dient ein Meldungssystem, der sog. Zusteller, der u.a. den Transfer von Meldungen zwischen Bearbeitern, verbunden mit Synchronisierung einerseits und Pufferung der Meldungen andererseits, durchführt.

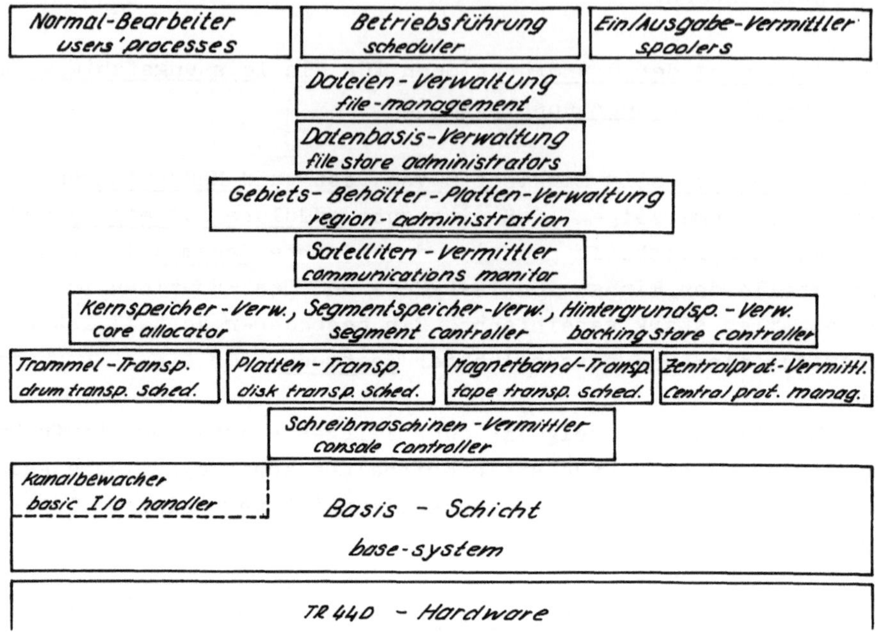

In dieser Schichtenstruktur der Systemteile (Bearbeiter) wird durch das Kommunikationssystem in der Basisschicht gewährleistet, daß Aufträge nur innerhalb derselben Schicht und in tiefer liegende Schichten gesendet werden können. Antworten (als Quittungen) werden in umgekehrter Richtung zurückgereicht. 1) 2). Zyklische Wartezustände sind daher nur innerhalb der gleichen Schicht möglich.

Anm.: Ein Bearbeiter ist eine Funktionseinheit, die selbständig Aufträge bearbeiten kann, für den ein eigener Adreßraum definiert ist, und dem noch gewisse Verwaltungsinformation zugeordnet ist. Diese Verwaltungsinformation ist in einem Speicherbereich, dem sog. Bearbeiterleitblock, nach einem festen Schema untergebracht.

---

1) siehe Aufsatz von K. Lagally: "Aufruf von Systemdienstleistungen in BSM, einem schichtenweise gegliederten Betriebssystem."

2) siehe Lit. [1]

2.3. Die Wünsche für Test- und Meßmöglichkeiten während und nach den Entwicklungsarbeiten von BSM sind:

- Primitiv-Dump
- Direkt-Abfrage von Speicherinhalten über Operateur-Konsolschreibmaschine
- Ereignisgesteuerter Universaldump
- Ereignismeldung mit Informationsablage
- ein- und ausschaltbare Ablaufregistrierung von Bearbeitern in vorgebbaren Befehlsbereichen.
- ein- und ausschaltbare Meßfunktionen in Systemteilen.

3. Die Realisierung der Grundeinrichtungen für Tests und Messungen im BSM

3.1. On-line-Informationsausgaben für Test- und Meßzwecke sind in einem System dieser Größenordnung und Aufgabenstellung nur als allerletzte Notmaßnahmen anzusetzen, die nur dann benötigt werden, wenn das System nicht mehr in der Lage ist "mit eigenen Kräften" Information über seinen Zustand abzugeben.
Für diesen Fall gibt es den TR440-Primitiv-Absolutdump, der nicht Bestandteil des Betriebssystemes ist. Nach Laden desselben können mit Absolutadressen angebbare Speicherbereiche direkt gedumpt werden.

3.2. Off-line Informationsausgaben setzen gewisse Mindestleistungen des Systems voraus.

Die direkte Abfrage oder Eingabe von Speicherinhalten via Operateur-Konsolschreibmaschine setzt in BSM das Funktionieren der Basisschicht und des Schreibmaschinenvermittlers voraus. Diese Möglichkeit der Abwicklung von Tests oder Messungen soll jedoch nur in Ausnahmefällen wahrgenommen werden und wird daher nicht besonders unterstützt.

Als Regelfall soll in BSM die Informationsablage und -ausgabe über ein oder mehrere Zentralprotokolle geschehen, die von einem Auswerte-Programm später ausgewertet werden können.

3.3. Das Zentralprotokoll (ZP) als zentraler Ablageort für Test- und Meßinformation ist ein Speicherbereich auf einem Hintergrundspeicher (Trommel, Platte, Magnetband). Ein Systemteil, der sog. Zentralprotokollvermittler (ZPV) hat die Aufgabe diese Speicherbereiche zu verwalten und es Bearbeitern zu ermöglichen bequem Information in das ZP absetzen zu können.

Die Hintergrundspeicherbereiche bekommt der ZPV von der Betriebsführung zugeteilt und gibt sie an diese auch wieder (auf Aufforderung oder bei voller Belegung) zur Auswertung zurück.

Ferner bekommt der ZPV mitgeteilt, welche Auftragsarten (Dump, Direkte Information, Trace, etc.) auf welche Hintergrundspeicherbereiche (falls mehrere eingerichtet wurden) geleitet werden müssen.

Unter diesen Voraussetzungen hat der ZPV die Auftragsannahme, die Erzeugung der ZP-Elemente, den Zusammenbau und das Senden der Transportaufträge und die Verwaltung der ihm zugeteilten Speicherbereiche durchzuführen.

Anm. 1: Eine Zuteilung und Rückgabe von ZP-Speicherbereichen sowie eine Änderung der Verteilung der Auftragsarten auf die ZP-Bereiche muß im lfd. Betrieb durchgeführt werden können!

Anm. 2: Ein ZP-Element ist eine selbstbeschreibende Eintragseinheit im ZP. Der Elementkopf enthält die Elementbeschreibung, der Rumpf die eigentliche Information.

Anm. 3: Nach Rückgabe eines ZP-Bereiches erfolgt dessen Auswertung durch Auswertungsprogramme, die als Benutzerprogramme laufen.

Die Einplanung eines derartigen ZPV in die Systemstruktur von BSM wurde im wesentlichen von zwei Kriterien bestimmt:

1. - Möglichst viele Systemteile sollen die Leistungen des ZPV in Anspruch nehmen können, damit muß sich der ZPV möglichst tief im Schichtenbild befinden.

2. - Der ZPV seinerseits benötigt die Leistungen der Hintergrund-Transporteure (Trommel-Tr., Platten-Tr., Magnetband-Tr.), daher muß er sich im Schichtenbild mindestens so hoch befinden wie diese Transporteure.

Damit ist der natürliche Ort des ZPV in der Schicht der Transporteure und damit haben alle Bearbeiter außer dem Schreibmaschinen-Vermittler und der Systembasis Zugang zu Zentralprotokolldiensten.

3.4. Skizzierung von Informationsgewinnungs- und Informationsablageverfahren in BSM

3.4.1. Ereignisgesteuerter Universaldump

Anwendung: Kopieren von Speicherbereichen größeren Umfanges (Listen, Variablenbereiche o.ä.) bei Auftreten von Fehlfunktionen eines Systemteiles, die er selbst bemerkt, Kopieren von Test- oder Meßdaten größeren Umfanges.

Initiierung: Durch Alarm-, Fehlerbehandlungs-, Test- oder Meßprogramme, die Bestandteil eines Systemteils (Bearbeiters) sind, und aufgrund von definierten Ereignissen angesprungen werden.

Auftragsform an ZPV: Angabe des Auftraggebers, Kennzeichen für das Ereignis (falls möglich), Angabe der zu dumpenden Adressbereiche im Adressraum des Auftraggebers.

Abwicklung der Info.Ablage: Der ZPV erzeugt pro Auftrag ein ZP-Element in dem für diese Auftragsart vorgesehenen Zentralprotokoll. Dafür wird aus der Auftragsbeschreibung unter Hinzufügung von notwendiger Verwaltungsinformation der Elementkopf zusammengestellt und durch Auftrag an den Transporteur auf den vorgesehenen Hintergrundspeicherbereich transportiert. Der Elementrumpf entsteht aus den zu dumpenden Speicherinhalten. Der ZPV stellt aus der Auftragsbeschreibung Transportaufträge für den Hintergrundtransporteur her, der die Inhalte der angegebenen Hauptspeicherbereiche in den angegebenen Hintergrundspeicherbereich transportiert. Nach Abwicklung des Dump-Auftrages bekommt der Auftraggeber eine Quittung und kann dann weiterarbeiten.

Bemerkung: Der Dumpauftrag kann aus einer Anzahl von Teilaufträgen für nicht notwendig zusammenhängende Speicherbereiche bestehen.

3.4.2. Ereignismeldung mit direkter Informationsablage

Anwendung: Ablegen von Informationsmengen kleineren Umfanges max. 30 Maschinenworte) bei definierten Fehler-, Test- oder Meßereignissen (z.B. Zählen, Werte von Variablen).

Initiierung: Durch Alarm-, Fehlerbehandlungs-, Test- oder Meßprogramme, die integrierter Bestandteil eines Bearbeiters sind und aufgrund definierter Ereignisse angesprungen werden.

Auftragsform an ZPV: Angabe des Auftraggebers, Kennzeichen für das Ereignis, Information.

Abwicklung der Info-Ablage: Aus dem Auftrag, der die Information direkt enthält, wird ein Zentralprotokollelement erzeugt, indem noch notwendige Verwaltungsinformation hinzugefügt wird. Dieses Element wird in einen Puffer gelegt, der für diese Auftragsart vorgesehen ist. Ein (mit evtl. mehreren derartigen Elementen) gefüllter Puffer wird vom ZPV mit Hilfe der Transportdienste auf den vorgesehenen Hintergrundspeicherbereich kopiert.

Bemerkung: Der Bearbeiter kann sofort nach Absenden des Auftrages für Informationsablage weiterarbeiten.

3.4.3. Ein- und ausschaltbare Ablaufregistrierung von Bearbeitern in angebbaren Befehlsbereichen

Anwendung: Schrittweise Registrierung des Ablaufs von Programmen oder Programmstücken zur Überwachung der Ausführung.

Initiierung: Ein Befehl wird im TR440 in den zwei Phasen: Abrufphase- Ausführungsphase durchgeführt. Nach jeder Phase werden die Alarmbits abgeprüft. (Alarme melden hardwaremäßig erkannte Zustände, die eine normale Fortsetzung der CPU-Aktionen nicht erlauben; z.B. Division durch Null.) Ein Bit "Stopalarm nach Abrufphase" führt dazu, daß in diesem Zustand die Registerinhalte gesichert werden und zu einer angegebenen Alarmadresse verzweigt wird. Das Bit kann von außen (Operateur) oder durch ein Steuermakro im Code des Bearbeiters gesetzt werden.

Auftragsform an den ZPV: Angabe des Auftraggebers, Registerinhalte nach Stop nach Abrufphase als Information.

Abwicklung der Info.-Ablage: Die Informationsablage wird nach einem Stopalarm nur dann durchgeführt, wenn im Leitblock des Bearbeiters eine Steuervariable gesetzt ist. Diese kann von außen gesetzt und gelöscht werden. Die Alarmbehandlung für diesen Alarm prüft diese Steuervariable und sendet, wenn sie gesetzt ist, an den ZPV eine Botschaft mit Bearbeiterangabe und Registerinhalten.
Bei der Vorbereitung der Ablaufregistrierung wird auch der ZPV benachrichtigt und es werden ihm Auftraggeber, die Adressbereiche, innerhalb derer eine Informationsablage erfolgen soll, und eine Adresse, bei der die Ablaufregistrierung abgeschaltet werden soll, angegeben.
Unter Beachtung dieser Information erzeugt der ZPV aus dem Auftrag ein ZP-Element, welches in den Puffer gestellt wird, und quittiert die Erledigung mit einer Antwort, in der angegeben wird, ob die Ablaufregistrierung fortgesetzt wird.
Die Alarmbehandlung, die die Botschaft sandte, bekommt die Antwort, löscht ggf. das Stopalarm-Bit und setzt den Bearbeiter mit der Befehlsausführungsphase fort. Das Stopalarm-Bit kann auch durch ein Steuermakro im Code des Bearbeiters gelöscht werden.

Bemerkung: Die Vorbereitung der Ablaufregistrierung soll sehr einfach durch ein Operateurkommando mit Angabe der nötigen Parameter geschehen.

3.4.4. Ein- und ausschaltbare Test- und Meßfunktionen in Bearbeitern

Anwendung: Zur bequemen Einrichtung einer Testvariante gegenüber einer Normallaufvariante eines Bearbeiters. Allgemein bei Test- und Meßfunktionen in Bearbeitern, die man bequem ein- oder ausschalten können soll.

Initiierung: Durch Leerbefehle, die nicht verdrahtet sind, sondern bei denen ein Systemunterprogramm angesprungen wird, wenn in der Verwaltungsinformation im Bearbeiterleitblock eine bestimmte Variable in definierter Weise besetzt ist. Sonst sind diese Leerbefehle wirkungslos. Die Steuervariable kann von außen gesetzt werden.

Fall 1: Der Leerbefehl hat nur eine Standardreaktion des Systemunterprogrammes zur Folge (z.B. Senden einer Botschaft an den ZPV mit Inhalt der Register).

Fall 2: Der Leerbefehl wird von dem Systemunterprogramm in einen Unterprogrammsprung umgewandelt. Das Sprungziel im Bearbeiter wird vor dem Leerbefehl in einem Befehlswerksregister bereitgestellt. In dem angesprungenen ("eingeschalteten") Unterprogramm können u.a. auch ZP-Einträge durch Dump oder direkte Informationsablage durchgeführt werden.

Bemerkung: Die Steuervariable soll einfach durch ein Operateur-Kommando gesetzt oder gelöscht werden.

4. Zusammenfassung

Die beschriebenen Verfahren und Einrichtungen zur Informationsgewinnung und -abspeicherung erlauben es, in einer breiten Palette von Anwendungen Information <u>bequem</u> aus dem System zum externen Gebrauch auszuschleusen.

Die Vorbereitung und Definition des "Ereignisses" bis zu dem Punkte: "Jetzt will ich diese Information zur Ausgabe abgespeichert haben" muß vom Interessenten jeweils im Einzelfall durchgeführt werden. Zur Auswertung seiner Ergebnisse können ihm gute Auswertungsprogramme zur Verfügung stehen.

Diese Erkenntnisse, die über Grundeinrichtungen für Messungen zum externen Gebrauch gewonnen werden, dienen nicht allein zur Fortentwicklung <u>dieser</u> Verfahren, sondern auch in zunehmendem Maße für <u>systeminterne</u> Messungen zur Erfassung und Transfer von Meßgrößen, die zur <u>internen Regelung</u> des Betriebsablaufes gebraucht werden.

Literatur-Referenzen:

1 G. Goos, J. Jürgens, K. Lagally:
The Operating System BSM, viewed as a Community of Parallel Processes.
T.U.-München, Abt. Mathematik, BS-Gruppe, Bericht 7208

2 P.C. Poole:
Debugging and Testing.
Advanced Course on Software Engineering.
T.U.-München, 1972

3 G. Mersmann:
Planung von Meßverfahren in einem Teilnehmerrechensystem.
NTG/GI-Fachtagung in Darmstadt, April 1972

ANALYSIS OF DEMAND PAGING ALGORITHMS

A.PALMBOOM

1. Introduction

In a memory hierarchy of two memories, named buffer and background memory, the traffic of information between buffer and background memory can be ruled by various algorithms. The information is organized in pages. A page is the smallest amount of information that can be transported separately. The processor is supposed always to see first in the buffer for a page, in which it needs some information. If an algorithm only moves pages if the processor does not find a needed page, then the algorithm is a DEMAND PAGING ALGORITHM. In this paper we make the assumption that all DEMANDS for PAGES of the PROCESSOR are independent, and the probability for each PAGE to be demanded is constant during the processing of a program. In [1] such a program behaviour is called stationary 0-order program behaviour. The sequence of all page addresses, generated by the demands of the processor, is named REFERENCE TRACE, the processor is said to make references to the pages. The probability that the processor finds the demanded page in the buffer is named HITRATE and the probability that it is not, MISRATE. So, HITRATE + MISRATE = 1.

In 2 we develop mathematical description of the stationary 0-order programs, assuming the total number of different pages very large.

In 4 the hitrate is derived from that program model, for the various DEMAND PAGING algorithms named FIFO, RO, LRU, OPT, CYCLE n and RO n, which are explained in 3. The algorithm SUBOPT is explained, and its hitrate is derived, in 2.

2. Mathematical description of the program behaviour

We suppose, as AHO e.a., [1], N = 1, ..., n are the pages of a given program. Each page has a probability, independent of time, that is, independent of the point on the reference trace. The probability of page i, to be referenced at one reference of the processor, is p_i, $1 \leqq i \leqq n$. $\sum_{i=1}^{n} p_i = 1$. We now assume n to be large, as molecules in 1 dm^3 gas.

The number of references in a reference trace is also large, even large compared with n. A single page is not suitable to be a measure for the total amount of pages, and neither is a single reference for the length of the trace. Therefore, we take as unit of amount of pages the total amount of pages of the program considered. This is also the unit of length of reference trace: a reference trace that contains each page of the program one time and only one time, has the unit length. The probability of one individual page in general is practically zero. Therefore, we caracterize the probabilities of the page by p_i x n; the mean of this for all pages is 1. p_i x n is the expectation of the number of times page i occurs in a part of unit length of the trace. In a large trace we may see it as the frequency of occurrence of page i, that is the number of times of occurrence divided by the length of the trace. We use the word DEMAND RATE and the symbol x for this frequency of occurrence. Now it is conceivable that all pages are arranged in order of non increasing DEMAND RATE. We then can define in the following two manners the distribution of DEMAND RATES of the pages, also called the program behaviour.

A. Define H(b) as follows, $0 \leq b \leq 1$:

   the range in order of non increasing DEMAND RATE is divided in two parts: one with size b and one with size 1-b. The one with size b contains the pages with greatest DEMAND RATES, each page of that part has greater DEMAND RATE than each page of the other part. The page with DEMAND RATE just equal to the critical dividing value, is said to have RANGE NUMBER b. That page may be reckoned to belong to one or the other part, as the size of one individual page is neglected. Hereafter we use "PAGES BETWEEN b_1 and b_2" for "PAGES WITH RANGE NUMBER BETWEEN b_1 and b_2". H(b) is defined now as the fraction of all references in the trace that are to the part of size b with the greatest DEMAND RATES. Clearly H(b) is a monotonic non-decreasing function of b, and H(0)=0 and H(1)=1.

   If, for example, $H(\frac{1}{10}) = \frac{19}{20}$, then 95% of all references is made to the 10% of the pages with greatest DEMAND RATE, and therefore only 5% of the references are made then to the remaining 90% of the pages.

B. F(x) is the fraction of all pages with DEMAND RATE less than x. Clearly F(x) is a monotonic non-decreasing function of x, and F(0)=0 and $F(\infty)=1$.

Now we explain a DEMAND PAGING algorithm, which we call SUBOPT.
In [1] an algorithm is described as Denning-Chen-Shedler optimal algorithm. It assumes all DEMAND RATES, at least their relative order, to be known, which is not true, in general. Then we always can, if the buffer is filled and a page outside the buffer is referenced, threw out the page that has, of all pages in the buffer, the smallest DEMAND RATE. When the program lasts very long, in the limiting, stationary state just all pages, total relative size = b = relative buffer size, with greatest DEMAND RATES are in the buffer. Apart of just one place, the same each time, of the

buffer, whose page changes if a page outside the buffer is referenced, there is no traffic between buffer and background memory. That one place has a size that can be neglected. So we may renounce of all traffic of pages, for this analysis: fill the buffer with the pages, in order of decreasing DEMAND RATE. Even in case a page outside the buffer is referenced, we do not exchange pages. The HITRATE now is the probability that a referenced page is found in the buffer. This is the probability of referencing one of the pages of the part of fraction b with the greatest DEMAND RATES. This just is H(b) as defined above. So H(b) is the HITRATE as function of the relative buffer size b, under the algorithm SUBOPT.

We now derive a relation between H(b) and F(x).
First we make the assumption that $\frac{dH}{db}$ and $\frac{d^2H}{db^2}$ exist and $\frac{d^2H}{db^2} \neq 0$ for $0 < b < 1$. Then we look at some cases that not all these conditions are satisfied.
Thus, now assume $\frac{dH}{db}$ and $\frac{d^2H}{db^2}$ exist and $\frac{d^2H}{db^2} \neq 0$.

$$\frac{dH(b)}{db} = \lim_{\Delta b \to 0} \frac{H(b+\Delta b)-H(b)}{\Delta b} =$$

$$\lim_{\Delta b \to 0} \frac{\text{fraction of all references, to pages between b and b+}\Delta b}{\Delta b} =$$

$$\lim_{\Delta b \to 0} \frac{\text{number of references per unit trace length, to pages between b and b+}\Delta b}{\text{number of pages between b and b+}\Delta b} =$$

$\lim_{\Delta b \to 0}$ mean DEMAND RATE of the pages between b and b+ Δb = DEMAND RATE of page with RANGE NUMBER b.

So: $\frac{dH}{db} = x$.

The range is made in order of non-increasing x, so $\frac{dH}{db}$ is non-increasing and $\frac{d^2H}{db^2} \leq 0$, if it exists.
With the first assumption we have $\frac{d^2H}{db^2} < 0$, and $x = \frac{dH}{db}$ is a monotonic decreasing function of b. So, this function can be inverted:
$b = b(x)$. The page with DEMAND RATE x has RANGE NUMBER $b = b(x)$, and

$$\frac{db}{dx} = \frac{1}{\frac{dx}{db}} = \frac{1}{\frac{d^2H}{db^2}} .$$

b(x) is the fraction of pages with DEMAND RATE not less than $x = \frac{dH}{db}$.
Therefore, $b(x) = 1-F(x)$ and $\frac{dF(x)}{dx} = -\frac{1}{\frac{d^2H}{db^2}}$ which is > 0 as $\frac{d^2H}{db^2} < 0$.

With $x = \frac{dH}{db}$ and the boundary conditions $H(0)=0$, $H(1)=1$, $F(0)=0$ and $F(\infty)=1$ this fixes the relation between $H(b)$ and $F(x)$.

$\frac{dF(x)}{dx}$ exists; we define $f(x) = \frac{dF(x)}{dx}$.

$f(x_1)dx$ is the fraction of all pages with DEMAND RATE between x_1 and x_1+dx.

The fraction of all references, made to the pages with DEMAND RATE between x_1 and x_1-dx is $-(\frac{dH}{dx})_{x=x_1} dx = -(\frac{dH}{db}\frac{db}{dx})_{x=x_1} dx = x_1 f(x_1)dx$.

Therefore, $\int_0^\infty f(x)dx=1$ and $\int_0^\infty xf(x)dx=1$.

Discontinuities of $f(x)$ may exist, they do not influence the derivation of the relations between $H(b)$ and $F(x)$.

In some generalized way these relations still hold under less stringent assumptions about differentiability. We do not give details here.

Example: $f(x) = e^{-x}$, $x > 0$.

$F(x) = \int_0^x e^{-u}du = 1-e^{-x}$, which satisfies the conditions $F(0) = 0$ and $F(\infty) = 1$.

$b(x) = 1-F(x)$ and further derivation gives:

$b(x) = e^{-x}$

$x(b) = -\ln b$

$\frac{dH}{db} = -\ln b$, which, with $H(0) = 0$, gives $H(b) = b(1-\ln b)$, which satisfies $H(1) = 1$.

3. The DEMAND PAGING ALGORITHMS

The algorithm SUBOPT was already explained in 2, owing to its close relation with the distribution functions of references and DEMAND RATES. Here the algorithms FIFO, RO, LRU, OPT, CYCLE n and RO n will be set forth. This is done in terms of a finite number of pages, say V and the number of page places in the buffer we call B.

So $b = \frac{B}{V}$.

All these algorithms are DEMAND PAGING algorithms:

only when the buffer is filled, that is, B pages are in the buffer, and a page outside the buffer is referenced, a page is thrown out of the buffer. The referenced page comes in the buffer then. Therefore, to describe the algorithms it is sufficient to describe how the algorithm indicates the page to be thrown out, in case this is needed.

FIFO, First In First Out.

The page that has remained the longest time in the buffer, is thrown out.

RO, Random Out.

The page to be thrown out is chosen at random. Each of the pages in the buffer has a probability $\frac{1}{B}$ to be thrown out.

LRU, Least Recently Used.
The page to which is made no reference (is not used) for the longest time, seeing back from the moment "NOW", that is seeing back from "now" on the reference trace, is thrown out. If the thrown out page was referenced the last time at a point, say t_1, on the reference trace, then between t_1 and "now" each other page that is in the buffer now, has been referenced at least one time.

OPT, optimal algorithm. This algorithm is still more unrealistic as SUBOPT, ch. 2. It assumes the whole reference trace to be known. This is not in contradiction with the definition of 0-order stationary state: we may think of a trace first generated following 0-order stationary state, and after that the algorithm is allowed to see at the whole trace, also forward, "in the future". The algorithm threws out the page which will not be referenced for the longest time, that is, does not occur the longest distance from now in forward direction on the trace. Note that each other page now in the buffer, will occur at least one time before the first occurrence of the chosen page.

CYCLE n.
We can describe FIFO by considering all buffer places arranged in a cycle; a pointer points to a place, the page on that place is the first to be replaced after now; if it is replaced, the pointer goes to the following buffer place in the cycle. With CYCLE n to each place is assigned a counter which can take the values 0, 1, ..., n, n is a nonnegative integer. As with FIFO, the places are arranged in a cycle and a pointer points to a place. If a page outside the buffer is referenced, the pointer looks at the counter of the place where it points to. If the counter has value 0, the page on that place can be thrown out and the referenced page is placed on that place. The counter remains 0, the pointer goes to the following place in the cycle, where it awaits the following reference to a page outside the buffer. If the counter has value greater than 0, the counter is diminished by 1, its page stays there, and the pointer goes to the following place in the cycle, where it looks again to the counter and acts exactly as at the first place. So, it goes on, diminishing counters that are greater than 0, up to the first counter it encounters that has value 0. The pointer always finds a counter with value 0 at last, for if first there is no counter with value 0, the pointer goes round the cycle as many times as necessary to set a counter 0 and find it 0 one round further. If a page in the buffer is referenced, the counter of its place increases 1. However, n is the maximum value of the counter; if it

is n then it remains n.
Obviously, CYCLE 0 is the same as FIFO.
CYCLE1 is known under the name SECOND CHANGE.

RO n.
This is an analogous generalization of RO as CYCLE n of FIFO. To each place in the buffer is assigned a counter again which can take the values 0, 1, ..., n, n is a nonnegative integer. If a page outside the buffer is referenced, and the buffer is filled, a page of the buffer is chosen at random, each page in the buffer has a probability $\frac{1}{B}$ to be chosen. If its counter has value 0, the page is replaced by the referenced page which starts its stay at the buffer with counter value 0. If the counter has value greater than 0, the counter is diminished by 1, the page stays, and another page is chosen at random. And so on, until a page is chosen with counter value 0, which then is replaced. If a page in the buffer is referenced, its counter increases 1. However, n is the maximum value of the counter; if it is n then it remains n.
Obviously, RO 0 is exactly RO.

4. MISRATE

In 2 the distribution function F(x) was introduced, the fraction of all pages with DEMAND RATE less than x. Of that pages, a part is in the buffer. We define G(x) as the fraction of all pages satisfying the two conditions: DEMAND RATE is less than x, page is in the buffer. Obviously $G(x) \leqq F(x)$, $dG(x) \leqq dF(x)$, $G(0)=0$ and $G(\infty)=b$, where b is again the relative buffer size. For all described algorithms, except OPT, the population in the buffer is independent of the further references on the trace. Therefore, for all algorithms except OPT:
HITRATE= $\int_0^\infty x dG(x)$ and MISRATE= $\int_0^\infty x d\{F(x)-G(x)\}$, these being the probabilities that a reference is made to a page in, or outside, the buffer respectively. For deriving relations between MISRATE and b, one can try to write down equations between streams of pages as a function of x. We assume without proof that all algorithms will reach a stationary state.
Another method is to consider one individual page A with DEMAND RATE x, and derive the number of times per unit trace length it is expected to go from outside the buffer into the buffer. This we call the INSTREAM RATE. It is a function of x. Integrating over all pages gives the MISRATE.

RO. The amount of pages going into the buffer per unit trace length, with DEMAND RATE between x and x+dx is proportional with the amount of pages outside the buffer with DEMAND RATE between x and x+dx, and proportional with the DEMAND RATE x. The amount of pages going out of the buffer per unit trace length, with DEMAND RATE between x and x+dx, is proportional to the amount of pages with such DEMAND RATE in the buffer, for the pages are chosen at random. Therefore

$$D\ x\{dF(x)-dG(x)\} = dG(x), \text{ so}$$

$$dG(x) = \frac{DxdF(x)}{1+Dx} \quad \text{and} \quad d\{F(x)-G(x)\} = \frac{dF(x)}{1+Dx}$$

The relation between MISRATE and b is now fixed by

$$b = \int_0^\infty \frac{DxdF(x)}{1+Dx} \quad \text{and} \quad \text{MISRATE} = \int_0^\infty \frac{xdF(x)}{1+Dx},$$

D may vary between 0 and ∞.

FIFO. In a natural way we chose in case of RO the stream equation method. Here we use the other, and look at one page A with DEMAND RATE x. The length of the reference trace corresponding with one stay of A in, resp. outside, the buffer, are random variables $\underline{li}$ and $\underline{lo}$ resp. $\underline{li}$ is obviously independent of x, we set $\underline{li}$ = D, constant in a stationary state. When A is thrown out, it stays outside the buffer until its next reference. The probability distribution of $\underline{lo}$ is independent of the foregoing, and on each moment the remainder of $\underline{lo}$ has the same distribution. This is a consequence of the model we are considering, the 0-order stationary state. In terms of conditional probabilities:

$$P\left\{\underline{lo}-a<c \mid \underline{lo}>a\right\} = P\left\{\underline{lo}<c\right\},\ c>0.$$

The only distribution with this property is the negative exponential distribution,

$$P\left\{\underline{lo}<c\right\} = 1-e^{-uc}, \text{ with expectation } E\left\{\underline{lo}\right\} = \frac{1}{u}$$

The frequency of occurrence in the trace of page A is x, see 2. Therefore the expectation of the length of interval until a next reference of A is $\frac{1}{x}$. So u=x and $P\left\{\underline{lo}<c\right\} = 1-e^{-xc}$ and $E\left\{\underline{lo}\right\} = \frac{1}{x}$.

Let $\underline{lc} = \underline{li}+\underline{lo}$; $\underline{li}$ and $\underline{lo}$ are independent random variables, therefore

$$E\left\{\underline{lc}\right\} = E\left\{\underline{li}\right\} + E\left\{\underline{lo}\right\} = D+\frac{1}{x}.$$

The INSTREAM RATE is

$$\frac{1}{E\left\{\underline{lc}\right\}} = \frac{x}{1+Dx} \quad \text{and MISRATE} = \int_0^\infty \frac{xdF(x)}{1+Dx}.$$

$$\text{Further: } \frac{dG(x)}{dF(x)} = \frac{E\left\{\underline{li}\right\}}{E\left\{\underline{lc}\right\}} = \frac{Dx}{1+Dx}, \text{ therefore}$$

$$b = \int_0^\infty dG(x) = \int_0^\infty \frac{DxdF(x)}{Dx+1}.$$

So we have the same relations as with RO, be it that D is introduced otherwise. In fact we could have used the second method for RO. $E\left\{\underline{li}\right\} = D$

again, the only difference is that with FIFO also $P\{\underline{li} = D\} = 1$, which does not hold with RO.

LRU. Here both methods can be applied. D is here introduced as the trace length on which the buffer fills up, with any demand paging algorithm. If during D a page in the buffer is not used, it will go out of the buffer, under the LRU algorithm. In the second method we see that $\underline{li}$ is built up out of reference intervals less than D. This equals the situation of the wait time problem of a pedestrian crossing a traffic lane. Only, here one interval with length D must be added. $E\{\underline{lo}\}$ is, as with FIFO, $\frac{1}{x}$.
$E\{\underline{li}\} = \frac{1}{x}(e^{xD}-1-xD)+D = \frac{1}{x}(e^{xD}-1)$, and $E\{\underline{lc}\} = E\{\underline{li}\} + E\{\underline{lo}\} = \frac{1}{x}e^{xD}$.
In the same way as in the case of FIFO we find

$$b = \int_0^\infty (1-e^{-xD})dF(x) \text{ and MISRATE } = \int_0^\infty xe^{-xD}dF(x).$$

The wait time problem of the crossing pedestrian we took from Stam, [4], VIII, 2, voorb. 12.

OPT. With the algorithm OPT the buffer population depends on the trace not yet referenced as well as on the trace already referenced. We may expect the pages with short interval between last reference before "here" and first reference after "here" in the buffer. This is analogous to the paradoxal example in Feller, [3]. Ch. I, 4, concerning the waiting time for next bus arrival. We derived here

$$b = \int_0^\infty \{1-(Dx+1)e^{-Dx}\} dF(x) \text{ and MISRATE } = \int_0^\infty xe^{-xD}dF(x)$$

CYCLE n. We set $dF(x)-dG(x) = f_0(x)$ and $dG(x) = f_1(x) + \dots + f_n(x)$. The population in the buffer is divided in n parts, to which the frequency functions $f_j(x)$ correspond. Page A belongs to part j if the last time the pointer passed, it decreased its counter from i to i-1. A page from outside the buffer comes into part 1.
The following equations can now be derived:

$$x\, f_0(x) = \frac{1}{D}e^{-xD}f_1(x),$$

$$f_j(x) = \sum_{k=1}^{j-1} \left\{f_k(x). \sum_{l=j-k+1}^{\infty} \frac{(xD)^l}{l!}\right\}, \quad j = 2, \dots, n$$

D is the length of reference trace during with the pointer in the buffer turns round one time. For CYCLE1, the SECOND CHANCE algorithm, we have

$$dG(x) = \frac{dF(x)}{1+xDe^{xD}} \quad \text{and thus}$$

$$b = \int_0^\infty \frac{dF(x)}{1+xDe^{xD}}, \quad \text{MISRATE} = \int_0^\infty \frac{x^2De^{xD}dF(x)}{1+xDe^{xD}}.$$

RO n. We now define n+1 parts in the buffer. Page A belongs to part i+1 if its counter is i, i = 0, 1, ..., n. Corresponding frequency functions are again $f_1(x)$, $f_2(x)$, ..., $f_{n+1}(x)$.
As with RO, that is RO 0, we have $Dxf_0(x) = f_1(x)$.
Similar equations now hold:

$$Dxf_i(x) = f_{i+1}(x),\ i = 1, \ldots, n,$$

with the same D, for the random choice is made out of the total population with frequency function $f_1(x) + \ldots + f_{n+1}(x)$.

Now $f(x) = \sum_{i=0}^{n+1} f_i(x) = \sum_{i=0}^{n+1} f_0(x)(xD)^i = f_0(x).\frac{1-(xD)^{n+2}}{1-xD}$,

and $f_0(x) = \frac{1-xD}{1-(xD)^{n+2}} f(x)$.

In this equation we can easy see at the limiting case $n \longrightarrow \infty$. We see that pages with $x > \frac{1}{D}$ have probability 1 to be in the buffer, for they have $f_0(x) = 0$.

Computations on some simple examples of F(x), with only two different values of x, suggest that LRU does better than FIFO and RO, but CYCLE1 better than LRU, with little difference. We state the guess that the limiting cases of CYCLE n and RO n for $n \longrightarrow \infty$ are the best algorithm under the assumption that only information is kept concerning references to pages now in the buffer, from the moment they came in. Superfluous to remind this concerns only the 0-order stationary state.

The basic ideas we took particularly from:

[1] Aho, Denning, Ullman.
Principles of optimal page replacement
Journal ACM, vol. 13, no. 1, Jan. 71 p.p. 80-93.

[2] Mattson, Gecsei, Slutz, Traiger.
Evaluation techniques for storage hierarchies.
IBM Systems Journal no. 2 1970 p.p. 78-117.

[3] W. Feller.
An Introduction to Probability Theory and Its Applications, volume II, sec. ed., Wiley, 1970.

[4] A.J. Stam.
Inleiding tot de waarschijnlijkheidsrekening.
Uitgeverij H. Stam, 1964.

The idea of streaming equations are due to C.P.J. Alewijnse, who developed with A. Palmboom the topic reported here.

EINIGE METHODEN ZUR VORHERSAGE DES VERHALTENS KLEINER SYSTEME MIT VIRTUELLEM SPEICHER

K.M.SCHULZ

Hintergrund

Unser Entwicklungsprojekt begann Ende 1970, als für das untere Ende der System /370 Modellreihe eine Programmierunterstützung der dynamischen Adreßumsetzung geplant wurde. Damals wurden verschiedene Möglichkeiten erörtert, und selbst während der Entwicklungsarbeiten machte das Projekt noch einige Veränderungen mit, beginnend mit einem sehr spezialisierten Entwurf und schließlich endend in einem sehr verallgemeinerten, wie er Mitte des Jahres angekündigt worden ist.

Die wesentlichen Eigenschaften sind:

- Mehrere virtuelle Programmbereiche in einem eindeutigen, virtuellen Adreßraum,
- der Hauptspeicher wird als ein Pool von Seitenrahmen für alle aktiven virtuellen Programme benutzt und enthält daneben den Supervisor.
- Eine Supervisorerweiterung enthält:
  - o Seitenverwaltungsroutinen, die Kontrolle erhalten, wennimmer eine Fehladressierung auftritt, die augenblicklich nicht im Hauptspeicher dargestellt werden kann. In diesem Fall wird eine andere Seite im Hauptspeicher durch diejenige ersetzt, die die referierte Adresse enthält.
  - o Kanalprogrammübersetzungsroutinen, die für jede Ein/Ausgabe-Operation das entsprechende virtuelle Kanalprogramm übersetzen, da die Kanäle sich nicht der dynamischen Adreßumsetzung bedienen.
  - o Seitenfestlegungsroutinen, die vorübergehend für jede Ein/Ausgabe-Operation die vom Kanal benötigten Bereiche sowie Kontrollblöcke festlegen.

Anfang 1971 war nun ein Plan entwickelt worden zur Beantwortung aller Fragen, die sich auf das Leistungsverhalten dieses Systems und natürlich der vorhergehenden Entwürfe bezogen; Fragen wie:

- welcher Entwurf,
- Seitenrahmenpool auf Programm- oder Systembasis,
- das Verhalten heutiger DOS Programme in einem virtuellen System,

- die Ausnutzung des Hauptspeichers und die Möglichkeit, mehr Programme parallel durchzuführen,
- der zusätzliche Zeitaufwand aufgrund der Adreßumsetzung in der Maschine und im Kontrollprogramm,
- das allgemeine Leistungsverhalten der virtuellen Speicherunterstützung im DOS in Abhängigkeit vom verfügbaren Hauptspeicher.

Verschiedene Fragen des Entwurfs, die sich im Leistungsverhalten niederschlagen, wurden ohne Modell oder anderen Mitteln, allein mit logischen Argumenten entschieden. Die wesentlichen Fragen jedoch, einschließlich Leistungszahlen, wurden im Leistungsplan beantwortet, wie er im folgenden beschrieben wird:

Leistungsplan:

Um gewisse Ergebnisse so früh wie möglich zu erhalten, wurde ein Stufenplan entwickelt, bestehend aus vier Stufen in folgender Reihenfolge:

1. Analytische Untersuchungen des Verhaltens von Programmen in einem virtuellen System mit der Voraussage des Leistungsabfalls.
2. Entwicklung eines Modells zur genaueren Erfassung der Gesichtspunkte überlappter Ein/Ausgabe-Operationen.
3. Untersuchung des Mehrprogrammbetriebs am Modell, d.h. die Hauptspeicherausnutzung im virtuellen Mehrprogrammbetrieb, wobei der Hauptspeicher aufgrund des augenblichlichen Bedarfs und nicht nach der maximalen Größe an die verschiedenen Programme verteilt wird.
4. Entwicklung eines experimentellen virtuellen DOS Systems (Prototyp) zum Zweck, echte Programme auf einem System /370 mit dynamischer Adreßumwandlung laufen zu lassen. Das erlaubt bereits, die Leistungsgrößen mit denen des endgültigen Produkts zu vergleichen, sofern man die nötigen Korrekturen berücksichtigt wegen Unterschieden im Entwurf.

Die Stufen 1 und 2 legten mehr Gewicht auf das Leistungsverhalten einzelner Programme, die Stufen 3 und 4 betonten die Eigenschaften des Mehrprogrammbetriebs. Insbesondere gewannen 3 und 4 an Bedeutung, nachdem man die Ergebnisse der vorhergehenden Stufen verstand.

Analytische Untersuchungen

Diese Untersuchungen basierten auf Programm-'Traces', die alle Adreßreferenzen eines einzelnen Programmes zusammen mit dem Supervisor enthielten, Diese Traces wurden durch ein spezielles Programm verwertet, das einen Seitenaustauschalgorithmus enthielt sowie gewisse Parameter wie Seitengrößen und verfügbaren Hauptspeicher. Das Programm erlaubt, einzelne Seiten dauernd festzuhalten und zwar solche, die den Supervisor und Ein/Ausgabebereiche enthalten.

Als Ergebnis dieser Auswertungen erhielt man die mittlere Anzahl ausgeführter Instruktionen eines Programmes zwischen zwei aufeinanderfolgenden Fehladressierungen in Abhängigkeit vom Überbelegungsfaktor, dem Verhältnis von verfügbarem Hauptspeicher zur Programmgröße. Figur 1 zeigt diese Abhängigkeit für einige DOS Programme.

Indem man die Zeit berücksichtigt, die anfällt, um eine Fehladressierung zu behandeln, also im wesentlichen die Zeit für einen Seitenwechsel sowie die Geschwindigkeit der einzelnen Systemelemente, könnte das Diagramm in ein Leistungsdiagramm übersetzt werden; allerdings mit gewissen Annäherungen besonders bezüglich des Ein/Ausgabeverhaltens.

Grobes Modell

Ein grobes Modell, das ebenfalls auf der mittleren Anzahl ausgeführter Instruktionen beruht, brachte bessere Ergebnisse, da es auch das richtige (überlappte) Ein/Ausgabeverhalten berücksichtigte. Figur 2 zeigt die Durchsatzbereiche für die untersuchten DOS-Programme als Funktion des Überbelegungsfaktors.

Die Ergebnisse dieser frühen Stufen zeigten, daß einige existierende DOS Programme eine Überbelegung des Speichers erlauben, daß jedoch für ihre Mehrzahl die Leistung stark abfällt, selbst wenn nur eine Seite weggenommen wird. Man beachte, daß diese Programme nicht angepaßt wurden an das virtuelle Konzept. Der Schluß war daher, daß vom Leistungsgesichtspunkt betrachtet, solche Programme normalerweise den Hauptspeicher nicht überbelegen dürfen. Diese Möglichkeit sollte für Sonderfälle existieren. Jedoch der Leistungsvorteil eines virtuellen Speichersystems sollte in der besseren Ausnutzung des Hauptspeichers liegen und damit in der Fähigkeit, den Grad des Mehrprogrammbetriebs bei schlecht genutztem System zu erhöhen.

Verschiedene Installationen wurden untersucht um festzustellen, inwieweit sie den Hauptspeicher heute ausnutzen. Figur 3 zeigt einige Ergebnisse. Sie sind typisch für ein System mit festen Programmbereichen, die auf die größten Programme zugeschnitten sind. Die nächste Methode berücksichtigt diesen Sachverhalt.

Mehrprogramm-Modell

Dieses Modell wurde gespeist mit Kurven, die die Programmbereichsausnutzung darstellten und bildete daraus eine Kurve für das System. Die mittlere Anzahl durchlaufener Instruktionen zwischen zwei Fehladdressierungen wurde berechnet und sodann wie beim vorher beschriebenen Modell fortgefahren. Figur 4 zeigt nun die so gewonnenen Durchsatzbereiche auf Systembasis im Gegensatz zu Figur 2 auf Auftragsbasis. Der Bereich ist schmäler und der Durchsatz fällt weniger ab für vergleichbare Speichergrößen.

Figur 5 versucht eine Erklärung dafür:
Zwei Auftragsfolgen, die jeweils in ihren Programmbereich passen, aber ein System, das zu jedem Zeitpunkt unbenutzten Hauptspeicher aufweist. Einer einzelnen Auftragsfolge Hauptspeicher wegzunehmen würde ihren Durchsatz verringern. Beim ganzen System hat das bis zu einer bestimmten Größe überhaupt keinen Einfluß. Diese Tatsache rechtfertigte die Einführung eines Seitenrahmenpools auf Systembasis im Gegensatz mehrerer auf Programmbasis, die keine bessere Hauptspeicherverwaltung bringen.

Prototyp

Schließlich wurde ein experimentelles virtuelles Speichersystem entwikkelt, indem ein früherer DOS Rel. modifiziert wurde, sodaß er nun Seitenwechsel, Kanalprogrammübersetzung und Seitenfestlegung auf einem System /370 durchführen konnte. Es handelte sich um kein richtiges virtuelles System. Um Probleme bei Fehladressierungen in ununterbrechbaren Supervisorzuständen zu vermeiden, befinden sich die Programme bei ihrer Ausführung stets vollkommen im Hauptspeicher. Jedoch sind sie nur teilweise adressierbar über die sog. Seitentabellen. Bei normaler Fehladressierung werden die Tabellen auf den neuesten Stand gebracht und eine realistische Ein/Ausgabeoperation durchgeführt. Andernfalls werden nur sofort die Tabellen verändert, jedoch die Ein/Ausgabeoperationen,der eigentliche Seitenwechsel, aufgeschoben, bis es der Supervisorzustand erlaubt, die Operation nachzuvollziehen. Da derartige Fehladressierungen nicht häufig auftreten und ihre Behandlung auch nur aufgeschoben wird, ist der Fehler vernachlässigbar.

Der Prototyp arbeitet mit einem FIFO-Seitenwechsel-Algorithmus. Kanalprogramme werden übersetzt,doch die ursprünglichen werden ausgeführt. Das Verfahren sorgt auch im Gegensatz zu den vorherigen Methoden für ein zeitlich realistisches, zeitweises Festlegen von Ein/Ausgabebereichen.

Die Programme, die über den Prototyp laufen sollten, wurden ausgewählt unter dem Gesichtspunkt, den Arbeitsanfall einer typischen DOS Installation darzustellen. Sie bildeten ein Gemisch aus

- *Übersetzungs- und Ausführungsarbeiten*
- *Wissenschaftlich/technische und kaufmännische Anwendungen*
- *FORTRAN/COBOL/PL/I/SORT*
- *Verschiedene Datenorganisationen*
- *Verschiedener Hauptspeicherbedarf*
- *Verschiedene Auslastung der Zentraleinheit*

Der so gebildete konstante Arbeitsanfall wurde unter verschiedenen Umständen gemessen:

- *In 1, 2 und 3 Programmbereichen*
- *Auf verschieden großen Maschinen*

Man beachte, daß die Auftragsfolgen in keiner Weise optimisiert waren bezüglich des Hauptspeicherbedarfs.

Figur 6 zeigt das Leistungsverhalten jener konstanten Auftragsmenge in verschieden großen S/370 Modellen 145. Verschiedene Maschinengrößen erlaubten stets einen gewissen Grad von Mehrfachprogrammierung, die Figur zeigt stets den günstigsten Fall, z.B. bei 128 K Hauptspeicher 2 reelle bzw. 3 virtuelle Programmbereiche.

Im allgemeinen erlaubt die Figur den Schluß, daß die Leistung unseres Systems annehmbar ist. Man beachte, daß die Leistungsfähigkeit eines Systems nicht allein durch die Anzahl von Aufträgen pro Zentraleinheit, sondern auch durch solche weniger meßbare Größen bestimmt ist wie: erforderlicher Programmier-, Planungs- und Handhabungsaufwand. Gerade in dieser Hinsicht bildet das System besondere Vorteile.

Schlußbemerkung

Der Vortrag versuchte die Methoden zu beschreiben, die wir benutzen, um ein Gefühl dafür zu bekommen, was die Leistung unseres Systems sein wird, wie wir versuchten, ein virtuelles System besser zu verstehen und wie wir unsere Betrachtungsweise änderten und den Mehrprogrammbetrieb später betonten. Die Ereignisse selbst wurden nur gestreift. Erwähnt sei, daß unsere Untersuchungen am endgültigen Produkt gute Übereinstimmung lieferten.

Fig. 1 Mittlere Instruktionszahl (MIZ) bei variablem Hauptspeicher

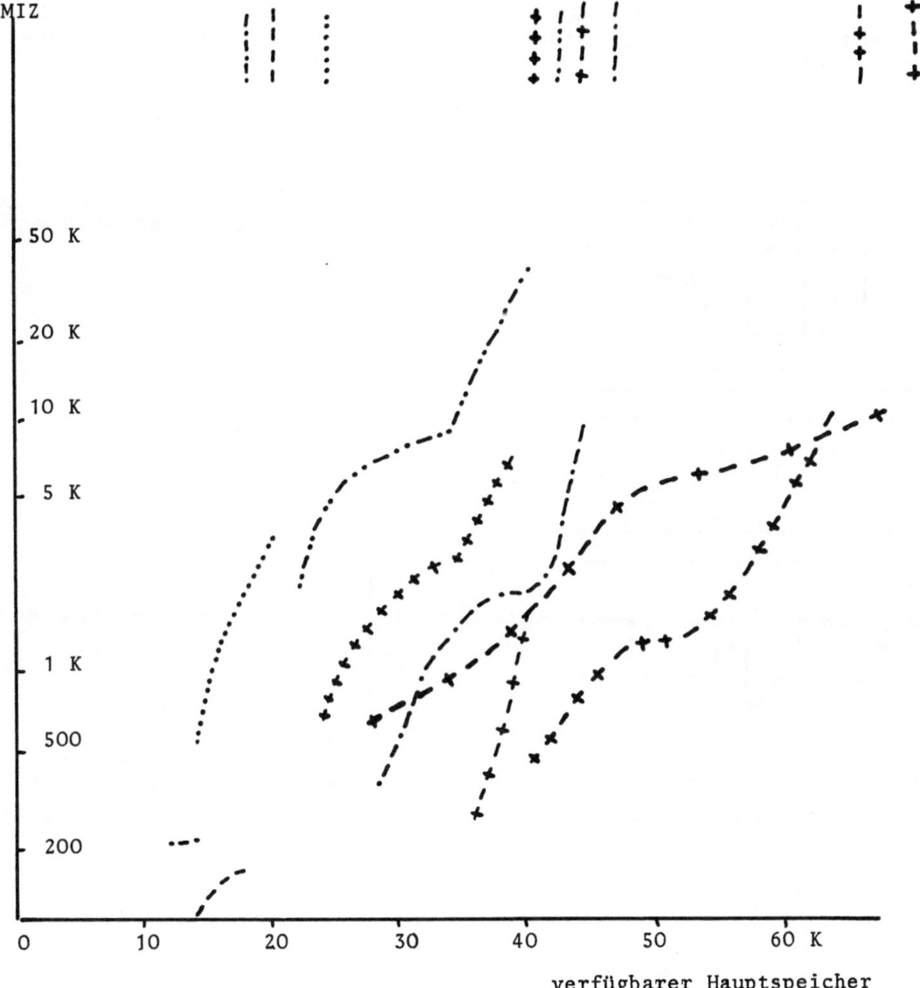

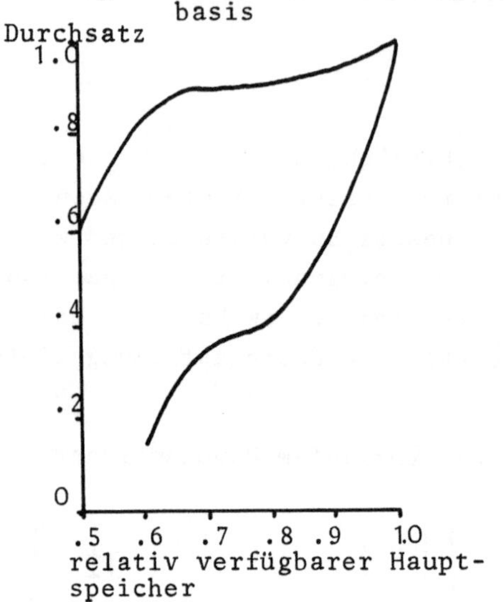

Fig. 2 Durchsatz auf Programmbasis

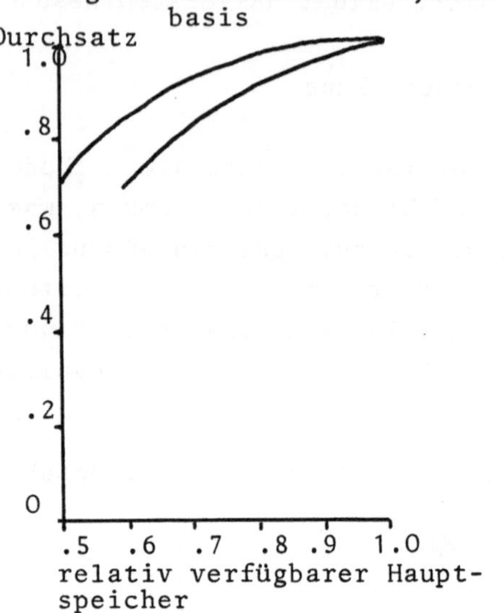

Fig. 4 Durchsatz auf Systembasis

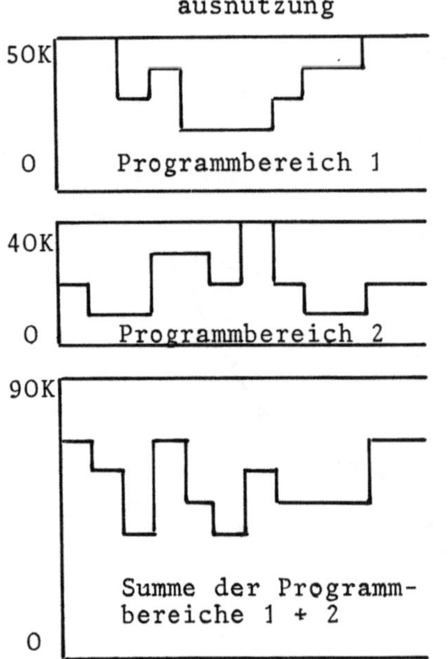

Fig. 5 Zeitliche Speicherausnutzung

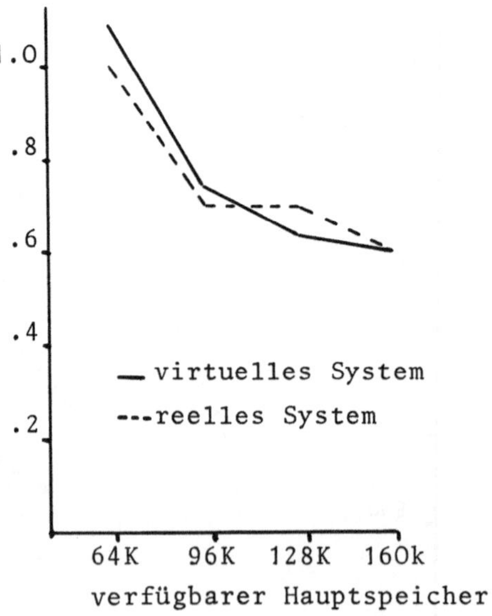

Fig. 6 Zeitbedarf einer konstanten Arbeitsmenge

Fig. 3
Wahrscheinlichkeit relativer Programmgrößen und Programmbereichsausnutzung

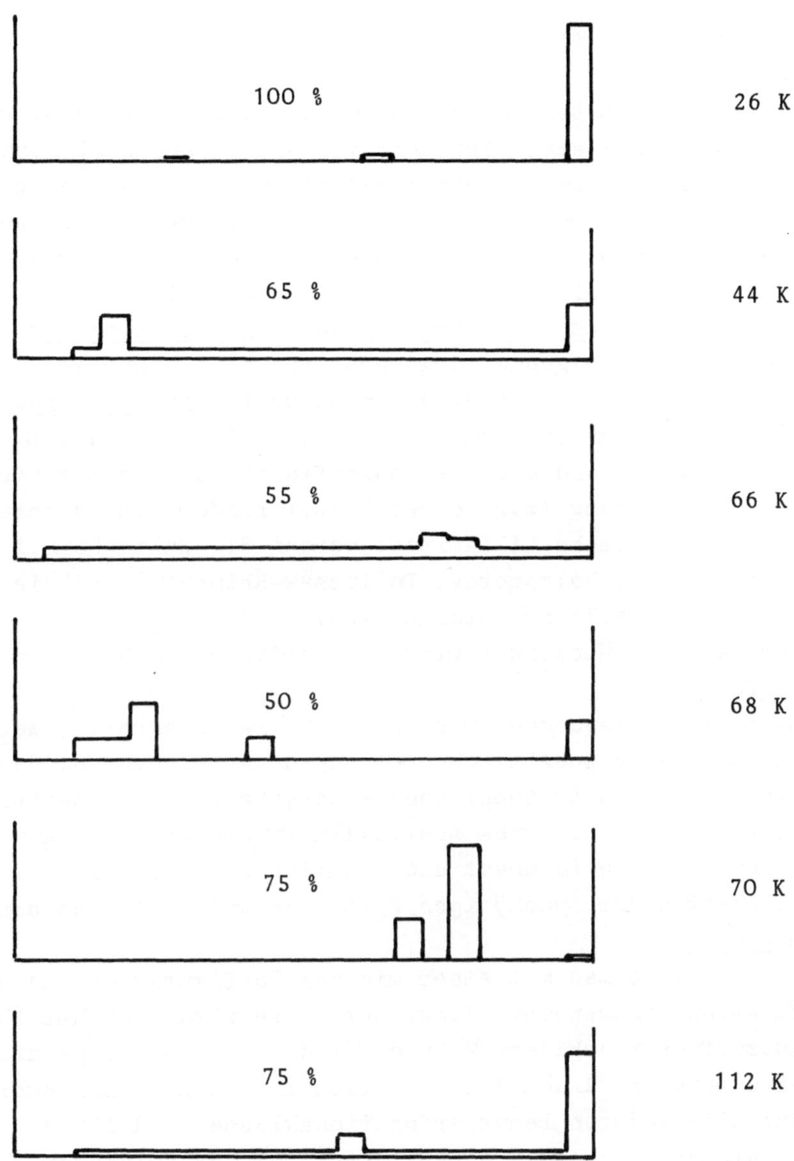

FUNKTIONSKLASSEN UND DYNAMISCHE SPEICHERVERWALTUNG IN REALZEIT - DATENVERARBEITUNGSSYSTEMEN

C.KUCK

1. Einleitung

Es wird eine Betriebssystemstruktur zugrunde gelegt, wie sie in dem Buch des Verfassers "Programmsysteme für Realzeitrechner" (Oldenbourg Verlag, München und Wien) beschrieben worden ist. Diese Struktur wird in diesem Aufsatz, den im Buch schon gegebenen Ansätzen folgend, mit Hilfe der Wahrscheinlichkeitsrechnung detaillierter beschrieben und mit der dynamischen Programmierung optimiert.

2. Ein Überblick über den Gedankengang des Aufsatzes

Das Ziel der folgenden Argumentation ist, einen Weg aufzuzeigen, die Kosten/Auftrag bei geforderten Antwortzeiten mit einem praktikablen Verfahren zu minimieren. Dabei hängen die Kosten z.B. von der Kernspeichergröße und der Plattenkonfiguration des Systems ab. Aber auch seine Auslastung (z.B. durch Hintergrundarbeiten) spielt eine Rolle. Als mathematische Hilfsmittel werden die Wahrscheinlichkeitsrechnung (Markov, Kolmogorov, Pollaczek-Khinchin) und die dynamische Optimierung (Bellman) herangezogen.

Zur besseren Übersicht wird das Verfahren in 7 Stufen gegliedert:

Stufe 1

Es soll zum bequemen praktischen Gebrauch erreicht werden, daß möglichst wenige spezifische Messungen ausreichen, um das Programmsystem für die Systemplanung eindeutig zu charakterisieren. Man mißt hierzu mit Hilfe eines speziellen Programms die Ankunfts- und Bedienraten für jede Datenart und Funktion so, als seien die Wahrscheinlichkeiten der zugehörigen Systemzustände 1 (Anschlußpunkt zur Praxis).

Stufe 2a

Dann beginnt man mit einer minimal Konfiguration und einer möglichen Funktionsklasseneinteilung. Für diese wird zunächst für eine Benutzerfunktionsklasse γ und für die von ihr aufgerufenen Prozesse eine Datenart A und eine Funktion B im System berücksichtigt, während für alle anderen Benutzerfunktionsklassen und für die von ihnen aufgerufenen Prozesse die Meßergebnisse nach folgender Vorschrift superponiert werden: "Man addiert die Ankunftsraten der primären Aufträge und mittelt die funktionsabhängigen Ankunfts- und Bedienraten (mit den Ankunftsraten ihrer primären Aufträge gewichtet). Die Bedienraten für die Dienstleistungen des Betriebssystems bleiben unverändert." - Das dazugehörige Kolmogorov-System wird aufgestellt und gelöst und

aus seiner Lösung werden die Übergangswahrscheinlichkeiten dafür berechnet, daß die Funktionsklasse X die Regie erhält, wenn die Datenart A von der Benutzerfunktion B in der Benutzerfunktionsklasse Y verarbeitet wird, und die Benutzerfunktionsklasse Y die Regie abgibt.Jetzt kommt ein weiterer Gedanke hinzu: Die Verwaltungszeit eines Betriebssystems kann sicher verringert werden, wenn es gelingt, den Verteiler so zu steuern, daß er mit größtmöglicher Wahrscheinlichkeit nur auf Prozesse trifft, für die er etwas tun kann,d.h. die Fälle in denen der Verteiler z.B. nach Aufruf der dynamischen Kernspeicherverwaltung feststellt, daß dem im Moment behandelten Prozess der erforderliche Kernspeicher nicht zur Verfügung gestellt werden kann, sollen möglichst nicht vorkommen.
Anschließend fährt man mit der nächsten Datenart und der gleichen Funktion, oder der nächsten Funktion in der gleichen oder nächsten Funktionsklasse fort, wobei die Berücksichtigung der Aufrufsabhängigkeit entfällt, sobald die Benutzerfunktionsklassen behandelt worden sind.

Stufe 2b

Wenn die Funktionsklasseneinteilung durchgerechnet ist, beginnt man wieder mit der ersten Datenart und Benutzerfunktion in der ersten Benutzerfunktionsklasse, berücksichtigt aber jetzt die errechnete Verteilung für die Wahrscheinlichkeiten R, daß sich der Verteiler mit dem Prozess Z befasst. Dies wird solange wiederholt, bis die Tabelle der Übergangswahrscheinlichkeiten (Entscheidungstabelle(Sprungverteiler)für den Verteiler) stabil ist.

Stufe 3

Dann wendet man auf die berechnete Entscheidungstabelle und ihre Zieltabelle die dynamische Optimierung nach Bellman an, um die Prioritätsverteilung in der Wartelistenorganisation zu bestimmen und so sicherzustellen, daß z.B. bei Überlauf der Durchsatz maximiert wird. In die Zieltabelle für die dynamische Optimierung werden nach Bedarf Werte eingesetzt, die den Anforderungen der Anwendung entsprechen. (Die Auswirkungen auf die Datenarten und Funktionen einer Funktionsklasse werden in späteren Arbeiten untersucht. Zunächst werden in diesem Aufsatz die statistischen Kenndaten der Funktionsklassen insgesamt berechnet).

Stufe 4

Anschließend superponiert man wie oben angegeben alle Meßergebnisse und berechnet die Verluste/Benutzerfunktionsklasse unter Berücksichtigung der ermittelten Verteilung für die Wahrscheinlichkeiten R, daß sich der Verteiler mit dem Prozess Z befasst.

Stufe 5 (Wiederholung von Stufe 2a und 2b)

Dann beginnt man wieder mit der Datenart A und der Funktion B in der

Benutzerfunktionsklasse Y,superponiert die Ankunfts- und Bedienraten aber jetzt zusätzlich unter Berücksichtigung der berechneten Prioritätsverteilung und der berechneten Verluste. Es ergibt sich wieder eine stabile Tabelle von Übergangswahrscheinlichkeiten und eine Verteilung für die Wahrscheinlichkeiten R, daß sich der Verteiler mit dem Prozess Z befasst.

Stufe 6 (Wiederholung von Stufe 3)

Auf die neue Entscheidungstabelle und ihre Zieltabelle wendet man wieder die dynamische Programmierung an, um die Prioritätsverteilung in der Wartelistenorganisation zu bestimmen.

Stufe 7

Es folgen Wiederholungen der Stufen 4, 5 und 6 bis die Prioritätsverteilung in der Wartelistenorganisation unter Berücksichtigung der Verluste und die Entscheidungstabelle für die statistische Verteilung durch die Bedienorganisation (Sprungverteiler) stabil sind. -
Das errechnete Preis/Leistungsverhältnis wird über den Antwortzeiten der Benutzerfunktionsklassen aufgetragen. -
Nachdem die Anfangsfunktionsklasseneinteilung durchgerechnet ist, werden die λ_i variiert. Wenn eine Konfiguration durchgerechnet ist, wird sie unter Berücksichtigung der Ergebnisse für die kleinere Konfiguration erweitert.
Die berechneten statistischen Kenndaten werden mit der Statistikfunktion des Betriebssystems nachgemessen (experimentelle Nachprüfung).
Zusammengefasst kann man sagen: Man berechnet

1. die Prioritätsverteilung in der Wartelistenorganisation unter Berücksichtigung der Verluste,
2. die Entscheidungstabelle für die statistische Verteilung durch die Bedienorganisation(Sprungverteiler),
3. die optimale Funktionsklasseneinteilung,
4. die minimale Konfiguration,

um ein optimales Preis/Leistungsverhältnis bei geforderten Antwortzeiten unter einer gegebenen Zielsetzung einzustellen.

3. Das erweiterte Kolmogorov-System des Programmsystems

Die Abb.2 zeigt 21 Gleichungen mit 21 Unbekannten pro Funktionsklasse und eine Normierungsbedingung für das ganze System. (siehe S.300)
Das Gleichungssystem 1 der Abb. 2 wird jetzt beschrieben:

Gl. 1-6

Die Gleichungen 1-6 beschreiben die Verhältnisse in der Wartelistenorganisation. W(I) bedeutet die Wahrscheinlichkeit dafür, daß sich I Elemente der Funktionsklasse X im System aufhalten. λ_p ist die mittlere primäre Ankunftsrate und μ die mittlere Bedienrate der Funktionsklasse X. Die λ_R müssen bei den Funktionsklassen, die von anderen aufgerufen werden, mit $\sum_{K=1}^{Y} P_K(3)$ multipliziert werden. Die $\sum_{K=1} P_K(3)$ ist die Wahrscheinlichkeit dafür, daß sich wenigstens einer der Prozesse, die den Prozess aufrufen können, im Zustand 3 befindet Die Unabhängigkeit der Ereignisse wird versuchsweise angenommen und muß durch die experimentelle Prüfung geprüft werden. Sie ist aber aufgrund der statistischen Eingriffe wahrscheinlich.

Gl. 7

Die Gl.7 sagt aus, daß man in den Prozesszustand 1 durch Normierung durch die eigene Task im Zustand 3, durch Normierung durch eine fremde Task im Zustand 5, beim Zurückholen eines verdrängten und in der Zwischenzeit normierten Prozesses, wenn die Regieverteilung sich mit diesem Prozess beschäftigt und durch Normierung durch eine fremde Task im Zustand 52 kommen kann. Der Term

$$\lambda(1,52) \cdot P(52) \cdot \sum_{K=1}^{Y} P_K(3)$$

sagt zum Beispiel aus, daß der eigene Prozess sich im Zustand 52 <u>und</u> wenigstens ein fremder Prozess, der die Normierung durchführen kann, sich im Zustand 3 befinden muß, wenn der Übergang stattfinden soll. - Die Unabhängigkeit der Prozesszustände verschiedener Funktionsklassen, die gemeinsam einen Übergang veranlassen, wird versuchsweise angenommen. Sie ist wegen der statistisch verteilten Ereignisse wahrscheinlich. Die linke Seite der Gl.7 beschreibt die Abgänge aus dem Prozesszustand P(1).

Gl. 8

Die linke Seite von Gl.8 sagt aus, daß ein bereiter Prozess in den Zustand "aktiv" übergeht, wenn sich der Verteiler mit dem Prozess beschäftigt (wobei den E/A-Funktionen das Gerät zur Verfügung stehen muß, Faktor G). Die rechte Seite gibt zunächst die Bereitstellung wartender Prozesse wieder, wenn der erforderliche Kernspeicher zur Verfügung steht und sich der Verteiler mit dem Prozess beschäftigt. F ist die Wahrscheinlichkeit dafür, daß die Kernspeicherverwaltung den Speicher liefern kann und R ist die Wahrscheinlichkeit dafür,daß sich der Verteiler mit dem Prozess beschäftigt. Dann folgt ein Term, der die Bereitstellung der eigenen Task wiedergibt und anschließend folgt die Bereitstellung eines Prozesses im Zustand 5 (gesperrt) durch einen fremden Prozess im Zustand 3. Ausserdem sind Bereitstellungen im Zustand 52 durch eine fremde Task oder beim Abschluß des Zurückholens eines verdrängten und bereiten Prozesses, wenn der Verteiler sich mit dem Prozess beschäftigt, möglich (letzter Summand der Gl.8.). Die linke Seite der Gl.8 beschreibt wieder die Abgänge aus dem Prozesszustand P(2).

Gl. 9

Die Gl.9 zeigt auf der linken Seite, daß die Regieverteilung unterbrochene Prozesse wieder aktiviert, wenn sie sich mit dem unterbrochenen Prozess beschäftigt. Der erste Summand auf der rechten Seite zeigt, daß sich die Prozesse selbst unterbrochen setzen können. Dann folgt die Aktivierung eines gesperrten Prozesses durch einen fremden Prozess im Zustand 3. Der letzte Summand berücksichtigt den Abschluß der Zurückholung eines unterbrochenen Prozesses, wenn sich der Verteiler mit diesem Prozess beschäftigt. Die linke Seite der Gl.9 beschreibt die Abgänge aus dem Prozesszustand P(4).

Für die detaillierte Beschreibung der restlichen Gleichungen fehlt hier leider der Platz.

3.1 Gradientenmethode zur Lösung des erweiterten Kolmogorov-Systems

Zur Lösung des erweiterten Kolmogorov-Systems wird die Gradientenmethode benutzt.

4. Die Berechnung der Übergangswahrscheinlichkeiten pij und der vermittelten Nachrichten rij und die Anwendung der dynamischen Optimierung

Aus der Lösung des erweiterten Kolmogorov-Systems werden die Übergangswahrscheinlichkeiten pij dafür, daß anschließend ein Prozess der Funktionsklasse k die Regie bekommt, wenn die Funktion j die Regie hatte und die Anzahl vermittelter Nachrichten rij, wenn ein Prozess der Funktionsklasse k die Regie bekommt, wenn die Funktion j die Regie hatte, berechnet.

4.1 Analytische Formulierung mit Hilfe der dynamischen Optimierung von Bellman

Es gilt (i= Prioritätenindex, j= Klassenindex, M= Anzahl Prioritäten, N= Anzahl Funktionsklassen):

$$f_n(i) = \max_q \left[\sum_{j=1}^{N} p_{ij}(q) \left(r_{ij}(q) + f_{n-1}(j) \right) \right] \qquad i = 1,2,3 \ldots M \qquad \text{Gl.1}$$

$p_{ij}(q)$ Übergangswahrscheinlichkeiten

$r_{ij}(q)$ Anzahl der vermittelten Nachrichten

Wir benutzen nun folgenden Satz 1: Für

$$f_n(i) = \max_q \left[b_i(q) + \sum_{j=1}^{N} a_{ij}(q) f_{n-1}(j) \right] \quad \text{mit}$$

$$b_i(q) \geqq 0 \text{ für alle } i \text{ und } q,$$

$$a_{ij}(q) \geqq 0 \text{ für alle } i, j \text{ und } q,$$

$$\sum_{j=1}^{N} a_{ij}(q) = 1 \qquad i = 1, 2, 3 \cdots M,$$

gilt für $n \longrightarrow \infty$ (asymptotisches Verhalten):

$$f_n(i) \sim n \cdot g \quad \text{mit}$$

$$g = \max_q \lim_{n \to \infty} \left[\frac{b(q) + A(q)\,b(q) + \cdots + A(q)^{n-1}\,b(q)}{n} \right] \text{ und}$$

$$b(q) = \begin{pmatrix} b_1 & (q) \\ b_2 & (q) \\ \vdots & \\ b_M & (q) \end{pmatrix}, \quad A(q) = (a_{ij}(q)).$$

Wir schreiben jetzt an Stelle von Gl.1:

$$V_i^{\,n} = \sum_{j=1}^{N} p_{ij} \left(r_{ij} + V_j^{\,n-1} \right) \qquad \text{Gl.2}$$

Für grosse n folgt aus Gl.2 <u>nach Satz 1:</u>

$$v_i + ng = \sum_{j=1}^{N} p_{ij} \left[r_{ij} + v_j + (n-1)g \right].$$

Da $\sum_{j=1}^{N} p_{ij} = 1$ ergibt sich:

$$g + v_i = \sum_{j=1}^{N} p_{ij} \left(r_{ij} + v_j \right) \qquad i = 1,2,3\ldots,M \qquad \text{Gl.3}$$

Gl.3 ist ein Gleichungssystem von M Gleichungen (Anzahl Prioritäten) mit M+1 Unbekannten, das iterativ optimiert wird. Wir wählen eine Anfangsstrategie (z.B. jede Funktionsklasse soll zuerst ihre Zeile 1 (Priorität) bedienen) und $v_M = 0$. Damit lösen wir Gl.3 auf. Es ergibt sich g und ein Satz v_i. Mit dieser Lösung berechnen wir für jede Zeile (Priorität) das $g + v_i$ und bestimmen für jede Funktionsklasse das Maximum:

$$\left(g + v_i \right)^{*} = \max \sum_{j=1}^{N} p_{ij} \left(r_{ij} + v_j \right) \qquad i = 1,2,3\ldots M \qquad \text{Gl.4}$$

Die Maxima ergeben eine neue Strategie, für die g und der Satz v_i wieder durch Auflösung der Gl.3 bestimmt wird. Dann berechnet man wieder die $g + v_i$ für jede Zeile und bestimmt wieder für jede Funktionsklasse das Maximum, usw. bis die Strategie stabil wird.

5. <u>Abgeleitete Ergebnisse</u>

<u>Die mittlere Antwortzeit</u>

Die mittlere Antwortzeit t_{wi} einer Funktionsklasse bei Poisson-Einströmung und exponentiell verteilten Bedienzeiten ist:

$$t_{w_i} = \frac{L_i}{\lambda_i} \qquad \text{Gl.1}$$

Dabei ist L_i die mittlere Anzahl Aufträge der Funktionsklasse i im System und λ_i die mittlere Ankunftsrate für diese Funktionsklasse. Es gilt, daß

$$L_i = \sum_{n=1}^{6} \left(n \cdot W(n) \cdot \sum (\text{alle Kombinationen})\right) + \sum_{K=1}^{14} P[1,K].$$

Die Verluste sind übrigens für unser Beispiel

$$V_i = W(6) \cdot \sum (\text{alle Kombinationen}).$$

Die reine Wartezeit in der Warteschlange ist bei Poisson-Einströmung und exponentiell verteilten Bedienzeiten:

$$t_{wq_i} = \frac{L_{q_i}}{W_i \cdot \lambda_i} \qquad \text{Gl.2}$$

Dabei ist L_{qi} die mittlere Anzahl Aufträge der Funktionsklasse i in der Wartelistenorganisation. Das λ_i muss in Gl.2 mit der Wahrscheinlichkeit W_i dafür multipliziert werden, daß ein Auftrag überhaupt warten muss, damit der Anteil unberücksichtigt bleibt, der sofort dran kommt. Es gilt, daß

$$L_{q_i} = \sum_{n=1}^{6} \left(n \cdot W(n) \cdot \sum (\text{alle Kombinationen})\right),$$

$$W_i = \sum_{n=1}^{5} \left(W(n) \cdot \sum (\text{alle Kombinationen})\right).$$

Es muß gelten

$$t_{W_i} - t_{Wq_i} = \frac{1}{\mu_i}.$$

<u>Die Ausführungs-, Tot- und Verwaltungszeit</u>

Die Ausführungszeit T_E (Execution time), Totzeit T_i (Idle time) und Verwaltungszeit T_r (Overhead time) lassen sich wie folgt errechnen:

$$T_E = \sum_{K=1}^{10} P_K(3)$$ aufgeschlüsselt nach Funktionsklassen und insgesamt

$$T_i = \sum_{K=1}^{10} W(0)$$ insgesamt (Reserve)

$T_V = 1 - T_E - T_i$ aufgeschlüsselt nach Funktionsklassen und insgesamt

6. Zusammenfassung

Die Berechnung des Verkehrsflusses in Datenverarbeitungsanlagen zur optimalen Auslegung ihrer hardware und software in Abhängigkeit der Parameter ihrer Anwendung gelingt mit Hilfe eines erweiterten Kolmogorov-Systems und mit Hilfe der Dynamischen Programmierung von Bellman. Die Kenngrößen des Programmsystems (Ausführungszeiten, Antwort-, Verwaltungs-, Totzeiten) lassen sich aus der Lösung des Kolmogorov-Systems ableiten.

$$\mu W(6) = \left(\lambda_P + \lambda_A \sum_{K=1}^{Y} P_K(3)\right) \cdot W(5) \qquad \text{Gl. } 1$$

$$\left(\lambda_P + \lambda_A \sum_{K=1}^{Y} P_K(3) + \mu\right) W(5) = \left(\lambda_P + \lambda_A \sum_{K=1}^{Y} P_K(3)\right) W(4) + \mu W(6) \qquad 2$$

$$\left(\lambda_P + \lambda_A \sum_{K=1}^{Y} P_K(3) + \mu\right) W(4) = \left(\lambda_P + \lambda_A \sum_{K=1}^{Y} P_K(3)\right) W(3) + \mu W(5) \qquad 3$$

$\lambda \sum_{K=1}^{Y} P_K(3)$ gilt für die abhängigen Aufrufe

$$\left(\lambda_P + \lambda_A \sum_{K=1}^{Y} P_K(3) + \mu\right) W(3) = \left(\lambda_P + \lambda_A \sum_{K=1}^{Y} P_K(3)\right) W(2) + \mu W(4) \qquad 4$$

$$\left(\lambda_P + \lambda_A \sum_{K=1}^{Y} P_K(3) + \mu\right) W(2) = \left(\lambda_P + \lambda_A \sum_{K=1}^{Y} P_K(3)\right) W(1) + \mu W(3) \qquad 5$$

$$\left(\lambda_P + \lambda_A \sum_{K=1}^{Y} P_K(3) + \mu\right) W(1) = \left(\lambda_P + \lambda_A \sum_{K=1}^{Y} P_K(3)\right) W(0) + \mu W(2) \qquad 6$$

$$\left(\mu(X,2,1) \cdot F(X) \cdot R(1) + \lambda(7,1) \cdot \sum_{K=1}^{Y} P_K(3)\right) \cdot P(1) = \lambda(1,3)\, P(3) + \lambda(1,5) \sum_{K=1}^{Y} P_K(3) \cdot P(5) + \mu(1,51) \cdot R(1) \cdot P(51) + \lambda(1,52) \cdot \sum_{K=1}^{Y} P_K(3) \cdot P(52) \qquad 7$$

$$\left(\mu(X,3,2) \cdot R(1) + \lambda(7,2) \cdot \sum_{K=1}^{Y} P_K(3)\right) \cdot P(2) = \mu(X,2,1) \cdot F(X) \cdot R(1) \cdot P(1) + \lambda(2,3) \cdot P(3) + \lambda(2,5) \cdot \sum_{K=1}^{Y} P_K(3) \cdot P(5) + \left(\lambda(2,52) \sum_{K=1}^{Y} P_K(3) + JN(1) \cdot G(1) + \mu(2,52) \cdot R(1)\right) \cdot P(52_{FKT}) \qquad 8$$

$$\mu(3,4) \cdot R(1) \cdot P(4) \cdot (\lambda_{31} + \lambda_{32} + \cdots \lambda_{3n} / \lambda_3) \cdot \sum_{J=1}^{14} P_3(J) - \left(\lambda(4,3) + \sum_{Z=1} JN(Z) \cdot G(Z)\right) P(3) + \lambda(4,5) \sum_{K=1}^{Y} P_K(3) \cdot P(5) + \mu(4,54) \cdot P(54) \cdot R(1) \qquad 9$$

$$\left((\lambda(1,5) + \lambda(2,5) + \lambda(4,5) + \lambda(7,5)) \sum_{K=1}^{Y} P_K(3)\right) P(5) = \lambda(5,3) \cdot P(3) + \mu(5,55) \cdot R(1) \cdot P(55) \qquad 10$$

$$\left((\mu(1,51) + \mu(61,51))\, R(1)\right) P(51) = \lambda(51,55) \sum_{K=1}^{Y} P_K(3)\, P(55) + \mu(51,61) \cdot F(X) \cdot R(1) \cdot P(61) \qquad 11$$

$$\left((\lambda(1,52) + \lambda(2,52)) \sum_{K=1}^{Y} P_K(3) + \mu(2,52) \cdot R(1)\right) \cdot P(52) = \lambda(52,2) \cdot \sum_{K=1}^{Y} P_K(3) \cdot P(2) + \lambda(52,3) \cdot P(3) + \lambda(52,55) \cdot \sum_{K=1}^{Y} P_K(3) \cdot P(55) + \mu(52,62) \cdot F(X) \cdot R(1) \cdot P(62) \qquad 12$$

$$\left((\mu(4,54) + \mu(64,54))\, R(1)\right) \cdot P(54) = \mu(54,4) \cdot PM \cdot \sum PA(1,K) \sum_{K=1}^{Y} P_K(1) \cdot R(1) \cdot P(4) + \lambda(54,55) \cdot \sum^{Y} P_K(3) \cdot P(55) + \mu(54,64) \cdot F(X) \cdot R(1) \cdot P(64) \qquad 13$$

$$\left((\mu(5,55) + \mu(65,55))\, R(1) + (\lambda(51,55) + \lambda(52,55) + \lambda(54,55)) \sum_{K=1}^{Y} P_K(3)\right) P(55) = \mu(55,5) \cdot PM \cdot \sum PA(1,K) \cdot \sum_{K=1}^{Y} P_K(1) \cdot R(1) \cdot P(5) + \mu(55,65) \cdot F(X) \cdot R(1) \cdot P(65) \qquad 14$$

$\mu(51,61)\cdot F(X)\cdot R(1)\cdot P(61) = \lambda(61,65)\sum_{K=1}^{Y} P_K(3)\cdot P(65) + \mu(61,51)\cdot R(1)\cdot P(51)$ Gl. 15

$\mu(52,62)\cdot F(X)\cdot R(1)\cdot P(62) = \mu(62,52)\cdot R(1)\cdot P(52) + \lambda(62,65)\cdot\sum_{K=1}^{Y} P_K(3)\cdot P(65)$ 16

$\mu(54,64)\cdot F(X)\cdot R(1)\cdot P(64) = \mu(64,54)\cdot R(1)\cdot P(54) + \lambda(64,65)\cdot\sum_{K=1}^{Y} P_K(3)\cdot P(65)$ 17

$\mu(55,65)\cdot F(X)\cdot R(1)\cdot P(65) = \mu(65,55)\cdot R(1)\cdot P(55)$ 18

$\mu(0,7)\cdot R(1)\cdot P(7) = \lambda(7,1)\cdot\sum_{K=1}^{Y} P_K(3)\,P(1) + \lambda(7,2)\cdot\sum_{K=1}^{Y} P_K(3)\,P(2) + [\lambda(7,3)+\mu(7,3)]\,P(3) + \lambda(7,5)\cdot$ 19
$\sum_{K=1}^{Y} P_K(3)\cdot P(5) + \sum_{\text{alle o.V}} \lambda(7,65)\cdot\sum_{K=1}^{Y} P_K(3)\cdot P(65)$

$\overline{S} = \sum_{K=1}^{10} (S(K)\cdot\sum_{i=2} P(1)), \quad M = \frac{S}{(\overline{S}/10)}$ alle o.V. = alle Prozesszustände ohne die der Verdrängung 20, 21

$\overline{\lambda} = \sum_{i=1}^{10} \lambda_i\,(P_i(1) + P_i(61) + P_i(62) + P_i(64) + P_i(65)), \quad \overline{\mu} = \sum_{i=1}^{10} \mu_i\,P_i(7)$ 22, 23

$P_M = \frac{(\overline{\lambda}/\overline{\mu})^M}{M!}\;\frac{e^{-\overline{\lambda}/\overline{\mu}}}{\sum_{m=0}^{M} \frac{(\overline{\lambda}/\overline{\mu})^m}{m!} e^{-\overline{\lambda}/\overline{\mu}}}$ *, $F = 1 - P_M$ $\quad \overline{\lambda}, \overline{\mu}$ Ankunfts- bezw. Bedienrate für die dynamische Kernspeicherverwaltung 24

$G = 1 - \sum_{i=3}^{\text{alle}} P(1)$ Wahrscheinlichkeit, daß ein Gerät frei ist 25

$\sum_{i=1}^{14} P(1) = \frac{\lambda}{\mu_{14}}$ 26

$1 - W(0) = \sum_{i=1} P(1)$ 27

$\sum_{i=1}^{\text{alle}} W(1) = 1$ Normierungsbedingung für das ganze Gleichungssystem 28

$\frac{1}{\mu(7,3)} = T_q = \frac{T_s}{1-q_m}\left[1 - \frac{q_m}{2}\left(1 - \frac{G_s^2}{T_s^2}\right)\right]$ * für Plattenprozesse 29

Abb.2 erweitertes Kolmogorov-System

$T_s = T_f + T_c + T_r, \quad T_r = T_v + T_d + T_o, \quad T_c = L_c/\lambda$ $\quad\lambda$ Ankunftsrate der Plattenaufträge 30 - 32

$L_c = \sum_{n=1}^{m} \left(n\cdot\frac{z^{(m-n)}}{(m-n)!}\left[\sum_{n=0}^{m}\frac{z^n}{n!}\right]^{-1}\right) - 1, \quad z = (W\cdot T_r)^{-1}$ $\quad m$ Anzahl Moduln der Platte 33, 34

MODELL EINES AUFTRAGSSYSTEMS FÜR DIE ZEITDIENSTVERWALTUNG EINES PROZESSRECHNERS

D.HILSE

1. Einführung

In Realzeitsystemen ist eine leistungsfähige Zeitdienstverwaltung von großer Bedeutung. Sie soll sich an der Erfüllung folgender Kriterien orientieren:

1. Klare logische Struktur mit definierter Schnittstelle.
2. Geringer Overhead.
3. Freizügigkeit bezüglich der Anzahl der Zeitdienstaufträge.

Im folgenden sollen unter Zeitdiensten die vielfältigsten Weckdienste sowohl zu bestimmten Tageszeiten (Absolutzeit) als auch nach Ablauf frei wählbarer periodischer Zeitintervalle (Relativzeit) verstanden werden.

Die vorliegende Zeitdienstverwaltung ist ein Modul des im Institut für Datenverarbeitung in der Technik der Gesellschaft für Kernforschung Karlsruhe konzipierten Realzeitbetriebssystems CALAS70 (Computer Aided Laboratory Automation System). Ihr liegt ein Zustandsmodell zugrunde, das im folgenden Abschnitt in einer allgemeinen Form beschrieben wird.

2. Ein Zustandsmodell

2.1. Begriffsdefinitionen

Unter einem Bearbeitungssystem wollen wir eine Menge von Objekten verstehen (z.B. Hard- und/oder Software-Module), die in der Lage sind, Systemaufträge entgegenzunehmen, zu bearbeiten und an ein Zielsystem weiterzuleiten.

Als Auftrag gelte ein von einem Auftraggeber in einer auftragsspezifischen Parameterliste eindeutig spezifizierter Bearbeitungswunsch.

Ein Auftraggeber ist in diesem Zusammenhang ein dem o. def. Bearbeitungssystem nicht angehörendes System.

2.2. Der Systemzustandsraum

Die Abwicklung voneinander unabhängiger Aufträge innerhalb eines Systems aufgrund vorgegebener Algorithmen läßt sich als eine schrittweise Änderung ihrer Bearbeitungszustände oder kürzer, ihrer Zustände, beschreiben. Die Zustandsänderungen werden entweder durch interne oder externe Ereignisse gesteuert. Die Konservierung eines geänderten Auftragszustandes geschieht in einem auftragsspezifischen Zustandsbeschreibungsblock.

Betrachten wir nun das System zu einem bestimmten Zeitpunkt t_1. Zu diesem Zeitpunkt befinden sich alle N von diesem System bearbeiteten Aufträge in einem eindeutig definierten Zustand $z\ (v_1,v_2,v_3,\ldots,v_d)$. Der aktuelle Zustand z_k des Auftrages A_k ist eine Funktion seiner im Zustandsbeschreibungsblock gespeicherten Zustandsvariablen $\{v_i\}$, i=1,,d. Es sind die Koordinaten eines Punktes z_k in einem d-dimensionalen Raum, dem Zustandsraum R des Systems.

Die Änderung des Zustandes eines der N unabhängigen Aufträge A_k bedeutet also die Änderung seiner Zustandsvariablen $\{v_i\}$, oder geometrisch, die Änderung seines Ortes im Zustandsraum R.

Der Zustandsraum R kann nun in eine Anzahl von Teilräumen R_i zerlegt werden

$$R_i \subseteq R \qquad i=0,1,2,\ldots,I \qquad (2.2.-1)$$

In einem Teilraum R_i werden diejenigen Aufträge A_k zusammengefaßt, die in mindestens einer Zustandsvariablen v_i übereinstimmen. Die Elemente $r_{i,j}$ des Teilraumes R_i sind also Aufträge mit den Zuständen $z(v_1,v_2,\ldots,v_i=\text{const},\ldots,v_d)$. R_i ist als Teilraum von R mit obiger Eigenschaft ein höchstens (d-1)-dimensionaler Raum.

Innerhalb eines Teilraumes R_i lassen sich jeweils bestimmte Grenzzustände G_i definieren. Nimmt ein Auftrag A_k im Verlauf seiner Zustandsänderungen diesen Grenzzustand ein, so wird eine grenzzustandsspezifische Aktivität gestartet (z.B. Statusmeldung an den Auftraggeber, Rückgriff auf eine auftragsspezifische Parameterliste u. dgl.).

2.3. Der Ereignis- und Filterfunktionenraum

Wie bereits angedeutet werden die Zustandsänderungen im Zustandsraum des Systems durch das Auftreten interner oder externer Ereignisse veranlaßt. Innerhalb des Systems ist jedem Ereignis eine Ereignisfunktion e_i fest zugeordnet, die die Änderungsart und -richtung bestimmt. Die Menge aller Ereignisfunktionen bildet den sog. Ereignis- oder E-Raum.

Die unmittelbare zustandsändernde Einwirkung der Ereignisfunktionen auf die Zustände oder eine Gruppe gleichartiger Zustände des Zustandsraumes (z.B. Zustände eines Teilraumes R_i) wird durch mit den entsprechenden Ereignisfunktionen verknüpfte Filterfunktionen gesteuert. Die Filterfunktionen sind Elemente m_i eines sog. Masken- oder M-Raumes. Ihr momentaner Wert ist vom aktuellen Zustand derjenigen Gruppe abhängig, auf die die zugeordnete Ereignisfunktion einwirken soll (Rückkopplung des Zustandsraumes R auf den Maskenraum).

$$f_{m_i} : R \supseteq R_i \longrightarrow M \tag{2.3.-1}$$

$$m_i = f_{m_i} \; (r_{i,j}) \tag{2.3.-2}$$

$$\text{für } i = 0,1,2,\ldots,I$$
$$j = 1,2,\ldots\ldots,J$$

wobei $r_{i,j} \varepsilon R_i$, $m_i \varepsilon M$, f_{m_i} = Abbildungsfunktion.

Die durch die Filterfunktionen beeinflußten Ereignisfunktionen wirken nun unmittelbar auf die Elemente $r_{i,j}$ entsprechender Teilräume R_i ein.

$$f_{R_i} : (E,M) \longrightarrow R_i \tag{2.3.-3}$$

$$r_{i,j} = f_{R_i} \; (e_i, m_i) \tag{2.3.-4}$$

mit $r_{i,j} \varepsilon R_i$, $e_i \varepsilon E$, $m_i \varepsilon M$, f_{R_i} = Abbildungsfunktion.

Die Abbildungsfunktion f_{R_i} führt den Zustand der Aufträge zum Zeitpunkt t_1 in einen neuen Zustand zum Zeitpunkt t_2 über.
In der Abb. 1 sind die gegenseitigen Abhängigkeiten der Elemente einzelner Räume dargestellt.

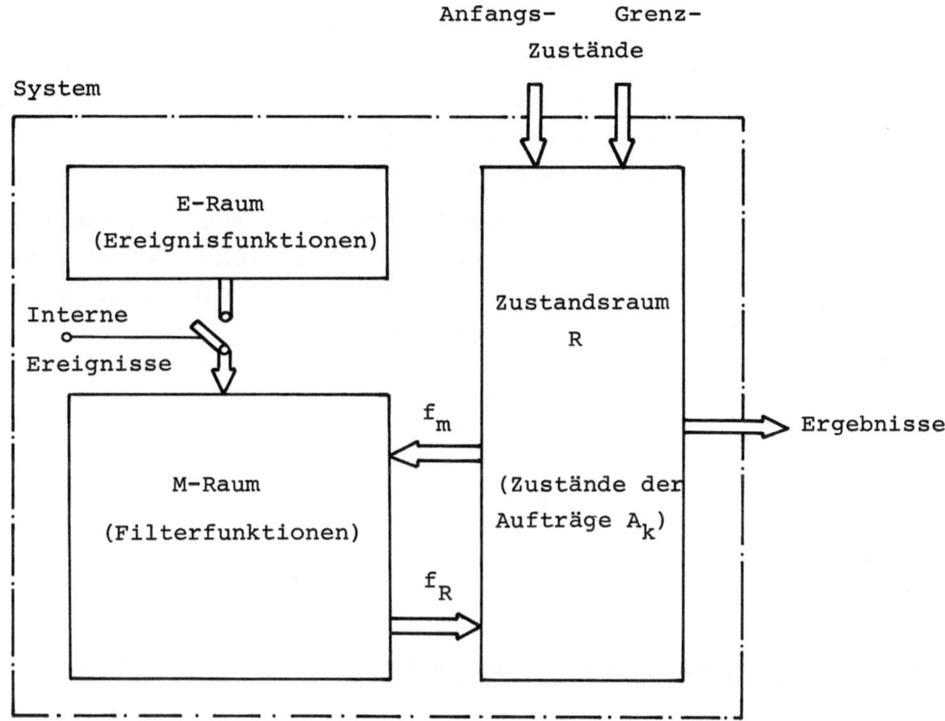

Abb. 1 Einwirkung der Elemente verschiedener Räume aufeinander

2.4. Zusammenstellung der Ergebnisse

Gemäß den Gleichungen (2.3.-2) und (2.3.-4) erhält man die Elemente $r_{i,j}^{t2}$ des Zustandsraumes R zum Zeitpunkt t_2 aus den Elementen $r_{i,j}^{t1}$ des Zustandsraumes R zum Zeitpunkt t_1 nach folgendem Algorithmus:

$$r_{i,j}^{t2} = f_{R_i} \quad (e_i, f_{m_i} \quad (r_{i,j}^{t1})) \tag{2.4.-1}$$

$$\text{für } i = 0,1,\ldots,I$$
$$j = 1,2,\ldots,J$$

Danach bewirkt das i-te Ereignis die Aktivierung der diesem Ereignis fest zugeordneten Ereignisfunktion e_i. Die funktionelle Verknüpfung von e_i mit der entsprechenden Filterfunktion m_i liefert die gefilterte Ereignisfunktion, die unmittelbar zustandsändernd auf die Zustände des Teilzustandsraumes R_i einwirkt. Die Zustandsänderung ruft über die Funktion f_{m_i} eine Änderung der Filterfunktion m_i hervor. Die Funktion f_{m_i} hat deshalb die Wirkung einer Rückkopplung des veränderten Zustandes auf die ihn verändernde Ereignisfunktion e_i.

Das Einbringen neuer Aufträge in den Systemzustandsraum (Anfangszustände) wird durch externe Ereignisse veranlaßt. Der sich dabei verändernde Zustand eines Teilzustandsraumes R_k beeinflußt über die zugehörige Abbildungsfunktion f_{m_k} die Filterfunktion m_k.

Für eine Veränderung der Elemente $r_{i,j}$ des Zustandsraumes R werden benötigt:

a) Die Abbildungsfunktionen f_{R_i} und f_{m_i}

b) Die Ereignisfunktionen e_i

c) Die Anfangs- und Grenzzustände

3. Anwendungsbeispiel: Realzeituhrverwaltung

3.1. Die Auftragsbeschreibung

Die vollständige Beschreibung eines an das System "UHR" gerichteten Auftrags A_k besteht in der Angabe mindestens eines der folgenden Punkte:

1. Absolutweckzeitpunkt AZ_k (Tageszeit),
2. Größe eines Zeitintervalls RZ_k (Relativzeit), evtl. mit Angabe der Periodizität WZ_k (Wiederholzahl),
3. Zielauftrag (Aktivierung nach Ablauf der vorgewählten Zeit),

in der auftragsspezifischen Parameterliste.

Das System arbeitet mit mehreren Grundzeiteinheiten (1 sec - 1 Tag). Die gewünschte Relativzeit RZ_k muß deshalb in diese "zugelassenen" Grundzeiteinheiten ε_i zerlegt

$$RZ_k = \sum_{i=0}^{I_k} T_i \cdot \varepsilon_i \qquad (3.1.-1)$$

und auf den Auftragsannahmezeitpunkt

$$t = \sum_i t_i \cdot \varepsilon_i$$

zwangssynchronisiert werden.

$$RZ_k = \sum_{i=0}^{I_k-1} (T_i+t_i) \cdot \varepsilon_i + T_{I_k} \cdot \varepsilon_{I_k} \qquad (3.1.-2)$$

Die Normierung der Zeitgrößen auf ihre Einheiten ε_i liefert einen (I_k+1)-dimensionalen korrigierten RZ_k-Vektor

$$RZ_k = \{\tau_i\}, \qquad i=0,1,\ldots,I_k \qquad (3.1.-3)$$

der als Bezugsgröße der Zustandsvariablen eines Auftrags A_k in der auftragsspezifischen Parameterliste gehalten wird.

3.2. Die Wahl der Zustandsvariablen und der Grenzzustände

Die Anzahl und Art der Zustandsvariablen sollte sich an einer eindeutigen Zustandsbeschreibung des k-ten Auftrags orientieren. Für den RZ-Auftrag genügt die Angabe

1. der Grundzeiteinheit ε_i bzw. i,
2. des Multiplikationsfaktors τ_i.

Der aktuelle Zustand eines Auftrags A_k wird also durch das Paar $(i,\tau_i)_k$ bestimmt; es stellt einen Punkt mit den Koordinaten $v_1=i$ und $v_2=\tau_i$ in einem zweidimensionalen Zustandsraum R dar.

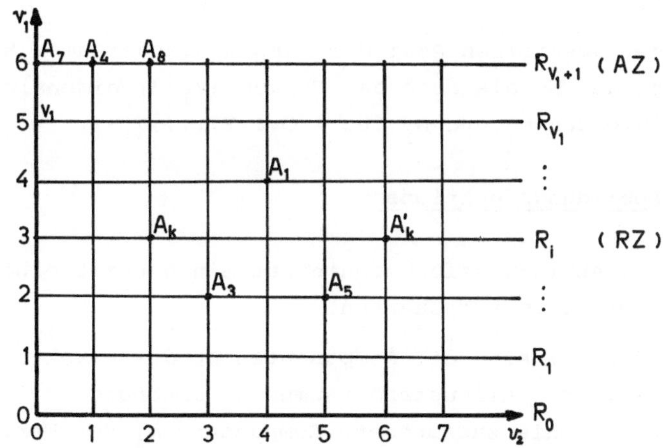

Abb. 2 Zweidimensionaler Zustandsraum R

Der Anfangszustand eines Auftrags (z.B. A_k') ist das Paar (I_k, τ_{I_k}), entsprechend der höchstwertigen Komponente des in seiner Parameterliste gespeicherten korrigierten RZ_k-Vektors. Wegen der Begrenzung der Anzahl unterscheidbarer Grundzeiteinheiten (Hardwarebedingung) kann die Zustandsvariable v_1 aller RZ-Aufträge höchstens den Wert V_1 annehmen, während die Zustandsvariable v_2 unbeschränkt bleibt (kein Limit bezüglich der Anzahl der Aufträge).

Der Zustandsraum R wird nun entsprechend $v_1 = const_i$ in Teilzustandsräume R_i, $i=0,1,\ldots,v_1+1$, eingeteilt. Alle Aufträge in R_i haben die Zustände $Z(v_1=const_i, v_2)$. Sie belegen die entsprechenden Elemente $r_{i,j}$ von R_i.

Die noch zu wählende Ereignisfunktion e_i verändert im Normalfall den Zustand des Auftrags A_k durch seine sukzessive Verschiebung nach links entlang der Waagerechten $v_1=const_i$ (siehe Abb. 2). Erreicht auf diese Weise ein Auftrag das Element $r_{i,0}$ (v_1-Achse), so hat er definitionsgemäß seinen Grenzzustand G_i eingenommen. Die hierbei aktivierte Grenzzustandsfunktion g_i entscheidet mittels Rückgriff auf die auftragsspezifische Parameterliste über einen neuen Auftragsstatus (bestimmter Folgezustand oder Beendigung).

Der Teilzustandsraum R_{v_1+1} ist ausschließlich für die AZ-Aufträge reserviert. Der Anfangszustand eines AZ-Auftrages ist eine Funktion des gewünschten Weckzeitpunktes AZ und der bei der Auftragsannahme aktuellen Uhrzeit. Der zeitlich aktuellste Auftrag befindet sich immer im Grenzzustand G_{v_1+1}. Er wird gemäß seiner Parameterliste aktiviert, sobald der Grenzzustandsfunktion g_{v_1+1} die Einwirkung auf $r_{v_1+1,0}$ erlaubt wird.

Aufgrund der speziellen Abbildung des Zustandsraumes R auf den M-Raum sind sowohl der M- als auch der E-Raum (V_1+2)-dimensionale Vektoren, mit den Elementen e_i und m_i für $i=0,1,2,\ldots,V_1+1$.

3.3. Die Abbildungsfunktionen

Die Wahl der Abbildungsfunktionen hat einen unmittelbaren Einfluß auf die Größe der Vektorkomponenten.

Nach Gl. (2.3.-2) sind die Komponenten m_i des M-Vektors vom Belegungszustand des i-ten Teilzustandsraumes R_i abhängig. Falls Teilraum $R_i=0$ (leer), bekommt die zugeordnete Komponente m_i den Wert 0, andernfalls den Wert 1. Ist außerdem noch der Grenzzustand G_i belegt, so nimmt m_i den Wert 2 an.

$$m_i = f_{m_i}(r_{i,j}) = \begin{cases} 0, \text{ falls } R_i=\emptyset \\ 1, \text{ falls } R_i\neq\emptyset \text{ und } G_i=\emptyset \\ 2, \text{ falls } R_i\neq\emptyset \text{ und } G_i\neq\emptyset \end{cases} \qquad (3.3.-1)$$

Nach Gl. (2.3.-4) ist für die Veränderung der Elemente $r_{i,j}$ des Zustandsteilraumes R_i die Funktion f_{R_i} verantwortlich. Die Veränderung soll aufgrund der Einwirkung der Ereignisfunktion, gesteuert durch die Elemente m_i des M-Vektors, erfolgen.

$$r_{i,j} = f_{R_i}(e_i,m_i) = e_i(m_i) = \begin{cases} 0, \text{ falls } m_i=0 \\ r_{i,j+1}, \text{ falls } m_i=1 \\ g_i(G_i), \text{ falls } m_i=2 \end{cases} \qquad (3.3.-2)$$

für $i=0,1,\ldots,V_1,V_1+1$

$j=0,1,2,\ldots,J$

Die Elemente $r_{i,j}$ des neuen Zustandsteilraumes R_i verändern sich nicht, solange der Parameter m_i den Wert 0 behält. Für $m_i=1$ erfolgt eine sukzessive Verschiebung aller Zustände belegter Elemente von R_i nach links in Richtung kleinerer Werte von v_2 (siehe Abb. 2). Bei Erreichung des Grenzzustandes $G_i = r_{i,0}$ $(m_i=2)$ wird sofort die Grenzzustandsfunktion g_i gestartet. Sie sorgt dafür, daß das Element $r_{i,0}$ mit dem nächstfolgenden Zustand belegt und der Auftrag, gemäß seiner auftragsspezifischen Parameterliste, einem neuen Element $r_{m,n}$ von R_m zugewiesen wird. Die Grenzzustandsfunktion g_i wird solange aufgerufen, bis alle in G_i befindlichen Aufträge entweder einen neuen Zustand innerhalb R eingenommen oder den Zustandsraum R verlassen haben. Der nun folgende Aufruf der Funktion f_{m_i} weist den Elementen m_i des M-Vektors neue Werte zu.

3.4. Die Grenzzustandsfunktionen g_i für $i=0,1,\ldots,V_1,V_1+1$

Die Grenzzustandsfunktionen können ihrer Wirkung nach in zwei Gruppen eingeteilt werden.

(1) g_{V_1+1} für den Teilraum R_{V_1+1} (AZ)

(2) g_i für die Teilräume R_i, $i=0,1,\ldots,V_1$ (RZ)

Bei der Aktivierung der Grenzzustandsfunktion g_{V_1+1} muß sich zumindest ein Auftrag A_k im Grenzzustand befinden. Die Wirkung der g_{V_1+1} auf den Zustand des Auftrags A_k beschreibt folgender Algorithmus.

1. Löse A_k aus dem AZ-Grenzzustand.
2. Rückgriff auf die auftragsspezifische Parameterliste (RZ_k-Vektor).
3. Relativzeit (RZ) gewünscht?

3.1. Nein (RZ_k-Vektor = $\{0\}$). Starte Zielaktivität. Beende Auftrag A_k.

3.2. Ja. Zeitkorrektur des RZ_k-Vektors (Gl. 3.1.-2 und 3.1.-3).

4. Rückgriff auf die I_k-te Komponente des RZ_k-Vektors.
5. Führe A_k vom Zustand $z(V_1+1,0)$ in den Zustand $z(I_k,\tau_{I_k})$ über.
6. Führe nächstfolgenden Auftrag, wenn vorhanden, in den Grenzzustand über.
7. Weise der (V_1+1)-Komponente des M-Vektors entsprechenden Wert zu.

Die Grenzzustandsfunktionen g_i, $i=0,1,\ldots,j\ldots,V_1$ sind identisch. Es genügt also die Angabe eines Algorithmus für die Funktion g_j.

1. Löse A_k aus dem j-ten Grenzzustand.
2. Rückgriff auf die auftragsspezifische Parameterliste.
3. Wahl der n-ten Komponente des RZ_k-Vektors (Gl. 3.1.-3) mit dem Wert $\tau_n \neq 0$, $n=j-1,j-2,\ldots,1,0$.
4. $\tau_n \neq \emptyset$ vorhanden?

4.1. Ja. Springe nach 8.

4.2. Nein. Starte Zielaktivität.

5. Wiederholung der Zielaktivität gewünscht?

5.1. Nein. Beende A_k.

5.2. Ja. Zeitkorrektur des RZ_k-Vektors (Gl. 3.1.-2 und 3.1.-3).

6. Wähle seine $n=I_k$-te Komponente mit dem Wert $\tau_n = \tau_{I_k}$ aus.

7. Verzögerung erforderlich? $((I_k > j) \wedge (\varepsilon_{I_k} \neq 0))$.

7.1. Ja. Weise τ_n den Wert $\tau_{I_k}+1$ zu.

8. Führe A_k in den Zustand $z(n,\tau_n)$ über.

4. Zusammenfassung

Die Einführung des Begriffes eines Zustandsraumes als Ordnungsprinzip für die Menge aller Zustände bearbeiteter Aufträge erlaubt in einfacher Weise die vollständige dynamische Beschreibung aller Aktivitäten in einer Zeitdienstverwaltung. Die Zustandsänderungen der Aufträge werden entweder durch interne oder externe Ereignisse veranlaßt. Jedem Ereignis ist eine Ereignisfunktion fest zugeordnet, die die Änderungsart und -richtung bestimmt. Die unmittelbare zustandsändernde Einwirkung der Ereignisfunktionen auf die Zustände des Zustandsraumes wird mit Hilfe von Filterfunktionen gesteuert. Der momentane Wert einer solchen Filterfunktion ist vom aktuellen Zustand derjenigen Gruppe abhängig, auf die die zugeordnete Ereignisfunktion einwirken soll. Diese Rückkopplungseigenschaft des veränderten Zustandsraumes auf die ihn verändernden Ereignisfunktionen läßt sich für eine adaptive Steuerung der Zeitdienstaufträge ausnutzen.

AUFTRAGSVERKEHR ÜBER EINEN GENERELLEN AUFTRAGSPUFFER BEI PROZESSRECHNERSYSTEMEN

J.BAUTZ

Problemstellung

Prozeßsysteme vom Typ II, wie sie auf der letzten NTG-Tagung in Darmstadt von Herrn H.-P. Rost definiert wurden, stellen extreme Ansprüche an das Auflösungsvermögen des benutzten Betriebssystems. Da die eintreffenden Ereignisse stochastisch auftreten, ist der Zeitpunkt des Auftretens des nächsten Ereignisses unbekannt. Unter Ereignis soll hier ein logisches Ereignis verstanden werden, wobei kein Unterschied zwischen einem externen (hardwaremäßigen) und einem internen (softwaremäßigen) Ereignis gemacht werden soll. Ein solches logisches Ereignis schlägt sich i.a. direkt oder auch indirekt in Form einer Programmbeauftragung nieder. Somit kann der Fall eintreten, daß ein Programm kurz hintereinander mit verschiedenen Parametersätzen beauftragt wird. Da der zeitliche Abstand der beiden Ereignisse unterhalb der Bearbeitungszeit durch das Programm liegen kann, dürfen die beiden Parametersätze nicht in das gleiche Parameterfeld geschrieben werden, da es sonst zu einem Informationsverlust oder -verfälschung kommen könnte.

Dieses beschriebene Problem ist ganz allgemein charakteristisch für den Auftragsverkehr in einem Typ II-Prozeßsystem:
Es werden für ein Programm ein oder mehrere neue Aufträge erzeugt, ehe es einen vorhergehenden Auftrag abgearbeitet hat. Bei externen Ereignissen wird die Mehrfachbeauftragung durch die Spontanität des Prozesses hervorgerufen. Betrachtet man die internen Ereignisse, so ist die Mehrfachbeauftragung Folge der Tatsache, daß die Programme Verzweigungen von Funktionsketten bilden, und es dadurch möglich ist, daß die Programme von mehreren Seiten quasi-gleichzeitig beauftragt werden.

Aus der Tatsache, daß für ein Programm zu einer Zeit u.U. mehrere Parametersätze zur Bearbeitung bereitstehen, ergibt sich die Forderung, die von einem Programm an ein weiteres Programm zu übergebenden Parameter - die noch nicht bearbeitet werden können - außerhalb des Programmkörpers abzulegen, da es sonst zu dem oben geschilderten Informationsverlust kommen könnte. Allein die Tatsache, daß man die Parametersätze außerhalb des Programmkörpers ablegt, ist jedoch noch kein Mittel gegen den Informationsverlust, wenn jedem Programm nur ein festzugeordneter Bereich zur

Aufnahme eines an ihn gerichteten Auftrages zur Verfügung steht. Ein geeignetes Betriebssystem wird daher also Systemdienste anbieten müssen, die dynamisch Arbeitsspeicherplatz zur Ablage von Parametersätzen bereitstellen.

Ein auftraggebendes Programm legt seinen Auftrag in einem solchen dynamisch zugeordneten Bereich ab, und der Auftragsempfänger kann ihn dort entnehmen. Somit besteht die Möglichkeit, daß mehrere Programme quasiparallel Aufträge für ein und dasselbe Programm erzeugen, indem sie sich jeweils dynamisch Arbeitsspeicherplatz von geeigneter Größe zuteilen lassen. Das Betriebssystem muß natürlich dann eine Kopplung der abgesetzten Aufträge vornehmen. Die erste resultierende Verbesserung für das Gesamtsystem ist die Tatsache, daß

1. keine Notwendigkeit besteht, daß das beauftragte Programm zur Zeit der Beauftragung im Arbeitsspeicher verfügbar ist und

2. das auftraggebende Programm in keinen Wartezustand übergeführt werden muß, wenn schon ein Auftrag für das beauftragte Programm existiert. Somit wird eine übermäßig lange Belegung von Betriebsmitteln, hervorgerufen durch die sonst eventuell notwendige Wartezeit, vermieden.

Die Größe der Parametersätze in einem Prozeßrechnersystem variiert sehr, übersteigt jedoch selten eine bestimmte Grenze, die weit unterhalb der durchschnittlichen Programmsegmentgrößen liegt. Aus diesem Grunde wird eine Arbeitsspeicherverwaltung wenig optimal sein, wenn an beliebigen Stellen im Arbeitsspeicher dynamisch erzeugte Parametersätze liegen und zwischen diesen "Inseln" die benötigten Segmente nichtresidenter Programme eingeplant werden müssen. In dem Moment, in dem die Parametersätze freigegeben werden, werden sie zu "Löchern", die ebenfalls nur sehr schwer oder erst wieder lange nach ihrer Freigabe in die Planung miteinbezogen werden können. Eine Berücksichtigung solcher Gegebenheiten würde nicht nur die Arbeitsspeicherverwaltung stark belasten, sondern könnte in Rechnern, wo keine geeigneten Möglichkeiten der Hardware existieren, zu Arbeitsspeicher-Verschränkungen führen.

Eine erste sehr einfache Lösungsmöglichkeit, die sich organisatorisch leicht durchführen ließe, wäre es, jedem Programm einen eigenen Auftragspuffer fester Länge (programmabhängig) zuzuordnen, in dem alle an das jeweilige Programm gerichteten Aufträge zwischengepuffert werden. Gegen die Lösung sprechen jedoch eine Reihe von Tatsachen. Erstens würde ein Großteil der programmbezogenen Auftragspuffer leerstehen, da zu einem Zeitpunkt immer nur ein Teil aller Programme beauftragt ist.

Zweitens müßte bei jedem Auftragspuffer getrennt die Dimensionierung und damit die Frage der Vermeidung von Engpässen gelöst werden. Aus diesen Gründen und den weiter unten erläuterten daraus resultierenden Möglichkeiten, ist der optimale Vorschlag der, einen einzigen zentralen Auftragspuffer zur Aufnahme aller im Programmsystem erzeugten Aufträge zu installieren.

Realisierungsmöglichkeiten

Die einfachste Organisation eines solchen zentralen Auftragspuffers wäre es, für jeden Auftrag einen Block der Maximallänge - d.h. der Länge des größten im System erzeugten Auftrags - zur Verfügung zu stellen. Wie jedoch schon vorher gesagt, variieren die in einem Prozeßsystem erzeugten Aufträge bzgl. ihrer Parameteranzahl recht beachtlich. Das hätte zur Folge, daß bei dieser zwar recht einfachen Organisation jedoch ein extrem hoher Anteil an nicht ausgenutztem Platz des Auftragspuffers vorliegen würde. Eine andere einfache Lösung wäre die, daß man in den Puffer alle eintreffenden Aufträge dicht legt und dabei alle an ein und dasselbe Programm gerichteten miteinander verkettet. Aber auch hier würde man bald einen beachtlichen Anteil des Puffers unter Umständen nicht ausnützen können, da die freiwerdenden Bereiche zu klein sein können für neue Aufträge. Die andere Möglichkeit, durch Zusammenschieben die Lücken zu einem geschlossenen Freibereich zusammenzusetzen, bringt einen nicht vertretbaren zeitlichen Verwaltungsaufwand mit sich.

Aus diesem Grunde sieht man die Einteilung des Auftragspuffers in Blöcke konstanter mittlerer Länge vor. Soll nun ein Auftrag abgelegt werden, der mehr Parameter enthält als in einen solchen Block konstanter Länge hineinpassen, so werden die notwendige Anzahl von Blöcken durch sog. Auftragszeiger miteinander verkettet. Wichtig für die Effektivität dieser aufgezeigten Lösung ist die Wahl einer geeigneten Blockgröße. Wird die Blocklänge sehr klein gewählt, so ist der Organisationsaufwand durch die Zeiger relativ hoch, die Ausnutzung des verfügbaren Pufferplatzes jedoch sehr gut, da es nur zu geringem Verschnitt kommt. Ist die Blocklänge verhältnismäßig groß, so entspricht dies fast dem Fall der oben genannten maximalen Blocklänge. Das bedeutet, daß zwar der Organisationsaufwand (Anteil der Zeiger) sehr klein ist, daß aber die Ausnutzung durch erhöhten Verschnitt recht gering ist. Durch eine geeignete Wahl der Blocklänge, die wegen der unterschiedlichen Auftragslängen in verschiedenen Systemen systemabhängig sein kann, kann ein Optimum an Effektivität erreicht werden, wobei sowohl der Verwaltungsaufwand (zeitlich gesehen) als auch der Arbeitsspeicherbedarf betrachtet werden müssen.

Im Normierungszustand, wenn der Auftragspuffer vollständig leer ist, sind sämtliche Blöcke als eine Kette verzeigert, die sog. Freikette. Wird nun ein Auftrag erzeugt, so werden die über die Auftragskette verketteten Blöcke an eine programmorientierte Liste gehängt. Diese Liste enthält einen Zeiger auf den ersten Block der durch Auftragszeiger gekoppelten Blöcke eines Auftrages. Somit hat man also ausgehend von dem in der Liste notierten Zeiger und unter Berücksichtigung der Auftragszeiger Zugriff zum gesamten Auftrag. Damit man nun aber bei der Programmierung die Blockung des Auftragspuffers nicht zu berücksichtigen braucht, werden sinnvollerweise vom Betriebssystem Systemdienste zur Verfügung gestellt, mit denen die Parameter aus dem Variablenbereich des Programms in den generellen Auftragspuffer (Auftragserteilung) bzw. in umgekehrter Richtung (Auftragsentgegennahme) übernommen werden.

Da wie oben geschildert, bei stochastischen Prozessen, mehrere Aufträge für ein und dasselbe Programm vorliegen können, muß die Möglichkeit vorgesehen werden, im Auftragspuffer mehrere unterschiedliche Aufträge für ein und dasselbe Programm miteinander zu verketten. Dabei sind diese Aufträge in einer gewissen zeitlichen Reihenfolge entstanden und sollten demgemäß auch in dieser Reihenfolge abgearbeitet werden. Daraus resultiert die Forderung, daß die Aufträge in zeitlicher Reihenfolge abgelegt werden. Die Lösung hierfür erreicht man mit Hilfe eines zweiten Zeigersystems. Mit den sog. Kettenzeigern werden die einzelnen Aufträge zu einer Programmauftragskette gekoppelt. In dieser Auftragskette werden an einem Ende die neuen Aufträge angehängt. Dadurch ergibt die Aufeinanderfolge der Auftragsblockketten in der Programmauftragskette die zeitliche Reihenfolge der Auftragsentstehungen. (Bild 1)

Mit Hilfe dieser beiden Zeigertypen ist es uns gelungen, die oben genannten Forderungen an den Auftragsverkehr in einem Prozeßsystem vom Typ II zu befriedigen. Wir sind durch die skizzierte Lösung in die Lage versetzt worden, Aufträge variabler Länge optimal in der Reihenfolge ihrer zeitlichen Erzeugung zu puffern, und gleichzeitig sicherzustellen, daß zu einer Zeit für ein Programm mehr als ein Auftrag existieren kann.

Erweiterungen

Das Vorhandensein eines solchen generellen Auftragspuffers mit der eben geschilderten Struktur, kann nun noch weiter ausgenutzt werden zur Koordinierung von Programmläufen, indem eine weitere Strukturierung des Puffers vorgenommen wird. Folgendes Problem stellt sich oft aus technologischen Gründen in einem Prozeßrechnersystem: Ein Programm P gibt Aufträge an die Programme P1 und P2. Aus technologischen Gründen soll auf jeden Fall sichergestellt werden, daß erst der Auftrag an P2 abgearbeitet wird und erst danach der von P1. Das läßt sich nicht immer ohne weiteres sicherstellen, z.B. wegen der unterschiedlichen Prioritäten der Programme oder der Verfügbarkeit benötigter Betriebsmittel. Sicherlich gibt es die Möglichkeit, daß das Programm P zunächst nur den Auftrag an P2 absetzt, auf dessen Abarbeitung wartet und erst danach den Auftrag an P1 erzeugt. Damit würde sich aber im Normalfall das Programm P selbst gegen die seinerseitige Abarbeitung eines neuen Auftrages verriegeln und es würden, eventuell überflüssigerweise, lange Betriebsmittel gebunden sein, auf deren Freigabe andere Programme ihrerseits warten.

Diese Problemstellung läßt sich dadurch lösen, daß man die beiden Aufträge zu einem geordneten Paar (allgemein zu einem Auftrags-n-tupel) zusammenfaßt. Die Ordnung der Auftrags-n-tupeln bildet eine neue dem bisherigen Auftragspuffer übergeordnete Struktur. Ein solches Auftrags-n-tupel bezeichnen wir als Folgeauftrag. Die einzelnen Aufträge, die zusammen einen Folgeauftrag bilden, sind über den sog. Folgezeiger miteinander verkettet. Der gesamte Folgeauftrag hängt in der Programmauftragskette desjenigen Programms, an das der erste Teilauftrag gerichtet ist. Erst nach Abarbeitung dieses Teilauftrages wird der Rest des Folgeauftrages in die Programmauftragskette des zweiten Teilauftrages gehängt usf. Damit ergibt sich eine Struktur wie sie in Bild 2 angedeutet ist.

Mit Hilfe dieser zusätzlichen Struktur und den entsprechenden Systemdiensten, die es ermöglichen, die skizzierten Eigenschaften auszunutzen, wird der Programmierer in die Lage versetzt, Einfluß auf die Reihenfolge der Abarbeitung der in seinem Programm erzeugten Aufträge zu nehmen.

Engpaßprobleme

Die Festlegung der Größe eines generellen Auftragspuffers ist systemspezifisch und geschieht bei der Installation. Dasselbe gilt für eine optimale Blockgröße. Damit nun keine Engpaßprobleme bzw. deadlocks auftreten, muß der Bedarf an Auftragspufferblöcken für einen Programmlauf als Betriebsmittel eingeplant werden. Diese Betriebsmittel müssen vor Beginn des Programmlaufs zur Verfügung stehen und reserviert werden. Damit kann sichergestellt werden, daß jeder Programmlauf bis zum Ende geführt werden kann, ohne daß das Betriebsmittel "Auftragspufferblöcke" fehlt. Verfolgt man diese angegebene Strategie zur Vermeidung von deadlocks, so muß vor dem Start eines Programms dessen maximal möglicher Bedarf an Auftragspufferplatz reserviert werden. Weicht nun der Maximalwert sehr stark vom Durchschnittswert ab, so kommt man normalerweise zu einer schlechten Ausnutzung des Auftragspuffers, da wesentlich mehr reserviert wird als meistens benötigt wird. Aus diesem Grunde stellt das Betriebssystem einen Systemdienst zur Verfügung, mit dessen Hilfe dynamisch Auftragspufferplatz nachgefordert werden kann. Bei Programmen, bei denen Maximalwert und Durchschnittswert stark differieren, wird man zunächst zum Start den Durchschnittsbedarf angeben. Stellt nun ein solches Programm dann fest, daß der seltene Fall eingetreten ist, daß ein höherer Bedarf als der reservierte benötigt wird, so kann es dynamisch die Differenz nachfordern. Das Programm muß sich natürlich dann darauf einstellen, daß der geforderte zusätzliche Bedarf zur Zeit nicht gedeckt werden kann.

Jedoch kann man mit dieser Strategie nicht vermeiden, daß der Auftragspuffer nur mit Aufträgen an solche Programme gefüllt ist, deren einzelner Bedarf an Auftragsblöcken nicht gedeckt werden kann. Dies würde dann zu einem Stillstand der Systemteile führen, da kein Programm aktiviert wird, das Aufträge dem Auftragspuffer entnimmt und somit zusätzliche Blöcke freimacht. Hier wird erkennbar, daß im Gegensatz zu anderen Betriebsmitteltypen, das Betriebsmittel "Auftragspufferblock" noch nicht wiederbenutzbar wird, wenn das benutzende Programm seinen Lauf beendet hat. Tritt nun der zuletzt geschilderte deadlock-Fall ein, so kann man sich dadurch helfen, daß man den Auftragspuffer kurzzeitig auf einen Hintergrundspeicher ausdehnt. Dabei wird man nur die Aufträge für Programme sehr niedriger Priorität auf dem Hintergrundspeicher zwischenpuffern. Mit Hilfe dieses erweiterten Auftragspuffers gelingt es, kurzzeitig auftauchende Spitzenbelastungen des Systems und somit des Puffers abzufangen.

Anwendung und Auswirkung auf das gesamte Programmsystem

Die positive Wirkung eines generellen Auftragspuffers auf die Struktur eines Programmsystems geht über das bisher beschriebene zentrale Ablegen von Aufträgen und deren Abarbeitung weit hinaus. Dabei sollte man im wesentlichen drei resultierende Vorteile nennen:

1. Programme, die wegen ihres Umfanges und nicht ausreichender Größe des verfügbaren Arbeitsspeichers segmentiert werden mußten, können auf einfache Art die

den Vorgang beschreibenden Daten - sofern es sich nur um kleinere Datenmengen handelt - an das nächste Segment weiterreichen.

2. Programmkomplexen kann ein Re-entry-Verhalten ermöglicht werden. Dabei kann man zwei unterschiedliche Strukturen eines solchen Programmkomplexes feststellen:

a) Das Programm ist zerlegbar in mehrere Teile, die zusammen eine sequentiell ablaufende Kette bilden. Hat ein Teil der Programmkette seine Aufgabe erledigt, so erteilt er dem nächsten Glied der Kette einen Auftrag zur Fortführung der Aufgabe. Da die dazu relevanten Daten Bestandteil des Auftrages sind, kann der Auftraggeber, egal ob das beauftragte Glied seine Arbeit sofort aufnehmen kann oder nicht, eine neue Aufgabe beginnen. Damit erreicht man ein Re-entry-Verhalten der gesamten Programmkette, wobei über die Laufzeit des ersten Teils der Kette hinweg quasi eine Re-entry-Sperre gesetzt ist. Ebenso können Vorgänge, die jeder für sich eine solche Programmkette durchlaufen, sich aber in einem Glied überschneiden, quasi-parallel ablaufen, d.h. der eine Vorgang kann schon in Angriff genommen werden ehe der andere beendet worden ist.

b) Läßt sich die oben erwähnte Zerlegung in eine sequentiell ablaufende Kette nicht durchführen, so besteht trotzdem die Möglichkeit, eine Re-entry-Verhalten mit den Mitteln des Auftragspuffers zu erreichen. Sind beim Ablauf in der Kette Schleifen enthalten, so ist es notwendig, alle für einen Vorgang relevanten Daten im Auftrag an den nächsten weiterzugeben und diese bei der Wiederaufnahme desselben Vorgangs zurückzuerhalten. Dadurch wird das Programm in die Lage versetzt, einen neuen Vorgang zu beginnen und später gegebenenfalls den alten wieder aufzunehmen.

3. Bei Wartevorgängen - z.B. infolge von selbst erzeugten Unteraufgaben - braucht der Wartende nicht in einen Wartezustand übergeführt zu werden, womit er eventuell Betriebsmittel blockieren würde. Die Rückmeldung und damit der Anstoß zur Fortführung bzw. Beendigung eines logischen Vorgangs wird ebenfalls über den generellen Auftragspuffer erfolgen. Dies wird wie beim Re-entry-Verhalten dadurch erreicht, daß man alle den Vorgang beschreibenden Größen mit in die Unteraufgaben notiert, diese bei der Rückmeldung wieder mitgeteilt bekommt, und damit den Vorgang fortführen kann.

Alle drei beschriebenen Auswirkungen eines generellen Auftragspuffers kommen nur dann zum Tragen, wenn der Umfang der zu übermittelnden Daten nicht zu groß ist.

Für umfangreichere Datenmengen wird man sich andere Strategien überlegen müssen. Jedoch kann man anhand der aufgezählten Auswirkungen auf das gesamte Programmsystem erkennen, daß der generelle Auftragspuffer zur vollständigen Entkopplung von Programmläufen beitragen kann. Dies erscheint uns der allerwesentlichste Vorteil des geschilderten Auftragsverkehrs zu sein.

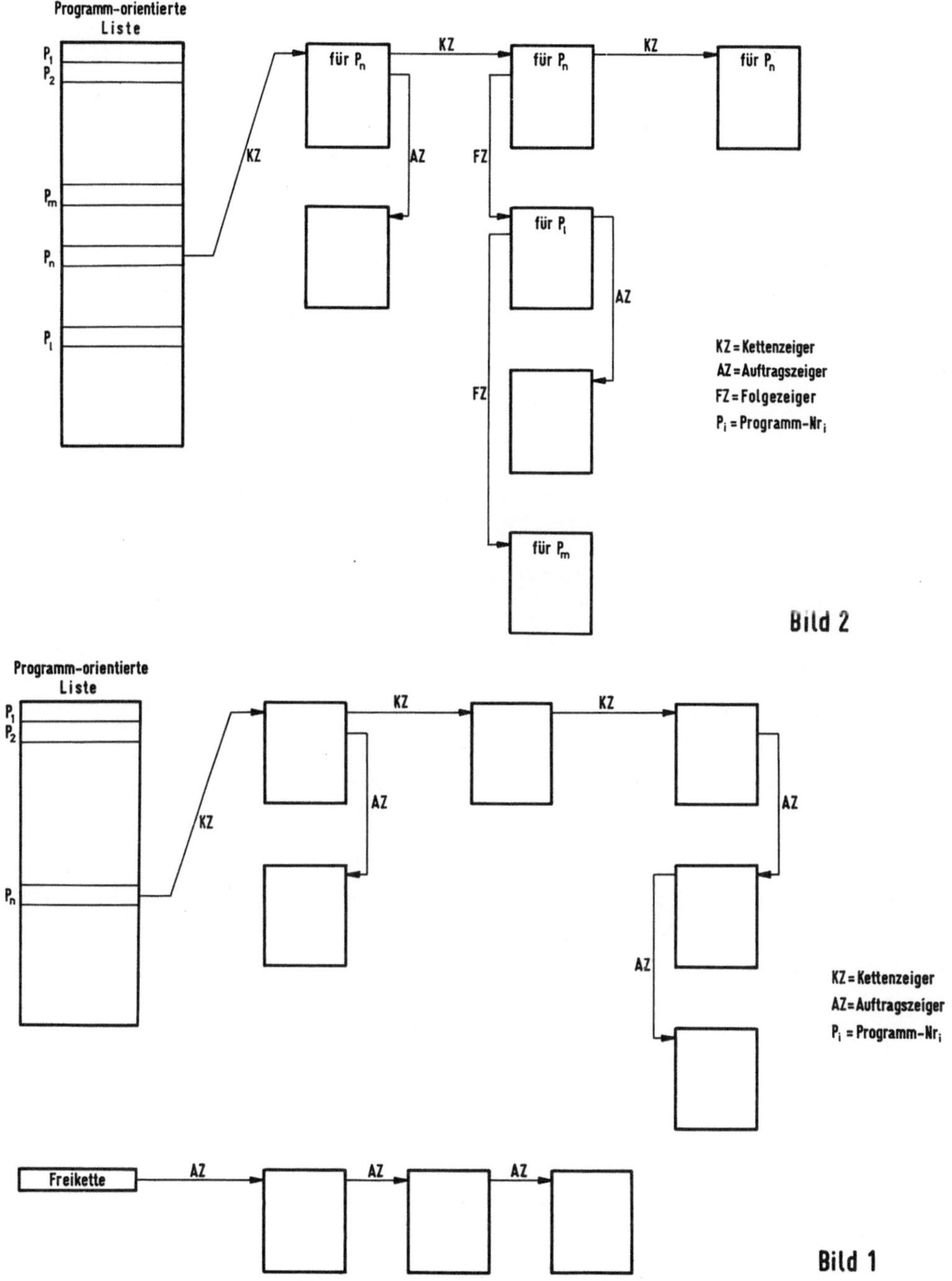

Bild 2

Bild 1

GRAPHISCHE SYSTEME

SPRACH- UND DATENSTRUKTUR DES SYSTEMS G R A P H I C

R.SCHUSTER, G.ENDERLE, K.LEINEMANN, E.G.SCHLECHTENDAHL, H.SCHNAUDER, U.SCHUMANN

1. Einleitung

Die Integration des Zeichnungswesens in den EDV-unterstützten Fertigungs-und Konstruktionsprozeß ist ein allgemein anerkanntes Ziel, unter anderem, weil das Zeichnen rund 30% der Arbeitszeit eines Konstrukteurs ausmacht [1]. Besonders elegant ist hier das interaktive Arbeiten mit einem Lichtgriffel am Display [2], jedoch entsteht hier eine gewisse Hardware-Abhängigkeit. Andererseits haben sich höhere Programmiersprachen zur Automatisierung von Berechnungsabläufen des technischen Entwurfs bewährt - wenngleich die direkte Anwendung dieser Sprache den nicht zum Programmierer ausgebildeten Ingenieur häufig überfordert. Die üblichen Programmiersprachen bieten jedoch dem Anwender keine Hilfsmittel, seine Zeichnungsprobleme zu formulieren. Die von Plotter-Herstellern gelieferte Software allein reicht nicht aus und komfortabelere Systeme wurden zwar bereits in ihren wünschenswerten Eigenschaften spezifiziert [3, 4] jedoch höchstens für Spezialbereiche (wie z.B. für elektrische Schaltkreise [5]) realisiert.

Wir haben daher im Rahmen von Arbeiten zu einem Projekt "Rechnergestützter Entwurf REGENT" [6] ein Programm GRAPHIC erstellt, das folgende wesentliche Aufgaben erfüllen kann:

1. Eingabe zur Erzeugung und Änderung graphischer Daten in einer Wortsprache mit Ausgabe auf Plottern,
2. Anschlußmöglichkeit an bestehende Programme, die eine starre Plotausgabe erzeugen und
3. Manipulationsmöglichkeit gespeicherter graphischer Informationen.

Die Festlegung auf eine Wortsprache bringt folgende Vorteile:

- Unabhängigkeit von nichtstandardisierter, teurer und wenig verbreiteter Hardware.
- Eingabe kann sowohl im Stapelbetrieb als auch interaktiv am Teletype erfolgen.
- Die Eingabe ist selbstdokumentierend.
- Die Koordinatenwerte u.ä. können genau eingegeben werden.
- Es kann eine für den Ingenieur leicht erlernbare, problemangepaßte Sprache verwendet werden.

Besonders wurde GRAPHIC darauf ausgelegt, den sonst sehr zeitraubenden Änderungsdienst an Strichzeichnungen in zwei Dimensionen zu vereinfachen. Durch ein klar definiertes Interface wurde eine weitgehende Unabhängigkeit vom Zeichengerät erreicht. Auch Ausgabe auf einem Displaygerät wäre realisierbar. GRAPHIC wurde unter dem Betriebssystem IBM-TSO bereits interaktiv betrieben.

Systemübersicht

Bevor auf spezielle Aspekte der Daten- und Sprachstruktur eingegangen wird, soll ein kurzer Überblick zum Konzept des Gesamtsystems gegeben werden.

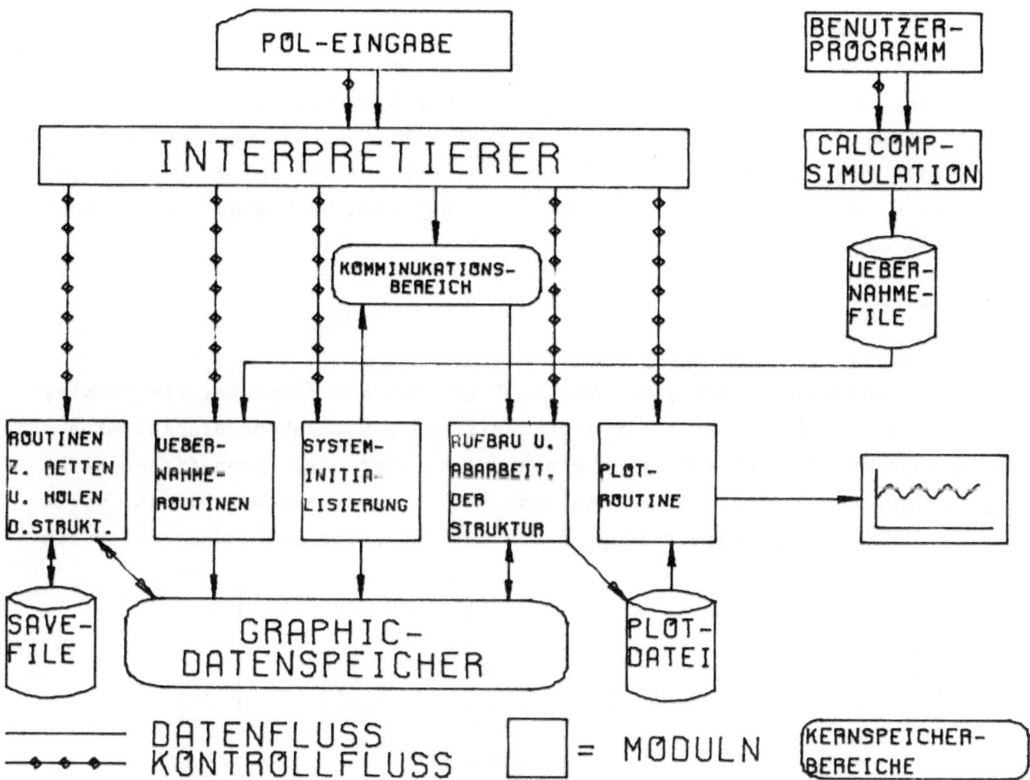

Abb.1: Hauptkomponenten des Systems GRAPHIC

Wie aus Abb.1 ersichtlich ist, besteht das System aus 4 Hauptkomponenten:

1. einem Interpretierer
2. einem Kommunikationsbereich
3. einem Modulpaket zur Strukturierung und Verarbeitung der Befehle und
4. einem graphischen Datenspeicher

Die Eingabe in der problemorientierten Sprache GRAPHIC wird von einem Inter-

pretierer analysiert, der dann durch den Aufruf bestimmter Moduln die Speicherung der Information in strukturierter Form im Kernspeicher veranlaßt oder die Manipulation bestehender Strukturen herbeiführt. Der graphische Datenspeicher enthält alle Objekte in ihrer internen Repräsentation. Eine Übergabe von Daten aus der GRAPHIC-Sprache erfolgt dabei über den Kommunikationsbereich.
Die Ausgabe graphischer Information erfolgt über eine Plot-Datei, die alle zum Zeichnen eines Objektes erforderlichen Angaben enthält. Diese Plot-Datei stellt ein klares Interface zur herstellerabhängigen Plotter-Hard- und Software dar. Wegen der Beschränkung auf elementare Eigenschaften der Zeichengeräte kann eine Umstellung schnell vollzogen werden. GRAPHIC wurde als Subsystem des Programmsystems ICES (Integrated Civil Engineering System)[7,8] implementiert. Dadurch konnte die Datenstruktur für graphische Objekte relativ leicht realisiert werden.ICES bietet außerdem mit seinem Subsystem CDL(Command Definition Language) eine Möglichkeit, problemorientierte Sprachen zu definieren. Einige Eigenheiten der GRAPHIC-Sprache, z.B.die Notwendigkeit, daß jede Anweisung (auch Zuweisungen) mit einem Wort der Sprache beginnen muß, resultieren aus der verwendeten CDL [8].

3. Datenstruktur

3.1 Graphische Objekt-Struktur

Eine Zeichnung besteht aus einer Vielzahl graphischer Elemente, wie Punkte, Linien, Texte usw., die in einem strukturierten Zusammenhang stehen. Eine Übersicht über Methoden zur Speicherung graphischer Strukturen findet sich in [9, 2]. Abb.2 zeigt die Darstellung der Struktur eines Dreiecks, wobei die Pfeile auf die Objekte zeigen, durch die das jeweilige Objekt definiert wird.

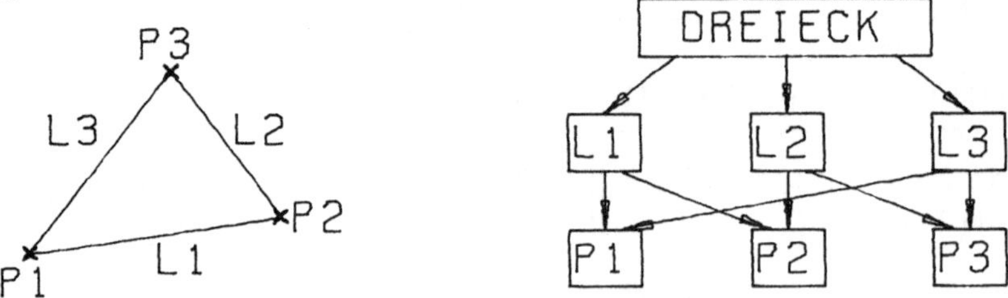

Abb.2: Datenstruktur für das Objekt "Dreieck"

Von jedem Objekt können nach oben und unten beliebig viele Striche ausgehen. Um derartige Strukturen flexibel speichern zu können, wurde die Aufgabe, zwei Objekte in der Struktur zu verbinden (ähnlich dem ASP-System [10]), sog. "Referenz-Objekten" übertragen, die ebenso gespeichert werden wie graphische Objekte. Die folgende Abbildung soll die Funktionsweise der Referenzen erläutern.

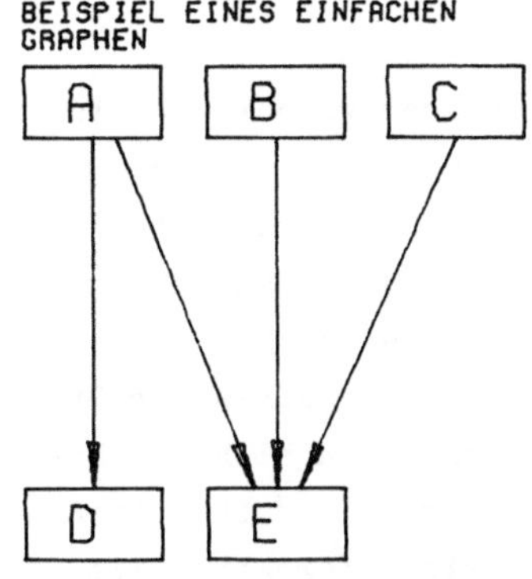

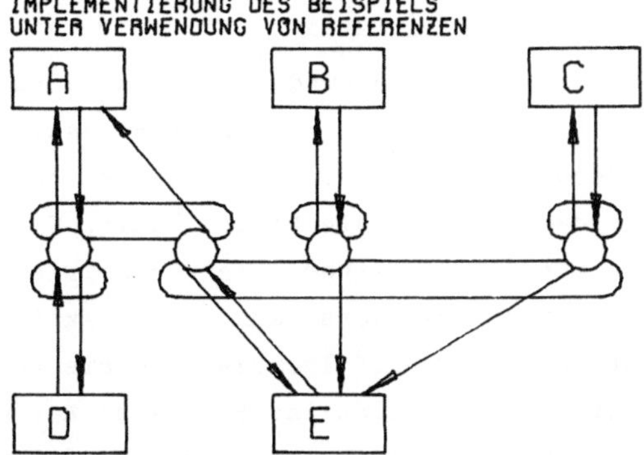

Abb.3: Referenzen

Die Einführung dieser Referenzobjekte führte zu einer starken Vereinheitlichung aller Verwaltungs- und Zugriffsalgorithmen für die Datenstruktur. Die graphischen Objekte enthalten außer der Information, die die Struktur beschreibt, noch einen Zeiger auf ein Feld mit den Attributen dieses Objektes. Bei einem Punkteelement sind in diesem Attributfeld z.B.die Punktekoordinaten gespeichert. Verschiedene Objekte unterscheiden sich allein in ihren Attributen.

3.2 Kollektionen in der GRAPHIC-Struktur

Für den Umgang mit graphischen Objekten ist es angenehm, wenn man logisch zusammenhängende Objekte zusammenfassen und mit einem Namen ansprechen kann. Wir nennen eine Zusammenfassung von graphischen Objekten eine graphische Kollektion. Die Linien eines Dreiecks mit der Beschriftung der Seiten und Eckpunkte könnten z.B. zu einer derartigen graphischen Kollektion zusammengefaßt werden.

3.3 Namen zur Identifizierung von Objekten und "undefinierte" Objekte

Zum Zwecke der Identifikation werden graphische Objekte mit einem Namen versehen. Er stellt die Verbindung zum bereits spezifizierten Objekt her oder dient als Platzhalter für noch undefinierte Objekte. Namen werden als Knoten in die Datenstruktur eingegliedert. Die gesamte Substruktur eines Namensobjektes wird mit diesem Namen angesprochen. Der Name selbst (also die Zeichenkette) ist ein Wert im Attributfeld eines Namensobjektes.
Werden während der Interpretation eines GRAPHIC-Programmes schon vorher definierte Namen referiert, so erfolgt der Zugriff auf das entsprechende Namensobjekt über eine Hash-Tabelle [13]. Zur Erhaltung der Konsistenz gibt es ein spezielles "undefiniertes Objekt" für nicht oder fehlerhaft definierte Objekte.

3.4 Graphische Elemente

Graphische Elemente sind Objekte zur Speicherung elementarer graphischer Information. Sie können ohne weitere Bearbeitung sofort gezeichnet werden. Häufig verwendete Bestandteile einer Zeichnung werden als Einheit betrachtet. So werden die Elemente Punkt, Linie, Kreisbogen, Text, Koordinatenachse, Schraffur usw. in einer ihrer Geometrie angemessenen Form gespeichert. Dies erweist sich besonders dann als effektiver als die Auflösung graphischer Objekte in eine Punktfolge bzw. die sie verbindenden Linien, wenn sich ein Benutzer nicht für einzelne Punkte seines Objektes,sondern z.B. nur für einen Polygonzug als ganzes interessiert oder wenn eine Lineartransformation mit allen Bestandteilen eines Objektes auszuführen ist. Andere realisierte Lösungen [2] benutzen hierarchisch gegliederte Strukturen von Punkten, Linien, Flächen und Körpern,die aus Punkten durch Zeiger- bzw. Ringlisten generiert werden; hier fungieren lediglich Punkte als Elemente in unserem Sinne.

3.5 Graphische Operationen

Eine graphische Operation verarbeitet graphische Objekte und erzeugt als Ergebnis ihrer Ausführung ein neues Objekt oder eine Kollektion von Objekten. Graphische Operationen erzeugen z.B. aus zwei Punkten eine Linie, durch drei Punkte einen Kreis oder führen Lineartransformationen durch. Hierbei muß der Anwender entscheiden, ob ein neues Objekt, das durch eine Operation aus anderen entsteht, sofort errechnet und einem Namen zugewiesen werden soll oder ob das Objekt durch die Operation in funktionalem Zusammenhang mit den Ausgangsobjekten bleiben soll.

In der Sprache kann der Benutzer zwischen diesen Möglichkeiten durch die Worte SETZE bzw. DEFINIERE unterscheiden und z.B.schreiben:

1) Im Falle der Zuweisung (Ausführungsmodus)
   SETZE 'L' ALS LINIE VON 'P1' NACH 'P2'
2) Im Falle der Funktionsdefinition (Programmiermodus)
   DEFINIERE 'L' ALS LINIE VON 'P1' NACH 'P2'

Im ersten Fall ist 'L' unabhängig von späteren Veränderungen der Punkte'P1' und 'P2', im zweiten Fall dagegen verändert sich 'L' automatisch entsprechend. Zur Realisierung dieser Fähigkeiten erwies es sich als zweckmäßig, alle Operationen als Knoten der Datenstruktur darzustellen. Jedes Operationsobjekt besitzt eine ihm zugehörige Prozedur, die ein Parserprogramm bei der Abarbeitung eines Operationsknotens aufruft. Die Objekte, mit denen Operationen ausgeführt werden, sind Subobjekte der Operation. Es gibt verschiedene Arten von Operationssubobjekten, ein Beispiel macht dies deutlich.Für "Linie von Punkt 'A' nach Punkt 'B' " müssen genau 2 Subobjekte vorhanden sein, die Reihenfolge dieser Objekte ist wichtig. Bei der Operation "Verschiebung eines Objektes"

dagegen kann das Objekt aus einer beliebigen Anzahl von Objekten bestehen, deren Reihenfolge unwichtig ist. Wir nennen die Subobjekte einer Operation, die in fester Anzahl und Reihenfolge auftreten, Argumente, diejenigen, deren Anzahl und Reihenfolge beliebig ist, Operanden des Operationsobjektes. Die Lineartransformation "Verdrehe ein Objekt O um einen Punkt P" hat sowohl ein Argument, den Drehpunkt P und eine Anzahl von Operanden, aus denen das Objekt O zusammengesetzt ist.
In der Datenstruktur werden Argumente und Operanden über unterschiedliche Abwärtszeiger erreicht. Abb.4 zeigt als Beispiel die Struktur der Operation "Drehung um Punkt".

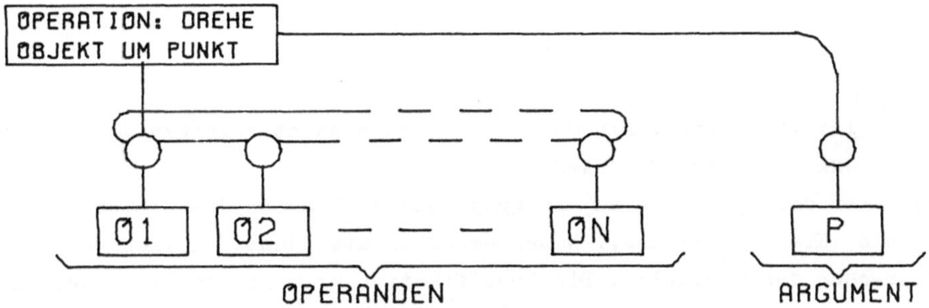

Abb.4: Argumente und Operanden einer Operation

Einige der in GRAPHIC möglichen graphischen Operationen sind:
- Lineartransformationen: Verdrehung, Verschiebung, Vergrößerung
- Kreis als Umkreis oder Inkreis eines Dreiecks
- Linie zu 2 Punkten
- Halbkreis über 2 Punkten
- Schnittpunkt zwischen Linien und Kreisen
- Schraffur innerhalb geschlossener Polygonzüge
- Erzeugung von Koordinatenachsen zu Polygonzügen

3.6 Kontrollobjekte und logisch-arithmetische Objekte

Kontrollobjekte steuern die Abarbeitung der Struktur. Sie entsprechen bestimmten Möglichkeiten der GRAPHIC-Sprache. Die Ausführung einer Struktur wird beispielsweise durch ein "Evaluiere-Objekt" ausgelöst. Andere Kontrollobjekte entsprechen den DO, IF oder PROCEDURE Anweisungen der Sprache. Sie fügen sich in die beschriebene Datenstruktur leicht ein. Die Anweisungen innerhalb eines Blocks können z.B. als Subobjekte eines Kollektionsobjektes in der Struktur repräsentiert sein.

Logisch-arithmetische Objekte erlauben z.B.die Realisierung der Kontrollvariablen von DO-Schleifen und der logischen Ausdrücke nach WHILE und IF.

4. Die Sprache des Systems GRAPHIC

4.1 Grundbestandteile der Sprache

Die GRAPHIC-Sprache soll dem Benutzer das Erzeugen, die Manipulation und die Ausgabe graphischer Objekte auf einfache Art ermöglichen. Durch eine Anlehnung an den üblichen Sprachgebrauch wird der Lernaufwand und die Anzahl der Eingabefehler reduziert. Für den geübten Programmierer besteht die Möglichkeit, die Eingabe auf wesentliche Syntaxelemente der Sprache zu beschränken, d.h. Worte der Sprache abzukürzen und Füllwörter wegzulassen. Die Befehle verlieren dann an Lesbarkeit, der Umfang der Eingabe wird aber stark vermindert.
Eine GRAPHIC-Anweisung lautet z.B. in ihrer vollständigen Form:

SETZE 'L' ALS LINIE VON 'P1' NACH 'P2'

und in ihrer kürzesten Form:

SET 'L' LIN 'P1' 'P2'

Die Eingabe ist formatfrei. Ein GRAPHIC-Programm steht zwischen den beiden Anweisungen GRAPHIC und ENDE GRAPHIC.
Die Konstanten der Sprache sind die graphischen Elemente des Systems GRAPHIC, Punkt, Linie, Kreis, Text usw.. Namen erlauben die Identifikation von Objekten, sie entsprechen den Variablen. Die Spezifikation graphischer Elemente, Namen und Operationen können zu Ausdrücken zusammengesetzt werden. Das Ergebnis der Ausführung eines Ausdruckes ist ein Element oder eine Kollektion von Elementen.

4.2 Aufbau von GRAPHIC-Anweisungen

Eine graphische Anweisung der allgemeinen Form

$$\left\{\begin{matrix}\underline{\text{SET}}\text{ZE}\\ \underline{\text{DEF}}\text{INIERE}\end{matrix}\right\} \quad \text{<name>} \quad \text{<objekt>}$$

bewirkt eine Zuordnung zwischen einem graphischen Objekt und einem Namen, über den das Objekt später angesprochen werden kann. SETZE bzw. DEFINIERE kennzeichnen den Ausführungsmodus,<name> erlaubt die Identifikation des Objektes, das durch <objekt> definiert ist. <objekt> ist eine Anweisung, deren allgemeiner Aufbau hier nicht beschrieben werden kann.
Innerhalb einer Anweisung kann eine beliebige Schachtelung der Spezifikation von Objekten auftreten, die in eine entsprechende Struktur umgesetzt wird. Diese Flexibilität demonstriert das folgende GRAPHIC-Programmbeispiel:

```
SETZE 'SP' SCHN LINIE VERS 1  1  'P1' SCHN POLY ( 'P2' 'P3' 'P4' ) -

LIN PUNKT 2  3  PUNKT 4  5 KREIS MITTELPUNKT 2  2  RADIUS 1
```

Jede Spezifikation beginnt dabei mit einem Prefix-Operator, der die Operationen <u>SCHN</u>ITTPUNKT, <u>LIN</u>IE, <u>VER</u>SCHIEBUNG und <u>POLY</u>GONZUG kennzeichnet. Die Linien im Beispiel sollen die Schachtelung der Spezifikation sichtbar machen.

4.3 Prozeduren

Die Deklaration von Prozeduren erlaubt eine Zusammenfassung von Anweisungen, deren Abspeicherung und eine spätere Ausführung:

PROCEDURE 'NAME' (parm,...,parm)

Prozeduren werden durch ihren Namen identifiziert und durch ein

CALL 'NAME' (obj,..,obj)

angesprochen. Auf Einzelheiten (z.B.Definition und Aufruf von Funktionsprozeduren und die Blockstruktur) kann hier nicht eingegangen werden.

4.4 Kontrollanweisungen

Zum Verlassen der sequentiellen Abarbeitung können IF-THEN-ELSE und DO-WHILE-Befehle verwendet werden, durch deren Schachtelung sich die gewünschten Verzweigungen erzielen lassen. Die wiederholte Ausführung einer Befehlsfolge wird durch das DO-Statement gestattet.

4.5 Systembefehle

Systembefehle sind GRAPHIC-Anweisungen, die nicht in eine Datenstruktur umgesetzt werden, sondern direkt eine Verarbeitung veranlassen. Ein wichtiger Systembefehl ist der UEBERNIMM-Befehl:

UEBERNIMM 'ZEICHN.1' VON FILE 15

Damit wird veranlaßt, daß der Inhalt einer Interface-Datei umgesetzt wird in GRAPHIC-Objekte. Diese Interface-Datei wurde vorher durch ein Programm gefüllt, das normalerweise eine starre Plotausgabe erzeugt. Die Aufrufe der Plotroutinen werden dabei abgefangen und die Interface-Datei wird mit der entsprechenden graphischen Information gefüllt. Nach Übernahme in GRAPHIC ist die gesamte Zeichnung unter dem angegebenen Namen, im Beispiel 'ZEICHN.1', ansprechbar. GRAPHIC generiert darüberhinaus für alle Einzelteile der Zeichnung (Linien, Punkte, Texte usw.) Namen, die auf Wunsch an die Objekte gezeichnet werden. Danach kann sowohl die gesamte Zeichnung als auch jedes Einzelteil in GRAPHIC manipuliert werden.

Außerdem gibt es Systembefehle zum Festlegen von Standardmaßeinheiten für Längenangaben, zur Fehlersuche und zum Testen von GRAPHIC-Programmoduln. Letztere drucken u.a.die gesamte Knotenliste mit den in [12] beschriebenen Routinen aus oder liefern einen Programmaufruf-Trace. Dies erleichtert die Erweiterung von GRAPHIC um neue Elementetypen und Operationen.

5. Ein GRAPHIC-Programm als Beispiel

Das folgende GRAPHIC-Programm erzeugt die Zeichnung in Abb.5. Auch alle anderen Abbildungen dieses Berichtes wurden mit GRAPHIC erzeugt.

```
GRAPHIC
EROEFFNE ZEICHNUNG AUF ABMESSUNGEN 20 CM 14 CM
SET 'SPRUNG' POLYGON 0 0 2 0 2 3 10 3 END
SET 'ANTWORT' POLYGON MIT 81 STUETZWERTEN GEMAESS
      TAU=1.
      DO 1 I=1,81
      X(I)=(I+19.)/10.
    1 Y(I)=3.*(1.-EXP(-(X(I)-2.)/TAU) )
      END
SET 'U1' TEXT 'U1' 1.2 1.5
SET 'U2' TEXT 'U2' 3.8 1.5
SET 'XAX' X-ACHSE BESCHRIFTUNG 'T (SEC)' ZU ( 'SPRUNG','ANTWORT' )
SET 'YAX' Y-ACHSE BESCHRIFTUNG 'U(V)' ZU ( 'SPRUNG','ANTWORT' )
SET 'TRANS' TRANSFORMATION ZU 'XAX' 'YAX' VON ( 'SPRUNG','ANTWORT','U1','U2',-
SCHRAFFUR ABSTAND 0.4 ZWISCHEN 'SPRUNG' UND 'ANTWORT' )
STANDARD EINHEIT CM
SET 'PFEIL' POLYGON 12.5 6.4 12.5 4.6 12.45 5.1 12.55 5.1 12.5 4.6 END
SET 'SCHALT.' ( 'PFEIL',TEX 'U1' 11.5 5.25,POL 12.5 6.5 13.5 6.5 13.5 6.35 14.5
6.35 14.5 6.65 13.5 6.65 13.5 6.5 END,POL 14.5 6.5 16.5 6.5 END,POL 15.5 6.5
15.5 5.6 15 5.6 16 5.6 15.5 5.6 END,POL 15.5 5.4 15 5.4 16 5.4 15.5 5.4 15.5
4.5 END,VERSCHIEBUNG 4 0 'PFEIL' TEX 'U2' 16.6 5.25,POL 16.5 4.5 12.5 4.5 END )
ZEICHNE ABBILDUNG VON ( 'XAX','YAX','TRANS','SCHALT.' )
RETTE 'ABB.5' 'KEY'
ENDE GRAPHIC
```

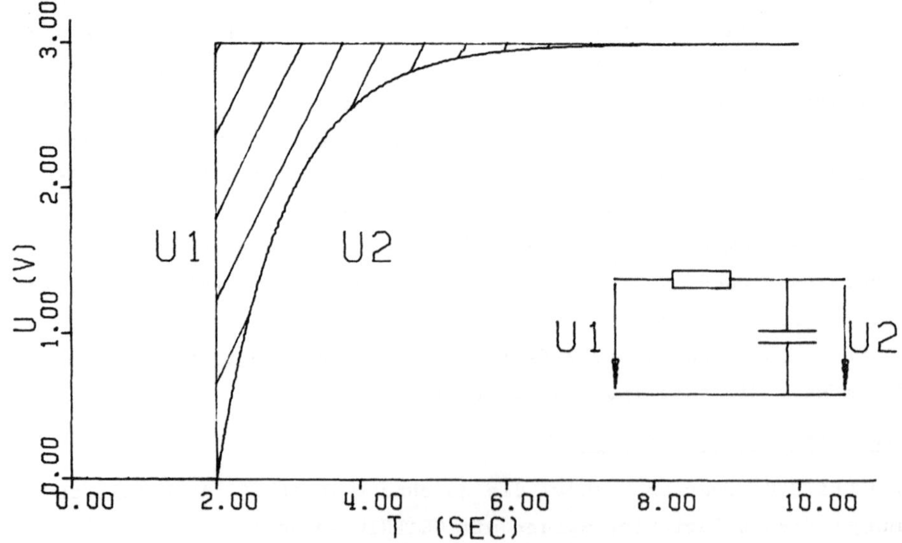

<u>Abb.5:</u> Beispiel einer mit GRAPHIC erstellten Zeichnung

6. L i t e r a t u r

[1] Simon, R.: Rechnerunterstütztes Konstruieren. Eine Möglichkeit zur Rationalisierung im Konstruktionsbereich. Diss.TH Aachen (1968)

[2] Encarnacao, J.: Untersuchungen zum Problem der rechnergesteuerten Darstellungen auf ebenen Bildschirmen. Diss. TU Berlin (1971)

[3] Comba, P.G.: A Language for Three-Dimensional-Geometry. IBM Syst.J. (1968), 292-307

[4] Kulsrud, H.E.: A General Purpose Graphic Language. CACM 11 (1968), 247-254

[5] Bracchi, G.: Ferrari, D.: A Language for Treating Geometric Patterns in a Two-dimensional Space. CACM 14 (1971), 26-32

[6] Enderle, G. et.al.: Erster REGENT-Halbjahresbericht.KFK - Externer Bericht 8/72-2 (Juni 1972)

[7] Roos, D.(ed.): ICES System-General Description. MIT, Department of Civil Engineering, R 67-49 (Sept.1967)

[8] Schlechtendahl, E.G.; Schumann, U.(ed.): Erfahrungen mit dem Programmsystem ICES bei ingenieurtechnischen Anwendungen. KFK 1506(Mai 1972)

[9] Williams, R.: A Survey of Data Structures for Computer Graphic Systems. Comp.Survey 3, No.1 (March 1971)

[10] Encarnacao, J.: Datenstrukturen für graphische Informationsverarbeitung, in W. Giloi (ed.): Symposium über Computer Graphics. Berlin (Okt.1971), 15-49

[11] Knuth, D.E.: The Art of Computer Programming, Vol.1, Addison-Wesley Publ.Co.(1968)

[12] Schumann, U.: E.G.Schlechtendahl: Algorithmen zur Verarbeitung von Baumstrukturen und ihre Anwendung in ICES, KFK 1536 (Jan.1972)

[13] Schumann, U.: Verwaltung von dynamischen Symboltabellen nach der HASH-Methode mit ICETRAN-Unterprogrammen. KFK-Externer Bericht 8/71-7 (Okt.1971)

DIE GRAPHIK - SOFTWARE DES TR 440

H.KÄÄB

1. Einführung

Im Teilnehmer-Rechensystem TR440 sind als Ein-, Ausgabegeräte auch Plotter, Sichtgeräte und Zeichentische teils direkt am TR440 teils über den Satellitenrechner TR86 anschliessbar. Das Ziel der Graphik-Software ist es, dem Benutzer, der den Rechner in einer höheren Programmiersprache betreibt, den Betrieb dieser Geräte in einer komfortablen Weise zu ermöglichen. Wie bei den anderen E/A-Geräten geschieht dies über Unterprogramme, die der Benutzer in seiner Programmiersprache aufruft. Die Prozeduren sind zum direkten Anschluss an FORTRAN erstellt, können aber mit Hilfe der Transferprozedur S&FTNA ohne Einschränkung auch in ALGOL-Programmen verwendet werden.

Vor der Schilderung der einzelnen Programmteile zunächst einige Angaben zur Hardware der verwendeten Geräte. Als Plotter können die Trommelplotter von Benson oder Calcomp mit 34 cm oder 75 cm Breite und Steuerung durch 8 Fahrbefehle in 45° Richtung verwendet werden. Der Anschluss von Mikrofilmplottern und Zeichentischen ist vorgesehen.
Als Sichtgerät wird das SIG100 von Telefunken verwendet. Mit diesem Sichtgerät können alphanumerische Zeichen und graphische Darstellungen ausgegeben werden. Hierzu dient ein Zeichen- und ein Vektorgenerator. Der Bildwiederholspeicher befindet sich im Satellitenrechner TR86, ist 617 Worte gross und wird mit 33 Hz ausgelesen. Dadurch können über 2000 Zeichen oder 614 Vektoren gezeichnet werden. Bei gleichzeitiger Ausgabe von Zeichen und Vektoren sind es entsprechend weniger. Maximal können bis zu 16 Sichtgeräte SIG100 an einem Kanal hängen.

Die Bildfläche beträgt 30x30 cm oder 512x512 Rasterpunkte. Vektoren können von jedem Rasterpunkt zu jedem Rasterpunkt führen. Der Vektorgenerator erzeugt zwischen zwei solchen beliebigen Rasterpunkten eine gerade Strecke.
Für die Eingabe steht eine Tastatur mit alphanumerischen Zeichen und Funktionstasten, sowie eine Rollkugel zur Verfügung. Mit der Rollkugel kann ein Fadenkreuz auf dem SIG100 bewegt werden. Dabei werden die Koordinaten an den TR86 und an das Benutzerprogramm zurückgegeben.

2.FOPLOT-Plottergrundsoftware

FOPLOT dient zum Zeichnen von Punkten, Strecken, Polygonzügen, Texten und Achsenkreuzen. Die Ansteuerung des Plotters geschieht über ein zentrales Unterprogramm. Durch geringfügige Modifikationen an diesem kann FOPLOT an verschiedene Plottertypen angepasst werden. Das Unterprogramm PLOSIG ermöglicht es, Zeichnungen wahlweise auf das Sichtgerät SIG100 oder den Plotter zu leiten. FOPLOT dient als Grundsoftware zu FUPLOT und anderen Programmpaketen.

3.FUPLOT-Funktionssoftware für wissenschaftliche Anwendungen

Aufbauend auf den FOPLOT-Programmen wurde ein Paket von Anwendungsprogrammen FUPLOT zum Zeichnen von Funktionen auf dem Plotter erstellt. In standardisierter Weise können damit beliebige Funktionen, die in analytischer Form oder durch Koordinatenpaare gegeben sind, gezeichnet werden. Der Benutzer braucht nur den Funktionsnamen, die Intervallgrenzen und drei Strings für Bild- und Achsenbeschriftung vorgeben. Mit einem Steuerparameter wird das gewünschte Format (DINA4 oder A3, hoch oder quer), sowie die Art der Bildachsen und der Skalierung (linear, logarithmisch, doppelt logarithmisch) angegeben. FUPLOT enthält Prozeduren zum Zeichnen von Funktionen oder Funktionenscharen in rechtwinkligen Koordinaten (ggf. mit Vertikalasymptoten), Polarkoordinaten oder in Parameterdarstellung $x=f(t)$, $y=g(t)$. Es können also auch mehrdeutige Funktionen wie Spiralen, Kardioiden usw. dargestellt werden. Seit kurzem steht auch ein Programm zur perspektivischen Darstellung von Funktionen von zwei Variablen $z=f(x,y)$, wahlweise mit oder ohne verdeckte Linien zur

Verfügung. Zum Leistungsumfang des Paketes gehört ferner eine Prozedur für die Interpolation von Datenpunkten, wobei eine Ausgleichsrechnung zusätzlich eingeschaltet werden kann.

Um den Komfort zu demonstrieren, den FUPLOT bietet, möge das folgende FORTRAN-Beispiel dienen, dessen Plotterausgabe im Anhang wiedergegeben ist:

```
      EXTERNAL SINH, COSH, TANH
      CALL PFUNC (SINH, -2., 2., -11,'Y=SINH(X)','X','Y')
      CALL PFUNC (COSH, 2., -2.,   0,'Y=COSH(X)','X','Y')
      CALL PFUNC (TANH,10.,-10.,   0,'Y=TANH(X)','X','Y')

C DER 2. UND 3. PARAM. SIND DIE INTERVALLGRENZEN, DER 4. PARAM.
C MACHT ANGABEN UEBER DAS LAYOUT DES BILDES.
C LAYOUT=0 BEDEUTET: KEIN NEUES ACHSENKREUZ
```

4. FOSIG - Interaktives graphisches System

In vielen Anwendungsbereichen im technisch-wissenschaftlichen Sektor, aber auch im rechnergestützten Unterricht und in der Verwaltung besteht der Bedarf, den Dialog zwischen Mensch und Computer mit graphischen Mitteln zu unterstützen.
Was man hier braucht, ist ein Zusammenspiel der Kreativität, Beurteilung und Entscheidung des Konstrukteurs einerseits und der Kapazität und Geschwindigkeit des Großrechners andererseits, mit dem Sichtgerät als Schnittstelle.
An dieser Schnittstelle ist eine anschauliche und kompakte, d.h. graphische Darstellung des aktuellen Standes des Entwurfs erforderlich.
Das Bild kann z.B. eine Turbinenschaufel, eine Tragwerkkonstruktion, ein Schaltkreis, ein Diagramm usw. sein. Dazu kommen Zahlenwerte (Eingangs- und Ausgangsgrössen) und TEXTE (Bildbeschriftungen, Aufforderungen). Die Regie hat das im Grossrechner laufende Anwendungsprogramm. Der am Sichtgerät sitzende Ingenieur kann nun Parameter eingeben und ändern, Bildelemente anzeigen (z.B. Tragwerkglieder, deren Verformung er sehen möchte), Berechnungs- und Bewertungsprogramme anschliessen und die Ergebnisse sofort in Form von graphischen Darstellungen und dazugehörenden Ausgangswerten anschauen. Auf diese Weise entstehen in kürzester Zeit optimale Entwürfe.

Das Programmpaket FOSIG enthält alle für solche interaktive Grafik benötigte Grundsoftware. FOSIG ermöglicht es dem Anwendungsprogrammierer, graphische Programme für die eben erwähnten Anwendungen in höheren Programmiersprachen zu erstellen. Das Programmpaket besteht aus etwa 40 eng zusammenarbeitenden Prozeduren zum Kreieren und Manipulieren von Bildern sowie zur Steuerung des interaktiven Programmablaufs. FOSIG setzt die Verwendung des Sichtgerätes SIG100 im Gespräch mit dem Grossrechner TR440 voraus. Dabei können sämtliche Hardwareeigenschaften des SIG100 ausgenutzt werden.

Diagramm 1
Bildhierarchie und Einteilung von Elementen

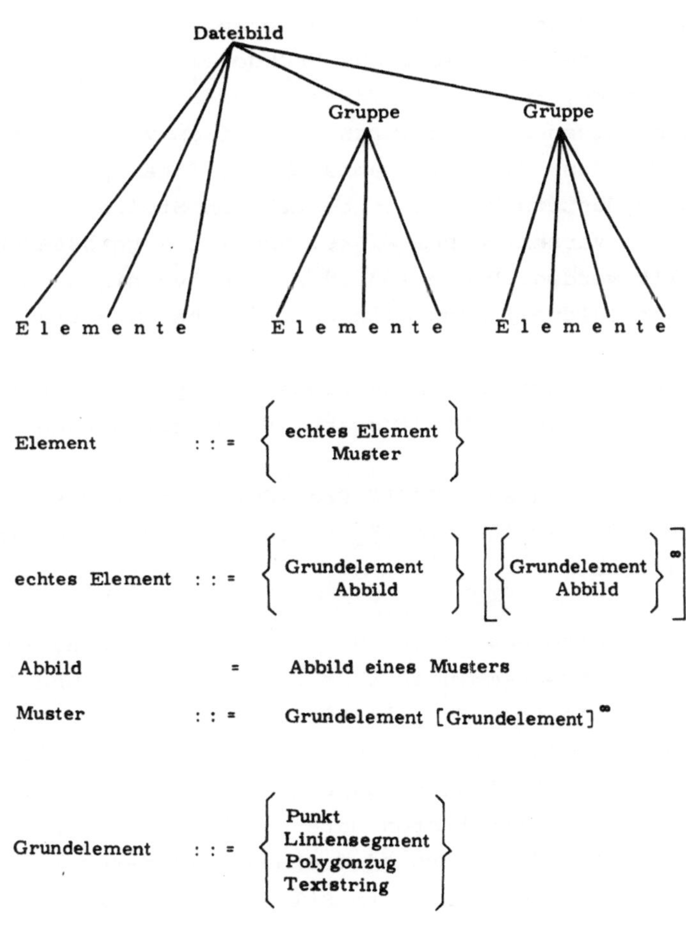

Die durch FOSIG erzeugte Graphik ist in einer dreistufigen Hierarchie gegliedert: Bild, Gruppe, Element. In einem Programmlauf können mehrere Bilder (Dateibilder) bearbeitet werden. Ein solches Dateibild ist eine Einheit sinnvoll zusammenhängender, graphischer Information von rechteckiger Form (Diagramm, Zeichnung, Tabelle, Leiterplatte). Ein Dateibild wird durch eine Nummer gekennzeichnet und besteht aus einzelnen Elementen. Zwischen Element und Dateibild kann noch wahlweise die Gruppe als dynamische Zwischenstufe liegen. Elemente sind die kleinsten Informationseinheiten, die durch das Anwendungsprogramm adressierbar sind. Wie beim Dateibild und der Gruppe geschieht die Adressierung über Nummern. Die Nummer ermöglicht eine Identifizierung des Elements durch Anzeigen mit der Rollkugel, wodurch anschliessend eine direkte Änderung durchführbar ist. Als Element kann z.B. ein Atommodell, ein Tragwerkstab, ein Flugprofil usw. auftreten.
Elemente sind selbst wieder aus Grundelementen zusammengesetzt: Punkte, Strecken, Kurven und Texte. Dieser Vorrat von Grundelementen kann anwendungsspezifisch durch Definition von Mustern beliebig erweitert werden (Flussdiagrammsymbole, Schaltplanzeichen usw.). Von solchen Mustern können an beliebigen Stellen des Bildes Abbilder unter verschiedenem Winkel und mit Vergrösserungsfaktor dargestellt werden. Diese Abbilder erhalten eigene Elementnummern und sind individuell manipulierbar. (Siehe auch Diagramm 1)

Das FOSIG-Paket ist in einige Prozedurgruppen unterteilt: Bildaufbau, Bildänderung, Bildausgabe, Eingabesteuerung und Archivierung.
Die Abhängigkeit dieser FOSIG-Prozeduren zeigt das Diagramm 2. Dabei geben die Pfeile die möglichen Richtungen des Informationsflusses wieder.

Die Bildaufbauprozeduren übernehmen die graphische Information vom Anwendungsprogramm über ihre Parameterliste und legen diese in geräteunabhängiger Form in einer Gebietsdatei, der Zwischendatei, auf dem Trommel- oder Plattenspeicher ab. Sie sind so gestaltet, dass der Anwendungsprogrammierer seine Bilder direkt aus einer problemorientierten Datenstruktur aufbauen kann. Er kann dazu den Sichtgeräteschirm oder einen Teil davon mit eigenen Koordinaten benennen. Die beim Bildaufbau zu verwendenden Koordinaten können sowohl absolut als auch inkrementell sein.

Diagramm 2
Abhängigkeit und Informationsfluß der FOSIG-Programme

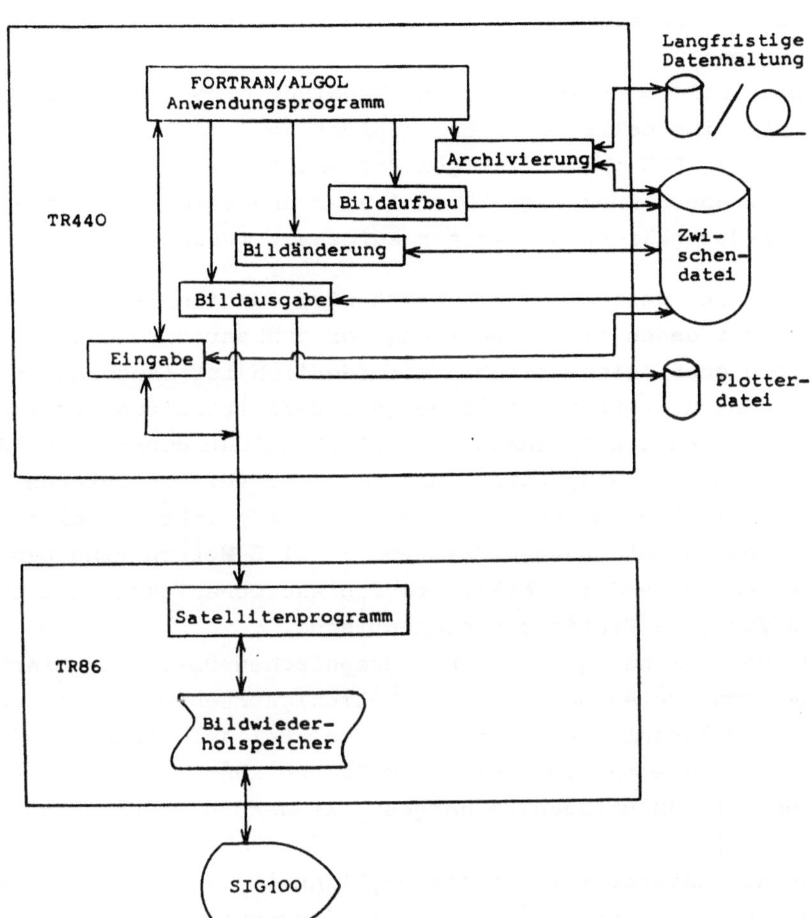

Auch Koordinaten, die in einem gemischten oder mehrfach dimensionierten Feld liegen, können direkt zum Bildaufbau verwendet werden.

Ausgehend von der Information, welche durch die Bildaufbauprozeduren in der Zwischendatei abgelegt wurden, können an beliebigen Stellen des Programms die Ausgabeprozeduren aufgerufen werden. Wegen der geräteunabhängigen Ablage der graphischen Information in der Zwischendatei kann sowohl eine Ausgabe auf dem Sichtgerät SIG100 als auch auf einem Zeichengerät (Plotter) erfolgen. Hierdurch wird die Möglichkeit gegeben, von dem jeweiligen Bildschirminhalt eine "hardcopy" zu erzeugen; die Entscheidung darüber kann

das Anwendungsprogramm dem Sichtgerätebenutzer überlassen. Die Ergebnisse eines graphischen Dialogs können auf diese Weise dokumentiert werden.
Als eine besondere Form der Ausgabe kann die Archivierung betrachtet werden:
Ein Dateibild kann in geräteunabhängiger Form aus der Zwischendatei in eine beliebige Datei kopiert werden. Diese Datei kann z.B. in der LFD (langfristigen Datenhaltung) auf dem Plattenspeicher oder einem Magnetband liegen und beim nächsten Programmlauf wieder geladen und weiter aufgebaut werden.

Ein weiterer wesentlicher Komfort wird für jene Anwendungen geboten, bei denen die Anfertigung von grösseren Zeichnungen auf Plottern oder Zeichentischen erforderlich ist (Autoindustrie, Maschinenbau, Petrochemie): Bei der Definition von "freien Dateibildern" kann die Zeichnung ohne Berücksichtigung der Bildschirmabmessungen und -kapazität aufgebaut werden. Die interne Ablage von Koordinaten in der Zwischendatei ermöglicht bei einer maximal erreichbaren Zeichnungsgrösse von 8 mal 8 Metern eine Genauigkeit von einem tausendstel Millimeter. Diese Genauigkeit ist ausreichend für alle Präzisionszeichentische.
Um solche Zeichnungen in einem graphischen Dialog zu bearbeiten, können von freien Dateibildern beliebige rechteckige Ausschnitte auf dem Bildschirm ausgegeben werden. Bei Aufteilung des Dateibildes in Ausschnitte geeigneter Grösse können auch die Beschriftungen auf dem Bildschirm dargestellt werden (durch den Zeichengenerator).
Besonders interessant ist die Möglichkeit, kritische Teile einer Zeichnung vergrössert darzustellen (Ausschnittsvergrösserung) und mit entsprechend höherer Genauigkeit zu bearbeiten.
Hierbei ist auch die Teilschirmausgabe zu erwähnen. Man kann einen Bildausschnitt auf einem Teil des Bildschirms ausgeben und auf einem zweiten Teil eine Liste von Tätigkeitskommandos erscheinen lassen. Der Sichtgerätebenutzer teilt dann dem Programm mit Hilfe der Rollkugel oder durch Tastatureingabe von zugeordneten Zeichen mit, welche Tätigkeit nun durchzuführen ist, z.B. Verschieben, Löschen, Drehen usw. (Menutechnik bei der Bildänderung).

Durch die Eingabeprozeduren kann der Sichtgerätebenutzer zur graphischen Eingabe der verschiedensten Arten aufgefordert werden:

Zahlen, logische Werte, Texte, Funktionstasten (für Programmverzweigungen), sowie zur Rollkugeleingabe,wobei ein Fadenkreuz über den Bildschirm bewegt wird.
Die Rollkugel kann auf zwei Weisen verwendet werden, zum Anzeigen bereits vorhandener Bildteile und zum Zeichnen von neuen Bildteilen. Durch das Anzeigen eines Elements wird dessen Element- und Gruppennummer automatisch dem Anwendungsprogramm übergeben. Diese Nummer kann dann für die Bildänderung verwendet werden. Um dem Benutzer am Sichtgerät zu zeigen, ob er das richtige Element angezeigt hat, kann dieses Element auf Wunsch flackernd dargestellt werden.
Die Toleranz, mit der das Anzeigen stattfinden darf, ist durch das Anwendungsprogramm je Dateibild voreinstellbar und zwar in Einheiten des Benutzerkoordinatensystems. Die Toleranz kann also anwendungsspezifisch definiert werden, wodurch bei Ausschnittsvergrösserung ein genaues Anzeigen möglich ist.
Für das freie Zeichnen mit der Rollkugel gibt es zwei wählbare Übersetzungsverhältnisse zwischen Rollkugel- und Fadenkreuzbewegung 1:2 (grob) und 4:1 (fein). Die Umschaltung geschieht mit Hilfe der Tastatur und wird unten am Sichtgerät angezeigt.
Geht man von einer 2.5 mm genauen Rollkugelpositionierung auf der Tischfläche aus, so erreicht man damit eine bis zu 0.6 mm genaue Fadenkreuzpositionierung, d.h. bis an die Grenze der durch das Bildschirmraster gegebenen Genauigkeit.
Da das Fadenkreuz auch durch die Tastatur bewegt werden kann, ist das Erzeugen von exakt waagerechten und senkrechten Linien leicht möglich, wobei die Anfangs- und Endpunkte auf Rastereinheiten genau festgelegt werden können.

Diese genaue Fadenkreuzpositionierung, sowie die anwendungsspezifische Toleranz machen die Rollkugeleingabe bei FOSIG zu einem leistungsfähigen und praxisnahen Hilfsmittel.

Anhang

Plotterausgabe des Beispiels von Seite 3

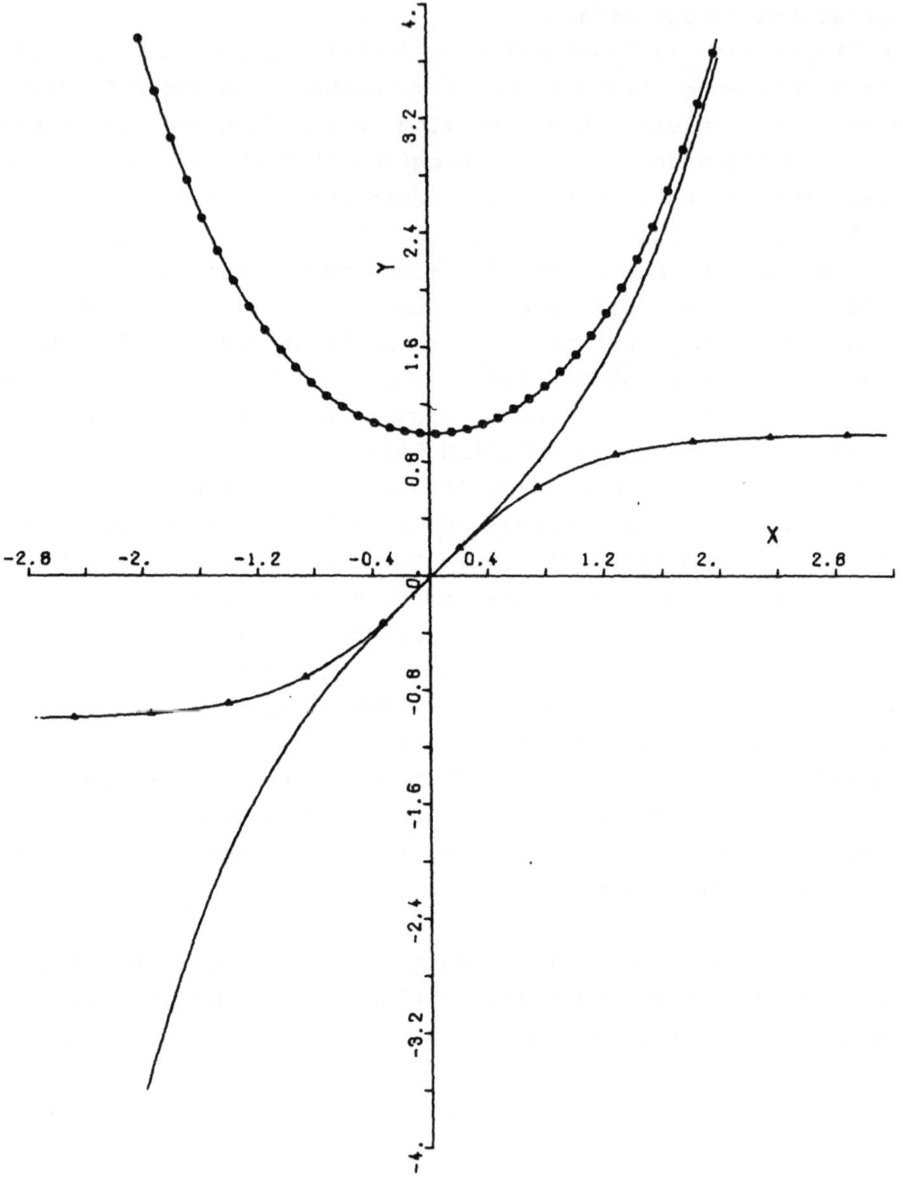

Y=SINH(X)

o Y=COSH(X)

▲ Y=TANH(X)

F I C H E - SOFTWARE UND C O M - PROGRAMMIERUNG

M.SCHWARZHUBER

A) 1 Ein Problem der kommerziellen Datenverarbeitung ist der ständig wachsende Papier-Output der EDV-Anlagen.

2 In der konventionellen Büro-Organisation hat man schon seit einiger Zeit die Papierberge abgetragen durch Übernahme der Informationen auf Mikrofilm. Diese Lösung bot sich natürlich auch für die von der EDVA ausgegebenen Informationen an.

3 Nach und nach kamen Geräte auf den Markt, die das aufwendige Abdrucken umgehen und die vom Computer kommenden Daten direkt online oder (via Magnetband) off-line gleich auf Mikrofilm ausgeben. Man kennt drei Formen dieses Computer-Output-on-Microfilm (COM)

- Rollfilm (meist 16 mm, manchmal auch 35 mm)
- Jackets (in Streifen geschnittener und in Sichthüllen konfektionierter Rollfilm)
- Fiche (Planfilm, meist in DIN A6, mit in 2 Ebenen angeordneten Bildern, Rows und Columns)

EY	EB	AL	LZ	EI	LE			
								INDEX SEITE

4 Bei den Fiches gibt es eine Reihe Besonderheiten in Ausstattung und Handhabung:

a) Normung: Es setzt sich immer mehr die NMA-Normung (NMA=National Microfilm Association) durch mit 24-facher Verkleinerung (72 Seiten pro Fiche) oder mit 42-facher Verkleinerung (224 Seiten pro Fiche)
Daneben existieren noch einige andere, weniger wichtige Formate.

b) Daten: Pro Bild wird eine gesamte Computer-Seite mit 64 Zeilen à 132 Zeichen ausgegeben. Jedes Bild erhält innerhalb des

Fiche Koordinaten, die ein Wiederauffinden der Daten erleichtern. Auf dieser Seite kann auch eine Zeichnung ausgegeben werden, ähnlich den bekannten Plottern.

c) Eyeballs: Da die Fiches als Einzelstücke vorliegen und in ein Rückvergrößerungs- bzw. Lesegerät eingelegt werden müssen, sollte man mit bloßem Auge feststellen können, welchen Inhalt der Fiche hat. Dazu werden große, mit bloßem Auge sichtbare Zeichen erstellt und in der obersten Reihe abgebildet. Pro Zeichen braucht man 1, 1/2 oder 1/4 Bild.
Vorteile dieser sog. Eyeballs:
   - Eindeutige Inhaltsbestimmung eines Fiches ohne Rückvergrößerungsgerät
   - Kontrolle über Vollständigkeit eines Bestandes von mehreren Fiches
   - Kontrolle des Datums, letzte Version von mehreren Ausgaben

   Nachteile: Eine ganze Datenzeile geht verloren und kann nicht anderweitig genutzt werden.

d) Index: Um jede Information auf dem Fiche schnell und sicher wieder zu finden, wird auf einer abschließenden Seite (Rechts unten) eine Indexseite aufgebaut. Der in der Sortierung niedrigste (oder höchste) Suchbegriff einer Datenseite wird mit seinen Koordinaten gespeichert.
Mit zwei Zugriffen kann man also jede Information auf ca. 207 Seiten finden (Seitenzahl je nach Format verschieden!)

Ziel dieses Vortrages ist nicht die Beschreibung der für COM notwendigen Geräte oder die Möglichkeiten einer Anwendung von COM, sondern die Programmierung von COM, ihre Möglichkeiten und Schwierigkeiten und die angebotenen Lösungen dafür.

B) I Problematik

1) Da die Bildgröße genormt ist, Papierformate andererseits in vielen Größen existieren und verwendet werden (z.B. 12'380, 8'380, 12'250) entsteht bei der Verwendung von Mikrofilm ein Normierungszwang. Mehr als 64 Zeilen zu je 132 Zeichen sind nur in Ausnahmefällen möglich. Werden mehr Zeilen als möglich gegeben, würde ein Papierdrucker auf das nächste Blatt schieben und dort weiterdrucken, als wäre nichts geschehen. Eine Mikrofilmkamera aber "schiebt" nicht zeilenweise, sondern höchstens bildweise. Da der Befehl "Schieben auf neues Bild = Frame Advance" aber nicht gegeben wurde, entsteht also ein sog. Overprint. Die letzten Zeilen des Bildes überschreiben

die ersten. Es kommt zum gleichen Effekt wie bei einer Doppelbelichtung in einem Photoapparat.
Umgekehrt: kommen zu wenig Zeilen, muß der restliche Platz des Bildes frei bleiben; man kann die Bilder nicht "zusammenschieben" oder ein anderes Format nehmen wie beim Papierdrucker. Dies gilt auch für kürzere Zeilen. Sie müssen mit Leerzeichen aufgefüllt werden bis zum Bildrand.

2) Alle COM-Anlagen (also die Verfilmungsanlagen) verarbeiten als Vorschubzeichen den sog. ASA-Code. Dies ist ein internationaler und firmenunabhängiger Code mit einem Vorrat für ein-, zwei- oder dreizeiligen Vorschub und Steuerung über Lochband für 9 sog. Kanäle. Daneben aber haben alle Computersysteme einen sog. Maschinencode, der normalerweise wesentlich umfangreicher ist. (IBM führt 32, Siemens sogar 54 Positionen an)
Bei druckaufbereiteten Bändern besteht nun eine große Schwierigkeit, wenn die Steuerzeichen nicht dem ASA-Code entsprechen. Man behilft sich damit, daß man im Hauptspeicher der CPU einen Drucker simuliert und auf diese Weise zu ASA-Steuerzeichen kommt. (Die Möglichkeit der direkten Konvertierung Maschinen-Code → ASA-Code ist sehr aufwendig).

Zusätzlich zu den Seiten- und Zeilensteuerzeichen braucht eine COM-Anlage weitere Steuerzeichen z.B. GOTO NEXT FRAME, GOTO NEXT COLUMN, Formulareinblendung usw. Diese Steuerzeichen werden meist dem ASA-Code angenähert, sind also Zeichen des druckbaren Vorrats. Das wirft dann große Probleme auf, wenn auf dem Band das Steuerzeichen aus irgendeinem Grund fehlt.

3) Das Index-Bild ist das letzte Bild rechts unten auf dem Fiche. Weil dieses Bild natürlich auch als letztes geschrieben werden muß, müssen die Koordinaten der Daten in einem Pool gesammelt werden. Pro Daten-Bild kann nur ein Eintrag gesammelt werden. Es muß also festgelegt werden, ob der niedrigste oder höchste Begriff einer Datenseite den Index darstellt. Die Daten müssen in einer logischen Folge liegen, sonst wird die Indicierung sinnlos.
Jedes Datenbild wird durch Koordinaten festgelegt (z.B. Bo5, E15). Diese Koordinaten werden im Indexbild dem Indexbegriff zugeordnet.

Die Schwierigkeit besteht nun darin, zum richtigen Zeitpunkt des Schreibens der Datenzeile den Indexbegriff den Koordinaten zuzuordnen und dem Pool einzuschreiben.

4) Eyeballs können je nach Kameratyp auf zwei Arten hergestellt werden:
- Der Elektronenstrahl wird gebündelt und entsprechend abgelenkt

- Die Eyeball-Zeichen werden aus normalen Zeichen zusammengefügt.

Im ersten Fall ergeben sich keine besonderen Schwierigkeiten. Durch entsprechende Steuerzeichen kann die übergebene Zeichenkette groß und mit bloßem Auge lesbar sein.
Im zweiten Fall muß eine eigene Routine vorhanden sein, die aus einem normal großen Zeichen (meist *) die Eyeballs "zeichnet". Da die Eyeball-Informationen aber von Fiche zu Fiche verschieden sind, muß diese Zusammenstellung immer wieder neu erfolgen. Eine andere Methode besteht darin, daß die gezeichneten Eyeballs auf einem Direktzugriffsspeicher einmal aufgebaut werden und dort entweder über Algorithmen oder über Indexleisten abgerufen und in das Fiche-Band eingebaut werden. Beide Methoden sind sehr zeitaufwendig. Trotzdem kann man auf Eyeballs fast nicht verzichten; es sei denn, man fügt sie nach Fertigstellung der Fiches mit Filzschreiber per Hand hinzu. Damit verliert man aber die Sicherheit über die Vollständigkeit des Fiche-Bestandes.

5) Bei einem sehr großen Datenbestand besteht bislang die Notwendigkeit, zuerst den betreffenden Fiche aufgrund der Eyeballs manuell auszuwählen, ihn in ein Lesegerät einzulegen und dann die betreffende Seite über die Indexseite aufzusuchen. Der erste Auswählschritt sollte nun natürlich auch noch maschinell erfolgen können. Dazu ist es notwendig, einen übergeordneten Index aufzubauen, zu warten und die Fiches diesem Index zuzuordnen.
Das Fiche-Sammel-Gerät wird über einen Zusatz an einen Computer angeschlossen. Der Bediener gibt auf einer Tastatur seine zu suchende Information ein. Der Computer sucht über die 1. Indexleiste den Fiche aus und legt ihn gleich ins Betrachtungsgerät mit der Indexseite so ein, daß der Bediener mit einem 2. Knopfdruck seine gesuchte Datenseite hat. Eine Beschreibung dieser Geräte würde hier zu weit führen. Aber für die Programmierung entsteht die Notwendigkeit, weiterführende Indices aufzubauen, zu warten und auf Direktzugriffsspeichern zur Verfügung zu stellen. Die ersten Einsatzversuche damit zeigten sehr vielversprechende Ergebnisse.

II Lösungsmöglichkeiten, um die oben geschilderten Schwierigkeiten zu meistern. Zwei Systeme und ihre Besonderheiten sollen vorgestellt werden.

1) Die COM-Anlage braucht eigens aufbereitete Bänder. In einem Computerlauf müssen also Bänder erstellt werden, die den Spezifikationen der COM-Anlage entsprechen. Die Software dafür

setzt sich aus drei Teilen zusammen.

a) Module:

Für jede Funktion (Schreiben einer Datenzeile, Einfügen eines Index, Kreieren eines Eyeballs usw.) wird dem Betriebssystem ein Modul eingefügt, der diese eine Funktion durchführt. Das hat den Vorteil, daß die Funktion allgemein einsetzbar ist und auf alle Möglichkeiten eingerichtet. Natürlich bläht das u.U. den Modul in seiner Größe ziemlich auf.

Einige Beispiele für solche Module:

aa) Initialisation:

Hier werden die Parameter für den gesamten Fichelauf festgelegt:
- Welche Fiche-Art? (Verkleinerungsfaktor)
- Sollen Eyeballs geschrieben werden oder nicht?
- Soll eine Indicierung durchgeführt werden oder nicht?
- Wo liegen die Eyeballs innerhalb eines Fiches?
- Wie lang ist der Indexbegriff?
- Welche Koordinaten haben die Reihen und Kolonnen?
- Soll ein Formulardia eingeblendet werden?
- Wie sehen die Steuerzeichen für die einzelnen Funktionen aus?

und noch vieles andere mehr.

bb) Schreiben einer Datenzeile

Folgende Prüfungen müssen dem Schreiben vorausgehen:
- Ist das Einzelbild noch aufnahmefähig?
- Wenn nein, ist die Kolonne noch aufnahmefähig?
- Wenn nein, ist die Reihe noch aufnahmefähig?
- Ist der gesamt Fiche noch aufnahmefähig?
- Wenn Bildvorschub festgestellt worden ist: muß der Eyeball-Generator aufgerufen werden?
- Muß evtl. der Index-Generator aufgerufen werden?
- Ist die Datenzeile durch Satzende-Steuerzeichen abgeschlossen?

und noch einige andere.

cc) Index schreiben

Entweder selbständig (d.h. von bb)-Modul aufgerufen!) oder durch direkte Anforderung des Anwenders angestoßen, muß der Modul u.a. folgende Funktionen durchführen:
- Feststellen der gerade aktuellen Koordinaten
- Index-Begriff und Koordinaten dem Pool einschreiben
- Prüfen, ob der Index-Pool ausgegeben werden soll
- Index-Pool formatisieren und auf das Fiche-Band schreiben

dd) Eyeball-Generator

Er muß folgende Funktionen ausführen:
- Erkennen des übergebenen Zeichens
- Entscheidung, ob das Zeichen generiert werden kann (nicht alle Zeichen sind im Vorrat enthalten!)
- Gegebenenfalls Substitution auf ein generierbares Zeichen
- Prüfen, ob 1, 2 oder 4 Zeichen pro Bild geschrieben werden sollen
- Zeichen generieren
- Zeichen ausgeben oder - im Fall mehrerer Zeichen pro Bild - einem Eyeball-Pool einschreiben
- Im Fall mehrerer Eyeballs pro Bild gegebenenfalls den Pool formatisieren und ausgeben.

ee) Abschluß

Dieser Modul muß für einen ordnungsgemäßen Abschluß sorgen, wenn der Anwender die Ausgabe beenden will:
- Ausgabe aller noch nicht abgeschlossenen Pools
- Abschluß des letzten Fiche
- Abschluß des Fiche-Bandes

Natürlich beinhalten die hier groß skizzierten Funktionen eine ganze Anzahl von Einzelaktionen. Die Software eines bestimmten COM-Systems z.B. enthält 13 solcher Module, die alle untereinander verzahnt sind. Sie sind alle in sich abgeschlossen und können Informationen von einem zum anderen weitergeben. Damit wird diese große Flexibilität erreicht.

b) Gerade diese Flexibilität ist es aber auch, die in der Anwendung der Module gewisse Schwierigkeiten mit sich bringt. Viele der genannten Funktionen werden immer gebraucht, manche selten, manche fast gar nie.

Um dem Anwender diese Schwierigkeiten zu ersparen oder wenigstens zu erleichtern, haben wir z.B. eine Reihe von Makros geschaffen. Sie implementieren die benötigten Funktionen selbständig, wenn sie immer gebraucht werden. Die fast nie gebrauchten werden nicht unterstützt, während der Anwender bei seltenen Funktionen über Parameter seine gewählten Funktionen bestimmen kann. Dazu einige Beispiele:

aa) Die Definition des sog. Control-Blocks, in dem alle für die Fiche-Software notwendigen Felder und Konstanten definiert sind, benötigt mindestens 25 Befehle. Das schließt natürlich die Gefahr des falschen Gebrauchs ein. Durch die Einführung des Makros FCNTRL (Fiche

Control) kommt der Anwender mit einem einzigen Aufruf aus. Sollte er allerdings ganz spezielle Anwendungsformen wünschen, muß er nach wie vor den Control-Block selbst definieren.

bb) Das gleiche gilt für die Initialisation eines Fiche-Laufes. Sie ist für einen Fiche-Typ immer gleich. Trotzdem verlangt es die Flexibilität der Fiche-Module, daß die ca. 10 Befehle immer wieder geschrieben werden müssen. Diese fehlerträchtige Arbeit nimmt der Makro FCHIN dem Anwender ab. Lediglich dann, wenn dem Anwender die Standardform nicht genügt, muß er die Initialisation selber vornehmen.

cc) Soll aufgrund der Datenstruktur ein neuer Fiche begonnen werden, ehe der vorhergehende voll ist, braucht der Benutzer nur eine Makroinstruktion zu geben. Andernfalls müßte er ca. 15 Befehle schreiben, um den vorzeitigen Fiche-Wechsel zu erreichen.

Neben einigen anderen Vorzügen haben diese Makros den Vorteil, daß sich der Benutzer nicht mehr mit den Besonderheiten und Eigenheiten der Fiche-Software herumschlagen muß, wenn er nicht spezielle Wünsche bezüglich der Fiche-Ausstattung hat. Die Makros können in etwa mit den Makros verglichen werden, die alle Hersteller von Computern für die Ein-/Ausgabe von Daten zur Verfügung stellen. (IOCS-Makros)
Den Gebrauch der Fiche-Makros kann der Anwender-Programmierer relativ schnell erlernen. Er muß sein Anwenderprogramm schreiben, wie gewohnt, und anstelle der IOCS-Makros für die Ausgabe auf Drucker muß er die entsprechenden Makros verwenden für die Ausgabe auf das Fiche-Band. Damit hat letztlich die Fiche-Programmierung viel von ihrem Schrecken verloren.

2) Um von einem herkömmlichen Computer unabhängig zu werden, gibt es inzwischen auch COM-Systeme, die mit eigenen kleinen Computern ausgerüstet sind. Meist ist das eine Ein-Adress-Maschine mit 4 bis 16 Kilobytes Speicherkapazität.
Hier muß nun nicht mehr ein fiche-aufbereitetes Band eingehängt werden, sondern es kann das druckaufbereitete Band sein oder sogar das Ausgangsband. Der COM-Computer bereitet die Daten fiche-gerecht auf und gibt sie gleich der Kamera weiter, die sie auf den Film bringt.
Meist liefert der COM-Hersteller als Software sog. Utilities, also Dienstprogramme, die die Aufbereitung übernehmen und denen über Parameter die auszuwählenden Funktionen mitgeteilt werden. Natürlich bleibt auch hier weiterhin die Mög-

lichkeit, den COM-Computer so zu programmieren, daß ein individuelles Anwenderprogramm die Datenaufbereitung übernimmt. Das aber ist relativ schwierig und in vielen Fällen auch gar nicht notwendig.

3) Ausgabe von Zeichnungen und dergl.
Was für die Datenflut im kommerziellen Bereich gilt, hat natürlich auch seine Gültigkeit im technisch-wissenschaftlichen Bereich. Es war also von der Idee her nur ein Schritt, auch die über Plotter ausgegebenen Zeichnungen, Konstruktionen u.ä. in die Ausgabe auf Mikrofilm einzubeziehen.
Es gibt heute schon Maschinen dafür. Sie "zeichnen" nicht auf Papier, sondern eben auf Mikrofilm Der Elektronenstrahl wird entsprechend gebündelt und abgelenkt und bringt damit die digitalisierten Daten in analoger Form zu Mikrofilm.
Die Programmierung dafür ist der Programmierung eines Plotter sehr stark ähnlich. Es wird mit Koordinaten auf der x- und y-Achse gearbeitet und der Elektronenstrahl von einer Koordinate zur anderen bewegt, entweder bei eingeschalteter Optik oder nicht eingeschalteter.
Alle Hersteller solcher COM-Anlagen haben dafür eine umfangreiche Software entwickelt, die meist auf der Verwendung von FORTRAN basiert. Sie nimmt dem Anwender die mühsame Kleinarbeit ab. Mit wenigen Aufrufen erreicht der Anwender die Darstellung von Geraden, Kreisen, Ellipsen u.s.w. Aus diesen Elementen kann er dann seine gewünschten Zeichnungen erstellen.

C) Zum Schluß ein ganz kurzer Ausblick in die Zukunft. Wir stehen vor einer sicher explosionsartigen Ausbreitung von COM. Das ergibt, daß die Anwendung und Programmierung in Zukunft einfacher werden wird. Vielleicht kommt es zu einer parallelen Entwicklung von immer höheren Sprachen für COM, ähnlich den Compilern für die Computer.

Auch eine andere Technik kündigt sich langsam an. Das Gegenstück zu COM wird CIM sein. (Computer-Input-of-Microfilm) Damit werden wir dann die Möglichkeit haben, von den auf Mikrofilm gespeicherten Daten wieder zu vom Computer verarbeitbaren Daten zu kommen. Oder mit anderen Worten: es wird eine einfache Möglichkeit geben, analoge Daten wieder zu digitalisieren.

ZENTRALEINHEITEN UND ENTWICKLUNGS-AUTOMATISIERUNG

DAS PROBLEM DER ASSOZIATIVSPEICHERDURCHLAUFZEIT BEI PAGING-VERFAHREN IM ZEHN-NANOSEKUNDENBEREICH

H.SCHECHER

In den kommenden Jahren dürfte der Halbleiterspeicher als Arbeitsspeicher in schnellen elektronischen Rechenanlagen zunehmend an Bedeutung gewinnen. Diese Speicher können ebensowenig wie die heutigen Kernspeicher zu beliebig großen Kapazitäten ausgebaut werden. Die Gründe dafür sind vor allem die hohen Kosten, außerdem steigt die Zugriffszeit immer etwas mit der Kapazität an. Es wird daher auch in Zukunft notwendig sein, einen Großkapazitätsspeicher im Hintergrund vorzusehen und nur die Seiten eines Programms in den Arbeitsspeicher zu verlegen, die unmittelbar gebraucht werden. Die Steuerung dieser Prozesse dürfte auch weiterhin nur wenig von der Art, wie sie heute durchgeführt wird, verschieden sein. Man wird also im wesentlichen das "paging"- bzw. das Segmentierungsverfahren anwenden. Durch beide Verfahren wird aber die Abarbeitung der Programme etwas verzögert.

Die Verzögerungen sind dadurch bedingt, daß zur Umsetzung der Seitennummer - wir wollen diesen Begriff im folgenden auch für die Kombination Segment-Seitennummer verwenden - in die Kachelnummer im günstigsten Fall eine Speicherzugriffszeit benötigt wird. Man kann diese Verzögerungen auf ein erträgliches Maß reduzieren, wenn man einen Assoziativspeicher einführt, in dem die gerade aktuellen Zuordnungen Seiten-Kachelnummer gespeichert sind. Bei einer Anlage mit Assoziativspeichern können bei der Abarbeitung von Befehlen drei verschieden lange Verzögerungszeiten auftreten:

1. Die Seite, auf die der Adreßteil des auszuführenden Befehls weist, befindet sich noch nicht im Arbeitsspeicher. Dieser Fall kommt bei vernünftigem Programmaufbau relativ selten vor. Tritt er ein, so muß durch das Betriebssystem die gewünschte Seite in den Arbeitsspeicher gebracht werden und die Einträge in die entsprechenden Listen durchgeführt werden. Er verursacht eine merkliche Verzögerung.

2. Die gewünschte Seite ist im Arbeitsspeicher, die Zuordnung Seitennummer - Kachelnummer jedoch nicht im Assoziativspeicher. Dieser Fall tritt bei Anlagen mit kleinem Assoziativspeicher relativ häufig auf. Hier wird die zur Seite gehörige Kachelnummer auf konventionelle Weise mit Hilfe der Seiten- Kachelzuord-

nungsliste bestimmt. Anschließend wird eine nach einem Alterungsmechanismus ausgewählte Zelle des Assoziativspeichers mit der gefundenen Seiten-Kachelnummer-Zuordnung überschrieben. Die durch diesen Prozeß hervorgerufene Verzögerung liegt in der Größenordnung eines oder zweier Kernspeicherzyklen.

3. Die gewünschte Seite wird im Assoziativspeicher gefunden. Jetzt ist die Verzögerungszeit gleich der Zugriffszeit des Assoziativspeichers, also einige zehn Nanosekunden. Dieser dritte Fall sollte, wenn die Maschine richtig konzipiert wurde, am häufigsten eintreten. Bei unseren heutigen Anlagen wird also durch das "paging" bzw. Segmentierungsverfahren bei den meisten Befehlen die Zugriffszeit zum Kernspeicher um ca. 10 % verlängert. Dieser Preis ist bei den Vorteilen, die diese Verfahren bieten, nicht zu hoch.

Ganz anders sind aber die Verhältnisse, wenn als Arbeitsspeicher ein Speicher verwendet wird, dessen Zugriffszeit in der Größenordnung der des Assoziativspeichers liegt. In diesem Fall liegen die Verlängerungen der Zugriffszeiten, die durch die Adreßtransformationen im Assoziativspeicher entstehen, bei 100 %. Damit wäre aber die Verwendung eines Assoziativspeichers zumindest beim "paging"-Verfahren sinnlos geworden, denn man kann jetzt mit der gleichen Verzögerungszeit die Kachelnummer direkt aus der Zuordnungsliste im Arbeitsspeicher holen. Selbst für die großen Vorteile, die das "paging"- bzw. das Segmentierungsverfahren bringen, ist der Preis der doppelten Speicherzugriffszeit zu hoch, es wäre daher wenig sinnvoll, diese Verfahren weiterhin anzuwenden.

In dieser Arbeit soll gezeigt werden, daß es bestimmte Eigenschaften der Halbleiterspeicher ermöglichen, den Assoziativspeicher so in die Adressierung des Arbeitsspeichers einzubauen, daß nun so gut wie keine Verzögerung durch die Adreßtransformation entsteht. Es wird sich weiterhin ergeben, daß obengenannter Fall 2. (eine Seite ist bereits im Arbeitsspeicher aber die Zuordnung Seiten-Kachelnummer steht nicht im Assoziativspeicher) nicht mehr auftreten kann. Außerdem können die sehr aufwendigen Schaltungen für den Alterungsmechanismus für die Neubesetzung des Assoziativspeichers entfallen.

Wir betrachten zuerst den Aufbau eines größeren Halbleiterspeichers. Er ist aus fertigungstechnischen Gründen wie ein Kernspeicher aus einzelnen Moduln aufgebaut. Die Modulgröße ist durch die Grenzen der Großintegration in einem Siliziumkristall gegeben, sie liegt bei ungefähr 1k. Die Tatsache, daß bei einem Halbleiterspeicher die Modulgröße ohne technische Schwierigkeiten aber auch ohne technisch etwas zu verschenken, der üblichen Seitengröße angepaßt werden kann, soll im folgenden benutzt werden.

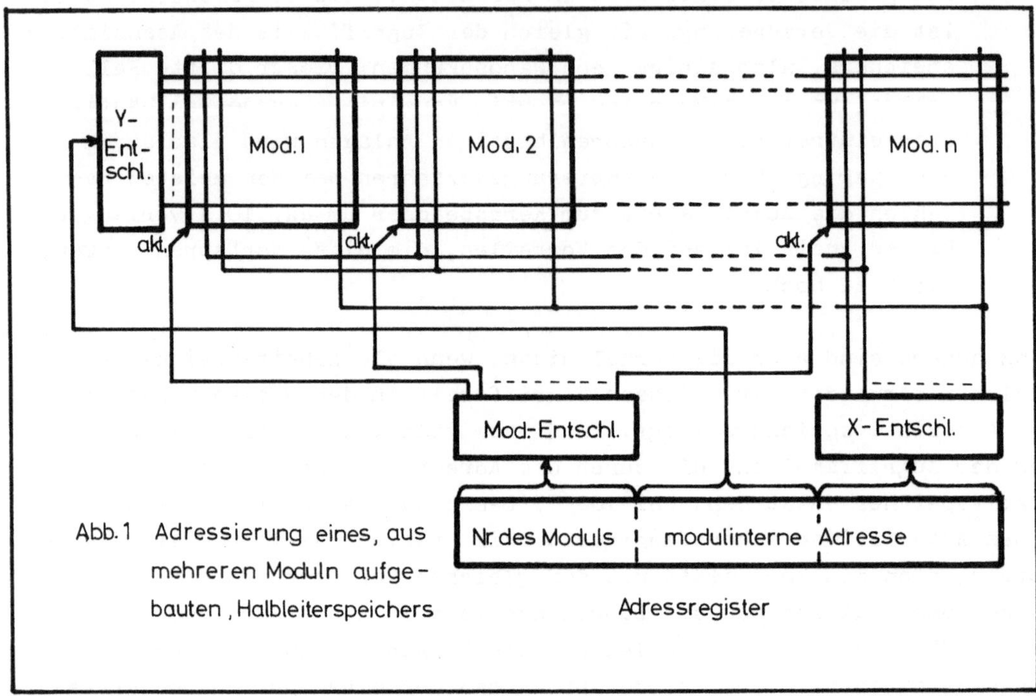

Abb. 1 Adressierung eines, aus mehreren Moduln aufgebauten, Halbleiterspeichers

Wie Abb. 1 zeigt, ordnet man die Zellen in den einzelnen Moduln eines größeren Halbleiterspeichers wie beim Kernspeicher zweckmäßig zweidimensional an. Das Adreßwort gliedert sich also in drei Teile. Der erste und zweite geben die Koordinaten innerhalb der Moduln, die Modulauswahl wird durch den dritten Teil besorgt. Durch die Zweiteilung der Anwahl ist es möglich, den Speicherzyklus grundsätzlich auf zwei verschiedene Arten ablaufen zu lassen. Nach der ersten wird erst der richtige Modul ausgewählt. Daraufhin werden die Eingänge seiner x- und y-Entschlüssler mit den Flip-Flop-Ausgängen des Adreßregisters verbunden, die die modulinterne Adresse der gewünschten Zelle enthalten (Abb. 2a). Dann erfolgt die Auswahl dieser Zelle. Bei diesem Verfahren wird also nur im ausgewählten Modul ein Anwahlprozess gestartet. Nach einem Anwahlprozeß braucht jeder Halbleiterspeichermodul eine gewisse Beruhigungszeit. Folgen im Mikroprogramm der auszuführenden Operation nach dem Speicherzugriff noch weitere Schritte, so können diese natürlich während der Erholphase des Speichers ausgeführt werden.

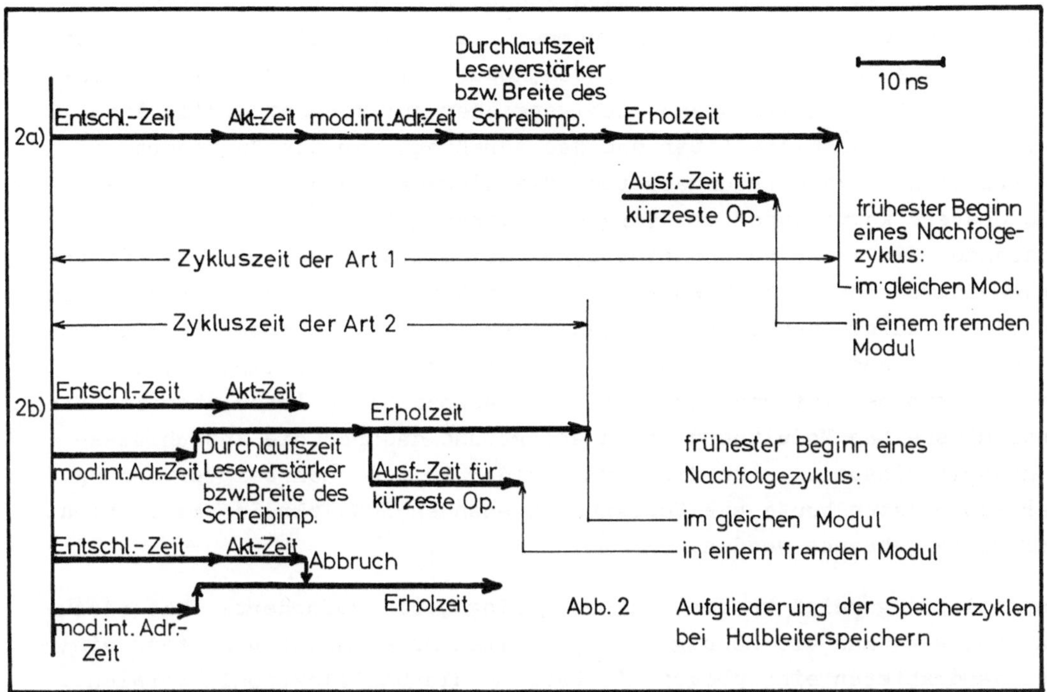

Abb. 2 Aufgliederung der Speicherzyklen bei Halbleiterspeichern

Nach der zweiten Art werden in allen Moduln des Speichers gleich zu Beginn eines Zyklus die Anwahlvorgänge für die Zelle gestartet (Abb.2b). Parallel dazu erfolgt die Modulauswahl. Nur derjenige Modul wird mit den Informationssammelschienen verbunden, der ausgewählt wurde. In allen anderen wird der Speicherzyklus abgebrochen. In diesen Moduln ergibt sich eine etwas kleinere Erholzeit. Man erkennt aus Abb. 2, daß der Speicherzyklus nach der zweiten Art zeitlich etwas günstiger liegt als der nach der ersten Art. Außerdem sieht man leicht, daß der Zeitgewinn, der durch die Überlappung von Speicherzyklen bei aufeinanderfolgenden Aufrufen in nicht gleichen Moduln im günstigen Fall erzielt werden kann, bei ca. 10 % der Zykluszeit liegt. Verglichen mit den Verhältnissen beim Kernspeicher, wo ca. 70 % der Zykluszeit überlappt werden können, ist dieser Wert klein. Deshalb spielt eine Adreßverschränkung, durch die man bekanntlich die Wahrscheinlichkeit, daß zwei aufeinanderfolgende Speicherzyklen in verschiedenen Moduln ablaufen, erhöhen kann, beim Halbleiterspeicher eine geringere Rolle. Im folgenden kann deshalb - das hier beschriebene Verfahren läßt sich nur ohne Adreßverschränkung durchführen - auf sie verzichtet werden, ohne daß dadurch größere zeitliche Einbußen entstünden.

Für beide Arten des Speicherzyklus steht, will man für die Transformation der Seiten- in die Kachelnummer keine zusätzliche Zeit investieren, nur die Durchschaltzeit auf den Modul, also ca. 20 ns zur Verfügung. Schaltet man einen Assoziativspeicher auf konventionelle Art zwischen das Befehlsregister und das Adreßregister des Speichers, so entstehen zwei Verzögerungszeiten, die Eingangs- und die Ausgangszeit. Die erstere kommt durch den Vergleichsvorgang im Assoziativspeicher zustande, die letztere entsteht durch die Laufzeit der Schaltfront vom ausgewählten Informationswort des Assoziativspeichers zum betreffenden Modul des Halbleiterspeichers. Dabei muß die gleiche Entschlüsselungsschaltung durchlaufen werden wie bei der direkten Modulanwahl. Selbst wenn man in den Informationsworten des Assoziativspeichers bereits die entschlüsselten Modulkoordinaten ablegt und dadurch die Entschlüsselungszeit einspart, kann die Summe beider Zeiten auch bei Verwendung der schnellsten heute zur Verfügung stehenden Schaltkreisfamilie nicht auf 20 ns gebracht werden.

Es soll nun gezeigt werden, daß es gelingt, die geforderte Zeit einzuhalten, wenn man die Modulgröße der Seitengröße anpaßt und statt einer festverdrahteten eine programmierbare Modulanwahlelektronik vorsieht.

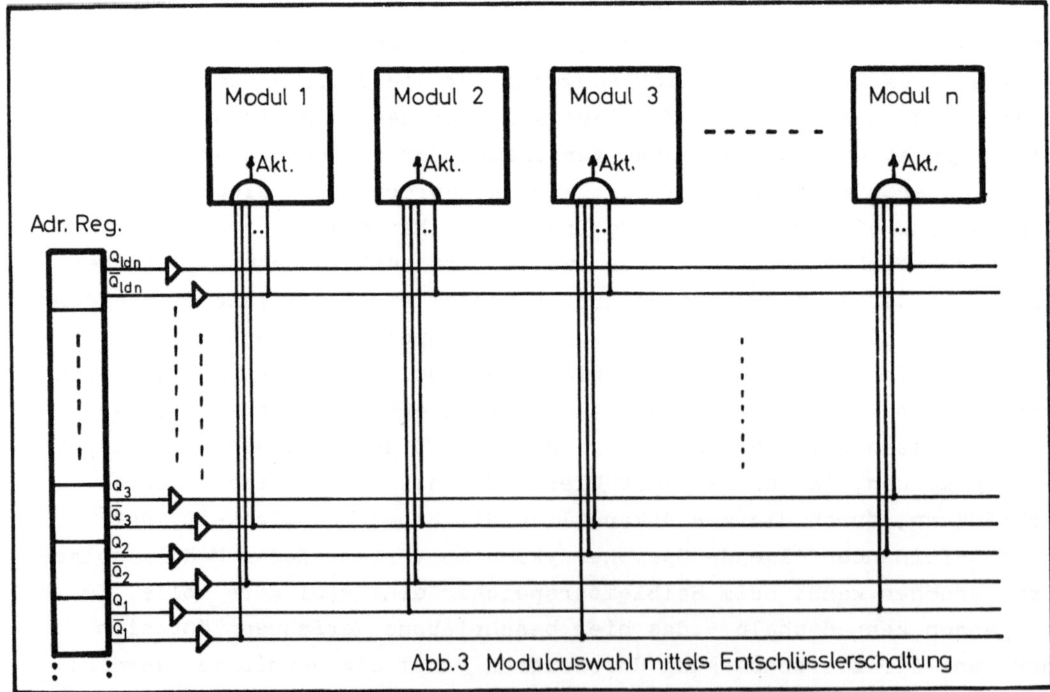

Abb.3 Modulauswahl mittels Entschlüsslerschaltung

Wir betrachten zuerst die festverdrahtete Anwahlelektronik. Hier ordnet man jedem Speichermodul ein Und-Glied mit ld n Eingängen zu (n = Anzahl der Moduln). Die Eingänge dieser Glieder sind so mit den Q bzw. $\overline{Q}$-Ausgängen der Flip-Flops des Adressenregisters verbunden, daß für jedes ankommende Bitmuster immer nur eines dieser Und-Glieder durchschaltet.

Die programmierbare Anwahlelektronik wird realisiert, indem man die Und-Glieder mit ld n Eingängen durch Assoziativregister, bestehend aus ld n Flip-Flops ersetzt. Diese Register sind über besondere, nur innerhalb des Betriebssystems benützte Befehle erreichbar. Hat das Betriebssystem einer bestimmten Seite s eine Kachel k zugewiesen, so setzt es in das Assoziativregister des Moduls k die Seitennummer s ein. Kommt nun ein Befehl mit der Seitennummer s zur Ausführung, so wird das im Adressenregister stehende s mit den Inhalten der Assoziativregister aller Moduln verglichen und nur der Modul an die Zellenanwahl bzw. an die Informationssammelschienen angeschaltet, dessen Assoziativregisterinhalt mit s übereinstimmt.

Es soll nun der Aufbau des Assoziativregisters beschrieben werden. Der Inhalt des ν ten Assoziativregisters stimmt mit dem des Adressenregisters überein, wenn folgende Bedingung den Wert "true" hat:

(1) $$T = \bigwedge_{\lambda = 1}^{\mathrm{ld}\, n} (Q_\lambda A_{\nu\lambda} + \overline{Q}_\lambda \overline{A}_{\nu\lambda})$$ n = Anzahl der Moduln (Zweierpotenz)

Die Q_λ sind dabei die Werte der Flip-Flop-Ausgänge des Adreßregisters, die $A_{\nu\lambda}$ die einer Assoziativzelle. Obige Bedingung führt auf folgende Schaltung, die für jedes Assoziativregister aufgebaut werden muß.

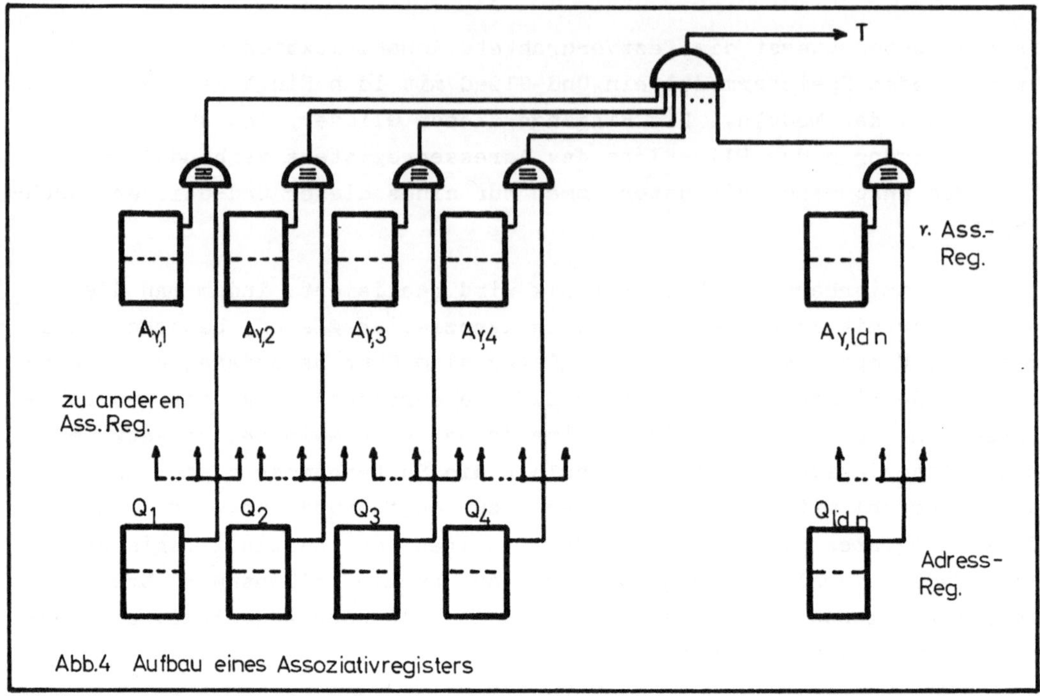

Abb.4 Aufbau eines Assoziativregisters

Man erhält die Trefferfunktion T und damit die Entscheidung, ob der Modul angeschaltet wird oder nicht nach einer Verzögerung von zwei Gatterlaufzeiten. Man kann jedoch Schaltelemente und Zeit einsparen, wenn zur Modulauswahl die negierte Trefferfunktion T verwendet wird.

$$\overline{T} = \overline{\bigwedge_{\lambda = 1}^{ld\,n} (Q_\lambda A_{\nu\lambda} + \overline{Q}_\lambda \overline{A}_{\nu\lambda})}$$

daraus ergibt sich durch Anwendung der de Morganschen Regel:

$$\overline{T} = \bigvee_{\lambda = 1}^{ld\,n} (Q_\lambda \overline{A_{\nu\lambda}} + \overline{Q}_\lambda A_{\nu\lambda})$$

Aus der Und-Verknüpfung mit ld n Eingängen ist eine Oder-Verknüpfung geworden, diese löst sich jedoch, werden ihre Eingangsvariablen, z.B.

durch Ströme dargestellt in einem einfachen Leitungsknoten auf. Aber auch die Äquivalenzglieder lassen sich eliminieren, wenn man die Variablen $A_{\nu\lambda}$ durch die Transistorströme der Flip-Flop der Assoziativregister und die Variablen Q_λ durch die Stellung gewisser Schalter darstellt.

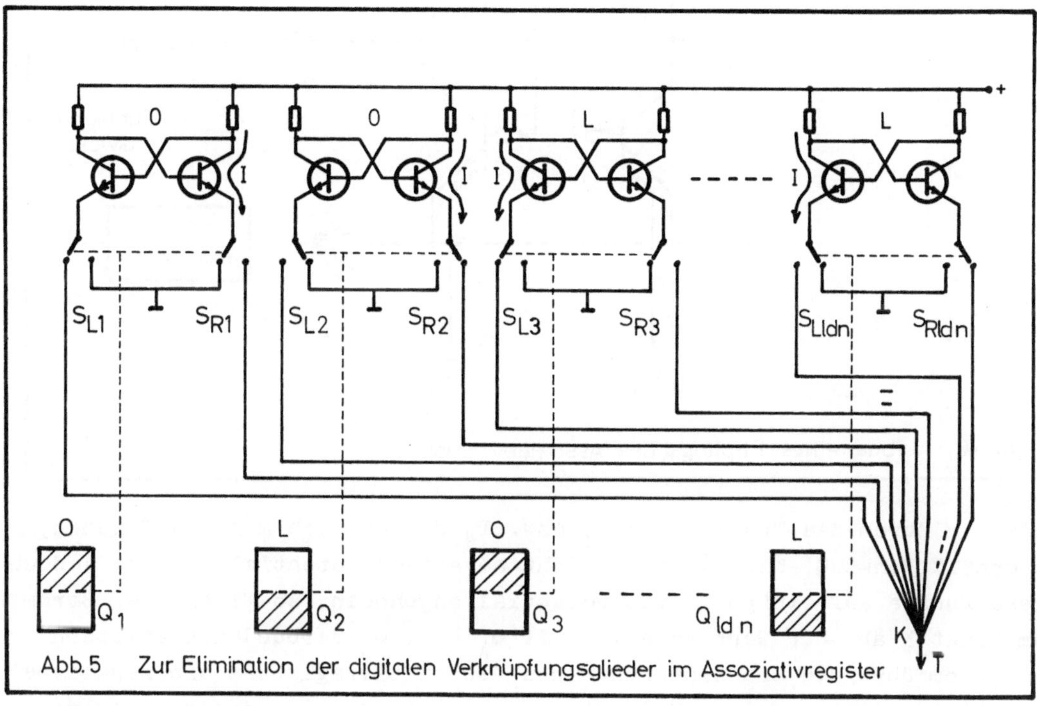

Abb. 5 Zur Elimination der digitalen Verknüpfungsglieder im Assoziativregister

Diese Schalter S_L und S_R werden zweckmäßigerweise durch Mehrfachemitter bei den Transistoren des Assoziativregisters realisiert. Da sich aber dadurch ein unsymmetrischer Betrieb der Register-Flip-Flops ergibt, der zu Unstabilitäten führen könnte, ist es notwendig, Trenntransistoren in den Flip-Flops vorzusehen. Wir kommen deshalb zu folgender Schaltung:

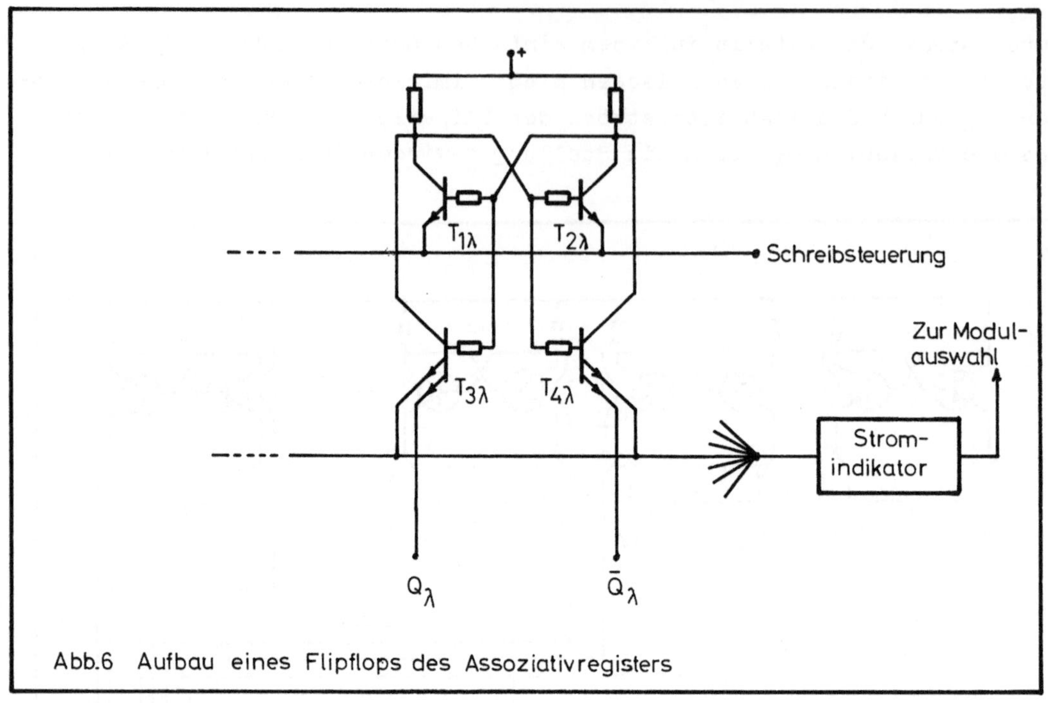

Abb.6 Aufbau eines Flipflops des Assoziativregisters

Soll der Strom des Transistors T_3 bzw. T_4 direkt nach Masse abfließen, so erhält Punkt Q_λ bzw. $\bar{Q}_\lambda$ ein leicht negatives Potential, werden jedoch diese Punkte auf ein positives Potential angehoben, so fließt der Strom zum Punkt K ab. Nur wenn an allen mit Q_λ bzw. $\bar{Q}_\lambda$ verbundenen Emittern der stromführenden Transistoren eines Assoziativregisters ein negatives Potential anliegt, fließt kein Strom zum Punkt K. Wird durch einen geeigneten Stromindikator, der an K angeschlossen ist, kein Strom festgestellt, so erfolgt die Anwahl des Moduls.

Soll in ein Assoziativregister eine neue Seitennummer eingeschrieben werden, so wird Punkt K an positives Potential gelegt, die Punkte Q_λ bzw. $\bar{Q}_\lambda$ werden mit den Bitwerten des einzuschreibenden Wortes verbunden und dann kurzzeitig die Schreibleitung auf positives Potential gehoben [2].

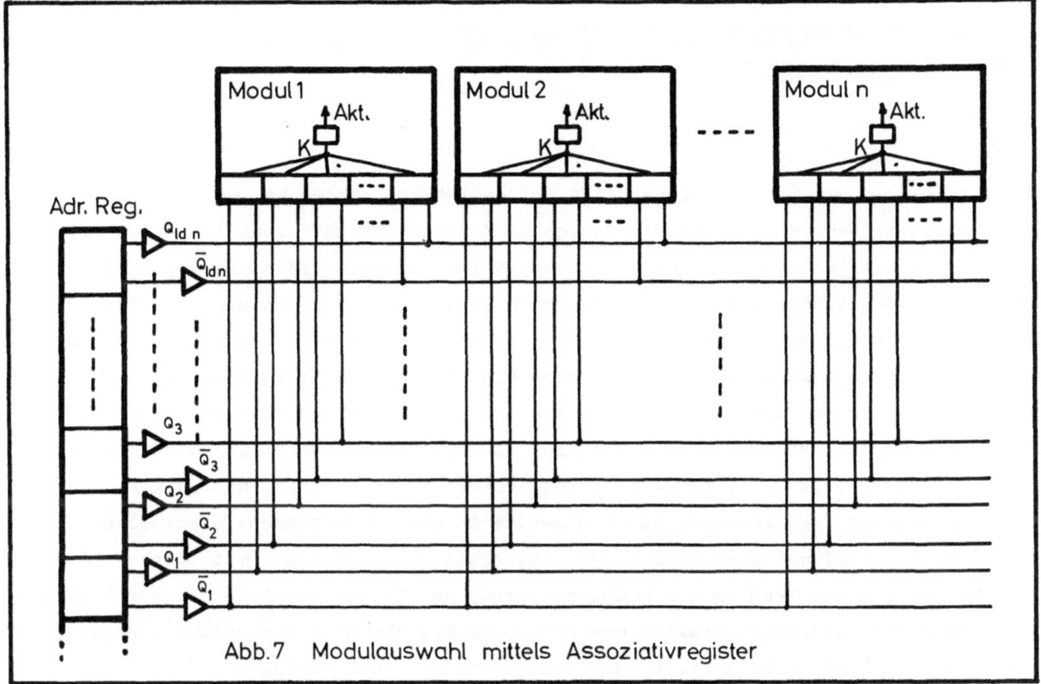

Abb.7 Modulauswahl mittels Assoziativregister

Abb. 7 zeigt das Gesamtschaltbild des Speichers. Die Spannungspegel, die zur Emitterumschaltung erforderlich sind, müssen von Leistungsverstärkern geliefert werden. Ähnliche Verstärker sind jedoch auch für die festverdrahteten Adressenentschlüssler notwendig.

Als verzögerndes Glied tritt jetzt an Stelle des Adressenentschlüsslers der Stromindikator, mit etwa der gleichen Verzögerungszeit. Alle anderen Schaltglieder in beiden Anordnungen sind gleich. Damit ist die gestellte Forderung, die Adreßtransformation während der Modulauswahlzeit zu erledigen, erfüllt.

Als Mehraufwand muß pro Kachel ein zusätzliches assoziatives Register mit ld n Stellen, welches aber ähnlich aufgebaut ist wie eine Speicherzelle, investiert werden.

Dafür kann jedoch ein besonderer Assoziativspeicher mit dem zugehörigen Alterungsmechanismus und die Seiten-Kachel-Zuordnungsliste entfallen.

LITERATUR

[1] Jerry Einbinder, Semiconductor Memories
Wiley Interscience New York-London-Sidney-Toronto

[2] Heinz Schecher, Ein schneller Assoziativspeicherarray in bipolarer Technik, Bericht Nr. 7213 der Technischen Universität München

EINIGE UNTERSUCHUNGEN ZUR HARDWARE-REALISIERUNG VON SOFTWARE-OPERATOREN

D.SCHMID

In der Entwicklung der Digitalrechner sind in den letzten Jahren besonders zwei Tendenzen hervorgetreten: Einerseits die steigende Komplexität und Immobilität der Software und andererseits die zunehmende Leistungsfähigkeit sowie die sinkenden Preise elektronischer Schaltungen. Es liegt nahe, nach Wegen zu suchen, um die günstige Tendenz der technologischen Entwicklung zur Entlastung der Software einzusetzen. Bisher sind bereits einige Ansätze zur Lösung dieses Problems bekannt geworden, die im wesentlichen entweder auf eine Realisierung spezieller Algorithmen oder auf eine verstärkte Anwendung der Mikroprogrammierung zur Interpretation von Programmiersprachen hinauslaufen, z.B. |1,2,3|. Eine weitere Möglichkeit besteht darin, häufig wiederkehrende umfangreichere Prozesse, beispielsweise in Systemprogrammen, speziellen Schaltwerken zur Ausführung zu übertragen. Abgesehen davon, daß man mit solchen Lösungen der erwünschten Tendenz zur Modularisierung der Betriebssysteme entgegenkommt, ist die Frage von Interesse, wieweit man mit einer Ausführung durch solche funktionsspezialisierten Schaltwerke Zeiteinsparungen gegenüber einer Ausführung durch spezielle Programme erzielen kann. Sie soll hier näher untersucht werden.

Gegenstand der hier behandelten Untersuchungen sind vor allem interne Sortierprozesse, da sie im Rahmen der Programmübersetzung und -ausführung einen erheblichen Raum einnehmen und sich deshalb besonders für eine schnelle Ausführung durch eine Schaltung anbieten.

Sortieren soll dabei das Ordnen von Datenbeständen nach einem bestimmten Ordnungskriterium bedeuten. Dieses Ordnungskriterium ist in der Regel eine Größenrelation, die aufgrund einer vorgegebenen Kollationsfolge zwischen den Sortiermerkmalen bzw. Kennbegriffen der zu sortierenden Daten hergestellt wird. Hier sei ausschließlich von einem Kriterium ausgegangen, das eine Ordnung der Sortiermerkmale in lexikalisch aufsteigender oder absteigender Reihenfolge erzeugt. Als Sortiermerkmal sei einheitlich eine Zahl, die sog. Schlüsselzahl, zugrunde gelegt, ohne weiter darauf einzugehen, aus welchen Kennbegriffen diese gebildet wird.

Die zahlreichen Sortierverfahren, die zur Herstellung einer solchen Ordnung entwickelt wurden, eignen sich nicht alle in gleicher Weise für eine schaltungstechnische Realisierung. Für eine Auswahl müssen vor allem drei Gesichtspunkt maßgebend sein:

1. Technischer Aufwand.
2. Erforderlicher Speicherplatz.
3. Eignung des Verfahrens für eine Ausführung durch eine

Schaltung (z.B. rekursiver Aufbau; Verwendung von Operationen, die eine einfache schaltungstechnische Umsetzung oder die Ausnutzung besonderer technischer Möglichkeiten gestatten usw.).

Legt man diese Kriterien zugrunde, so stellen sich die folgenden Verfahren als besonders geeignet heraus:

Sortieren durch Einordnen |4|:

Ausgangspunkt ist eine Liste der Länge L, deren Elemente in aufsteigender Reihenfolge sortiert werden sollen. Der Sortiervorgang erfolgt derart, daß aus der zu sortierenden Liste die Schlüsselzahlen nacheinander ausgelesen und in eine neue Liste an richtiger Stelle eingeordnet werden.

Das Verfahren ist relativ einfach: eine neue Schlüsselzahl wird jeweils, beginnend am Anfang oder Ende der bis dahin aufgebauten Liste, mit den Schlüsselzahlen dieser Liste so lange verglichen, bis ihre richtige relative Position ermittelt ist. Die bereits eingeordneten Schlüsselzahlen, die größer als die einzuordnende Zahl sind, werden verschoben, um Platz für die neu hinzugekommene Zahl zu schaffen.

Beispiel:

zu sortierende Liste:	Durchläufe 1.	2.	3.	4.	5.	6.
27	27	8	8	8	8	2
8	8	27	10	10	10	8
10	10	10	27	27	20	10
30	30	30	30	30	27	20
20	20	20	20	20	30	27
2	2	2	2	2	2	30

Bild 1: Beispiel zum Sortieren durch Einordnen

Es bedeuten: Y, X: Vergleich von X mit Y

Z, Y, X: Abspeicherung von X anstelle von Z und Verschiebung von Y und Z

Für die Sortierung einer Liste der Länge L benötigt man L Durchläufe. Die Anzahl der Operationen pro Durchlauf hängt von der Vorsortierung der Liste ab. Nimmt man die Länge der bereits geordneten Teilliste mit q an, so werden im Mittel q/2 Aufrufe und Vergleiche zur Einordnung einer weiteren Schlüsselzahl erforderlich sein. Die Anzahl der erforderlichen Aufrufe und Vergleichsoperationen ergibt sich also im Mittel zu

$$A_E = \sum_{q=2}^{L} q/2 \approx L^2/4 \qquad (1)$$

Das Verfahren ist wegen der quadratischen Abhängigkeit der Zahl der Operationen von der Listenlänge für das Sortieren langer Listen schlecht geeignet, aber vorteilhaft zum Vorsortieren kürzerer Listen einsetzbar, die dann auf andere Weise fertig sortiert bzw. gemischt werden können. Es benötigt keinen zusätzlichen Speicherplatz, wenn man die geordnete Liste in den freiwerdenden Plätzen der aufgerufenen Schlüsselzahlen aufbaut und kann außerdem durch eine relativ einfache Schaltung ausgeführt werden. Diese Schaltung ist in ein Operationswerk, welches die Operationen ausführt und ein Steuerwerk, welches die Steuerung des Ablaufs übernimmt, untergliedert. Es verursacht folgenden Aufwand:

Operationswerk:	2 Register (Wortlänge)	Steuerwerk: 4 Flipflops
	2 Zähler	Verknüpfungsglieder
	2 Adreßregister	
	1 Vergleichsschaltung	
	Verknüpfungsglieder	

Die Einzelheiten des Entwurfs solcher Schaltwerke sind in der Literatur ausreichend angegeben, so daß hier darauf verzichtet werden kann, sie genauer zu erläutern. |5,6|.

Ein weiteres Verfahren, das sich vor allem wegen seiner hohen Sortiergeschwindigkeit anbietet, wurde 1959 von Shell angegeben. |7|.

Shell - Sort:

Bei diesem Verfahren werden durch fortgesetzte Halbierung der zu sortierenden Listen Teillisten erzeugt. (Bei ungeradzahliger Anzahl von Schlüsselzahlen in einer Liste ist die der Hälfte benachbarte nächstkleinere ganze Zahl als neue Teillistenlänge zu wählen.) Nach jeder Halbierung werden nur diejenigen Schlüsselzahlen, die in aufeinanderfolgenden Teillisten gleiche Positionen einnehmen, miteinander verglichen. Ihre Plätze sind zu tauschen, wenn die Schlüsselzahl in der betrachteten Teilliste größer ist als die mit ihr verglichene Schlüsselzahl der nachfolgenden Teilliste. Das Verfahren ist solange weiterzuführen, bis keine weitere Halbierung mehr möglich ist, weil die zuletzt bearbeiteten Teillisten jeweils nur noch ein Element enthalten. Die Liste liegt spätestens dann sortiert vor. (Bild 2).

Sind bei der Abarbeitung von Teillisten, die an zweiter oder höherer Stelle stehen, Vertauschungen erforderlich, beispielsweise, weil eine in der dritten Teilliste stehende Zahl B größer ist als die mit ihr verglichene Zahl A der vierten Teilliste, so ist das nunmehr in die dritte Teilliste wandernde Element A in einem rückwärts gerichteten Vergleich mit seinem Pendant in der vorhergehenden (zweiten) Teilliste zu vergleichen und gegebenenfalls zu vertauschen. Ist ein Tausch mit dem Element in der zweiten Teilliste erforderlich, so ist der rückwärts gerichtete Vergleich mit dem betreffenden Element der vorhergehenden ersten Teilliste zu wiederholen. (Vgl. Einordnung der Zahl 2 in der 13. Spalte von Bild 2.) Generell gilt, daß im Falle eines Platztauschs bei rückwärts gerichteten Vergleichen der Vergleich und evtl. Austausch so lange mit den betreffenden Elementen der vorhergehenden Teillisten zu wiederholen ist, bis keine Vertauschung mehr erforderlich ist oder die erste Teilliste erreicht wurde. Der Prozeß des Vorwärts- und Rückwärts-Vertauschens bewirkt, daß die Schlüsselzahlen mit einer Schrittweite, welche der jeweiligen Teillistenlänge entspricht, relativ schnell an ihren Platz in der sortierten Teilliste wandern.

Bild 2 demonstriert das Verfahren an einem Beispiel:

	Sortierlauf																	
Zu sort. Liste	1. (Teillisten-länge 5:		2. (Teillistenlänge:2)						3. (Teillistenlänge:1)									
7	7	1	1	1	1	1	1	1	1	1	1	1	1	1	1	1	1	1
10	10	5	5	4	4	4	4	4	5	3	3	3	2	2	2	2	2	2
3	3	3	3	3	2	2	2	2	3	5	4	4	3	3	3	3	3	3
4	4	4	4	5	5	5	5	5	4		5	2	4	4	4	4	4	4
2	2	2	2		3	3	3	3	2			5	5	5	5	5	5	5
1	1	7	7			7	6	6	7					7	7	6	6	6
5	5	10	10				10	8	10					10	6	7	7	7
6	6	6	6				7	7	6						10	10	8	8
8	8	8	8					10	8								10	9
9	9	9	9					9	9									10

Es bedeuten: X┐ Y┘ Vergleich zwischen X und Y; X◄┐ Y┘ Platztausch von X und Y

Bild 2: Beispiel zum Sortieren nach dem Shell-Sort-Verfahren

Aufwand: Operationswerk: 2 Register (Wortlänge)
2 Register (Adressenlänge)
3 Adreßregister
3 Vergleichsschaltungen
Verknüpfungsglieder

Steuerwerk: 4 Flipflops
Verknüpfungsglieder

Das Verfahren ist sehr schnell und hat außerdem den Vorteil, keinen zusätzlichen Speicherplatz zu benötigen. Bei der Ausführung durch eine Schaltung ist der Zeitbedarf im wesentlichen von der Zahl der erforderlichen Speicherzugriffe abhängig. Bestimmt man die Mindestzahl dieser Zugriffe, so ergibt sich mit guter Näherung folgende Abhängigkeit von der Listenlänge:

$$A_S \approx 2L(\alpha-1) \qquad (2)$$

mit L = Listenlänge

$\alpha = \lfloor \mathrm{ld}\ L \rfloor$, wobei $\lfloor\ \rfloor$ bedeuten soll, daß die in ld L enthaltene größte ganze Zahl zu wählen ist.

Aus Gleichung(2) ergibt sich eine Sortierzeit von mindestens

$$t_{S_{min}} \approx 2L(\alpha-1)(t_Z+t_V) \qquad (3)$$

(mit t_Z = Zugriffszeit und t_V = Zeit zur Ausführung eines Vergleichs.)

Die mittlere Sortierzeit liegt etwa um den Faktor 1,2 über dem Minimalwert:

$$t_{S_{mittel}} \approx 2,4 \cdot L(\alpha-1)(t_Z+t_V) \qquad (4)$$

Bemerkungen zu den bisherigen Verfahren:

Bei den beiden bis jetzt behandelten Verfahren wurde eine direkte Umsetzung der Sortieralgorithmen in Schaltungen vorgenommen. Dieses Vorgehen ist naheliegend, läßt aber spezifische Vorteile außer acht, die sich aus der direkten Realisierung der Verfahren durch Schaltungen ergeben können. Als solche Vorteile wären vor allem zu nennen:

- Paralleler Ablauf voneinander unabhängiger Teilprozesse und
- Einsatz von Baugruppen, die Funktionen ausführen, welche durch Programme nicht in äquivalenter Weise zu realisieren sind.

Als Baugruppen, die Vorteile im zuletzt genannten Punkt für Sortierprozesse bieten, wären vor allem Klassifikatoren zu nennen. |8,9|. Schaltungen dieser Art haben die Fähigkeit, aus einem Satz von f Schlüsselzahlen die größte in relativ kurzer Zeit herauszusuchen. So sind bei einem linearen Klassifikator für f = 32 Schlüsselzahlen einer Länge von 4 Byte ohne größere technologische Schwierigkeiten Klassifikationszeiten von etwa 0,5 μs erreichbar.

In Anbetracht dieser Eigenschaft ist es zweckmäßig, neue Sortierprozesse zu entwickeln oder bereits bekannte so zu modifizieren, daß die spezifischen Vorteile der Klassifikatoren ausgenutzt werden. Es seien im folgenden zwei derartige Prozesse vorgestellt:

Sortieren durch Aufspalten und Auswählen

Bei diesem Verfahren sind zwei Phasen unterscheidbar: in einem ersten Abschnitt wird die zu sortierende Liste in Teillisten der Länge f (und eine evtl. Rest-Teilliste < f) unterteilt und mit Hilfe des Klassifikators teillistenweise sortiert. In der zweiten Phase wird der Klassifikator mit den auf den Plätzen f, 2f, 3f,...ff stehenden größten Schlüsselzahlen der ersten f Teillisten gefüllt, um unter diesen die größte zu ermitteln. Diese wird aus dem Klassifikator ausgelagert und am Ende einer Pufferliste der Länge f^2 abgespeichert. Danach wird der Selektionsvorgang wiederholt, nachdem anstelle des selektierten Elements die nächstgrößte Zahl aus derjenigen Teilliste in den Klassifikator nachgeschoben wurde, aus der die ausgelagerte Schlüsselzahl stammte. Nachdem auf diese Weise die ersten f Teillisten abgearbeitet sind und eine sortierte Pufferliste der Länge f^2 gebildet wurde, wird das Verfahren auf die nächsten f Teillisten angewendet und damit eine zweite Pufferliste der Länge f^2 aufgebaut. Dieses Vorgehen ist so lange fortzusetzen, bis die ursprüngliche Liste abgearbeitet ist. Danach ist der Vorgang zu wiederholen, wobei anstelle der oben genannten Teillisten jetzt die zuletzt gebildeten Pufferlisten verwendet werden. Der Sortiervorgang ist abgeschlossen, sowie nach i Stufen nur noch eine einzige Pufferliste der Länge f^i entsteht, also gilt:

$$f^i \geq L \tag{5}$$

(mit $i = \lceil \log_f L \rceil$, wobei $\lceil\ \rceil$ bedeuten soll, daß $i = \log_f L$ gilt, falls $\log_f L$ ganzzahlig ist; anderenfalls ist die nächstgrößere ganze Zahl zu wählen.)

Bild 3 zeigt den Ablauf des Verfahrens:

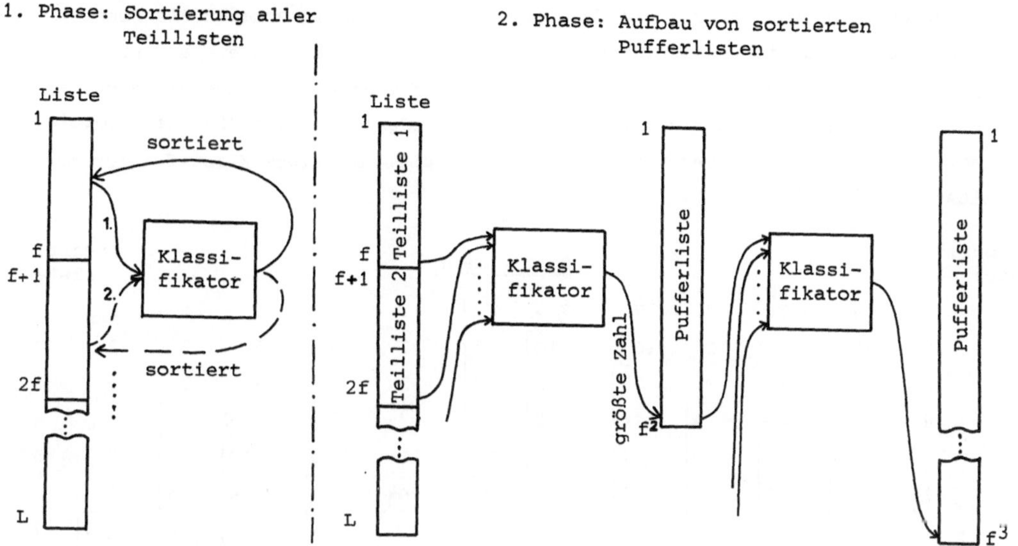

Bild 3: Schema des Verfahrens "Sortieren durch Aufspalten und Auswählen".

Die Zeit zur Ausführung der Sortierung ist bei diesem Verfahren im wesentlichen von der Länge L der zu sortierenden Liste und von der Zahl i der Stufen abhängig, die durchlaufen werden müssen, um die gesamte Liste zu sortieren:

$$t_A \approx iL(t_Z+t_K) \tag{6}$$

(mit $i = \lceil \log_f L \rceil$, t_Z = Zugriffszeit, t_K = Klassifikationszeit.)

Bild 5 zeigt den Zeitbedarf des Verfahrens in Abhängigkeit von der Listenlänge L für eine Klassifikatorkapazität von f = 32 und $t_Z = t_K = 0{,}5\,\mu s$.

Das Verfahren stellt sich als außerordentlich schnell heraus. Die erforderliche Schaltung ist allerdings relativ kompliziert und umfangreich. Sie verursacht folgenden Aufwand:

Operationswerk: 1 Register (Wortlänge),
6 Register (Bytelänge),
5 Adreßregister,
14 Vergleicher,
32 Zähler,
1 Klassifikator,
Schaltglieder.

Steuerwerk: 5 Flipflops
Schaltglieder.

Das Verfahren benötigt ferner zur Unterbringung der Pufferliste zusätzlichen Speicherplatz von Listenlänge. Beide Nachteile vermeidet das folgende Verfahren:

Zonenschmelzverfahren:

Dieses Verfahren beruht darauf, daß der Klassifikator - gewissermaßen als Fenster - von unten nach oben über die zu sortierende Liste wandert, indem er stets am unteren Ende sein größtes Element an die Liste zurückgibt und dafür am oberen Ende ein neues Element aufnimmt. Diese Durchläufe sind so lange zu wiederholen, bis die Liste sortiert vorliegt. Bild 4 zeigt das Verfahren an einem Beispiel mit einem Klassifikator der Kapazität 4:

Zu sort. Liste:							Sortierlauf								sort. Liste:
7	7	7	7	7	7	7	7	1	1	1	1	1	1	1	1
10	10	10	10	10	10	10	3	2	2	2	2	2	2	2	2
3	3	3	3	3	3	3	2	3	3	3	3	3	3	3	3
4	4	4	4	4	4	2	1	7	7	7	7	7	4	4	4
2	2	2	2	2	2	1	10	10	10	10	10	4	5	5	5
1	1	1	1	1	1	4	4	4	4	4	4	5	6	6	6
5	5	5	5	5	5	5	5	5	5	5	5	6	7	7	7
6	6	6	6	6	6	6	6	6	6	6	6	10	10	10	8
8	8	8	8	8	8	8	8	8	8	8	8	8	8	8	9
9	9	9	9	9	9	9	9	9	9	9	9	9	9	9	10

Klassifikator

Bild 4:Beispiel zum Sortieren nach dem Zonenschmelzverfahren

Der Klassifikator führt bei diesem Verfahren einen Transport der Listenelemente aus, wobei sich zeigen läßt, daß bei zufälliger Verteilung der Schlüsselzahlen pro Listenelement eine mittlere Transportlänge von L/4 auftritt. Man kann ferner zeigen, daß pro Durchlauf mindestens (f-1) Schlüsselzahlen am Listenanfang und im Mittel insgesamt 4 f Zahlen in der Liste richtig eingeordnet werden, wenn f die Kapazität des Klassifikators ist. Daraus läßt sich ableiten, daß die Liste im Mittel nach

$$A_{Zs_{mittel}} = n \cdot L \left\{ 1 - \frac{(f-1)\cdot(n-1)}{2L} \right\} \qquad (7)$$

Zugriffen sortiert vorliegt, wobei $n = \lceil \frac{L}{4f} \rceil$ ist.

Bei paralleler Abwicklung der Lese-, Schreib- und Klassifikationsoperationen ergibt sich folgende mittlere Sortierzeit:

$$t_{Zs_{mittel}} = t_Z\, n\, L \left\{1 - \frac{(f-1)\cdot(n-1)}{2L}\right\}; \qquad n = \left\lceil\frac{L}{4f}\right\rceil \tag{8}$$

Im ungünstigsten Fall kann diese Zeit bis auf maximal

$$t_{Zs_{max}} = t_Z L \left\{1 + \frac{L}{2(f-1)}\right\} \tag{9}$$

ansteigen. Im günstigsten Fall kann sie (bei bereits sortierter Liste) bis auf

$$t_{Zs_{min}} \approx L\cdot t_Z \tag{10}$$

abnehmen. Bild 5 zeigt den Verlauf der Sortierzeiten in Abhängigkeit von der Listenlänge bei einer Klassifikatorkapazität von $f = 32$ und einer Zugriffszeit von 0,5 µs. Das Verfahren ist bei längeren Listen im Mittel etwas langsamer als das Sortieren durch Aufspalten und Auswählen. Es benötigt jedoch im Gegensatz zu diesem Verfahren keinen zusätzlichen Speicherplatz, sondern kommt mit dem Platz der zu sortierenden Liste im Arbeitspeicher aus.

Schaltungsaufwand:

Operationswerk: 2 Register (Wortlänge)
3 Adreßregister
1 Zähler
1 Vergleichsschaltung
1 Klassifikator
Verknüpfungselemente

Steuerwerk: 4 Flipflops
Verknüpfungselemente

Vergleich der Sortierzeiten mit der Laufzeit von Sortierprogrammen

Um die ermittelten Sortierzeiten mit den Laufzeiten von Sortierprogrammen vergleichen zu können, wurden die beiden ersten Verfahren für eine Anlage CDC 3300 programmiert und die Ausführungszeiten bestimmt. |10|. Es ergab sich bei einer Programmierung in Maschinensprache folgende Abhängigkeit von der Listenlänge:

Sortieren durch Einordnen:

$$t_{P_1} \approx \left\{23(L-1) + 7{,}5(L-1)^2\right\} \mu s$$

Shell-Sort:

$$t_{P_2} \approx 58\cdot L^{1{,}226} \; \mu s$$

Bild 5 zeigt einen Vergleich der verschiedenen Sortierzeiten.

Es ergibt sich bei der Ausführung der Sortierung durch die schnellsten der betrachteten Schaltungen eine Verkürzung der Sortierzeit auf 1/200 bis 1/300 der Laufzeit der Sortierprogramme. Dieser Wert könnte vor allem durch technologische Maßnahmen noch verbessert werden.

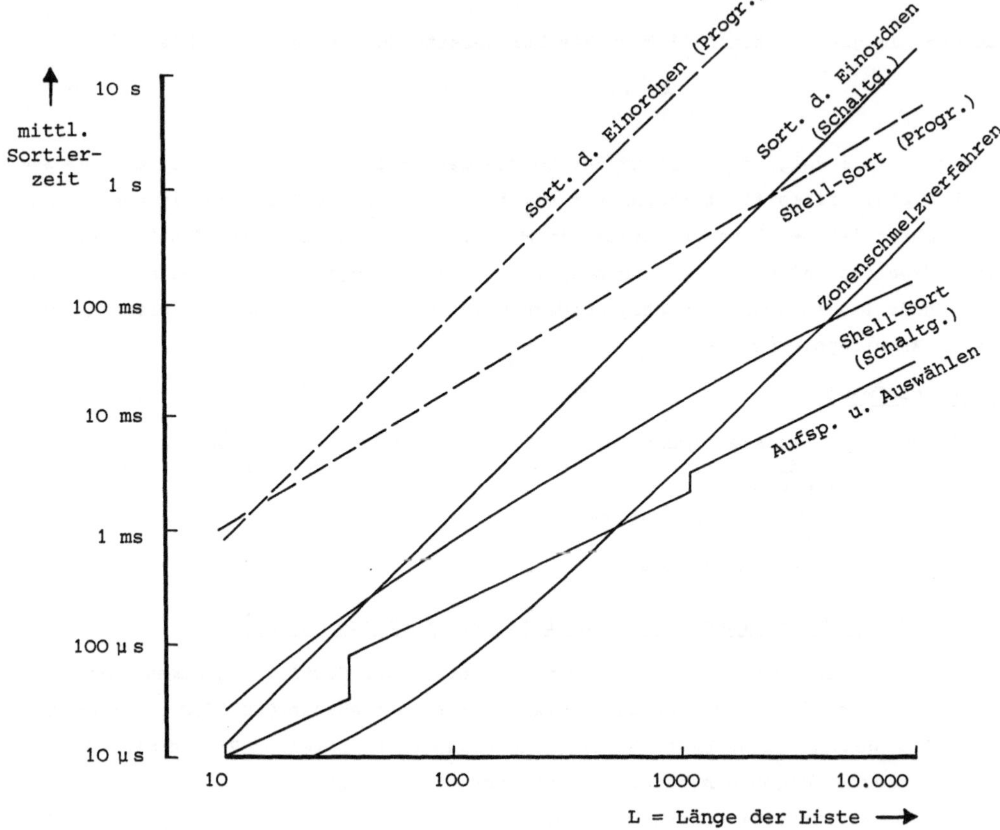

Bild 5: Mittlere Sortierzeiten der betrachteten Schaltungen und Programme.

(Parameter der Sortierschaltungen: Zugriffszeit = 0,5 µs, Klassifikatorkapazität = 32 Schlüsselzahlen.
Programme in Maschinensprache auf CD 3300)

|1| Berkling, K.J.: A Computing Machine Based on Tree Structures.
IEEE Trans. on C., Vol. C-20, No.4, Apr. 1971, pp. 404-418

|2| Weber, H.: A Microprogrammed Implementation of EULER on IBM System/360 Model 30
Comm. ACM, Vol. 10, No. 9, Sept. 1967

|3| Batcher, K.E.: Sorting networks and their applications.
Proc. Spring Joint Comp. Conf. 1968, pp. 307-314

|4| Wedekind, H.: Datenorganisation.
de Gruyter, Berlin, 1970

|5| Wendt, S.: Eine Methode zum Entwurf komplexer Schaltwerke unter Verwendung spezieller Ablaufdiagramme.
Elektron. Rechenanl. 12 (1970), H.6, S. 314-323

|6| Schmid, D.; Senger, D.; Wojtkowiak, H.: Technische Informatik, Teil 1.
Oldenbourg, München 1972

|7| Shell, D.L.: A High-Speed Sorting Procedure.
Comm. ACM 2, No.7 (1959), pp. 30-32

|8| Schmid, D.: Untersuchungen an Klassifikatoren mit Hilfe eines mathematischen Modells.
Nachrichtentechn. Zeitschr. NTZ 1970, H.3, S. 151-157

|9| Schmid, D.: Eine Schaltung zum Aufbau schneller Klassifikatoren für binäre und nichtbinäre Muster.
Nachrichtentechn. Zeitschr. NTZ 1970, H.4, S. 185-188

|10| Knieper, D.: Untersuchung zur Hardware-Realisierung von Software-Operatoren.
Diplomarbeit am Institut für Informatik, Forschungsgruppe Rechnerorganisation; Universität Karlsruhe 1971

PERFORMANCE EVALUATION OF PROCESSOR DESIGN

L.J.ZECKENDORF

Summary

Performance evaluation is one of many aspects of computer system design. Analytic models and simulation models each have their own merits as evaluation tools.

The present paper deals with software simulation of the hardware elements of a computer system; the performance evaluation of operating system and application software is not discussed here. This does not mean that the characteristics of the software are ignored; indeed, the behaviour of the software has an important effect on the hardware performance and measurements on running systems constitute a major source of simulation input.

Section 1 of this paper presents a definition of levels of hardware design at which performance evaluation by software simulation has been proven feasible and useful.

Section 2 describes a programming technique which has succesfully been used, especially in simulation models which are developed in parallel with the design of the systems being simulated. This technique facilitates the model to be kept up-to-date with the hardware design.

The application of the technique is not restricted to simulation models; its principles can be used in the development of programs of any type.

1. Levels of simulation

Figure 1 shows a generalized configuration of the hardware elements of a computer system.

The performance of the hardware is presently evaluated at three distinct levels. The definition of "performance" depends on the level; the quantities by which the performance is expressed are called the performance measures.

It should be noted that this section is restricted to simulation models for performance evaluation only; other simulations, e.g. to test the correctness of a design, or to estimate its reliability, are not discussed here.

1.1 The Buffer Memory level (figure 2)

The performance measure at the Buffer Memory level is the hitrate (average number of read accesses to data in buffer relative to total number of read accesses).

Various buffer memory designs and replacement algorithms are evaluated, using address traces measured on actually running systems.

The results of this simulation are used as input at the next level.

1.2 The Processor level (figure 3)

The performance measure at the Processor level is the average instruction execution time.

The calculation of processor speed is no trivial matter for processors designed with look-ahead and/or buffer memory, because in these cases the execution time of an instruction may depend on previously executed instructions.

Input to the Processor model includes:

- processor cycle time(s);
- cycle time, access time and hitrate of buffer memory (if present);
- main memory cycle and access times;
- instruction mix.

In case of a processor with look-ahead a two-dimensional instruction mix is used, in which P(i,j) is the probability that an instruction of type i is followed by an instruction of type j. This instruction mix is obtained from measurements on actually running systems.

A secondary result of the simulation, namely the main memory load, is used as input at the next level.

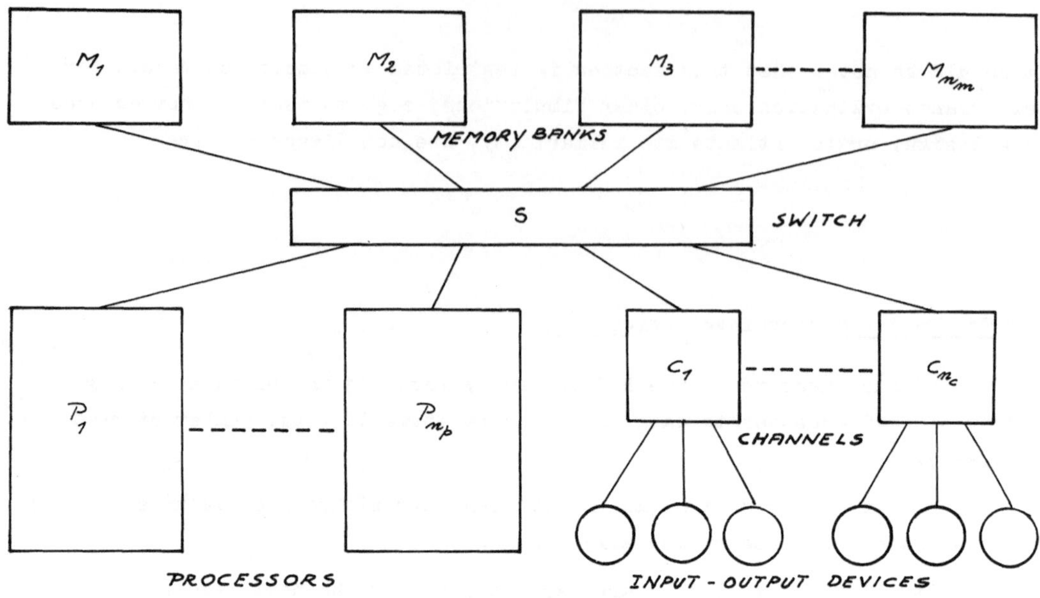

Figure 1. Generalized hardware configuration of a computer system.

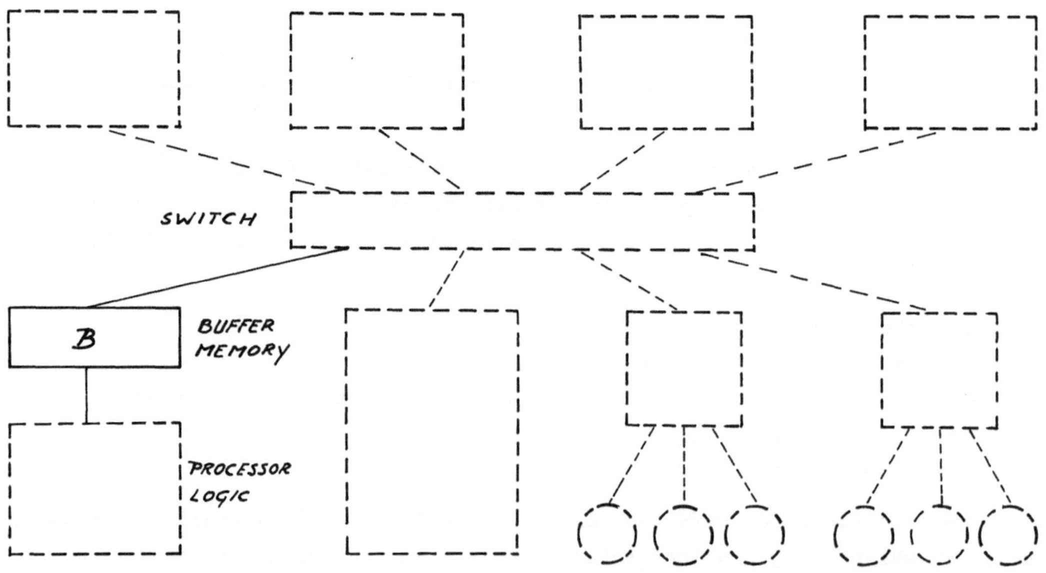

Figure 2. Configuration at the Buffer Memory level. The Buffer Memory is the only relevant element at this level. The processor logic is represented by an Address Trace in the simulation.

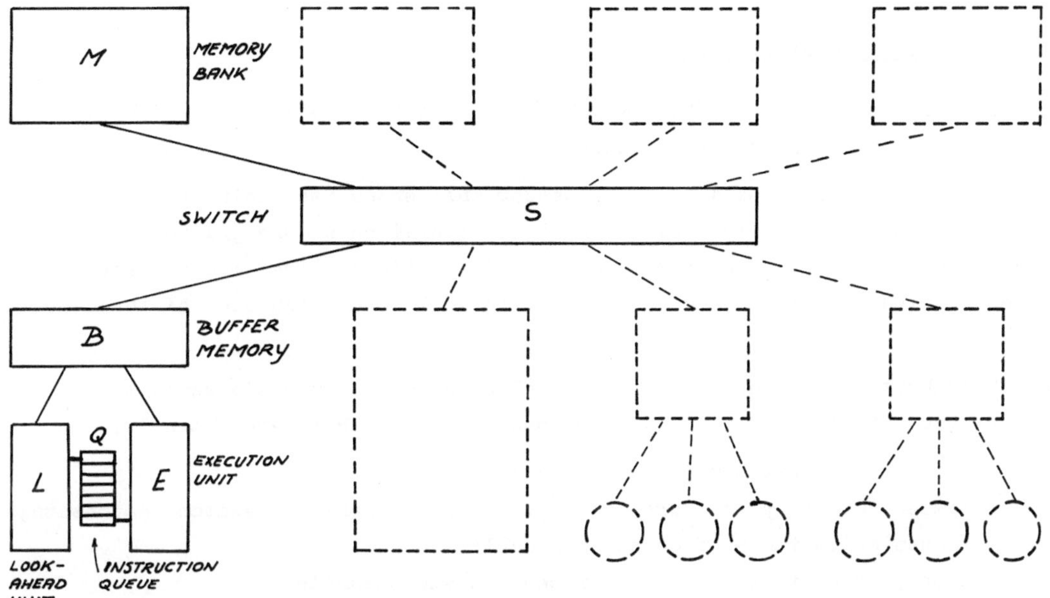

Figure 3. Configuration at the Processor level. The elements which are relevant at this level are indicated by solid lines. The processor structure in this example is one with Look-ahead and Buffer Memory.

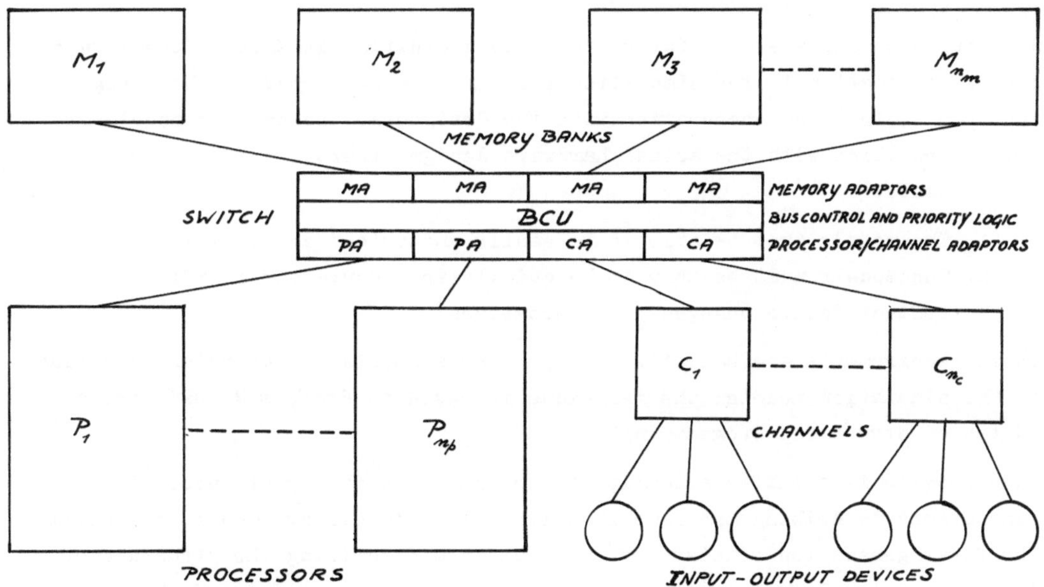

Figure 4. Configuration at the Switch level. All elements are relevant at this level. A particular type of switch is shown in more detail as an example.

1.3 The Switch level (figure 4)

The performance measure at the Switch level is the effective memory speed experienced by processors and channels.

The effective memory speed for a processor influences its instruction execution rate and may be used as input for iteration at the previous level. The effective memory speed for a channel, in particular the memory response time distribution, is a measure for the probability of occurence of throughput errors.

(A throughput error occurs when a channel needs a memory cycle while the memory has not yet processed the previous cycle for that same channel).

The input for the Switch model consists of:

- timing data of processors, channels, memory banks and switch components;
- transmission times of connecting cables;
- memory load distribution of processors and channels.

2. Programming Technique

Simulation models are used for performance evaluation at each of the levels defined in section 1. The simulation programs are developed in the design department, in close cooperation with the designers. Because the models are made in parallel with the actual hardware design, there are two major requirements:

A. The models must be able to be easily understood and verified.

B. The models must be able to be quickly and accurately modified to reflect design changes or alternatives.

These requirements are satisfied by applying a special programming technique to the simulation models; the technique is based on Prof. E.W. Dijkstra's "Notes on Structured Programming".

Each program is actually a family of programs, consisting of successive generations describing the same algorithm with increasing amount of detail. The first generation consists of only comments describing the structure of the program in plain language. Each later generation consists of the program text of the preceding generation, in which additional comments and/or program statements are inserted to provide the additional detail. This principle is schematically illustrated by figure 5.

A particular generation is identified by a list of version numbers; the generation number is equal to the number of elements in this list. The last generation of a program is actually compiled and executed; preceding generations are kept as documentation and - their main purpose - are used as means of communication between model programmer and design engineer, when the model is verified or changes are discussed.

Design changes and alternatives are introduced in the model by developing alternative versions of existing generations. This is the reason why a generation is identified by a list rather than a single number. A family of generations with alternative versions has the structure of a tree, as illustrated by figure 6.

When a design change is discussed by the programmer and the designer, they look for the generation which contains sufficiently little detail so that it is invariant with respect to the change. If this generation cannot be found, they define a new version of generation one. Otherwise, when generation n is invariant, they define a new version of generation n+1, and corresponding new versions of later generations. The result is that the tree is extended with a new branch.

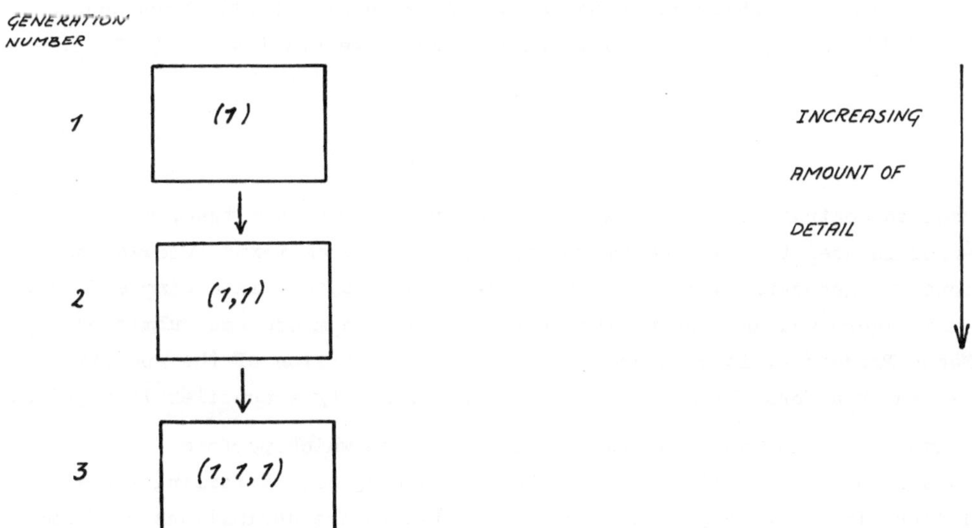

Figure 5. Example of family of programs consisting of three generations. Each rectangle represents a version of the program.

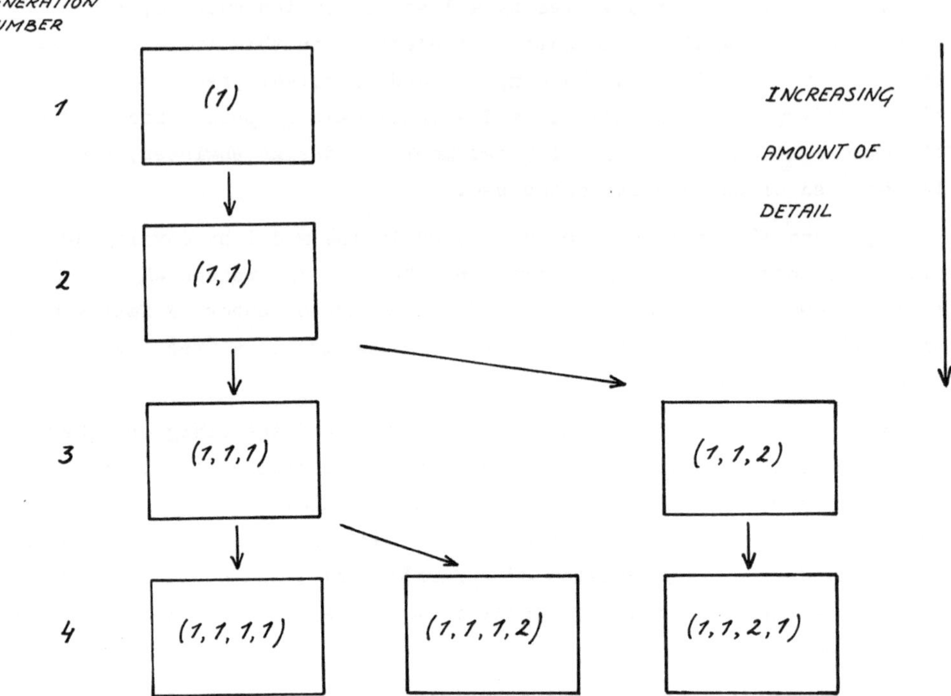

Figure 6. Example of tree of programs. Versions (1,1,1) and (1,1,2) are alternatives which are both derived from version (1,1). Versions (1,1,1,1) and (1,1,1,2) are alternative fourth generations of (1,1,1).

In order to control the consistency of the generations in a tree, a Macro Processor is used to generate the versions. All program texts relevant to the versions and generations of a complete tree are contained in a single Macro. When this Macro and an appropriate list of version numbers are submitted to the Macro Processor, it will produce the intended version of the specified generation in a form which can be further processed by a compiler if required.

Each simulation program consists of a main program which performs initialization and input-output only, and a number of subprograms performing the actual simulation. In order to prevent inconsistencies in the definitions of Common Blocks and External Procedures, the program statements defining these external objects are contained in separate Macros which are invoked inside the Macros used to generate the programs.

The method described in the two preceding paragraphs insures that a piece of program text which must be repeated in several generations of the same program, or in several different programs (subprograms), is indeed the same piece of text wherever it is required. No single comment or statement which is used more than once in a program need be written more than once. This application of the Macro Processor is a great help in maintenance.

3. Examples

The presentation of this paper is illustrated by some practical examples.

Reference

Dijkstra, E.W.: Notes on Structured Programming.
T.H. Eindhoven, 1970.

ZUR OPTIMIERUNG VON ZUVERLÄSSIGKEIT UND NUTZUNGSGRAD VON SYSTEMEN MIT SELBSTDIAGNOSE

W.SCHNEEWEISS

Es werden komplexe Systeme, insbesondere Digitalrechner mit der Fähigkeit zu Selbstüberwachung und Fehlerdiagnose betrachtet. Durch die dabei nötigen Prüfprogramme wird zwar i.allg. der Nutzungsgrad verringert, aber über die verkürzte Ausfallzeit wird die Verfügbarkeit erhöht. Bei Kenntnis des Zusammenhangs zwischen mittlerem Diagnoseaufwand und mittlerer Ausfalldauer kann jeweils angegeben werden, ob ein System für ein Gütekriterium bezüglich Nutzungsgrad (mittlerer prozentualer Arbeitskapazität für den Benutzer) und Verfügbarkeit (Zuverlässigkeit) optimal ist. Für den Fall eines hyperbolischen Zusammenhangs zwischen beiden Größen wird zu mehreren einfachen Gütekriterien das Betriebsoptimum bestimmt. Es liegt meist bei der geforderten Mindestverfügbarkeit.

1. Einführung

Offensichtlich ist bei komplexen Systemen wie Rechnern eine Erhöhung der Verfügbarkeit (z.B. durch Selbstdiagnose) meist mit einer Verringerung der Effektivität verbunden. Dabei ist jedoch ohne genauere Analyse nicht klar, wie viel Überwachungsaufwand optimal ist. Hier folgt ein Beitrag zu dieser Analyse.

Nun werden einige der zu benutzenden Begriffe so weit präzisiert, daß aus ihnen eine mathematisch behandelbare Fragestellung gewonnen werden kann: Als Denkmodell soll ein Prozeßrechner dienen, in dem — zeitlich verschachtelt mit Anwender - (Benutzer-)Programmen — Testprogramme laufen können. Erwünscht ist ein hoher Nutzungsgrad (relative Kapazität)

$$K = \frac{\mathrm{MTFU}}{\mathrm{MTBF+MTTR}}$$

mit MTBF [1] (Mean Time Between Failures): Mittlere ausfallfreie Betriebsdauer,

MTTR [1] (Mean Time To Repair): Mittlere Ausfalldauer und

MTFU (Mean Time For User): Mittlere Nutzungsdauer d.h. die mittlere Summe aller Zeitspannen innerhalb eines Betriebszyklus [2] (Betrieb und Ausfall), während der Benutzerprogramme laufen.

1 Übliche Abkürzung.
2 Die Betriebszyklen haben die mittlere Länge MTBF+MTTR,

Da nicht nur falsche Ergebnisse, sondern auch ausfallbedingte größere zeitliche Lücken in vielen Anwenderprogrammen gerade beim Echtzeit (on-line)-Betrieb eines Prozeßrechners unerwünscht sind, möchte man zusätzlich eine hohe Verfügbarkeit (im stationären Zustand)

$$V := \frac{MTBF}{MTBF+MTTR}$$

erzielen. Bei den ständig mitlaufenden Test-Programmen wird angenommen, daß sie durch geeignete Vergabe von Prioritäten den Echtzeitbetrieb nur unerheblich stören. Rechenzeit beanspruchen sie natürlich nach wie vor!

Neben K und V sollen folgende Symbole benutzt werden, wobei E die Bildung des mathematischen Erwartungswertes bezeichnet:

EA : mittlere Ausfalldauer (MTTR),
EB : mittlere Betriebsdauer (MTBF) zwischen zwei Ausfällen,
EN : mittlere Nutzungsdauer zwischen zwei Ausfällen,
ED : mittlere Test- und Diagnosedauer zwischen zwei Ausfällen.

ED ist nicht als Teil von EA gemeint, sondern es soll

$$EB = EN + ED \tag{1}$$

gelten. Jedoch soll EA mit steigendem ED sinken.
Da man über diesen Zusammenhang heute noch recht wenig weiß, geht es darum, eine einigermaßen flexible Annahme zu machen. Ein Beispiel ist der hyperbolische Zusammenhang nach Bild 1, bei dem noch über die Parameter a und b frei verfügt werden kann. Eine größere Steilheit bei kleinen ED scheint überflüssig zu sein, da jedes Anwenderprogramm eine Reihe schwerer Ausfälle anzeigt.

Gesucht ist nun ein Maximum eines Gütekriteriums

$$G(K,V);\ K \leq K_{min},\quad V \leq V_{min}, \tag{2}$$

wobei K und V Kleinstwerte nicht unterschreiten dürfen.

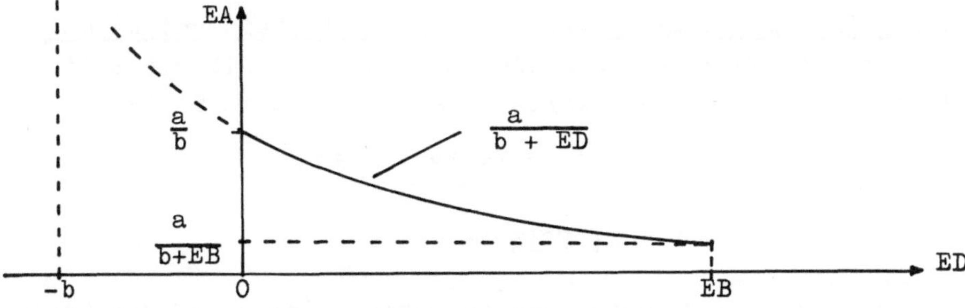

Bild 1 Angenommene Abhängigkeit der mittleren Ausfalldauer EA von der mittleren Diagnosedauer ED.

2. Zusammenhang zwischen Verfügbarkeit und Nutzungsgrad

Mit den oben erklärten Abkürzungen lauten die Definitionsgleichungen für K und V

$$K = \frac{EB - ED}{EB + EA}^{1)} \tag{3}$$

und

$$V = \frac{EB}{EB + EA}\ .^{1)} \tag{4}$$

Also ist immer $K \leq V$.

Aus Gl.(4) folgt unmittelbar als Alternative zu Gl.(3)

$$K = V(1 - \frac{ED}{EB}). \tag{3a}$$

Die MTBF EB soll im folgenden als Konstante angenommen werden, während EA durch Testprogramme verkürzt werden kann. Genauer soll z.B. angenommen werden, daß (vgl. Bild 1)

$$EA = \frac{a}{b + ED}\ ; \quad a,b = \text{const.},\ a,b > 0. \tag{5}$$

Interessant ist nun die Abhängigkeit zwischen V und K: Allgemein ist nach Gl.(4) einerseits

$$EA = \frac{EB}{V} - EB = EB(\ \frac{1}{V} - 1). \tag{6}$$

Andererseits ist nach Gl.(5) speziell

$$ED = \frac{a}{EA} - b, \tag{7}$$

und nach Einsetzen für EA aus Gl. (6)

$$ED = \frac{a}{EB(\frac{1}{V}-1)} - b. \tag{7a}$$

Also wird beim Einsetzen von Gl.(7a) in Gl.(3a) (für EB=const.)

$$K = V - \frac{V}{EB} \cdot \left[\frac{a\ V}{EB(1-V)} - b \right] =: h(V). \tag{8}$$

Nun ist im Bereich $V_{min} \leq V < 1$, $K_{min} \leq K < 1$ das Maximum von $G(K,V) = G\ [h(V),\ V\ ] =: \tilde{G}(V)$ zu bestimmen; genauer das optimale $V=V_o$ dort.

3. Bestimmung optimaler Werte für Verfügbarkeit und Kapazität

Zur Vereinfachung der folgenden Rechnungen, soll die Zeiteinheit gleich der MTBF gewählt werden. Dann gilt statt Gl.(8)

$$K = h(V) := V(1+b- \frac{a\ V}{1-V}\ ) \tag{8a}$$

mit

$$V = \frac{1}{1 + EA}\ . \tag{4a}$$

---

1 Die einzelnen Erwartungswerte beziehen sich auf das Gesamtsystem. Dieses kann, muß aber nicht aus redundanten oder teilredundanten Untersystemen bestehen.

Da EA zwischen a/b und a/(b+1) liegt (vgl. Bild 1 für EB=1), ist (mit OS für obere Schranke, US für untere)

$$V_{OS} > V > V_{US}. \tag{9}$$

Mit

$$V_{OS} := \frac{1}{1+\frac{a}{b+1}} = \frac{b+1}{1+a+b} = 1 - \frac{a}{1+a+b} \tag{10}$$

und

$$V_{US} := \frac{1}{1+\frac{a}{b}} = \frac{b}{a+b} = 1 - \frac{a}{a+b} \tag{10a}$$

gilt statt Gl.(9)

$$\frac{a}{1+a+b} < 1-V < \frac{a}{a+b}. \tag{9a}$$

Sinnvollerweise sei stets $V_{OS} > V_{min}$; jedoch ist nicht unbedingt $V_{US} > V_{min}$.

Als Gütekriterium benutzen wir zunächst

$$G_1(K,V) := K + cV, \tag{11}$$

wobei durch den Parameter c noch Gewichtungen vorgenommen werden können. Eine zweite Möglichkeit ist

$$G_2(K,V) := KV. \tag{12}$$

Für G_1 und G_2 werden Maxima gesucht. Schließlich werden wir

$$G_3(K,V) := (1-K)(1-V) = 1-K-V+KV \tag{13}$$

betrachten, wobei das Produkt aus Kapazitätsausfall und Nichtverfügbarkeit zu einem Minimum zu machen ist.

Kriterium 1: $G_1 = K + cV$:

Mit dem h(V) von Gl.(8a) ist nach Gl.(11)

$$G_1(K,V) := \tilde{G}_1(V) = h(V) + cV = V\left(1+b+c-\frac{aV}{1-V}\right). \tag{14}$$

Es wird zunächst ein relatives Maximum gesucht: Dazu wird

$$\tilde{G}'_1(V) = 1+b+c-a\,\frac{V(2-V)}{(1-V)^2}\;;\quad \tilde{G}''_1(V) = -2a\,\frac{(1-V)^2+V(2-V)}{(1-V)^3}$$

gebildet. Zwischen 0 und 1 ist stets $\tilde{G}''_1(V) < 0$, so daß jedes relative Extremum ein Maximum ist. Für ein relatives Extremum bei $V_{o,r}$ ist $\tilde{G}'_1(V_{o,r}) = 0$. Die Lösung dieser quadratischen Gleichung lautet

$$V_{o,r} = 1 - \sqrt{\frac{a}{1+a+b+c}}, \tag{15}$$

wobei wegen der Forderung $V_o < 1$ das andere Vorzeichen der Wurzel nicht interessiert.

Damit $V_{o,r}$ im zulässigen Bereich liegt, also ein (optimales) V_o ist, muß nach Gl.(9a)

$$\frac{a}{1+a+b} < \sqrt{\frac{a}{1+a+b+c}} < \frac{a}{a+b} \qquad (16)$$

gelten. Für hinreichend kleine c ist jedoch wegen $x < \sqrt{x}$; $x < 1$ nur der rechte Teil der Ungleichung interessant; für hinreichend große c nur der linke.
Für V_o von Gl.(15) ist über Gl.(8a) das optimale $K=K_o=h(V_{o,r})$ leicht auszurechnen.

Nun wird der Fall untersucht, daß $\tilde{G}_1(V)$ im theoretisch zulässigen Bereich (V_{US}, V_{OS}) kein relatives Maximum hat:

Wenn $V_{o,r} < V_{US}$ ist, ist das optimale V das kleinste zulässige, d.h. unter Beachtung der Nebenbedingung $V > V_{min}$ ist

$$V_o = \max(V_{US}, V_{min}) \; ; \quad V_{min} < V_{OS} \, , \qquad (17)$$

denn $\tilde{G}_1$ fällt im zulässigen Bereich monoton. Wie lautet hier K_o ?
Wenn man bedenkt, daß für V_{US} gerade ED=0 ist, folgt aus Gl.(3a) (für EB=1) K=V. Daher wird nach Gln.(10a) und (8a)

$$K_o = \begin{cases} \frac{b}{a+b} \text{ für } V_{US} > V_{min}, \\ V_{min}\left(1+b- \frac{a\,V_{min}}{1-V_{min}}\right) \text{ für } V_{US} < V_{min}. \end{cases} \qquad (18)$$

Wenn $V_{o,r} > V_{OS}$ wäre, dann wäre $\tilde{G}_1(V)$ im zulässigen Bereich monoton steigend, so daß $V_o = \tilde{G}_1(V_{OS})$ wäre. Da aber nach Definition von K Gl.(3) die Funktion K = h(V) bei V_{OS} wegen ED=EB verschwindet, liegt bei $V_{o,r} > V_{OS}$ eine Entartung vor.

Kriterium 2: $G_2 = KV$:
Hier ist nach Gl.(8a)

$$G_2(K,V) = \tilde{G}_2(V) = Vh(V) = V^2\left(1+b- \frac{a\,V}{1-V}\right). \qquad (19)$$

Die Gl.

$$\tilde{G}'_2(V) = V\left[2(1+b)- aV\,\frac{3-2V}{(1-V)^2}\right] = 0$$

für ein relatives Extremum ist wieder quadratisch. Die Lösung lautet

$$V_{o,r}=1-\frac{a+\sqrt{a[8(1+a+b)+a]}}{4(1+a+b)} . \tag{20}$$

Dabei muß wieder wegen der Forderung $V_{o,r} < 1$ das eine Vorzeichen der Wurzel ausgeschlossen werden.
Es ist noch zu prüfen, ob bei $V_{o,r}$ ein relatives Maximum liegt: Das direkte Prüfen, ob $\tilde{G}''_2(V_{o,r}) < 0$, ist mühsam. Einfacher ist es zu zeigen, daß $\tilde{G}'_2(V)$ bei $V=1-0$ negativ ist und daher bis zum Extremum bei $V < 1$ negativ bleibt. Tatsächlich hat $\tilde{G}'_2(V)$ bei 1 eine Polstelle, in deren engeren Nachbarschaft $\tilde{G}''_2(V)$ negativ ist.

Weiterhin werden wieder Bedingungen dafür gesucht, daß das relative Maximum im zulässigen Bereich liegt. Aus den Gln.(9a) und (20) ergibt sich in Analogie zu Gl.(16)

$$\frac{a}{1+a+b} < \frac{a+\sqrt{a(9a+8b+8)}}{4(1+a+b)} < \frac{a}{a+b} . \tag{21}$$

Da die Wurzel $> 3a$ ist, ist nur der rechte Teil dieser Ungl. interessant. Die maximale Kapazität ist also im Falle, daß Ungl.(21) erfüllt ist, mit $V=V_{o,r}$ aus Gl.(8a) zu bestimmen. Für $V_{o,r} < V_{US}$ gelten wieder Gln. (17), (18).

<u>Kriterium 3:</u> $G_3 = (1-K)(1-V)$:
Mit $h(V)$ von Gl.(8a) ist nach Gl.(13)

$$\tilde{G}_3(V) = 1-V\,[2+b-V(1+a+b)] . \tag{22}$$

Zur Bestimmung eines relativen Minimums wird wieder differenziert:

$$\tilde{G}'_3(V) = -2-b+2V(1+a+b),\quad \tilde{G}''_3(V) = 2(1+a+b).$$

Bei

$$V_{o,r} = \frac{2+b}{2(1+a+b)} = 1-\frac{2a+b}{2(1+a+b)} \tag{23}$$

liegt also ein relatives Minimum von $\tilde{G}_3$. Zwar ist $V_{o,r} < 1$, aber es ist wieder nötig zu untersuchen, ob $V_{US} < V_{o,r} < V_{OS}$ oder - nach Gl. (9a) - ob

$$\frac{a}{1+a+b} < \frac{2a+b}{2(1+a+b)} < \frac{a}{a+b} . \tag{24}$$

Nicht trivial ist jedoch nur der rechte Teil dieser Ungleichung.
Aus Gl.(8a) folgt hier das optimale K zu

$$K_o = \frac{b(2+b)}{2(2a+b)} . \tag{25}$$

Wenn $V_o < V_{US}$, folgen V_o und K_o wieder aus Gln. (17), (18).

4. Diskussion der Ergebnisse

Damit für ein nicht zu schlechtes System die Verfügbarkeit $V \approx 1$ ist, muß nach Bild 1 (für EB=1) $a/b \ll 1$ sein.
Um außerdem eine einigermaßen wirksame Diagnose zu haben, welche die Nichtverfügbarkeit wenigstens auf die Hälfte reduzieren kann, muß $b < 1$ sein. Insgesamt gilt für die Parameter a, b demnach

$$0 < a \ll b < 1. \tag{26}$$

Wir wollen nun untersuchen, ob es unter dieser der Praxis entnommenen Bedingung für a und b leicht, d.h. für einen großen Anteil der möglichen Parameter a und b zu einem relativen Extremum kommt:

Kriterium 1: Aus dem rechten Teil von Ungl.(16) folgt rasch

$$a < \frac{b^2}{1 + c - b} \text{ für } b > 1 + c; \; a > \frac{b^2}{1 + c - b} \text{ für } 0<b<1+c. \tag{27}$$

Die erste Bedingung ist, da die rechte Seite negativ ist und nur $a > 0$ interessiert, irrelevant. Mit der zweiten Bedingung läßt sich Ungl.(26) eventuell erfüllen; jedoch muß offenbar außerdem

$$1 + c - b \gg 1$$

sein. Das führt wiederum zur Forderung $c \gg 1$, mit der leicht der linke Teil von Ungl.(16) verletzt wird.

Kriterium 2: Aus dem rechten Teil von Ungl.(21) folgt nach einiger Zwischenrechnung

$$a < \frac{b^2}{2 - b} \text{ für } b > 2; \quad a > \frac{b^2}{2 - b} \text{ für } 0 < b < 2. \tag{28}$$

Wieder interessieren nur positive a, also nur die rechte Bedingung für a. Für $0 < b < 2$ gilt die vergröberte Abschätzung

$$a > b^2/2. \tag{29}$$

Auch hier ist - bei wirksamen Prüfprogrammen gemäß Ungl.(26) - ein relatives Extremum eines Gütekriteriums nur in einem engen Parameterbereich möglich, da bei einigermaßen brauchbaren Systemen $a \ll b$ sein soll. Zur Veranschaulichung dient Bild 2, wo in dem kleinen schraffierten Bereich die Parameterpaare a, b liegen, die die Ungl. (26) und (29) erfüllen, falls man b/10 als wesentlich kleiner als b ansieht.

Kriterium 3: Aus dem rechten Teil von Ungl. (24) folgt unmittelbar Ungl. (28), also dieselbe Bedingung wie bei Kriterium 2. Ungl. (29) garantiert dabei, daß K_o von Gl.(25) unter 1 bleibt. Daraus

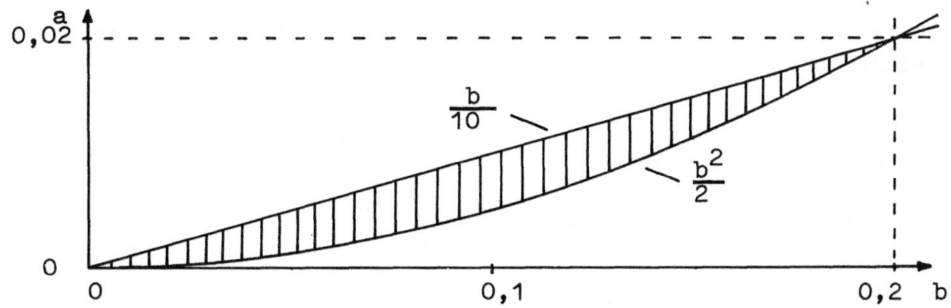

Bild 2 Bereich der Erfüllung von Ungln.(26) und (29)

ergibt sich folgende Empfehlung für die Praxis: Bei Systemen, die nach den hier untersuchten oder ähnlichen Kriterien optimiert werden sollen und für die wirksame Prüfprogramme zur Verfügung stehen, wird sich oft die Mühe der Einstellung des Systems auf das relative Extremum des gewählten Gütekriteriums, d.h. eine genaue Dosierung des Testaufwandes nicht bezahlt machen. Im Zweifelsfalle kann man z.B. das Verhältnis $\tilde{G}(V_{o,r})/\tilde{G}\ [\max(V_{U\ S}, V_{min})]$ bilden, um zu sehen, ob es sich lohnt, über die Mindestverfügbarkeit hinauszugehen. Insbesondere ist bei $V_{US} \geq V_{min}$ zu überlegen, ob überhaupt spezielle Prüfprogramme laufen sollen. Z.B. erhält man bei Kriterium 3 dazu nach Gl. (23)

$$\frac{\tilde{G}_3(V_{o,r})}{\tilde{G}_3(V_{US})} = \frac{(4a-b^2)(a+b)^2}{4a^2(1+a+b)} .$$

In vielen Fällen wird die optimale Verfügbarkeit diejenige sein, die sich ohne Test ergibt (nämlich bei $V_{min} \leq V_{US}$) oder aber die minimal geforderte (wenn $V_{min} \geq V_{US}$), die jedoch nur mittels eines gewissen laufenden Prüfaufwandes zu erreichen sein wird.

Wir wollen jetzt noch zeigen, daß man zu Kriteriun des oben untersuchten Typs auch aus etwas allgemeineren Überlegungen kommen kann: Es ist zweifellos erstrebenswert, sowohl EA als auch ED möglichst klein zu machen. Da die Benutzerkapazität durch EA und ED geschmälert wird, scheint es sinnvoll, die Summe zu minimieren. Nun ist (wieder für EB=1) nach Gln. (6) und (3a)

$$EA + ED = \frac{1-K}{V} .$$

Das führt auf Kriterium 4

$$G_4(K,V) = \frac{1-K}{V} ,$$

das sich nicht wesentlich von den oben behandelten Kriteriun 1 bis 3 unterscheidet! Interessant ist hier jedoch, daß die Lage des relativen Minimums von

$$\tilde{G}_4(V) = \frac{1}{V} - 1 + \frac{aV}{1-V} - b$$

nicht von b abhängt. Aus

$$\tilde{G}'_4(V) = -\frac{1}{V^2} + \frac{a}{(1-V)^2} \; ; \; \tilde{G}''_4(V) = \frac{2}{V^3} + \frac{2a}{(1-V)^3}$$

folgt nämlich ein relatives Minimum bei

$$V_{o,r} = \frac{1}{1+\sqrt{a}} \quad .$$

Aber auch hier zeigt ein Blick auf Ungl.(9a), daß ein relatives Minimum die Ausnahme sein wird.

Abschließend sei noch bemerkt, daß man neben den optimalen Werten von Verfügbarkeit V, Kapazität K und "Gütezahl" G_i auch die optimale mittlere Diagnosedauer ED ausrechnen kann, z.B. über Gl.(7a). ED wäre eine Kennzahl, nach der man in Zukunft vielleicht Testprogrammpakete klassifizieren könnte. Die Erstellung und die wissenschaftliche Durchdringung solcher größerer gestuft einsetzbarer Testprogramme ist das eigentliche Problem, für dessen Bearbeitung hier nur einige Motivierungshilfen gegeben werden sollten.

REALISIERUNG DES STREAMING - KONZEPTS

W.J.PAUL

I.Einleitung

Ein Computer besteht unter anderem aus Schaltwerk und Kernspeicher. Die Register des Schaltwerks arbeiten mit Flipflops,die viel schneller sind als die Ringkerne des Speichers.Durch dieses Mißverhältnis der Schaltzeiten entstehen im Schaltwerk Wartezeiten, in denen das Schaltwerk auf neue Daten aus dem Speicher wartet oder Daten nicht wegspeichern lassen kann, weil der Speicher noch mit dem vorhergehenden Lese- oder Schreibbefehl beschäftigt ist.Um dem abzuhelfen,unterteilt man den Speicher in mehrere selbständige Speicherwerke, in denen man gleichzeitig lesen oder schreiben kann (Speicherverschränkung).Bei einigen Listenoperationen ist es möglich, den Datenfluß zwischen Speicherwerken und Schaltwerk so zu organisieren, daß im Schaltwerk keine Wartezeiten entstehen.Hierbei werden Makrobefehle auf Hardwareebene realisiert.Das ist das Streamingkonzept.

Wir testen dieses Konzept an der folgenden charakteristischen Aufgabe: Gesucht ist die Realisierung eines Maschinenbefehls,der folgendes tut:

Im Speicher steht auf N aufeinanderfolgenden Speicherplätzen die Liste $A = A_1,\dots,A_N$, auf anderen N aufeinanderfolgenden Plätzen eine Liste $B = B_1,\dots,B_N$ .Für eine Liste $C = C_1,\dots,C_N$ sind weitere N aufeinanderfolgende Plätze reserviert.Wir schreiben dem Schaltwerk die Adressen von A_1, B_1, C_1 in die Indexregister I_1, I_2, I_3 sowie die Listenlänge N in ein spezielles Register.

Dann soll eine Liste $A_1 * B_1,\dots,A_N * B_N$ berechnet und auf den Plätzen $C_1,\dots,C_N$ abgespeichert werden. $*$ ist eine binäre Operation, die im Rechenwerk ausgeführt werden kann und deren Ausführungszeit von den Operanden abhängt.Im Rechenwerk dürfen hierbei vom Beginn der Berechnung von C_1 bis zum Ende der Rechnung für C_N keine Wartezeiten entstehen.

Wir werden folgendes ausrechnen:

i) Minimale Anzahl von Speicherwerken
ii) Obere und untere Schranken für den Bedarf an Pufferspeicher zwischen Speicher und Rechenwerk
iii) Aufwand und zeitlicher Gewinnfaktor

II. Modelle für Rechenwerk und Speicher

Wir betrachten das Rechenwerk als Verbraucher und Lieferanten von Daten.In den Akkumulator AC und den Hilfsakkumulator AH werden

Daten a und b geschrieben, und eine Rechnung, die AC:=AC*AH bewirkt,wird gestartet.Nach einer Anzahl von Schaltwerktakten t(a,b) steht im Akkumulator a*b.Wir bezeichnen die Mindestzeit zur Berechnung eines Elements C_i mit $tmin := \underset{a,b}{Min}\{t(a,b)\}$

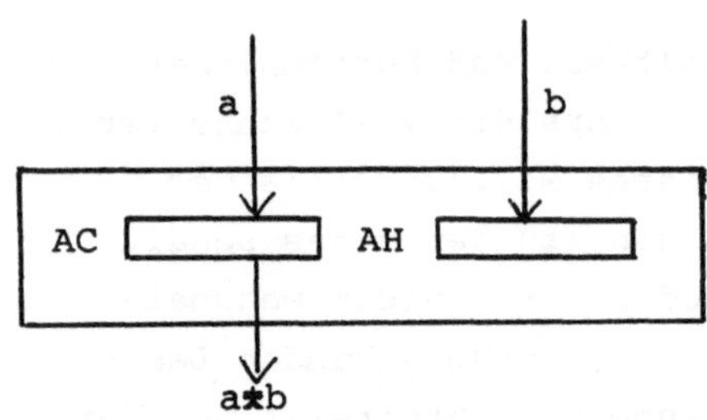

Wir bemerken: wenn wir unseren Makrobefehl für die Operation * realisieren können,dann können wir ihn auch mit einer binären Operation als Parameter realisieren,sofern nur die minimale Ausführungszeit der zulässigen Operationen $\geq$ tmin ist.

Ein Speicherwerk betrachten wir als Folge von M adressierbaren Zellen mit langer Zugriffszeit und ein schnelles Ein-Ausgaberegister E,das so schnell ist wie die Register des Schaltwerks.Ergeht an das Speicherwerk ein Lese- oder Schreibbefehl,wird ein Taktimpuls angeworfen,mit dem der Befehl ausgeführt wird.Nach einer Periode des Taktimpulses ist der Befehl ausgeführt.Diese Speicherzykluszeit ist ein Vielfaches eines Schaltwerktakts.Wir nennen dieses Vielfache F.

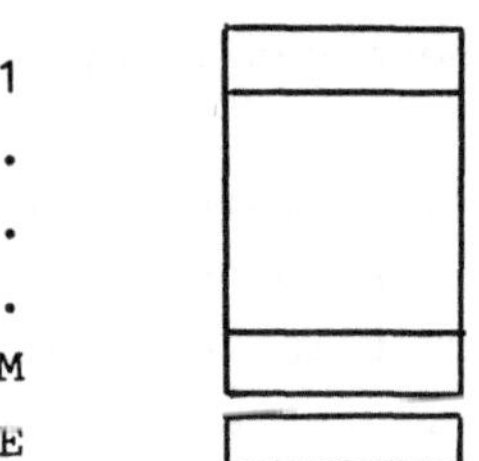

(F $\approx$ 1o bei heutigen Maschinen).Wir setzen $q := \lceil F/tmin \rceil$;das ist die maximale Anzahl von Elementen C_i,die während eines Speicherzyklus berechnet werden kann.

III. Minimaler Bedarf an Speicherwerken

Satz 1: Der minimale Bedarf an Speicherwerken zur Lösung unserer Aufgabe ist 3q.

Beweis über zwei Lemmata:

Lemma 1: Man braucht mindestens 3q Speicherwerke

Beweis: Man wähle a,b mit t(a,b)=tmin und setze A=a,a,... ,B=b,b,... mit genügend großer Listenlänge N.Alle F Takte verbraucht das Rechenwerk 2q Daten und liefert q Daten zum wegspeichern.Da ein Speicherwerk in F Takten nur ein Datum liefern oder wegspeichern kann,braucht man mindestens 3q Speicherwerke.

Lemma 2: Man kommt mit 3q Speicherwerken aus

Beweis: Man muß eine Realisierung mit 3q Speicherwerken angeben.

Wir unterteilen den Speicher in 3 Gruppen zu je q Speicherwerken. Die Adresse einer Zelle im Gesamtspeicher ist gegeben durch ein Tripel (g,s,a) mit:

g: Speichergruppe, $g \in \{1,2,3\}$

s: Speicherwerk in der Speichergruppe, $s \in [1:q]$

a: Adresse der Zelle im Speicherwerk, $a \in [1:M]$

Wir erklären die Nachfolgeradresse

$$N(g,s,a) = \begin{cases} (g,s+1,a) & \text{für } s \neq q \\ (g,1,a+1) & \text{für } s=q \end{cases}$$

Durch diese Anordnung der Adressen kann stets auf q aufeinanderfolgende Zellen gleichzeitig zugegriffen werden.

Beispiel einer Liste, die in einer Speichergruppe abgespeichert ist:

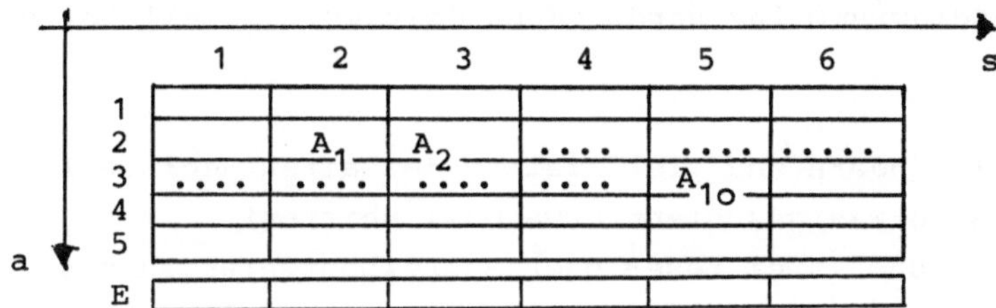

M=5, q=6, N=1o

Bezeichnung: Ein Indexregister I_j enthalte die Adresse (g,s,a). (g,s) bezeichnet ein Speicherwerk, a eine Adresse darin. Wir bezeichnen mit $E(I_j)$ das E-Register des Speicherwerks (g,s).

Folgende Indexregisterbefehle werden benutzt:

$I_j:=N(I_j)$:Nachfolgeradresse ins Indexregister schreiben

Lesen(I_j) :$E(I_j)$:=Inhalt der Speicherzelle a im Speicherwerk (g,s)

Schreiben(I_j):Inhalt der Zelle a im Speicherwerk (g,s):=$E(I_j)$

Die beiden letzten Befehle sind erst F Takte, nachdem sie gegeben wurden, ausgeführt.

In einer Speichergruppe stehe nun Liste A. Die Daten aus den E-Registern dieser Speichergruppe werden von AC werbraucht. In einer anderen Speichergruppe steht Liste B. Die E-Register dieser Gruppe geben ihre Daten an AH weiter. Liste C wird in der dritten Gruppe abgespeichert werden. In die E-Register dieser Gruppe werden die berechneten Daten C_i aus AC geschrieben.

Die Listen sind also auf die drei Speichergruppen verteilt. Um das zu erreichen, muß evtl. Liste A oder B umgespeichert werden. Man vermeidet aber hierdurch,daß an ein Speicherwerk gleichzeitig zwei Lese- oder Schreibbefehle gegeben werden,die verschiedene Listen betreffen.

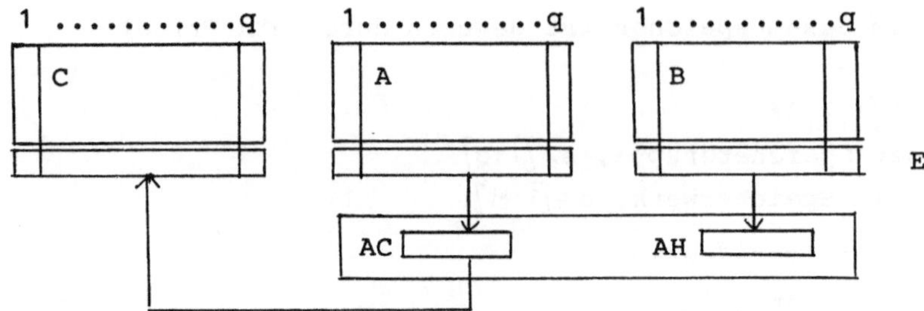

Wir realisieren unseren Makrobefehl nach dem Flußdiagramm auf der nächsten Seite.Was in einem stark eingerahmten Kästchen steht,soll während eines Schaltwerktakts ausgeführt werden.Es ist hier zu beachten, daß es sich um ein Flußdiagramm für Hardware handelt,wo speziell folgendes möglich ist:

i) Parallelarbeit
ii) einen Registerinhalt ändern und gleichzeitig den alten Registerinhalt weitergeben (so etwas geschieht etwa beim shiften)

Man wird erkennen: zwischen zwei Lese- oder Schreibbefehlen an das gleiche Speicherwerk werden stets q Daten C_i berechnet.Das dauert $\geqslant$ q.tmin $\geqslant$F Takte.Ein Speicherwerk ist also stets mit dem vorigen Befehl fertig,wenn ein neuer Befehl an es gegeben wird.Damit ist Satz 1 bewiesen.

Die Kosten zur Realisierung des Flußdiagramms sind etwa die des Festpunktmultiplizierwerks aus [I] ,Kapitel 4.3. Hinzu kommen die Kosten für das Aufspalten des Speichers in 3q kleine Speicherwerke.

Es wurden keine zusätzlichen Register zum Zwischenspeichern von Daten benötigt.

IV. Bedarf an Pufferspeicher

Hat man statt den vorne beschriebenen Speicherwerken,deren Speicherzyklus nach Belieben gestartet werden kann,Speicherwerke mit stehendem Speichertakt,wo ein Befehlszyklus nur alle F Takte beginnen kann - selbst wenn das Speicherwerk gerade nicht arbeitet -,dann läßt sich folgendes zeigen:

Satz 1: Die minimale Anzahl von Speicherwerken zur Lösung unserer Aufgabe ist 3q

Um mit 3q von diesen Speicherwerken unseren Makrobefehl zu realisieren, braucht man allerdings schnelle Register zum Zwischenspeichern von

Flußdiagramm:

b ist ein Zähler

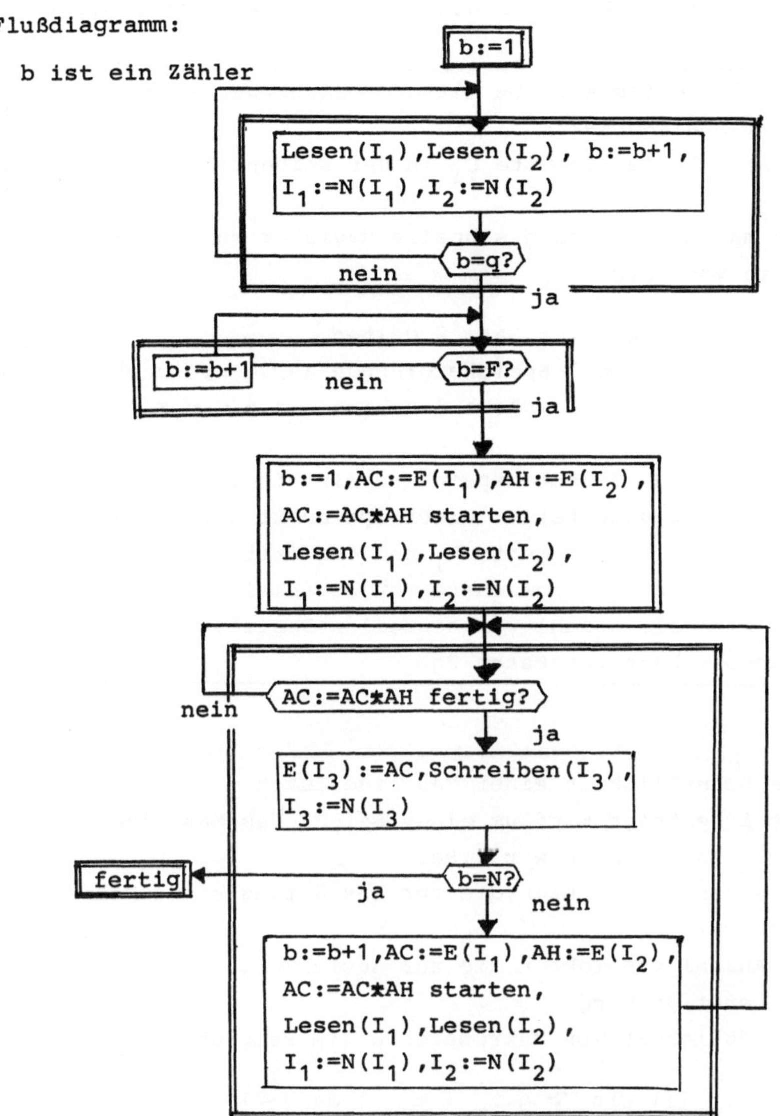

Daten(schnell ist wieder zu verstehen als:so schnell wie die Register des Schaltwerks).

Satz 2: i)man löst die obige Aufgabe mit 3q Speicherwerken mit stehendem Speichertakt

ii)man berechnet die Elemente C_i in der Reihenfolge ihrer Indizes

dann braucht man mindestens q schnelle Register zum Zwischenspeichern von Daten

Satz 3: i)die Voraussetzungen von Satz 2 gelten

ii)der Speicher ist in 3 Speichergruppen zu 3q Speicherwerken aufgeteilt,auf welche die Listen A,B,C verteilt sind

iii) die Register zum Zwischenspeichern sind in drei kleine Pufferspeicher unterteilt: einer speichert nur Elemente A_i,ein zweiter nur Elemente B_i und der dritte nur Elemente C_i(das ist am einfachsten zu organisieren)

dann ist die minimale Anzahl von schnellen Registern zum Zwischenspeichern von Daten 2q

V.Zeitgewinn

Wir erklären die Schnelligkeit einer Maschine durch die Anzahl von Takten,die im Mittel benötigt wird,um einen Befehl des Maschinencodes abzuarbeiten.Diese Anzahl nennen wir t.Sei

t_m die mittlere Anzahl von Takten,die zur Ausführung eines Makrobefehls benötigt wird

t_n die mittlere Anzahl von Takten,die zur Ausführung eines nicht-Makrobefehls benötigt wird

g die relative Häufigkeit von Makrobefehlen im Programm

so ergibt sich:

$$t= g.t_m +(1-g)t_n \approx g.t_m + t_n \quad \text{da } g \ll 1$$

Wir berechnen t für eine Maschine E mit nur einem Speicherwerk und für eine Maschine S' mit verschränktem Speicher,die diesen aber nur bei der Ausführung von Makrobefehlen der Art C:=A*B ausnutzt.

Wir machen dazu folgende Hypothesen:

i) t_n=2F für E und S'

ii) die Rechnung für AC:=AC*AH dauert stets F Takte

Bemerkungen:

ad i) um ein Befehlswort abzuarbeiten,muß i.A. zwei mal auf den Speicher zugegriffen werden: einmal,um das Befehlswort ins Befehlsregister zu holen;dann,um ein Datum aus dem Speicher zu holen oder hineinzuschreiben,das durch das Befehlswort bezeichnet wird.Das dauert 2F Takte.Zwischendurch können anfallende Rechnungen stattfinden.

ad ii) Unter * werden hauptsächlich arithmetische Operationen vorkommen.Die Ausführung arithmetischer Operationen dauert bei modernen Maschinen etwa so lang wie ein Speicherzyklus.

Berechnung von t_m für S':

Es müssen I_1, I_2, I_3,N,* vorbesetzt werden. Dazu sind 5 Befehle notwendig	1oF Takte
Berechnung von Liste C	N.F Takte
Vorher vergehen F Takte,bis A_1 und B_1 verfügbar sind.Nachher muß man F Takte warten, bis C_N weggespeichert ist.	2F Takte
Die Wahrscheinlichkeit,daß Liste A und B in der gleichen Speichergruppe stehen,ist 1/3.Also muß bei jedem dritten Makrobefehl zusätzlich eine Liste umgespeichert werden.Das kann man auf Hardwareebene wieder als Makrobefehl realisieren.Jedes Datum,das umgespeichert wird,bleibt nur einen Takt in AC (tmin=1,q=F).	1/3(N+2F) Takte

Insgesamt ergibt sich bei mittlerer Listenlänge $\overline{N}$:

$$t_{mS'} = 12{,}7F + \overline{N}(F+1/3)$$

Berechnung von t_m für E:

Simuliert man C:=A*B auf einer Einadreßmaschine,wird im Mittel $\overline{N}$ mal folgende Befehlsfolge durchlaufen:

1) Befehl AC:=A_i lesen und ausführen	2F Takte
2) Befehl AC:=AC*B_i lesen und ausführen	2F Takte
3) Befehl AC wegspeichern lesen und ausführen	2F Takte
4) Befehl,abzufragen,ob man fertig ist,lesen	F Takte
5) Abfragen,ob man fertig ist.Das kann man mit Indexregistern machen.Kein Speicherzugriff nötig	-
6) drei Befehle lesen,Adressen zu erhöhen,um richtig auf die nächsten Listenelemente zuzugreifen bzw. richrig abzuspeichern	3F Takte
7) die drei Adressen erhöhen;mir Indexregistern	-
8) Befehl lesen,den in 5) abgefragten Zähler zu andern	F Takte
9) Zähler ändern (Indexregister)	-

Insgesamt: $t_{mE} = 11F\overline{N}$

Man erhält einen Gewinnfaktor

$$G_{S'/E}=\frac{t_E}{t_{S'}} = \frac{11gF\overline{N} + 2F}{g((F+1/3)\overline{N} + 12{,}7F) + 2F}$$

Sei V eine schnellere Maschine als E mit verschränktem Speicher,so daß $t_{nV} = a.t_{nE} = 2aF$ mit $a<1$.Die Größe von a hängt davon ab,wie gut der verschränkte Speicher ausgenutzt ist.Sei weiter S eine Maschine,bei der das Streamingkonzept realisiert ist und die außerdem mit ihrem verschränkten Speicher den gleichen Zeitgewinn erzielt wie V,d.h. $t_{nS}=2aF$.

Dann erhält man $t_V = a.t_E$

$$t_{mS} = g((F+1/3)N + 2{,}7F + 1oaF) + 2aF$$

$$\boxed{G_{S/V}= \frac{11gFN + 2F}{g((F+1/3)N/a + 2{,}7F/a + 1oF) + 2F}}$$

Beispiel: a=3/4 , g=1/2o, N=1o, F=1o ; dann ist $G_{S/V}=2{,}2$;$G_{S'/E}=2{,}4$

Beim Streaming wurde der verschränkte Speicher dazu benutzt,Makrobefehle auf Hardwareebene so zu realisieren,daß im Rechenwerk keine Wartezeiten auftraten.Als Alternative A böte sich an,die Makrobefehle zwar auf Hardwareebene zu verdrahten,womit man den Zeitverlust bei der Schleifenverwaltung umgeht, und die Forderung,daß keine Wartezeiten entstehen, fallenzulassen.Zur Berechnung eines Elements C_i wären 3 Speicherzugriffe nötig,weitere F Takte dauert die eigentliche Rechnung AC:=AC*AH.Man kommt also auf $t_{mA}= 4NF + 1oF$,denn man hat ja noch $I_1,\dots,N$ vorzubesetzen.

Es ist $$G_{A/E}= \frac{11gFN + 2F}{g(4NF + 1oF) + 2F}$$

Beispiel mit den obigen Zahlenwerten: $G_{A/E}= 1{,}5$

Die Organisation hiervon kostet etwa die Hälfte des vorne zitierten Festpunktmultiplizierwerks.Außerdem muß man den Speicher nicht in so viele Speicherwerke aufteilen,wie das beim Streaming nötig ist.

VI.Literatur

[I] G.Hotz:
Informatik:Rechenanlagen
Teubner Studienbücher Informatik

[II] W.J.Paul:
Verschiedene Realisierungen des Streamingkonzepts und damit verbundene Optimierungsfragen; Diplomarbeit am Institut für Informatik der Universität des Saarlandes

DURCHSATZSTEIGERUNG IN RECHENANLAGEN BEI VERWENDUNG VON KLEINEN PUFFERSPEICHERN

A. BÄCHLE

Zusammenfassung

Bei Verwendung schneller Pufferspeicher kann man die Zeiten für das Bereitstellen von Befehlen und Operanden für die Zentraleinheit einer Rechenanlage verkürzen. Anstelle eines gemeinsamen Pufferspeichers für Befehle und Operanden werden hier getrennte Pufferspeicher untersucht. Als weitere beschleunigende Maßnahme wird ein Befehls-Lookahead betrachtet.

Die Eigenschaften der Pufferspeicher und des Befehls-Lookahead wird durch Simulation mit dynamischen Befehlsfolgen ermittelt. Mit Hilfe eines Modells einer Zentraleinheit wird dann der Durchsatz bestimmt, wenn man diese Puffer verwendet. Neben der Puffergröße werden auch die Zugriffszeit des Puffers und die Befehlsausführungszeit in der Zentraleinheit berücksichtigt.

1. Einleitung

Bei schnellen Rechenanlagen besteht ein deutlicher Unterschied zwischen der Zeit für die Befehlsausführung und der Zugriffszeit zum Zentralspeicher für das Holen der Befehle und Operanden. Während man z. B. eine Festkomma-Addition in 50 bis 100 ns ausführen kann, liegen die Zugriffszeiten vom zentralen Prozessor auf einen Zentralspeicher mit z. B. 512 k Worten im Bereich von 400 ns bis 1000 ns. Dies bedeutet, daß die Befehlsausführungszeit ohne beschleunigende Maßnahmen im wesentlichen von der Speicherzugriffszeit bestimmt wird.

Es ist bekannt, daß innerhalb bestimmter Zeiten Zugriffe zu einzelnen Bereichen des Zentralspeichers (ZS) mit sehr unterschiedlichen Häufigkeiten auftreten. Wenn man häufig benützte Bereiche des Zentralspeichers in einem Zwischenspeicher mit kurzer Zugriffszeit (z. B. 50 bis 200 ns) puffert, dann kann man einen großen Teil der Speicherzugriffe aus diesem Pufferspeicher in kurzer Zeit bedienen. Zugriffe zum langsamen Zentralspeicher treten dann nur noch selten auf. Die Wahrscheinlichkeit, daß bei einem Zugriff zum Puffer die gewünschte Größe dort nicht gefunden wird, wird im folgenden mit Fehlrate h bezeichnet. In einigen Veröffentlichungen (/1/ bis /3/) wird der Einfluß der Puffergröße, seine Verwaltungsart und die Adressenstatistik der Programme auf die Fehlrate des Puffers untersucht.

Während bei diesen Untersuchungen Pufferspeicher betrachtet wurden, die sowohl Befehle als auch Operanden enthalten, werden hier getrennte Pufferspeicher für Befehle und Operanden untersucht. Zusätzlich zu diesen Puffern wird noch ein Befehls-Lookahead betrachtet, der während der Verarbeitung eines Befehlsworts das im Speicher folgende Befehlswort bereitstellt.

Die Wirkungsweise der Pufferspeicher und des Befehls-Lookahead werden in Abschnitt 2 beschrieben. In Abschnitt 3 werden die Ergebnisse der Simulation und das Verhalten der Puffer diskutiert. In Abschnitt 4 wird dann für ein einfaches Modell einer Zentraleinheit der Durchsatz berechnet, wenn man einen Befehlspuffer, einen Operandenpuffer und einen Befehls-Lookahead verwendet. Die Ergebnisse werden in Abschnitt 5 mit den Durchsatzwerten verglichen, die man bei einem allgemeinen Pufferspeicher für Befehle und Operanden erhält.

2. Beschreibung der untersuchten Pufferspeicher

Die Aufgabe der Pufferspeicher ist es, die im dynamischen Befehlsablauf bereits benutzten Befehle und Operanden aufzubewahren. Sie werden so verwaltet, daß sie bevorzugt häufig benutzte Größen enthalten. Wenn bei einem Zugriff die gewünschte Größe nicht im Puffer ist, muß sie aus dem Zentralspeicher (ZS) geholt werden. Im allgemeinen wird man nicht nur die gewünschte Größe auslesen, sondern einen Block mit mehreren aufeinander folgenden Befehlen bzw. Operanden. Ein solcher Block wird im folgenden Nachladeeinheit (NE) genannt.

Für die untersuchten Puffer werden unterschiedliche Größen für die Nachladeeinheiten gewählt. Beim Befehlspuffer (BP) enthält eine NE zwei Befehle, sie ist identisch mit einem Speicherwort. Beim Operandenpuffer (OP) enthält die Nachladeeinheit einen Operanden. In den OP werden Konstante, einfache Variable und indizierte Variable eingelagert. Beim allgemeinen Puffer (AP) wird eine NE mit 8 Befehlen bzw. 4 Operanden gewählt.

Wenn beim Holen einer NE aus dem Zentralspeicher der Puffer bereits gefüllt ist, dann muß eine andere NE aus dem Puffer verdrängt werden. Diese NE kann nach verschiedenen Gesichtspunkten ausgewählt werden /1/. Bei den hier untersuchten Puffern wird immer die am längsten nicht benutzte NE verdrängt. Man bezeichnet dieses Prinzip auch als strenge Alterung.

Für die Ablage einer NE im Pufferspeicher kann man Einschränkungen machen, z. B. kann man Nachladeeinheiten aus einem bestimmten ZS-Bereich nur in einem bestimmten Bereich des Puffers ablegen. Dadurch wird die Adressierung und das Absuchen der Puffer vereinfacht. In solchen Fällen bezieht sich der Verdrängungsmechanismus nur auf NE'n im zugelassenen Pufferbereich. Hier dagegen werden solche Einschränkungen nicht gemacht, es wird immer die am längsten nicht benutzte NE im gesamten Pufferspeicher verdrängt.

Bei Speicherzugriffen muß man zwischen Abspeichern und Holen von Operanden unterscheiden. Bei den Simulationen werden nur Lesezugriffe berücksichtigt, da sich bei ihnen die Fehlrate der Puffer in der Befehlsdauer voll auswirkt. Schreibzugriffe gehen immer zum ZS, da er die aktuellen Daten enthalten muß. Falls der zu schreibende Operand auch im Puffer vorhanden ist, wird der Schreibbefehl auch dort ausgeführt. Diese Vorgänge können jedoch parallel zur Ausführung der folgenden Befehle ablaufen. Bei anderen Messungen von Pufferspeichern, bei denen auch Schreibzugriffe den Puffer laden, ergaben sich nur geringfügige Unterschiede bei der Fehlrate.

Zusammen mit dem Befehlspuffer kann noch ein Befehls-Lookahead arbeiten, der während der Bearbeitung eines Befehls das statisch folgende Befehlswort bereitstellt. Dadurch können alle Befehle, mit Ausnahme von Sprungzielen, rechtzeitig bereitgestellt werden. Die Zugriffszeit zum Puffer wirkt sich also nur dann aus, wenn der letzte Befehl ein ausgeführter Sprungbefehl war.

3. Diskussion der Meßergebnisse

Die Fehlrate der Pufferspeicher wurde durch Simulation mit dynamischen Befehlsfolgen gemessen, die während eines Programmlaufs in der Rechenanlage TR 4 auf Magnetbänder aufgezeichnet wurden. Als Datenmaterial wurden 6 Algol-Programme, 5 Fortranprogramme, 3 Algol-Übersetzerläufe und 3 Fortran-Übersetzerläufe verwendet. Aus diesen Programmläufen wurden 60 Stichproben mit insgesamt 2 Millionen Befehlen ausgewertet.

In den Diagrammen 1 und 2 ist die Fehlrate der Pufferspeicher über der Puffergröße aufgetragen. Die Puffergröße ist in Ganzworten (Speicherworten) angegeben, wobei ein Ganzwort zwei Befehle oder einen Operanden enthalten kann. Die Fehlrate ist das Verhältnis der nicht erfüllbaren Zugriffswünsche bezogen auf alle Zugriffswünsche zu dem betrachteten Puffer.

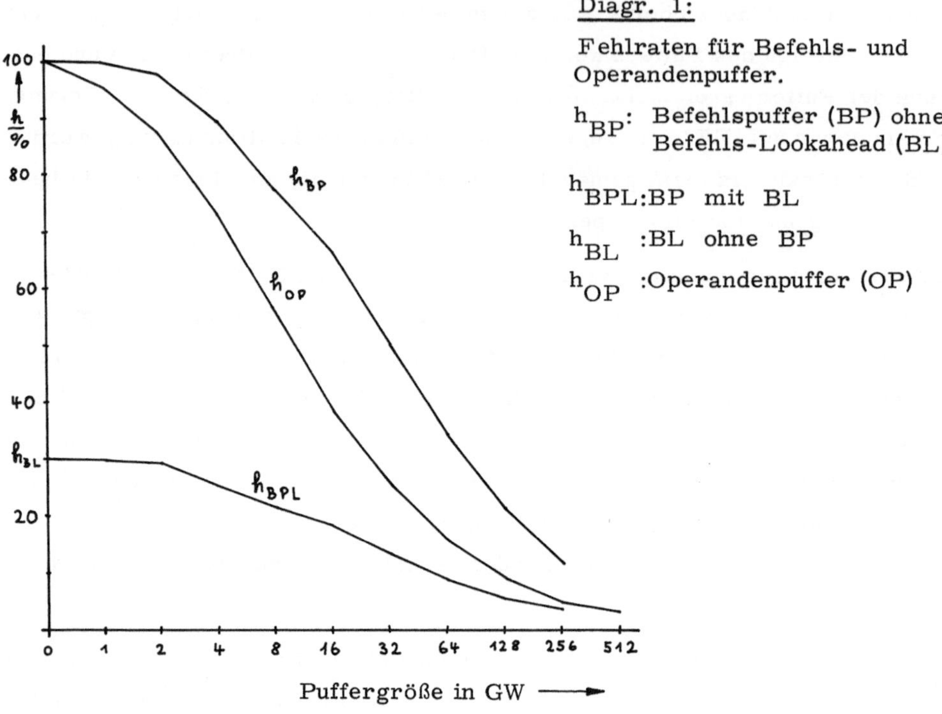

Diagr. 1:

Fehlraten für Befehls- und Operandenpuffer.

h_{BP}: Befehlspuffer (BP) ohne Befehls-Lookahead (BL)

h_{BPL}:BP mit BL

h_{BL} :BL ohne BP

h_{OP} :Operandenpuffer (OP)

Beim Befehlspuffer ohne Befehls-Lookahead (Diagr. 1) fällt auf, daß die Fehlrate mit der Puffergröße zunächst nur sehr langsam abnimmt. Bei 16 Ganzworten (32 Befehlen) liegt sie noch über 60 % . Bei noch größeren Puffern nimmt sie dann stärker ab. Man kann daraus schließen, daß ein kleiner Befehlspuffer mit weniger als 64 Befehlen (32 GW) nur eine geringfügige Leistungssteigerung ermöglichen wird. Ein wesentlich günstigeres Verhalten zeigt ein Befehlspuffer mit Befehls-Lookahead. Die Fehlrate h_{BL} des Befehls-Lookahead allein kann man aus Diagr. 1 für die Puffergröße 0 entnehmen; sie beträgt 31 % . Dies bedeutet, daß der Befehls-Lookahead allein fast 70 % aller Befehlszugriffe rechtzeitig bereitstellen kann. Um die Fehlrate des BL allein zu erreichen, müßte ein BP ohne BL mehr als 64 Ganzworte besitzen.

Neben der Fehlrate des BP ist in Diagr. 1 auch die Fehlrate eines Operandenpuffers mit einer Nachladeeinheit von 1 GW eingetragen.

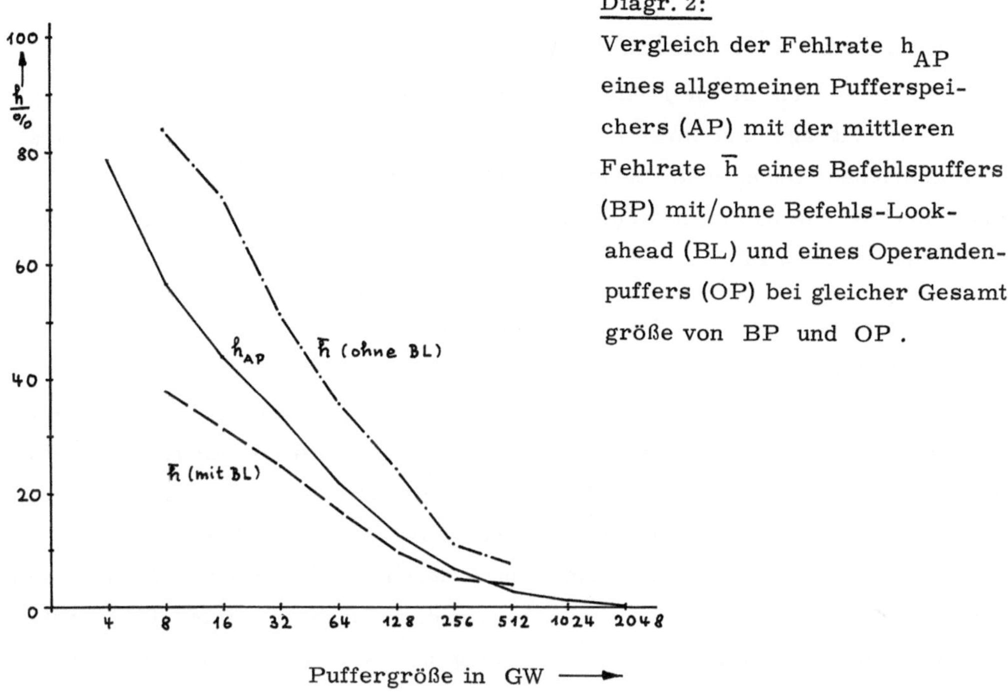

Diagr. 2:
Vergleich der Fehlrate h_{AP} eines allgemeinen Pufferspeichers (AP) mit der mittleren Fehlrate $\overline{h}$ eines Befehlspuffers (BP) mit/ohne Befehls-Lookahead (BL) und eines Operandenpuffers (OP) bei gleicher Gesamtgröße von BP und OP.

In Diagr. 2 ist die Fehlrate des allgemeinen Pufferspeichers mit einer Nachladeeinheit von 8 Befehlen bzw. 4 Operanden aufgetragen. Als Vergleich wird die mittlere Fehlrate $\overline{h}$ eines BP und eines OP gleicher Gesamtgröße angegeben, wobei zusätzlich noch ein Befehls-Lookahead wahlweise unterstellt ist. Die Puffergröße l_{BP} des BP und l_{OP} des OP werden so gewählt, daß die mittlere Fehlrate $\overline{h} = w_B^* \cdot h_{BP}(l_{BP}) + w_O^* \; h_{OP}(l_{OP})$ bei $l_{BP} + l_{OP}$ = konst. ein Minimum wird. Dabei sind w_B^* und w_O^* die auf die Gesamtzahl der Zugriffe bezogenen Anteile der Befehls- und Operandenzugriffe. Die Fehlrate von BP und OP ohne BL ist größer als die des AP. Dies wird wahrscheinlich durch die feste Aufteilung in einen Befehls- und einen Operandenbereich verursacht, die sich gegenseitig nicht mit Speicherplätzen aushelfen können. Beim AP dagegen wird nicht zwischen Befehlen und Operanden unterschieden. Ein weiterer Grund ist die grössere Nachladeeinheit beim AP, durch die ähnlich wie bei einem BL Befehle und Operanden vorausschauend in den Puffer gebracht werden. Verwendet man dagegen neben dem BP und dem OP noch einen BL, dann erhält man eine kleinere Fehlrate als beim AP. Dies wird durch die wesentlich kleinere Fehlrate des BP mit BL verursacht (Vgl Diagr. 1).

4. Berechnung des Durchsatzes einer Zentraleinheit mit Pufferspeichern

Aus den Meßwerten für die Fehlrate der Pufferspeicher kann man noch keine unmittelbare Aussage über ihren Einfluß auf den Befehlsdurchsatz in einer Zentraleinheit machen. Deshalb soll jetzt ein einfaches Modell für die Zentraleinheit eines Rechners beschrieben werden, mit dem eine Abschätzung der mittleren Befehlsdauer möglich ist.

4.1 Beschreibung des Modells einer Zentraleinheit

Ein Befehl wird in vier Schritten verarbeitet: Befehl Holen, Adreßrechnung, Operand Holen und Ausführung bzw. Rechnen. Alle 4 Schritte sollen sequentiell ablaufen, wobei folgende Annahmen gemacht werden: Es wird immer ein Befehlswort mit zwei Befehlen aus dem Puffer bzw. dem ZS ausgelesen. Dadurch entfällt bei jedem zweiten Befehl die "Befehls-Holphase" Eine Ausnahme bilden jedoch die ausgeführten Sprungbefehle, nach denen immer ein Befehlswort geholt werden muß. Die "Adreßrechnungs"-Phase und die "Operand-Hole"-Phase entfallen bei Befehlen, die keine Adreßrechnung bzw. keinen Operand benötigen.

Bei den folgenden Berechnungen wird die Zugriffszeit T zum ZS als Zeiteinheit gewählt. In dieser Zeit sollen auch die Verzögerungszeiten durch die Übertragungsleitungen und durch das Speicher-Vorrangwerk enthalten sein. Für das Ausführen eines Befehls wird als Näherung eine für alle Befehle konstante Zeit $\tau_R = t_R/T$ angenommen. Ebensolange soll auch die Zeit für eine Adreßrechnung sein. Schreibzugriffe sollen eine halbe Speicherzugriffszeit erfordern, es ist also $\tau_S = t_S/T = 0,5$.

Für die Berechnungen werden die Häufigkeiten für Befehl Holen, Operand Holen, Adreß-Rechnung und für Schreibbefehle benötigt, die für das oben angegebene Datenmaterial gemessen wurden. Sie werden auf die Zahl der ausgewerteten Befehle bezogen und sind in folgender Tabelle zusammengestellt:

Häufigkeit für	Abkürzung	Meßwert in %
Befehlswort Holen	w_B	61
Operand Holen	w_O	30
Operand Schreiben	w_S	13
Adreßrechnung	w_A	24

Betrachtet man eine Zentraleinheit ohne Pufferspeicher, dann ist die mittlere Bearbeitungsdauer eines Befehls gleich der Summe der Zeiten für Befehl Holen, Adreßrechnung, Operand Holen und Schreiben und der Ausführungszeit. Die ersten vier Zeitanteile müssen natürlich mit der Häufigkeit für das jeweilige Ereignis multipliziert werden, da sich z. B. bei einem Befehl, der keine Adreßrechnung benötigt, die Bearbeitungsdauer um den Zeitanteil τ_R für Adreßrechnung verkürzt Man erhält damit für die mittlere Bearbeitungsdauer eines Befehls:

$$\tau_{Bef0} = w_B \cdot 1 + w_O \cdot 1 + w_A \cdot \tau_R + w_S \cdot 0,5 + \tau_R$$

Die Anzahl der je Speicherzugriffszeit T von einer Zentraleinheit ausgeführten Befehle wird mit Befehlsdurchsatz D bezeichnet. Er ist der Reziprokwert der mittleren Bearbeitungsdauer τ_{Bef} $D = 1/\tau_{Bef}$. Der Durchsatz einer ZE mit einem Pufferspeicher wird auf den Durchsatzwert $D_0 = 1/\tau_{Bef0}$ bezogen.

4.2 Befehlsausführungszeit bei Verwendung von Pufferspeichern

Bei Verwendung von Pufferspeichern werden die Zeitanteile für Befehl Holen und Operand Holen verkürzt. Dabei wird angenommen, daß während des assoziativen Suchens einer Größe im Puffer ein eventuell möglicher Zugriff zum Zentralspeicher schon vorbereitet wird. Außerdem soll die Zeit für "Befehl Holen" null sein, wenn das Befehlswort vom BL bereitgestellt werden kann. Bezeichnet man mit τ_{BP} die Zugriffszeit zum BP, dann benötigt man bei dem vom BL nicht bereitstellbaren Anteil h_{BL} der Zugriffe die Zeit τ_{BP}, und bei dem aus dem Puffer nicht erfüllbaren Anteil h_{BPL} der Zugriffe zusätzlich noch die Zeit $(1-\tau_{BP})$. Damit erhält man als mittlere Zeit für das Bereitstellen eines Befehlswortes $w_B [h_{BL} \cdot \tau_{BP} + h_{BPL}(1-\tau_{BP})]$. Verwendet man einen BP ohne BL, dann gehen alle Befehlszugriffe direkt zum BP, d. h. $h_{BL} = 1$. Anstelle der Fehlrate h_{BPL} des BP mit BL muß jetzt natürlich mit der Fehlrate h_{BP} des BP ohne BL gerechnet werden (vgl. Diagr. 1). Die Zeit für das Bereitstellen eines Befehlsworts ist dann $w_B[\tau_{BP} + h_{BP}(1 - \tau_{BP})]$. In entsprechender Weise erhält man bei einem Operandenpuffer mit der Fehlrate h_{OP} und einer Zugriffszeit τ_{OP} als mittlere Zeit für das Holen eines Operanden $w_O[\tau_{OP}+h_{OP}(1-\tau_{OP})]$. Die mittlere Bearbeitungsdauer eines Befehls wird damit:

$$\tau_{Bef} = w_B [h_{BL} \cdot \tau_{BP} + h_{BPL}(1 - \tau_{BP})] + w_O[\tau_{OP} + h_{OP}(1-\tau_{OP})] + w_S \cdot 0,5 + (1 + w_A)\, \tau_R$$

In dieser Gleichung sind auch die Fälle enthalten, daß kein BP oder kein OP vorhanden ist. Es ist dann $h_{BPL} = h_{BL}$ bzw. $h_{BP} = 1$ oder $h_{OP} = 1$.

Anstelle von getrennten Pufferspeichern kann man auch einen allgemeinen Puffer für Befehle und Operanden mit einer Zugriffszeit τ_{AP} und einer Fehlrate h_{AP} betrachten. Verwendet man außerdem noch einen Befehls-Lookahead mit einer Fehlrate h_{BL}, dann ist die mittlere Bearbeitungsdauer eines Befehls:

$$\tau_{Bef} = (w_B \cdot h_{BL} + w_O)[\tau_{AP} + h_{AP} (1 - \tau_{AP})] + w_S \cdot 0,5 + (1 + w_A) \tau_R$$

Da ein AP mit einem BL zusammen nicht durch Simulation untersucht wurde, wird hier als Näherung angenommen, daß die Fehlraten h_{BL} des BL und h_{AP} des AP unabhängig sind. Wie die Meßergebnisse für den BP (Diagr. 1) zeigen, gilt dort in guter Näherung:

$$h_{BPL} \approx h_{BL} \cdot h_{BP}$$

5. Einige Beispiele für die Durchsatzsteigerung

An einigen Beispielen wird die Wirksamkeit der Pufferspeicher diskutiert. Als Maß für die Leistungszunahme wird die Durchsatzsteigerung gewählt, die man gegenüber einer Zentraleinheit (ZE) ohne Pufferspeicher aber sonst gleichen Eigenschaften erhält. Der Durchsatz der ZE ist gleich der Zahl der im Mittel pro Zugriffszeit T bearbeiteten Befehle.

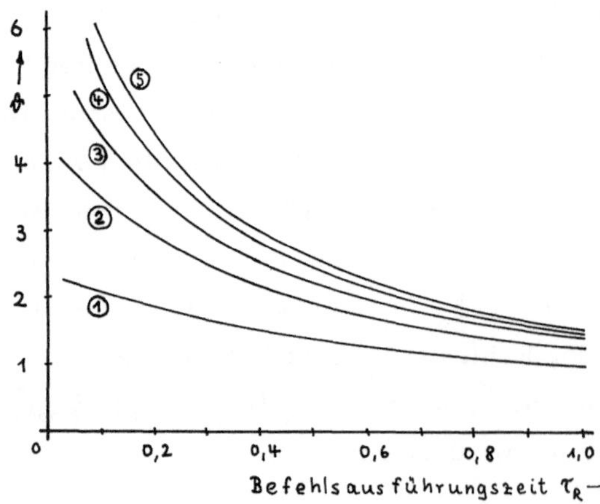

Diagr. 3:
Durchsatzerhöhung ϑ in Abhängigkeit von der Befehlsausführungszeit τ_R bei einer Zentraleinheit mit einem allgemeinen Pufferspeicher (AP) mit Größe l_{AP} und Zugriffszeit τ_{AP}.

	l_{AP}	τ_{AP}
①	0	-
②	2048	0,5
③	128	0,25
④	2048	0,25
⑤	128	0,10

Diagr. 3 zeigt den Einfluß der Ausführungszeit τ_R auf den Durchsatz. Der Durchsatz ist hier bezogen auf eine Vergleichsmaschine ohne Puffer mit $\tau_R = 1$. Zur

Beschleunigung der ZE wird ein allgemeiner Puffer betrachtet, dessen Größe l_{AP} und Zugriffszeit τ_{AP} Parameter der Kurvenschar sind. Man kann aus dem Diagramm folgendes entnehmen:

a) Bei einer ZE ohne AP (Kurve 1) bringt auch eine starke Verkürzung von τ_R eine vergleichsweise geringe Durchsatzsteigerung, da die Zeiten für das Holen von Befehlen und Operanden nicht beeinflußt werden.

b) Bei einer großen Ausführungszeit τ_R wirkt sich die Fehlrate der Puffer auf den Durchsatz nur wenig aus, weil das Ausführen der Befehle den Engpaß bildet.

c) Einen starken Einfluß auf den Durchsatz hat die Zugriffszeit τ_{AP} des Pufferspeichers.

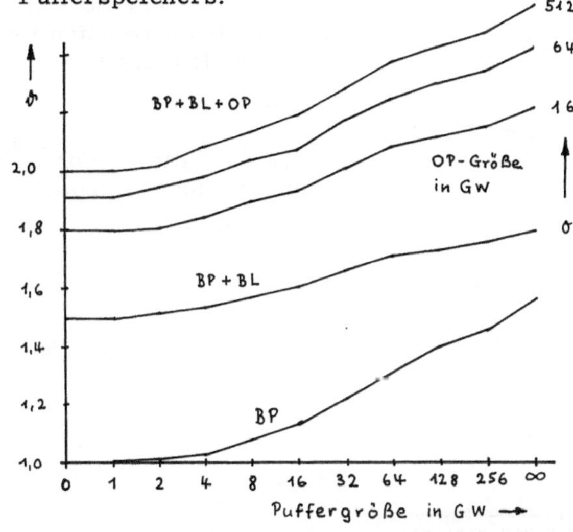

Diagr. 4:

Durchsatzerhöhung ϑ bei einem Befehlspuffer (BP), Befehls-Lookahead (BL) und Operandenpuffer (OP). Zugriffszeit zu den Puffern:

$\tau_{BP} = \tau_{OP} = 0.25$

Befehlsausführungszeit:

$\tau_R = 0.25$

Die Durchsatzsteigerung durch einen Befehlspuffer ist in Diagr. 4 aufgetragen. Es werden 3 Fälle betrachtet, der BP allein, der BP mit BL und der BP mit BL und einem OP. Beim Modell mit Puffer und auch beim Vergleichsmodell ohne Puffer ist die Ausführungszeit τ_R=0,25. Man sieht aus Diagr. 4, daß der BP allein nur eine geringe Durchsatzsteigerung ermöglicht. Eine wesentliche Verbesserung erhält man durch einen Befehls-Lookahead. Die Durchsatzsteigerung des BL ohne BP kann man aus Diagr. 4 für die Puffergröße 0 entnehmen. Der Durchsatz nimmt bei einem BP mit BL mit der Puffergröße langsamer zu, da nur bei Sprungbefehlen zum BP zugegriffen wird. Eine weitere Erhöhung des Durchsatzes ist durch einen zusätzlichen Operandenpuffer möglich.

In Diagr. 5 wird der Durchsatz des allgemeinen Puffers mit dem der getrennten Puffer bei gleicher Gesamtgröße verglichen. Die Größen von BP und OP werden so gewählt, daß die mittlere Fehlrate pro Zugriff ein Minimum wird (vgl. Diagr. 2). Obwohl sich die Fehlraten von AP und BP + BL + OP (Diagr. 2) mit zunehmender Puffergröße annähern, erhält man beim Durchsatz einen deutlichen Unterschied. Der Grund dafür ist, daß für das Auslesen aus dem AP immer die Zeit τ_{AP} benötigt wird, während der BL bei Nicht-Sprungbefehlen das folgende Befehlswort ohne Zeitbedarf bereitstellt. Die mit getrennten Puffern möglichen Durchsatzwerte erreichen fast die Werte eines AP mit BL.

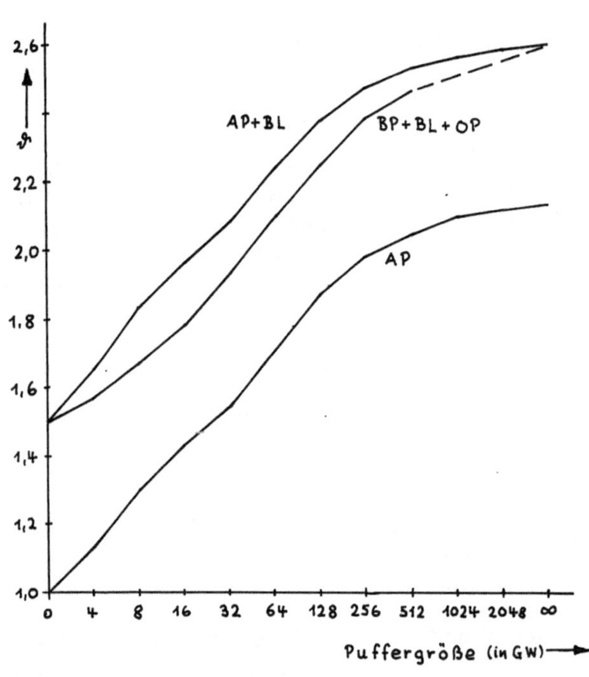

Diagr. 5:

Durchsatzsteigerung ϑ bei einem allgemeinen Puffer (AP) mit/ohne Befehls-Lookahead (BL) und bei getrennten Pufferspeichern (BP und OP)

Zugriffszeiten:

$\tau_{AP} = \tau_{BP} = \tau_{OP} = 0.25$

Befehlsausführungszeit:

$\tau_R = 0.25$

Die Ergebnisse lassen sich in folgenden Punkten zusammenfassen:

1. Die Zugriffszeit zu einem Pufferspeicher hat einen gegenüber der Puffergröße starken Einfluß auf den Durchsatz.
2. Der Durchsatz erhöht sich nur noch wenig , wenn man durch Vergrößern des Puffers die Fehlrate auf Werte unter 5 % reduziert.
3. Kleine Pufferspeicher für z. B. 32 Befehle (16 GW) oder 16 Operanden brin-

gen je für sich eine Durchsatzsteigerung von höchstens 20 %.

4. Die Wirkung dieser Puffer kann man durch einen Befehls-Lookahead so weit verbessern, daß man den Durchsatz eines AP ohne BL erreicht, jedoch bei einer wesentlich kleineren Puffergröße. Bsp.: Ein BP + BL + OP mit je 32 GW hat denselben Durchsatz wie ein AP ohne BL mit 1024 GW.

Literatur

/1/ D. H. Gibson: Considerations in block-oriented systems design, AFIPS Proc., Vol. 30, SJCC 1967, 75 - 80

/2/ F. F. Lee: Study of "look-aside" memory, IEEE Trans., Vol. C-18, No. 11, 1062 - 1064

/3/ R. M. Meade: On memory system design, AFIPS Proc., Vol. 37, FJCC 1970, 33 - 43

EXPERIMENTIERSYSTEM FÜR EIN TECHNISCHES INFORMATIKPRAKTIKUM

R.HARTENSTEIN

Zum Studienplan für Informatik an der Universität Karlsruhe gehört als Pflichtveranstaltung ein Hardware-Praktikum. Praktika ähnlichen stofflichen Inhaltes sind an sich nichts neues. Ein vergleichbares Praktikum wird beispielsweise hier in Karlsruhe an der Fakultät für Elektrotechnik angeboten für Nachrichtentechniker im 7. Semester. Der wesentliche Unterschied zum Hardware-Praktikum für Informatiker liegt in der Zielsetzung. Nachrichtentechniker im 7. Semester bringen über das Stoffgebiet ihres Praktikums ein sehr umfangreiches Wissen mit, das sich erstreckt über elektronische Bauelemente und Baugruppen, digitale Schaltungen, elektrische Meßtechnik, Hochfrequenztechnik, Theorie der Wechselströme und Netzwerkstheorie. Hingegen verfügen die Informatiker des 4. Semesters über weniger umfangreiche elektrotechnische Grundlagenkenntnisse, als dies bei Nachrichtentechnikern im 7. Semester der Fall ist. Ziel des Hardware-Praktikums für Informatiker ist es, dem Informatikstudenten frühzeitig die Möglichkeit zum praktischen Umgang mit modernen Bauelementen zu geben, ohne übermäßig tiefgehende Spezialkenntnisse aus Nachbardisziplinen, wie etwa über Laplace-Transformation oder harmonische Analyse, vorauszusetzen. Der Praktikums-Teilnehmer wird hier vor allem als systemorientiert denkender künftiger Anwender betrachtet. Ein weiteres Ziel des Hardware-Praktikums für Informatiker besteht darin, die Grundlagen zu vertiefen für eine Beschäftigung mit Technischer Informatik auch nach dem Vordiplom.

Zunächst soll eine Übersicht gegeben werden über die zur Auswahl stehenden Typen an Praktikumseinrichtungen. In der Regel wendet eine solche digitale Experimentiereinrichtung dem Studenten eine Programmiertafel zu (auch "Steckbrett" genannt, englisch: patch-board), auf welcher über einfache Buchsen die Ein- und Ausgänge der vorhandenen Bausteine zugänglich sind. Der Praktikums-Teilnehmer kann nun durch Stecken von Verbindungen auf der Programmiertafel Schaltungen realisieren. Hierzu sind passende Experimentierkabel vorhanden, meist einpolige Miniaturkabel in verschiedenen Längen und mit 2-mm-Bananensteckern.

Einrichtungen für Hardware-Praktika lassen sich u.a. nach der Flexibilität ihrer Struktur gliedern (Bild 1). Zwei Extremfälle auf der Flexibilitätsskala sind hierbei der Typ *Meßobjekt mit starrer Struktur* (Typ A) und der Typ *Baukastensystem mit veränderlichem Bausteinvorrat* (Typ C). Irgendwo zwischen den beiden liegt der Typ *Baukastensystem mit festem Bausteinvorrat* (Typ B). Nach der Form des Einsatzes ist folgende Gliederung möglich:

(1) Jeder Arbeitsplatz besitzt eine eigene selbständige Einrichtung.

(2) Viele Arbeitsplätze haben Anteil an einer zentralen Hardware-Einrichtung.

Im letzteren Fall verfügt jeder Arbeitsplatz über eine Dokumentation zur Zentraleinrichtung und z.B. eine an diese anschließbare Programmiertafel. Ein Beispiel hierfür ist das DEG (Digitales Experimentiergerät), welches hier in Karlsruhe in der Fakultät für Elektrotechnik vor etwa 4 Jahren entwickelt wurde |1|, und zum Typ B.2 gehört. Wegen der relativ hohen Kosten für integrierte Schaltungen waren zu dieser Zeit nur bei kleinem Bausteinvorrat der Typ B.1 und bei größerem Bausteinvorrat der Typ B.2 vorzuziehen. Ein Nachteil des Typ B.1 (ein Beispiel ist in |2| beschrieben) ist geringe Flexibilität. Nachteile des Typ B.2 sind der höhere Abstraktionsgrad bei der Benutzung und die Tatsache, daß nicht mehrere Arbeitsgruppen gleichzeitig Zugang zu der Zentraleinrichtung haben.

In der Zwischenzeit sind integrierte Bausteine sehr viel billiger geworden. Außerdem gibt es inzwischen integrierte Schaltungen, die wesentlich mehr Funktionen in einem Baustein vereinigen, als dies bei früher erhältlichen Typen möglich war. Weitere wichtige Aspekte der Entwicklung des Marktes für integrierte Digitalbausteine sind folgende:

1. In weiten Anwendungsbereichen haben sich die Signal-Spezifikationen der TTL-Bausteinfamilie wie eine inoffizielle Norm durchgesetzt und der Bauteile-Markt bietet hier ein ständig wachsendes Typenspektrum;
2. viele Bausteine anderer Familien sind in TTL-kompatiblen Versionen erhältlich;
3. praktisch alle wichtigen Bausteine sind in einer Version mit einer *dual-in-line*-Anordnung der Anschlußstifte erhältlich, bei welcher ebenfalls von einer inoffiziellen Norm gesprochen werden kann. Für solche *dual-in-line*-Bausteine gibt es sehr preiswerte Stecksockel.

Unter *dual-in-line* (DIL) wird eine Anordnung der Anschlüsse in zwei Reihen verstanden, wobei sich an jeder Breitseite des rechteckigen Bausteingehäuses eine der beiden Reihen befindet. Solche DIL-Bauteile sind gegenüber Stecksockeln aufwärtskompatibel, d.h., daß Bauteile mit weniger Anschlußstiften in Sockel mit einer größeren Zahl von Anschlußstiften gesteckt werden können.

Die durch die geschilderte Marktentwicklung entstandenen neuen Möglichkeiten wurden ausgenützt zur Entwicklung des Experimentiersystems für das *Technische Informatik Praktikum (TIP)* in Karlsruhe, welches zum Typ C.1 zu rechnen ist. Die hier zugehörigen Experimentiereinrichtungen seien im folgenden beschrieben.

Zur besseren Veranschaulichung seien zunächst Einrichtungen vom Typ B und vom Typ C miteinander verglichen. Bei Experimentiereinrichtungen mit festem Bausteinvorrat (Typ B) sind nur die Experimentierbuchsen auf der Programmiertafel von außen zugänglich. Der Rest des Systemes, der aus dem Bausteinvorrat und der Verdrahtung besteht, ist hierbei nicht von außen zugänglich. Einrichtungen vom Typ C (variabler Bausteinvorrat) unterscheiden sich hiervon grundlegend. Die Bausteine befinden sich nicht im unzugänglichen Inneren des Gerätes. Vielmehr ist neben den Experimentierbuchsen eine zweite Klasse von Buchsen ("Bausteinfassungen") von außen zugänglich, welche dem Anschluß der ausgewählten Bausteine dient (siehe Bild 3). Die Bausteine können je nach Form direkt in die Bausteinfassung gesteckt werden (z.B. integrierte Schaltungen), oder über ein Kabel an die Bausteinfassung angeschlossen werden (z.B. andere Experimentieraufbauten oder Peripheriegeräte). Die eigentliche Experimentiereinrichtung reduziert sich bei Typ C gegenüber Typ B auf eine gedruckte Schaltung, bestehend aus mehreren gleichen Teilschaltungen nach dem Muster in Bild 2: Jeder Anschluß einer DIL-Bausteinfassung ist mit einer 2mm-Buchse verbunden. Das Experimentierbrett nach Bild 3 enthält beispielsweise 15 solcher Teilschaltungen. Zu umfangreicheren Aufbauten können mehrere solcher Experimentierbretter zu größeren Einheiten zusammengesteckt werden.

Im folgenden sei kurz der praktische Einsatz dieser Experimentierbretter geschildert. Vor Beginn der Veranstaltung werden die Experimentiergeräte (z.B. Bild 3) von Betreuern mit Bauteilen bestückt. Der Student erhält in der Versuchsanleitung zu jeder aufgesteckten integrierten Schaltung einen kleinen Schaltplan, der auch über die Anschlußbelegung Auskunft gibt (Schema gemäß Bild 2).

Eine Erweiterung der didaktischen Möglichkeiten ergibt sich durch folgende weitere Einsatzart. Durch eine beschriftete und mit Schaltplänen illustrierte Abdeckplatte (z.B. in Bild 4) kann das System in eine Assistentenebene und eine Studentenebene unterteilt werden. Zur Herabsetzung des Komplexitätsgrades der vom Studenten zu steckenden Verdrahtung kann ein Teil der Verdrahtung in der Ebene unterhalb der Abdeckplatte (Assistentenebene) vom Betreuerpersonal im voraus realisiert werden. Die Anzahl der durch den Studenten zugänglichen 2mm-Buchsen wird hierdurch stark reduziert. Die Herstellung der Abdeckplatte ist mit einem Minimum an Werkzeug möglich, wenn eine hierzu käuflich erhältliche Rasterplatte verwendet wird. Zur Ausrüstung unseres Anfängerpraktikums gehören neben den beschriebenen Experimentierbrettern:

1. *Konsolgeräte*, auf welchen ein Vorrat von Schaltern, Tasten und Lampen zugänglich ist. Diese Konsolgeräte (ein Beispiel in Bild 5) ermöglichen die manuelle Eingabe (Schalterreihe S und Tasten in Bild 5) und die Ausgabe (Lampenreihen L in Bild 5) logischer Variablen;

2. ein *Bauteile-Lager* an integrierten Schaltungen der TTL-Familie und sonstigen TTL-kompatiblen Bauteilen, die auf DIL-Fassungen steckbar sind, wie Schiebeschalter, Wippenschalter, Relais, Lampenanzeigen, 7-Segmentanzeigen für Ziffern, alpha-numerische 5 x 7-Rasteranzeigen, Verzögerungsleitungen, Dioden, Transistoren, Potentiometer, Digital-Analog-Wandler, Operationsverstärker und andere Analogbausteine. Zur Selbstanfertigung einfacher Schaltungen mittels diskreter Bauelemente stehen DIL-Leergehäuse zur Verfügung, die je nach Volumen der erstellten Schaltung mit oder ohne Deckel verwendet werden.

3. Ein *Gerätepark* an Impulsgebern (zwei verschiedene Standardtypen), Zweistrahloszillographen und Spannungsversorgungsgeräten.

Für das Anfängerpraktikum stehen folgende Stückzahlen an Geräten zur Verfügung: 20 Konsolgeräte, 50 Steckbretter mit je 10 bis 15 DIL-Fassungen, 40 Spannungsversorgungsgeräte, 20 Oszillographen, 20 Impulsgeber und 30 Drehspulmultimeter. Unter der Annahme, daß Veranstaltungstermine von Versuchen sich überschneiden mit Vorbereitungszeiten für andere Versuche, können mit dieser Ausstattung an einem einzigen Veranstaltungstermin gleichzeitig 20 Versuche gefahren werden. Bei drei Teilnehmern je Arbeitsgruppe und 2 Parallelveranstaltungen wurde hierbei eine Kapazität von 120 Informatikstudenten erreicht. Zur Betreuung der 20 Arbeitsgruppen eines Veranstaltungstermins wurden je nach Schwierigkeitsgrad des Versuches 3 bis 4 studentische Tutoren zur Betreuung eingesetzt. Insbesondere bei Problemen meßtechnischer Art ist dieser relativ hoch erscheinende Betreueraufwand notwendig. Der im Praktikum behandelte Stoff läßt sich etwa wie folgt in Stichworten angeben:

Zweipole und Zweipol-Netze, deren statische Eigenschaften, Analyse und Synthese, Meßtechnik bei Gleichstrom, Vorzeichenregeln;

RC-Netzwerke, deren Sprungsantwort-Verhalten, Analyse und Synthese, Meßtechnik mit Oszillographen;

Elektronische Schaltstufen, elektrische Analogsignale als Träger logischer Variablen, technische Probleme der Realisierung (Toleranzen, Belastung, Zeitprobleme);

Logische Schaltungen, Formen der elektrischen Realisierung logischer Operationen, praktischer Gebrauch der Schaltalgebra, Eigenschaften und Gebrauch von: Schaltungen mit diskreten Bauteilen, integrierten Schaltungen, Eingabeschaltern, Anzeigelampen;

Schaltnetze, Problemformulierung, logischer Entwurf, Minimisierung, Realisierung bei vorgegebener Schaltkreisfamilie, Schnittstellenprobleme, Übergänge zwischen verschiedenen Logiktypen;

Rückgekoppelte Schaltnetze, Laufzeiteffekte, Asynchrone Schaltwerke, deren Analyse und Synthese, Realisierung von Flipflops aus logischen Schaltungen, Gegenüberstellung verschiedener Flipfloptypen und Taktsteuerungsarten;

Laufzeitprobleme bei Schaltnetzen, Hazard-Probleme und deren Lösung, Messung des Zeitverhaltens von Schaltnetzen;

Register, Realisierung von Registern, Zählern und Schieberegistern mittels integrierter Flipflop-Bausteine, Verwendung verschiedener Taktungsarten, praktischer Gebrauch binär codierter Zahlendarstellungen und deren Konversion;

Register-Transfer-Strukturen, Anwendung integrierter Register, (De-)Multiplexer und Schaltnetze zur Realisierung arithmetisch-logischer Operationen, praktischer Gebrauch binär codierter Zahlendarstellungen, technische Probleme der Ablaufsteuerung (Taktungsprobleme u.a.);

Synchrone Schaltwerke, Hardware-Implementierung von Ablaufdiagrammen, Prinzipien der Funktion von Leitwerken, klassischer Schaltwerksentwurf.

Mit den Experimentiereinrichtungen wurden in didaktischer Hinsicht im allgemeinen gute Erfahrungen gemacht. Bei komplexeren Versuchsaufbauten läßt sich die Durchsichtigkeit des zu steckenden "Drahtverhau" dadurch steuern, daß ein Teil der Verdrahtung in die Assistentenebene verlegt wird. Die Anleitungsskripten und Aufgabenblätter sind bei einem Teil der Versuche noch stark verbesserungsbedürftig. Eine didaktische Erfolgskontrolle wird bei unserem Praktikum im wesentlichen durch drei verschiedene Informationskanäle möglich. Zu jedem Praktikumsversuch erhält jede Arbeitsgruppe ein Kritikformular mit der Bitte um Beantwortung von Fragen und Niederschrift von kritischen Bemerkungen und Verbesserungsvorschlägen. Darüber hinaus wird für jede Praktikumsgruppe durchschnittlich zu jedem zweiten Praktikumstermin ein Gespräch mit einem Angehörigen des Lehrkörpers anberaumt. Dieses Gespräch gibt den Praktikums-Teilnehmern Gelegenheit, das Arbeiten ihrer Schaltung zu demonstrieren und zu beschreiben. Bei diesem Gespräch werden Fragen an die Praktikums-Teilnehmer gestellt. Hier wird beispielsweise gefragt nach der Funktion der Schaltung, wenn eine bestimmte Komponente fehlerhaft ist, oder falsch eingebaut wurde, usw.. Fragen dieser Art geben einen Eindruck darüber, welchen Grad von Verständnis die Teilnehmer der Gruppe inzwischen erreicht haben. Weiteren Aufschluß über den didaktischen Erfolg des Praktikums ergibt das Gespräch mit den studentischen Tutoren, die während der Praktikumsveranstaltung ständig in den Praktikumsräumen anwesend sind.

Zur Zeit wird die Veranstaltung eines Fortgeschrittenen-Praktikums diskutiert. Hierzu eignen sich kleine, einfache Tischmodelle folgender Ein/Ausgabe- und Speichereinheiten: Kassetten-Magnetbandspeicher, Kernspeicher, Zifferndrucker, Lochkartenleser, Bildschirmgerät, Fernschreiber, u.ä.. Als Stoff für ein solches Fortgeschrittenen-Praktikum bieten sich Themen an, die wie folgt in Stichworten skizziert seien: Datensammelleitungen, Kanalwerke, Datenübertragung, Speicherorganisations-Hardware, Koordinierung konkurrierender Prozessoren, Digital-Analog-Wandlung, Analog-Digital-Wandlung, Hardware der Bildschirm-Ein-Ausgabe, Mikroprogrammsteuerungen, Anwendung von Assoziativspeichern, Steuerung von Peripheriegeraten, Hardware-Realisierung verschiedener Algorithmen (z.B. Such-, Sortier- oder Lade-Algorithmen u.a.m.).

Für ein solches Fortgeschrittenen-Praktikum erscheint uns ein Konzept für erstrebenswert, das aus Lösungen zu mehreren Teilaufgaben gegen Ende des Praktikums die Synthese einer interessanten Prozessorkonfiguration ermöglicht. Der Erfahrungsbericht über den *UHC-1-Computer* (s. |3|) demonstriert, daß ein vergleichbares Projekt selbst unter sehr viel schwierigeren Umständen innerhalb eines einzigen Semesters durchgezogen werden kann. Einen genügend niedrigen Komplexitätsgrad verspricht die Einhaltung folgender Bedingungen:

1. Ein einziger DMA-Kanal koordiniert alle Moduln des Systems;
2. Fortfall von Formatierung und Konversion, wenn nur im Dual- und Oktal-Code

verarbeitet, sowie ein- und ausgegeben wird;

3. Eliminierung schwierigerer Konfliktprobleme bei Betriebsmittelvergabe durch manuelle Eingriffe;
4. nur ca. 10 bis 12 Mikrobefehle werden angewandt (womit sich alles prinzipiell wichtige realisieren läßt);
5. Verwendung eines einheitlichen Wortformates (kleine Kernspeichermoduln mit 16 und mehr Bit Wortlänge sind sehr preiswert käuflich zu erwerben).

Eine naheliegende Organisationsform für ein solches Fortgeschrittenen-Praktikum wäre die Form der Projektorganisation: Einzelne Gruppen bauen anhand von Pflichtenheften einzelne Moduln auf, die später zusammengeschaltet werden. Diese Organisationsform bietet ausgiebig Gelegenheit zur Übung der Kooperation von Gruppen.

Literaturhinweise:

|1| H.M. Lipp; P. Muth; S. Wendt: *Digitales Experimentier-System.* Elektron. Rechenanl. 12 (1970), H. 5, S. 269-277.

|2| T.L. Hughes: *DIGITAL Computer lab workbook.* Digital Equipment Coporation, 1969.

|3| F.F. Kuo: *A Case Study on a Student-Designed Digital Computer.* IEEE Trans. E-14 (1971), 4, S. 217-220.

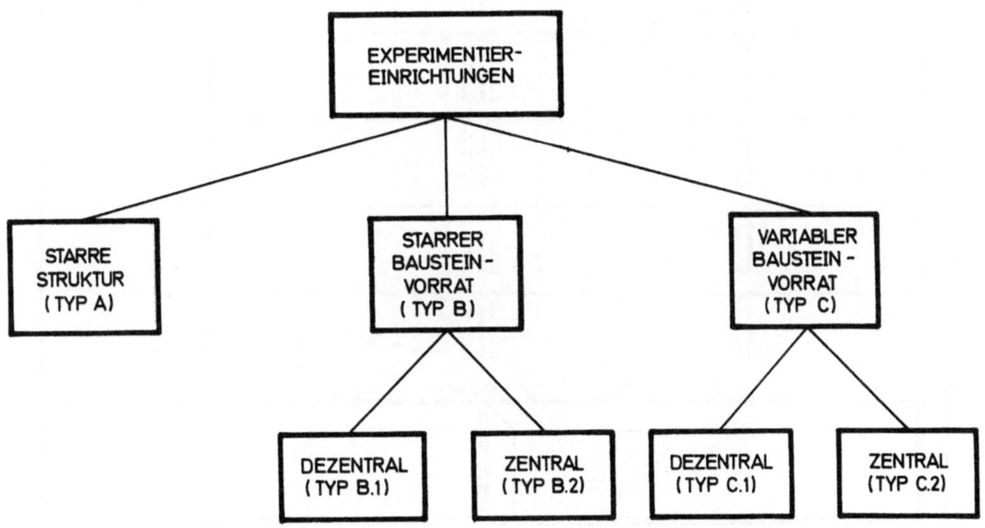

Bild 1: Gliederung von Experimentiereinrichtungen für Hardware-Praktika

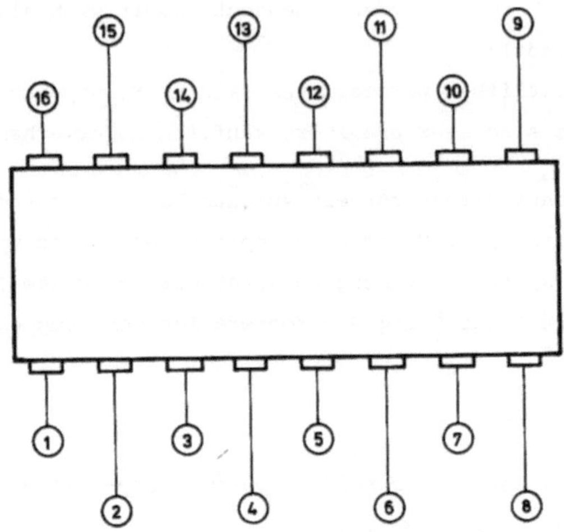

Bild 2: Teilverdrahtung eines Experimentierbrettes
(Typ C.1) mit DIL-Bausteinfassungen

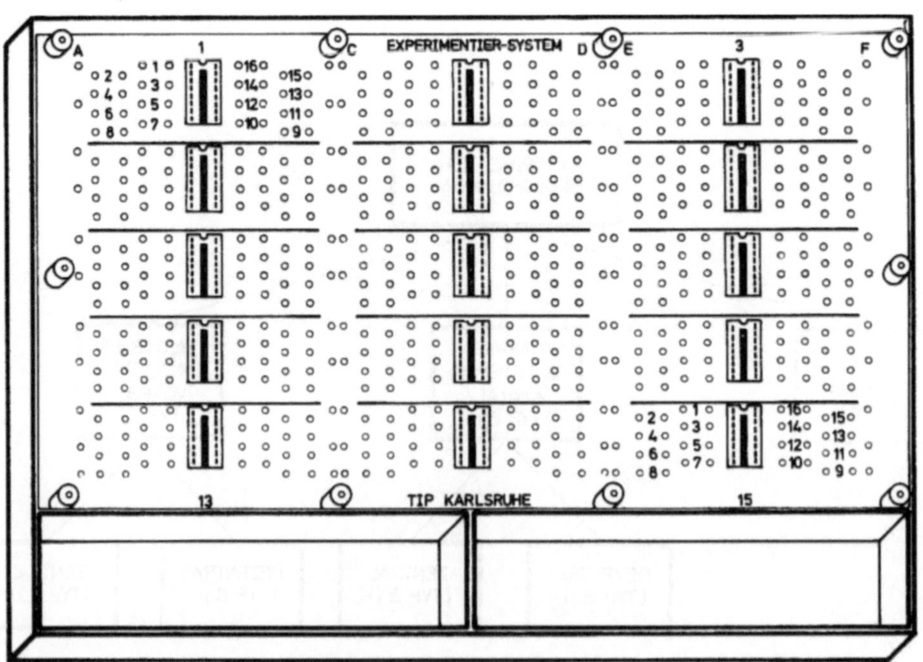

Bild 3: Experimentiereinrichtung* von Typ C.1
mit DIL-Bausteinfassungen

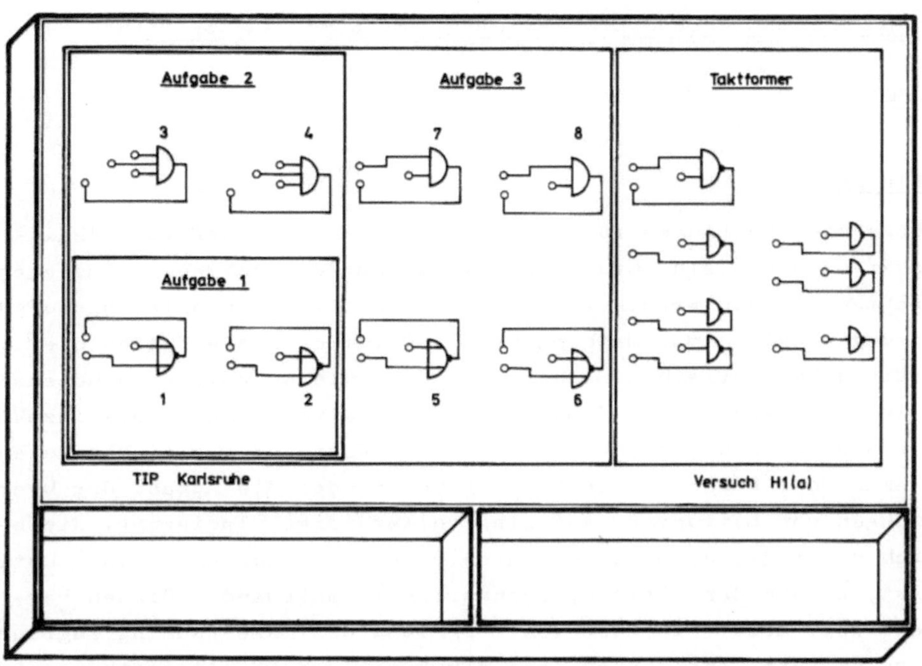

Bild 4: Zwei-Ebenen-Version (mit Abdeckplatte) der Experimentier-einrichtung* in Bild 3

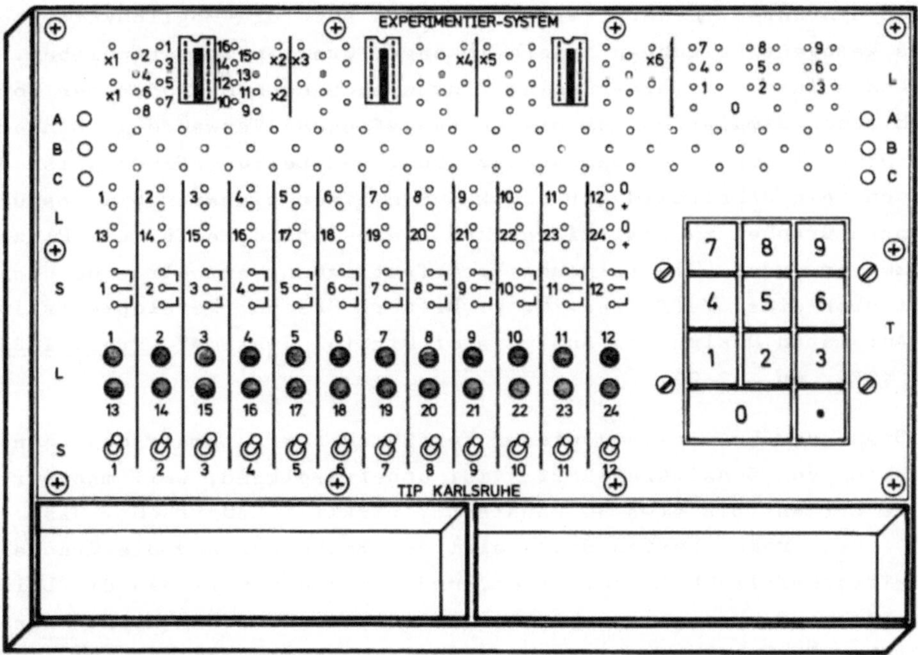

Bild 5: Konsolgerät* für manuelle Eingabe und optische Ausgabe logischer Variablen bei digitalen Experimentiergeräten.

PLAZIEREN UND PSEUDOLEITUNGSFINDEN BEI SCHALTKREISKARTEN

K.GROTZ

1. Einleitung

Die bekannten Verfahren für den automatischen Entwurf von Schaltkreiskarten haben eine Grundidee gemeinsam: die Aufgaben Plazieren und Leitungsfinden werden getrennt behandelt. Die Plazierungsaufgabe wird gewöhnlich mit mathematischen Optimierungsverfahren oder mit iterativen heuristischen Methoden gelöst. Die wesentlichen Gütemaße für die Optimierung sind dabei die Gesamtleitungslänge, die Anzahl der erforderlichen Ebenenwechsel auf der Karte oder gleichbedeutend die Anzahl der Ecken in den Leitungszügen oder die Anzahl der Überkreuzungen von Leitungen. Auf eine vollständige Plazierung, die bezüglich einer dieser oben genannten Gütemaße (näherungsweise) optimal ist, werden dann Leitungssuchverfahren angewandt. Diesen Verfahren liegt meist die Idee von LEE/MOORE des maze-running zugrunde. Die später veröffentlichten, auf der Basis des LEE-Algorithmus aufbauenden Verfahren versuchen den Leitungssuchprozeß abzukürzen, indem sie die Feinheit des Gitternetzes vergröbern oder Vorzugsrichtungen einführen. Neuere Verfahren haben auch die Möglichkeit, bereits gezogene Leitungen innerhalb enger Grenzen zu verschieben. Neben LEE's Idee des maze-running finden auch noch Methoden der Topographischen Simulation für die Leitungsfindung Verwendung. Ein erster Schritt zur gemeinsamen Plazierung und Leitungsfindung ist der Versuch, ein Schaltbild der Logik durch einen planaren bzw. pseudoplanaren Graphen zu realisieren und diese Topologie für die Plazierung zu verwenden. Die folgende Veröffentlichung enthält eine Übersicht über diese Verfahren: M. A. Breuer, "Recent Developments in the Automated Design and Analysis of Digital Systems", Proc. IEEE, Jan. 1972, pp. 12-27.

Der Stand der Entwicklung dieser Verfahren zur automatischen Konstruktion von Schaltkreiskarten ist unbefriedigend, weil man nur kleine Karten (bis etwa 50 Bausteine) wirklich beherrscht. Das heißt, bei großen Karten übersteigt der Rechenaufwand die Grenze der Wirtschaftlichkeit zum einen, und zum anderen finden die Leitungssuchverfahren gar nicht alle Leitungen. Zu einem nicht unerheblichen Teil kommen die Schwierigkeiten sicher daher, daß dem Verfahren zur Leitungssuche eine vollständige Plazierung angeboten wird, die mit Optimierungskriterien gefunden wurde, welche die Problematik der Leitungsfindung nur zu einem sehr geringen Teil erfassen.

Die vorliegende Arbeit beschreibt ein Verfahren, das die Aufgaben Plazieren und Leitungsfinden koppelt. Darin kann die Leitungsführung von der Freiheit der Platzvergabe für Bausteine Gebrauch machen. Der Algorithmus findet mit konstruktiv heuristischen Methoden eine vollständige Plazierung und eine Grobform der Leitungen, d. h., die Leitungen werden bis in unmittelbare Nachbarschaft der zu verbindenden Bausteine gezogen. Es fehlen die Verbindungen zu den Kontakten. Zu deren Ergänzung müssen später nur noch die lokalen Verhältnisse am Baustein berücksichtigt werden.

Der Algorithmus wurde auf zweiseitig, gleichmäßig mit Flatpacks bestückte Karten angewandt. Dabei konnten folgende Ergebnisse erzielt werden:

	Beispiel 1	Beispiel 2
Anzahl der Bausteine (MECL 1)	135	198
Anzahl der Plätze	182	224
Prozentsatz der Pseudoleitungen	99,1 %	96,2 %
Rechenzeit auf TR 440	389 s	711 s

2. Formale Beschreibung der Schaltkreiskarte und Definition der Pseudoleitungen

Gegeben sei eine Schaltung, d. h. eine Menge $\mathcal{B}$ von p Bausteinen (AND-Gates, OR-Gates, Flipflops, usw.) und eine Vorschrift, die angibt, welche Kontakte der Bausteine miteinander zu verbinden sind. Verbindungen gleichen elektrischen Potentials heißen Signale und werden in der Signalmenge Γ zusammengefaßt. Mit $B(s)$ werde die Menge der Bausteine bezeichnet, die durch das Signal $s \in \Gamma$ verbunden werden und mit $S(b)$ die Menge der Signale, die an die verschiedenen Kontakte von $b \in \mathcal{B}$ geführt werden. Die Realisierung eines Signals als gedruckte Leiterbahnen auf der Schaltkreiskarte heißt Leitung.

Die Schaltkreiskarten, die dieser Arbeit zugrunde liegen, sind rechteckig und geometrisch gleichmäßig mit Bausteinen bestückbar. Abb. 1 veranschaulicht das Schema, nach dem die Karten symmetrisch zweiseitig mit Bausteinen bestückt werden.

Die Rasterung, die hierbei entsteht, wird dazu verwendet, die Karte in Teilflächen (i,k) aufzuteilen und die darin enthaltenen Bestandteile der Schaltung in einer Matrix

$$\mathfrak{F} = (f_{ik}) \qquad \begin{array}{l} i = 0(1)n \\ k = 1(1)m \end{array}$$

zu beschreiben. Daher sind n und m immer ungerade.

Zur genaueren Definition der Elemente f_{ik} von $\mathfrak{F}$ sind noch einige Vorbereitungen nötig. Entsprechend Abb. 1 sind auf den Teilflächen mit geraden i und k Bausteine untergebracht, und zwar möglicherweise auf beiden Kartenseiten. Jedem Baustein b wird eine Zahl t(b) zugeordnet, die eine Aussage über seinen Platzbedarf macht, und jede Teilfläche (i,k) kann Bausteine entsprechend einer festen Kapazität τ_{ik} aufnehmen. Es ist $\tau_{ik} > 0$ für i und k gerade, und $\tau_{ik} = 0$ sonst. Sei die Karte z. B. zweiseitig mit lauter gleichgroßen Flatpacks bestückt, so ist t(b) = 1 für alle $b \in \mathfrak{B}$. Jede Fläche f_{ik} mit i und k gerade kann zwei Bausteine aufnehmen, je einen auf den Kartenseiten. Es ist also $\tau_{ik} = 2$ für i und k gerade. Gibt es Bausteine verschiedener Größe, so werden die Zusammenhänge etwas komplizierter.

Die nicht von Bausteinen belegten Teilflächen dienen der Aufnahme von Leitungen für Signale. Die gewählte Anordnung der Bausteine läßt ganze Zeilen und Spalten von Teilflächen für die Leitungsführung frei. Im folgenden heißen die Zeilen, die senkrecht zur Steckerkante verlaufen, senkrechte Autobahnen, und die Spalten, die parallel zur Steckerkante verlaufen, waagerechte Autobahnen. Die Leitungen verlaufen in den senkrechten Autobahnen auf der einen Kartenseite und in den waagerechten Autobahnen auf der anderen Kartenseite.

In Abhängigkeit vom Mindestabstand der Leitungen untereinander und von der Breite einer Autobahn kann diese eine bestimmte Anzahl von Leitungen in Spuren parallel führen. Die Autobahnen werden entsprechend ihrer Überdeckung durch Teilflächen in Abschnitte eingeteilt. Die Autobahnen und ihre Abschnitte werden so numeriert, daß gilt:

- Die Teilfläche (2g -1,k) überdeckt den k-ten Abschnitt der g-ten waagerechten Autobahn.
- Die Teilfläche (i,2h -1) überdeckt den i-ten Abschnitt der h-ten senkrechten Autobahn.

Der Autobahnbegriff führt auf die Definition der Pseudoleitung, wie sie später im Plazierungsalgorithmus verwirklicht werden soll. Seien b und b' Bausteine, die durch ein Signal s verbunden sind; b sei auf (i,k) und b' auf (i',k') plaziert. Eine Pseudoleitung $\sigma_s(i,k;i',k')$ für diese Verbindung belegt Spuren in Abschnitten von waagerechten und senkrechten Autobahnen. Die Auswahl der waagrechten Autobahn richtet sich danach, auf welcher Bausteinseite das Signal s einen Kontakt berührt. (Bei der späteren Konstruktion der echten Leitungen sind abhängig vom Bausteintyp noch Kontakte auf dieser Bausteinseite vertauschbar). Berührt s an b einen Kontakt auf der steckerzugewandten Bausteinseite, so wird die waagrechte Autobahn $j = i/2$ ausgewählt; im anderen Fall die waagrechte Autobahn $j = (i/2)+1$. Dann ist eine Pseudoleitung $\sigma_s(i,k;\ i',k')$ die Belegung je einer freien Spur in den Abschnitten k bis k'-1 oder k'+1 der waagerechten Autobahn j und die Belegung je einer freien Spur in den Abschnitten i-1 (bzw. i+1 in Abhängigkeit von der Nummer der waagerechten Autobahn) bis i' der senkrechten Autobahn k'/2 oder (k'/2)+1, je nachdem, wo die Belegung der waagerechten Autobahn endet. Wird in dieser Definition i mit i' und k mit k' vertauscht, so ist das Ergebnis eine weitere Pseudoleitung $\sigma_s(i,k;\ i',k')$. Im allgemeinen gibt es also für eine Pseudoleitung vier Möglichkeiten. Abb. 1 zeigt diese an einem Beispiel.

In Sonderfällen können Pseudoleitungen einfachere Formen annehmen.

Obige Definition einer Pseudoleitung zwischen zwei Punkten läßt nur die L-Form für den Weg der Leitung zu. Treppen- und Mäanderformen sind algorithmisch nicht vorgesehen und können allenfalls bei einer manuellen Nacharbeitung Verwendung finden. Dies vereinfacht nicht nur das Leitungssuchverfahren, sondern begünstigt auch die Übersichtlichkeit, die für Fehlersuche und Änderungen sehr erstrebenswert ist.

Wie bereits angedeutet, wird der Prozess der Pseudoleitungsfindung in den Plaziervorgang miteinbezogen werden. Deshalb werden zur Definition der Matrixelemente f_{ik}, die die Belegungsmatrix bilden, neben

B_{ik} = Menge der Bausteine, die auf (i,k) plaziert sind,

auch Signalmengen miteinbezogen:

SW_{ik} (SS_{ik}) = Menge der Signale, die eine Spur in dem Abschnitt der waagerechten (senkrechten) Autobahn belegen, der von der Teilfläche (i,k) überdeckt wird.

Damit sei

$$f_{ik} = B_{ik} \cup SW_{ik} \cup SS_{ik}.$$

Gewisse geometrische Randbedingungen spiegeln sich im Aufbau der f_{ik} wieder. So muß stets gelten

$$\sum_{b \in B_{ik}} t(b) \leq \tau_{ik} \qquad \text{und } \tau_{ik} = 0 \quad \text{für i oder k ungerade.}$$

In jedem Autobahnabschnitt stehen nur eine beschränkte Anzahl von Spuren zur Verfügung. Die Anzahl der Spuren, die ein Autobahnabschnitt enthält, der von der Teilfläche (i,k) überdeckt ist, wird mit ξ_{ik} für die waagerechten und mit η_{ik} für die senkrechten Autobahnen angegeben. Es muß stets gelten:

$$|SW_{ik}| \leq \xi_{ik} \text{ und } \xi_{ik} = 0 \text{ für } i \text{ gerade,}$$

$$|SS_{ik}| \leq \eta_{ik} \text{ und } \eta_{ik} = 0 \text{ für } k \text{ gerade.}$$

3. Das Modell des konstruktiven Plazierungsalgorithmus

Besteht die Schaltung aus p Bausteinen, so läuft der Algorithmus in p Schritten ab. Im μ-ten Schritt werde der Baustein b_μ plaziert. Es sei also

$$B_\mu = \{b_1,\ldots,b_\mu\}$$

die Menge der Bausteine, die nach dem μ-ten Schritt plaziert sind.

Nach dem in Abschnitt 2. Gesagten setzt sich die Menge der Teilflächen $\mathcal{R}$, die Bausteine aufnehmen können, wie folgt zusammen:

$$\mathcal{R} = \{ (i,k) \ / \ i \text{ gerade und } k \text{ gerade.} \}$$

Die Menge der vor dem μ-ten Schritt für Bausteine des Platzbedarfs $\leq$ t noch freien Teilflächen sei

$$P_\mu(t) = \{ (i,k) \in \mathcal{R} \ / (\tau_{ik} - \sum_{b \in B_{\mu-1} \cap B_{ik}} t(b)) \geq t \}.$$

Es sind dies genau diejenigen Teilflächen, die nach dem $(\mu-1)$-ten Schritt noch frei von Bausteinen sind oder nur soweit von Bausteinen belegt sind, daß ein Baustein vom Platzbedarf t noch zusätzlich auf ihnen untergebracht werden kann.

Im μ-ten Schritt $(1 \leq \mu \leq p)$ des Algorithmus laufen zwei Teilschritte ab.

Im

1. T e i l s c h r i t t wird der zu plazierende Baustein b_μ gefunden. Gegeben ist eine Folge von reellwertigen Gütemaßen

$$\varphi_\mu = \varphi_{\mu,1},\ldots, \quad \varphi_{\mu,v} \ .$$

Diese erzeugt ausgehend von $B^c_{\mu-1} = \mathcal{L} \setminus B_{\mu-1}$ eine absteigende Folge von Bausteinmengen

$$B^c_{\mu-1} = B_{\mu,1} \supseteq B_{\mu,2} \supseteq \ldots \supseteq B_{\mu,v} = \{b_\mu\} \ .$$

Die $\varphi_{\mu,j}$ sind Abbildungen von $B_{\mu,j}$ in die reellen Zahlen.

Die Erzeugung der Bausteinmengen erfolgt nach der Vorschrift

$$B_{\mu,j+1} = \left\{ b \in B_{\mu,j} / \varphi_{\mu,j}(b) \leq \varphi_{\mu,j}(b') \text{ für alle } b' \in B_{\mu,j} \right\} .$$

b_μ ist dann der Baustein, der im μ-ten Schritt plaziert wird.

Die Eindeutigkeit von b_μ, d. h. $|B_{\mu,v}| = 1$ wird notfalls durch eine Zufallsauswahl erzwungen.

In jeder der v Stufen werden die Bausteine aus $B_{\mu,j}$ nach dem Gütemaß $\varphi_{\mu,j}$ sortiert und nur die besten in die Menge $B_{\mu,j+1}$ übertragen.

Der Platz für b_μ wird im
2. Teilschritt gefunden. Gegeben ist eine Folge von reellwertigen Gütemaßen

$$\psi_\mu = \psi_{\mu,1}, \ldots, \psi_{\mu,w}.$$

Diese erzeugt, ausgehend von $P_\mu(t(b\ ))$, eine absteigende Folge von Mengen aus Teilflächen

$$P_\mu(t(b_\mu)) = P_{\mu,1} \supseteq P_{\mu,2} \supseteq \ldots \supseteq P_{\mu,w} = \left\{ (i_\mu, k_\mu) \right\}.$$

Die $\psi_{\mu,j}$ sind Abb. von $B_{\mu,j}$ in die reellen Zahlen und die Erzeugung der Mengen $P_{\mu,j}$ erfolgt analog der Erzeugung der Bausteinmengen im 1. Teilschritt. $(i_\mu,\ k_\mu)$ ist dann die Teilfläche, auf die b_μ plaziert wird. Wie im 1. Teilschritt wird gegebenenfalls auch hier die Eindeutigkeit erzwungen.

4. Die Elemente des Algorithmus

4.1. Die Auswahl eines Bausteines

Im 1. Teilschritt des μ-ten Schritts im Konstruktionsvorgang wird der zu plazierende Baustein b_μ ausgewählt.

Die Leitungssuche wird sicher erleichtert, wenn Bausteine mit gemeinsamen Signalen, die also durch Leitungen verbunden werden müssen, möglichst nahe beieinander auf der Karte plaziert werden. Hiermit wird die Voraussetzung für kürzere Leitungen geschaffen, die in wenigen Autobahnabschnitten Spuren in Anspruch mehmen und damit mehr Freiheiten für andere Leitungen lassen. Dieses Argument gilt allerdings nicht in aller Strenge: die beschränkte Kapazität der Autobahnen setzt natürliche Grenzen.

Sei

$$U(B_\mu) = \bigcup_{b \in B_\mu} S(b)$$

der Signalumfang aller nach dem μ-ten Schritt plazierten Bausteine. Die Menge der nach dem μ-ten Schritt "offenen" Signale

$$O_\mu = U(B_\mu) \cap U(B_\mu^c)$$

besteht aus den Signalen, die sowohl an Bausteinen anliegen, die schon plaziert sind, als auch an solchen, die noch nicht plaziert sind. Das Bestreben ist, die Menge der offenen Signale möglichst klein zu halten. Lange Signale werden naturgemäß für die Dauer vieler Schritte in der Menge der offenen Signale verbleiben. Deshalb müssen die kurzen Signale ein höheres Gewicht erhalten, um für sie die naturgemäß kurze mögliche Aufenthaltsdauer in den O_μ zu realisieren. In Zusammenhang mit der Aufenthaltsdauer eines Signals in den Mengen O_μ steht auch die Länge der Leitung für dieses Signal. Notwendige Bedingung für eine kurze Leitung ist eine kurze Aufenthaltsdauer. Während einer großen Aufenthaltsdauer können Plätze belegt werden, die eine kurze Leitung ermöglicht hätten. Aus diesem Zusammenhang läßt sich eine bessere Bewertung kurzer Signale noch einmal in einer anderen Weise motivieren: lange Signale benötigen naturgemäß längere Leitungen, da sie viele Bausteine berühren. Deshalb müssen wenigstens kurze Signale möglichst auch durch kurze Leitungen realisiert werden, um den vorhandenen Platz auf der Karte wirtschaftlich zu nutzen.

Bei dem Auswahlvorgang sind eigentlich für die Berechnung der Signallänge die bereits plazierten Bausteine eines Signals s nicht mehr relevant. Vielmehr interessiert nur noch seine Restlänge

$|B(s) \cap B^c_{\mu-1}|$, d. h. die Anzahl der Bausteine, die noch nicht plaziert sind, aber von s berührt werden. Ein langes Signal s, für das im μ-ten Schritt einer der letzten Bausteine aus B(s) plaziert werden kann, sollte genau so gut bewertet werden wie ein kurzes Signal.

Bisher wurden nur die Signale betrachtet, die in der Menge der bereits plazierten Bausteine vorkommen. Für die anderen, die Fremdsignale $s \in O_\mu^c$, mit $O_\mu^c = \Gamma \setminus O_\mu$, gilt ein ähnlicher Sachverhalt. Auch hier erscheint eine stärkere Bewertung der kurzen Signale angebracht. Diese werden den Umfang der Menge der offenen Signale nur über wenige Schritte mitbestimmen und belasten.

Für Gütemaße zur Realisierung eines so gesteuerten Auswahlprozesses gibt es viele Möglichkeiten. Mit dem folgenden wurden die besten Ergebnisse erzielt:

$$\varphi_{\mu,1} : b \mapsto \frac{-1}{S(b)} \left(\sum_{s \in S(b) \cap O_{\mu-1}} 100/|B(s) \cap B^c_{\mu-1}| - \sum_{s \in S(b) \cap O^c_{\mu-1}} |B(s)| \right).$$

Dabei werden Signale, die kurz vor dem Abschluß stehen, sehr hoch bewertet. Den Signalen, die nach dem μ-ten Schritt neu in die Menge der offenen Signale aufgenommen werden müssen, kommt geringere Bedeutung zu. Durch den Faktor 100 in der ersten Summe wird das Hauptgewicht auf die Signale $s \in O_{\mu-1}$ gelegt. Diese Zahl hat in Versuchen die besten Ergebnisse geliefert. Der Faktor $1/|S(b)|$ verhindert eine Bevorzugung von Bausteinen, an denen nur wenige Signale anliegen.

Ein Zufallszahlengenerator $\varphi_{\mu,2}$ erzwingt notfalls die Eindeutigkeit der Auswahl.

4.2. Die Auswahl eines Platzes

Im 2. Teilschritt des konstruktiven Plazierungsalgorithmus wird ein Platz für den im 1. Teilschritt ausgewählten Baustein b_μ gesucht. Die Pseudoleitungsführung wird die Auswahl des Platzes in dominierender Weise steuern. Bis auf kleine Varianten im Detail erscheint nur eine Vorgehensweise vernünftig. Der Baustein b_μ wird versuchsweise auf alle für ihn bezüglich seines Platzbedarfs möglichen Plätze gesetzt. Für Signale des Bausteins b_μ, die bereits Kontaktpunkte (Bausteine oder Pseudoleitungen) aus vorhergegangenen Schritten auf der Karte haben, werden die kürzest möglichen Pseudoleitungen versuchsweise gezogen. Derjenige Platz wird den Vorzug erhalten, bei dem für ein Maximum an Signalen die Pseudoleitungen auf freien Autobahnspuren untergebracht werden können. Ist diese Auswahl nicht eindeutig, so wird die Länge der Pseudoleitungen als weiteres Gütemaß hinzugezogen. Ein Gütemaß, das diese Strategie realisiert, kann wie folgt aussehen:

$$\psi_{\mu,2} : (i,k) \mapsto \sum_{s \in S(b_\mu) \cap O_{\mu-1}} \min_{(i',k')} \left(\sigma_s(i,k;i',k') + c \cdot \ell(i,k;i',k';s) \right)$$

Die einzelnen Komponenten dieser Formel bedürfen nun einer Definition und Erläuterung.

Der Leitungsbaum zum Signal s im μ-ten Schritt

$$L_\mu(s) = \left\{ (i,k) / s \in \bigcup_{b \in B^\mu_{ik}} S(b) \quad \text{oder } s \in SW^\mu_{ik} \quad \text{oder } s \in SS^\mu_{ik} \right\}$$

ist die Menge der Teilflächen, in denen für das Signal s nach dem μ-ten Schritt Kontaktpunkte vorhanden sind. In einer Teilfläche (i,k) existiert nach dem μ-ten Schritt ein Kontaktpunkt für ein

Signal s, wenn auf (i,k) in den ersten μ Schritten ein Baustein plaziert wurde, an dem das Signal s anliegt, oder wenn eine Autobahnspur in (i,k) für eine Pseudoleitung für das Signal s belegt wurde. Als kleine Zusatzinformation sei hier bemerkt, daß nach jedem Schritt die Mengen B^{μ}_{ik}, SW^{μ}_{ik}, SS^{μ}_{ik} auf den aktuellen Stand gebracht werden, indem die Vorgänge des μ-ten Schrittes in diesen Mengen archiviert werden. Die Mengen B^{μ}_{ik}, SW^{μ}_{ik}, SS^{μ}_{ik} repräsentieren dann den Stand der Plazierung und Leitungsfindung nach dem μ-ten Schritt.

Die Länge einer Pseudoleitung $\sigma_s(i',k';\ i'',k'')$ werde mit $|\sigma_s(i',k';i'',k'')|$ bezeichnet.

Die zweite Komponente im Gütemaß $\psi_{\mu,2}$ bewertet den Fall, ob eine geplante Pseudoleitung in freien Autobahnspuren möglich ist oder nicht. Dazu sei

$$c \gg \sum_{i=1}^{n} \sum_{k=1}^{m} (\xi_{ik} + \eta_{ik})$$

eine sehr große Konstante, die die theoretisch möglichen Längen von Pseudoleitungen bei weitem übersteigt. Für die Funktion ℓ gilt:

$$\ell(i,k;\ i',k';s) = \begin{cases} 0 & \text{wenn die Pseudoleitung } \sigma_s(i,k;i',k') \text{ möglich ist,} \\ 1 & \text{sonst.} \end{cases}$$

Dabei wird auch der Fall berücksichtigt, ob 2 oder mehr Signale des Bausteins in gleichen Autobahnabschnitten Spuren benötigen, diese jedoch nur noch für einen Teil der Signale ausreichen.

Die Beschaffenheit von $\psi_{\mu,2}$ läßt es sinnvoll erscheinen, nicht alle Plätze aus $P_{\mu}(t(b_{\mu}))$ zu betrachten, sondern nur den Rand des schon von Bausteinen belegten Raumes. Genau sind dies diejenigen Teilflächen, die schon von Bausteinen belegt sind, aber noch einen Baustein vom Platzbedarf $t(b_{\mu})$ zusätzlich aufnehmen können, und die Teilflächen in der unmittelbaren Nachbarschaft von solchen Teilflächen, die einen Baustein vom Platzbedarf $t(b_{\mu})$ nicht mehr aufnehmen können.

Formal ist dies die Menge

$$R_{\mu}(t) = \Big\{ (i,k) \in P_{\mu}(t) \ / \big(t < \sum_{b \in B^{\mu}_{ik}} t(b) + t \leq \tau_{ik}\big) \ \text{oder(es existiert ein} \ (i',k') \in \mathcal{R} \ \text{mit} \ |i'-i| + |k'-k| = 2 \ \text{und} \ \tau_{i'k'} < \sum_{b \in B^{\mu}_{i'k'}} t(b) + t) \Big\},$$

die kurz freier Kranz im μ-ten Schritt zum Platzbedarf t heißen soll. Die Plätze aus $P_\mu(t) \setminus R_\mu(t)$ bringen offensichtlich keine neue Situation bezüglich der Anzahl der offenen Signale, für die Pseudoleitungen möglich sind und verkürzen die Längen dieser Pseudoleitungen sicher nicht.

Für den Auswahlvorgang tritt also $\psi_{\mu,1}$ in der Funktionenfolge vor das Gütemaß $\psi_{\mu,2}$ mit

$$\psi_{\mu,1} : (i,k) \mapsto \left\{ \begin{matrix} 0 \\ 1 \end{matrix} \text{ für } (i,k) \begin{matrix} \in R_\mu(t(b_\mu)), \\ \in P_\mu(t(b_\mu)) \setminus R_\mu(t(b_\mu)). \end{matrix} \right\}$$

Ein Zufallszahlengenerator $\psi_{\mu,3}$ erzwingt notfalls die Eindeutigkeit der Auswahl.

5. Schlußbemerkung

Der Autor möchte an dieser Stelle Frau Dr. Beyer für viele wertvolle Hinweise und für ihre ständige Diskussionsbereitschaft herzlich danken.

Abb. 1

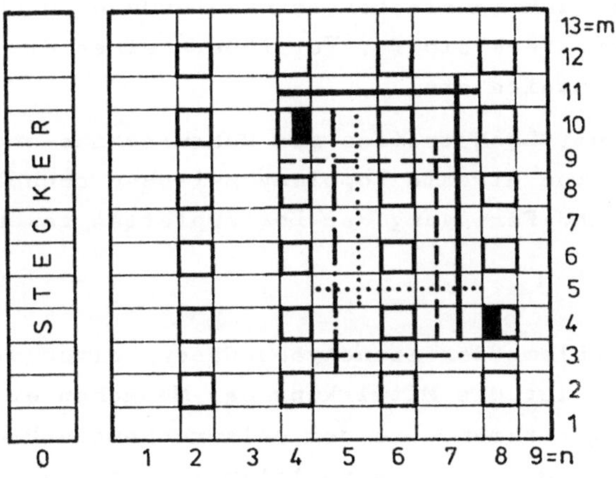

INTERAKTIVER EINSATZ VON SICHTGERÄTEN BEIM RECHNERUNTERSTÜTZTEN ENTWURF VON GROSSRECHNER-LEITERPLATTEN MIT HILFE DES PROGRAMMSYSTEMS ZEISIG

K.HORN

Zusammenfassung

Mit Hilfe des Programmsystems ZEISIG ist der direkte Eingriff des Menschen zur Lösung der Probleme der ebenengebundenen Leitungsführung und der Abänderung bereits fertig vorliegender Leiterplatten möglich.
ZEISIG stellt ein dialogfähiges graphisches Programmsystem dar, mit dem das Bild einer Leiterplatte auf dem Bildschirm dargestellt und durch Eingabe graphischer Daten verändert werden kann.
Folgende Programmleistungen ermöglichen einen wirkungsvollen Dialog:

- Auswahl der auf dem Bildschirm darzustellenden Bildelemente (Leitungen, Anschlüsse, Bohrungen, Sperrgebiete etc.).
- Aufruf von Auskunfteidiensten über den graphischen und logischen Inhalt einer Leiterplatte.
- Veränderungen der graphischen Daten der Bildelemente (Löschen, Neuzeichnen).

Zu diesen den Inhalt des Bildschirmbildes bestimmenden Kommandos treten verschiedene über Funktionstasten anzuwählende Bildschirmmanipulation wie Verschieben, Verkleinern, Vergrößern eines Bildausschnittes, Wechsel der Kartenseite etc.

Durch Ausgabe der Steuer-Lochstreifen für Bohrmaschine und Zeichentisch ist mit ZEISIG eine direkte Kopplung zwischen rechnerunterstützter Entwicklung und Fertigung der Leiterplatten gewährleistet.

1. Einleitung

Bei der Lösung des Problems der ebenengebundenen Leitungsführung auf einer Leiterplatte ist die Mitwirkung des Menschen erforderlich, weil die bekannten Algorithmen, die den entsprechenden Programmen zugrunde liegen, in der Regel keine vollständige Lösung liefern. Dies gilt vor allem dann, wenn sehr hohe Forderungen gestellt werden (repräsentative Werte für eine TR 440-Leiterplatte: 208 IC-Bauelemente, 86 Steckeranschlüsse, 480 cm^2 Fläche, zwei Ebenen für Leitungsführung).

Das Problem kann jedoch optimal mit dem Einsatz eines Sichtgerätes gelöst werden: das Bild einer Leiterplatte, wie es als Ergebnis eines Leitungsfindungsprogramms vorliegt, wird auf dem Bildschirm dargestellt; es kann dort vom Benutzer verändert werden: entweder ergänzt er alle noch fehlenden Leitungen oder er modifiziert das Leiterplattenbild derart, daß nach Rückgabe der Daten an das Leitungsfindungsprogramm die Leiterplatte von diesem fertiggestellt werden kann.

Die meisten bekannten Computer-Grafik-Systeme sind jedoch für die LSI-Technik entwickelt worden und lassen sich deshalb nur beschränkt auf die Probleme der Leiterplattenkonstruktion anwenden. Wir haben uns deshalb bei TELEFUNKEN COMPUTER entschlossen, selbst ein derartiges Programm namens ZEISIG ("Zeichne auf dem Sichtgerät") zu entwickeln.

2. ZEISIG-Manipulationen

Die von ZEISIG zu erbringenden Leistungen können angefordert werden

(a) durch Betätigung von Funktionstasten

(b) durch Eingabe von Kommandos über die Tastatur

Dieser gerätemäßigen Unterscheidung entspricht auch eine bedeutungsmäßige:

mit (a): Veränderung des auf dem Bildschirm gezeigten Teiles der Leiterplatte ("Fenster") in seiner Lage und Größe.

mit (b): Veränderung des Fensterinhaltes.

2.1. Funktionstastenbefehle

Der Benutzer wird nur in Ausnahmefällen an der Darstellung der gesamten Leiterplatte interessiert sein, da dann wegen der extrem hohen Datendichte Veränderungen des Bildes sehr schwierig auszuführen sind und leicht fehlerhaft werden. Er wird vielmehr einen bequemen Maßstab wählen, bei dem die einzelnen Bildelemente deutlich voneinander getrennt sind, wobei dann allerdings nur mehr ein Ausschnitt aus dem Bild der Leiterplatte gezeigt werden kann: er schaut gleichsam durch ein Fenster auf die Leiterplatte.

Mit Hilfe von Funktionstasten kann nun der Benutzer die Lage des Fensters nach oben, unten, links und rechts verschieben, er kann von einer Seite der Leiterplatte auf die andere wechseln, das Fenster verkleinern oder vergrößern. Damit er bei diesen Manipulationen niemals die Übersicht verliert, kann er von der Darstellung des Fensters auf die des "Übersichtsbildes" umstellen, auf dem die Leiterplatte

als Ganzes (jedoch nicht mit allen, sondern nur mit einigen die Orientierung unterstützenden Bildelementen) und darauf die augenblickliche Lage des Fensters gezeigt wird.
Bei einigen Befehlen ist es sinnvoll, zusätzlich zur betreffenden Funktionstaste auch noch die Repetitionstaste zu drücken: dies bewirkt eine fortlaufende Wiederholung des angewählten Auftrages.

2.2. Tastaturkommandos

2.2.1. Struktur der Kommandosprache

Die einzelnen Anweisungen ermöglichen es dem Benutzer, in einen Dialog mit dem Programm zu treten, indem er die von ihm gewünschte Programmleistung aufruft und nach seinen Angaben zur Ausführung bringt.

Die möglichen Kommandos sind in zwei Ebenen angeordnet: Durch die Kommandos der ersten Ebene ("primären Kommandos") erfolgt die Auswahl eines Oberbegriffes der zu erbringenden Leistung. Die Gesamtheit der primären Kommandos wird "primäres Menü" genannt.
Jedem primären Kommando ist eine Menge von Kommandos der zweiten Ebene ("sekundären Kommandos") zugeordnet, mit denen die zu erbringende Leistung spezifiziert wird. Die Menge der zum primären Kommando K_i gehörenden sekundären Kommando wird "zu K_i gehörendes sekundäres Menü" genannt.
Eine vom Programm zu erbringende Leistung ist erst dann ausreichend spezifiziert, wenn die primären und die sekundären Kommandos angegeben worden sind.

2.2.2. Vorhandene primäre und sekundäre Kommandos

Nach dem Laden des entsprechenden ZEISIG-Moduls erscheint auf dem Bildschirm in der ersten Zeile das primäre Menü, bestehend aus folgenden primären Kommandos:

DARSTELLUNG: Ausgabe der auf dem Bildschirm darzustellenden Bildelemente (koordinatenorientiertes Arbeiten).

INFORMATION: Aufruf diverser Auskunfteidienste, mit denen ein signalorientiertes Arbeiten unterstützt wird.

VERAENDERUNG: Veränderungen der graphischen Daten.

ARCHIVIERUNG: Abänderung des Archivs aufgrund der mit den V-Kommandos durchgeführten Änderungen.

Der Benutzer wählt ein primäres Kommando durch Eingabe des entsprechenden Buchstabens in die Tastatur an. Danach erscheint in der

zweiten Zeile das zum angewählten primären Kommando gehörende sekundäre Menü.
Zu den einzelnen primären Kommandos sind dies folgende sekundären Kommandos:

(D) DARSTELLUNG

- Darstellung aller Leitungen, aller Anschlüsse, aller Bohrungen, aller Sperrgebiete innerhalb des Fensters.
- Darstellung aller Bildelemente innerhalb des Fensters.

(I) INFORMATION

- Darstellung aller Bildelemente, die zu speziell angewählten Signalen gehören.
- Ausgabe des Namens desjenigen Signals, das das mit der Rollkugel markierte Bildelement enthält.
- Ausgabe der Länge des Leitungsnetzes desjenigen Signals, dessen Namen eingegeben wurde oder das das mit der Rollkugel markierte Bildelemente enthält.
- Die Bildelemente eines Signals flackern, wenn noch nicht alle Teile des Leitungsnetzes miteinander verbunden sind.
- Ausgabe der Namen derjenigen Signale, deren Netze noch nicht vollständig verbunden sind.

(V) VERAENDERUNG

- Löschen eines Polygonzuges zwischen zwei markierten Endpunkte einschließlich der dazwischenliegenden Bohrungen.
- Löschen einer Bohrung.
- Löschen aller Figuren eines Signalnetzes.
- Neuzeichnen eines Streckenzuges.
- Neuzeichnen einer Bohrung (anschließend Wechsel der Seite der Leiterplatte).
- Einschalten des Rasterkorrekturprogramms: bei Neuzeichne-Kommandos wird automatisch im Kartenraster gezeichnet: die eingegebenen Koordinaten werden auf den nächsten Rasterpunkt gelegt.

Bei Neuzeichne-Manipulationen wird auf Kreuzungsfreiheit überprüft; Meldung wenn eine andere Figur geschnitten wird.

(C) ARCHIVIERUNG

- Zeigen des "neuen Zustandes" = Zustand nach Abschluß der vorausgegangenen V-Manipulationen.

- Zeigen des "alten Zustandes" = Zustand vor Beginn der V-Manipulationen, d. h. nach der letzten Archivierung.
- Die Archivierung (Abänderung der Daten im Archiv entsprechend der ausgeführten V-Manipulationen) erfolgt erst dann, wenn bei der Darstellung des neuen Zustandes der Benutzer die Richtigkeit der Änderungen bestätigt.

2.2.3. Dateneingabe

Bei einigen Kommandos werden Daten benötigt. Im allgemeinen kann für diese Dateneingabe eine Auswahl unter verschiedenen Geräten getroffen werden (Tastatur, Rollkugel, Verschiebepfeile auf Tastatur). So kann z. B. für die Anforderung der Signallänge entweder der Namen des Signals über die Tastatur eingegeben werden oder der Benutzer kann mit der Rollkugel einen Punkt auf einem zum Leitungsnetz des Signals gehörenden Bildelement markieren. Die Verschiebepfeile dienen zur bequemen Eingabe von Linienzügen in horizontaler oder vertikaler Richtung.

2.2.4. Datensicherung

Damit durch unachtsame Lösche- und Neuzeichne-Manipulationen nicht ungewollt Daten zerstört werden, sind folgende Maßnahmen zur Datensicherung vorhanden:

(1) Jede Änderung wird zunächst nur auf dem Bildschirm ausgeführt.

(2) Durch Eingabe von + oder - wird diese Änderung bestätigt (und in eine Änderungsdatei eingetragen) oder rückgängig gemacht.

(3) Die Daten der bestätigten Manipulationen können nicht innerhalb des sekundären Menüs zu VERAENDERUNG in das Archiv eingetragen werden; es muß vielmehr erst das primäre Kommando ARCHIVIERUNG aufgerufen werden.

3. Archivaufbau

Eine wesentliche Voraussetzung für das erfolgreiche Arbeiten mit einnem Sichtgerät ist eine dem jeweiligen Problem optimal angepaßte Anordnung der Daten in einer Datei, dem sog. "Archiv". Im Zusammenhang mit der Leiterplattenkonstruktion ergeben sich folgende Forderungen, die im Archivaufbau realisiert sein müssen:

(a) Änderungsfreundlichkeit: Hinzufügen und Löschen von Bild-Elementen und von Teilen von Bildelementen.

(b) Orientierung nach Signalen: Im allgemeinen sind bei der rechnerunterstützten Entwicklung von Leiterplatten die Daten nach den auf der Leiterplatte vorhandenen Signalen angeordnet. Der Benutzer möchte deshalb schnell alle Bildelemente erkennen, die zu einem Signal gehören; ferner wünscht er eine Auskunft darüber, ob alle Anschlußpunkte des Signals miteinander verbunden sind oder noch nicht; ist dies der Fall, so möchte er alle noch zu verbindenden Punkte markiert sehen, damit er durch entsprechende Manipulation das Leitungsnetz vervollständigen kann.

(c) Orientierung nach Koordinaten: alle Bildelemente sowie die dazugehörigen Signale können durch Markierung eines beliebigen Punktes auf dem Element mit der Rollkugel angesprochen werden.

(d) Kurze Anwortzeiten im Dialog Benutzer - Programm beim Arbeiten am Sichtgerät.

Alle oben genannten Forderungen werden im ZEISIG-Archiv erfüllt.

Das Archiv gliedert sich in zwei strukturell stark voneinander abweichende Teile:

- in ein signalorientiertes Archiv ("Figurenarchiv")
- in ein koordinatenorientiertes Archiv ("Koordinatenarchiv").

3.1. Figurenarchiv

Das Figurenarchiv ist aufgebaut aus den darzustellenden Bildelementen, wobei der "Figur" (Streckenzug, Bohrung, Lötauge) eine grundlegende Bedeutung zukommt. Die Organisation erfolgt nach dem Gesichtspunkt, die zwischen den Bildelementen vorhandenen geometrischen und logischen Relationen zu erfassen und einen schnellen Zugriff von einem Element zu dem nächsten ihm inhaltlich verwandten zu gewährleisten.

Das Figurenarchiv besteht deshalb aus einem Wald von Bäumen, wobei jeweils ein Baum alle zu einem Siganl gehörenden Bildelemente enthält. Die Bildelemente, die Knoten, sind in den drei Ebenen der Signale, Teilnetze und Figuren angeordnet. Die Kanten geben die Zusammenfassung von Figuren zu einem Teilnetz (alle Figuren eines Teilnetzes sind untereinander verbunden; ein noch nicht verbundener Anschlußpunkt eines Signals bildet ein - aus einer Figur bestehendes - Teilnetz) sowie die der Teilnetze zum gesamten Leitungsnetz eines

Signals wieder (das Leitungsnetz eines Signals ist genau dann vollständig verbunden, wenn es aus nur einem Teilnetz besteht).

Diese Struktur wird durch folgende Kettenorganisation realisiert:
Es treten zwei Kettentypen auf:
Im ersten schließen sich an den Ankersatz des Signals die Kettenglieder der zugehörigen Teilnetzsätze an. Der Signalsatz enthält zusätzliche Informationen über den Signalnamen und die Länge des Leitungsnetzes.
Jeder Teilnetzsatz ist Anker für den zweiten Kettentyp; die dazugehörigen Kettenglieder sind die Sätze der das Teilnetz bildenden Figuren. Im Figurensatz ist die graphische Information enthalten.
Die Verkettung der Gliedsätze erfolgt über einen Vorgänger- und Nachfolger-Zeiger, die im Falle des ersten bzw. letzten Kettengliedes auf den Ankersatz verweisen. Vom Ankersatz weist je ein Zeiger auf das erste und letzte Kettenglied.

Infolge der großen Datenmenge, die zur vollständigen Beschreibung des Bildes einer Leiterplatte notwendig ist, kann das Archiv nicht als Ganzes im Kernspeicher belassen werden: es wird vielmehr in Plattendateien abgelegt. Lediglich der Teil des Archivs, der die notwendigen Daten für die gerade durchgeführte Manipulation enthält, wird als "aktueller Archiv-Auszug" (AAA) im Kernspeicher gehalten: es sind dies

- bei D-Kommandos: alle Figuren innerhalb des Fensters und dessen nächster Umgebung
- bei I-Kommandos: alle Figuren zum angewählten Signal auf der ganzen Leiterplatte.

Mit der AAA-Konzeption wird die Zahl der Plattenzugriffe minimal gehalten, und es können deshalb günstige Antwortzeiten erreicht werden.

3.2. Koordinatenarchiv

Das Koordinatenarchiv besteht aus einer hierarchischen Struktur von Grob- und Feintabellen, mit deren Hilfe die Adresse derjenigen Figur im Figurenarchiv gefunden wird, die dem Punkt, dessen Koordinaten (z. B. mit der Rollkugel) eingegeben worden sind, zugeordnet werden kann.

4. Einsatz in der Leiterplattenkonstruktion

Die Herstellung von Leiterplatten ist ein langer und mühseliger Weg: werden die Leitungen manuell am Reißbrett konstruiert, geklebt, mit einem Digitalisierungsgerät aufgenommen und wird schließlich die Leiterplatte mit den notwendigen Kontrolläufen gezeichnet. so kann eine längere Zeitspanne vergehen zwischen der Abgabe der Unterlagen des Entwicklers an die Konstruktion und der Lieferung der fertigen bestückten Leiterplatte. Es sind deshalb energische Anstrengungen notwendig, um eine Durchlaufverkürzung zu erreichen: dies gelingt durch technische Vereinheitlichung (z. B. festes Bohrbild) und durch strukturelle Veränderungen im Ablauf.

Eine solche Änderung wäre der Übergang von der manuellen zur halbautomatischen Methode unter Einsatz von ZEISIG mit folgenden Schritten:

(1) Plazierung der Bausteine auf der Leiterplatte mit einem Plazierungsprogramm.

(2) Ermittlung der Leitungen per Programm.

(3) Vervollständigung des Leiterplattenbildes am Sichtgerät mit ZEISIG.

(4) Vergleich des Ist- mit dem Soll-Zustand per Programm.

(5) Bei Abweichungen: Abänderungen mit ZEISIG, so daß Soll- und Ist-Zustand übereinstimmen.

(6) ZEISIG: Ausgabe der Steuerlochstreifen für Zeichentisch und Bohrmaschine.

Es ist somit ein Einsatz von ZEISIG an zwei Stellen möglich:

- im Zusammenhang mit der Leitungsfindung
- beim Änderungsdienst in der Zeichenstelle.

DIE GRUNDLAGEN DES PROGRAMMS A T E D I S

K.PFEUFFER

1. Einleitung

Bevor hier auf das Thema dieses Vortrags eingegangen werden kann, muß zunächst etwas darüber gesagt werden, was sich hinter dem Begriff ATEDIS verbirgt. Der Name ist eine Abkürzung für "Automatische Testerstellung bei digitalen Schaltwerken". ATEDIS steht damit stellvertretend für die Aufgabe, Programme zu entwickeln, die direkt als Prüfprogrammgeneratoren arbeiten oder entsprechende Zuarbeit für solche Generatoren leisten. Das bedeutet, daß es sich bei ATEDIS um eine Reihe von geplanten bzw. vorhandenen Operatoren handelt, wobei wir unter Operator immer ein Programm verstehen, das autonom auf dem Rechner läuft, d. h. also mit einem STARTE-Kommando in Gang gesetzt werden kann.

Alle bisher entstandenen Operatoren sind in FORTRAN codiert. Davon sind fertiggestellt und mit folgenden Leistungen ausgestattet:

a) Operator S1:
   Erzeugt Steuerlochstreifen für den TFK-Testautomaten KAPA für kombinatorische oder streng synchrone Schaltwerke auf der Basis der Einfachsensibilisierung.

b) Operator S10:
   Leistung wie S1, aber Ausgabe von Steuerlochstreifen für das Prüfsystem NC 820.

c) Operator ASS2:
   Erzeugt Steuerlochstreifen für KAPA und NC 820 für asynchrone Schaltwerke mit Einfach- und Mehrfachsensibilisierung und Überprüfung der erstellten Tests auf Hasardfreiheit durch logisch fünfwertige Simulation. Außerdem wird die Zahl der zu sensibilisierenden Wege dadurch optimiert, daß vor jeder Testberechnung geprüft wird, ob der zu prüfende Weg nicht schon durch andere Tests überprüft wird.

d) Operator HAKORR(1):
Ermöglicht eine manuelle Umsortierung von Testschritten, wenn der betreffende Testsatz vom Operator ASS2 als hasardbehaftet erkannt worden ist.

Zur Vorstellung der Größe solcher Operatoren mögen die folgenden Angaben des Operators ASS2 dienen:

a) Befehlsumfang: ca. 10 000 FORTRAN-Statements

b) Kernspeicherbedarf: 75 K

c) Hintergrundspeicherbedarf: 1400 K

d) Laufzeiten: zwischen 5 und 200 Minuten

e) Schaltwerksgröße: 800 Ausgangsfunktionen mit 9 Eingängen (bei mehr Eingängen entsprechend weniger Ausgangsfunktionen).

2. Die Grundlagen des ATEDIS-Verfahrens

2.1. Die Wegsensibilisierung

Um sicherzugehen, daß kein Fehler in einem Schaltwerk vorliegt, muß man eigentlich das zu prüfende Schaltwerk alle seine möglichen Zustände durchlaufen lassen. Dies führt jedoch in der Praxis bei der Größe heutiger Schaltwerke zu nicht mehr vertretbarem Zeit- und Rechenaufwand. Dieser wird durch die Wegsensibilisierungsverfahren sinnvoll eingeschränkt, wobei allerdings auch das Fehlererkennungsvermögen des Verfahrens in gewisser Weise verringert wird. Alle Wegsensibilisierungsverfahren vermögen nämlich sogenannte "topologisch aktive Fehler" nicht mit Sicherheit zu entdecken, da sie bei der Testerstellung ja gerade von der Soll-Topologie des Schaltwerks ausgehen und topologische Erweiterungen, die durch Fehler entstanden sind, nicht in Rechnung stellen können. Einschränkungen durch Fehler gegenüber der Soll-Topologie werden selbstverständlich erkannt. Was bedeutet nun überhaupt "Wegsensibilisierung"? Man versteht unter Wegsensibilisierung folgenden Vorgang: In einem Schaltwerk wird durch eine Menge von Eingangssignalen dafür gesorgt, daß ein bestimmter Schaltwerksausgang im fehlerfreien Fall nur noch eine Funktion eines einzigen Eingangssignals ist. Der Signalweg von diesem Eingang (primary input) zu dem Ausgang (observable output) heißt dann sensibilisierter Weg. Wenn wir ein simples Beispiel nehmen wollen:
Bei einem NOR-Gatter wird der Weg von einem Eingang zum Ausgang dadurch sensibilisiert, daß alle übrigen Eingänge auf logisch Null gelegt werden.

Das mathematische Hilfsmittel mit dem man derartige Sensibilisierungsbelegungen berechnen kann, ist bei ATEDIS die sogenannte "Boolesche Differenz".

Darunter versteht man folgendes:
Die Boolesche Differenz einer Booleschen Funktion $F(X1,X2,\ldots,Xi,\ldots Xn)$ bezüglich einer Variablen Xi ist das Exklusive ODER der Funktion mit sich selbst, wobei jedoch die Variable Xi einmal negiert wird. In Formeln also:

$$\frac{dF}{dXi} = F(X1,X2,\ldots,Xi,\ldots,Xn) \oplus F(X1,X2,\ldots,\overline{Xi},\ldots,Xn)$$

Man kann zeigen, daß die Funktion dF/dXi von Xi unabhängig ist.

$$F(X1,X2,\ldots,Xi,\ldots Xn) = F1 \cdot Xi + F2 \cdot \overline{Xi} + F3$$

$$\frac{dF}{dXi} = (F1 \cdot Xi + F2 \cdot \overline{Xi} + F3) \oplus (F1 \cdot \overline{Xi} + F2 \cdot Xi + F3)$$

$$= \overline{F3}(F1 \oplus F2)$$

Macht man andererseits die Funktion dF/dXi durch entsprechende Wahl der $Xj (j \neq i)$ "wahr", dann bedeutet das, daß $F(X1,X2,\ldots Xi,\ldots Xn)$ nur noch von Xi abhängt, denn beim Übergang von $Xi \rightarrow \overline{Xi}$ ändert sich auch F, sonst wäre p. Def. das Exklusive ODER nicht "wahr".

Bildet man also die Boolesche Differenz eines Schaltwerkausgangs bezüglich einer Eingangsvariablen und macht diese Boolesche Differenz wahr, so erhält man die Sensibilisierungsbedingungen für den Signalweg von dem betreffenden Eingang zum Ausgang.

Die Voraussetzung für einen Einsatz der Booleschen Differenz ist natürlich der, daß in ihr nur noch Schaltwerkeingangsvariable vorkommen, da für die Prüfautomaten das Schaltwerk nur über Steckerkontakte zugänglich sein soll.

Diese Bedingung beschränkte den Einsatz der Booleschen Differenz zur Testerstellung zunächst auf kombinatorische Schaltwerke für deren Ausgangsfunktion tatsächlich eine Zurückführung auf Eingangsvariable möglich ist. Das waren die Ergebnisse, die in der Arbeit [2] veröffentlicht worden sind. Ende 1969 haben Dr. Hsiao und ich,unabhängig voneinander,einen Algorithmus entdeckt, der es ermöglicht, Boolesche Differenzen auch für sequentielle Schaltwerke zu erstellen.
Der Wegsensibilisierungsalgorithmus bei ATEDIS unterscheidet dabei zwei Sensibilierungsarten.

2.2. Einfachsensibilisierung

Die Sensibilisierungsbedingung für jedes Wegstück muß wahr gemacht werden, damit das betreffende Wegstück per Definition sensibilisiert wird. Um einen ganzen Weg von einem Stecker-Eingang zu einem beobachtbaren Ausgang zu sensibilisieren, muß also die konjunktive Verknüpfung aller Wegstück-Sensibilisierungsbedingungen geschaffen werden, d. h. aber, man bildet die Konjunktion der Booleschen Differenzen aller Wegstücke, d. h. der Bausteinteilfunktionen, die zu dem betreffenden Wegstück gehören. Zum Beweis dieser Behauptung genügt es, anzunehmen, es seien auf einem sensibilisierten Weg nicht alle Wegstück-Sensibilisierungsbedingungen wahr. Dies führt sofort zum Widerspruch, da der Weg per Definition nur dann sensibilisiert ist, wenn alle seine Wegstücke sensibilisiert sind.

Andererseits haben wir gezeigt, daß die Boolesche Differenz einer Booleschen Funktion bezüglich einer Eingangsvariablen gerade diese Eingangsvariable nicht enthält. Bildet man deshalb die Boolesche Differenz eines Weges nach dem oben beschriebenen Verfahren (Kettenregel) so ist aus dem Ergebnis jeder Term zu entfernen, der die Wegeingangsvariable enthält. Derartige Fälle treten nur beim sogenannten "reconverging fanout" auf. Ein solcher Fall bedeutet, daß aus der Menge der Sensibilisierungskonjunktionen eines Wegstückes nicht alle Elemente dieser Menge für die Gesamtwegsensibiliserung herangezogen werden können, sondern gerade nur jene Elemente, die beim "reconverging fanout" nicht mit dem zu sensibilisierenden Weg verknüpft sind. Damit kommen wir zur nächsten Sensibilisierungsart.

2.3. Mehrfachsensibilisierung

Gibt es nämlich für eine nach der "Kettenregel" erstellte Boolesche Differenz keinen einzigen Term ohne die Wegeingangsvariable, so führt das nach unserem Algorithmus zum identischen Verschwinden der Booleschen Differenz des Gesamtweges, d. h. jedoch, dieser Weg ist nicht sensibilisierbar, genauer gesagt ist er nicht allein sensibilisierbar, sondern nur zusammen mit einem oder mehreren anderen Wegen. Dabei handelt es sich jedoch wohlgemerkt stets um Wege, die den Stecker-Eingang und den beobachtbaren Ausgang gemeinsam haben! Dies ist z. B. der Fall bei eingebauter Redundanz, aber auch in Schaltungen der folgenden Art, die im Rechner TR 440 recht häufig vorkommen.

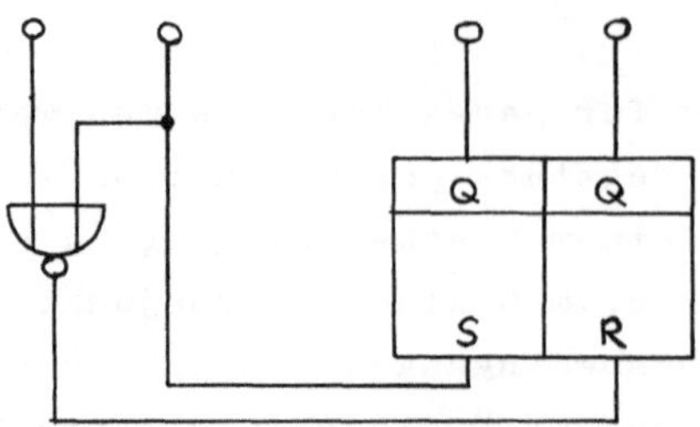

Die Tatsache, daß jeder Term der nach der Kettenregel erstellten Booleschen Differenz noch die Wegeingangsvariable enthält, stellt folgenden Sachverhalt dar: Es gibt auf dem zu sensibilisierenden Weg mindestens ein Bauelement, bei dem zur Sensibilisierung ein Signal verwendet werden muß, das über einen Fanout von unserem Prüfsignal herrührt. Da jeder Term der Booleschen Differenz dieses Signal enthält, ist keine andere Lösung als die einer Mehrfachsensibilisierung möglich. In diesem Fall wird jetzt jedoch in jedem Term die Eingangsvariable wahr gemacht, d. h. einfach weggelassen und nicht wie vorher der ganze Term verworfen.

2.4. Testerstellung für asynchrone Schaltwerke

Zum Schluß soll noch das Problem der asynchronen Schaltwerke angeschnitten werden. Bei der Testerstellung mit Hilfe der Booleschen Differenzen, die nach der Kettenregel erzeugt werden, können auch speichernde Elemente verarbeitet werden. Dazu teilt das Programm das Schaltwerk und den betreffenden Weg in Zeitbereiche ein, wobei topologisch hintereinanderliegende Speicherbausteine nicht in denselben Zeitbereich gehören. Was an Ansteuerung innerhalb eines Zeitbereiches berechnet wird, ist also gleichzeitig zu betrachten, d. h. es werden keine Laufzeiten und Verzögerungen in Betracht gezogen. Das bedeutet aber, daß die so erstellten Tests nur bei streng synchronen Schaltwerken einwandfrei arbeiten, bei asynchronen dagegen Hasards erzeugen können. Um dennoch das Verfahren für asynchrone Schaltwerke anwenden zu können, wurde folgender Weg eingeschlagen: Der Testautomat steuert das Schaltwerk sequentiell, d. h. Belegung für Belegung in relativ langsamer Reihenfolge an (ca. 130 µs). Damit wird für die Schaltwerksteile, die reine Baumstruktur haben, die Lage einfach, für Teile mit "reconverging fanout" dagegen nicht. Um das einwandfreie Arbeiten der Tests zu gewährleisten, wird nun jeder erstellte Test simuliert, und zwar wird die sequentielle Arbeitsweise des Testautomaten simuliert. Ausgegangen wird dabei davon, daß das Schaltwerk sich in einem unbekannten Zustand befindet, was bei der Simulation durch den Wert - 1 ausgedrückt wird. Durch die sequentielle Belegungsweise erhält man bei reiner Baumstruktur eine eindeutige Zuordnung von Hasards zum entsprechenden Test. Bei "reconverging fanout" haben wir dagegen ein "worst-case-Verfahren" zur Simulation herangezogen, das einen Hasard anzeigt, wenn er prinzipiell möglich ist. Dazu werden die verschiedenen Zweige des "reconverging-fanout" nacheinander gerechnet, und zwar zuerst die topologisch kürzeren. Führt ein Test zu einem essentiellen Hasard, weil ein Speicherbaustein sich im falschen Zustand befindet, so wird das vom Simulator bemerkt, da er die Ist- mit den Soll-Zuständen vergleicht. Der Simulator bearbeitet übrigens nur den Teil des Schaltwerks, der zu dem beobachtbaren Ausgang führt und von diesem Teil werden nur die Bausteinausgänge neu berechnet, bei denen sich mindestens ein Eingangssignal geändert hat.

Da die Belegungsfolgefrequenz des Testautomaten hinreichend niedrig gewählt wurde, kann davon ausgegangen werden, daß das Schaltwerk sich bereits in Ruhe befindet wenn der nächste Belegungswechsel stattfindet, es sei denn, das Schaltwerk ist durch die Art der Belegung instabil geworden. Genau das wird auch vom Simulator überprüft, der Instabilität meldet, wenn das Schaltwerk nach einer Belegungsänderung in irgendeinem Teil oszilliert.

Der eingangs erwähnte Operator HAKORR(1) gestattet uns die Reihenfolge der Belegungen eines Zeitbereiches, für die es vom Verfahren her zunächst keine Hinweise gibt, sondern die vom Programm willkürlich angenommen wird, beim Auftreten eines Hasards zu permutieren, so daß der Hasard vermieden wird, was wiederum durch Simulation überprüft wird.

3. Beispiele

Die folgenden Beispiele stammen von einem Lauf des Operators ASS2 mit den Daten der Kanalwerk-Steckeinheit KW2 des TR 440. Der Stromlaufplan in Abb. 1 gibt den 8. Teil der Steckeinheit wieder. Anhand der folgenden Originalausdrucke kann der Verlauf der Sensibilisierung und des Prüfsignals (9999) leicht nachvollzogen werden.

1. Beispiel:

```
ZEILE DER WEGLISTE  89
TESTSATZ NR.:  43
EINGANG  103: AUSGANG  70:

 1.TESTSATZVORSCHLAG
INTERNE EXTREMWERTE DER BELEGUNGSZEITEBENEN:
 MAXIMUM =     4 : MINIMUM =     1

D-DURCHLAUF VOM AUSGANG ZUM EINGANG:
       70       248       247       244 1100244       245       229       103
        1        -1         2        -2        -2         2         3         3
ZEIT- UND BELEGUNGSSORTIERTER TESTSATZ
ENDEKRITERIEN:  TAKTE:=L:-1  :TAKTE=O:-2  : DATEN=L:-3  : DATEN=O:-4
ZEITEBENENGRENZE:-5
       74        66        -3       103        73        69        76        -4
-5        73        76        -3        95        75        86        -4     9999
    -3        -5        69        95        66        -3        76        -4        -5
  66        -3        -5
```

2. Beispiel:

```
ZEILE DER WEGLISTE  52
TESTSATZ NR.:  28
EINGANG 138:  AUSGANG  67:

 1. TESTSATZVORSCHLAG
INTERNE EXTREMWERTE DER BELEGUNGSZEITEBENEN:
 MAXIMUM =     4 : MINIMUM =     1

D-DURCHLAUF VOM AUSGANG ZUM EINGANG:
       67       255       459       371 1100371       369       367       364
       -1        -1         1        -2        -2         2         3        -3
  1000364       237       232       138
       -3         3        -3         3

ZEIT -UND BELEGUNGSSORTIERTER TESTSATZ
ENDEKRITERIEN:: TAKTE=L:-1 : TAKTE=O:-2 : DATEN=L:-3 : DATEN=O:-4
ZEITEBENENGRENZE:-5
      112        84         3        71        87       120       138        -4
       -5       137
       84       112        -3        71        87       120        -4      9999
       -4        -5
      120       103        73        -3       112        87        86        -4
       -5       139        -3        68        -4        -5
```

4. Literaturhinweise

[1] Arthur D. Friedman, Premachandran R. Menon, "Fault Detection in Digital Circuits", Prentice-Hall, Inc., Englewood Cliffs, New Jersey

[2] F. F. Sellers, M. Y. Hsiao, L. W. Bearnson, "Analyzing errors with the Boolean Difference", IEEE Trans. Comp. Vol. C. 17. No 7, July 1968, p.p. 676-683

[3] K. Pfeuffer, Prüf- und Diagnosetests für sequentielle Schaltwerke, AEG-Telefunken DBS 2700271

[4] I. P. Roth, "Diagnosis of automata failures: a calculus and a method", IBM J. Res. Rev. Vol. 10, July 1966, p.p. 278-291

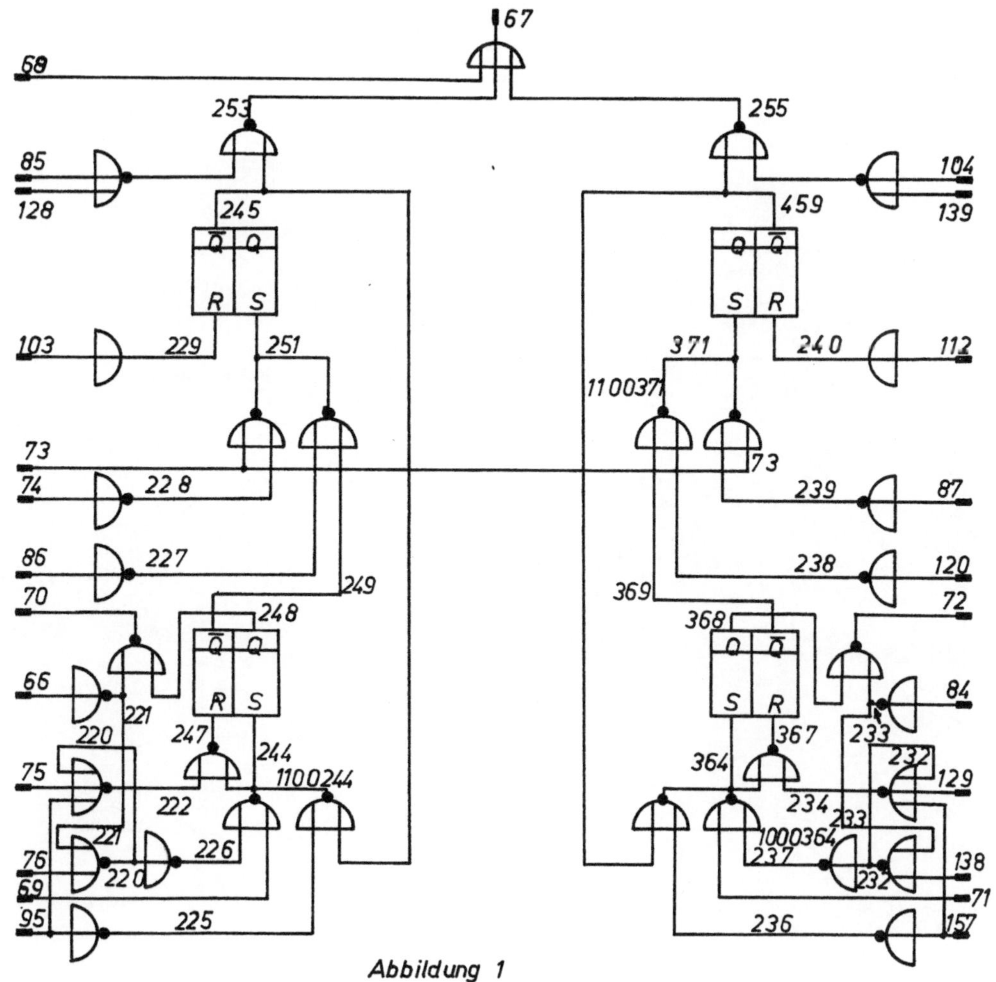

Abbildung 1

INFORMATIONSSYSTEME

N E O S - EIN ANSATZ ZUR LÖSUNG EINIGER OFFENER PROBLEME BEI DER KONZEPTION VON DATENBANKSYSTEMEN

E.FALKENBERG ET AL.

O. Einführung

Bei der Konzeption von Datenbanksystemen[1] kann man folgende fünf Hauptproblemkreise unterscheiden:

Sprachliche Mittel für den Benutzer
Operationen an Datenbeständen auf logischer Ebene
Physikalischer Zugriff und Speicherung
Datenstrukturen
Datenschutz und Datensicherung

Das vorliegende Papier beschränkt sich auf die Kurzdarstellung einiger Ansätze betreffend die Problemkreise Datenstrukturen und Operationen an Datenbeständen auf logischer Ebene. Außerdem wird ein Überblick über den Gesamtaufbau des Systems gegeben.

1. Zielsetzungen von NEOS

Beim Aufbau von computergestützten Informationssystemen tritt das Problem auf, Teile der Wirklichkeit möglichst exakt auf ein Datensystem[2] abzubilden. Der Forderung nach Exaktheit (insbesondere Vermeidung von Informationsverlusten) und nach Redundanzfreiheit werden bei komplexen Informationssystemen in den meisten Fällen nur Datensysteme von der Struktur eines allgemeinen endlichen Graphen (Netzwerke) gerecht. Deshalb sollten Datenbanksysteme netzwerkartige Datenstrukturen ohne jede Restriktion nicht nur zulassen, sondern auch generalisierte, effiziente, selbständige Funktionen zur problemorientierten und benutzerfreundlichen Handhabung solcher Netzwerke bereitstellen.
Dies ist die Hauptintention des vorliegenden Konzepts des Netzwerkoperationssystems NEOS.

---

1) Wir verstehen unter Datenbanksystemen (Generalized Data Base Management Systems) Softwaresysteme, mit deren Hilfe sich die Datenbanken von computergestützten Informationssystemen erzeugen, strukturieren, manipulieren und abfragen lassen.

2) Wir verstehen unter einem Datensystem ein strukturiertes System von Daten auf logischer Ebene.

Beim Entwurf eines speziellen Datensystems für eine Datenbank[3)] stößt man häufig auf Informationen, die Attribute eines bestimmten Gegenstandstyps sind und für alle Gegenstände dieses Typs denselben Inhalt haben. NEOS bietet eine Möglichkeit, eine Vielfachspeicherung solcher Informationen zu vermeiden.

Ein Datensystem enthält oft gewisse Daten, deren Inhalt oder Struktur von den Inhalten oder Strukturen anderer Daten abhängig sind. Bei der Änderung dieser Daten müssen jene einer Folgeänderung unterworfen werden. Mit Hilfe von NEOS kann man solche Folgeänderungen vorprogrammieren (Schneeballeffekt).

Es gibt verschiedene Typen von Benutzern, die auf eine Datenbank zugreifen. Grob unterscheidet man den Datenadministrator, den Anwendungsprogrammierer und den Nichtprogrammierer. Jeder möchte seinen Zugriffswunsch zur Datenbank auf eine ihm und seinem Problem adäquate Weise formulieren. Da es noch keine Sprache gibt, die allen Benutzertypen optimal angepaßt ist, erscheint es angeraten, bei einem Datenbanksystem verschiedene Sprachebenen zur Auswahl zur Verfügung zu stellen.

2. NEOS-Datenstrukturen

Beschränkt man sich zunächst, wie bei der klassischen Datenbank üblich, bei der Bildung eines Datensystems auf Zustände als Teile der Wirklichkeit, so ergibt sich die folgende Abbildung: Gegenstände werden durch Knoten, Relationen zwischen den Gegenständen werden durch Kanten repräsentiert. Es gibt zwei- und höherwertige Relationen. Die Knoten und im allgemeinen auch die Kanten sind mit Daten versehen, die Attribute der Gegenstände bzw. Relationen repräsentieren.

2.1 Bausteinkonzept

Um die Handhabung der Menge von Knoten und Kanten, die das Netzwerk bilden, zu vereinfachen, empfiehlt sich die Einführung eines einheitlichen Strukturelements, das sich folgendermaßen definieren läßt: Sind ungerichtete Kanten vorhanden, zerlegt man sie in entgegengesetzt gerichtete Kanten. Dann faßt man jeweils einen Knoten und alle von ihm weg gerichteten Kanten, den Verweisen, zugriffsmäßig zu einem solchen einheitlichen Element, einem Baustein, zusammen (s.Abb.1 und 2). Die Menge aller Bausteine bildet das Netzwerk. Ein Baustein repräsentiert die Informationen über einen Gegenstand und seine Beziehungen zu anderen Gegenständen. Bausteine, die dieselbe Datenstrukturbeschreibung (s.2.4) aufweisen, sind zu einer Datei zusammengefaßt.

---

3) Wir verstehen unter einer Datenbank die physikalische Realisierung eines Datensystems.

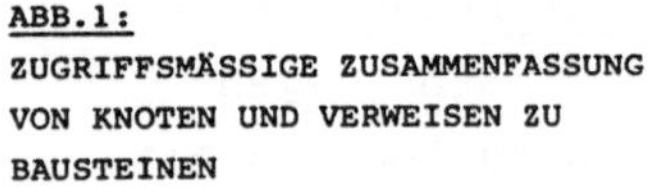

ABB.1:
ZUGRIFFSMÄSSIGE ZUSAMMENFASSUNG VON KNOTEN UND VERWEISEN ZU BAUSTEINEN

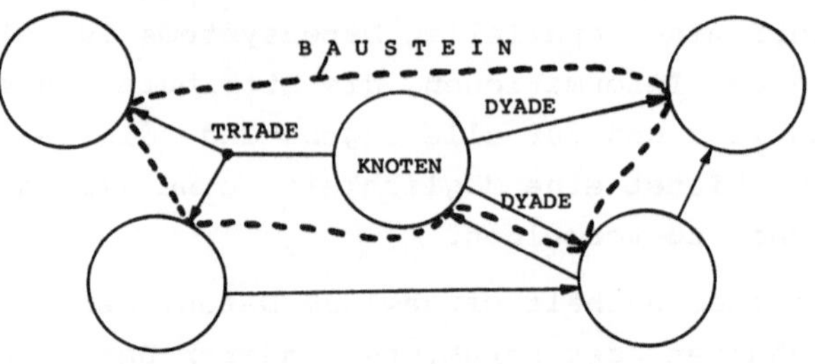

ABB.2:
BEISPIEL FÜR EINEN BAUSTEIN (PERSONALDATEI)

KNOTEN				VERWEIS (TRIADE)				VERWEIS (DYADE)			
12345	MAIER	KARL	01.01.40	A	10	XXXXXX	YYYYYY	B	1960	1970	ZZZZZZ
PERS.NR.	NAME	VORNAME	GEBURTSTAG		STD./WOCHE	POINTER NACH PROJEKT X	POINTER NACH PERSON Y		VON	BIS	POINTER NACH VORBILDUNG Z

ARBEITET AN PROJEKT (X) UNTER ANLEITUNG VON PERSON (Y) — HAT VORBILDUNG (Z)

Ein Knoten oder Verweis kann sich in mehrere Datengruppen gliedern.Eine Datengruppe ist eine Zusammenfassung derjenigen Daten, die bezüglich der Begriffe unbedingt oder bedingt, einmalig oder wiederholbar gleich zu behandeln sind. Diese Behandlung erfordert einen gewissen Speicher- und Organisationsaufwand, der nicht bei jedem einzelnen Datum, sondern nur bei einer Datengruppe aufgebracht werden muß.

2.2 Extraktkonzept

Informationen, die nicht nur einen bestimmten Gegenstand betreffen, sondern für alle Gegenstände eines Typs gleich sind, bedürfen einer Sonderbehandlung, wenn man sie nicht platzaufwendig in jedem Baustein einer Datei ablegen will. Und zwar kann man Daten bzw. Verweise, die solchen Informationen entsprechen, extrahieren und in einem Extraktbaustein zusammenfassen (s.Abb.3). Pro Datei ist ein Extraktbaustein vorgesehen, auf den bei Zugriffen zu anderen Bausteinen der Datei (Grundbausteine) stets auch zugegriffen wird, damit man die Information über einen Gegenstand und seine Beziehungen zu anderen Gegenständen vollständig zur Verfügung hat (s.Abb.4).

ABB.3:
BEISPIEL FÜR EINEN EXTRAKTBAUSTEIN (PERSONALDATEI)

KNOTEN		VERWEIS
GESAMTANZAHL DER PERSONEN	ALLGEMEINE RECHTE UND PFLICHTEN	UNTERSTEHT ORGANISATIONSEINHEIT

ABB.4:
AUFBAU EINER DATEI

EXTRAKTBAUSTEIN				
GRUNDBAUSTEIN 1	GRUNDBAUSTEIN 2	GRUNDBAUSTEIN 3	GRUNDBAUSTEIN 4	......

2.3 Folgeänderungskonzept

Daten, deren Inhalt oder Struktur von den Inhalten oder Strukturen anderer Daten abhängig ist, müssen bei der Änderung dieser Daten einer Folgeänderung unterworfen werden. Die Durchführung einer solchen Folgeänderung überläßt man entweder der Verantwortung des Datenadministrators oder einem Programm, das nach Durchführung der Primäränderung angesprungen wird und die Folgeänderung vornimmt.
Folgeänderungsprogramme sind eine besondere Art von gerichteten Beziehungen innerhalb eines Netzwerks und gehören logisch zur Beschreibung der Datenstruktur. Daten, deren Änderung Folgeänderungen auslösen soll, müssen eine Strukturbeschreibung besitzen, die ein Folgeänderungsprogramm oder einen Hinweis darauf enthält. Ein Anwendungsbeispiel dieses Konzepts ist die laufende selbsttätige Korrektur von akkumulierten Daten. (s.Abb.5).

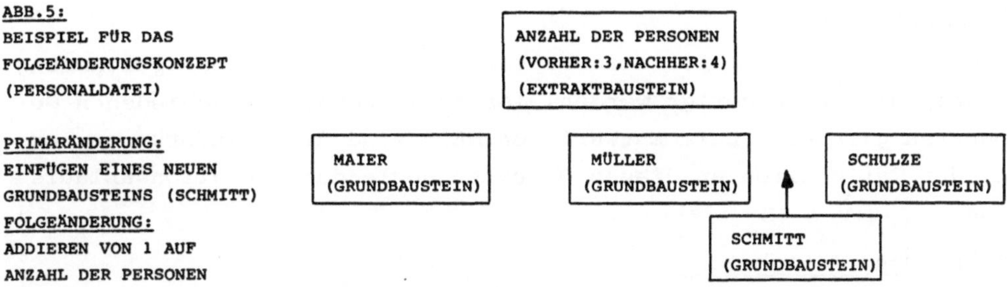

2.4 Strukturbeschreibung (Schema)

Das Schema gliedert sich in die Beschreibung der Speicherungs- und Zugriffsform und in die der Netzwerkstruktur. Erstere ist nicht fest vorgegeben, sondern kann vom Benutzer in einem vorgegebenen Rahmen gewählt werden. Vorgesehen sind die sequentielle, die index-sequentielle und die indirekt gestreute Speicherungs- und Zugriffsform sowie Kombinationen davon.
Die Netzwerkstrukturbeschreibung besteht aus den einzelnen Dateischemata. Diese gliedern sich jeweils in drei Teile, und zwar in einen allgemeinen Teil (Dateiname, Identifierbeschreibungen), einen Teil zur Beschreibung des Bausteinaufbaus (Knoten- und Verweisbeschreibungen) und einen Teil zur Beschreibung der Ordnung der verschiedenen Daten des Bausteins (zugriffsmäßigen Zusammenfassungen verschiedener Daten des Bausteins unter Kollektionsnamen). (s.Abb.6).

Enthält eine Datei einen Extraktbaustein, so gliedert sich die Beschreibung des Bausteinaufbaus in einen Teil für den Extraktbaustein und einen für die Grundbausteine.

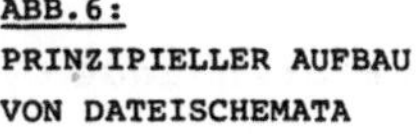
ABB.6:
PRINZIPIELLER AUFBAU
VON DATEISCHEMATA

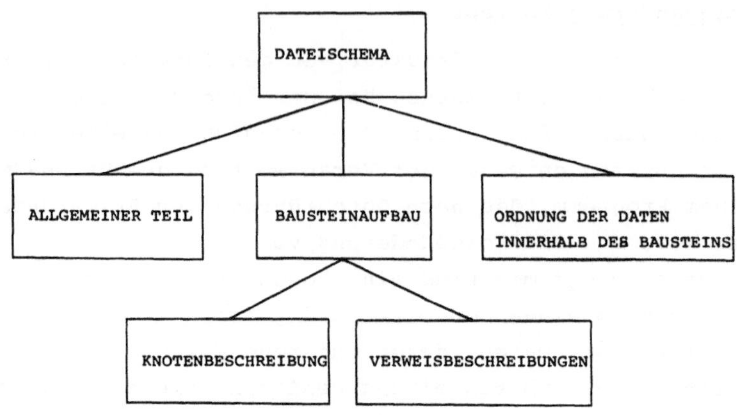

3. NEOS-Operationen

Operationen, wie sie in Informationssystemen zur Informationsspeicherung und -wiedergewinnung benötigt werden, lassen sich nach verschiedenen Gesichtspunkten gliedern. Beim Entwurf von NEOS sind die Gliederungen der Objekte, der Tätigkeiten an diesen Objekten sowie des Operationsablaufs maßgebend.

3.1 Objekte und Tätigkeiten

Man muß unterscheiden zwischen Operationen, die den Verkehr mit der Datenbank durchführen und solchen, die die Aufbereitung und Weiterverarbeitung der Daten betreffen. Die hier angeführte Gliederung gilt für die ersteren. Für die Objekte Schema, Instance, Struktur und Inhalt gelten folgende Definitionen (vgl.Abb.7):

Eine Datenmenge bedarf eines Behälters zu ihrer Aufbewahrung. Jeder Behälter besitzt eine Struktur. Man unterscheidet eine interne Struktur (Strukturierung des Behälters in seinem Inneren) und eine externe Struktur (Einbettung des Behälters in seine Umgebung). Der Behälter wird im allgemeinen mit einem Inhalt, der Datenmenge, aufgefüllt. Existiert von dem Behälter nicht nur eine Beschreibung, sondern ist er auch explizit vorhanden, wird er als Instance bezeichnet. Die Beschreibung der Struktur des Behälters heißt Schema. Man unterscheidet entsprechend der internen und externen Struktur ein internes und externes Schema.

An den so definierten Objekten sind gewisse Tätigkeiten durchzuführen, nämlich Erzeugen, Vernichten und Abfragen. Diese Tätigkeiten werden als Grundoperationen bezeichnet, weil sich Datenbankoperationen wie Einfügen, Löschen, Ändern, Abfragen aus ihnen zusammensetzen.

ABB.7:
OBJEKTE UND TÄTIGKEITEN

OBJEKTE \ TÄTIGKEITEN			BEEINFLUSSEN		ABFRAGEN
			ERZEUGEN	VERNICHTEN	
SCHEMA		INTERN / EXTERN	1	1	2,3,4,5,6,7
INSTANCE	STRUKTUR	INTERN / EXTERN	2	3	2,3,4,5,6,7
INSTANCE	INHALT		2,5,6	4	5,7

An einigen Beispielen wird gezeigt, wie sich herkömmliche Datenbankoperationen aus den oben angegebenen Grundoperationen zusammensetzen lassen (s.Abb.7):

1: Datenstrukturdefinition
2: Einfügen von Behältern
3: Löschen von Behältern
4: Löschen von Inhalten
5: Ändern von Inhalten in Abhängigkeit von anderen Inhalten
6: Überschreiben von Inhalten
7: Abfragen von Inhalten

3.2 Operationsablauf

Zu Beginn einer Operation steht häufig das Suchen in der Datenbank. Was gesucht werden soll, wird durch eine Prämisse definiert. Weitere Vorgänge im Operationsablauf sind das Abspeichern in die Datenbank, die Eingabe und die Ausgabe sowie die Transformation von Daten (z.B.Ändern, Aggregieren).(s.Abb.8).

Eine solche Gliederung bietet sich für den modularen Aufbau der Operationen an, da sich klare und einfache Schnittstellen ergeben.

Da Instance und Schema verschiedenartig strukturiert sind, muß man Vorgänge, die das Instance betreffen, und solche, die das Schema betreffen, unterscheiden.

ABB.8:
VORGÄNGE IM OPERATIONSABLAUF UND IHRE MÖGLICHE AUFEINANDERFOLGE

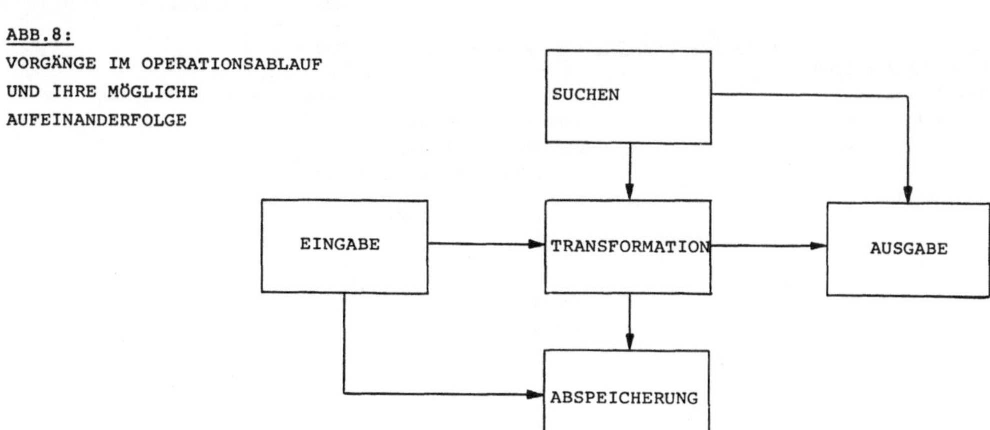

Nicht alle genannten Vorgänge treten gemeinsam bei jeder Operation auf. An einigen Beispielen wird gezeigt, wie sich herkömmliche Datenbankoperationen aus diesen Vorgängen zusammensetzen lassen (nur Instances betreffend):

Einfügen von Behältern: Eingabe, Abspeicherung
Löschen von Behältern : Suchen, Transformation, Abspeicherung
Ändern von Inhalten : Suchen + Eingabe, Transformation, Abspeicherung
Abfragen von Inhalten : Suchen, Ausgabe.

3.3 Suchen in NEOS-Netzwerken

Bei jedem Suchvorgang sind einer oder mehrere Bausteine einer Datei als Ausgangsbausteine ausgezeichnet. Der Ausgangsbaustein ist nicht statisch definiert, sondern wird erst durch die Suchfrage festgelegt.

Zunächst wird der erste Ausgangsbaustein gesucht. Falls die Prämisse dies verlangt, wird mit Hilfe der Verweise im Ausgangsbaustein auf weitere Bausteine zugegriffen. Der jeweilige Ausgangsbaustein und alle zu ihm gehörigen sonstigen Bausteine werden in einem Arbeitsspeicher als Basisergebnis zur weiteren Verarbeitung abgelegt. Falls mehrere Ausgangsbausteine vorhanden sind, wiederholt sich dieser Vorgang mit dem jeweils nächsten Ausgangsbaustein.

Die Formulierung der Prämisse erfolgt durch ein Prämissenschema. Dieses stellt einen Ausschnitt aus dem Schema dar. Eventuelle Schleifen, die im Schema vorkommen, sind im Prämissenschema durch Mehrfachangabe der betreffenden Knoten aufgelöst. Dadurch kann das Prämissenschema als Baum dargestellt werden. Die Wurzel dieses Baumes definiert die Ausgangsbausteine, die übrigen Knoten definieren die weiteren Bausteine.

ABB.9:
BEISPIEL FÜR EIN PRÄMISSENSCHEMA

SUCHFRAGE:
WELCHE PERSONEN ARBEITEN AM PROJEKT A JEWEILS UNTER WESSEN ANLEITUNG? WELCHE VORBILDUNG HABEN DIE PERSONEN, DIE AM PROJEKT A ARBEITEN?

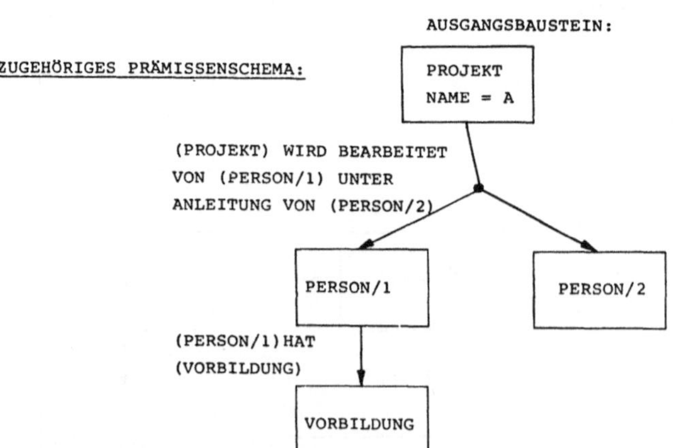

Das Ergebnis einer Prämisse läßt sich in folgende drei Stufen gliedern:

Das <u>Gesamtergebnis</u> enthält alle durch die Prämisse angesprochenen Bausteine.

Ein <u>Basisergebnis</u> enthält einen Ausgangsbaustein und alle zu ihm gehörigen Bausteine.

Ein <u>Teilergebnis</u> enthält einen Ausgangsbaustein und von allen zu ihm gehörigen sonstigen Bausteintypen je ein Exemplar.

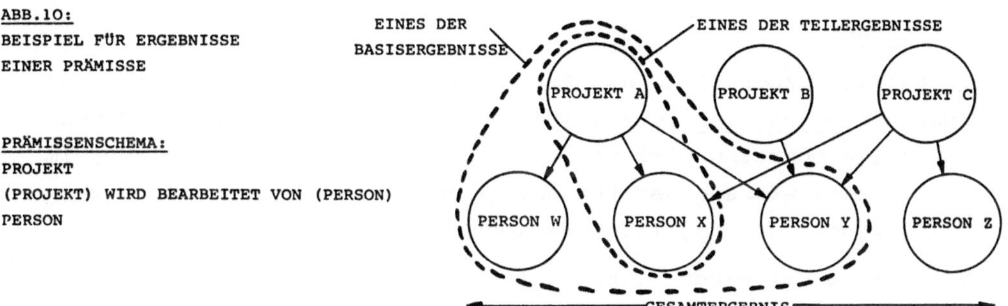

ABB.10:
BEISPIEL FÜR ERGEBNISSE
EINER PRÄMISSE

PRÄMISSENSCHEMA:
PROJEKT
(PROJEKT) WIRD BEARBEITET VON (PERSON)
PERSON

4. Aufbau von NEOS

Der Entwurf von NEOS zielt u.a. darauf ab, verschiedene Problemkreise herauszukristallisieren und auch aufbaumäßig auseinanderzuhalten. Die verschiedenen Benutzer einer Datenbank wollen ihre Zugriffswünsche in einer möglichst bequemen und problemgerechten Weise formulieren. Hierzu sind mehrere Benutzersprachebenen nötig. Damit die die Zugriffswünsche ausführenden Operatoren nicht für jede Benutzersprachebene anders arbeiten müssen, ist eine interne Sprachebene zwischengeschaltet, welche die Zugriffswünsche formalisiert darstellt.

An Operatoren unterscheidet man zwei Sorten; die einen realisieren einnen logischen Zugriff, der von den anderen in einen physikalischen Zugriff zum Speicher umgesetzt wird. Die Einführung der logischen Zugriffsebene dient dazu, die Möglichkeit der Verwendung verschiedener Speicherzugriffstechniken offenzuhalten.

ABB.11:
GLIEDERUNG DES AUFBAUS VON NEOS, SPRACH- UND ZUGRIFFSEBENEN

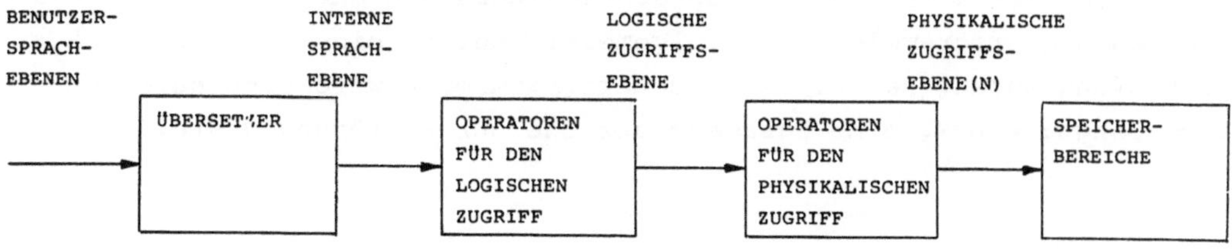

4.1 Speicherbereiche

NEOS kennt im wesentlichen folgende Speicherbereiche (s.Abb.12):

Die Datenbank und ihr Schema befinden sich auf Externspeicher. Beide besitzen einen Arbeitsspeicherbereich im Kernspeicher, der die aktuellen Bausteine bzw. Bausteinschemata aufnimmt. Wie ein Bausteinschema strukturiert ist, steht als Schema des Schemas in einem gesonderten Bereich. Diese zweistufige Beschreibungshierarchie dient dazu, die Flexibilität des Systems bei der Einführung neuer Strukturelemente zu erhöhen.

4.2 Operatoren

Der physikalische Zugriff zu den Externspeichern wird von den beiden Externspeicher-Operatoren durchgeführt.(s.Abb.12). Der für die Datenbank zuständige Operator wird von der Speicherstrukturbeschreibung im Schema gesteuert, während der für das Schema zuständige Operator nur eine Speicherungs- und Zugriffsform kennt.

Die Durchführung der eigentlichen Netzwerkoperationen obliegt dem Instance-Operator, der im Bedarfsfall Dienste des Schema-Operators in Anspruch nimmt. Beide Operatoren weisen wegen der prinzipiell gleichen Aufgabenstellung dieselbe Einteilung entsprechend der Gliederung des Operationsablaufs auf:

Der Such-Operator besorgt das Suchen (s.3.3); das Gegenstück ist der Abspeicher-Operator, der Informationen z.B. aufgrund einer Eingabe auf Datenbank oder Schema ablegt.

Der Transformations-Operator dient zur Veränderung von Informationen, die im Arbeitsspeicher stehen.

Der Eingabe-Operator transportiert eingegebene Informationen in den jeweiligen Arbeitsspeicher, während der Ausgabe-Operator Informationen aus dem Arbeitsspeicher in eine Ausgabeform überführt und im Ausgabespeicher ablegt.

4.3 Benutzersprachebenen

Durch die Einführung der internen Sprachebene (s.Abb.11)ist es möglich, den verschiedenen Benutzertypen verschiedene Sprachebenen bereitzustellen. Dem Datenadministrator und Anwendungsprogrammierer wird man eine problemorientierte Sprache mit Spracherweiterungen anbieten, dabei wird der Anwendungsprogrammierer im allgemeinen nur zu einem eingeschränkten Sprachumfang Zugang haben. Dem Nichtprogrammierer wird eine self-contained language bzw. eine Parametersprache zur Verfügung gestellt.

ABB.12:
ÜBERSICHT ÜBER DEN AUFBAU VON NEOS

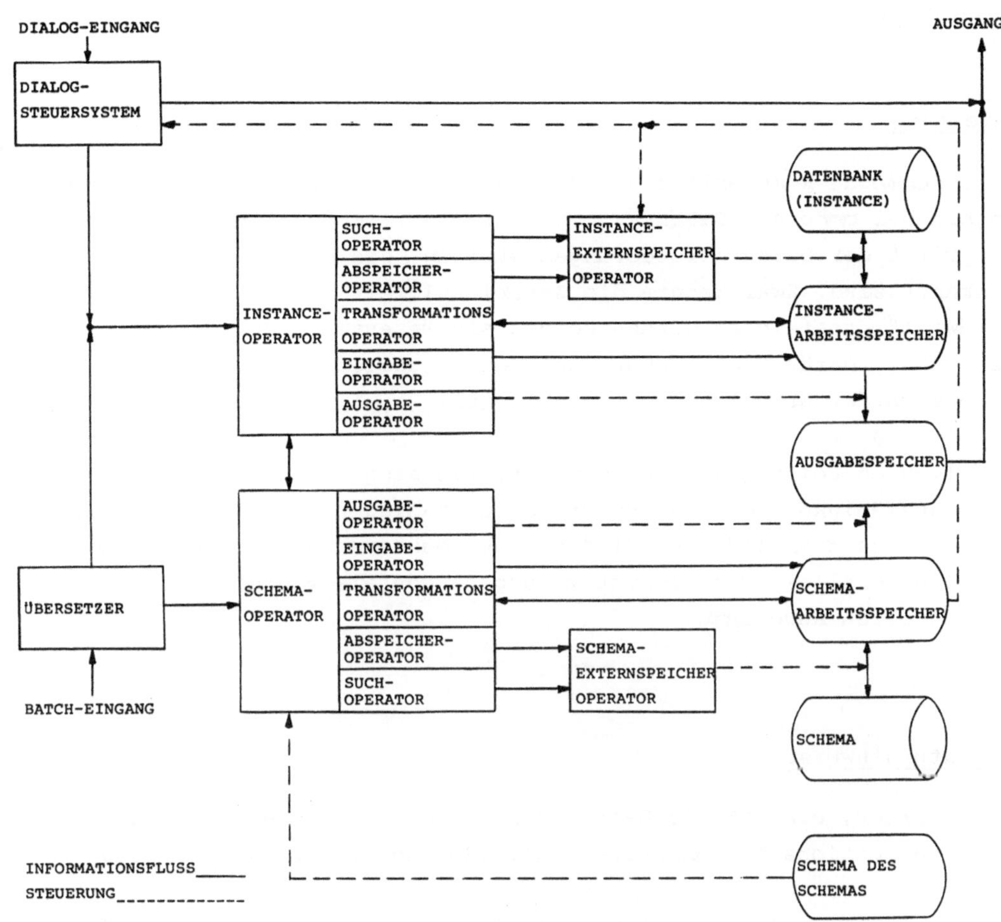

5. Literatur

CODASYL Systems Committee:
Feature Analysis of Generalized Data Base Management Systems
Technical Report, New York, Mai 1971

CODASYL Data Base Task Group:
CODASYL Data Base Task Group Report
Technical Report, New York, April 1971

Olle, T. William:
An assessment of how the CODASLY Data Base Task Group Proposal
meets the Guide-Share Requirements
Norwegian Computing Center, Oslo, April 1972

VERFAHREN ZUR SICHERUNG UND WIEDERHERSTELLUNG VON DATENBESTÄNDEN

D.F.JUNG

Einleitung

Die zunehmende Komplexität und der enorme Umfang von Datenbeständen, wie sie bei modernen Datensystemen anfallen, werden zukünfig an die Integrität der Daten Anforderungen stellen, die heute noch weitgehend unbekannt sind. Zwar konnte die Zuverlässigkeit der Maschinen, der "Hardware", gesteigert werden so daß sie wesentlich unanfälliger sind als früher, dafür treten aber neue Fehlerquellen auf, die vornehmlich im Bereich der Maschinenbedienung liegen.

Im folgenden Beitrag wird untersucht, wie sich die vervielfachte Leistungsfähigkeit der Datenverarbeitungsanlagen zur Sicherung der Dateien einsetzen läßt. Es wird hierbei mehr von den Anforderungen an ein generelles Journal-System ausgegangen als von einer individuellen Anwendung.

Literaturhinweise

W. C. Carter, e.a. "Logic Design for Dynamic and Interactive Recovery", IEEE Transactions on Computers, Vol. C20, No 11, Noo 71, p. 1300

D. C. Burnstine, "Transaction Journaling in Information Systems", IBM System Development Division Poughkeepsie, TR 00.2277, March 13,1972

R. G. Fraser, "Integrity of a Mass Storage Filing System", Computer Journal (British), February 1969

P. C. Lockemann and W. D. Knutsen, "Recovery of Disk Contents After System Failure", Communications of ACM, Vol. 11, No. 8, August 1968

C. T. Davis, Jr. "A Recovery Architecture for a Data System", IBM Programming Center San Jose, October 13, 1971.

Grundsätze eines Journal-Systems

Effizienz

Die primäre Aufgabe eines Journal-Systems ist, den Verlust von Daten durch Maschinen- oder Programmierfehler zu verhindern. Dies kann erreicht werden durch die Aufzeichnung von redundanten Daten in einem Journal. Wenn wir annehmen, daß ein Datenverarbeitungssystem, Maschinen sowohl als auch Programme, bis zu einem gewissen Grade zuverlässig ist, können wir davon ausgehen, daß die Daten eines Journals relativ selten verwendet werden. Andererseits muß jede Änderung einer Datei im Journal vermerkt werden, daß heißt, für jede Ausgabe eines neuen oder Änderung eines schon bestehenden Satzes muß eine zusätzliche Ausgabeoperation gestartet werden.

Diese beiden Voraussetzungen führen zu der Forderung, daß ein Journal-System sehr effektiv in der Datenaufzeichnung sein muß. Dagegen ist die Verarbeitungsgeschwindigkeit von Journaldaten von untergeordneter Bedeutung.

Datenträger

Welcher Datenträger soll verwendet werden? Wir müssen damit rechnen, daß ein Journal erheblich größer wird als eine Datei. Normalerweise sind Plattenspeicher hierfür zu teuer. Es bieten sich Magnetbänder an, zumal sie noch den zusätzlichen Vorteil haben, daß sie, sequentiell verarbeitet, schneller sind als Platten. Andererseits sind Platten sicherer als Bänder. Es kommt häufiger vor, daß ein Band zerreißt, als daß eine Platte mechanisch zerstört wird.

Ein Journal-System muß also hauptsächlich für Bänder ausgelegt werden, muß aber auch Platten verarbeiten können.

Ein-Mehr-Journal Methode

Um die Vollständigkeit eines Journals zu gewährleisten, sollte ein Betriebssystem nur ein Journal haben. Dadurch wird vermieden, daß bei der Verarbeitung des Journals, also bei der Wiedererstellung einer Datei, ein Teilstück vergessen wird. Das trifft in besonderem Maße für ein Multiprogramming System zu, bei dem eine Datei simultan von mehreren Programmen verarbeitet werden kann. Ein Journal, das gleichzeitig von mehreren Programmen benutzt wird, bildet aber einen Engpaß für ein System. Es müssen hier individuell für jede Anwendung die Vor- und Nachteile abgewogen werden.

Ein Journal-System muß beide Verfahren, die Ein-Journal und die Mehr-Journal Methode, unterstützen.

Audit Trail

Ein weiterer Aspekt der Datensicherung ist die Verfolgung der Zustandsänderung (Audit Trail) einer Datei. Besonders in Datenbank/Datenkommunikationssystemen, wo einander unbekannte Benutzer dieselbe Datei verwenden, wird ein Verfahren benötigt das erlaubt, die Ursache einer Information und deren Änderung zu verfolgen. Die Probleme des Audit trails sind jedoch so vielschichtig, daß eine generelle Systemlösung nicht gefunden werden kann, vielmehr wird jede Anwendung ein individuelles Verfahren entwickeln müssen.

Aufgabe eines Journal-Systems ist es, dem Benutzer die Möglichkeit zu geben, unabhängig von einer Zustandsänderung jede beliebige Information auf ein Journal zu schreiben. Es ist dabei selbstverständlich, daß der Benutzer auch selbstverantwortlich ist für die Verarbeitung dieser Information.

Fehlerquellen

Für die Untersuchung eines Journal-Systems ist es notwendig, die Fehlerquellen eines Datenverarbeitungssystems zu kennen. Grundsätzlich können vier Quellen unterschieden werden:

1. Physikalische Zerstörung. Eine Datei wird so beschädigt, daß sie teilweise oder gänzlich nicht mehr lesbar ist. Bevor weitere Operationen möglich sind, muß der Inhalt der Datei wieder hergestellt werden.

2. Falsche Programme. Eine Datei wird durch ein Programm fehlerhaft verändert. Sie muß in den Zustand zurückversetzt werden, den sie vor dem Start des fehlerhaften Programmes hatte.

3. Falsche Eingabedaten. Einzelne Sätze werden durch falsche Eingabedaten verändert. Die fehlerhaften Sätze müssen erkannt und verbessert werden.

4. Programmunterbrechung. Eine Datei wird zwar richtig aber nicht vollständig verändert. Sie muß in einen Zustand zurückversetzt werden, so daß das unterbrochene Programm weiterlaufen kann.

Methoden der Wiederherstellung

Je nach Betriebsart, Fehlerquellen und Sicherungsaufwand können unterschiedliche Methoden der Wiederherstellung einer Datei angewendet werden.

1. Backup

Die einfachste Art ist das Backup. Die Dateien werden in regelmäßigen Zeitintervallen kopiert. Bei Verlust wird die Kopie an Stelle des Originals verwendet. Diese Methode bedarf keines speziellen Journals, hat aber den Nachteil, daß alle Änderungen, die nach dem Kopieren an einer Datei vorgenommen werden, verloren sind. Die entsprechenden Programme müssen nochmals ausgeführt werden.

2. Recovery

Diese Art ist eine Fortführung des Backup. Auch hier werden regelmäßig Kopien erstellt, aber zusätzlich alle Zustandsänderungen auf einem Journal vermerkt. Bei Bedarf kann dann die Kopie mit Hilfe des Journals auf den letzten Stand des Originals gebracht werden. Diese Methode ist besonders dann notwendig, wenn die Eingabedaten, die zur Änderung der Datei geführt haben, nicht mehr verfügbar sind, so daß ein Wiederholungslauf der Programme nicht ausgeführt werden kann.

3. Reset

Während Backup und Recovery angewendet werden um physikalische Fehler, also die Zerstörung einer Datei, zu beheben, korrigiert Reset logische Fehler, hervorgerufen durch fehlerhafte Eingabedaten oder Programme.

Die Korrektur kann auf zwei Arten durchgeführt werden. Das fehlerhafte aber noch lesbare Original wird mit Hilfe des Journals zurückgesetzt zu einem Zustand, der zeitlich vor dem Fehler liegt. Für diese Art des Reset ist es notwendig, im Journal den Zustand (eine Zustandsänderung) vor der Änderung zu vermerken.

Die andere Möglichkeit ist, eine Kopie der Datei weiterzuschreiben ebenfalls bis zum Zustand vor dem Fehler. Hierfür muß im Journal der Zustand (eine Zustandsänderung) nach der Änderung eingetragen werden.

4. Checkpoint/Restart

Bei langlaufenden Programmen werden regelmäßig sogenannte Checkpoints durchgeführt. Diese sollen verhindern, daß bei einer Unterbrechung das Programm von Anfang an wiederholt werden muß. Checkpoints erlauben, ein unterbrochenes Programm von diesem Punkt an weiterlaufen zu lassen.

Wenn zwischen Checkpoint und Unterbrechung Änderungen an einer Datei vorgenommen wurden, so müssen diese Änderungen in den meisten Fällen rückgängig gemacht werden, soll das Programm vom Checkpoint an fehlerfrei weiterlaufen. Hierfür können beide Arten des Reset angewendet werden.

Datensicherheit und Preis der Sicherung

Ein Journal-System ist natürlich bestrebt, die absolute Sicherheit der Dateien zu gewährleisten, jedoch müssen wir zunächst untersuchen, welchen Grad der Sicherheit wir erreichen können und zu welchen Kosten. Der Preis der hier von Interesse ist, ist der Verlust an Leistung, also der Verarbeitunggeschwindigkeit eines Gesamtsystems.

Der Grad der Sicherheit einer Datei hängt ab von der Vollständigkeit des Journals. Ist kein Journal vorhanden, ist auch keine Sicherheit gegeben. Ist ein Journal absolut vollständig, so ist die Datei absolut sicher. Zwischen diesen beiden Extremen der Sicherheit und damit auch des Leistungsverlustes gibt es mehrere Abstufungen.

Die Vollständigkeit eines Journals ist besonders durch einen Systemzusammenbruch gefährdet, weil hierbei alle Sätze verloren gehen, die zwar schon zur Ausgabe aufbereitet sind, aber noch im Kernspeicher stehen. Gerade hierbei ist eine absolute Sicherheit nicht erreichbar. Folgende Betriebsarten sind möglich:

1. Ungeblockte synchrone Journal Ausgabe.
   Diese Betriebsart bietet die bestmögliche Sicherheit. Die Sätze des Journals sind ungeblockt. Das Anwendungsprogramm erhält die Kontrolle erst dann zurück, wenn die Ausgabe zum Journal fehlerfrei abgeschlossen ist. Dadurch kann nur der letzte verarbeitete Satz verloren gehen im Falle eines Systemzusammenbruches. Der Leistungsabfall jedoch ist erheblich. Die Ausgabezeit eines Satzes kann sich um ein mehrfaches der Zeit, die ohne Journal benötigt wird, verlängern.

2. Geblockte synchrone Journal Ausgabe.
   Bei dieser Betriebsart werden die Sätze des Journals geblockt. Das Anwendungsprogramm erhält die Kontrolle zurück, wenn der Journal-Satz in den entsprechenden Puffer gestellt wurde. Die Synchronisierung des Journals mit der Datei wird dadurch erreicht, daß ein Journalblock immer <u>vor</u> einem Datenblock geschrieben wird. Das kann bedeuten, daß ein Journalblock unter Umständen nicht voll ist.

   Bei einem Systemzusammenbruch gehen alle Sätze im Puffer verloren jedoch ist der Journal immer auf einem neueren Stand, also vollständiger als die Datei. Der Leistungsabfall wird durch das Blocken der Journal Sätze vermindert.

3. Geblockte asynchrone Journal Ausgabe.
   Wie bei der Betriebsart 2 sind die Sätze des Journals geblockt. Die Ausgabe erfolgt aber asynchron zur Datenausgabe immer dann, wenn ein Journalblock vollständig ist. Das hat zur Folge, daß eine Datei Sätze enthalten kann, die im Journal nicht verzeichnet sind. Bei einem späteren Reset kann dies zu erheblichen Schwierigkeiten führen.
   Der Leistungsabfall ist geringer, da nur vollständige Journal Blöcke geschrieben werden.

4. Backup als Journal
   Wird auf das Führen eines Journals verzichtet und zur Datensicherung nur ein Backup erstellt, ist der Leistungsabfall minimal und beträgt nur die Zeit, die für das Kopieren benötigt wird. Die Daten sind aber nur gesichert bis zum Backup, alle späteren Änderungen sind gefährdet.

   Im Anhang sind für eine ISAM Datei Ausgabezeiten für die verschiedenen Betriebsarten zustammengestellt.

Journal Aufbau

Bei einer Veränderung eines Satzes wird selten der ganze Satz geändert. Meistens sind nur einzelne Felder im Satz betroffen. Theoretisch würde es ausreichen, nur die geänderten Felder im Journal zu verzeichnen, praktisch führt das jedoch zu großen Schwierigkeiten. Die Felder müßten betreffs ihrer Länge und Position genau beschrieben werden, was zusätzliche Information im Journal bedeuten würde. In vielen Fällen ist diese Zusatzinformation umfangreicher als die geänderten Daten selbst. Außerdem ist ein Journal-System nicht in der Lage, diese Zusatzinformation selbständig zu erstellen. Eine Unterstützung durch den Benutzer wäre erforderlich. Deshalb ist es zweckmäßiger, den gesamten geänderten Satz im Journal einzutragen.

Wie oben angeführt, sind, je nach Anwendung, für einen geänderten Satz zwei Arten von Journaleinträgen möglich. Einmal kann der Satz vor der Änderung genommen werden. Dies ist notwendig für Reset. Für Recovery muß der Satz nach der Änderung eingetragen werden. Bei Bedarf können beide Arten geschrieben werden.

Von der Natur her ist ein Journal immer chronologisch aufgebaut, das heißt, alle Änderungen einer Datei sind in der zeitlichen Reihenfolge ihres Auftretens vermerkt. Diese Zeitabhängigkeit ist außerordentlich wichtig. Wenn ein Satz mehrmals geändert wurde, kann nur so der letzte gültige Zustand gefunden werden. Auch beim Zurücksetzen einer Datei ist in den meisten Fällen der Zeitpunkt ausschlaggebend. Deshalb bekommt jeder Journalrecord eine Zeitmarke angefügt.

Neben der Zustandsänderung und ihrer Zeitabhängigkeit sind gewisse Ereignisse für eine Datei wichtig, selbst wenn sie keine Änderungen bewirken. Solche Ereignisse wie Öffnen (OPEN) und Schließen (CLOSE) einer Datei, sowie Checkpoint werden ebenfalls im Journal eingetragen.

Eine weitere Gruppe von Journaldaten sind Daten, die der Benutzer einträgt aus Gründen, die vom System nicht mehr zu kontrollieren sind. Dem Benutzer stehen zwei Wege zur Verfügung. Einmal kann er jedem Journalsatz individuell Daten hinzufügen, zum Anderen kann er ganze Sätze schreiben, ohne daß eine Dateiänderung damit verbunden ist. Beim Lesen eines Journals müssen diese Daten vom Benutzer verarbeitet werden.

Satz Format

Im Folgenden werden die einzelnen Felder eines Journal Satzes detailliert beschrieben. Die Reihenfolge der Felder ist willkürlich und ebenso wie der Inhalt nur als mögliches Beispiel gedacht.

1. Typ: Beschreibt den Datentype des Satzes.
   Folgende Typen sind möglich:

   Datensatz vor der Änderung
   Datensatz nach der Änderung
   Benutzer Satz
   System Marke für OPEN / CLOSE / Checkpoint

2. Activität: Markierungsfeld. Beschreibt die Ursache für den Satz.

   Änderung eines existierenden Satzes
   Hinzufügen eines neuen Satzes
   Entfernen eines alten Satzes

3. Zeit: Zeitfeld. Speichert die Zeit zu der der Satz im Journal geschrieben wurde.

4. R. Adr.: Relative Adresse der Benutzerinformation und der Daten im Journal Satz.

5. Phys.Adr.: Physikalische Adresse des Daten Satzes auf der Platte.

6. Datei: Name der Datei zu der der Satz gehört.

7. Länge: Länge der Benutzerinformation

8. BI: Benutzerinformation

9. Länge: Länge des Daten Satzes

10. Daten: Daten Satz

Wenn der Typ einen Datensatz vor der Änderung bezeichnet und die Aktivität ist Hinzufügen, dann enthält der Journal Satz keinen Datenteil.

Wenn der Typ einen Datenrecord nach der Änderung bezeichnet und die Aktivität ist Entfernen, dann enthält der Journal Satz keinen Datenteil.

Wenn der Typ eine System Marke bezeichnet, dann enthält der Datenteil den Jobnamen.

Wenn der Typ einen Benutzer Satz bezeichnet, dann entfallen die Felder 4 bis 9.

Implementierung

Eine der Grundvoraussetzungen für die Implementierung ist die Unabhängigkeit der Anwendungsprogramme vom Journal-System. Mit anderen Worten, das System muß eingeführt werden können, ohne daß bestehende Programme geändert werden müssen. Das läßt sich erreichen für alle Fälle, in denen der Benutzer nicht eigene Daten auf das Journal schreiben will. Eingriffe in das übergeordnete Betriebssystem sind allerdings nicht ganz vermeidbar.

Beim Betrieb eines Journals sind folgende Schritte zu durchlaufen:

Zur Startzeit eines Programmes wird ein Journal und seine Beziehung zur Datei definiert. Es ist durchaus möglich, mehrere Dateien auf ein Journal zu beziehen. Als Attribute einer Datei, nicht des Journals, wird definiert, ob ein Satz vor oder nach einer Änderung oder beide Male im Journal einzutragen ist, Block Faktor, synchroner oder asynchroner Betrieb und Ähnliches mehr. Aus dieser Information baut Job Control die notwendigen Kontrollblöcke auf und lädt die entsprechenden Routinen des Journal-Systems. Die Datenzugriffsroutinen (z.B. ISAM) überwachen den Verkehr des Programmes mit einer Datei. Wenn notwendig, werden von hier die Routinen des Journal-Systems aufgerufen.

Natürlich ist auch eine Implementierung möglich, bei der nicht das Betriebssystem, sondern die Anwendungsprogramme geändert werden. In diesem Fall müssen die Routinen des Journal-Systems über ensprechende Befehle im Anwendungsprogramm aufgerufen werden.

Neben den Routinen für das Aufzeichnen eines Journals, werden Programme für dessen Verarbeitung benötigt. So gehören zu einem Journal-System Programme für Recovery oder Reset von Dateien und für Restart von Programmen. Diese Systemprogramme haben Anschlußpunkte für vom Benutzer zu schreibende Routinen, die die Verarbeitung der Benutzerdaten im Journal übernehmen.

Zeitabschätzungen für eine ISAM Datei ohne und mit Journal

Die betrachtete ISAM Datei hat die folgenden Kennzeichen:

Zentraler Rechner	360/50
Platteneinheit	2314, Model 1
Dateigröße	10.000 Sätze
Logische Satzlänge	200 bytes (konstant)
Blockgröße	2200 bytes
Index Größe (Key)	8 bytes
Puffer	2
Prüfleser	ja
Index im Speicher	ja
Zylinder Überlauf	3 Spuren pro Zylinder
Arbeitsweise	Move Mode
Operating System	DOS Release 25

Die Datei ist af 22 zusammenhängenden Zylindern gespeichert. Hierbei sind 3 Zylinder als unabhängige Überlaufzylinder eingeschlossen. Die Datei ist neu aufgebaut, das heißt es sind noch keine neuen Sätze hinzugefügt worden.

Es wurde die mittlere Reaktionszeit pro Satz ohne Journal gemessen für folgende Betriebsarten:

Sequentielles Lesen (SL)	3,5 ms
Sequentielles Ändern (SA)	7,7 ms
Direktes Lesen (DL)	81,9 ms
Direktes Ändern (DA)	132,5 ms
Hinzufügen (H)	314,4 ms

Für das Journal wurden folgende Annahmen gemacht:

- Datei und Journal sind auf verschiedenen Einheiten.
  Das ist die normale Anwendung, da sonst im Falle der Zerstörung eines Plattenstapels sowohl Datei als auch Journal verloren wären.

- Die Ausgabezeit für einen ungeblockten Journalsatz beträgt 14,5 ms. Diese Zeit enthält die mittlere Verzögerung auf Grund der Plattenrotation (12,5 ms) und eine gleichmäßig verteilte Zeit für den Zylinderzugriff (1 ms). Diese Zeit ist maßgebend für den synchronen Journal.

- Die Ausgabezeit für einen geblockten Journalsatz beträgt 4,3 ms und entspricht der mittleren Zeit für eine SAM Datei.

Für eine Datei mit synchronem ungeblocktem Journal ergeben sich folgende Verhältnisse:

	Seq. Ändern	Dir. Ändern	Hinzufügen
Ohne Journal	7,7	132,5	314,4
Mit Journal	22,2	147,5	328,9
Faktor	2,95	1,11	1,05

Für eine Datei mit asynchronem Journal ergeben sich folgende Verhältnisse:

	Seq. Ändern	Dir. Ändern	Hinzufügen
Ohne Journal	7,7	132,5	314,4
Mit Journal	12,0	136,8	318,7
Faktor	1,56	1,03	1,01

Aus den Zahlen geht klar hervor, daß der Leistungsverlust für sequentielle Verarbeitung am größten ist. Bei sequentieller Ausgabe zur Datei und synchronem ungeblocktem Journal verdreifacht sich etwa die Ausgabezeit pro Satz. Für direkten Zugriff ist der Leistungsverlust aber erheblich geringer und beträgt nur noch zwischen 1 und 10 %.

JURISTISCHES INFORMATIONSSYSTEM: EINE FALLSTUDIE FÜR EIN INFORMATIONSSYSTEM GROSSEN UMFANGS

F.GEBHARDT, P.C.LOCKEMANN

1. Einleitung

Seit Jahren gibt es mahnende Stimmen, die von einer Beeinträchtigung der Rechtsordnung in der Bundesrepublik (und in anderen Ländern) durch ein immer erdrückenderes Angebot an juristischen Publikationen - Gesetzen und Verordnungen, Gerichtsentscheidungen, Literatur - warnen. Zu dieser Entwicklung tragen in gleicher Weise die steigende Technisierung und Spezialisierung unserer Gesellschaft, die zunehmenden Fürsorgepflichten des Staates und die wachsende internationale Verflechtung bei. Es ist daher schon vor einigen Jahren sowohl von der Bundesregierung als auch aus Kreisen juristischer Standesorganisationen und der Rechtswissenschaft vorgeschlagen worden, zur Bewältigung der Informationsflut im Rechtswesen neue und geeignete Instrumente, insbesondere auch die elektronische Datenverarbeitung, heranzuziehen. Im Jahre 1970 wurde deshalb eine Arbeitsgruppe, bestehend aus Mitgliedern des Bundesjustizministeriums, der Gesellschaft für Mathematik und Datenverarbeitung Bonn und der C-E-I-R GmbH beauftragt, ein Systemkonzept für die Einrichtung eines juristischen Informationssystems zu erarbeiten. Der abschließende Bericht dieser Arbeitsgruppe liegt seit einigen Monaten vor [1].

Im vorliegenden Beitrag soll versucht werden, einen kurzen Einblick in die Arbeiten der Gruppe zu geben. Dabei wollen wir das Augenmerk des Lesers auf einige Probleme lenken, deren Lösung der Arbeitsgruppe besondere Schwierigkeiten bereitete und die uns symptomatisch für umfangreiche Informationssysteme erscheinen, die mehr als nur die Mechanisierung von Routineaufgaben zum Ziel haben.

2. Fragen zur Vorgehensweise

Die Einrichtung von Informationssystemen hat ihren Ausgang im Bereich der Wehrtechnik und der innerbetrieblichen Organisation von Unternehmen genommen. Die Ansätze zu einer Systematik für Planung und Einrichtung solcher Systeme haben sich daher aus diesen Bereichen heraus entwickelt. Typischerweise wird ein Vorgehen in folgenden Stufen empfohlen [2]:

(1) Voruntersuchung (Prüfung, ob ein DV-System eingeführt werden soll):
  - Aufnahme des Istzustandes
  - Zielsetzung
  - Grobanalyse
  - Entscheidung über Fortführung
(2) Erstellung der Grundkonzeption:
  - Detailanalyse
  - System-Synthese
  - Kapazitätserfordernisse
  - Wirtschaftlichkeitsberechnung
  - Realisierungsplan
  - Entscheidung über Verwirklichung
(3) Vorbereitung (Schaffung der konkreten Voraussetzungen für die Realisierung)
(4) Realisierung

Die klare Gliederung täuscht freilich darüber hinweg, daß sich manche Stufen nur mit unzureichenden Mitteln bearbeiten lassen. Besondere Schwierigkeiten zeigen sich bei der Beschreibung der Informationsflüsse innerhalb einer betrieblichen Organisation [3] und der Erkenntnisprozesse beim vorgesehenen Benutzer [4]; diese haben ihrerseits Rückwirkungen auf die Bestimmung der Kapazitätserfordernisse und auf die Wirtschaftlichkeitsberechnungen.

Die Frage der Einführung von Informationssystemen in der öffentlichen Verwaltung ist sehr viel neueren Datums. Die öffentliche Verwaltung befaßt sich mit sehr viel größeren und weniger scharf umrissenen Segmenten unserer Gesellschaft und in mehr Aspekten, als dies ein Unternehmen tut; zudem ist der Behördenapparat oftmals groß und geographisch verstreut, und häufig sind seine Ziele wenig konkret (z.B. "soziale Sicherung", "Chancengleichheit", "Rechtssicherheit"). Daher kann es nicht überraschen, daß die erwähnten Schwierigkeiten sich bei ihren Informationssystemen in sehr viel ernsthafterer Weise bemerkbar machen können. Die Frage ist sogar berechtigt, ob nicht für derartige Informationssysteme andere Methoden zu entwickeln und andere Bewertungsmaßstäbe anzulegen sind als bei betrieblichen Informationssystemen (wie läßt sich z.B. "Wirtschaftlichkeit" oder "Nutzen" eines Systems der öffentlichen Verwaltung definieren, wenn es mit der Verfolgung gesellschaftspolitischer Ziele verbunden ist?).

Trotzdem hat sich die Arbeitsgruppe weitgehend an die übliche Vorgehensweise gehalten. Als erstes hatte sie dabei Schwierigkeiten zu meistern, die mit ihrer personellen Zusammensetzung zusammenhängen. Es bedurfte einer längeren Anlaufzeit, vieler Geduld und guten Willens, bis die Verständigungsschwierigkeiten zwischen Spezialisten aus zwei so verschiedenartigen Berufsgruppen wie Rechtswesen und Datenverarbeitungstechnik überwunden waren und sich eine gedeihliche Zusammenarbeit entwickelte.

3. Zielanalyse

Eine wesentliche Schwierigkeit bei der Entwicklung der Zielvorstellungen muß sich notwendigerweise ergeben, wenn dem Auftrag nicht viel mehr als die politische Willensäußerung zugrunde liegt, auch angesichts der Informationsfülle eine soziale und humane Rechtsordnung zu gewährleisten, und sich zur Erfüllung dieser Aufgabe insbesondere der elektronischen Datenverarbeitung zu bedienen.

Die Arbeitsgruppe mußte aus dieser weitgespannten Äußerung heraus konkrete Einzelziele entwickeln, die sie zur Grundlage der weiteren Projektarbeit machen konnte. Sie identifizierte unter diesen schließlich drei Bereiche, in denen Maßnahmen zu einer Verbesserung der derzeitigen Situation ansetzen könnten:

(1) Sammlung und Auswertung sog."Sozialdaten", um rasch und wirkungsvoll auf gesellschaftliche Veränderungen reagieren zu können.

(2) Vereinheitlichung der juristischen Vorgehensweise.

(3) Gezielte Maßnahmen zur Verbesserung des Nachrichtenaustausches innerhalb des Rechtswesens.

Nicht nur stehen Forderungen (1) und (2) in einem gewissen Widerspruch zueinander; die Gruppe mußte auch erkennen, daß kaum Untersuchungen zu den damit verbundenen Problemen existieren. Insbesondere zeigte sich auch, daß die Rechtswissenschaft erst beginnt, sich über die Definition und Verwendbarkeit von Sozialdaten Gedanken zu machen und daß eine Vereinheitlichung der juristischen Vorgehensweise im Allgemeinen weder lösbar erscheint noch wünschenswert ist. Daher konnte allein Forderung (3) die Grundlage der weiteren Arbeit bilden.

4. Analyse der Systemumwelt

Welcher Personenkreis ist am Nachrichtenaustausch innerhalb des Rechts-

wesens beteiligt? Unser Rechtssystem ist keine wohlabgegrenzte Organisation, für die sich ohne weiteres sagen läßt, wer innerhalb und wer außerhalb steht. Unzweifelhaft sind die an der Gesetzgebung beteiligten Institutionen (Parlamente, Ministerien) wesentlich am Nachrichtenaustausch beteiligt, unzweifelhaft auch die höheren Gerichte und zentralen Verwaltungsbehörden. Schwieriger zu entscheiden ist bereits die Frage, in welchem Ausmaß sämtliche Gerichte, alle rechtswissenschaftlichen Institutionen, Industrie, Handel und Verbände am Nachrichtenaustausch teilnehmen, ob und auf welche Weise sie von der Informationsnot betroffen sind oder sich betroffen fühlen. Schließlich ist zu fragen, ob nicht sogar jeder einzelne Staatsbürger als Teilhaber am Nachrichtenaustausch zu betrachten ist. Selbst wenn man sich auf einen Personenkreis mit juristischer Vorbildung beschränkt, bewegt man sich in Größenordnungen von mehr als 100.000 Personen in 40.000 selbstständigen Institutionen. Drastische Einschränkungen sind also unvermeidlich.
Es bedarf noch einer detaillierten Analyse der vielen beteiligten Institutionen, Personengruppen und Rechtsbereiche, um diejenigen Einrichtungen zu identifizieren, bei denen eine Verbesserung des Nachrichtenflusses am vordringlichsten ist und den größten Nutzen verspricht."Vordringlichkeit" und "Nutzen" wiederum sind nicht allein rechnerische Fragen, ihre Definition fällt zum gleichen Teil auch in den gesellschaftspolitischen Bereich.

Die hohe Zahl juristischer Publikationen und Dokumente steht in ursächlichem Zusammenhang mit der Nichterfüllbarkeit der Forderung (2) oben; die langsame und raumaufwendige Verbreitung ist in der Übertragung durch das geschriebene Wort auf dem körperlichen Medium Papier begründet. Soll die Verbreitung nur noch auf Bedarf hin und mittels der Datenverarbeitung erfolgen, so ist als nächstes festzustellen, welches Material innerhalb des Informationssystems verfügungsbereit gehalten werden muß. Die Entscheidung darüber ist noch schwerwiegender als die über den in die Untersuchung einzubeziehenden Personenkreis, da nicht erfaßte Personen ja keineswegs von der Benutzung ausgeschlossen sind. Läßt sich schon der Benutzerkreis nicht scharf umreißen, so muß dies auch Auswirkungen auf die Auswahl des Materials haben. Zweifellos sind alle Gesetze und Verordnungen, auch ihre älteren Fassungen und bereits ungültige Gesetze, im System zu speichern und möglicherweise fortzuschreiben, ebenso alle wesentlichen Entscheidungen höherer Gerichte. Aber wann liegt liegt eine "wesentliche Entscheidung" vor? Sollten die Entscheidungen in ungekürzter oder gekürzter Form eingebracht werden? Können nicht auch Entscheidungen unterer Instanzen von

Bedeutung sein? Sind auch die von rechtsfähigen Organisationen, von Tarifpartnern, von kommunalen Parlamenten erlassenen Rechtsnormen mit einzubeziehen? Zählen zu den Nachrichten nicht auch der Schriftwechsel innerhalb von Gerichten oder zwischen streitenden Parteien? Welche Teile der rechtswissenschaftlichen Literatur sollen erfaßt werden? Die Auswahl muß sich letzten Endes orientieren an den technischen Möglichkeiten, an den Anforderungen zur Datenerfassung, am gewählten Benutzerkreis, am allgemeinen Interesse, das an einem Dokument existiert, und an der Häufigkeit, mit der es gebraucht wird, an anderen Alternativen für seine Bereitstellung und am dann notwendigen Aufwand bei seiner Beschaffung. Selbst wenn man sich auf Gesetze und Verordnungen von Bund und Ländern, Verwaltungsvorschriften zentraler Behörden, wichtige Entscheidungen vorwiegend der höheren Instanzen und eine Auswahl aus der Rechtsliteratur beschränkt, fällt neben einem nachträglich zu erfassenden Dokomentenbestand mit 1 bis 3 Mrd. Zeichen jährlich rd.1 Mrd. Zeichen neu an.

5. Benutzerverhalten

Durch bloße Verlagerung des Nachrichtenaustausches auf ein Medium, das für rasche Verbreitung und bequemen Zugriff sorgt, ist die Informationsnot des einzelnen Benutzers nicht unbedingt behoben - es besteht die Gefahr, daß ein Zuwenig an Material nur durch ein Zuviel an Material ersetzt wird. Daher muß die Bestimmung von Auswahlmethoden, die den Problemen und dem Problemlösungsverhalten der Benutzer angepaßt sind, das nächste Ziel sein. Voraussetzung hier wäre eine genaue Kenntnis des Verhaltens von juristisch geschulten Personen, wenn sie sich vor ein juristischen Problem gestellt sehen. In welcher Weise zerlegen sie ein Problem, in welchen Schritten lösen sie es, welche Lernprozesse spielen sich ab, wie oft und aufgrund welcher Informationen iterieren sie zwischen diesen Schritten, welches Material ziehen sie in den verschiedenen Schritten jeweils heran, welche Techniken wenden sie an? Lassen sich verschiedene Benutzergruppen mit unterschiedlichem Problemlösungsverhalten angeben? Wiederum mußte die Arbeitsgruppe feststellen, daß Untersuchungen dieser Art kaum existieren und daher allgemeingültige Aussagen noch nicht möglich sind; sie entwickelte wenigstens einige Ansätze zur Beschreibung des Problemlösungsverhaltens. In jedem Fall spielen dabei nicht näher formalisierbare menschliche Entscheidungsprozesse die bedeutsamste Rolle. Juristen selbst sehen ihre Arbeit als in hohem Maß individuell an und dürften daher technischen Neuerungen abwartend gegenüberstehen. Darüberhinaus jedoch erscheint selbst bei stark eingeschränktem Systemumfang der Benutzerkreis sehr heterogen.

Die Arbeitsgruppe hat daraus den Schluß gezogen, daß ein juristisches Informationssystem zunächst nicht mehr als ein Dokumentationssystem sein kann. Allerdings sollte es möglichst weitreichende, dem juristischen Verhalten angepaßte Hilfen bei der Suche und Erschließung juristischer Dokumente bieten. Dabei muß das System in mehrerlei Hinsicht über die herkömmlichen Dokumentationssysteme hinausgehen: Die formalen Angaben zu den Dokumenten sind sehr umfangreich [5]; Beispiele sind Normgeber, Zeitangaben, Überschriften, Fundstellen, Verweisungen, Änderungen bei Normen; Spruchkörper, Fundstellen, vor- und nachgehende Entscheidungen, Leitsatz, Normenkette bei Entscheidungen. Die Dokumenttexte sind im Hinblick auf Verarbeitungszwecke stark untergliedert, bei Normen bis hinab zu Halbsätzen. Zwischen den Dokumenten besteht eine Vielfalt wechselseitiger Beziehungen wie Verweisungen, Zitierungen, Änderungen, hierarchische Anordnungen. Diese Anforderungen lassen sich unschwer aus dem heutigen Aufbau juristischer Dokumente herleiten. Angesichts der weitgehend iterativen Vorgehensweise mit ihren menschlichen Entscheidungsprozessen wurde schließlich gefolgert, daß das juristische Informationssystem im Grundsatz ein Teilnehmersystem sein sollte.

6. Technische Möglichkeiten

Im bisherigen Verlauf wurden Anforderungen aus rechtpolitischen und systemanalytischen Erwägungen hergeleitet; die technischen Möglichkeiten gaben nicht mehr als einen groben Rahmen ab. Die Anforderungen sind nunmehr in Einklang zu bringen mit den Eigenschaften vorhandener oder in naher Zukunft zu erwartender technischer Einrichtungen und mit den vorhandenen personellen und finanziellen Mitteln.

Zunächst ist festzustellen, ob existierende Informationssysteme als Vorbild für das geplante System dienen können. Die Arbeitsgruppe hat zu diesem Zweck zahlreiche Dokumentationssysteme im In- und Ausland, insbesondere auch solche für juristische Anwendungen, untersucht. Es zeigt sich, daß heute vorhandene Dokumentationssysteme kaum über einen Umfang von einigen 100 Mio Zeichen hinausgehen, daß juristische Dokumentationssysteme mit wenigen Ausnahmen weit unter diesem Umfang liegen und großenteils experimenteller Natur sind, und daß nur wenige Dokumentationssysteme Zugriff im Dialogverkehr erlauben. Selbst bei erheblicher Einschränkung der Anforderungen wird ein juristisches Informationssystem also in technisches Neuland vorstoßen.

Die bei der Dokumentensuche ablaufenden Verarbeitungsprozesse sind zugleich rechenaufwendig und aktiv bezüglich interner Ein- und Ausgabe. Detaillierte Berechnungen zeigten, daß die Zahl der im Teilnehmerverkehr gleichzeitig bearbeitbaren Anfragen nach dem heutigen Stand der Technik - selbst unter Verwendung leistungsfähiger DV-Anlagen und maßgeschneiderter Software - 50 kaum übersteigen kann. Zwar ist unbekannt, wie häufig ein einzelner Benutzer zum System zugreifen wird, aber es erscheint unrealistisch, einen Kreis regelmäßiger Kunden von mehr als wenigen 1000 Juristen zuzulassen.

Die Forderung nach Dialogverkehr bringt den Zwang zur Datenhaltung auf direkt zugreifbaren Speichern mit sich, zumindest was die für Verarbeitungszwecke benötigten Dateien (z.B. Umkehrdateien, Thesauri) anbetrifft. Für diese Zwecke kommen heute nur Plattenspeicher in Frage. Trotz großer Fortschritte in den letzten Jahren erlegen Zugriffszeit, Speicherkapazität und Speicherkosten auch hier erhebliche Einschränkungen auf. Billigere, aber langsamere Sonderanfertigungen existieren oder stehen vor der Auslieferung (Chip Store, Videobänder, Laser-Massenspeicher). Neue, vielversprechende Techniken (Magneto-optische Speicher, Magnetblasen- und Tiefsttemperaturspeicher) werden noch im Labor erprobt. Wir mußten also davon ausgehen, daß zumindest in nächster Zukunft nicht mit grundlegenden speichertechnischen Neuerungen gerechnet werden kann.

Die größten Anforderungen in personeller und finanzieller Hinsicht sind nicht durch die technischen Einrichtungen bedingt. Vielmehr beansprucht die maschinengerechte Erfassung und Aufbereitung der Dokumente rd. 60 bis 80% der finanziellen und personellen Aufwendungen (über 10 Mio DM/ Jahr bei 1 Mrd Zeichen). Für den einzelnen Benutzer oder die Institution wiederum wiegen die Kosten für Miete der Datenstation und für Datenübertragung am schwersten. Sie liegen monatlich zwischen einigen 100 DM in Ortsverkehr und bis zu 5000 DM bei großen Entfernungen, hoher Benutzungsdauer und komfortabler Geräteausstattung. Da die Höhe dieser Kosten zu einer unerwünschten Auslese beim Kundenkreis führen kann, scheinen hier neben wirtschaftlichen auch rechtspolitische Überlegungen notwendig.

7. Entwicklungssystem

Wünsche und Wirklichkeit klaffen also in vieler Hinsicht weit auseinander. Sollte die Arbeitsgruppe deshalb von einer Einrichtung eines juristischen Informationssystems abraten? Wir waren der Ansicht, daß ein gegenüber den Maximalforderungen in der Größe stark eingeschränktes System ("Entwicklungssystem ") eingerichtet werden sollte. Hauptsächliche Gründe sind:

- Ein Informationsnotstand liegt vor. Ihn nicht überall beseitigen zu können darf nicht heißen, ihn nirgendwo zu beseitigen.
- Das Problemlösungsverhalten des Benutzers hat entscheidenden Einfluß auf die Systemkonzeption. Bevor ein umfangreicheres juristisches Informationssystem erstellt wird, sollten in kleinerem Rahmen Erfahrungen gesammelt werden.
- Die geforderten Eigenschaften des Systems gehen teilweise über die herkömmlicher Dokumentationssysteme hinaus. Auch hier müssen zunächst in kleinerem Rahmen Erfahrungen mit ihrer Realisierung und Brauchbarkeit gesammelt werden.
- Die rechtspolitischen Auswirkungen eines juristischen Informationssystems sind schwer abzuschätzen. Ein vorhandenes System kann konkrete und wertvolle Anhaltspunkte zur öffentlichen Diskussion beitragen.

Andererseits muß ein solches Informationssystem von einer Größe sein, die neben einer sinnvollen Anwendung auch brauchbare Aussagen im Hinblick auf ein später mögliches umfassenderes System und dessen Eigenschaften erlaubt. Die Arbeitsgruppe hat daher vorgeschlagen, daß das Entwicklungssystem im Endausbau aus zwei Sachgebieten Dokumente im Umfang von je 1 Mrd Zeichen umfassen und in der Lage sein soll, im Höchstfall 50 Anfragen gleichzeitig zu beantworten. Damit liegt dieses System immer noch oberhalb der Größe vergleichbarer Dokumentationssysteme. Augenblicklich versucht man, einen Benutzerkreis zu finden, der auch ein beschränktes System sinnvoll einsetzen kann und dessen Erfahrungen wichtige Anhaltspunkte für das weitere Vorgehen liefern werden.

Mit diesem Beitrag hoffen die Autoren, einige der Probleme und Überlegungen aufgezeigt zu haben, die bei der Einrichtung von großen Informationssystemen der öffentlichen Verwaltung zu erwarten sind. Manche der geschilderten Probleme sind allerdings mehr eine Folge der Forderung nach einem System, das konkrete Hilfestellung in Entscheidungsprozessen zu leisten vermag, und der zu weit gefaßten und unklar abgegrenzten Größenordnung. Vor allem scheinen uns die Ergebnisse der Projektstudie eine Aufforderung, die Erarbeitung systematischer Grundlagen zu intensivieren, insbesondere solche zur Analyse von Verwaltungsorganisationen und -objekten, zur Beschreibung von Vorgehensweisen bei der Problemlösung und zur technischen Einsatzplanung.

Literatur

[1] Das Juristische Informationssystem - Analyse, Planung,- Vorschlage; Bundesministerium der Justiz (Hrsg.), Januar 1972; Vertrieb: C.F. Müller, Karlsruhe.

[2] E. Parisini, O. Wächter, Organisations-Handbuch bei der Einführung von ADV- Systemen; Walter de Gruyter & Co, Berlin 1971.

[3] A. Schulz, Strukturanalyse der maschinellen betrieblichen Informationsbearbeitung; Walter de Gruyter & Co, Berlin 1970.

[4] W. Kirsch, Entscheidungsprozesse, 3 Bände; Betriebswirtschaftlicher Verlag Dr. Th. Gabler, Wiesbaden 1971.

[5] Allgemeiner Datenerhebungskatalog für die Dokumentation in der Bundesverwaltung (ADEK); Bundesministerium des Innern (Hrsg.), 29. März 1972.

DAS "PFLEGEPROBLEM" BEI INFORMATION-RETRIEVAL-SYSTEMEN

J.MARTIN, P.SCHNUPP

Zusammenfassung

Information-Retrieval-Systeme verwalten in der Regel neben dem Primärdatenbestand (Datensätze, Dokumente) Sekundärdatenbestände (Thesauri, invertierte Listen o.ä.), die eine Verweisstruktur über den Primärdatenbestand legen und damit das gezielte Auffinden von Informationen ermöglichen. Will man den Primärdatenbestand vollständig überdecken (d.h. jeden beliebigen Feldinhalt in jedem Satz des Primärbestandes als Deskriptor zulassen), so bedeutet dies nicht nur eine beträchtliche Erhöhung des benötigten Externspeicherplatzes, sondern auch ein den praktischen Systemeinsatz stark behinderndes Pflegeproblem bei großer Änderungshäufigkeit. Jede Änderung verlangt ja nicht mehr lediglich einen Update des eigentlichen Datensatzes, sondern zwei weitere Updates der invertierten Listen für jedes geänderte Feld (Austragen des alten und Eintragen des neuen Deskriptors).

Wird der Änderungsdienst manuell vorgenommen, so führt dies nicht nur zu einer oft nicht mehr tragbaren Überlastung des mit der Pflege der Datenbestände betrauten Personals, sondern auch zu unvermeidlichen Irrtümern und Versehen, welche eine stetig wachsende Inkonsistenz zwischen primären und sekundären Datenbestand verursachen.

Es wird ein bereits praktisch eingesetztes Verfahren beschrieben, welches die Durchführung des Folgeänderungsdienstes der invertierten Listen automatisiert und damit für den Benutzer transparent macht.

1. Invertierte Listen

Die Grundaufgabe jeden Information-Retrieval-System ist es, aus größeren, meist wahlfrei zugreifbar gespeicherten Beständen von Datensätzen (Dokumenten) durch Eingabe einer Suchanfrage bestimmte wieder herausfinden zu können. Im einfachsten Fall besteht die Suchanfrage nur aus einem einzigen, einen Datensatz eindeutig beschreibenden Begriff - etwa einer Materialnummer in einer Materialdatei. Wird zur Datei immer nur über diesen einen Begriff zugegriffen, ist die Aufgabe fast trivial: man kann bei Erstellung und Update den Datenbestand indexsequentiell nach diesem Begriff speichern oder sich aus diesem Begriff die Adresse des jeweiligen Datensatzes auf den Externspeicher errechnen [1]. Information- Retrieval verlangt jedoch mehr: Datensätze sollen durch verschiedenartige Suchbegriffe ansprechbar sein, und es sollen in einer Anfragesprache auch komplizierte logische Ausdrücke zur Beschreibung des gewünschten Datensatzes formulierbar sein.

Die meisten Information- Retrieval- Systeme benutzen für die Realisierung dieser Forderung das Verfahren der " invertierten Listen " [2] . Für jedes bei Anfragen interessierende Datenfeld im Satz wird eine invertierte Datei erstellt, die für jeden mindestens einmal vorhandenen Wert Verweise auf alle Sätze aufführt, in welchen das betreffende Datenfeld diesen Wert hat. Sind diese Verweisliste und in ihnen die Verweise zudem sortiert, sind Algorithmen für die üblichen logischen Verknüpfungen UND, ODER, UND NICHT sowie Anfragen bezüglich Wertebereichen u.ä. sehr einfach zu implementieren.

2. Der Update- Aufwand bei total invertierten Dateien

Die Probleme stecken auch hier wie so oft in den Details der praktischen Realisierung und Anwendung [3] : soll der Inhalt jedes Feldes eines jeden Satzes potentieller Suchbegriff sein, d.h. wünscht man eine " totale Invertierung " der Primärdatei, so führt dies zu beträchtlichem Aufwand.

Die sich ständig vergrößernde Kapazität und die sinkenden Kosten der Großspeicher lassen dabei die eine, früher dominierende Seite des Aufwandaspektes - den für die invertierten Listen benötigten Speicherplatz - etwas in den Hintergrund treten. Um so fühlbarer wird jedoch der zeitliche Aufwand bei Erstellung und Update einer voll invertierten Datenbasis. Die Änderung eines Satzes des Primärdatenbestandes erfordert ja zusätzlich für jedes geänderte Datenfeld ein Austragen und Neueintragen des Verweises auf diesen Satz in den zugehörige invertierten Listen, wobei zudem noch (um weiterhin eine rationelle Verarbeitung auch von logisch komplexeren Suchanfragen garantieren zu können) auf eine Beibehaltung der Sortierung der invertierten Listen geachtet werden muß.

Dies führt einmal dazu, daß eine vollständige Update- Bearbeitung so viele Plattenoperationen verlangt, daß an eine Realzeit- Verarbeitung eines Update-Wunsches oft nicht zu denken ist. Vielmehr wird man in der Praxis meist zumindest die notwendigen Änderungen der invertierten Listen über ein Hintergrundprogramm abwickeln. Dies führt natürlich dazu, daß die Verweise in den invertierten Listen nicht mehr den gleichen Aktualitätsgrad wie der Primärbestand haben. Bei vielen Anwendungen ist dies jedoch tragbar: bei einer Suchanfrage werden Sätze, deren Feldinhalte erst kürzlich die gewünschten Werte angenommen haben, eben noch nicht ausgewiesen, und gegen die Ausgabe von Sätzen, bei denen inzwischen nicht mehr der gesuchte Wert im Datenfeld steht, kann man sich durch ein einfaches Nachprüfen des tatsächlichen Feldinhaltes vor der Ausgabe schützen. Wichtig ist lediglich, daß überhaupt in vertretbarer Zeit - was darunter zu verstehen ist, hängt von der jeweiligen Anwendung ab - sämtliche Änderungen auch in der invertierten Listenstruktur richtig nachgetragen werden.

Dies ist jedoch der Punkt, an dem die praktische Anwendung häufig scheitert. Wenn nicht jede Änderung eines Satzes der Primärdatei vollautomatisch den Update sämtlicher auf ihn bezogenen Verweise in den invertierten Listen anstößt, sondern irgendwelche Arbeiten dazwischengeschaltet sind (z.B. Ablochen von Änderungskarten für die invertierten Listen, periodisches Aufsetzen von Änderungläufen mit diesen Karten u.ä.), so entstehen durch die damit verbundenen " Handling" - Probleme (Falschlochen, Vergessen von Folgeänderungen etc.) bald immer größere permanente Abweichungen zwischen Primär- und Verweisdatenbestand, die nach einiger Zeit die Benutzung des Systems ernstlich in Frage stellen können.

3. Systemanforderungen für einen automatischen Folge - Update

Eine Automatisierung dieses Vorganges ist jedoch vor allem dann nicht ganz einfach, wenn die primären Änderungen zwar On- Line durch ein Realzeit- Auskunfts- und Änderungsprogramm - etwa über Terminals - erfolgen, die Folgeänderungen der invertierten Listen aber etwa zu Zeiten geringer Systembelastung im Hintergrund durchgeführt werden sollen.

In diesem Fall steht der Implementierer des Realzeit- Änderungsdienstes vor zwei Problemen: das Programm muß

- erkennen, welche Änderungen auch in den invertierten Listen vermerkt werden müssen und
- zu einem späteren Termin die Aktivierung eines Hintergrundprogrammes zur Wartung der invertierten Listen veranlassen und diesem Aufträge hinterlassen können.

Die erste der beiden Aufgaben ist leicht zu lösen, sofern der Primärdatenbestand als " Datenbank " organisiert ist, d.h. das System intern Beschreibungstafeln der Datenstrukturen führt. Im Falle einer vollständigen Invertierung kann das Realzeit- Update- Programm zur Versorgung des Wartungsprogramms für invertierte Listen für jedes geänderte Feld einfach auf die betreffenden Feldbeschreibungen in diesen Tafeln verweisen. Ist die Invertierung nicht vollständig, sondern bezieht sie sich lediglich auf einen Teil der Datenfelder eines Satztyps, so kann man - wie etwa im DBTG- Proposal [4] - in der Datenbankbeschreibungssprache die Möglichkeit vorsehen, für jedes Datenfeld den Wunsch nach einer Indexerstellung über diesem Feld explizit in den Datenbeschreibungstafeln zu vermerken.

Das einzige verbleibende Problem ist die Aktivierung des Hintergrundprogramms und die Realisierung einer einfachen Kommunikationsmöglichkeit mit diesem. Diese Aufgabe ist deshalb nicht ganz einfach, weil praktisch alle gegenwärtig angebotenen Hersteller- Betriebssysteme keine bequeme Einrichtung zur längerfristigen Kommunikation eines laufenden Programms (Prozesses) mit der Ablaufsteuerung und zu späteren Zeitpunkten aktivierten Prozessen bereitstellen (eine Ausnahme werden die " Auftragsvariablen " des geplanten Betriebssystems BSR für die Siemens 4004 - Anlagen bilden [5]).

4. Die dynamische Datenbasis

Ein sehr leistungsfähiges Mittel für die Realisierung dieser Kommunikationsaufgabe bietet jedoch das gegenwärtig bereits im Einsatz befindliche HALAIS (Halberg Aktives Informations- System) der Halbergerhütte [6] mit der Bereitstellung einer für Ablaufsteuerung und Arbeitsprogramme zugänglichen längerfristigen dynamischen Datenbasis.

4.1 Benutzer- und Systemschnittstelle

Die Grundvorstellung ist, neben der eigentlichen langfristigen Datenhaltung (der "Datenbank ") noch eine"dynamische" Datenhaltung einzuführen, welche alle Daten enthält, die zwar in das System eingegeben wurden, jedoch noch auf die eigentliche Verarbeitung zu einem späteren Termin warten (das in vielen Systemen vorhandene SPOOL kann als ein primitiver Vorläufer dieser Idee angesehen werden). Dazu existiert ein Realzeit- Datenannahme- Programm, welches jederzeit " Lochkartenbilder" entgegennehmen und speichern kann. Diese Lochkartenbilder sind in zwei Felder aufgeteilt. Das erste, einige Zeichen lange Felde enthält einen Namen, die " Kartenart ", welche Art und Typ des jeweiligen

Datums angibt; für den Inhalt des zweiten Feldes, des eigentlichen Datenfeldes, gibt es vom System aus keinerlei Einschränkungen. Syntax und Interpretation des Inhalts dieses Feldes sind abhängig von der Art und damit vom Namen des Datums. Diese Daten-Kartenbilder haben Meldungs- oder Auftrags-Charakter und entsprechen damit in gewissem Sinne den " Messages " in vielen Multiprogramming-Systemen (vgl. z.B. [7]). Sie werden jedoch nicht im Kernspeicher gehalten und haben damit eine wesentlich längere potentielle Lebensdauer.

Sie können nun einerseits von peripheren Geräten (z.B. Kartenleser, Terminals) stammen andererseits aber auch von jedem laufenden Realzeit- oder Hintergrundprogramm generiert und über einen Systemmakro an die Datenannahme gereicht werden. Vom Zeitpunkt der Übergabe ist die Herkunft eines Datenkartenbildes für das System uninteressant geworden - die diesbezügliche Schnittstelle eines " menschlichen " Benutzers des HALAIS-Systems unterscheidet sich somit in nichts von der, die ein unter HALAIS laufendes Programm gegenüber dem restlichen System sieht.

Existiert nun - wie unter HALAIS - überhaupt ein Programm zur (manuellen, d.h. vom menschlichen Benutzer aus gesteuerten) Änderung von invertierten Listen, so verschwindet das oben dargestellte Kommunikationsproblem : das Realzeit-Update-Programm für den Primärdatenbestand muß lediglich Auftragskarten zur späteren Pflege der invertierten Liste generieren und diese an die Datenannahme weiterreichen. Wie die termingerechte Aktivierung und Versorgung dieses Pflegeprogrammes vor sich geht, braucht es im übrigen ebensowenig zu kümmern wie einen menschlichen Anwender - trotzdem soll das Verfahren im folgenden beschrieben werden.

4.2 Struktur der dynamischen Datenbasis und Ablaufsteuerung

Ein zu irgendeinem Zeitpunkt der dynamischen Datenbasis übergebenes Kartenbild ist zunächst einmal lediglich nichts weiter als zwei Zeichenstrings, der Name ("Kartenart") und der eigentlich relevante, zu verarbeitende Karteninhalt (das Datenfeld). Das Datenfeld interessiert die Datenannahme und die Ablaufsteuerung nicht - seine Interpretation ist die Aufgabe der Verarbeitungsprogramme für Daten dieser Art. Allerdings ist es zweckmäßig, bereits bei der Datenannahme eine vorläufige Syntax-Prüfung dieses Feldes vorzunehmen, um vor allem bei von peripheren Geräten eingelesenen Daten syntaktisch fehlerhafte sofort abweisen zu können.

Die Aufgabe der dynamischen Datenbasis ist lediglich die Herstellung einer " Bindung " des Datennamens an die für die spätere Verarbeitung wesentliche Information, eine Liste von (Verarbeitungsprogramm- Termin) - Paaren. Die Datenannahme verfügt für jeden erlaubten Datennamen über eine - vom Systemorganisator jederzeit änderbare - derartige Liste. Darin kann der zu jedem Verarbeitungsprogramm gehörende Termin sowohl relativ (" sofort ", " nach 14 Tagen ") oder auch absolut (" täglich um 20 ^{00} Uhr ", " an jedem 28. eines Monats ") angegeben sein. Die einzige Aufgabe der Datenannahme ist es, jedes ihr übergebene Datum in die Warteschlange vor der zum Datentyp gehörenden Verarbeitungsprogramm-Liste einzureihen.

Die Ablaufsteuerung prüft nun laufend, für welche Daten einer oder mehrere der in dieser Liste angegebenen Verarbeitungstermine bereits erreicht sind; für diese aktiviert sie dann die betreffenden Arbeitsprogramme und stellt diesen (ähnlich wie Datenkartenstapel in einem herkömmlichen SPOOL) alle für sie bestimmten Kartenbilder zur sequentiellen Verarbeitung zur Verfügung. Hierbei berücksichtigt die Ablaufsteuerung noch ggf. vorhandene " Programmaktivierungsinformationen ", die z.B. eine Vorsortierung der Datenkarten nach beliebigen Unterfeldern im Datenfeld verlangen können.

5. Zusammenfassung und Erfahrungen

So einfach das Prinzip der langfristigen, vollautomatischen Systemablaufsteuerung über eine dynamische Datenbasis auch ist, so nützlich ist es schon ganz allgemein durch die Entlastung von Organisatoren, Programmierern und Operateuren von den Aufgaben der Arbeitsvorbereitung und - steuerung eines größeren Datenverarbeitungssystems. Fast unentbehrlich wird ein derartiger Systemdienst jedoch, wenn zwei oder mehrere Programme zu unterschiedlichen Terminen zusammenwirken müssen, um ein bestimmtes Ziel zu erreichen, und Kommunikationsstörungen zwischen diesen Programmen durch menschliche Fehlleistungen nicht in Kauf genommen werden dürfen. Ein Beispiel hierfür ist die Pflege von Verweisstrukturen über dem Primärdatenbestand in Informationssystemen - eine Aufgabe, die im HALAIS- System gegenwärtig vollautomatisch mit hoher Sicherheit vorgenommen wird und für den Systembenutzer und - bediener völlig transparent geworden ist.

LITERATUR

[1] R.Morris,
"Scatter Storage Techniques "
Comm. ACM, 11 (1968), 38

[2] D.Lefkovitz
" File Structure für On- Line Systems "
Ch. 7, Spartan, New York (1969)

[3] G.F. Coulomis, J.M. Evans, R.W. Mitchell
" Towards Content- Adressing in Data Bases "
Comm.J. 15 (1972), 95

[4] CODASYL Data Base Task Group Report,
April 1971, ACM New York (1971)

[5] H.L. Wieler
" Das Betriebssystem OS 4004 "
Vortrag vor dem German Chapter of the ACM
am 9.7.1970, TH München

[6] J.Martin, P.Schnupp
" Die datengetriebene Programmablauf- Steuerung als
Basis zur Rechnerintegration im Verwaltungsbereich "
HMD, (Mai 1972) 2/7/3

[7] P.B.Hansen
" The Nucleus of a Multiprogramming System "
Comm. ACM 13 (1970) 238

FORMALISIEREN VON INHALT NATÜRLICHER SPRACHEN DURCH DEUTERVALENZEN UND DEUTERKRITERIEN

P.KÜMMEL

1.0 Numerisieren von Inhaltseinheiten (1.1 - 1.5)

1.1 Deuter und seine Valenzen

Erhebliche Schwierigkeiten beim Trennen sprachlichen Ausdrucks von seinem Inhalt bedingen ein vergleichendes Bewerten unterschiedlicher Sprachsysteme. Der Inhaltsschatz in Form eines Wissensbestandes läßt sich durch mannigfaltige sprachliche Trägersysteme und Zeichenrepertoires zum Ausdruck bringen ((1) S. 234 ff). Dabei offenbaren Ausdruckssysteme für die visuelle Sinneswahrnehmung den größten Inhaltsbezug ((2) S. 101 ff u. S. 122 ff). Das Repertoire der chinesischen Schriftzeichen läßt erkennen, daß bei beliebigen künstlichen Restriktionen des Zeichenschatzes immer der Klassifikationsaspekt nach Deutern oder Wurzelzeichen erhalten bleibt ((3) S. 36 ff). Diese Gliederungsmöglichkeit nach Deutern weist in ihrer Funktion direkt auf den sprachlichen Inhalt ((2) S. 16 ff). Ein umfangreicher Teil der Zeichen ist heteroexpressiv, d.h. mindestens aus zwei oder mehr Komponenten zusammengesetzt. Dabei bildet jede Komponente für sich im gleichen Zeichenrepertoire wieder eine voll funktionstüchtige Ausdruckseinheit. Die Komponente "Baum" hat beispielsweise häufiger Anteil an der Bildung von Kompositivzeichen als die Komponenten "Stein" oder "Ohr". Der Schatz von Ausdruckseinheiten eines Sprachsystems zerfällt in monoexpressive und heteroexpressive Träger von Inhalt. Vergleicht man die Ausdruckseinheiten chinesischer Schriftzeichen mit dem Wortschatz europäischer Sprachen ((3) S. 55 ff u. S. 58 ff), so kann man die chinesischen Kompositivzeichen mit Heteronomen in Relation bringen:

1.	Glove	(Mononom)
2.	Handschuh	(Heteronom als Binom)
3.	Handschuhfach	(Heteronom als Trinom)

Wird der Bedeutungsschatz eines Sprachrepertoires auf zehn Einheiten beschränkt, dienen folgende Termini als Beispiele: a) Auto, b) Autobahn, c) Bahn, d) Eisenbahn, e) Handschuh, f) Hausschuh, g) Holzschuh, h) Polizeiauto, i) Schuh und j) Seilbahn. Die Bedeutung des Terminus "Schuh" weist in diesem verknappten Sprachschatz die größte Relativverflechtung auf. Sie erscheint dreimal, nämlich unter e),f) und g). Position i) erhält somit die Deutervalenz (3). Ihr folgen die Inhaltseinheiten der Termini: "Bahn" (3) und "Auto" (2) mit ihren Verflechtungen zu anderen Bedeutungen des gleichen Schatzes. Jene Einheiten besitzen die Deutervalenzen (3) und (2). Alle Einheiten des Bedeutungsschatzes menschlichen Wissens lassen sich numerisch nicht nur nach den bislang bekannten allgemeinen und relativen Frequenzen, sondern auch nach Deutervalenzen bewerten. Für die bildliche Darstellung des Verflechtungsausmaßes als Deutervalenz hat sich die Vorstellungsstütze von Fasersträngen mit Ösen bewährt. Wird ein Inhaltsschatz auf drei Einheiten beschränkt, ergibt sich in Anlehnung an das Ausdruckssystem der deutschen Nationalsprache nachstehende Darstellung. Die Deutervalenz, in Klammern geschrieben, ist mit der Anzahl von Deuterfasern weiterer Deuter in der betreffenden Deuteröse identisch. Die Deuterziffer, in Dezimalbrüchen angegeben, wird nach dem Prinzip der Dezimalklassifikation eingeordnet (Abb 1). Diese Abbildung enthält in einem begrenzten Modell neun Deuter.

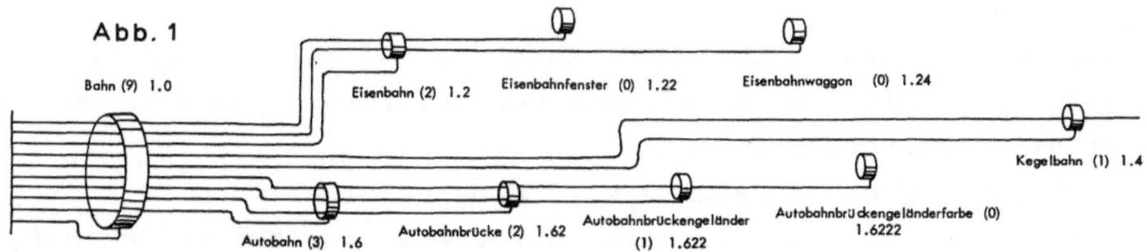

An den ersten Ziffern lassen sich gewisse Sparten des Wissensschatzes, an den letzten wahre und unwahre Sachverhalte ablesen. Inhaltsschätze größeren Ausmaßes erzeugen schwammartige Gebilde aus Fasersträngen und Ösen. Sie sind mit Kabelbäumen der Hardware zu vergleichen. Alle Fasern eines Deuterschwammes gehen von der Wurzelwand aus, die wiederum als Grunddeuter ausgebildet sein kann.

1.2 Definition: D e u t e r

Ein Deuter, unter Orientalisten auch Wurzelzeichen oder Radikal genannt, stellt eine Inhaltseinheit bzw. eine Bedeutung des Schatzes natürlicher Sprachen und damit eine Informationseinheit dar. Als Klassifikationsphänomen ursprünglich visuellen sprachlichen Ausdrucks zeichnet sich der Deuter durch seine relative Valenz, die anteilige Verflechtung zu weiteren Bedeutungen, im gleichen Einheitenschatz aus. Durch sie wird Einblick in Inhaltserscheinungen gewährleistet, den der auditiv wahrgenommene Ausdruck versagt.

1.3 Die fünf Deuterkriterien

Der Weg zum Ursprung einer Bedeutung - ihrer Entstehung - führt zur wissenschaftlichen Forschung und dem Patentwesen ((3) S. 23 ff). Sowohl eine Entdeckung wie eine Erfindung bedingen neue Benennungen im Ausdruck. Diese Erscheinung weist auf die tatsächliche Neugeburt einer Inhaltseinheit hin. Beim Recherchierverfahren des Patentwesens, das dem Iststandermitteln der wissenschaftlichen Dokumentation entspricht, treten folgende Kriterien ((3) S. 63) zum möglichen Numerisieren auf:

1. Man ermittelt mit einer sogenannten "Offensichtlichkeitsprüfung", ob es sich bei der Anmeldung um ernstgemeinte, wahrhaftige Erfindungen handelt, die den bestehenden Gesetzen nicht widersprechen. Das Kriterium lautet: Wahrheit.
2. Man sucht die zugehörige Klasse und Gruppe einer neuen zu prüfenden Erfindung auf, um weitere bewertende Vergleiche mit dem bisherigen Aufkommen des Kenntnisschatzes vornehmen zu können. Das Kriterium lautet: Identität.
3. Man legt die allgemein anzuerkennende Geburtszeit der Erfindung durch den perforierten Eingangsstempel mit Datum fest. Das Kriterium lautet: Alter.
4. Nach der Geburt einer Erfindung kann die allgemeine und relative Benutzung und damit die Häufigkeit des Auftretens gemessen werden. Das Kriterium lautet: Frequenz.
5. Für die Erteilung eines Patents wird eine erforderliche Erfindungshöhe und die Fortschrittlichkeit bewertet. Das Kriterium lautet: Vorrang.

Kriterium Nr. 4 berührt das Prüfungs- und Recherchierverfahren nicht, ist aber zum Bewerten einer Information wichtig. Die Kriterien 4 und 5, Frequenz und Vorrang, weisen Bezug zur Deutervalenz auf. Es läßt sich zusätzlich zum Deuterschwamm ein Frequenzschwamm mit Deutern konzipieren, dessen Faserstränge mit wachsender Frequenz stärker werden. Nach der Informationstheorie (SHANNON/WEAVER) würden dann die Deuterösen an den dünnsten Fasersträngen den größten Informationsgehalt aufweisen. Der Informationswert konzipiert sich jedoch aus mehreren Grössen, (siehe unten 1.5!).

1.4 Deuterschwamm zum Numerisieren der fünf Deuterkriterien

Um die fünf Deuterkriterien zu formalisieren, wird eine mehrdimensionale aber mindestens zweidimensionale Veranschaulichung erforderlich ((3) S. 64 ff).Der unter 1.1 erwähnte Deuterschwamm, in dem die Valenzen bildlich dargestellt sind, dient diesem Zweck. Jede Deuteröse ist mit allen Deuterwerten (Abb 1) zu versehen. Das Kriterium Wahrheit (Abb 3) wird durch die Deuterziffer charakterisiert, indem die Wahrheit der Sache oder des Sachverhalts mit geraden und die Unwahrheit mit ungeraden Dezimalbrüchen am Deuter zu implementieren ist. Die Iden tität wird ebenfalls durch die Deuterziffer bewertet. Das Alter bestimmt sich nach der Geburtsziffer, welche zum fortlaufenden Numerisie ren der Ösen des Deuterschatzes dient. Die Frequenzen, allgemeine und relative, werden in gemeinen Brüchen angegeben, wobei die größte Auftretenshäufigkeit mit 1 zu bemessen ist ((2) S. 119 ff). Allgemeine Frequenzen bemessen die Häufigkeit des Auftretens seit Existenzbeginn des Deuters, relative Frequenzen die Auftretenshäufigkeit in Bezug zu weiteren Einheiten des Schatzes. Der Vorrang bestimmt sich durch die Spannungsziffer in Prozenten, deren Wert durch Unregelmässigkeiten an der Peripherie des Schwammgewächses gegeben ist (Abb 2). Wird die unregelmässig gewachsene Einbuchtung an der Schwammperipherie groß, kann der Wert der Spannungsziffer bis zu 100% betragen. Deuter, die sich an der harmonisch gewachsenen Peripherie befinden, weisen Größen auf, die dicht bei 0 % liegen.

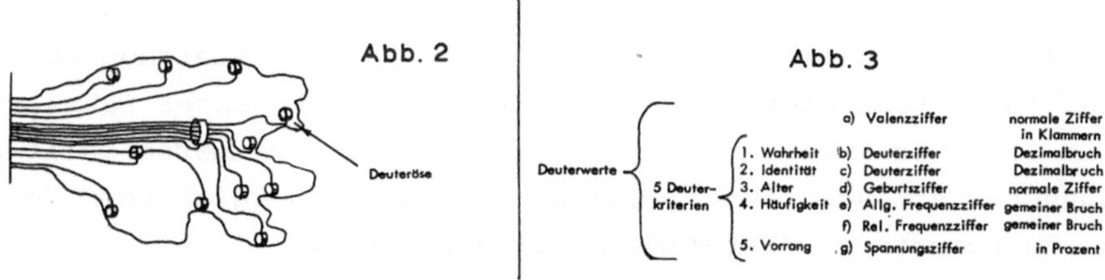

1.5 Definition: Informationseinheit oder: Inhaltseinheit sprachlichen Ausdrucks

Die Inhaltseinheit ((3) S. 69 f), auch Bedeutung genannt, ist 1.unzerteilbar, 2. nicht durch weitere Einheiten des Repertoires ersetzbar, weist 3. als Konkretum dreidimensionale und als Abstraktum vierdimensionale Charakteristika in der mnestischen Vorstellung auf, ist 4. immer heterogenetisch in dem Sinne, daß auch bei einem Wert der relativen Deutervalenz (0) eine geschlossene Einheit zwischen Faserwurzel an der Wurzelwand und Deuteröse durch die verbindende Faserstruktur gegeben ist, besitzt 5. eine relative Valenz, die bei leerer Deuteröse Null beträgt und mit jedem zusätzlichen, in der Öse befindlichen Faserstrang um 1 wächst, wird 6. durch die fünf Deuterkriterien: I Wahrheit, II Identität, III Alter, IV Frequenz und V Vorrang charakterisiert, wobei sich Wahrheit und Identität durch die Deuterziffer, das Alter durch die Geburtsziffer, die Häufigkeit durch allg. und rel. Frequenzwerte in Relation zur Deutervalenzziffer und der Vorrang durch die Spannungsziffer bestimmen.

2.0 NUMERISIEREN VON SÄTZEN DURCH IHRE REDUKTION AUF INHALTSEINHEITEN MIT HILFE EINER FORMALGRAMMATIK

2.1 Definition: Natürliche Sprachen

Natürliche Sprachen sind Teil des willkürlichen Ausdrucks ((1) S.233f) der sich in zwei Bereiche, 1. natürliche und 2. künstliche Sprachen, zergliedert. Natürliche Sprachsysteme schließen ehemals künstlich gewesene nur dann nicht aus, wenn diese sich durch lang andauerndes Bestehen zu natürlichen Sprachen weiter entwickeln konnten. Natürliche Sprachen stellen Ausdruckssysteme dar, deren Benutzung a) über einer Mindestdauer liegt (etwa der Lebenszeit eines Individuums der Betreffenden Sprachgemeinschaft oder mehr) und b), deren allgemeine Verständlichkeit einen Individuenkreis umfaßt, welcher die Ausmaße eines nationalen Sprachbereiches nicht unterschreitet. Den Kriterien a) und b) gemäß lassen sich Kinder- und Ausländersprachen (Gastarbeiterdeutsch) wie unter gewissen Voraussetzungen der syntaktisch verknappte Sprechfunk bei der Verkehrsfliegerei noch zu den natürlichen Sprachen zählen.

2.2 Auf Heteronome reduzierte Sätze als Inhaltseinheit

Inhalt natürlicher Sprachen gelangt gewöhnlich durch vollständige Sätze zum Ausdruck. Jeder dieser Sätze läßt sich als Heteronom konzipieren ((2) S. 101). Konkreter Inhalt: Verkleidungsbezug einer Lehne des Sessels im Direktorzimmer: Als Heteronom: "Direktorzimmersessellehnenverkleidungsbezug". Abstrakter Inhalt: Der Vater übergibt dem Sohn das Geld: als Heteronom: /Vater/Sohn/Geldübergabe/.

2.3 Das Prädikat als Inhaltseinheit abstrakter Sätze

Die Satzaussage, durch das Prädikat bestimmt, verkörpert das grammatische Zentrum eines Satzes. Für einige europäische Nationalsprachen gilt daher auch die Folge: Subjekt-Prädikat-Objekt. Beispiel: "Der Schüler liest das Buch". Andere, wie etwa asiatische Nationalsprachen, benutzen die Folge: Subjekt-Objekt-Prädikat. "Seito ga hon wo yomimasu" Die Objekte als Konkreta stehen an Bedeutung hinter dem Prädikat als Abstraktum zurück. Es handelt sich beim Inhalt der Aussage des vorstehenden Beispielsatzes primär um den Vorgang des Lesens. Erst von entfernterer Wichtigkeit sind die Zusätze: "Wer liest?" und "Was wird gelesen?" Man kann den ganzen Inhalt des Satzes als Lesevorgang bezeichnen. 1. Lesen, 2. Buchlesen und 3. /Schüler/Buch/Lesen/.

2.4 Das Endnomen als Einheitenrepräsentant des Satzes

Heteronome konkreten Inhalts stellen Inhaltseinheiten ausschließlich des Endnomens dar. Gemäß 2.2 handelt es sich um einen Bezug bzw. eine Verkleidung. Die nähere Beschreibung der Bedeutung geht aus den davor befindlichen Nomina hervor. Das gleiche gilt für abstrakte Einheiten, deren Prädikat das letzte Nomen im Heteronom darstellt. Weitere Einzelheiten des Prädikates ergeben sich gleichwohl aus den davor befindlichen Nomenfolgen.

2.5 Umkehr der Nomenfolgen eines Heteronoms zum Numerisieren im Deuterschwamm

Die als Beispiel dienende Bedeutung der "Anspitzerklingenbefesti - gungsschraube" eines "Vierfachnomens" stellt eine durch Nomenfolgen-vorsatz näher beschriebene Schraube dar ((3) S. 60 f). Sie wird wie folgt in den Deuterschwamm implementiert:

Abb. 4

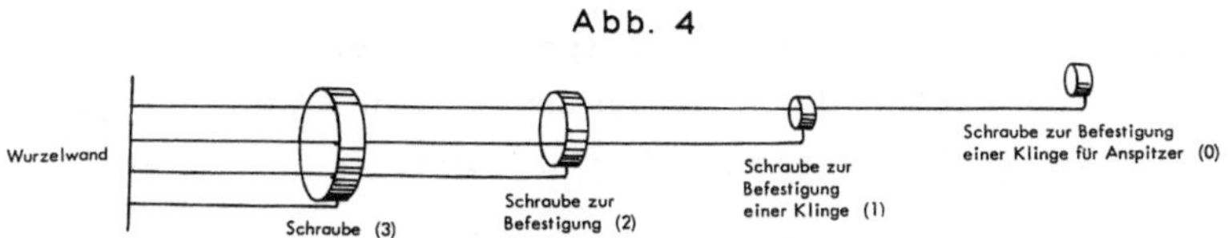

2.6 Grundregeln der Formalgrammatik

Die Formal- oder Deuterfolgengrammatik enthält Richtlinien für ei - nen Satzbau, nach denen jeder Satz als Heteronom zu konzipieren ist.Es gelten u.a. folgende Grundregeln ((3) S. 76 f):

§ 1 Aller Ausdruck sprachlichen Inhalts ist in Deuterfolgen nach Art eines Heteronoms zu konzipieren, in dem Verben und Adjektiva zu substantivieren sind. Beispiel: "...übergibt das Geld" = Geldüber gabe, oder "...sonniger Tag" = Sonnentag.

§ 2 Bei abstrakten Inhalten ist die Folge: Subjekt-Objekt-Prädikat einzuhalten.

§ 3 Die Deuterfolgen sollen ohne Partikel auf fünf Einheiten in Form eines "Fünffachnomens" begrenzt bleiben.

§ 4 Nach dem Kettenstichverfahren können lange Sätze in kleinere Heteronome, höchstens jedoch in ein Fünffachnomen, aufgelöst werden. Partikel eines Heteronoms (§5) sind nicht als Nomen zu zählen. Die Prädikateinheit der vorhergehenden Deuterfolge wird mit in die nächste Einheit verkettet: "Der Vater, der in Hamburg wohnt, übergibt dem in München studierenden Sohn das Geld": 1. Heteronom als Vierfachnomen: /Vater/Hamburg/Wohnen/Geldübergabe/, 2. Heteronom als Fünffachnomen: /Vater/Sohn/München/Studium/Geldübergabe/.

§ 5 Erforderliche Partikel für Zeit, Frage usw., die in Klammern zu schreiben sind, kommen vor dem Endnomen zu stehen: 1.) "Der Vater gab dem Sohn das Geld"; /Vater/Sohn/(Prät.)/Geldübergabe/ oder : "Fährt der Zug um 12:30 Uhr ab?"; /Zug/12:30Uhr/(Quest.)/Abfahrt/.

§ 6 Das Pronomen oder Fürwort, das gewöhnlich ein Substantiv vertritt, ist immer durch das ursprünglich zu vertretende Substantiv zu er-setzen. 1. Beispiel: Der kleine Max sagt nicht:"Iche möchte essen", sondern;"Max möchte essen". 2. Beispiel: Der Pilot sagt zur Abkür-zung nicht: "Ich bitte um Startfreigabe", sondern;"D-ECMO erbit-tet Startfreigabe".

3.0 ANWENDUNGSBEREICHE DER FORMALISIERUNG

3.1 Deuterschwamm zur Konzeption eines Assoziativspeichers

Der Deuterschwamm kann in seiner numerisierten Struktur durch konventionelle Compilersprachen implementiert werden. Geeigneter ist jedoch ein Assoziativspeicher. Wie mit einer Schablone werden elektrisch Speicherzellen abgedeckt, um den gesuchten Inhalt zu finden. Der gespeicherte Inhalt der Deuterwerte dient gleichzeitig als Suchadresse. Zum weiteren Klassifizieren sind stufenweise Markierungen möglich (Abb 5). Nach der Transformation des Dualsystems in das Dezimalsystem können die Deuterwerte gemäß Abb 3 eingegeben werden:

Abb. 5

●	○	●	○	○	○	–	
○	●	●	○	○	●	–	
●	○	●	○	●	●	+	
●	●	●	○	●	●	–	
○	●	●	●	○	○	–	
	○	●	○				doppelt gefilterter Eingang
▨							2. Stufe der Maskierung
○	○	●	○				einmal gefilterter Eingang
				▨	▨		1. Stufe der Maskierung
○	○	●	○	○	●		ursprünglicher Eingang

Um einen winzigen Teil des menschlichen Wissens in Form eines Deuterschwammes abzuspeichern, sind große Speicherkapazitäten erforderlich , denen nur noch Fotospeicher bzw. COM - Systeme gerecht werden. Vorausgesetzt, daß nur die Wahrheit abgespeichert wird, ist ein Löschen des implementierten Bestandes nicht notwendig.

3.2 Faktenretrieval sowie automatisches Recherchieren und Übersetzen für die Dokumentation

Über das Nachforschen nach Literaturhinweisen und Publikationstitel des "Document-Retrieval" hinaus werden beim Faktenretrieval Inhalte gesucht und aufgefunden. Für das automatische Recherchieren ((3)S 71f) mit möglicher Anwendung im Patentwesen und bei der wissenschaftlichen Dokumentation gelten die gleichen Richtlinien wie beim Faktenretrieval. Die Vorgänge sind mit jenen des automatischen Übersetzens artverwandt. Die aufzusuchenden Inhalte werden mit Deuterwerten in den Deu terschwamm eines Assoziativspeichers implementiert. Die Sucheingabe in der einfachsten Form bringt den Suchterminus des Fragestellers, dessen Deuterziffer der Maschine bekannt ist. Nach automatischem Auffinden des gespeicherten Deuters werden alle Deuterwerte ausgedruckt. Bei Bedarf können angrenzende Deuter mit ihren Termini, Valenzen und Deuterkriterien ausgegeben werden.

Für das automatische Übersetzen sind zusätzliche Bezifferungen erforderlich. Würde ein Begrenzen auf den Bedarf des EWG - Areals erfolgen, könnten die Nationalsprachen 1. Deutsch, 2. Englisch, 3. Französisch, 4. Holländisch und 5. Italienisch jeweils mit den betreffenden Ziffern

1 bis 5 versehen werden. Beim Ausdehnen der Benutzung auf die restlichen Weltsprachen ist dieser Ziffernbestand der Sprachgemeinschaftsziffern (SPG - Ziffern) nach einer alphabetischen Reihenfolge zu erweitern. Gemäß den Leitsätzen der Formalgrammatik (2.6) sind sowohl bei der Ein- wie bei der Ausgabe mit Hilfe der zugehörigen SPG - Ziffern Deuterfolgen in Form von Heteronomen beliebiger Nationalsprachen zu erstellen. Der jeweilige sprachliche Inhalt bleibt unverändert. Es werden multilinguale Recherchier- und Übersetzungsprozeduren gemäß der Formalgrammatik (2.6) automatisch gewährleistet. Beispiele:Kon kretum: /Anspitzer/Klingen/Befestigungs/Schraube/ = /Pencilsharpener/ /Nife/Fastener/Screw/, Abstraktum: /Vater/Sohn/Geldübergabe/ = /Father/ /Son/Moneytransfer/.

3.3 Implementierungsbeispiel des Deuters "Sanduhr"

Nachstehend ist der Deuter Sanduhr als Beispiel in den Schwamm des Assoziativspeichers implementiert. Die Sanduhr, zuweilen noch als Eier uhr benutzt, ist als Totobjekt anzusehen. Ihre strukturelle und anwendungsbezogene Entwicklung ist abgeschlossen. Im Deuterschwamm wachsen fast keine neuen Knospen nach, wodurch sich die Deutervalenz kaum ändert. Eine mutmaßliche Einteilung des menschlichen Wissens zergliedert den Bestand der Naturkonkreta auf 10, der Künstlichkonkreta abermals auf 10 und den Rest der Abstrakta auf 80%. Die Sanduhr ist der Wurzelwand der Künstlichkonkreta anzuhängen. Das gegenwärtige menschliche Wissen bestehe beispielsweise aus drei Millionen Bedeutungen. Die Sanduhr erhält dann folgende Deuterwerte zugeordnet:

a) Valenzziffer	(28)	d) Allgemeine Frequenzziffer	1/2 833 697
b) Deuterziffer	303 728	e) Relative Frequenzziffer	1/1 379 236
c) Geburtsziffer	96 003	f) Spannungsziffer	2 %

Abb. 6

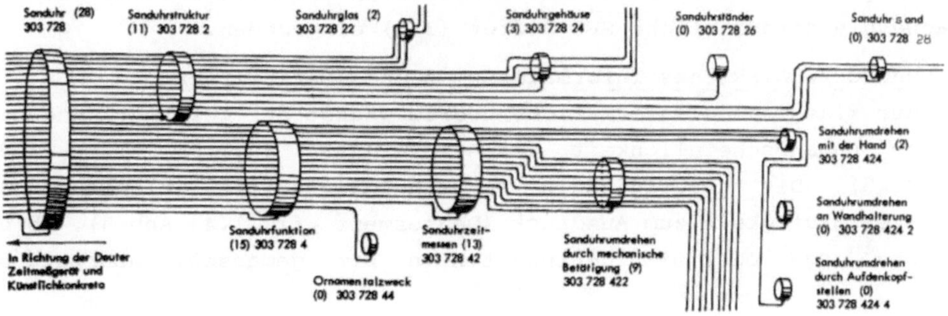

Alle zugehörigen Deuterwerte sind für den Inhalt "Sanduhr" in den Deuterschwamm des Assoziativspeichers oder behelfsweise in den Speicher eines herkömmlichen EDV-Geräts zu implementieren. Ist einem Benutzer die Bedeutung des Terminus "Sanduhr" unbekannt, wird durch die Eingabe automatisch die Deuterziffer des Deuters Sanduhr aufgerufen. Dabei unterteilen sich die Sucheingaben 1. in "deuterintern" und 2. in "deuterextern". Eine deuterinterne Sucheingabe erfragt gemäß den fünf Deuterkriterien und der Valenz einzelne oder alle Deuterwerte. Es handelt sich um eine Suchprozedur 1. Ordnung (Abb 7). Fehlt dem Benutzer immer noch der erforderliche Zusammenhang zu seiner unvollständigen Wissensvorstellung, erfolgt die Sucheingabe 2. Ordnung (Abb 8). Durch sie wird der nächste in Richtung Wurzelwand angeordnete Deuter mit seinen Deuterwerten befragt. Es handelt sich beispielsweise um den Deuter des Terminus: "Zeitmeßgerät". Eine Sucheingabe 3. Ordnung läßt alle Deuterwerte der in Richtung Schwammperipherie benachbarten Deuter ausdrucken (Abb 9).

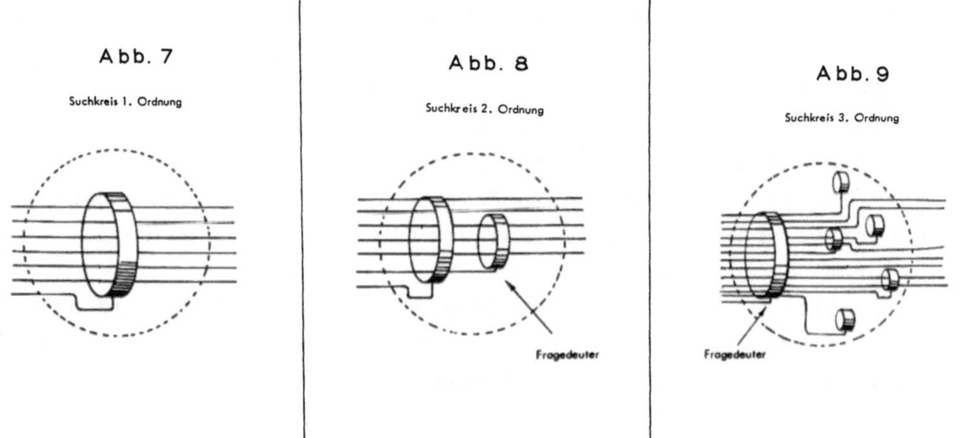

Diese Sucheingaben sind sowohl für das automatische Recherchieren, wie das Faktenretrieval gedacht und daher für beide Prozeduren identisch. Beim Vorgang des automatischen Übersetzens wird mit der gewünschten Sprache die erforderliche SPG-Ziffer (3.2) eingegeben.

3.4 SHANNON/WEAVERsches Informationsmaß und Deuterziffern

Nach der klassischen Informationstheorie wächst der Informationsgehalt mit der Unwahrscheinlichkeit des Auftretens: $I\ (a_i) = -ld\ p_i$ Bit ((3) S. 5). Die aufzufindenden Wahrscheinlichkeiten gelangen in der relativen Häufigkeit zum Ausdruck (Deuterwert f), 1.4, Abb 3). Ob dekadisch ^{10}log- oder mit ld-Einheiten in Bit gemessen, mehr als die relative Frequenz der Information läßt sich mit der Informationstheorie nicht ermitteln. Es fehlt das Bestimmen der übrigen Deuterwerte a) bis g) minus f) , (1.4, Abb 3).

Ausblick:

1. Die Vorgänge des automatischen Übersetzens, Recherchierens und Faktenretrievals sind in ihrem Wesen gleich und bedingen das Numerisieren von Inhalt natürlicher Sprachen (3.2).
2. Inhalt natürlicher Sprachen (2.1) ist in seiner Erscheinung als I n f o r m a t i o n anzusprechen (1.5).
3. Die SHANNON/WEAVERsche Informationstheorie sowie die Größe Bit sind für eine Informationsmetrik unzureichend (3.4).
4. Das Numerisieren von Information ist nur durch Ermitteln von Deuterwerten (1.4) und das vorläufige Anwenden einer verknappten Syntax nach den Grundregeln der Formalgrammatik möglich (2.6).
5. Ein präzises Ermitteln der Deuterwerte (1.4) ist mit auditiv-phonographisch erfolgendem sprachlichen Ausdruck nicht realisierbar, sondern nur durch Vergleiche mit Sprachsystemen visueller Sinneswahrnehmung wie Gebärden, Ideo- und Piktographie (1.1).
6. Ein fruchtbares Programmieren und Implementieren für die automatische Übersetzung kann erst nach präzisem Bestimmen der Deuterwerte (1.4) erfolgen.
7. Für das Eingeben von Deuterwerten in die EDV-Hardware sind Assoziativspeicher geeigneter als herkömmliche Adressenspeicher (3.1).

L i t e r a t u r :

KÜMMEL Peter; Betrachtungen zur Ausdrucksanalyse, in: Zeitschrift für Sprachwissenschaft Phonetik und Kommunikationswissenschaft, (13 Seiten), Akademie - Verlag, Bd. 21, Heft 3/4 Berlin, 1968

KÜMMEL Peter; Struktur und Funktion sichtbarer Zeichen, (223 Seiten), Verlag Schnelle GmbH, Quickborn bei Hamburg, 1969

KÜMMEL Peter; Wertbestimmung von Information, Zur qualitativen Analyse des Inhalts natürlicher Sprachen, Grundlagen der Nichtnumerik, (90 Seiten), Max Niemeyer Verlag, Tübingen, 1972

WORTSTAMM - RETRIEVAL IN T E L D O K 4 4 0

D.L.HOLMBERG, B.S.MÜLLER

1. Beschreibung von Wortstammretrieval

In Dokumentationssystemen finden an verschiedenen Stellen Wortstammmethoden Anwendung. Wortstammretrieval ist eine dieser Methoden. Wortstammethoden dienen dazu

- den Umfang des Thesaurus zu verringern
- die Handhabung für den Benutzer des Systems zu vereinfachen
- die Retrievalergebnisse zu verbessern.

Wortstammethoden arbeiten auf verschiedene Weise mit Teilwörtern, mit den sogenannten Wortstämmen. Den Wörtern Schuld, Schulden, Schuldner, schuldig, schuldhaft z.B. ist der Wortstamm SCHULD gemeinsam; den Wörtern Arbeit, arbeitsam, Arbeiter der Stamm ARBEIT. Anstatt mit den Wörtern selbst kann mit den Wortstämmen gearbeitet werden.

Der Umfang eines Thesaurus kann erheblich verringert werden, wenn für mehrere Wörter ein Wortstamm eingesetzt wird. Solche Thesauruseintragungen werden Stammwörter genannt, um sie von den Wortstämmen im linguistischen Sinne zu unterscheiden, da eine Thesauruseintragung sowohl ein Wortstamm, wie SCHULD, als auch ein verstümmeltes oder ganzes Wort wie SCHULDN oder SCHULDNER, oder eine Wortgruppe wie BUNDESKANZLER WILLY BRANDT sein kann.

Eine einzige Stammeintragung im Thesaurus, wie z.B. ARBEIT, kann für mehrere Wörter, wie z.B. Arbeit, arbeiten, arbeitsam und Arbeiter stehen. Es ist einleuchtend, daß ein Thesaurus, der nach dieser Methode aufgebaut wird, verhältnismäßig klein gehalten werden kann.

Das ist einer der Gründe dafür, daß Telefunken Computer den Benutzern von TELDOK 440 Wortstammethoden anbieten will. Der zweite Grund betrifft die Benutzerfreundlichkeit. Mit Hilfe von Wortstammmethoden kann der Benutzer seine Suchanfrage in natürlicher Sprache formulieren, und wird auf diese Weise von dem Zwang befreit, die genaue Terminologie des Thesaurus in seiner Suchanfrage zu gebrauchen. Durch die im System vorhandenen Leistungen können die Wörter seiner Frage wie Wortstämme behandelt werden, und auf dieser Basis mit der Deskriptorliste verglichen werden. Dadurch können Retrievalergebnisse verbessert werden. Informationen, die dem Benutzer durch seine ungenaue Fragestellung verloren gegangen wären, werden ihm durch Wortstammethoden zugänglich gemacht.

2. Methoden des Wortstammretrievals

Mit Wortstammethoden will man hauptsächlich zweierlei leisten:

- Wörter mit dem gleichen Stamm als gleichwertig erkennen
- zusammengesetzte Wörter in ihre Teile zerlegen *).

Wörter mit dem gleichen Stamm erkennen heißt, sowohl Flexionsendungen wie z.B. das finale n in Maßnahmen, als auch Suffixe im allgemeinen wie z.B. das -ung in Stabilisierung behandeln zu können. Ein zusammengesetztes Wort wie Währungstabilisierungsmaßnahmen will man in die Teile: Währung, stabilisier und maßnahme zerlegen, damit ein Benutzer im Retrievalprozess sowohl nach Information zur Währungsstabilisierungsmaßnahmen als auch nach Maßnahmen zur Stabilisierung der Währung fragen kann.

Es gibt mehrere Methoden, die angewendet werden, um Wortstämme in Retrievalsystemen zu bearbeiten. Welche Methode benutzt wird, ist hauptsächlich von der Form des Thesaurus abhängig.

Aus der Sicht des Wortstammretrievals kann man von 3 Thesaurustypen reden:

- von Thesauri mit Stammwörtern als Eintragungen
- von Thesauri mit Stammwörtern, zu denen Suffixinformation zugeordnet wird
- von Thesauri mit Textwörtern.

Es gibt, allgemein gesprochen, fünf Vergleichs- und Matchingmethoden, die einzeln und in Kombination für die Recherche gebraucht werden. Die Zuordnung zwischen Leistung, Thesaurustyp, und Matching-Methode zeigt Tabelle I.

Methode (1), längstes Match, analog zu englisch \`longest match´, wird in Zusammenhang mit einem Thesaurus gebraucht, der Stammwörter mit oder ohne zusätzliche Suffixinformation als Eintragungen enthält. So werden Fragewörter wie Ventilator und Ventilation mit einem Stammwort wie z.B. VENTILAT gematcht, oder verschlüsseln und Verschlüsselung mit dem Stammwort VERSCHLÜSS. Das IBM-Patentdokumentationssystem **) verwendet einen Thesaurus mit Stammwortein-

*) wird nicht von allen Systemen angestrebt

**) s. Bibliographie (1),(2),(3)

tragungen, ohne zusätzliche Suffixinformation, und sucht das längste Match zu einem Fragewort im Thesaurus.

Die zweite und dritte Matchingmethode werden bei Thesauri angewendet, die Textwörter als Eintragungen haben wie z.B. das IBM-System STAIRS. *) Für Methode (2), Match mit dem Anfang eines Deskriptors, sollte der Benutzer sinnvollerweise versuchen, seine Suchanfrage mit Stammwörtern zu stellen. Dann wird das Fragewort mit dem Anfang der im Thesaurus enthaltenen Deskriptoren verglichen bis ein Match gefunden wird.

Bei der dritten Matchingmethode werden durch Einführung eines sogenannten Universalzeichens Teile des Frageworts ausgeblendet. So kann z.B. mit dem Fragewort Bundeskanzl** sowohl der Deskriptor BUNDESKANZLER als auch der Deskriptor BUNDESKANZLEI gematcht werden.

Die Matchingmethoden (4) und (5) dienen zur Verfeinerung der Methode (1). Für Methode (4) muß jedem Stammwort im Thesaurus Suffixinformation zugeordnet werden. Das längste Match wird gefunden, und dann wird der verbleibende Teil des Frageworts mit den für dieses Stammwort möglichen Suffixen verglichen. Erst wenn auch hier ein Match gefunden wird, werden Fragewort und Deskriptor als gleichwertig angesehen. Für das geplante kombinierte System GOLEM/PASSAT **) von SIEMENS, werden Methoden (1) und (4) auf diese Weise Anwendung finden

Methode (5) wird genau wie Methode (4) angewendet, nur wird hier mit einer allgemeinen Suffixliste verglichen, anstatt mit einer Liste, die dem Stammwort zugeordnet wurde. Der Vergleich mit der Suffixliste kann wiederholt werden, um mehrere Suffixe erkennen zu können. Die Suffixliste kann auch Fugenelemente, wie das n in Sonnenschein enthalten. Die Kombination von Methoden (1) und (5) wird neben vielen anderen Methoden in Saltons Retrievalsystem SMART angewendet. ***)

Zusammengesetzte Wörter können durch wiederholte Anwendung der Methoden (1) und (4) oder (1) und (5) in ihre Teile zerlegt werden. Nehmen wir als Beispiel das zusammengesetzte Wort Währungsstabilisierung. Durch Anwendung von Methode (1) wird das längste Match für

*) s. Bibliographie (8)

**) s. Bibliographie (4),(5)

***) s. Bibliographie (6),(7)

	THESAURUSEINTRAGUNG		
MATCHINGMETHODE	Stammwort	Stammwort und Suffix	Textwort
1. längstes Match	X	X	
2. Match mit Anfang eines Deskriptors			X
3. Fragewort mit Universalzeichen	X		X
4. Suffixe für einzelnes Wort		X	
5. Suffixliste	X		
LEISTUNG			
1. Wörter mit gleichem Stamm erkennen	1, 3, 1 und 5	1 und 4	2,3
2. Zusammengesetzte Wörter zerlegen	1 und 5	1 und 4	

Tabelle I. Matchingmethoden, die mit verschiedenen Thesauri angewendet werden, mit erbrachter Leistung.

den ersten Teil des Wortes gefunden. In diesem Fall wäre das Währung. Dann wird das S durch Vergleich mit der Suffixliste als Fuge erkannt, und der Wortteil stabilisierung wird erneut mit dem Thesaurus für das längste Match, wahrscheinlich stabilisier, verglichen. -ung wird als Suffix erkannt. Auf diese Weise wird das Wort in Währung s stabilisier ung zerlegt, und die Teile sind für weitere Verarbeitung erkannt. Dieses Verfahren ist im IBM-Patentdokumentationssystem und im SIEMENS-System GOLEM/PASSAT möglich.
Es ist leider zur Zeit nicht möglich einer der hier dargestellten Wortstammretrievalmethoden den Vorrang zu geben, da keine Ergebnisse von Vergleichstests vorliegen. Um diese Lücke zu füllen sollen verschiedene Methoden in TELDOK 440 realisiert werden. Eine Evaluation der Resultate bei Anwendung an einen größeren Datenbestand soll dies ermöglichen.

3. Wortstammretrieval in TELDOK 440

Die Entwicklung des Wortstammretrievals für TELDOK 440 findet in zwei Phasen statt, wie in Abbildung 3.1. dargestellt wird.

Studien/Test	Implementierung in TELDOK 440
- mit Stammliste	- Wortstamm I
- ohne Stammliste	- Wortstamm II
- andere Wortstammethoden	
- Evaluation	

Abbildung 3.1. Wortstammretrieval für TELDOK 440

Zur Phase Studien/Test gehören Vorstudien und Testsysteme für Wortstammethoden, die mit Stammwortlisten arbeiten. Die Stammwortliste übernimmt teilweise die Funktion der im Kapitel 2 erwähnten Thesauri mit Stammworteintragungen. Die dort beschriebenen Methoden werden angewendet.
Zur Phase Studien/Test gehört zusätzlich der Versuch mit einer neuen Wortstammethode die ohne Stammwortliste arbeitet. Ein Algorithmus wird komponierte und nichtkomponierte Wörter auf die in ihnen enthaltenen Stämme zurückführen. Die Analyse wird anhand eines großen Datenbestands, bestehend aus mehr als 14.000 Komposita aus der Duden Rechtschreibung und aus mehreren Millionen laufende Wörter deutscher Zeitungssprache durchgeführt.

Falls es möglich ist einen solchen Algorithmus zu finden, hätte diese Methode über den bisher erwähnten den Vorteil, jedes beliebige Wort zerlegen zu können. Das Aufstellen und Erweitern (updating) einer Stammwortliste wäre nicht notwendig.

Zu den anderen Wortstammethoden zählen die in Kapitel 2 erwähnten Methoden (2) und (3), nämlich das Match mit dem Anfang eines Deskriptors und der Vergleich mit Fragewörtern, die Universalzeichen enthalten. Mit ihnen werden Evaluationstests durchgeführt.

In der allgemein zugänglichen Literatur sind keine ausreichenden Evaluationen der angewendeten Methoden erwähnt. Für Bewertungszwecke stehen TELDOK 440 folgende Datenbestände zur Verfügung:

- Datenbank des Dokumentationsrings Elektrotechnik
- Juristischer Datenbestand
- allgemeine Zeitungssprache.

Bei der Evaluation wird das Problem der Erhöhung der Homonymie durch Wortstammethoden mit berücksichtigt werden. Bei automatischen Wortstammanalyseverfahren könnten die Wörter BERGE, BERGEN (Dativ Plural), BERGEN (Infinitiv), BERGUNG alle auf dem Stamm BERG zurückgeführt werden, wodurch ein Bedeutungsverlust stattfinden könnte. Die Auswirkungen dieses Effekts sind unter echten Arbeitsbedingungen noch nicht ausreichend geprüft worden.

Das in Abbildung 3.1. aufgeführte Arbeitsphase 'Implementierung in TELDOK 440' bezieht sich auf die verschiedenen Ausbaustufen des Wortstammretrievals in TELDOK 440. Hier soll hauptsächlich von Wortstamm I in TELDOK 440 die Rede sein.

Wortstamm I verwendet eine Stammwortliste, die in die Datenbank integriert wird. Ein Stammwort verweist auf einen oder mehrere Deskriptoren, der auf ein oder mehrere Dokumente verweist, wie in Abbildung 3.2.

Abbildung 3.2. Schematische Datenbankstruktur

Flexibilität und Umschaltbarkeit der Retrievalmethode werden dadurch gewährleistet, daß der Benutzer durch ein Kommando den Wortstammprozess einleitet. Durch das Kommando ERWEITERN*) wird der Rahmen der nachfolgenden Suchanfragen erweitert. Für Wortstamm I in TELDOK 440 hat das Kommando ERWEITERN 4 Parameter : *ERWEITERN (p_1,p_2,p_3,p_4). p_1: = EIN|AUS dient zum Ein- und Ausstellen verschiedener Retrievalarten. p_2:= VOLLWORT|STAMM gibt dem Benutzer die Möglichkeit zwischen der Recherche mit oder ohne Stammwortmethoden zu wählen. p_3:= S(ynonyme)|H(omonyme)|F(semantisches Feld)|A(ntonyme)|O(berbegriffe)|U(nterbegriffe) erlaubt die Erweiterung der Suchanfrage durch semantische Verknüpfungen. p_4:= 1|2|...|10 gibt die Stufentiefe an bis zu der die semantischen Verknüpfungen verfolgt werden sollen.

Man kann sich die Wirkung beispielsweise des Kommandos

*ERWEITERN (EIN,STAMM,O,2)

in Zusammenhang mit der Suchanfrage

A: DESKR1, DESKR2, DESKR3,...

wie folgt vorstellen. Mit dem Kommando wird verlangt, daß die Suchanfrage mit Wortstammethoden bearbeitet wird, und daß die Oberbegriffe, die mit den gefundenen Thesaurusdeskriptoren verknüpft sind, bis zur 2. Stufe mit in die Recherche einbezogen werden sollen. (s. Abbildung 3.3.)

Ergebnis der Wortstammanalyse. Erweiterung durch die Oberbegriffe

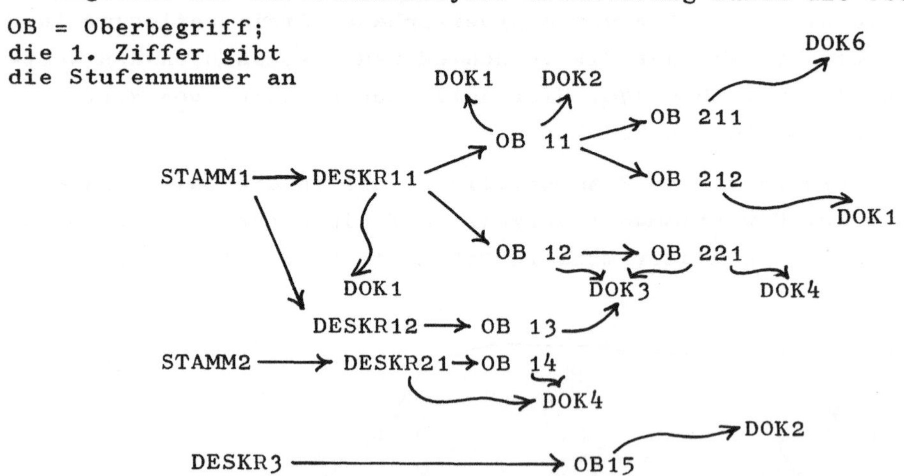

Abbildung 3.3. Beispiel für die Erweiterung einer Suchanfrage bei Wortstammretrieval unter Berücksichtigung von Oberbegriffen bis zur 2. Stufe

*) s. Bibliographie (9)

Das Kommando bewirkt, daß die Deskriptoren der Suchanfrage zunächst durch Anwendung der Stammwortliste in Stämme und Suffixe zerlegt werden. Wenn ein Deskriptor einer Suchanfrage nicht zerlegt werden kann, wird er in dem nachfolgenden Suchprozess nicht wie ein Stamm sondern wie ein normaler Vollwortdeskriptor behandelt.

Mit Hilfe des Kommandos GIBSTAMM können die Zuordnungen zwischen Stämmen und Deskriptoren (Vollwörtern) dem Benutzer gezeigt werden. Das Kommando GIBSTAMM hat einen Parameter:

*GIBSTAMM (p)

Der Parameter hat folgende Bedeutungen:

p=EIN. Einstellen des Kommandos GIBSTAMM für die nachfolgenden Suchanfragen

p=AUS. Ausstellen des Kommandos GIBSTAMM

p=Suchanfragennummer. Ausgabe des Ergebnisses der Wortstammanalyse für die Deskriptoren einer bestimmten Suchanfrage

p=*Deskriptor. Ausgabe des Ergebnisses der Wortstammanalyse für einen bestimmten Deskriptor

p=+Stamm. Ausgabe der einem bestimmten Stamm zugeordneten Deskriptoren.

Für die weiteren Ausbaustufen der Wortstammethodik in TELDOK 440 werden die Ergebnisse der Studien und Tests Berücksichtigung finden. Unter anderem wird eventuell die Möglichkeit geschaffen, Stämme in der Datenbank semantisch miteinander zu verknüpfen (vgl. das Kommando ERWEITERN).

Zum Aufbau der Stammwortliste und zur Korrektur desselben wird ein autonomes Programm erstellt.

Die Indizierung von Dokumenten mit Hilfe der Wortstammanalyse-algorithmen und die anschließende Einrichtung der Datenbank geschieht ebenfalls durch autonome Programme.

Darüberhinaus stehen die allgemeinen Moduln zum on-line updating im Dialog in späteren TELDOK-Ausbaustufen zur Verfügung.

Bibliographie

(1) BÖHME, Franz. "Das Volltext-Suchverfahren für die Patentdokumentation bei der IBM Deutschland".
In: IBM Nachrichten, Nr. 205, 21 Tg., Feb. 1971

(2) WILLIAMS, J.H., Jr. "BROWSER-an Automatic Indexing On-Line Text Retrieval System", Federal Systems Division, IBM Gaithersburg, Maryland, Sept. 1969. Veröffentlicht als Report AD 693143 durch U.S. Department of Commerce, Clearinghouse for Federal Scientific an Technical Information.

(3) ————, and PERRIENS, M.P. "Automatic Full Text Indexing and Searching System", IBM Federal Systems Division Information Systems. Symposium, Sept. 4-6,1968, Washington, D.C.

(4) HOFFMANN/JAHL/QUANDT/WEIGAND. "Automatische Textanalyse mit PASSAT". In: Zeitschrift für Datenverarbeitung 1971, 495-504

(5) ————, "PASSAT-Überlegungen und Versuche zur automatischen Textanalyse als Vorbedingung für thesaurusorientierte maschinelle Informations- und Dokumentationssysteme".
In: Nachrichten für Dokumentation 22 (1971) Nr. 6, 241-251

(6) SALTON, Gerard. Automatic Information Organization and Retrieval
New York: Mac Graw-Hill, 1968

(7) ———— The SMART Retrieval System. Experiments in Automatic Document Processing.
Englewood Cliffs, N.J.: Prentice-Hall, 1971.

(8) IBM Deutschland. STAIRS. Storage and Information Retrieval System. Ein IBM Dokumentationssystem. Stichworte und Abbildungen zu einem Referat.
IBM Form M12-1016-0. 1971.

(9) TELDOK Handbuch. TELEFUNKEN COMPUTER GmbH. Druckschrift 440.G0.02. Ausgabe 0872-VK10. August 1972

DYNAMISCHE DOKUMENTENRÄUME

E.KONRAD

Zusammenfassung: Um die Effektivität von Dokument-Retrieval-Systemen zu verbessern, sind eine Reihe von Verfahren entwickelt worden, welche Relevanzurteile von Benutzern als Feedback-Information verwenden. Dabei werden hauptsächlich Strategien angewandt, die auf der Iteration von Suchfragen beruhen und einen statischen Dokumentenraum voraussetzen. Eine radikale Strategie besteht darin, nicht die Suchfrage, sondern den gesamten Dokumentenraum zu ändern, d.h. einen dynamischen Dokumentenraum zu benutzen. In der vorliegenden Arbeit wird eine hybride Strategie beschrieben, die sowohl mit der Iteration der Suchfrage als auch einem dynamischen Dokumentenraum operiert.

1. Einleitung

Dokument-Retrieval-Systeme beantworten Fragen eines Benutzers mit Hinweisen auf Dokumente. Wir legen unseren Überlegungen folgendes Modell zugrunde:

(a) Dokumente und Suchfragen in natürlicher Sprache werden umgewandelt in mehrdimensionale Vektoren eines abstrakten Raumes. Jedes Dokument wird dabei überführt in einen Vektor $x=(x_1,x_2,...,x_N)$ und jede Suchfrage in einen Vektor $q=(q_1,q_2,...,q_N)$. Die Vektorkomponenten bedeuten nichtnegative Gewichtszahlen; x_i z.B. ist das Gewicht des Deskriptors i im Dokumentenvektor x . Die Gesamtheit der Dokumentenvektoren wird Dokumentenraum genannt.

(b) Der Dokumentenraum wird durchsucht, indem der Suchfragenvektor q mit jedem Dokumentenvektor x verglichen wird. Dabei wird jedesmal ein Korrelationskoeffizient K(q,x) berechnet.

(c) Die Dokumentenvektoren werden nach absteigender Größe von K(q,x) geordnet. Die Ordnungszahl von x bezüglich q wird Rang von x genannt.

(d) Nach Wahl eines Schnittes S in der Menge der Korrelationskoeffizienten nennt das System als Antwort eine Menge A von Dokumenten (Relevanzvorschlag des Systems). Die Dokumente von A werden vom Benutzer auf Relevanz geprüft.

Erfahrungen mit Retrieval-Systemen haben in der Vergangenheit gezeigt, daß der Benutzer in einem einzigen Suchvorgang i.a. keine befriedigenden Ergebnisse erzielt. Verbesserungen lassen sich durch Feedback-Strategien erreichen.

2. Feedback-Strategien

Bequem für den Benutzer sind Feedback-Verfahren, die nach Angabe der relevanten und nichtrelevanten Dokumente in der Antwortmenge A die Suchfrage bzw. den Dokumentenraum automatisch korrigieren. Solche Verfahren sind insbesondere im System SMART /6/ realisiert und experimentell überprüft worden. Bewertungstests mit den Maßen Recall und Precision haben ergeben, daß die Verfahren zur Änderung der Suchfrage /4/, /5/ den Verfahren zur Änderung des Dokumentenraumes /1/, /2/, /3/ deutlich unterlegen sind.

Die Iteration einer Suchfrage q in einem statischen Dokumentenraum geschieht dadurch, daß q in jedem Schritt an als relevant identifizierte Dokumente herangerückt und von als nichtrelevant identifizierten Dokumenten entfernt wird. Umgekehrt kann man die Suchfrage konstant lassen und den Dokumentenraum transformieren, d.h. relevante Dokumente werden an die Suchfrage q herangerückt und nichtrelevante von q entfernt. Diese Methode, die einen dynamischen Dokumentenraum benutzt, ist radikaler als die Suchfrageniteration; denn ihr liegt die Vorstellung zugrunde, daß schlechte Retrievalergebnisse nicht dem Benutzer, sondern dem System anzulasten sind. Insbesondere lassen sich mit diesem Verfahren relevante Dokumente finden, die im Dokumentenraum weit entfernt voneinander liegen. Da andererseits die Änderung des Dokumentenraumes wesentlich aufwendiger ist als die Änderung der Suchfrage, schlagen wir eine hybride Strategie vor.

Der Benutzer iteriert zunächst die Suchfrage und erst anschließend den Dokumentenraum. Sind die Ergebnisse via Änderung der Suchfrage hinreichend gut, so kann auf eine Änderung des Dokumentenraumes verzichtet werden.

Für die hybride Strategie geben wir abschließend einen Algorithmus an.

3. Implementierung

Implementierungen beginnen mit der Erstellung von Algorithmen. Im folgenden wird ein Algorithmus beschrieben, welcher Bestandteil des Systems FAKYR (Fachbereich-Kybernetik-Retrievalsystem) ist. FAKYR wird an der TU Berlin im Rahmen von Diplomarbeiten von den Herren Bock, Hausen, Hennings und Zuse auf einer IBM 360/67 implementiert.

Wir stellen die auszuführenden Schritte der hybriden Strategie dar:

(a) Ein Suchfragenvektor $q^{(o)}$ (Anfangsfrage) wird eingegeben und iteriert.

Die Iteration geschieht im Anschluß an Rocchio /4/ mit Hilfe der Formel

$$q^{(m+1)} = r_m s_m q^{(m)} + s_m \sum_{k=1}^{r_m} \frac{x^{(k)}}{|x^{(k)}|} - r_m \sum_{k=1}^{s_m} \frac{y^{(k)}}{|y^{(k)}|} \quad ; \quad m=0,1,\ldots,p.$$

$q^{(m)}$ ist der Suchfragenvektor, der nach dem m-ten Schritt entsteht; r_m ist die Anzahl der relevanten und s_m die Anzahl der nichtrelevanten Dokumente in der Antwort A_m auf die Suchfrage $q^{(m)}$; $x^{(k)}$ und $y^{(k)}$ sind die Vektoren der relevanten bzw. nichtrelevanten Dokumente; $|x^{(k)}|$ ist die Länge von $x^{(k)}$, entsprechend $|y^{(k)}|$ von $y^{(k)}$.
Für den Fall, daß in $q^{(m+1)}$ negative Komponenten auftreten, sei $q^{(m+1)}$ gleich dem Nullvektor.
Bricht der Benutzer die Iteration nach dem p-ten Schritt ab, so hat er als Gesamtantwortmenge A die Vereinigung der Mengen $A_o, A_1, \ldots, A_p$.
(b) Es sei r die Anzahl der relevanten und s die Anzahl der nichtrelevanten Dokumente in A. Dann berechnet sich die Trennschärfe T_i des Deskriptors i aus

$$T_i = \frac{1}{r}\sum_{j=1}^{r} x_i^{(j)} - \frac{1}{s}\sum_{j=1}^{s} y_i^{(j)} \quad .$$

$x^{(j)}$ und $y^{(j)}$ sind Vektoren von relevanten bzw. nichtrelevanten Dokumenten aus A.
(c) Nach Wahl eines Schnittes t im Bereich der Trennschärfen T_i $(i=1,\ldots,N)$, werden diejenigen Deskriptoren i bestimmt, für welche $|T_i|>t$ gilt.
Diese Deskriptorenmenge wird durch Hinzunahme von Deskriptoren, die im Suchfragenvektor $q^{(o)}$ ein von Null verschiedenes Gewicht haben, zu einer Menge M ergänzt. Die Deskriptoren von M haben die Eigenschaft, relevante von nichtrelevanten Dokumenten zu trennen.
(d) Für die Deskriptoren i aus M werden die Größen S_i, R_i und N_i berechnet:

$$S_i = \frac{q_i^{(o)}}{\sum_{j=1}^{N} q_j^{(o)}}$$

mit $q_i^{(o)}$ bzw. $q_j^{(o)}$ als i-ter bzw. j-ter Komponente des Suchfragenvektors $q^{(o)}$;

$$R_i = \frac{\sum_{j=1}^{r} x_i^{(j)}}{\sum_{i,j=1}^{N,r} x_i^{(j)}} \quad \text{und} \quad N_i = \frac{\sum_{j=1}^{s} y_i^{(j)}}{\sum_{i,j=1}^{N,s} y_i^{(j)}} \quad .$$

Diese drei Größen sind resp. Maße für die Bedeutung des Deskriptors i in der Suchfrage, in den relevanten und nichtrelevanten Dokumenten von A.
(e) Für jeden Deskriptor i aus M berechnet man den Änderungsfaktor L_i.
Es sei $L_i = S_i + R_i$, wenn $T_i > t$ oder wenn der Deskriptor i im Suchfragenvektor $q^{(o)}$ ein von Null verschiedenes Gewicht hat.
Es sei $L_i = -N_i$, wenn $T_i < t$ und wenn der Deskriptor i in $q^{(o)}$ das Gewicht Null hat.
(f) Der Dokumentenraum wird nun wie folgt transformiert:
Alle Vektoren von nichtrelevanten Dokumenten (Benutzerurteil) werden durch den

Nullvektor ersetzt. Dadurch werden die nichtrelevanten Dokumente so weit wie möglich von der Suchfrage entfernt.
In allen übrigen Dokumentenvektoren $x^{(j)}$ werden die Komponenten $x_i^{(j)}$ durch $x_i^{(j)}+L_i x_i^{(j)}$ $(i=1,\ldots,N)$ ersetzt.
Die Suchfrage $q^{(o)}$ wird schließlich im geänderten Dokumentenraum verarbeitet.
Die Schritte (b) bis (f) werden wiederholt bis der Benutzer mit der Anwort des Systems zufrieden ist.
Die vorstehend beschriebene Feedback-Strategie unterscheidet sich von dem Verfahren in /3/ durch Einbeziehung der Suchfrageniteration und von dem Verfahren in /1/ durch Berücksichtigung der Gewichte im Suchfragenvektor.
Um das Verfahren bezüglich Recall und Precision zu optimieren, können in den Änderungsfaktor L_i Parameter a und b eingeführt werden: $L_i = aS_i+bR_i$ und $L_i = -bN_i$.
Die Bestimmung der Werte von a und b jedoch muß experimentellen Untersuchungen vorbehalten bleiben.

Literatur

/1/ Brauen,T.L.: Document Vector Modification, in G. Salton (Editor): The SMART Retrieval System, Prentice Hall 1971,S.456-484

/2/ Ide,E;Salton,G.: Interactive Search Strategies and Dynamic File Organization in Information Retrieval, a.a.O. S.373-393.

/3/ Friedman,S.R.;Maceyak,J.A.;Weiss,S.F.: A Relevance Feedback System based on Document Transformations, a.a.O. S.447-455.

/4/ Rocchio,J.J.Jr.: Relevance Feedback in Information Retrieval, a.a.O. S.313-323.

/5/ Salton,G.: Relevance Feedback and the Optimization of Retrieval Effektiveness, a.a.O. S.324-336.

/6/ Salton,G.: The SMART Project - Status Report and Plans, a.a.O, S.3-11.

B I B L I S - EIN BIBLIOTHEKS-, INFORMATIONS- UND VERWALTUNGSSYSTEM

H.-J.SCHNEIDER, G.SIEWERT ET AL.

0 Einführung

Das Anliegen dieser Präsentation ist es nicht, Neues aus bibliothekarischer Sicht zu bringen, es soll vielmehr gezeigt werden, wie Software-Engineering-Mittel (Informatik-Mittel) konsequent bei automatischen Bibliothekssystemen angewendet werden können. Auf diese Weise werden Charakteristika wie gute Anpassbarkeit, Änderungsfreundlichkeit und Flexibilität bei automatischen Bibliothekssystemen erreicht, wie sie bei heute existenten Systemen kaum vorhanden sind.

Im ersten Teil wird eine kurze Übersicht über den Stand der Technik gegeben. Anschließend folgt unter 2 eine kurze Beschreibung des Systems, wobei die Maximen der Systementwicklung besonders hervorgehoben werden. Ein Anwendungsbeispiel einer Titelaufnahme wird unter 3 gegeben, schließlich ist unter 4 eine kleine Literaturzusammenstellung angehängt.

1 Stand der Technik

Da der Rahmen dieser Arbeit durch eine ausführliche Behandlung des jetzigen Standes auf diesem Gebiet völlig gesprengt werden würde, wird nur kurz auf die Hauptgesichtspunkte eingegangen.

Alphabetische Katalogisierung

Die Preussischen Instruktionen sollen im deutschsprachigen Raum allmählich durch die sich besser zur mechanischen Verarbeitung eignenden Regeln für die Alphabetische Katalogisierung (RAK) ersetzt werden [8].

Logische Datenerfassungsschemata

Von der Library of Congress (LC) und der British National Bibliography (BNB) wurde gemeinsam ein logisches Datenerfassungsschema MARC II entwickelt [3]. Dieses Schema wird von den meisten heute verwendeten Datenerfassungsschemata als Grundlage genommen. Besonders hervorzuheben im deutschsprachigen Raum sind das von der Bayerischen Staatsbibliothek in München entwickelte Schema [4] und das von einer Arbeitsgruppe im Auftrag der Deutschen Forschungsgemeinschaft entwickelte sogenannte "DFG-Schema" [2] (dieses Kategorieschema wurde bei der BIBLIS-Implementierung zugrunde gelegt).

Austauschschemata

Die International Federation of Library Associations (IFLA) hat 1971 einen Normungsvorschlag zum Austausch bibliographischer Informationen zwischen Institutionen unterschiedlicher Sprachgebiete gemacht [5]. Zur Zeit sind unter anderem noch weitere Entwicklungen bei der International Standards Organization (ISO) und beim Deutschen Normenausschuß (MARC D) im Gange.

Automatisierungsbestrebungen

An vielen deutschen Universitätsbibliotheken sind Automatisierungsbestrebungen festzustellen. Leider konnte man sich noch nicht auf ein einziges logisches System einigen.

Gesamtsysteme

Bei einigen Programmsystemen sind von den möglichen Bibliotheksfunktionen

Erwerbung (Bestellung, Inventarisierung)
Nachweis (Titelaufnahme, Katalogisierung, Katalogerstellung)
Bereitstellung (Ausleihe)
Statistikenerstellung

alle bis auf Titelaufnahme und Katalogisierung automatisiert. Hervorzuheben sind die Systeme LMS [1] und ILS [7].

2. Beschreibung des Systems

2.1 Zweck und Aufgabe. Stand des Projektes

Zweck des Programmiersystems BIBLIS ist es, Informationen über bibliographische Einheiten (BE) einzulesen, abzuspeichern, den Bibliothekar bzw. den Benutzer der Bibliothek über das Vorhandensein bzw. Nichtvorhandensein von BEs zu informieren und dem Bibliothekar alle Arbeiten, die mit dem Erwerb von BEs zusammenhängen, abzunehmen bzw. wesentlich zu erleichtern.

Bibliographische Einheit (BE)

wird in diesem Zusammenhang als Oberbegriff verwendet für

selbständige Literatur (Monographie, Stücktitel, Hochschulschrift, Report, Konferenzpapier),
Gesamtheit (Sammelwerk, Reihe, Zeitschrift, zeitschriftenartige Reihe) und
unselbständige Literatur (Zeitschriftaufsatz, Kapitel aus selbständiger Literatur).

Die aufzunehmenden Informationen über die BEs umfassen alle sogenannten Kennzeichnungsdaten (wie Personennamen, Körperschaftsnamen, Sachtitel, Informationen über übergeordnete Gesamtheiten, Auflagenbezeichnungen, also die Daten zur formalen Beschreibung). Inhaltsdaten (Deskriptoren, also Daten der Sacherschließung), werden noch keine aufgenommen; deren Aufnahme ist aber in Kürze vorgesehen.

Wie schon oben erwähnt, wurde bei der BIBLIS-Implementierung das DFG-Schema in teilweise abgeänderter Form zugrunde gelegt. BIBLIS ist aber so flexibel, daß auch andere Schemata verwendet werden können.

Verwirklicht bzw. im Testendstadium der Programmierung sind bis jetzt folgende Aufgaben:

Eingabe von bibliographischen Einheiten

- Einlesen, Prüfen, Kontrollprotokollieren und Abspeichern von BEs (s. Abb.1)
- Löschen ganzer BEs
- Löschen, Ersetzen und Einfügen von Kategorien

Ausgabe von Katalogen

- Arbeitskatalog (enthält die gesamten eingegebenen BE-Informationen in entschlüsselter Form, s. Abb.2)
- Gesamtkatalog (alphabetischer Katalog aller BEs, aber nur mit für den Benutzer relevanten Informationen. Eintragungen unter Namen von Personen, unter Namen von Körperschaften und unter Sachtiteln treten gemischt im Katalog auf.)
- Katalog zur Kurzinformation
- Titelkatalog
- Autorenkatalog für selbständige und unselbständige Literatur
- Gesamtheitenkatalog

Verwaltungsaufgaben

- Bestellung zur Ansicht bzw. fest von BEs beim Buchhändler
- Mahnen der Buchaußenstände
- Buchführen der akkumulierten Ausgaben für die Bibliothek eventuell nach Kostenstellen getrennt
- Schreiben einer Inventarliste für die Universitätsverw.(s.Abb.3)
- Aufstellen der Liste der bestellten, aber noch nicht gelieferten BEs
- Allgemeine Adressenverwaltung

Geplant ist weiter

- Umstellen des Systems von TR4 auf TR440 (batch auf on-line)
- Umstellen von ALGOL 60 auf BCPL (bessere effektive Transportfähigkeit)
- On-line-Korrektur
- On-line-Ausleihe
- Verarbeitung von Inhaltsdaten (Dokumentation)

Einige der geplanten Problemkreise konnten bis jetzt noch nicht mit der Programmierung in Angriff genommen werden, da die dafür benötigte Computerausstattung erst Ende 1972 zur Verfügung steht.

2.2 Software-Engineering-Maximen

Im folgenden werden die bei der Systementwicklung im Vordergrund stehenden Maximen beschrieben.

Redundanzfreiheit

Die aufzunehmenden BEs dürfen variabel lang sein, dasselbe gilt auch für die meisten Kategorieninhalte. Bei der Aufnahme und Speicherung wird, wenn möglich und praktikabel, mit Schlüsseln gearbeitet (z.B.für aufnehmende Stelle, Abschlußvermerk, bibliographische Ebene, Erscheinungsland, Sprache des Textes). Logische Adressen bezeichnen Informationseinheiten, in denen ausführliche Informationen über die verschlüsselten Objekte stehen (z.B. Adresse des Stammbuchhändlers).

Anpassbarkeit (adaptability)

Dadurch daß alle wesentlichen Teile des Programmsystems tabellengesteuert angelegt sind, kann der Systemmanager auf einfache und flexible Weise auf die verschiedenartigen Benutzerwünsche reagieren.

Das beginnt bei der Eingabe. Durch Code-Tabellen können unterschiedliche Interpretationen der Eingabe-Bitmuster erreicht werden.

Man unterscheidet grundsätzlich den einzugebenden Code (zur Zeit Flexowriter 8-Kanal-Code, Groß-Klein-Schreibung), den internen bibliographischen Code und den auszugebenden Code (zur Zeit TR4-Code, s.Abb.4). Die einzelnen BEs sind in Kategorien unterteilt, die ihrerseits jeweils verschiedene logische Informationseinheiten aufnehmen. Das Einlesen der BEs wird von Tabellen gesteuert, die Informationen über den Aufbau und die Art der Kategorien enthalten.

Die Datenstruktur einer BE (Vorhandensein einzelner Kategorien) hängt im allgemeinen vom Inhalt bzw. vom Vorhandensein einzelner Kategorien ab. Die Zulässigkeit einer Datenstruktur wird mittels eines tabellengesteuerten Programmes überprüft (s.Abb.5).

Bei der Sortierung der BEs wird eine Sortierwerttabelle verwendet. Dies geschieht erst bei der Verarbeitung der BEs, z.B. bei der Katalogerstellung.

Das Ausgabeformat der Kataloge wird auch durch Tabellen gesteuert. Die Steuerung wird getrennt nach den verschiedenen Katalogen und nach den drei Typen von BEs vorgenommen (s.Abb.6). Die verschlüsselten Informationen werden über Referenzlisten (die auch jederzeit geändert werden können) entschlüsselt (s.Abb.7). Häufig auftretende Informationen, z.B. über Adressen der Stammbuchhändler, der Hauptverlage, der wesentlichen Körperschaften und über Zeitschriften) können über die dazugehörige logische Adresse abgerufen werden. Dabei werden im allgemeinen Inhalte von mehreren Kategorien zuerst ersetzt und dann ausgedruckt.

Maintenance

Das System ist modulartig aufgebaut. Die einzelnen Funktionen sind in Prozeduren (ohne globale Größen) formuliert, die weitgehend tabellengesteuert sind. Dadurch wurde der Programmieraufwand verhältnismäßig gering gehalten, die Programme sind durchsichtig und daher leicht zu pflegen. Es wurde beim Entwurf darauf geachtet, möglichst wenig Kategorietypen einzuführen. Dadurch bedingt wird man ein bißchen mehr Aufwand bei der Aufnahme in Kauf nehmen müssen; bei einer Abschätzung des Gesamtaufwandes und der Zuverlässigkeit des Systems wird sich dies aber positiv auswirken.

Transportfähigkeit (transportability)

Das System soll, sobald der Telefunken-Computer TR440 in Stuttgart installiert ist, auf die Implementierungssprache (low level language) BCPL umgestellt werden. Der BCPL-Compiler ist zu ca. 80 % in BCPL geschrieben, der Rest, die Schnittstelle zum Betriebssystem und der Code-Generator, müssen in Assembler-Sprache geschrieben werden. Darüberhinaus ist BCPL schon auf vielen Maschinen verschiedener Hersteller implementiert.

Abbildungen

```
--------
051            233
053   I
054   11.71
057   M
061   US
062   US
065           1388
067    3C 269
068              2
072   A
800   K
805   FLACH
810   FRANKFURT
820   13. 8.71
840     65.80
110   M|A|CKEEMAN, W.M.
310   A COMPILER GENERATOR
313   S
314   US
400   PRENTICE HALL SERIES IN AUTOMATIC COMPUTATION
510   ENGLEWOOD CLIFFS, N.J.
520     11    527
540     45 LITERATURANGABEN
110   HORNING, J.J. (2)
110   WORTMAN, D.B. (3)
511   PRENTICE HALL
```

Abb.1

Kontrollprotokoll

```
*233,                    1388,              3C 269,
MCKEEMAN, W.M., SANTA CRUZ, UNIVERSITY OF CALIFORNIA,
(VERF.),
HORNING, J.J., TORONTO, UNIVERSITY, (VERF.),
WORTMAN, D.B., STANFORD, UNIVERSITY, (VERF.),
A COMPILER GENERATOR,
SACHBUCH, ENGLISCH,
PRENTICE HALL SERIES IN AUTOMATIC COMPUTATION,
ZAHLREICHE ABB.,
45 LITERATURANGABEN,
ENGLEWOOD CLIFFS, N.J., PRENTICE HALL,
1970, S. 11-527,
IFI, 11.71, ABGESCHL., SELBST.LIT., USA, ENGLISCH, H, 2,
GEBUNDEN, MONOGRAPHIE,
GEKAUFT BEI, FLACH, FRANKFURT,
25.5.71, 13.8.71, 7452891,
65.80 DM,
```

Abb.2 Ausdruck Arbeitskatalog

BIBLIOTHEKSVERZEICHNIS DES INSTITUTS FUER INFORMATIK

FORTL. NR	GEGENSTAND	ANSCHAFFUNG JAHR	DM	SIGNATUR	BEZUGSQUELLE RECHNUNGSDATUM
1388	MCKEEMAN, W.M. A COMPILER GENERATOR	1971	65.80	3C 269	FLACH R.V. 13.08.71

Abb.3 Inventarliste

CODE-TABELLE - BIBLIOTHEKSAUTOMATISIERUNG

binäre Werte	kl. Flexowriter gr.	interner Bibl. Code	TR 4-Hexade	Druck	Bemerkungen
32	0)	0 55	0 55	0)	
1	1 '	1 56	1 56	1 '	
2	2 τ	2 129	2	2	
19	3 >	3 58	3 58	3 >	
4	4 σ	4 128	4	4	

Abb.4 Eingabe/Ausgabe-Code-Tabelle

$$\langle \text{Monographie} \rangle ::= \langle 051\rangle\ \langle 053\rangle\ \langle 054\rangle\ \langle 056\rangle\ \langle 057\rangle\ \{\langle 061\rangle\}\ldots\ \{\langle 062\rangle\}\ldots$$

$$(\langle 800\rangle \neq 1\ : \langle 065\rangle)\ \langle 066\rangle\ \langle 067\rangle\ [\langle 068\rangle]\ \{\langle 071\rangle\}\ldots\ \{\langle 072\rangle\}\ldots\ [\langle 073\rangle]$$

$$\left\{\left[\begin{Bmatrix}\langle 110\rangle\\ \langle 200\rangle\end{Bmatrix}\right]\right\}\ldots\ \left\{\left[\begin{Bmatrix}\langle 110\rangle\\ \langle 210\rangle\end{Bmatrix}\right]\right\}\ldots\ \{(e(\langle 110\rangle) : [\langle 112\rangle])\ (e(\langle 110\rangle) : \left[\begin{Bmatrix}\langle 150\rangle\\ \langle 114\rangle\end{Bmatrix}\right])$$

$$(e(\langle 110\rangle) : \langle 117\rangle)\}\ldots\ \left\{\left[\begin{Bmatrix}\langle 200\rangle\\ \langle 210\rangle\end{Bmatrix}\right]\right\}\ldots\ \{(e(\langle 210\rangle) : [\langle 214\rangle])(e(\langle 210\rangle) : [\langle 218\rangle])$$

$$(e(\langle 210\rangle) : [\langle 220\rangle])\ (e(\langle 210\rangle) : \left[\begin{Bmatrix}\langle 230\rangle\\ \langle 221\rangle\end{Bmatrix}\right])\ (e(\langle 230\rangle) : [\langle 223\rangle])$$

$$(e(\langle 221\rangle) : [\langle 223\rangle])\}\ldots\ \{\langle 310\rangle\ [\langle 312\rangle]\ [\langle 313\rangle]\ [\langle 314\rangle]\ [\langle 315\rangle]$$

$$[\langle 317\rangle]\ (e(\langle 317\rangle) : [\langle 318\rangle])\}\ldots\ [\langle 319\rangle]\ [\langle 320\rangle]\ [\langle 330\rangle]$$

$$\left[\begin{Bmatrix}\langle 401\rangle\\ \langle 400\rangle\end{Bmatrix}\right]\quad [\langle 460\rangle]$$

$$[\langle 501\rangle]\quad [\langle 502\rangle]\quad \left\{\left[\left[\begin{Bmatrix}\langle 570\rangle\\ \langle 511\rangle\end{Bmatrix}\right]\right]\right\}\ldots\quad \{(e(\langle 511\rangle):\langle 510\rangle)\}\ldots\quad [\langle 512\rangle]$$

$$(\langle 072\rangle = q : [\langle 515\rangle])\quad (\langle 072\rangle = q : [\langle 516\rangle])\quad \langle 520\rangle\quad \{[\langle 521\rangle]\}\ldots\quad [\langle 530\rangle]$$

$$[\langle 532\rangle]\quad [\langle 540\rangle]$$

$$(\langle 072\rangle = q : [\langle 601\rangle])\quad (\langle 072\rangle = m : [\langle 620\rangle])\quad (\langle 072\rangle = m : [\langle 621\rangle])\quad (\langle 072\rangle = b : [\langle 630\rangle])\quad (e(\langle 630\rangle):[\langle 631\rangle])\quad (e(\langle 630\rangle):[\langle 632\rangle])(\langle 072\rangle = q:\begin{Bmatrix}\langle 641\rangle\\ \langle 640\rangle\end{Bmatrix})$$

$$\langle 800\rangle\quad \begin{Bmatrix}\langle 806\rangle\\ \langle 805\rangle\end{Bmatrix}\quad (e(\langle 805\rangle):\langle 810\rangle)\quad [\langle 815\rangle]\quad (\langle 800\rangle = k :\langle 820\rangle)$$

$$(\langle 800\rangle = k : [\langle 830\rangle])\quad (\langle 800\rangle = k :\langle 840\rangle)\quad (\langle 800\rangle = 1 :\langle 850\rangle)$$

Abb.5 Zulässige Datenstruktur Monographie

TABELLE FUER MONOGRAPHIEN

51	0	2	0	0
65	0	21	0	0
67	1	41	0	0
110	2	2	210	9999
112	2	0	2005	0
114	2	0	0	0
117	1	0	1117	110
210	2	2	310	9999
214	2	0	2005	0
220	1	0	1220	0
218	2	2	0	0
221	2	2	0	0
223	2	0	2005	210
310	2	2	0	9999

Abb.6 Tabelle Ausgabe-Format

56
A × ABGESCHL. ×
B × FEST BESTELLT ×
C × ZUR ANSICHT BESTELLT ×
N × NICHT ABGESCHL. ×
W × NICHT LIEFERBAR ×
Y × FEST BESTELLEN ×
Z × ZUR ANSICHT BESTELLEN ×

57
A × UNSELBST.LIT. ×
C × SAMML. ×
M × SELBST.LIT. ×
S × REIHE ×
T × ZEITSCHRIFTENARTIGE REIHE ×
Z × ZEITSCHRIFT ×

62
FR × FRANZOESISCH ×
GE × DEUTSCH ×
UR × RUSSISCH ×
US × ENGLISCH ×

71
A × MIKROFILM ×
B × MIKROFICHE ×
C × FOTO ×
D × FOTOKOPIE ×
E × XEROGRAPHIE ×
F × FILMMATERIAL ×
G × DIA ×
H × TONBAND ×
I × SCHALLPLATTE ×

Abb.7 Referenzlisten

3 Anwendungsbeispiel einer Titelaufnahme

Zur Verdeutlichung des BIBLIS soll zum Schluß ein Beispiel stehen. Hierfür wurde "McKeeman, A Compiler Generator" gewählt. Dabei wurden nicht alle Kategorien ausgefüllt.

Es handelt sich um eine Monographie, eine selbständige bibliographische Einheit (BE), die gleichzeitig Teil einer ungezählten Reihe ist.

Kategoriegruppe 0 : Allgemeine Codes

Idn.-Nr.	(6D)	▲$_{10}$051	000233
Aufn.Stelle	(A)	$_{10}$053	i
Datum Speicher	(4D)	$_{10}$054	1171
Abschlußvermerk	(A)	$_{10}$056	a
Ebene d.bibl.Bes.	(A)	$_{10}$057	m
Ersch.Land	(2A)	$_{10}$061	us
Sprache d.Text.	(2A)	$_{10}$062	us
Akzessions-Nr.	(6D)	$_{10}$065	001388
Standort	(A)	$_{10}$066	h
Signatur	(2DA4D)	$_{10}$067	3C 269
Anzahl d.vorh. Exemplare	(2D)	$_{10}$068	2
Physik.Form	(A)	$_{10}$071	o
Veröffentl.Art	(A)	$_{10}$072	a

Die Kategorien 051 - 072 sind verwaltungstechnischer Art. Angaben über Erscheinungsland und Sprache sind für eine grobe Einteilung notwendig. Hier werden bei der Aufnahme Schlüssel verwendet, um Schreibarbeit zu ersparen.

Kategoriegruppe 1 : Personennamen

In 110 - 117 werden Name, Funktion und Körperschaft des Verfassers festgehalten. Im vorliegenden Beispiel sind drei Verfasser angegeben.

Personenname	(vA)	$_{10}$110	M|a|cKeeman, W.M.
Körpersch.Pers.	(vA)	$_{10}$114	Santa Cruz, University of California
Relator	(A)	$_{10}$117	a
		$_{10}$110(2)	Horning, J.J.
		$_{10}$114(2)	Toronto, University
		$_{10}$117(2)	a
		$_{10}$110(3)	Wortman, D.B.
		$_{10}$114(3)	Stanford, University
		$_{10}$117(3)	a

Kategoriegruppe 2 : Körperschaft

Da als Verfasser oder Herausgeber keine Körperschaft angegeben ist, werden die Kategorien nicht abgelocht.

Kategoriegruppe 3 : Sachtitel

Sachtitel	(vA)	$_{10}310$	A Compiler Generator
Relator, Sachtit.	(A)	$_{10}313$	s
Sprachbez.d.Tit.	(2A)	$_{10}314$	us

Der Titel des vorliegenden Buches hat keine weiteren Zusätze, so daß hier nur die angegebenen Kategorien aufgenommen werden müssen.

Kategoriegruppe 4 : Übergeordnete Gesamtheit

Überg.Gesamth.	(vA)	$_{10}400$	Prentice Hall Series in Automatic Computation

In der Kategorie 400 wird vermerkt, daß das Buch "A Compiler Generator" Teil der ungezählten Reihe "Prentice Hall Series in Automatic Computation" ist.

Kategoriegruppe 5 : Auflagenbezeichnung

Verlag	(vA)	$_{10}511$	Prentice Hall
Verlagsort	(vA)	$_{10}510$	Englewood Cliffs, N.J.
Ersch.jahr	(4D)	$_{10}512$	1970
Kollation	([4D]→4D→[4D])	$_{10}520$	11→ 527→
Beigab.verm.	(A3D)	$_{10}521$	b999
Bibl.Angaben	(4DvA)	$_{10}540$	45 Literaturangaben

Die 5. Kategorie enthält den vollständigen Erscheinungsvermerk und die Kollation. Zusätzlich können in dieser Rubrik Angaben über eventuell vorhandene Bibliographie und Beigaben wie Abbildungen und Tabellen gemacht werden, die auch in Schlüsseln ausgedrückt werden.

Kategoriegruppe 6 : Zusätzl.Angaben zu besonderen Publikationsformen

Diese Kategorien sind für bibliographisch unselbständige Literatur, Reports, Konferenzberichte, Hochschul- und Patentschriften vorgesehen, da diese Literatur spezielle Aufnahmeanforderungen stellt.

Kategoriegruppe 7 : Inhaltsdaten

Diese Kategorie ist für die Sacherschließung vorgesehen.

Kategoriegruppe 8 : Erwerbsdaten

Erwerbsart	(A)	$_{10}800$	k
Name d.Buchhdl.	(vA)	$_{10}805$	Flach
Ort d.Buchhdl.	(vA)	$_{10}810$	Frankfurt
Rechnungsdatum	(6D)	$_{10}820$	130871

Rechnungs-Nr.	(vA)	$_{10}830$	7452891
Preis	(4D.2D)	$_{10}840$	65.80

Hier findet man die für die Führung der Inventarisierungsliste und den Verkehr mit dem Buchhändler wichtigen Daten.

4 Literaturzusammenstellung

[1] ALEXANDER, R.W. : Library management system (LMS): Descriptive specifications for an on-line, real-time integrated library system
IBM Laboratory Report, 1968

[2] ARBEITSSTELLE FÜR BIBLIOTHEKSTECHNIK BEI DER STAATSBIBLIOTHEK PREUSSISCHER KULTURBESITZ: Entwurf eines Kategorienschemas zur Erfassung bibliographischer Daten (DFG-Schema)
Informationen (3) 3.Auflage, 25.6.71 -
Entwurf eines normierten Kataloges von bibliographischen Datenelementen, 25.2.72

[3] AVRAM, H.D.; KNAPP, J.F.; RATHER, L.R.: The MARC II format. A communication format for bibliographic data
Washington, D.C.: Libr.Congress Inf.Systems Office, 1968

[4] BAYERISCHE STAATSBIBLIOTHEK MÜNCHEN: Maschinelle Datenorganisation der Bibliothek München, 4.4.1972

[5] INTERNATIONAL FEDERATION OF LIBRARY ASSOCIATIONS (IFLA):COMMITTEE ON CATALOGING: International Standard Bibliographic Description (ISBD), 1971

[6] NIEWALDA, P.: Datenverarbeitung im Bibliothekswesen
Verlag Dokumentation, 1971

[7] PETRUCCI, A.: The integrated library system - programming considerations
1968 Meeting of European librarians working in the nuclear field
EURATOM 1969, EUR 4256e

[8] VEREIN DEUTSCHER BIBLIOTHEKARE: KOMMISSION ALPHABETISCHE KATALOGISIERUNG: Regeln für die alphabetische Katalogisierung (RAK), Vorabdruck 1969-72

PROZESSINFORMATIK

AUFBAU BETRIEBSSICHERER UND BEDIENUNGSFREUNDLICHER MEHRRECHNERSYSTEME ZUR PROZESSÜBERWACHUNG

H.WILDPANER

Zusammenfassung:

Die Forderungen an Mehrrechnersysteme für die Prozeßautomation werden genannt. Als typische Systemstrukturen werden das Satellitensystem und das mehrfach-modular-redundante System kurz erläutert. Für ein Satellitensystem und ein redundantes System wird eine Zuverlässigkeitsabschätzung durchgeführt.

1. Einleitung

Um das Jahr 1960 wurden die ersten Pilotanlagen für Prozeßsteuerungen mit Rechenanlagen errichtet. Seit etwa 1965 werden Prozeßrechner in immer größerem Maße für Überwachungs-, Regel- und Steueraufgaben in industriellen Prozessen verwendet. Je umfangreicher die Aufgaben von Prozeßrechenanlagen werden, umso größere Anforderungen werden an ihre Betriebssicherheit bzw. ihre Zuverlässigkeit gestellt, da Produktionsausfälle aufgrund von Totalausfällen von Prozeßrechnern möglichst vermieden werden sollen. Die Betriebssicherheit kann in Mehrrechnersystemen durch die Verteilung des Ausfallrisikos auf mehrere weitgehend autonom arbeitende Prozeßrechner oder durch den Aufbau von redundanten Systemen erhöht werden (1).

In den letzten Jahren wurde zusätzlich die Forderung nach einer funktionellen, d. h. bedienungsfreundlichen Gestaltung der Schnittstelle zwischen Mensch und Prozeßrechensystem immer wichtiger (2) (3).

2. Forderungen an Mehrrechnersysteme

An Mehrrechnersysteme werden zusammen mit den bereits erwähnten eine Reihe von Forderungen gestellt wie:

- Betriebssicherheit und Zuverlässigkeit
- Bedienungsfreundlichkeit
- Wartungs- und Reparaturfreundlichkeit
- übersichtlicher Aufbau von Hardware und Software
- autonomer Betrieb von einzelnen Teilen des Mehrrechnersystems
- Erweiterungsmöglichkeit
- günstiges Preis-/Leistungsverhältnis.

2.1. Betriebssicherheit und Zuverlässigkeit

Die Definition der Begriffe Betriebssicherheit und Zuverlässigkeit ist nicht ganz einheitlich. Unter Betriebssicherheit soll die Gewähr verstanden werden, daß der Produktionsablauf nicht beeinträchtigt wird durch unvermeidbare Störungen, die von außen kommen, die in der Anlage selbst auftreten oder die durch die Bedienung verursacht werden. Unter Zuverlässigkeit soll die Wahrscheinlichkeit verstanden werden, daß ein System während einer bestimmten Zeit oder für eine bestimmte Anzahl von Funktionen fehlerfrei arbeitet.
Die Betriebssicherheit bzw. die Zuverlässigkeit können u. a. durch folgende Maßnahmen verbessert werden:

- Auslegung des Systems (Struktur) nach Zuverlässigkeitsgesichtspunkten (z. B. modulare Redundanz auf Untersystemebene)
- Komponentenauswahl, Konstruktion (z. B. Unterlastung von Schaltkreisen) und Fertigung
- ausreichende Erprobungszeit
- Einhalten der zulässigen physikalischen Umgebungsbedingungen (z. B. Temperatur, Feuchte, Staubgehalt)
- Back-up-Vorrichtungen für den Störfall
- Vorhandensein von Prüfeinrichtungen zur Fehlerlokalisierung
- Wartungs- und Reparaturdienst.

2.2. Bedienungsfreundlichkeit

Die Betriebssicherheit eines Automationssystems ist auch vom Bedienungspersonal abhängig. Die Bedienung erfolgt mit umso geringerer Fehlerwahrscheinlichkeit und kritische Situationen, Störungen und Gefahrenmomente werden umso besser beherrscht, je funktionsgerechter die Schnittstelle zwischen Mensch und Maschine gestaltet ist. Die bei der Auslegung des Mensch-Maschine-Systems auftretenden Fragen werden im Rahmen des Forschungsgebietes Anthropotechnik behandelt (2) (3). Die wichtigsten Schnittstellen zwischen Bedienungspersonal und Prozeßrechensystem sind Bedienungspulte und Anzeigen wie z. B. Sichtgeräte.

Ein Beispiel für ein Bedienungspult ist aus der Abb. 1 ersichtlich. Die Bedienungselemente sind Funktionstasten zur Anwahl bestimmter Rechnerfunktionen, Rändelschalter zur Einstellung von Meßstellennummern, ein Schlüsselschalter. Mit digitalen Leuchtanzeigen wird der Meßwert dargestellt.

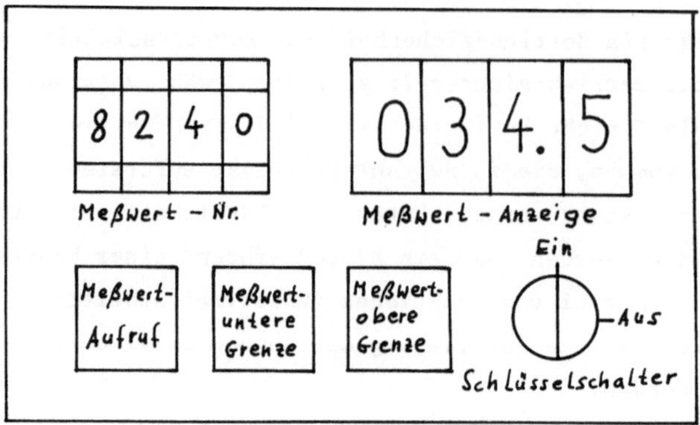

Abb. 1 - Bedienungspult

2.3. Wartungsfreundlichkeit und Reparaturfreundlichkeit

Zur Unterstützung der Wartung und Fehlerlokalisierung ist es vorteilhaft, wenn die einzlenen Einheiten eines Mehrrechnersystems wie Prozeßperipherie, Satellitenrechner und Hauptrechner mit Prüf- und Anzeigeeinrichtungen ausgestattet sind. Die Fehlerlokalisierung und die Rekonstruktion von Fehlerfällen (aus einem "Logbuch") sollte softwaremäßig unterstützt werden.

2.4. Übersichtlicher Aufbau von Hardware und Software

Zur Erleichterung der Planung, Beurteilung der Betriebssicherheit und Betriebszuverlässigkeit, Inbetriebnahme, Wartung und Fehlersuche sollte das System möglichst übersichtlich aufgebaut sein. Es ist daher günstig, kompakte Bausteine der Hardware und Software zu verwenden.

2.5. Autonomer Betrieb von einzelnen Teilen des Mehrrechnersystems

Ist ein autonomer Betrieb von einzelnen Untersystemen wie z. B. von Satellitenrechnern möglich, dann können diese für sich in Betrieb genommen werden. Bei Störung in einem der Untersysteme bleiben die anderen weiter funktionsfähig. Das Wiedereinfügen (Rekonfiguration) eines reparierten Untersystems in das Gesamtsystem soll störungsfrei vor sich gehen.

2.6. Erweiterbarkeit

Die Erweiterbarkeit der Hardware und Software sollte für den späteren Ausbau geplant sein.

2.7. Preis/Leistungsverhältnis

Zur Erreichung einer vorgegebenen Betriebssicherheit bzw. Zuverlässigkeit können meistens verschiedene Varianten von Mehrrechnersystemen angegeben werden. Die Entscheidung für ein System wird u. a. durch die Kosten der Hardware, Software und der Inbetriebnahme, Instandhaltung und von Folgeschäden (z. B. Produktionsausfälle) bestimmt (s. Abb. 2).

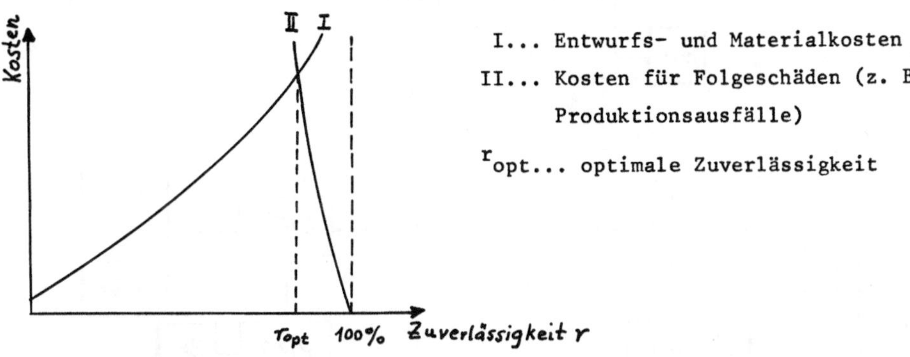

Abb. 2: Kostenfunktion von Seriensystemen in Abhängigkeit von der gewünschten Zuverlässigkeit (5)

3. Systemstrukturen

Je nach den Anforderungen an ein Mehrrechnersystem können verschiedene Systemstrukturen für die Realisierung in Frage kommen. Als Grundtypen sollen folgende zwei Strukturen betrachtet werden:

- Satellitensysteme (hierarchische Systeme)
- mehrfach-modular-redundante Systeme

Neben der Hardware erfordern Mehrrechnersysteme, die im Realzeitbetrieb arbeiten, ein gut durchdachtes Softwaresystem. Besondere Anforderungen werden an die Fehleranalyse und die Reaktion im Fehlerfalle gestellt.

3.1. Satellitensystem (hierarchisches System)

Ein Beispiel für ein Satellitensystem ist in der Abb. 3 dargestellt. An einen Hauptrechner mit Standardperipherie, Anzeigegeräten und Bedienungspult sind mehrere Satellitenrechner angeschlossen. Diese sind ihrer jeweiligen Aufgabe in Verbindung mit einem Prozeß angepaßt. Die Satelliten besitzen jeweils ein Anzeigegerät und ein Bedienungspult für den autonomen Betrieb während der Inbetriebnahmephase oder während eines Störungsfalles im System. Die Prozeßperipherie ist mit einer Prüfanzeige ausgestattet. Die Zustandsmeldelampen ermöglichen einen schnellen Überblick über das System.

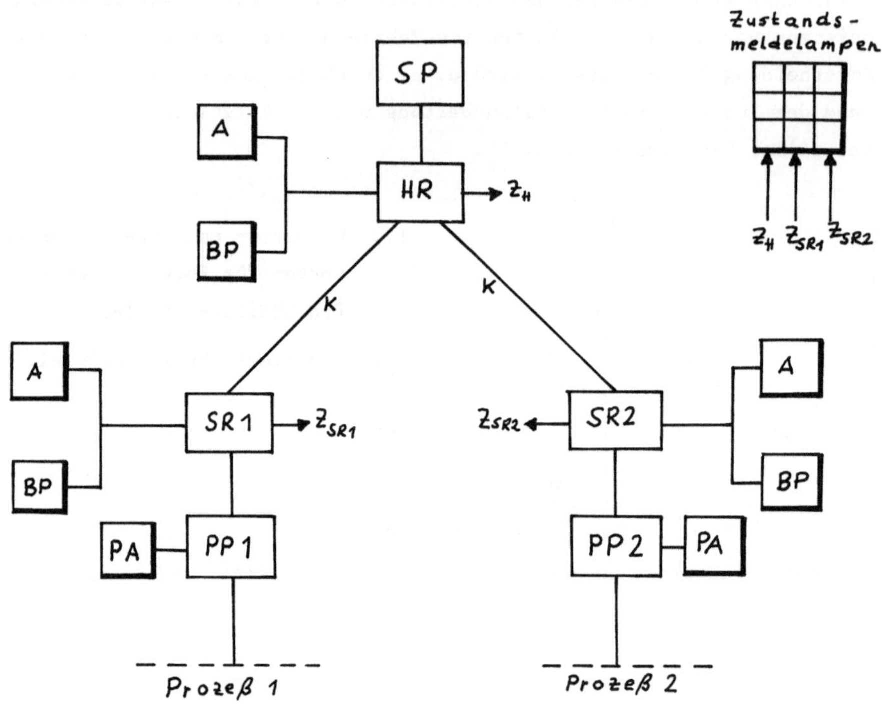

Abb. 3: Satellitensystem

Zeichenerklärung:

SP:	Standardperipherie	A:	Anzeige
HR:	Hauptrechner	BP:	Bedienungspult
SR1-2:	Satellitenrechner 1 - 2	PA:	Prüfanzeige
K:	Rechner-Rechner-Kopplung	Z_H, Z_{SR1}, Z_{SR2}:	Zustandsmeldung von Rechnern
PP1-2:	Prozeßperipherie 1 - 2		

3.3. Mehrfach-modular-redundantes System

Mehrfach-modular-redundante Systeme werden bei sehr hohen Anforderungen an die Betriebssicherheit bzw. Zuverlässigkeit verwendet. In diesen Systemen sind einzelne Moduln wie z. B. Einheiten der Standard- und Prozeßperipherie und Zentraleinheiten mehrfach (redundant) vorhanden. Die einzelnen Moduln sind miteinander so verbunden, daß bei Ausfall eines Moduls auf einen anderen gleichartigen Modul umgeschaltet werden kann (s. Abb. 4).

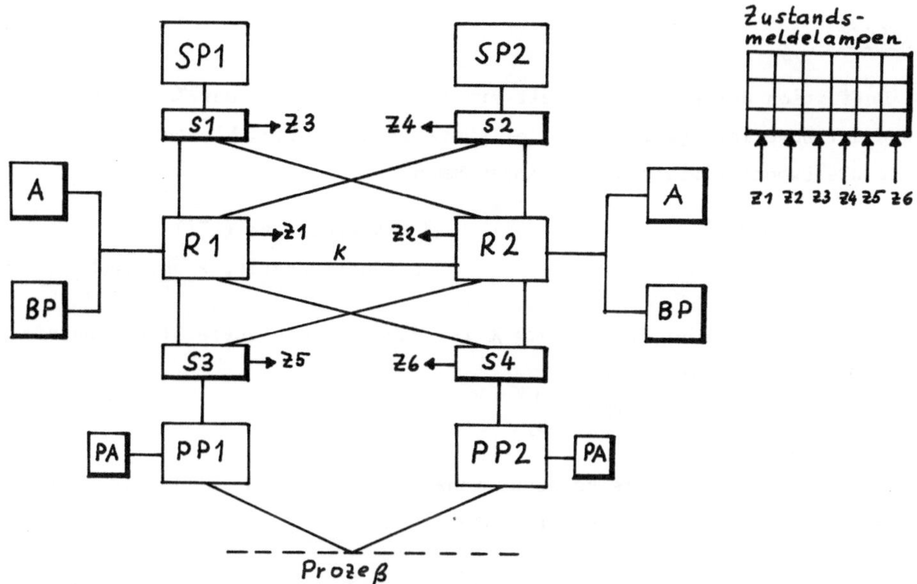

Abb. 4: Zweifach-modular-redundantes System

Zeichenerklärung:

R1-2: Rechner 1 - 2
S1-S4: Schalter 1 - 4 für Mehrfachzugriff zur Peripherie
Z1-6: Zustandsmeldungen
sonst s. Abb. 3

Der in Abb. 4 eingezeichnete Schalter für Mehrfachzugriff ist ein für den Aufbau von Mehrrechnersystemen wichtiges Element. Neben der Eigenschaft des Mehrfachzugriffs werden von diesem Schalter u. a. verlangt: hohe Zuverlässigkeit, Selbstprüfeinrichtungen und Prüfeinrichtungen für die übertragenen Daten.

4. Zuverlässigkeitsschätzung

Die Bestimmung der mit einer bestimmten Struktur erreichbaren Zuverlässigkeit kann sehr aufwendig sein. Zur Unterstützung der Zuverlässigkeitsanalyse werden z. B. Simulationsprogramme, die auf der Monte-Carlo-Methode beruhen, verwendet.

Nachfolgend soll eine Abschätzung der mittleren ausfallfreien Betriebszeit eines Satellitensystems und der Zuverlässigkeit eines redundanten Systems gemacht werden.

4.1. Begriffe

Die Definition der Zuverlässigkeit erfolgte in Pt. 2.1. Der Zusammenhang zwischen der Zuverlässigkeit r und der Ausfallrate λ eines Elements wird idealisiert als Exponentialverteilung angenommen.

$$r = e^{-\lambda \cdot t}$$

λ : Ausfallrate (h^{-1})
t: Betriebszeit, z. B. in h

Der reziproke Wert der Ausfallrate λ ist die mittlere ausfallfreie Betriebszeit (MTBF) eines Elementes.

$$MTBF = \frac{1}{\lambda}$$

Die Ausfallrate λ wird als konstant innerhalb der wirtschaftlichen Betriebszeit eines Elementes oder Systems betrachtet (4).

4.2. Mittlere ausfallfreie Betriebszeit eines Satellitensystems

Wie aus Abb. 5 ersichtlich, sind in die Struktur des Satellitensystems die geschätzten mittleren ausfallfreien Betriebszeiten (MTBF) der einzelnen Einheiten eingetragen.

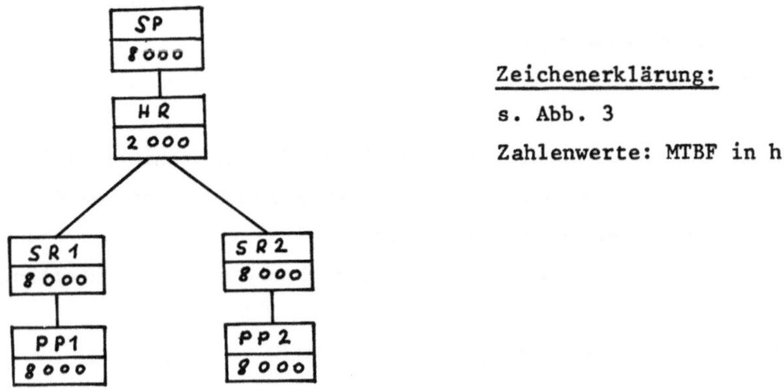

Abb. 5: Vereinfachtes Blockschema eines Satellitensystems

Aus dieser Struktur ergeben sich folgende mittlere ausfallfreie Betriebszeiten gemäß dem Gesetz, daß die Gesamtausfallrate in einem Seriensystem +) sich aus der Summe der Einzelausfallraten der Untersysteme zusammensetzt (5):

+) Anmerkung: Im Seriensystem ist im Gegensatz zum Parallelsystem die Funktion aller Einheiten für den Betrieb des Gesamtsystems notwendig. Für die Zuverlässigkeitsabschätzung wird das Satellitensystem als Seriensystem betrachtet.

Für 1 Satellitenstrang:

$$\lambda = \frac{1}{\text{MTBF}} = \frac{1}{8000} + \frac{1}{8000} = \frac{1}{4000}\ h^{-1}$$

<u>MTBF = 4000 h</u>

Für das Gesamtsystem:

$$\lambda = \frac{1}{\text{MTBF}} = \frac{1}{4000} + \frac{1}{4000} + \frac{1}{2000} + \frac{1}{8000} = \frac{9}{8000}\ h^{-1}$$

<u>MTBF ≈ 890 h</u>

4.3. Zuverlässigkeit eines redundanten Systems

Der Abschätzung liegt ein zweifach-redundantes System zugrunde (Abb. 6). Dabei wird vorausgesetzt, daß bei Ausfall eines Systems das 2. System die geforderte Funktion aufrecht erhält.

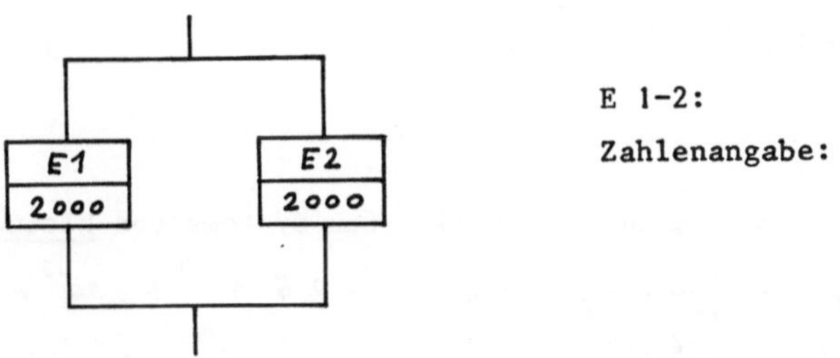

E 1-2: Einheit 1 - 2
Zahlenangabe: MTBF in h

Abb. 6: Zweifach-redundantes System

Gemäß der Literatur (5) ergibt sich für ein redundantes System folgende Ausfallrate λ_p:

$$\lambda_p = r \cdot \lambda \cdot \left(1 - \frac{1-(1-e^{-\lambda t})^{r-1}}{1-(1-e^{-\lambda t})^{r}}\right)$$

mit

r: Anzahl der parallelen Einheiten
λ: Ausfallrate einer Einheit

Für ein System mit einem Kontrollabstand von z. B. 10 h bzw. der Instandsetzung einer ausgefallenen Einheit innerhalb von 10 h fällt die Ausfallrate nach dieser Zeit jeweils auf 0 zurück. Es ergibt sich laut (5) die Sägezahnkurve in Abb. 7.

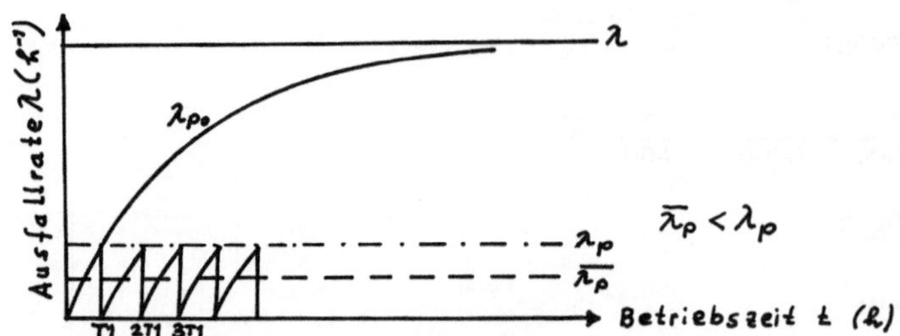

Abb. 7: Ausfallrate eines redundanten Systems

Zeichenerklärung:

T_1: Kontrollabstand

λ: Ausfallrate des Einzelelementes

λ_{p0}: Ausfallrate des nicht kontrollierten Systems

$\overline{\lambda}_p$: mittlere Ausfallrate des kontrollierten Systems

Nach der obigen Formel ergibt sich mit

$$\left.\begin{array}{l} t = 10\,h \text{(Kontrollabstand)} \\ \lambda = \frac{1}{2000\ h} = 5 \cdot 10^{-4}\ h^{-1} \end{array}\right\} \lambda . t << 1$$

$r = 2$

eine mittlere Ausfallrate $\overline{\lambda}_p$ des kontrollierten Systems von <u>kleiner als</u>

$$\overline{\lambda}_p < \lambda_p \approx r.\lambda.\left(1 - \frac{1-\lambda.t}{1-\lambda^2 t^2}\right) \approx r.\lambda.\lambda.t = 2.5.10^{-4}.5.10^{-3} =$$
$$= 50.10^{-7} = \underline{5.10^{-6}\ h^{-1}}$$

Daraus ergeben sich für das redundante System nach 10.000 h bzw. 20.000 h Betriebszeit folgende Zuverlässigkeiten r_p:

$$r_p = e^{-\overline{\lambda}_p . t} > e^{-\lambda_p . t} \approx 1 - \lambda_p . t \qquad \text{für } \lambda_p . t << 1$$

$$\underline{\underline{r_p\ (10^4\ h)}} > 1 - 5 \cdot 10^{-6} \cdot 10^4 = 1 - 5 \cdot 10^{-2} = 0{,}95 = \underline{\underline{95\ \%}}$$

$$\underline{\underline{r_p\ (2 \cdot 10^4\ h)}} > 1 - 2 \cdot 5 \cdot 10^{-6} \cdot 10^4 = 1 - 10^{-1} = 0{,}90 = \underline{\underline{90\ \%}}$$

Im Gegensatz zum redundanten System sinkt die Zuverlässigkeit des Einzelsystems bereits nach 200 h Betriebszeit auf

$$r_e\ (200\ h) \approx 1 - 5 \cdot 10^{-4} \cdot 2 \cdot 10^2 = 1 - 10^{-1} = 0{,}90 = \underline{\underline{90\ \%}}$$

ab.

5. Literatur

(1) R. E. Kuehn, Computer Redundancy: Design, Performance and Future, IEEE Transactions on Reliability, Vol. C - 18, No. 1, Febr. 1969 pp. 3 - 11

(2) G. Geiser, Anthropotechnische Gesichtspunkte der Prozeßautomatisierung, Reglungstechnische Praxis und Prozeß-Rechentechnik 6 (1970), S. 208 - 212

(3) G. Quietzsch, Der Prozeßrechner und die Betriebserfordernisse in der chemischen Industrie, Überlegungen eines Anwenders, Regelungstechnische Praxis und Prozeß-Rechentechnik 2 (1971), S. 45 - 52

(4) W. Angst und V. Wohler, Betriebssicherheit automatischer Steuerungssysteme, Interkama 1971, Kongreßvorträge, Oldenbourg München - Wien 1972, S. 379 - 385

(5) P. Hummitz, Zuverlässigkeit von Systemen, 2. Auflage, Reihe Automatisierungstechnik Bd. 28, Fr. Vieweg & Sohn, Braunschweig.

K O S E - EINE DIALOGSPRACHE FÜR PROZESSRECHNER

M.ABEL

1. Einleitung

Vom System bereitgestellte Leistungen werden oftmals vom Benutzer in Form eines Dialoges Mensch-Maschine angefordert. Ein solcher Dialog läuft i.a. auf einem Korrespondenzgerät (z.B. Fernschreiber, Display) ab. Der Ablauf eines Dialoges wird durch eine oder mehrere Tabellen festgelegt, die von einem zentralen Entschlüsslerprogramm verarbeitet werden.

Beispiele für Dialoge findet man nicht nur im Bedienungssystem (Lade- und Abzugsprogramme, Dokumentationsprogramme, etc.) auch das Prozesssystem kommt ohne Dialoge nicht aus. So gehören z.B. in der Lagersteuerung Dialoge wie manuelles Ein- bzw. Auslagern (manuell bedeutet hier z.B. unabhängig von einer angeschlossenen Fertigungssteuerung) und Störung bzw. Entstörung von Regalförderzeugen zur Durchführung der Wartungsarbeiten zum Standard.

Um eine leicht lesbare und dokumentationsfreundliche Formulierung dieser Dialoge zu ermöglichen,wurde die Dialogsprache KOSE (=KOrrespondenz SprachE) geschaffen.

2. Ablauf eines Dialoges

Ein KOSE-Programm zerfällt in 3 Teile, den Definitions-, den Deklarations- und den Anweisungsteil. Die Funktion der einzelnen Teile kann am besten durch die Schilderung des Dialogablaufes erläutert werden.

1. Phase, Dialoganwahl

Nach Betätigung einer Funktionstaste kann der Dialog durch Angabe seines Namens auf dem Korrespondenzgerät angewählt werden. Anhand interner Listen prüft der Entschlüssler, ob die Dialoganwahl gestattet ist. Dabei muß der angegebene Dialogname bekannt und die Anwahl von dem gewählten Gerät gestattet sein. Weiter darf kein Dialog laufen, demgegenüber der angewählte gesperrt ist,und auf dem Anwahlgerät darf kein Dialog höherer Priorität laufen. Diese für diese Prüfungen relevanten Daten stehen in der Dialogdefinition.

2. Phase, Dialogaktivierung und -lauf

Sind alle Bedingungen zur Dialogaktivierung erfüllt, so wird dem Dialog ein Aktivierungssatz fester Länge zugeteilt. Dieser Aktivierungssatz kann vom Programmierer aufgeteilt werden, dies geschieht durch dynamische Deklarationen. Dann wird die den Dialogablauf formulierende Tabelle vom Entschlüssler interpretativ abgearbeitet. Diese Tabelle enthält neben dem durch Anweisungen definierten Teil (dieser bestimmt den Ablauf) noch statische Teile wie Texte, die ebenfalls im Deklarationsteil definiert wurden.

Die Erfahrung zeigt, daß die in einem Dialog anfallenden Aufgaben häufig gleichartig sind. So werden angeforderte und eingegebene Daten meist geprüft,bevor sie weiterverarbeitet werden. Fasst man diese Prüfungsroutinen an zentraler Stelle zusammen, so können diese von allen Dialogen verwendet werden. Diese Zusammenfassung ist nur bei der Verarbeitung der Dialoge an zentraler Stelle möglich, daher ist ein zentraler Entschlüssler der dezentralisierten Dialogverarbeitung vorzuziehen. Mehr über diese zentral zusammengefassten Routinen findet man im Abschnitt 6 Standardfunktionen.

3. KOSE-Programme als Teile des Gesamtsystems

Aus den vorigen Abschnitten geht hervor, daß wir Dialoge nicht als selbständige Programme, sondern nur als Teil eines größeren Programmsystems sehen. KOSE ist daher auch nicht eine selbständige Programmiersprache, sondern nur in Verbindung mit dem gesamten Programmsystem zu benutzen. Dies wird besonders bei den in 4.2 definierten Externdeklarationen deutlich.

4. Syntaxelemente von KOSE

Wir geben eine Aufzählung der wichtigsten Syntaxelemente von KOSE in der Notation von (1).

KOSE-Programm ::= 'BEGIN' [<Dialogbeschreibung> ;]$_{1-\infty}$;

[<Deklaration> ;]$_{1-\infty}$;

[<Anweisung> ;]$_{1-\infty}$

'END'

Ein KOSE-Programm besteht somit aus einer Folge von Dialogbeschreibungen, einer Folge von Deklarationen und einer Folge von Anweisungen. Das Ganze ist in 'BEGIN' und 'END' eingeschlossen und die einzelnen Folgenglieder sind durch ";" getrennt.

4.1 Dialogbeschreibungen

<Dialogbeschreibung> ::= 'DIALOG' <Identifier> , 'ENTRY' <Identifier>

{, 'DEVICE' <Deviceliste>}

{, 'BAR' [<Identifier> ,] 1-∞ }

{, 'PRIORITY' <Zahl ohne Vorzeichen>}

In einem KOSE-Programm können mehrere Dialoge programmiert werden. Jedem Dialog ist eine Dialogbeschreibung zugeordnet. Diese enthält den Dialognamen, den Entrypoint in der Folge der Anweisungen, die Namen der zur Anwahl zugelassenen Geräte (die Namen der einzelnen Geräte werden dabei durch Komma getrennt), die gegen Parallellauf gesperrten Dialoge und die Priorität des Dialoges. Die letzten drei Angaben sind optional, fehlen sie, so gilt jeweils die Vereinbarung, die Anwahl ist von allen Korrespondenzgeräten gestattet, der Dialog ist gegenüber keinem anderen gegen Parallellauf gesperrt, der Dialog hat die niedrigste Prioritätsstufe (=Priorität 0).

4.2 Deklarationen

Wir kennen in KOSE keine verschiedenen Datentypen. Es werden immer nur Bitmuster gehandelt, der "Typ" ergibt sich dabei aus der jeweiligen Verwendung. Somit sind z.B. auch Ausdrücke wie 3+'TRUE' gültig und der Programmierer muß selbst dafür sorgen, daß solche sinnlosen Ausdrücke nicht auftreten. Aufgrund der Erfahrungen, die wir mit diesem Konzept bei der Anwendung von BCPL (2) gemacht haben, schien uns dies sinnvoll, zumal die Erfahrung zeigt, daß hauptsächlich Strings und Integergrößen in einem Dialog gehandelt werden.

Mit den oben erwähnten statischen Deklarationen können Einzeltexte, Texttabellen, Intervalle und Formate deklariert werden. Auf die Bedeutung der einzelnen Elemente gehen wir später ein. Als syntaktisches Beispiel hier eine

<Einzeltextdeklaration> ::= 'LET' <Identifier> = 'TEXT' <Zeichenkette>

{ 'STANDARD' <Zeichenkette> }

Mit den dynamischen Deklarationen

<Vektordeklaration> ::= 'VECTOR' [<Identifier> (<Konstante>)] 1-∞

<Variablendeklaration> ::= 'VARIABLE' [<Identifier>] 1-∞

können vom Beginn an im Aktivierungssatz einzelne Zellen bzw. Felder mit Namen versehen werden. Auf diese kann dann im Anweisungsteil gezielt zugegriffen werden. Der vom Programmierer nicht durch eigene Deklarationen ausgenützte Teil des Aktivierungssatzes wird als Stack verwaltet und ist unter dem Identifier STACK zu erreichen.

Weiter kennen wir noch die

<Manifestdeklaration> ::= 'MANIFEST' [<Identifier> = <Konstante>] 1-∞

mit der Konstantengrößen deklariert werden können. Die Verwaltung von symbolischen Konstantengrößen hat den Vorteil, daß bei einer Änderung derselben nur die entsprechenden Manifestdeklarationen ausgetauscht werden müssen, das übrige Programm aber vollständig invariant bleibt. Dies ist z.B. bei der Anpassung an verschiedene Systeme nötig.

Die Verbindung zu außerhalb des Programmes deklarierten Größen wird über die

<Externdeklaration> ::= 'EXTERN' { 'FROM' <Identifier> , }

[<Identifier>] 1-∞

hergestellt. Die hier aufgeführte Größe wird aus dem Bibliotheksadressbuch bezogen, dabei muß die Größe dort vollständig definiert sein, insbesondere muß bekannt sein, ob es sich um eine Konstante, Variable, ein Feld bzw. eine Procedur handelt.

5. Anweisungen

In den Anweisungen ist der eigentliche Ablauf des Dialoges festgelegt. Da alle diese Anweisungen in einer Tabelle verschlüsselt und dann vom Entschlüssler interpretativ abgearbeitet werden, haben wir uns entschlossen, den Anweisungsteil möglichst klein zu halten. Dies gilt in erster Linie für die zugelassenen Ausdrücke.

5.1 Ausgabe- und Anforderungsanweisungen

<Ausgabeanweisung> ::= 'WRITE' { (<Identifier>) } [<Adressausdruck> ,] 1-∞

<Anforderungsanweisung> ::= 'REQUEST' { (<Identifier>) }

[<Adressausdruck> ,] 1-∞

Den größten Anteil an einem Dialog bilden die Ausgabe- und Anforderungsanweisungen. Die Ausgabe kann bei beiden formatiert werden. Wir kennen die Formate T=Text, D=Dezimal-, O=Oktal-, H=Hexadezimalzahl und A=Allgemein. Zusätzlich kann ein G für gesperrt gedruckt sowie X für Leerstellen und / für Zeilenwechsel angegeben werden. Die Ausgabe beginnt grundsätzlich am Zeilenanfang und die einzelnen Elemente der Ausgabeliste werden entsprechend dem angegebenen Format zeichendicht ausgegeben. Alle Texte die ausgegeben werden, müssen vorher durch eine Textdeklaration definiert sein.

Bei der Anforderungsanweisung wird nach der Ausgabe eine Eingabe vom Operator erwartet. Diese Eingabe wird durch Zeilenwechsel beendet und steht dem Dialog dann in einem generellen Feld mit der Bezeichnung INPUT zur Verfügung. Innerhalb eines Dialoges darf aus diesem Feld nur gelesen werden.

5.2 Assignanweisung

<Assignanweisung> ::= <Adressausdruck> := <Ausdruck>

<Adressausdruck> ::= <Identifier> | <Identifier> ! <Index>

<Ausdruck> ::= <mon.Op.> <Primausdruck> |

<Primausdruck> <2OP> <Primausdruck>

<Primausdruck> ::= <Konstante> | <Adressausdruck> | <Funktionsausdruck>

Wie schon vorher bemerkt, haben wir die zugelassenen Ausdrücke stark eingeschränkt, um eine Aufblähung der interpretativ abgearbeiteten Tabellen zu verhindern. Zugelassen sind höchstens zwei durch einen Operator verbundene Primausdrücke. An Operatoren kennen wir eine Integer-Arithmetik, Vergleichsoperatoren, logische Operatoren und Shiftoperatoren. Über Funktionsausdrücke können entschlüsslerinterne Standardfunktionen angeschlossen werden.

5.3 Sonstige Anweisungen

Weiter kennen wir in KOSE eine

<einfache Sprunganweisung> ::= 'GOTO' <Identifier>

sowie eine

<indizierte Sprunganweisung> ::= 'GOTO' (<Adressausdruck>)

[<Identifier>] ,
2-∞

Bei der indizierten Sprunganweisung wird zunächst der Adressausdruck als Index ausgewertet und dann der entsprechende einfache Sprung ausgeführt. Liegt der Index nicht in dem durch die Zahl der Identifier definierten Intervall, so wird vom Entschlüssler ein Alarm erzeugt. Da die Auswertung logischer Ausdrücke wegen der fehlenden Kennzeichnung der Datentypen gewisse Schwierigkeiten bringt, haben wir drei verschiedene bedingte Anweisungen geschaffen, die

<IF-Anweisung> ::= 'IF' <Ausdruck> 'DO' <TRUE-Anweisung>

die

<UNLESS-Anweisung> ::= 'UNLESS' <Ausdruck> 'DO' <FALSE-Anweisung>

sowie die

<TEST-Anweisung> ::= 'TEST' <Ausdruck>

'THEN' <TRUE-Anweisung>

'ELSE' <FALSE-Anweisung>

Bei der Testanweisung wird ein Alarm ausgelöst, wenn der ausgewertete Ausdruck weder TRUE noch FALSE (im Sinn der Interndarstellung) ist.

Die folgend definierte Switchanweisung wurde hauptsächlich deshalb geschaffen, weil aufgrund der bisherigen Erfahrungen solche Anweisungen häufiger Bestandteil von Dialogen sind.

<Switchanweisung> ::= 'SWITCHON' <Adressausdruck> 'INTO' 'BEGIN'

[['CASE' <Konstante> : <Anweisung>]; 1-∞]; 1-∞

{ ; 'DEFAULT' : [<Anweisung>]; 1-∞ } 'END'

Mit dieser Anweisung können in einfacher und übersichtlicher Art z.B. Sprungverteiler programmiert werden.

6. Standardfunktionen

Die auf Anforderungen vom Operator eingegebenen Daten liegen in INPUT stets in Form von Strings vor. Zur Convertierung z.B. in eine Zahl, liegen Standardfunktionen vor. Weitere Standardfunktionen gibt es für Prüfungen von Eingabedaten. Vorgesehen sind hier eine Tabellenprüfung und eine Intervallprüfung. Bei der Tabellenprüfung wird der durch den Parameter bestimmte Text (dies ist in den meisten Fällen der Eingabetext) mit den Texten einer Texttabelle verglichen, und bei Übereinstimmung der entsprechende Index als Prüfungsergebnis geliefert. Bei der Intervallprüfung wird geprüft, ob die durch den Parameter bestimmte Date eine Zahl darstellt und in einem angegebenen

Intervall liegt. Die Texttabelle bzw. das Intervall müssen dabei im Deklarationsteil definiert werden. Beide Prüfungen existieren auch als logische Funktionen, deren Ergebnis je nach Ausgang der Prüfung 'TRUE' bzw. 'FALSE' ist. Damit können verschiedene Prüfungsergebnisse logisch miteinander verknüpft werden. Für die Bearbeitung von Strings sind weitere Standardfunktionen vorgesehen.

7. Prozedurverkehr

Für den Prozedurverkehr wurde eine Aufrufanweisung geschaffen:

```
<Aufrufanweisung> ::= 'CALL' <Identifier> ( [<Parameter> ,] 0-∞ )

<Parameter> ::= <Konstante> | <Adressausdruck>
```

Bei einem Prozeduraufruf muß der Prozedurname vorher durch eine Externdeklaration deklariert worden sein, weiter muß aus dem entsprechenden Bibliotheksadressbuch hervorgegangen sein, daß es sich dabei um einen Prozedurnamen handelt.

Mit einer Aufrufanweisung wird vom Entschlüssler die entsprechende Prozedur angestossen und die Abarbeitung des Dialoges unterbrochen. Nach Ablauf der Prozedur kann der Dialog an der Stelle nach der Aufrufanweisung fortgesetzt werden. Von der Prozedur mitgelieferte Parameter werden im INPUT zurückgeliefert.

8. Übersetzungssystem

Das gesamte Übersetzungssystem ist in mehrere Einzelteile zerlegt. Die ersten beiden Teile sind maschinenunabhängig, die restlichen Teile sind maschinenabhängig.

Der erste Lauf des Compilers leistet die syntaktische Analyse des eingelesenen Quellprogramms, dabei wird dieses gleichzeitig in eine Plexstruktur umgesetzt.

Der zweite Lauf des Compilers leistet die semantische Analyse des vom ersten Lauf erstellten Plex. Es wird ein Strom von maschinenunabhängigen "Entschlüsslerbefehlen" generiert. Bis hierher ist der KOSE-Compiler noch vollständig maschinenunabhängig und somit müssen bei einer Neuimplementierung nur die folgenden Teile neu geschrieben werden.

Der dritte Compilerlauf erstellt aus dem Strom der "Entschlüsslerbefehle" ein ladefähiges Objekt, dieses wird dann vom Ladeprogramm in den Rechner eingebaut und danach kann dann der Dialog angewählt werden.

Das gesamte System wurde versuchsweise in BCPL geschrieben und ist somit auch von dieser Seite her maschinenunabhängig.

Literaturangaben

(1) H.Bock, B.Schinzel,

Strukturtreue Syntaxkompression und zugehörige Parserprozeduren,
Gesellschaft für Informatik Bericht Nr. 4, Saarbrücken 1972

(2) M.Richards,

The BCPL Reference Manual,
Technical Memorandum No 69/1, Univ. Cambridge 1969

INFORMATIONSDARSTELLUNG AUF SICHTGERÄTEN

C.BENZ

Zusammenfassung

Es wird ein Verfahren zum Entwurf von bildlichen Darstellungen von Prozeßinformation auf Sichtgeräten beschrieben. Dabei wird die Grundstruktur der natürlichen Sprache in die bildliche Darstellung übernommen und es werden wahrnehmungspsychologische Gesetzmäßigkeiten berücksichtigt. Das Verfahren wird an Beispielen aus dem Kraftwerksbereich erläutert.

1. Einleitung

In verfahrenstechnischen Warten werden dem Bedienungsmann Informationen über den Zustand eines technologischen Prozesses dargeboten. Dies geschah vor der Entwicklung von Sichtgeräten ausschließlich mit Hilfe von Analoganzeigern, Digitalanzeigern, Lampen, Leuchtfeldern, Schreibern usw. Mit der Einführung von Sichtgeräten ergaben sich neue Möglichkeiten, Prozeßinformation darzustellen. Dabei sind für den Einsatz in Prozeßwarten aus Kostengründen neben alphanumerischen Sichtgeräten vor allem Sichtgeräte auf Fernsehbasis interessant. Mit derartigen preiswerten "Fernsehsichtgeräten" läßt sich Prozeßinformation unter anderem durch Bildzeichen (Symbole [1]) darstellen. Derartige Bildzeichen haben den Vorteil, daß ihre Bedeutung rasch erkannt wird und sie wenig Platz benötigen.

In der vorliegenden Arbeit wird ein Verfahren beschrieben, mit dem man bildliche Darstellungen von Prozeßinformation entwerfen kann. Es beruht darauf, daß die Grundstruktur der natürlichen Sprache in die bildliche Darstellung übernommen wird, und daß beim Entwurf der Bildzeichen wahrnehmungspsychologische Gesetzmäßigkeiten beachtet werden. Dabei sind für die einzelnen Beispiele selbstverständlich auch andere Bildzeichen vorstellbar. Wesentlich ist nur das Verfahren, das mit den Beispielen erläutert wird. In /1/ sind auf ähnliche Weise Darstellungen für ein Universalsichtgerät entworfen worden.

---

1 Nach DIN 30 600 werden derartige Darstellungen nicht "Symbole" sondern "Bildzeichen" genannt. Diese Bezeichnung wird daher im folgenden immer benutzt.

2. Wahrnehmungspsychologische Gesichtspunkte

Für den Entwurf von Bildzeichen ist es nützlich, die Gesetzmäßigkeiten der visuellen Wahrnehmung zu kennen. Diese wurden besonders in der Gestaltpsychologie untersucht. Da aus Platzgründen hier nicht näher auf eine Behandlung der Gestaltgesetze eingegangen werden kann, muß auf die einschlägige Literatur verwiesen werden /2,3/. Neben den Gestaltgesetzen ist beim Entwurf der Bildzeichen darauf zu achten, daß diese einander nicht zu ähnlich sehen, damit sie nicht miteinander verwechselt werden. Außerdem sollte sich die Bedeutung der Bildzeichen leicht mit ihrer Form assoziieren lassen.

3. Sprachaufbau und bildliche Darstellung

Wie bereits erwähnt, soll die Grundstruktur der natürlichen Sprache in eine bildliche Darstellung übertragen werden. Wenn das gelingt, werden derartige Darstellungen besonders leicht zu erlernen und zu "lesen" sein, denn wir haben seit unserer Kindheit gelernt und üben es täglich neu, Informationen, die entsprechend dem Aufbau unserer Sprache gegliedert sind, aufzunehmen.

In der natürlichen Sprache wird jede Sinneinheit durch einen Satz dargestellt. So lautet z.B. eine Information, die dem Bedienungsmann in der Warte übermittelt wird, als Satz formuliert: "Die Temperatur ist über der oberen Warngrenze". Dieser Satz läßt sich, wie alle Sätze der indogermanischen Sprachen, aufspalten in einen Teil, über den etwas ausgesagt wird (die Temperatur) und einen Teil, der die Aussage über den ersten Teil enthält (ist über der oberen Warngrenze). Der erste Teil wird in der traditionellen Schulgrammatik (Dudengrammatik) Subjekt, der zweite Teil Prädikat genannt /4,5,6,7/. In der generativen Grammatik /8/ ist es üblich, einen Satz durch einen sogenannten Strukturbaum darzustellen. Eine solche Anordnung zeigt den hierarchischen Aufbau eines Satzes aus sogenannten Konstituenten. Was man unter einer Konstituente und unter einem Strukturbaum versteht, sei am Beispiel des Satzes: "Die Temparatur ist über der oberen Warngrenze" erklärt. Um festzustellen, welche Beziehungen zwischen den Worten eines Satzes bestehen, teilt man den Satz schrittweise in immer kleinere zusammengehörige Wortgruppen auf, solange, bis man bei den einzelnen Worten angelangt ist. Diese einzelnen Wortgruppen heißen Konstituenten. In Bild 1 ist der zu untersuchende Satz in Konstituenten aufgeteilt und als Strukturbaum dargestellt. "Die Temperatur" und "ist über der oberen Warngrenze" sind die unmittelbaren Konstituenten des Satzes. Konstituenten, die nicht weiter in unmittelbare Konstituenten aufgespaltet werden können, heißen terminale Konstituenten; hier also: die, Temperatur, ist, über usw. (Genau genommen sind auch Wörter aus morphologischen Konstituenten aufgebaut.) Zur Konstituentenanalyse eines Satzes gibt es eine Reihe von Verfahren, die hier aber nicht näher beschrieben werden können. Wichtig ist, daß die Worte, aus denen eine Konstituente besteht, eng zusammengehören. Die Wortgruppe "ist über der" ist z.B. sicher keine Konstituente, denn der Artikel "der" gehört auf jeden Fall zum Substantiv "Warngrenze" und nicht zum Hilfsverb "ist". Will man nun einen in Worten formulierten Satz bildlich darstellen, dann kann das auf verschiedene Weise geschehen. Man kann einmal den ganzen Satz durch ein einziges Bildzeichen darstellen. Man kann aber auch für die Konstituenten Bildzeichen entwerfen und einen Satz aus mehreren Bildzeichen zusammensetzen. Dabei muß man um so mehr Konstituenten durch Bildzeichen ersetzen, je weiter man in der Hierarchie des Strukturbaumes nach unten geht. Wie später noch gezeigt wird, ist es für die hier zu behandelnden Informationen sinnvoll, für Konstituenten der 2. Hierarchiestufe des Strukturbaumes Bildzeichen zu entwerfen. Es werden also die in der traditionellen Grammatik "Subjekt" und "Prädikat" genannten Satzteile durch Bildzeichen ersetzt. Diese Bildzeichen sind dann die terminalen Konstituenten des bildlichen Satzes. Benutzt man "S" als Abkürzung für einen Satz, "Su" für eine Konstituente, die dem Subjekt entspricht, und "Pr" für eine Konstituente, die dem Prädikat entspricht, dann sieht der Strukturbaum von Sätzen wie dem oben behandelten entsprechend Bild 2 aus.

Su und Pr bezeichnen verschiedene Kategorien von Konstituenten. In der natürlichen Sprache, wo man bis auf die Ebene der Worte den Satz aufgliedert, entsprechen ihnen die "lexikalischen Kategorien" Artikel, Nomen, Verb usw.

Formuliert man einige Prozeßinformationen als Sätze und zerlegt diese in die Konstituenten der Kategorien Su und Pr, so zeigt sich, daß man nicht alle Konstituenten der Kategorie Su mit allen Konstituenten der Kategorie Pr entsprechend Bild 2 kombinieren darf. Die Konstituente "ist geschlossen", die Teil des Satzes "das Ventil ist geschlossen" ist, darf z.B. nicht mit der Konstituente "die Temperatur" zusammengefügt werden, sonst entsteht der unsinnige Satz "die Temperatur ist geschlossen". Die Konstituenten der gleichen Kategorie müssen daher so in Subkategorien unterteilt werden, daß die einzelnen Konstituenten der gleichen Subkategorie gegeneinander ausgetauscht werden können. In der natürlichen Sprache werden die Subkategorien

durch sogenannte "komplexe Symbole" gekennzeichnet, die z.B. bei einem Nomen (Hauptwort) ausdrücken, ob es konkret oder abstrakt, belebt oder unbelebt usw. ist. In dieser Prozeßbildsprache werden die Subkategorien durch Bezeichnungen wie Su1, Su2, Pr1, Pr2 usw. gekennzeichnet. Der Strukturbaum von Sätzen wie "die Temperatur ist über der oberen Warngrenze" sieht dann entsprechend Bild 3 aus.
Im folgenden sind einige Konstituenten der Kategorie Su und Pr angegeben, die alle den Subkategorien Su1 bzw. Pr1 angehören.

SU1 = die Temperatur,
der Druck,
der Höhenstand,
der Durchfluß,
der pH-Wert.

Pr1 = ist innerhalb des Gutbereiches,
ist über der oberen Warngrenze,
ist über der oberen Gefahrengrenze,
ist unter der unteren Warngrenze,
ist unter der unteren Gefahrengrenze,
steigt schwach,
steigt stark,
steigt sehr stark,
sinkt schwach,
sinkt stark,
sinkt sehr stark.

Man kann nun jede Konstituente der Subkategorie Su1 mit jeder Konstituente der Subkategorie Pr1 entsprechend dem Strukturbaum nach Bild 3 kombinieren und erhält immer einen sinnvollen Satz. Insgesamt erhält man mit den angegebenen 16 Konstituenten auf diese Weise 55 verschiedene Sätze. Würde man jeden Satz durch ein Bildzeichen ersetzen, müßte man also 55 Bildzeichen entwerfen. Führt man den Übergang auf eine bildliche Darstellung auf der Ebene der Konstituenten der Kategorien Su und Pr durch, benötigt man nur 16 Bildzeichen. Würde man bis auf die Ebene der Worte gehen, wären 23 Bildzeichen notwendig. Die Sätze würden dann aber aus 4 bis 7 Bildzeichen bestehen, während sie mit den Konstituenten der Kategorien Su und Pr nur 2 Bildzeichen enthalten. Neben der Tatsache, daß eine Gliederung in Subjekt und Prädikat eine markante Eigenschaft des indogermanischen Satzes ist, sprechen also auch die obigen Überlegungen für einen Übergang auf eine bildliche Darstellung auf der Ebene der Konstituenten der Kategorien Su und Pr.

Wie bereits erwähnt, sollen die Bildzeichen auf einem "Fernsehsichtgerät" dargestellt werden. Es wird angenommen, daß für jedes Bildzeichen ein Raster von 7 x 9 Punkten zur Verfügung steht. Dieses kann aber nicht immer voll ausgenutzt werden, da Zwischenräume zwischen den Zeichen vorgesehen werden müssen. In Bild 4 sind Bildzeichen für die Konstituenten der Subkategorien Su1 und Pr1 dargestellt. Für physikalische Größen wurden Buchstaben verwendet. Da diese bereits für Textdarstellungen vorhanden sind, wird damit die Zahl der notwendigen Bildzeichen reduziert. Bild 5 zeigt einige Beispiele für Bildzeichensätze, die aus den Konstituenten der Subkategorien Su1 und Su2 entsprechend dem Strukturbaum nach Bild 3 gebildet wurden.

Mit den Konstituenten der Subkategorien Su1 und Pr1 lassen sich auch Sätze wie "die Temperatur ist innerhalb des Gutbereichs (und) steigt" bilden. Der Strukturbaum solcher Sätze wird in Bild 6 gezeigt. Die Konstituenten der Subkategorie Pr1 müssen dabei nochmals in zwei neue Subkategorien Pr2 und Pr3 unterteilt werden, die ebenfalls in Bild 6 dargestellt sind. Geschieht dies nicht, dann können widersprüchliche Sätze wie "die Temperatur ist innerhalb der zulässigen Grenzen (und) über der oberen Warngrenze" entstehen. Innerhalb der Subkategorien Pr2 und Pr3 sind aber wieder alle Konstituenten austauschbar. Mit der Struktur gemäß Bild 6 lassen sich insgesamt 150 Sätze bilden, ohne daß ein einziges neues Bildzeichen entworfen werden muß. Wollte man jeden Satz durch ein eigenes Bildzeichen darstellen, dann wären zusammen mit den 55 Bildzeichen für die Sätze gemäß Bild 5 insgesamt bereits 205 Bildzeichen notwendig.

In Bild 7 sind ein weiterer Strukturbaum und Konstituenten der Subkategorien Su2 und Pr4 angegeben, die zum Verständnis von Bild 8 noch benötigt werden.

Die bisher gezeigten bildlichen Sätze werden in der Regel nicht isoliert benötigt, sondern es sind im allgemeinen mehrere Bildsätze notwendig, um über einen Anlagenteil einen Überblick zu bekommen. Es ist in der Wartentechnik üblich, die Zusammenhänge in einem Prozeß durch ein sogenanntes Fließbild darzustellen. In Bild 8 ist ein Ausschnitt aus einem Kraftwerksblock in einer fließbildähnlichen Darstellung gezeigt, die im wesentlichen aus bildlichen Sätzen besteht. Wie man sieht, ist das ohne Schwierigkeiten möglich.

4. Schluß

Es kann wohl mit Sicherheit gesagt werden, daß bildliche Darstellungen, die nach der Struktur der natürlichen Sprache aufgebaut und die unter Berücksichtigung der Gestaltgesetze entworfen werden, schneller erlernbar und besser zu "lesen" sind als solche, die nur intuitiv und ohne bewußte Anwendung solcher Gesetze entstehen. Außerdem gelangt man nach einem solchen Verfahren sehr viel schneller zu guten Lösungen.

5. Literaturverzeichnis

/1/ Benz, C.: "Methoden zum Entwurf von Symbolen zur Darstellung von Prozeßinformation in Warten". 5.Interkama 1971, Oldenbourg Verlag, S.192 - 197.

/2/ Metzger, W.: "Gesetze des Sehens". Waldemar Kramer, Frankfurt/Main (1953).

/3/ Metzger, W.: "Handbuch der Psychologie". Band I/I: "Figural-Wahrnehmung". Verlag für Psychologie, Dr.C.J.Hogrete, Göttingen (1966).

/4/ Grebe, P.(Hg.): "Duden-Grammatik". Bibliografisches Institut Mannheim (1959).

/5/ Moser, H.(Hg.): "Das Ringen um eine neue deutsche Grammatik". Wissenschaftliche Buchgesellschaft, Darmstadt (1965).

/6/ Hörmann, H.: "Psychologie der Sprache". (1967).

/7/ Bühler, K.: "Sprachtheorie". Gustav Fischer Verlag, Stuttgart (1965).

/8/ Bechert, J., Clement, P., Thümmel, W., Wagner, K.H.: "Einführung in die generative Transformationsgrammatik". Max Hueber Verlag, München (1970).

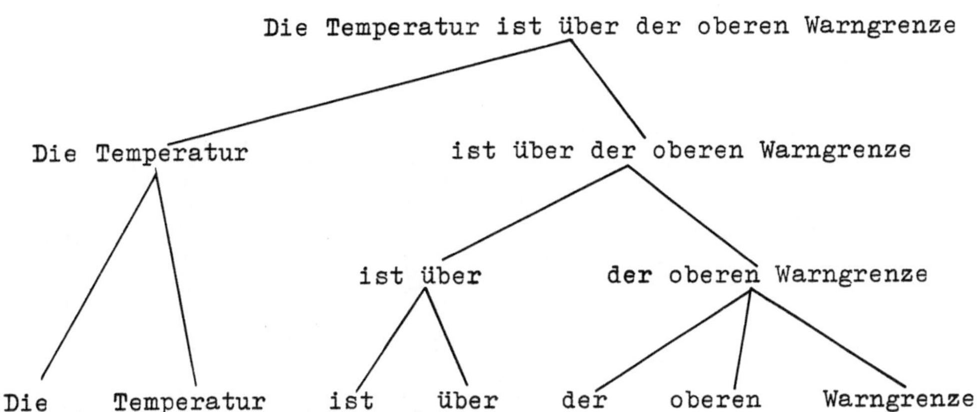

Bild 1 Spezieller Strukturbaum eines Satzes. Die terminalen Konstituenten gehören den lexikalischen Kategorien Artikel, Nomen, Verb usw. an.

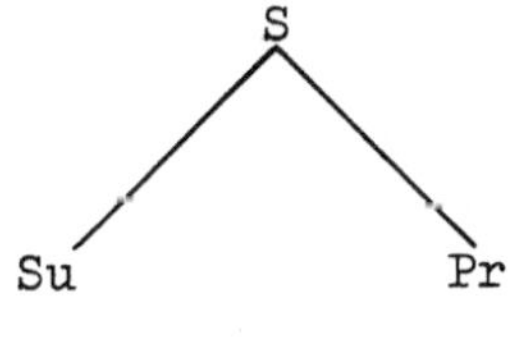

Bild 2 Allgemeiner Strukturbaum von Sätzen mit einer Struktur entsprechend Bild 1. Die terminalen Konstituenten gehören den Kategorien Su (Subjekt) und Pr (Prädikat) an.

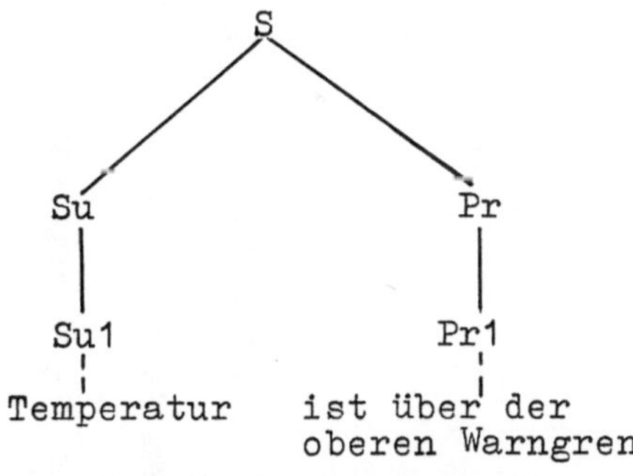

Bild 3 Allgemeiner Strukturbaum von Sätzen mit einer Struktur entsprechend Bild 1. Die terminalen Konstituenten der Kategorien Su und Pr gehören den Subkategorien Su1 und Pr1 an.

Su1 { T = die Temperatur
P = der Druck
L = der Höhenstand
F = der Durchfluß
Q = der pH-Wert }

Pr1 { = ist innerhalb des Gutbereiches
= ist über der oberen Warngrenze
= ist über der oberen Gefahrengrenze
= ist unter der unteren Warngrenze
= ist unter der unteren Gefahrengrenze

= steigt schwach
= steigt stark
= steigt sehr stark

= sinkt schwach
= sinkt stark
= sinkt sehr stark }

Bild 4 Bildzeichen für die Konstituenten der Subkategorien Su1 und Pr1

S
Su Pr
Su1 Pr1

T Die Temperatur ist über der oberen Warngrenze

P Der Druck sinkt schwach

L Der Höhenstand ist unter der unteren Gefahrengrenze

Q Der pH-Wert ist innerhalb des Gutbereichs

F Der Durchfluß steigt stark

Bild 5 Beispiele von Bildzeichensätzen

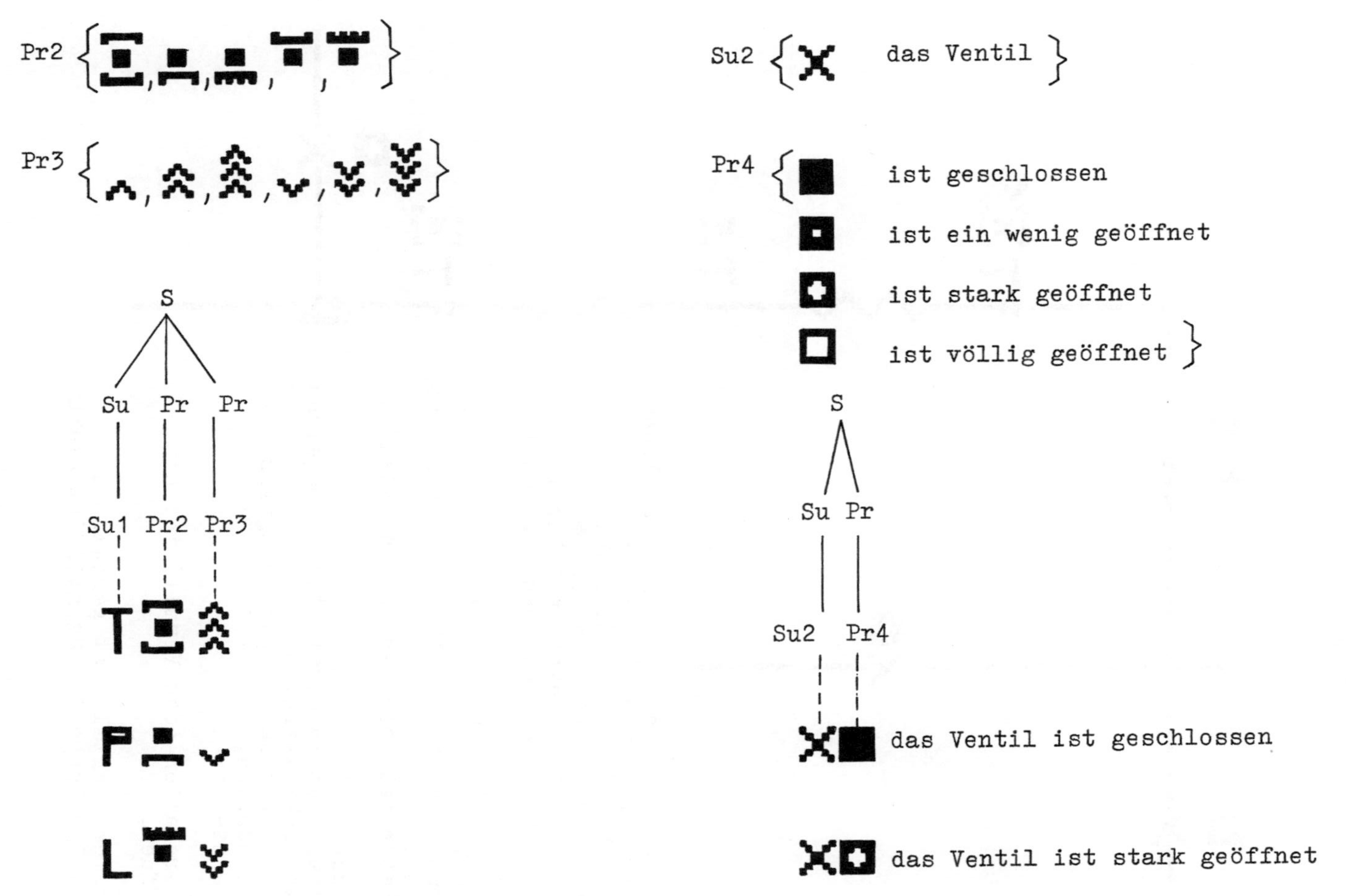

<u>Bild 6</u> Bildzeichen für die Konstituenten der Subkategorien Pr2 und Pr3 (Bedeutungen siehe Bild 4) und Beispiele von Bildzeichensätzen

<u>Bild 7</u> Bildzeichen für die Konstituenten der Subkategorien Su2 und Pr4 und Beispiele von Bildzeichensätzen

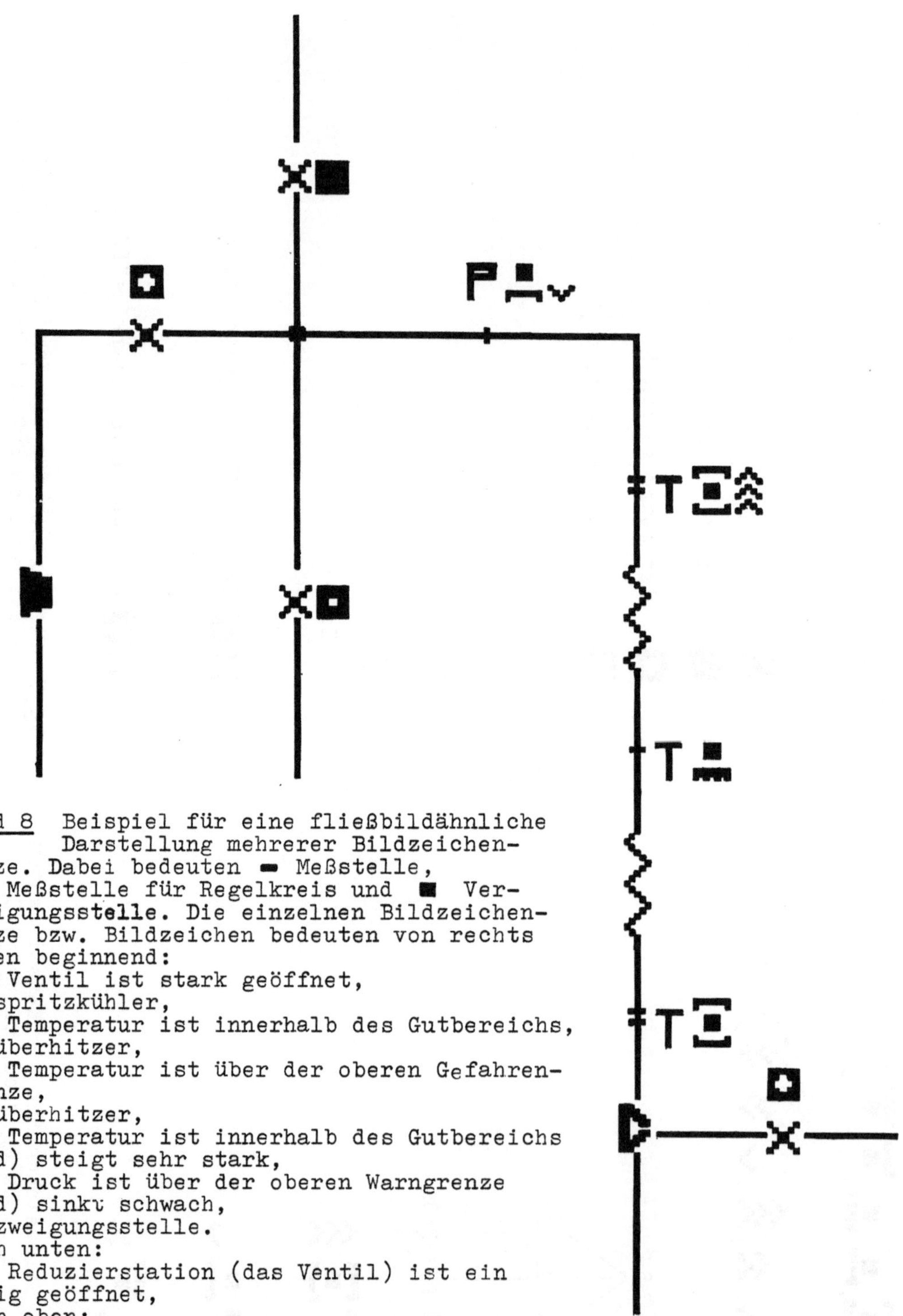

Bild 8 Beispiel für eine fließbildähnliche Darstellung mehrerer Bildzeichensätze. Dabei bedeuten ▬ Meßstelle, 〓 Meßstelle für Regelkreis und ■ Verzweigungsstelle. Die einzelnen Bildzeichensätze bzw. Bildzeichen bedeuten von rechts unten beginnend:
Das Ventil ist stark geöffnet,
Einspritzkühler,
die Temperatur ist innerhalb des Gutbereichs,
Endüberhitzer,
die Temperatur ist über der oberen Gefahrengrenze,
Endüberhitzer,
die Temperatur ist innerhalb des Gutbereichs (und) steigt sehr stark,
der Druck ist über der oberen Warngrenze (und) sinkt schwach,
Verzweigungsstelle.
Nach unten:
Die Reduzierstation (das Ventil) ist ein wenig geöffnet,
nach oben:
Der Bypass (das Ventil) ist geschlossen,
nach links: Das Turboeinlaßventil ist stark geöffnet,
Turbine.

DER GROSSRECHNER ALS HILFSMITTEL BEIM ERSTELLEN UND TESTEN LAUFFÄHIGER PROGRAMME FÜR PROZESSRECHNER

B.KRÜGER

Ein Prozeßrechner dient zur Führung eines technischen Prozesses. Um dies zu ermöglichen, muß er mit Programmen versorgt werden. Diese Programme sind das Ergebnis einer ausführlichen Systemanalyse und einer oft langwierigen Testarbeit. Soll ein neues Programm für einen schon in Betrieb befindlichen Prozeßrechner erstellt werden, so steht hierfür meist nicht genug Zeit auf dem Prozeßrechner zur Verfügung. Hier taucht zum ersten Mal der Wunsch auf, Anwenderprogramme auf einer anderen Anlage - nach Möglichkeit einer Großrechenanlage - zu erstellen und zu testen, ohne den laufenden Betrieb des Prozeßrechners zu stören.

Die gleiche Problematik ergibt sich auch noch in zwei weiteren Fällen:

1. Soll ein bereits installierter Prozeßrechner in seiner Hardware-Ausstattung erweitert werden, so ist es häufig wünschenswert, parallel zur Erweiterung der Hardware die neuen Anwenderprogramme zu erstellen und weitestgehend auszutesten.

2. Wird ein Prozeßrechnersystem neu entwickelt, und greift man hierbei nicht auf Rechnertypen mit gleichem Befehlsvorrat zurück, so ist es meist unmöglich, die Systemprogramme (Kompiler, Linkage Editor, Verwaltungsprogramme u. ä.) vor der Fertigstellung der Hardware zu testen.

Drei Gesichtspunkte sprechen also bei der Benutzung eines Prozeßrechners für die Unterstützung durch einen Großrechner.

1. Der Prozeßrechner ist in einem Prozeß integriert, und es können aus Zeit oder Kernspeichergründen keine neuen Anwenderprogramme ausgetestet werden.

2. Der Prozeßrechner soll erweitert werden. Die von den Anwenderprogrammen zusätzlich benötigte Hardware ist noch nicht verfügbar.

3. Systemprogramme können nicht ausgetestet werden, da die Hardware noch nicht fertig entwickelt ist.

Bei der Entwicklung der problemorientierten Prozeßrechnersprache PAS1/PL1 |1, 2, 3| für das Prozeßrechnersystem DP 1000 wurde auf diese Problematik Rücksicht genommen.

Entwicklung von Systemprogrammen

Die im DP 1000-System verwendete Sprache ist eine problemorientierte Prozeßrechnersprache, deren Vorteil gegenüber einer Programmierung in Assembler hier nicht zur Diskussion gestellt werden soll. Bei der Entwicklung einer Prozeßrechnersprache wie PAS1/PL1 ist es zweckmäßig, eine der aus dem Gebiet des technisch-wissenschaftlichen Rechnens bekannten Sprachen als Ausgangspunkt zu verwenden.

Nach eingehenden Untersuchungen stellte sich PL1 als geeignet heraus. Kriterien für diese Entscheidung waren u. a. Multitasking, Bit- und Zeichenkettenverarbeitung, Ereignisse und die Verfügbarkeit eines Kompilers.

Aufbauend auf dieser Systemsprache PL1 mußten für die Prozeßrechnersprache PAS1/PL1 Teile zur Beschreibung des Equipments, zum Austausch von Prozeßdaten und zur zeitlichen und logischen Verknüpfung von Tasks hinzugefügt werden.

Der wesentliche Vorteil, eine bereits eingeführte Sprache als Basis für eine Neuentwicklung zu verwenden, liegt darin, daß es für diese Sprache allgemein zugängliche Kompiler und Hilfsprogramme in Rechenzentren gibt. Dadurch ist es möglich, die Systemprogramme des neuen Rechnersystems (hier DP 1000) selbst in einer höheren Programmiersprache zu schreiben und zu testen, ohne vom Zustand der Zielmaschine abhängig zu sein. Es ist noch dabei zu beachten, daß vom neu erstellten Kompiler übersetzte Programme in einer maschinenunabhängigen Sprache (MUS) zwischengespeichert werden können. In einem abschließenden Schritt erfolgt die Umsetzung in den Code der Zielmaschine anhand von

Tabellen. Die Arbeitsweise eines solchen Kompilers ist im Bild 1 dargestellt.

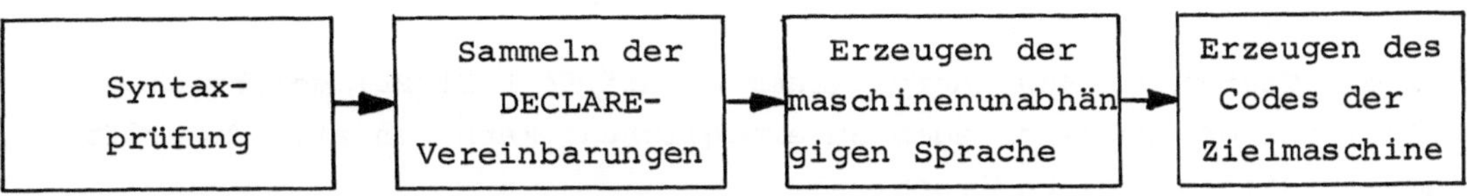

Bild 1

Erstellen und Testen von Anwenderprogrammen

Die Möglichkeiten zum Testen von Prozeßrechnerprogrammen auf fremden Rechnern werden von Fall zu Fall verschieden sein. Es kann daher hier nur gezeigt werden, welche Möglichkeiten im DP 1000-System vorhanden sind.

Im hier behandelten System können die Anwenderprogramme prozedurorientiert kompiliert werden. Es werden fünf wesentliche Prozedurtypen unterschieden.

Die REALTIMEPRØCEDURE dient zur Beschreibung des Equipmentteiles, dem Austausch von Prozeßdaten und zur zeitlichen und logischen Verknüpfung von Tasks.

EICH- und KØNTRØLL-Prozeduren dienen zur Kontrolle und Verarbeitung von Meßgrößen und Steuergrößen verschiedenster Art.

BEDIEN-Prozeduren ermöglichen es, Tasks über die Konsolschreibmaschine mit Parametern zu versorgen und mit hoher Priorität ablaufen zu lassen.

Die ØPTIØNS(MAIN)-Prozeduren und alle restlichen UNTERPRØZEDUREN werden i. a. zur Beschreibung mathematischer Zusammenhänge mit unterschiedlichsten Datentypen und für Protokollierungsaufgaben benötigt.

Die Anwenderprogrammteile, die den vier letztgenannten Prozedurtypen zuzuordnen sind, werden vom Anwender in einem PL1-Subset geschrieben und können daher auf jedem Großrechner, der über einen PL1-Kompiler verfügt, kompiliert und getestet werden. Nur die REALTIMEPRØCEDURE hat eine von PL1 abweichende Sprachform.

Um das Testen von Anwenderprogrammen, die in PAS1/PL1 geschrieben sind, auf Großrechenanlagen zu ermöglichen, kann man sich daher folgender Hilfsmittel bedienen:

1. Einführen von Kommentarzeichen, die auf verschiedenen Systemen unterschiedlich interpretiert werden.

2. Ersetzen der REALTIMEPRØCEDURE durch eine Prozedur vom Typ ØPTIØNS (MAIN) oder eine Unterprozedur, die die wesentlichen Teile wie z. B. Verknüpfung externer Größen und nicht zeitgetreue Ein- und Ausgabe von Meßgrößen sowie deren Bearbeitung übernimmt.

3. Teilweises Ersetzen der Ablaufsteuerung mit Ereignissen durch CALL-Aufrufe.

An einem Beispiel soll dies erläutert werden.

A u f g a b e

Fünf Analogmeßwerte sind alle 3 sec abzufragen, zu eichen und auf Grenzwerte zu überprüfen. Die Analogkanäle können einzeln oder gemeinsam durch einen Digitalschalter angewählt werden.

Digitalschalter-stellung	Angewählter Kanal 1	2	3	4	5
0	x	x	x	x	x
1	x				
2		x			
3			x		
4				x	
5					x
6 - 9	verboten				

Die physikalischen Meßwerte, die Digitalschalterstellungen und die Grenzwertüberschreitungen sind zu protokollieren.

L ö s u n g

Das Problem wird durch die drei Prozeduren PAS1ECHT, CHECK, PRØTØKØLL (s. Anhang) beschrieben. Zur Prüfung der Programmlogik auf einem Großrechner wurde die Realtimeprozedur PAS1ECHT durch die Prozedure PAS1SIM ersetzt.

Zusammenladen von Anwenderprogrammen

Eine weitere Arbeit, die nicht immer auf einem Prozeßrechner ausgeführt werden kann, ist das Zusammenladen von Prozeduren zu einem auf einem Prozeßrechner lauffähigen Programmpaket. Auch diese Aufgabe kann leicht durch einen Großrechner ausgeführt werden.

Im günstigsten Fall steht auf dem Großrechner soviel Kernspeicher zur Verfügung, daß der vom Anwenderprogramm im Prozeßrechner benötigte Kernspeicherplatz vollständig auf dem Großrechner simuliert werden kann. Diese Vorgehensweise wird immer dann optimalere Programme hinsichtlich der Laufzeit und eventuell sogar der Kernspeicherbelegung ergeben, wenn die Zielmaschine ein Rechner ist, bei dem mit direkter Adressierung nicht der gesamte Kernspeicher überstrichen werden kann.

Die Eingabedaten für einen solchen Linkage Editor, der auf einem Großrechner Programme für Prozeßrechner zusammenlädt, können auf unterschiedlichste Weise erzeugt und eingegeben werden, z. B. über Bibliotheken mit Standardprogrammen, Kompilate des PAS1/PL1-Kompilers auf dem Großrechner oder auf dem Prozeßrechner, dessen Ergebnisse auf Zwischenträgern (Karte, Lochstreifen, Band) abgelegt sind (Bild 2).

Liegt ein Anwenderprogramm im simulierten Kernspeicher vollständig vor, sind alle notwendigen Arbeiten hinsichtlich Erstellung externer Referenzen, Bereitstellung von Arbeitsspeicher für die einzelnen Tasks erfüllt, so kann der Inhalt des simulierten Kernspeichers des Prozeßrechners auf einen Zwischenträger ausgegeben und anschließend als lauffähiges Programmpaket in den Prozeßrechner eingelesen und dort ohne jede Änderung gestartet und ausgeführt werden.

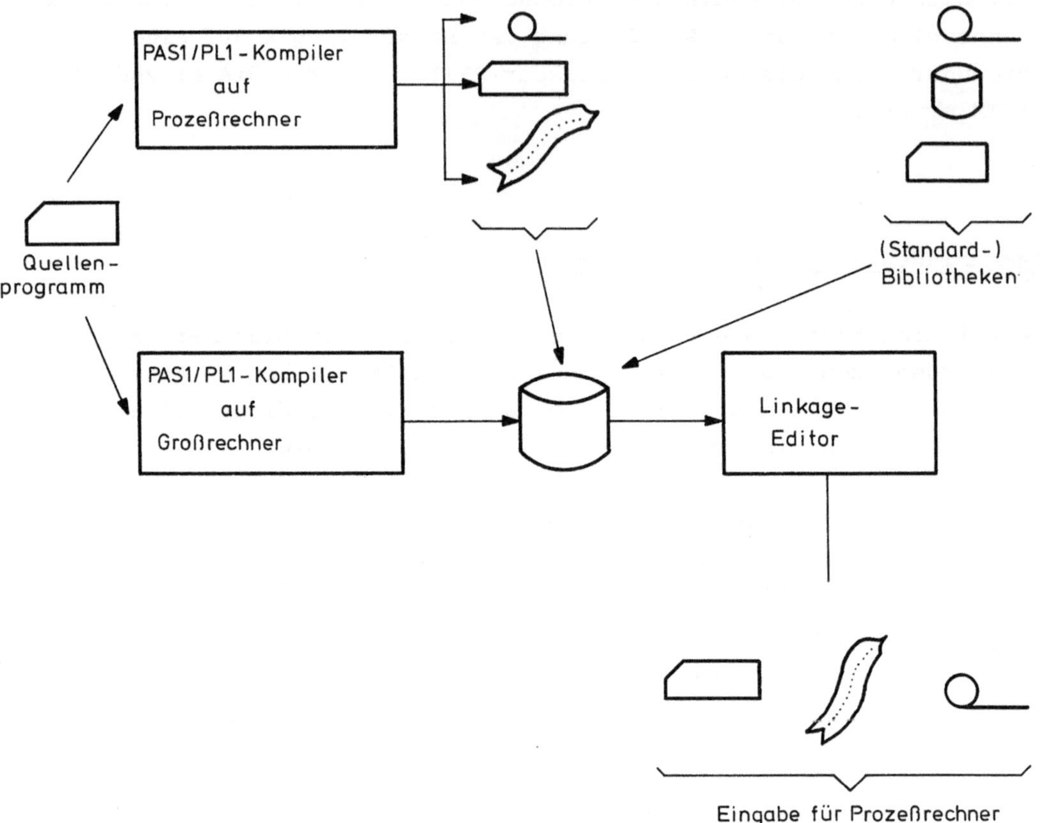

Bild 2 Laden auf einem Großrechner

Zusammenfassung

Ein Großrechner kann bei der Erstellung der Software eines neuen Prozeßrechners, beim Erstellen und Testen von Anwenderprogrammen und beim Zusammenladen lauffähiger Programmpakete für einen Prozeßrechner herangezogen werden. Derart erzeugte Prozeßrechnerprogramme können einen kleineren Kernspeicherbedarf oder eine kürzere Ausführungszeit haben als vergleichbare Programme, die auf einem Prozeßrechner erzeugt wurden, da auf einem Großrechner häufig Optimierungsstrategien und auch viel Kernspeicher zur Simulation des Prozeßrechnerkernspeichers zur Verfügung steht. Es wurde ein in der problemorientierten Prozeßrechnersprache PAS1/PL1 geschriebenes Programm erläutert.

<u>Literatur</u>

1 G. KOCH:

Die Software des Systems DP 1000
Sonderheft "Prozeß-Datenverarbeitung" der Fa. BBC Mannheim 1971

2 G. MÜLLER:

Compiler für das System DP 1000
Sonderheft "Prozeß-Datenverarbeitung" der Fa. BBC Mannheim 1971

3 K. BINGE, G. KOCH:

Interpretierende, problemorientierte und objektgebundene Programmsysteme für Prozeßrechner
Tagung anläßlich der "5. INTERKAMA 1971" in Düsseldorf.


```
 1        .PASIECHT: REALTIMEPROC;                                              .
 2        .          /*********************************************************** .
 2        .           *                                                       * .
 2        .           * TEST EINES DP 1000 - PROGRAMMS AUF EINER IBM 370/360   * .
 2        .           * 0.TEIL:  ECHTE MESSWERTAUFNAHME                        * .
 2        .           * BBC - MANNHEIM    ABT. ED      SEPTEMBER 1972 B.KRUEGER * .
 2        .           *                                                       * .
 2        .           *********************************************************/.
 2        .         EQUIPMENT;                                                  .
 3        .            WORD,0,DP 1005* DIGSWITCH = 512.5.4;                     .
 5        .            WORD,1,DP 1003,READYINT(10)* MODE(21)*                   .
 7        .                 GROUP(5): LOGVAL-1000;                              .
 8        .                                                                     .
 8        .         DECLARATIONS;                                               .
 9        .            GAUGE CHECK(1,1);                                        .
10        .            CORRESPONDENCE TO CHECK*                                 .
11        .               READWRITE LOGVAL;                                     .
12        .                                                                     .
12        .         EVENTS;                                                     .
13        .            PRIORITYRANGE (220:225);                                 .
14        .               PRIORITY (225);          EMESS EVERY 3 SEC;           .
16        .               PRIORITY (224);          EPROT;                       .
18        .               PRIORITY (223);          ESTART = CONJUNCT(EMESS, ¬EPROT);.
20        .         ACTIONS;                                                    .
21        .            ON ESTART SEQDO;                                         .
23    1   .NEXT:          IN DIGSWITCH;                                         .
24    1   .               IF DIGSWITCH > 5 THEN DO; SET EPROT; GOTO NEXT; END;  .
29    1   .               DO I=1 BY 1 TO 4; IN LOGVAL(I); END;                  .
32    1   .               IN LOGVAL(5),CHECK(1);                                .
33    1   .                     END;                                            .
34        .         END;  /* PASIECHT */                                        .
34       /.                                                                     .
```

```
STMT LEVEL NEST

   1              PAS1SIM: PROCEDURE OPTIONS (MAIN);
                           /**************************************************************
                            *                                                             *
                            * TEST EINES DP 1000 - PROGRAMMS AUF EINER IBM 370/360        *
                            * 1.TEIL:  SIMULATION DER MESSWERTAUFNAHME                    *
                            * BBC - MANNHEIM    ABT. ED      SEPTEMBER 1972 B.KRUEGER     *
                            *                                                             *
                            **************************************************************/
   2     1        DCL DIGSWITCH  /* WERT AM DIGITALSCHALTER    */ BIN FIXED(15)
                                                                  EXT /*? PROTOKOLL */;
   3     1        DCL (PARM,I)   /* HILFSGROESSE               */ BIN FIXED(15);
   4     1        DCL LOGVAL( 5) /* MESSGROESSEN               */ BIN FIXED(15)STATIC EXT;
   5     1        DCL PROTOKOLL  /* PROTOKOLLIEREN             */ ENTRY;
   6     1        DCL CHECK      /* EICH- & KONTROLLPROZEDURE */ ENTRY (BIN FIXED(15));
                  /******* ENDE DES DECLARE-TEILS ****************************************/

   7     1                 ON ENDFILE(SYSIN) GOTO ENDE;
   8     1        NEXT:    GET COPY EDIT(DIGSWITCH)(COL(1),F(10));
   9     1                 IF DIGSWITCH > 5 THEN DO; CALL PROTOKOLL; GOTO NEXT; END;
  14     1                    DO I=1 BY 1 TO 5;
  15     1     1                 GET COPY EDIT(LOGVAL(I))(F(10));
  16     1     1              END;
  17     1                 CALL CHECK(PARM);
  18     1                 GOTO NEXT;
  19     1        ENDE:    END;  /* PAS1SIM */

******************  LOGISCHES PROGRAMMENDE  ***************************************************
```

```
STMT LEVEL NEST

   1                 CHECK:  PROCEDURE(PARM) /*? CHECK */;
                             /***************************************************************
                              *                                                              *
                              * TEST EINES DP 1000 - PROGRAMMS AUF EINER IBM 370/360         *
                              * 2.TEIL:  GRENZWERT-UEBERWACHUNG UND WANDLUNG IN              *
                              *              PHYSIKALISCHE WERTE                             *
                              * BBC - MANNHEIM     ABT. ED      SEPTEMBER 1972 B.KRUEGER     *
                              *                                                              *
                              ***************************************************************/
   2     1           DCL (DIGSWITCH,/* WERT AM DIGITALSCHALTER     */
                          ERRORFLAG) /* PRUEFUNG                    */ BIN FIXED(15)
                                                                       EXT /*? PROTOKOLL */;
   3     1           DCL MWPHY(5)    /* PHYSIKALISCHER MESSWERT     */ BIN FIXED(30)
                                                                       EXT /*? PROTOKOLL */;
   4     1           DCL MB          /* MESSBEREICH                 */ BIN FIXED(15) STATIC EXT
                                                    INIT(500 /* MV */) /*? NAME.CHANGE */;
   5     1           DCL GRENZE(2)   /* OBERER/UNTERER GRENZWERT  */ BIN FIXED(15) STATIC EXT
                                                    INIT(-400,300) /*? NAME.CHANGE */;
   6     1           DCL (K,         /* HILFSGROESSE                */
                          PARM)      /* PARAMETER DER EICHPROZEDUR*/ BIN FIXED(15);
   7     1           /*? DCL EPROT                                     EVENT EXT PAS1 */;
                                     /* EREIGNIS STARTET PROTOKOLL*/
   8     1           DCL PROTOKOLL   /* PROTOKOLLIEREN              */ ENTRY;
   9     1           DCL LOGVAL( 5)  /* MESSGROESSEN                */ BIN FIXED(15)
                                                                       EXT /*? PAS1 */;
                     /******* ENDE DES DECLARE-TEILS ***************************************/

  10     1                   ERRORFLAG=0;
  11     1                   DO K=1 BY 1 TO 5;
  12     1     1                IF DIGSWITCH > 0 THEN IF K ¬= DIGSWITCH THEN DO;
  15     1     2                   MWPHY(K)=0; GOTO DOEND;                       END;
  18     1     1                MWPHY(K)=LOGVAL(K)*MB/20000;
  19     1     1                IF     MWPHY(K) > GRENZE(1) THEN
  20     1     1                   IF MWPHY(K) <=GRENZE(2) THEN ERRORFLAG=ERRORFLAG+1;
  22     1     1     DOEND:  END;
  23     1                      /*? COMPLETION(EPROT)='1'B;*/
                                /**/CALL PROTOKOLL;        /**/
  24     1                   END;  /* CHECK */
```

```
 1                /*?  PROTOKOLL: PROCEDURE OPTIONS (MAIN);          */
                  /**/ PROTOKOLL: PROCEDURE ;                      /**/
                        /***********************************************************
                         *                                                         *
                         * TEST EINES DP 1000 - PROGRAMMS AUF EINER IBM 360/370    *
                         * 3.TEIL PROTOKOLLIERUNG DER MESSWERTE                    *
                         * BBC - MANNHEIM     ABT. ED     SEPTEMBER 1972 B.KRUEGER *
                         *                                                         *
                         ***********************************************************/

 2    1           DCL I           /* HILFSGROESSE                  */ BIN FIXED(15);
 3    1           DCL (DIGSWITCH,/* WERT AM DIGITALSCHALTER        */
                      ERRORFLAG) /* PRUEFUNG                       */ BIN FIXED(15)STATIC EXT;
 4    1           DCL TEXT.       /* UEBERSCHRIFTEN                */ CHAR(49);
 5    1           DCL MWPHY(5)    /* PHYS. MESSWERT                */ BIN FIXED(30)STATIC EXT;
 6    1           DCL (MB,        /* MESSBEREICH                   */
                      GRENZE(2)) /* GRENZWERTE                     */ BIN FIXED(15)
                                                                      EXT /*? CHECK */;
 7    1           /*?  DCL EPROT                                      EVENT EXT PAS1 */;
                                  /* EREIGNIS STARTET PROTOKOLL*/
                  /******* ENDE DES DECLARE - TEILES ***********************************/

 8    1                  /*? CALL PASINI; CALL PASRUN; WAIT (EPROT);        */
11    1                  TEXT=' ';
12    1                  IF DIGSWITCH >5 THEN DO;
14    1    1                TEXT='FALSCHE STELLUNG DES DIGITALSCHALTERS'; GOTO DRUCK;
16    1    1                                END;
17    1                  IF DIGSWITCH = 0 THEN IF ERRORFLAG < 5 THEN GOTO FEHLER;
20    1                                                         ELSE;
21    1                                 ELSE IF ERRORFLAG = 0 THEN
22    1           FEHLER:     TEXT=  'GRENZWERT-UEBERSCHREIT. BEI DER FOLGENDEN MESSUNG';
23    1           DRUCK:  IF TEXT ¬= ' ' THEN  PUT EDIT(TEXT)(SKIP,A(49));
25    1                  IF DIGSWITCH > 5 THEN GOTO NEXT;
27    1                     PUT EDIT('DIGITALSCHALTERSTELLUNG:',DIGSWITCH,'MESSBEREICH:'
                              ,MB,'UNTERER GRENZWERT:',GRENZE(1),'OBERER GRENZWERT:',
                             GRENZE(2))(SKIP(5),(4)(SKIP,X(10),A(24),F(10)));
28    1                  PUT SKIP(2);
29    1                  DO I=1 BY 1 TO 5;
30    1    1             PUT EDIT('PHYSIKALISCHER WERT: ',MWPHY(I),' MV')
                            (SKIP,X(5),A(21),F(10),A(3));
31    1    1             END;
32    1           NEXT:   /*?  COMPLETICN(EPROT)='0'B;    */
33    1                  END;      /* PROTOKOLL */
```

DIE PROZESSPROGRAMMIERSPRACHE P E A R L
- SYSTEMBESCHREIBUNG UND E/A KONZEPT -

B.EICHENAUER

0. Einleitung

Der kostenwirksame Einsatz von digitalen Rechensystemen bei der Lösung von kommerziellen und technisch-wissenschaftlichen Aufgaben bereitet heute auch dem Anwender, dem die Funktionsweise von Digitalrechnern nur wenig vertraut ist, bei Verwendung höherer Programmiersprachen wie ALGOL, FORTRAN, PL/1 keine Schwierigkeiten mehr. Dagegen muß der Anwender, der Digitalrechner bei der Lösung von Prozeßautomationsaufgaben oder in der Experimentsteuerung einsetzen will, umfangreiche Erfahrung im Umgang mit den zum Einsatz kommenden Rechnertypen besitzen und sehr viel Zeit für die Erstellung von Automationsprogrammen aufwenden.

Um den Einsatz von Digitalrechnern bei der Automation technischer Prozesse zu vereinfachen, wurde seit etwa 3 Jahren in einem Arbeitskreis, an dem Mitarbeiter aus deutschen Forschungsinstituten und Industriefirmen teilnahmen*), die Prozeßprogrammiersprache PEARL (Process and Experiment Automation Realtime Language) entwickelt. Die Spezifikation von PEARL wird in Kürze im Rahmen des Projekts PDV bei der GFK, Karlsruhe erscheinen.

1. Überblick

PEARL ist eine prozedurorientierte Programmiersprache von mittlerem Sprachniveau, die außer konventionellen Ausdrucksmitteln, wie sie auch zur Formulierung kommerzieller und technisch-wissenschaftlicher Programme eingesetzt werden, Ausdrucksmittel zur problemangemessenen Darstellung von Realzeit-Aufgaben bietet.

In den algorithmischen Teil und den Ein/Ausgabeteil von PEARL wurden die Elemente moderner höherer Programmiersprachen wie PL/1, ALGOL68, soweit sie für die Realzeitprogrammierung geeignet sind, aufgenommen. Beispielsweise ist in

*) PEARL Arbeitskreis:
J. Brandes, TU, Karlsruhe / B. Eichenauer, ESG, München / S. Eichentopf, AEG-Telefunken, Konstanz / P. Elzer, Univ. Erlangen / L. Frevert, GFK, Karlsruhe / V. Haase, Unicomp, Blankenloch / P. Holleczek, Univ. Erlangen / K. Kreuter, SAG, Karlsruhe / G. Müller, BBC, Mannheim / K. Pfeiffer, KFA, Jülich / P. Rieder, SAG, Karlsruhe / B. Schürlein, CERN, Genf / K. Timmesfeld, IDAS, Limburg.

PEARL die Deklaration und einfache Handhabung von Bitketten, von Zeichenketten, von Zeigern und von Strukturen möglich. Durch Definition neuer Datentypen und zugeordneter Operatoren kann die Sprache erweitert werden. Anweisungen für die Mensch-Maschine-Kommunikation und für die Handhabung von Files sind vorgesehen. u. s. w.

Bekanntlich reichen die angeführten Ausdrucksmittel für die angemessene Formulierung von Automationsprogrammen nicht aus. Deshalb wurden in PEARL Sprachelemente

- o für die Definition und Handhabung von parallel ablauffähigen Programmteilen (Tasking),
- o für die logische und zeitliche Synchronisation von Tasks (Synchronisation und Timing),
- o für die Beschreibung des Aufbaus von Prozeßrechensystemen (Systembeschreibung),
- o für den systeminternen Datenaustausch und für die Kommunikation zwischen Prozeßrechensystem und nicht standardisierten Systemendstellen (Prozeß-E/A)

vorgesehen.

In diesem und dem nachfolgenden Vortrag sollen diese Sprachelemente, die PEARL zu einer universellen Realzeit-Programmiersprache machen, umrissen werden.

2. Systembeschreibung

Bei der Automation technischer Prozesse werden normalerweise neben wenigen Standardgeräten (z. B. Blattschreiber, Display, Digitaleingabe) zahlreiche nicht standardisierten Geräte, Meßwertgeber und Stellglieder eingesetzt. Während die Bedienung der Standardgeräte durch Funktionen des Betriebssystems wahrgenommen wird, muß die der nicht standardisierten Geräte im Rahmen des Automationsprogramms beschrieben werden.

Um das Automationsproblem trotz der Vielzahl der anzusprechenden Endstellen unabhängig von den Eigenschaften von Peripheriegeräten und vom physikalischen Anschluß der Meßwertgeber und Stellglieder formulieren zu können, wird in PEARL die Konfiguration des Prozeßrechensystems in einem eigenen Programmteil, dem sog. Systemteil, dargestellt. Dabei werden alle Geräte und Endstellen, die bei der Problembeschreibung - im sog. Problemteil - angesprochen werden sollen, durch Namen identifiziert.

Durch die Systembeschreibung werden dem PEARL-Übersetzer die zur Ausführung des Automationsprogramms erforderlichen anlagenabhängigen I/O-Handler und Treiberroutinen bekannt gemacht. Die Entwicklung zusätzlicher Job-Control-

Sprachen für die Gerätezuweisung erübrigt sich.

Die Syntax des Systemteils wurde so konzipiert, daß die Übertragung von Verdrahtungsplänen in eine maschinell lesbare Form leicht ausgeführt werden kann:

a) Anschluß von Standardgeräten:

Die Kopplung von Standardgeräten wird durch Angabe der herstellerspezifischen Gerätenamen mit zugelassener Richtung des Datenflusses beschrieben.

```
Beispiel:     COMP           <->      MUXCHAN;
              MUXCHAN * 1     ->      DIGOUT;
```

An den Rechner COMP ist das Kanalwerk MUXCHAN angeschlossen. Der Datenaustausch zwischen COMP und MUXCHAN kann in beiden Richtungen erfolgen. An Kanal 1 von MUXCHAN ist die Digitalausgabe DIGOUT angeschlossen.

Werden mehrere Geräte des gleichen Typs eingesetzt, so werden sie durch Indizierung unterschieden.

```
Beispiel:     MUXCHAN * 2    <-       DIGIN(1);
                      * 5    <-       DIGIN(2);
```

b) Bezeichnung von Endstellen:

Durch Bezeichner mit nachfolgendem Doppelpunkt werden Anschlüsse und Geräte, die im Problemteil explizite angesprochen werden, identifiziert.

```
Beispiel:     MUXCHAN * 4     <-> CONSOLE: SCHREIBM-TYP2;
       START: INTKLEMME(7)    <-  ;
       KONTAKT:                -> DIGIN(2) * 2 * 2,5;
       DRUCK:                  -> ANAIN * 27;
```

Die Schreibmaschine SCHREIBM-TYP2 wird im Problemteil unter dem Namen CONSOLE angesprochen. An Kanal 2, Bit 2 bis Bit 6 der Digitaleingabe DIGIN(2) ist KONTAKT angeschlossen. DRUCK ist an Kanal 27 der Analogeingabe ANAIN angeschlossen.

Mehrere Endstellen gleicher Kanalbreite dürfen zu einem Feld zusammengefasst werden.

```
Beispiel:   TEMPERATUR(1:10)    -> ANAIN * (7:15) & ANAIN * 20;
```

3. Kommunikation

In PEARL wird zwischen Mensch-Maschine-Kommunikation und systeminterner Kommunikation unterschieden.

a) Mensch-Maschine-Kommunikation:

Die formatierte E/A enthält die bekannten Anweisungstypen für die Character-I/O:

```
WRITE  [FROM]   quelle   TO     senke    FORMAT   format;
READ   [TO]     senke    FROM   quelle   FORMAT   format;
```

Beispiel: WRITE ('MESSWERT = ',SPANNUNG) TO CONSOLE
FORMAT (S(13),,) ;

Außerdem wurden wegen der zunehmenden Bedeutung graphischer Ein/Ausgabegeräte Anweisungen für die graphische E/A vorgesehen:

```
DRAW [FROM]  quelle   TO     senke    FORMAT   format;
SEE  [TO]    senke    FROM   quelle   FORMAT   format;
```

Als graphische Formatelemente wurden nur Grundelemente wie Punkt, Gerade, Winkel, Intensität, Farbe standardisiert. Der Einbau von Formatprozeduren in die graphischen Formate ist möglich.

b) Systeminterne Kommunikation:
Für den systeminternen Datenaustausch dienen die Anweisungen:

```
{ MOVE     }
{ TRANSFER }   quelle   TO   senke   [ GAUGE  eichprozedur ] ;
```

Mit der MOVE-Anweisung wird der nicht organisierte Datenaustausch zwischen Systemendstellen beschrieben.

Beispiel: MOVE KONTAKT TO BITSTRING;
FOR I TO 10 DO MOVE TEMPERATUR(I) TO VARIABLE(I)
CELSIUS (.007,.102,1.3); DONE;

Die TRANSFER-Anweisung dient zur organisierten Übertragung von Daten.

Beispiel: TRANSFER FILE1 TO FILE2;

Bei Angabe einer Eichprozedur wird der Meßwert nach der Übernahme gewandelt. Der sog. physikalische Wert wird bereitgestellt.

4. Programmbeispiel

Der Einsatz der skizzierten Sprachelemente soll im folgenden anhand eines vereinfachten Anwendungsbeispiels erläutert werden.

4.1 Aufgabenstellung

Betrachtet wird die in Abb. 1 dargestellte Testinstallation, die aus zwei Teststationen gleichen Aufbaus und aus einer programmierbaren Stromversorgung besteht. Mit den Teststationen sollen vier verschiedene Diodentypen auf Funktionstüchtigkeit überprüft werden.

Bei Testbeginn wird die Typennummer der zu prüfenden Diode über das Bediengerät der Teststation eingegeben. Danach soll die Stromversorgung eingeschaltet (Ausgabe an POWERSUPPLY) und die dem zu prüfenden Diodentyp zugeordnete Sperrspannung eingestellt werden (Ausgabe an VOLTAGESELECTOR).

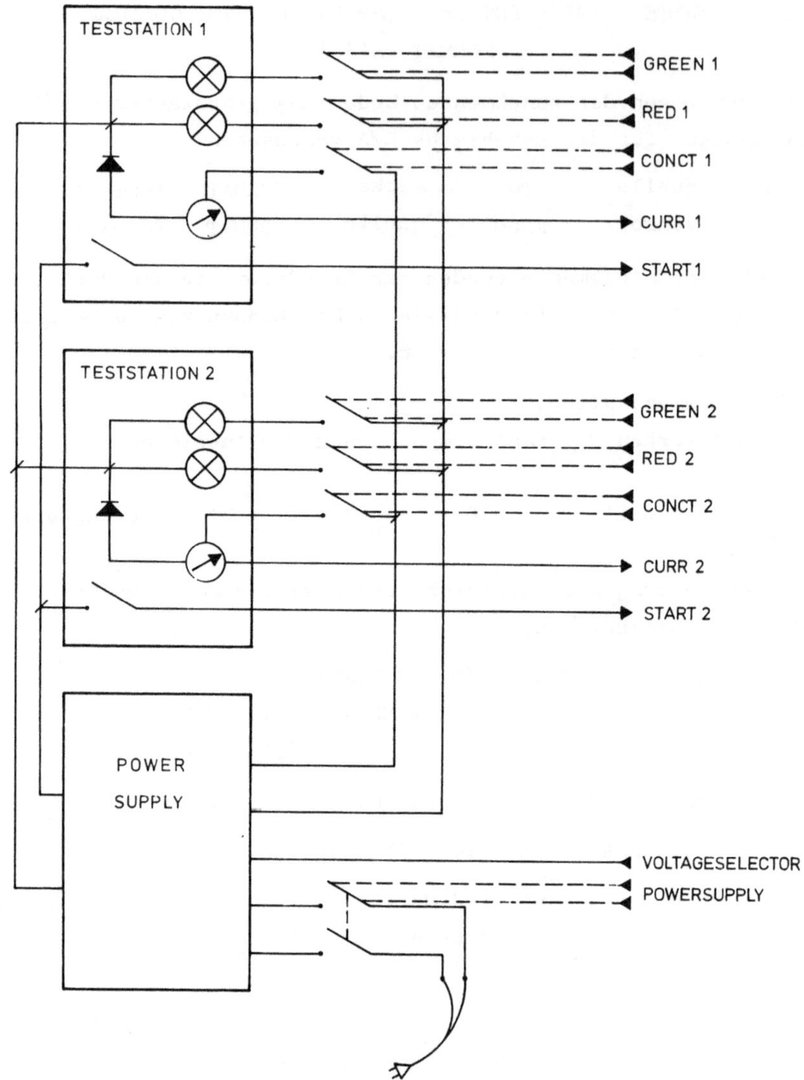

Abb. 1 Testinstallation

Nach Anschluß einer Diode an eine der Teststationen wird der Funktionstest durch Drücken der Starttaste der Teststation (START1 bzw. START2) ausgelöst.

Das Testprogramm legt die Sperrspannung an die Diode an (Schließen des Kontakts CONCT1 bzw. CONCT2), übernimmt den Sperrstrom (Einlesen von CURR1 bzw. CURR2) und schaltet die Sperrspannung wieder ab (Öffnen von CONCT1 bzw. CONCT2).

Falls der gemessene Sperrstrom oberhalb des zugelassenen typenabhängigen Maximalstroms liegt,soll für 2 Sekunden eine rote Lampe auf dem Bedienfeld der Teststation aufleuchten (Ausgabe an RED1 bzw. RED2). Die Funktionstüchtigkeit soll durch Aufleuchten einer grünen Lampe angezeigt werden (Ausgabe an GREEN1 bzw. GREEN2).

Bei Testende soll die Zahl der mit jeder Teststation geprüften Dioden und die Zahl der nicht funktionstüchtigen Dioden auf dem Blattschreiber ausgegeben werden.

4.2 Konfiguration des Prozeßrechensystems

In Abb. 2 ist der Aufbau eines hypothetischen Prozeßrechensystems dargestellt, an das die Testinstallation angeschlossen sei. COMP, CHAN, DIGOUT, ADCMUX und TTY seien Bezeichner für Standardgeräte.

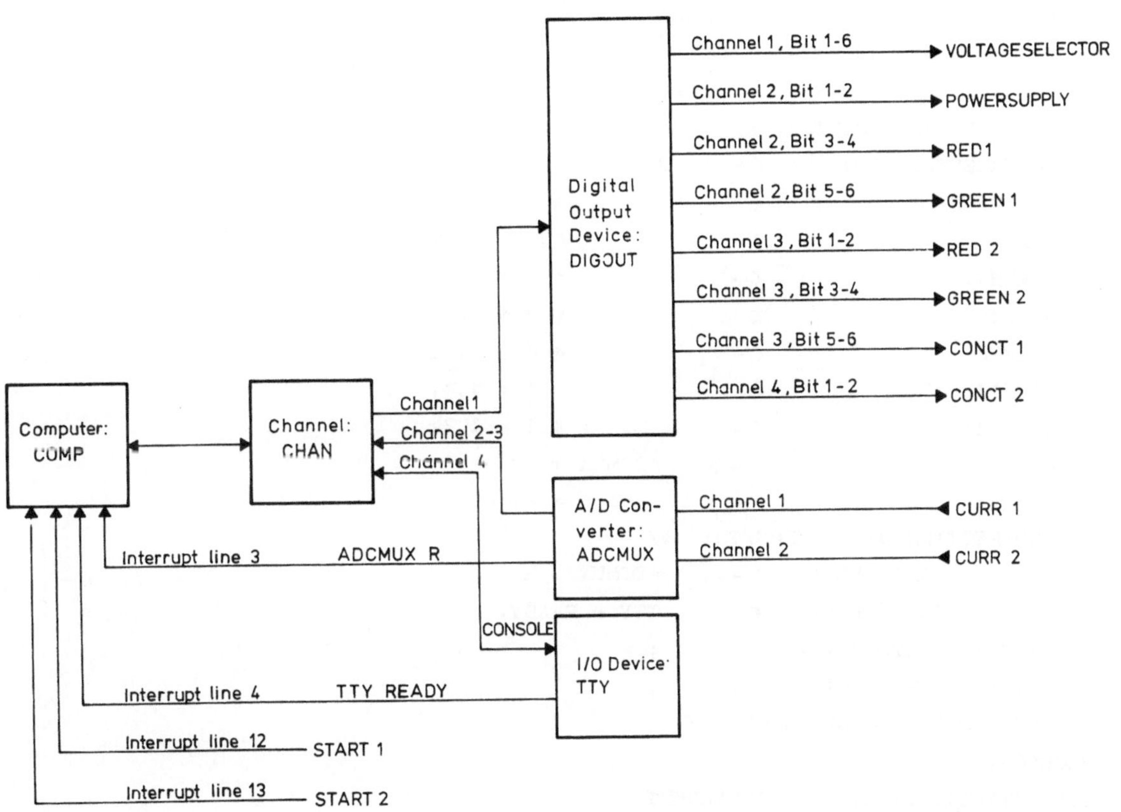

Abb. 2 Konfiguration des Prozeßrechensystems

4.3 Automationsprogramm

Das Automationsprogramm für die Testinstallation wurde in die drei quasiparallel ablauffähigen Programmteile TESTPROB, TEST1 und TEST2 aufgeteilt.

Die Haupttask TESTPROB wird bei Testbeginn vom Operateur über das Bediengerät CONSOLE aktiviert (z. B. mit der Bedienanweisung: ACTIVATE TESTPROB PRIO 3).

Um den Parallelbetrieb der Prozeßperipherie bei der Bedienung der beiden Teststationen zu ermöglichen, wurden die Bedienungsprogramme durch Einführung der Tasks TEST1 und TEST2 voneinander entkoppelt. TEST1 bzw. TEST2 wird nach Eintreffen des Interrupts START1 bzw. START2 aktiviert.

```
MODULE LIBRARY DIODETEST;
      /* PEARL EXAMPLE PROGRAM:  FUNCTION TEST PROBLEM  */
SYSTEM;
/* CONNECTION OF STANDARD DEVICES:  */
   COMP              <->   CHAN;
   CHAN * 1           ->   DIGOUT;
        * 2 * 1,12   <-    ADCMUX;
        * 4          <->   CONSOLE:  TTY;
/* PROCESS END POINTS:  */
   VOLTAGESELECTOR:       <-     DIGOUT * 1 * 1,6;
   POWERSUPPLY:           <-            * 2 * 1,2;
   RED1:                  <-            * 2 * 3,2;
   GREEN1:                <-            * 2 * 5,2;
   RED2:                  <-            * 3 * 1,2;
   GREEN2:                <-            * 3 * 3,2;
   CONCT1:                <-            * 3 * 5,2;
   CONCT2:                <-            * 4 * 1,2;
   CURR1:                   ->   ADCMUX * 1;
   CURR2:                   ->          * 2;
/* CONNECTION OF INTERRUPTS:  */
           CONTACT(3)    <-    ADCMUX * R;
           CONTACT(4)    <-    TTY * READY;
   START1: CONTACT(12)   <-    ;
   START2: CONTACT(13)   <-    ;
/* END OF SYSTEM DIVISION  */
PROBLEM;
DCL (START1,START2) VAL INTERRUPT;
TASK TESTPROB GLOBAL HANDLE:
  BEGIN
  DCL             /* STANDARD OUTPUT DEVICE:  */
      STANDARDWRITE VAL DVC  =  CONSOLE,
                  /* VARIABLES TO COUNT THE NUMBER OF TESTOBJECTS:  */
      (TOTAL1,TOTAL2,NOGO1,NOGO2) INT := 0,
                  /* VARIABLE TO STORE THE UPPER LIMIT OF REVERSE CURRENT:  */
      TYPECURR INT,
                  /* STRINGS TO ADJUST THE POWERSUPPLY TO REVERSE VOLTAGE:  */
```

```
    ADJUST(1:4) VAL BIN(6)  =  ('1000'B,'100'B,'10'B,'1'B),
              /* UPPER LIMITS OF REVERSE CURRENT:  */
    MAXCURR(1:4) VAL INT  =  (50,35,28,20),
              /* COMMON CHARACTER STRINGS:  */
    TEXT1 VAL CHAR(13)  =  'TEST STATION ',
    TEXT2 VAL CHAR(28)  =  ': NUMBER OF TESTED DIODES = ',
    TEXT3 VAL CHAR(27)  =  'NUMBER OF INFERIOR GOODS = ',
              /* COMMON FORMATS:  */
    COM1 VAL FORMAT  =  F'S(13),S(1),S(28),,L',
    COM2 VAL FORMAT  =  F'(16)C,S(27)';
              /* TEST PROCEDURE:  */
DCL  TEST PROC REENTRANT =
  ((UAMP,CONNECTOR,REDLAMP,GREENLAMP) VAL DVC,(TOTALNUMBER,NOGONUMBER) INT)
    BEGIN  DCL CURRENT INT;
           TOTALNUMBER := TOTALNUMBER + 1;
                  /* MEASURE REVERSE CURRENT:  */
           MOVE '1'B TO CONNECTOR;
           MOVE UAMP TO CURRENT;
           MOVE '10'B TO CONNECTOR;
                  /* CONTROL OF REVERSE CURRENT:  */
           IF CURRENT > TYPECURR OR CURRENT < 2 THEN
                  /* NOGO BRANCH:  */  MOVE '1'B TO REDLAMP;
                                       DELAY 2 SEC;
                                       MOVE '10'B TO REDLAMP;
                                       NOGONUMBER := NOGONUMBER + 1;
                                                 ELSE
                  /* GO BRANCH:  */    MOVE '1'B TO GREENLAMP;
                                       DELAY 2 SEC;
                                       MOVE '10'B TO GREENLAMP;      FI;
    END  /*  OF TEST PROCEDURE  */ ;
              /* DECLARATION OF TASKS TO CONTROL THE TEST STATIONS:  */
TASK TEST1:  CALL TEST(CURR1,CONCT1,RED1,GREEN1,TOTAL1,NOGO1);
TASK TEST2:  CALL TEST(CURR2,CONCT2,RED2,GREEN2,TOTAL2,NOGO2);
              /* GET THE TYPENUMBER OF DIODE UNDER TEST:  */
TYPEDEF:  WRITE (DATE,TIME,'TYPENUMBER := ') FORMAT((2)(,(2)C),S(14));
          READ TYPECURR FROM CONSOLE FORMAT(,(2)L);
          IF TYPECURR < 1 OR TYPECURR > 4 THEN
             WRITE 'INPUT ERROR: UNDEFINED TYPE' FORMAT((10)C,S(34),(2)L);
             GOTO TYPEDEF;            FI;
```

```
                /*  SWITCH ON AND ADJUST POWERSUPPLY:  */
  MOVE '1'B TO POWERSUPPLY;
  DELAY 2 MIN;
  MOVE ADJUST(TYPECURR) TO VOLTAGESELECTOR;
                /*  STORE LIMIT OF REVERSE CURRENT AND INDICATE TEST BEGIN:*/
  TYPECURR := MAXCURR(TYPECURR);
  WRITE (TIME, 'TEST BEGIN') FORMAT (,S(10),(2)L);
                /*  CONNECT START INTERRUPTS TO CONTROL TASKS:  */
  ON START1 ACTIVATE TEST1;
  ON START2 ACTIVATE TEST2;
                /*  SUSPEND MAIN TASK TESTPROB UNTIL OPERATORS COMMAND:
                    CONTINUE TESTPROB    */
  SUSPEND EXEPT TEST1,TEST2;
                /*  RECORD OF TEST RESULTS:  */
  WRITE (TIME,'  TEST RESULTS:',TEXT1,'1',TEXT2,TOTAL1,TEXT3,NOGO1,
                               TEXT1,'2',TEXT2,TOTAL2,TEXT3,NOGO2)
          FORMAT (,S(15),(2)((2)L,COM1,COM2),P);
  END  /*  OF MAIN TASK TESTPROB  */ ;
MODEND  /*  OF MODULE DIODETEST  */ ;
```

DAS TASK- UND TIMING- KONZEPT VON PEARL

P.RIEDER

1. Einleitung

Ein größeres wissenschaftliches Experiment und erst recht ein umfangreicher industrieller Prozeß zerfallen normalerweise immer in eine Anzahl Teilprozesse, die zwar gelegentlich miteinander koordiniert werden müssen, im übrigen aber autonom sind. Für eine Sprache zur Prozeßautomatisierung sind daher Elemente unerläßlich, mit denen die Überwachung und Steuerung derartiger Vorgänge in asynchron zu einander durchzuführende Aufgaben ("Task") eingeteilt und der Ablauf dieser Aufgaben zur rechten Zeit ("Timing") angestoßen, unterbrochen, fortgesetzt und beendet werden kann.

Wie dieser Bericht zeigen wird, besitzt PEARL solche Sprachelemente in reicher Auswahl. Allerdings geht es im folgenden mehr um eine Erörterung einiger grundlegender Konzepte und damit verbundener Probleme als um eine vollständige Aufzählung aller sprachlichen Möglichkeiten auf diesem Gebiet. Auf die Angabe syntaktischer Formeln wird ganz verzichtet.

2. Taskorganisation

2.1. Taskbegriff

Zu den Grundkonzeptionen von PEARL gehört es, daß es ein Programm im üblichen Sinn, das übersetzt, geladen und gestartet wird, nicht gibt. Einheit für die Compilierung ist der sog. Modul; ein Modul als solcher kann jedoch nicht ausgeführt werden, er besteht ausschließlich aus Deklarationen. Um wirklich Aktionen der Rechenanlage auszulösen, muß man eine oder mehrere sog. Tasks, die als solche in einem Modul vereinbart wurden, "aktivieren". Dies geschieht entweder vom Bedienungspult aus, wobei PEARL über Einzelheiten nichts aussagt, oder programmgesteuert durch eine schon laufende Task.

* PEARL wurde von einem Gremium aus Vertretern deutscher Elektrofirmen, Softwarehäuser und Forschungsinstitute gemeinsam entwickelt. Zur Konzeption der im folgenden beschriebenen Sprachelemente haben besonders die Herren B.Schürlein und K.H.Timmesfeld wesentlich beigetragen.

Eine Task im Sinne von PEARL liegt immer dann vor, wenn die Ausführung einer gegebenen Folge von Anweisungen eine in sich abgeschlossene Aufgabe darstellt, die asynchron und möglicherweise simultan zu allen sonstigen Operationen der Rechenanlage zu erledigen ist. Dabei spielt weder die Art der auszuführenden Anweisungen noch der Grund für ihre Ausführung eine Rolle. Das Taskkonzept überdeckt sowohl E/A-Operationen, die parallel zu irgendwelchen Rechnungen ablaufen sollen, als auch Reaktionen auf besondere Ereignisse in dem zu kontrollierenden Prozeß. Es kommt nur darauf an, daß die sequentielle Bearbeitung bestimmter Anweisungen dynamisch als Einheit betrachtet und gesteuert wird.

Dabei ist zu beachten, daß die auszuführende Anweisungsfolge wesentlicher Bestandteil der Taskdefinition ist, daß also die Bearbeitung unterschiedlicher Anweisungsfolgen nie die gleiche Task sein kann. Dagegen handelt es sich bei mehrfacher Durchführung der selben Anweisungen um die gleiche Task.

2.2. Erzeugung von Tasks

Wie andere Objekte der Sprache muß auch eine Task ausdrücklich vereinbart werden. Was in der Task getan werden soll, wird dabei in einem taskspezifischen Stück PEARL-Text angegeben, dem sog. Segment. Eine Taskdeklaration hat damit die Form

```
TASK T: /* SEGMENT */;
```

(/* und */ sind in PEARL Klammern um Kommentar, d.h. Stücke Quelltext, die nur zur besseren Verständlichkeit des Programms dienen, aber nicht mitübersetzt werden sollen).

Die Information über die von der Task durchzuführenden Operationen kann einfach darin bestehen, daß man unmittelbar im Segment alle Anweisungen niederschreibt, die man zu durchlaufen wünscht. Es ist aber ebenso gut möglich, das Segment auf einen einzigen Prozeduraufruf zusammenschrumpfen zu lassen und die eigentlich auszuführenden Statements in diese Prozedur zu legen. Dazwischen gibt es alle Übergänge; ein Segment kann syntaktisch aus einem einzelnen Statement, aus einer Gruppe von Statements oder aus einem Block bestehen. Semantisch wird jedoch verlangt, daß im Code einer Task, d.h. in ihrem Segment sowie allen Prozeduren, die von diesem direkt oder indirekt aufgerufen werden, keine Sprünge vorkommen, die auf Ziele außerhalb dieses Codes führen könnten.

Die Bearbeitung einer derart vereinbarten Task wird durch ein Statement

```
ACTIVATE T;
```

angestoßen.

Neben Tasks gibt es in PEARL noch Tasknamen, mit denen nacheinander verschiedene Tasks belegt und angesprochen werden können. Sie werden in der Form

TASKNAME TN;

vereinbart. Mit einem solchen Tasknamen kann allerdings nur dadurch eine Task verbunden werden, daß man sie aktiviert. Dies geschieht durch Anweisungen nach dem Muster

ACTIVATE TN: P(X,Y);

das Segment der betreffenden Task wird also erst bei der Aktivierung angegeben. Daß es sich dabei nicht einfach um eine Zuweisung des Segments an eine entsprechende Variable handelt, zeigt sich darin, daß die Verknüpfung zwischen Task und Tasknamen nach Beendigung der Task wieder aufgehoben ist: Will man die selbe Task unter dem gleichen Tasknamen nochmals aktivieren, so darf man nicht ACTIVATE TN; schreiben, man muß vielmehr auch das Segment wiederholen.

2.3. Taskoperationen

Man kann in PEARL aber nicht nur neue Tasks erzeugen, sondern auch in schon laufende eingreifen. Zur Beendigung von Tasks dienen Anweisungen der Form

TERMINATE T;

wo T ein beliebiger Task- oder Tasknamen-Bezeichner ist. Läßt man diesen Bezeichner weg, so beendet die betreffende Task sich selbst. Es ist allerdings nicht nötig, TERMINATE; zu schreiben, um eine Task nach planmäßigem Durchlaufen aller Statements abzubrechen; am (räumlichen) Ende ihres Segments wird automatisch eine entsprechende Anweisung impliziert.

Beenden einer Task von außen wird im wesentlichen für Fehler und ähnliche Sonderfälle benötigt. Weil dabei alle in der Task benutzten Größen in undefiniertem Zustand hinterlassen werden, ist eine andere Verwendung kaum sinnvoll.

TERMINATE auf eine nicht aktivierte Task wird als Leeroperation interpretiert.

Will man die Bearbeitung einer Task einstellen, später jedoch an der Unterbrechungsstelle weitermachen, so bedient man sich des Statements

SUSPEND T;

Auch hier bedeutet Weglassen des Bezeichners, daß eine Task sich selbst anhält. Die Suspendierung läßt sich durch

CONTINUE T;

leicht rückgängig machen, natürlich nur von einer anderen Task aus.

SUSPEND auf eine nicht aktivierte sowie CONTINUE auf eine nicht suspendierte Task werden als Leeroperationen aufgefaßt.

3. Zeitplanung

3.1. Asynchrone Reaktionen

Wie schon angedeutet, werden in PEARL auch die Reaktionen auf externe Interrupts als Tasks aktiviert. Die Verbindung zwischen einer solchen Task und dem Interrupt, durch den sie angestoßen werden soll, wird beim Durchlaufen eines Aktivierungsstatements der besonderen Form

ON ITT ACTIVATE T;

hergestellt. ITT muß vorher im Systemteil mit einem Interrupt identifiziert und im Problemteil als solcher spezifiziert werden. Nach Durchlaufen dieser Anweisung wird bei jedem Auftreten von ITT die Task T aktiviert.

Tritt der Interrupt erneut auf, bevor die Task T nach der vorhergehenden Aktivierung beendet ist, so wird mindestens eine weitere Aktivierung zwischengepuffert. Dies hat den Sinn, das Programmsystem gegen gelegentlich auftretende kleine zeitliche Verschiebungen unempfindlich zu machen. Implizit wird dabei natürlich vorausgesetzt, daß die Registrierung und Speicherung von Interrupts schon vom Betriebssystem erledigt wird.

Neben Interrupts gibt es auch Ereignisse, die zwar ebenfalls sporadisch auftreten, aber nur dann, wenn eine ganz bestimmte Task ganz bestimmte Operationen auszuführen versucht. Wenn das Auftreten dieses Ereignisses dann gleichzeitig impliziert, daß die auslösende Task nicht mehr sequentiell weiterlaufen kann, so liegt ein sog. Signal vor, auf das ausnahmsweise nicht durch Aktivierung einer neuen, sondern durch irreguläre Fortsetzung der alten Task reagiert wird. Die gewünschte Antwort wird durch eine Anweisung der Form

RESPONSE SGNL: /* REAKTION */;

mit dem betreffenden Signal (hier SGNL) verknüpft. Wenn das Signal auftritt, so wird, vereinfacht ausgedrückt, von der Stelle, wo sich die auslösende Task gerade befindet, an den Anfang der Signalreaktion gesprungen.

Reaktionen auf Signale sind blockspezifisch, sie werden bei Eintritt in den jeweiligen Block aktualisiert und bei Verlassen des Blocks durch die im umfassenderen Block spezifizierten ersetzt.

3.2. Zeitgrößen

In PEARL sind Zeiten unmittelbar als Objekte der Sprache zugänglich. Es gibt Konstante und Variable vom Typ CLOCK für Uhrzeiten und vom Typ DURATION für Zeitspannen sowie entsprechende arithmetische Operatoren. Zeitspannen können addiert, subtrahiert, mit REAL-Zahlen multipliziert und durch REAL-Zahlen dividiert werden. Bei Uhrzeiten sind Addition und Subtraktion einer Zeitspanne definiert; die Differenz zweier Uhrzeiten liefert eine Zeitspanne.

Zeitkonstanten haben in PEARL praktisch die aus dem täglichen Leben gewohnte Form. CLOCK-Konstanten beziehen sich auf eine 24-Stunden-Uhr und bestehen aus drei durch Doppelpunkt getrennten Zahlen, die Stunden, Minuten und Sekunden bedeuten. Dabei müssen Stunden und Minuten ganzzahlig angegeben werden, bei Sekunden dürfen auch Bruchteile geschrieben werden. Zulässige Zeitangaben sind also z.B.

8:30:0,   16:00:00,   17:23:14.4,   22:22:22,   0:0:0.5

Die Angaben für Minuten und Sekunden müssen kleiner als 60 sein. Die Zahl für die Stunden ist beliebig, wird aber Modulo 24 interpretiert.

DURATION-Konstanten haben Formen wie

6.5 HRS,   2 HRS 72 MIN,   1 HRS 25 SEC,   17 HRS 2 MIN 12.8 SEC,
35 MIN,   8.2 MIN 13 SEC,   22 SEC,   0.1 SEC,   0.02 SEC

Als Zahlenangaben für Stunden, Minuten und Sekunden können beliebige INTEGER- oder REAL-Werte stehen; die gesamte Zeitspanne ergibt sich dann einfach durch Addition.

Zeitgrößen dienen z.B. dazu, Laufzeiten überwachungsbedürftiger Vorgänge festzustellen. Wesentliches Hilfsmittel dabei ist eine Standardfunktion NOW, die als Resultat den Stand der rechnerinternen Uhr als Wert vom Typ CLOCK liefert.

Eine andere Anwendung von Zeitvariabeln besteht darin, eine Task bis zu einer bestimmten Uhrzeit oder für eine gewisse Zeitspanne anzuhalten. Schreibt man z.B.

DELAY T UNTIL 11:0:0   oder   DELAY T DURING 5 HRS,

so wird die Task T erst dann fortgesetzt, wenn der angegebene Zeitpunkt erreicht bzw. die angegebene Zeitspanne abgelaufen ist. Werden vorher weitere DELAY-Operationen für die gleiche Task ausgeführt, so wird diese erst fortgesetzt, wenn alle Verzögerungszeiten abgelaufen sind.

3.3. Einplanungslisten

Der wichtigste Anwendungsfall für Größen vom Typ CLOCK oder DURATION sind sog. Einplanungsvorschriften, mit denen im voraus festgelegt wird, wann eine Taskoperation ausgeführt werden soll. Sie werden einfach vor den entsprechenden Operator gesetzt. Schreibt man z.B.

AFTER 10 MIN ACTIVATE T;

so wird T nicht beim Durchlaufen dieser Anweisung, sondern erst 10 Min. danach aktiviert.

Einplanungsvorschriften gibt es in PEARL in vielfältigen Formen. Auch die schon erwähnte Verknüpfung einer Taskoperation mit einem Interrupt mittels ON ist ein Spezialfall davon. Neben ON und AFTER können noch die Schlüsselwörter ALL, AT, DURING, EVERY und UNTIL zur Bildung von Einplanungsvorschriften herangezogen werden. Hinter AT und UNTIL müssen dabei Ausdrücke vom Typ CLOCK, hinter AFTER, ALL, DURING und EVERY solche vom Typ DURATION stehen. Mögliche Einplanungsvorschriften sind z.B.

ALL 5 MIN, AT 7:0:0, AFTER 12 MIN ALL 2 SEC DURING 1 HRS,

AT 8:0:0 EVERY 15 MIN UNTIL 16:0:0, AT 8:0:0 ALL 15 MIN DURING 8 HRS

Bei Einplanungen mittels AFTER, ALL und DURING wird die genannte Zeitspanne, bei AT und UNTIL der angegebene und bei EVERY schließlich der aus dem vorhergehenden errechnete Zeitpunkt möglichst genau eingehalten. Dies ist dann wichtig, wenn bei der Synchronisation eine Mißweisung der rechnerinternen Uhr festgestellt wird. Um Zeitpunkte genau zu treffen, muß ein Vor- oder Nachgehen der internen Uhr in vollem Umfang ausgeglichen werden; zur exakten Einhaltung geplanter Zeitabstände wird die Abweichung dagegen nur dann und in dem Maß berücksichtigt, wie sie im laufenden Zeitintervall neu aufgetreten ist.

Vor jede Taskoperation kann man nicht nur eine, sondern, durch Kommata getrennt, beliebig viele solcher Einplanungsvorschriften setzen. Die Operation wird dann bei allen Anlässen ausgeführt, die in dieser sog. Einplanungsliste enthalten sind.

Einplanungen bleiben wirksam, bis sie abgearbeitet sind, durch neue ersetzt oder ausdrücklich gelöscht werden. Das Ersetzen von Einplanungen erfolgt dabei nicht nur task-, sondern auch operationsspezifisch, und zwar immer dann, wenn eine Anweisung durchlaufen wird, die die gleiche Operation für die selbe Task enthält. Eine leere Einplanungsliste wird wie AT NOW oder AFTER 0 SEC interpretiert.

Zum expliziten Löschen von Einplanungen gibt es die spezielle Taskoperation

PREVENT T;

Durch Ausführung dieser Operation werden alle Einplanungen gelöscht, die sich auf irgend eine Operation mit der Task T beziehen.

4. Beziehungen zwischen Tasks

4.1. Taskhierarchie

Ob eine Task von einer anderen aus überhaupt beeinflußt werden kann, richtet sich danach, wo ihr Bezeichner bekannt ist,und damit nach der Blockstruktur innerhalb des jeweiligen Moduls. In diese Blockstruktur sind die Segmente von Tasks in der gleichen Weise eingebettet wie etwa die Rümpfe von Prozeduren. Der Modul selbst spielt die Rolle eines äußersten Blocks.

Dynamisch bewirkt die Einbettung eines Tasksegments in einen Block, daß die entsprechende Task dem Block zugeordnet (attached) wird, sobald ihr Aktivierungsstatement durchlaufen wird, und von da ab als asynchron durchzuführender Teil der Bearbeitung dieses Blocks gilt. Diese Zuordnung endet erst, wenn die fragliche Task beendet ist und keine weiteren Aktivierungen mehr eingeplant sind. Praktisch bedeutet Zuordnung, daß am Blockende auf alle dem Block zugeordneten Tasks gewartet wird.

Da die statische Einbettung der Tasksegmente über mehrere Stufen gehen kann, ergibt sich daraus dynamisch letztlich eine ganze Taskhierarchie. Eine Task ist "Subtask" einer andern, ihrer "Mastertask", wenn das Segment der Subtask von einem Block umschlossen wird, der zum Code der Mastertask gehört. Vereinfacht ausgedrückt ist eine Task da Subtask, wo ihr Code steht.
Zu beachten ist, daß diese Taskhierarchie zwar erst dynamisch durch Einplanung oder Aktivierung der beteiligten Tasks aufgebaut wird, daß ihre Struktur aber nicht davon abhängt, wo die zugehörigen Aktivierungsstatements liegen. Tasks, die parallel zu einander vereinbart sind, bleiben auch dann unabhängig von einander, wenn eine innerhalb einer andern aktiviert wird. Dies gilt insbesondere für die oberste Stufe der Hierarchie, die auf Modulebene vereinbarten Tasks. Hat man einmal die erste davon aktiviert, - wie dies geht, wird in PEARL nicht definiert,- so können von dieser aus alle übrigen angestoßen werden, ohne daß dadurch irgendwelche Abhängigkeiten eingeschleppt würden.

Eine einfache Taskhierarchie zeigt das Beispiel

```
MODUL; PROBLEM;
     TASK TA1: BEGIN /* BLOCK 1 */ ... ACTIVATE TA2; ...
               END; ...
```

```
    TASK TA2: BEGIN /* BLOCK 2 */ ... TASKNAME TA3; ...
                  BEGIN /* BLOCK 2.1 */ ...
                       ACTIVATE TA3: BEGIN /* BLOCK 2.1.1 */ ...
                                     END; ...
                  END; ...
              END; ...
MODEND;
```

Da die Task TA2 parallel zu TA1 auf Modulebene vereinbart ist, wird sie ungeachtet ihrer Aktivierung in Block 1 nicht Subtask von TA1. Die mit dem Tasknamen TA3 bezeichnete Task ist zwar Subtask von TA2, aber nicht dem Block 2, sondern dem Block 2.1 zugeordnet.

4.2. Kommunikation zwischen Tasks

Aus der Einbeziehung der Tasksegmente in die Blockstruktur ergibt sich ein einfacher und sehr allgemeiner Weg für die Kommunikation zwischen Tasks, nämlich die Verwendung von Größen, die in einem alle interessierten Tasks umfassenden Block vereinbart sind. Bei Tasks, die dem Modul selbst zugeordnet sind, gehören dazu alle ebenfalls auf Modulebene vereinbarten Variabeln, bei Subtasks sämtliche Variabeln der Mastertask. Wie eine Art asynchron ausgeführter Block arbeitet jede Task direkt mit allen darin angesprochenen Variabeln.
Auch in einem Statement wie

```
ACTIVATE TN: P(X,Y);
```

wo P eine Prozedur bezeichne, die als Parameter zwei INTEGER-Werte benötigt, werden die aktuellen Werte von X und Y nicht bei der Aktivierung an die Task TN weitergegeben, sondern erst während des Ablaufs von TN direkt von der aufgerufenen Prozedur P übernommen.

Die naheliegende Alternative, solche Wertparameter durch das Betriebssystem zwischenspeichern zu lassen, bis sie in der zu aktivierenden Task gebraucht werden, hätte zwar den Vorteil, daß man an Variable, von denen in einer Task nur die bei der Aktivierung aktuellen Werte benützt werden,in einer dazu parallelen Task sofort nach Durchlaufen des Aktivierungsstatements neue Werte zuweisen könnte. Wenn man sie aber auf den allgemeinen Fall übertragen wollte und einfach alle Variabeln als Wertparameter ansieht, von denen in der Task nur die Werte verwendet werden, so würde dies zu der obskuren Konstruktion führen, daß im Code einer Task plötzlich gewisse Bezeichner wie eine Art formaler Parameter interpretiert würden und nicht mehr die im umgebenden vereinbarten Variabeln, sondern deren bei der Aktivierung zwischengespeicherte Werte bedeuteten. In

ACTIVATE TN ... P(X,Y); ... P(X,Y); ...

kann eine zeitlich zwischen den beiden Aufrufen von P liegende Zuweisung an X oder Y durch eine zu TN simultane Task nur dann ohne Einfluß auf das Resultat von TN sein, wenn darin eben X und Y formale Parameter sind, für die nur bei der Aktivierung von TN die aktuellen Werte der Variabeln gleichen Namens eingesetzt werden.

Will man in PEARL die Werte gewisser Variabeln an eine neu aktivierte Task übergeben und anschließend in einer simultanen Task ändern, so gibt es dafür zwei Wege: Man kann entweder noch vor der Aktivierung der neuen Task Kopien der aktuellen Werte als globalere Größen sicherstellen, oder man hält die Task, von der die Werte geändert werden, so lange auf, bis diese an lokale Größen der neuen Task übertragen sind.

4.3. Prioritäten

Die Zusammenarbeit zwischen Tasks wird dadurch kompliziert, daß in einer Installation normalerweise nicht genügend Betriebsmittel wie Zentraleinheiten und Arbeitsspeicher zur Verfügung stehen, um alle anstehenden Tasks simultan zu einander durchzuführen. Man muß die vorhandenen Betriebsmittel daher nach irgendwelchen Gesichtspunkten an die konkurrierenden Tasks verteilen. In PEARL wird diese Aufgabe prinzipiell dem Betriebssystem überlassen; nur in solchen Fällen, wo mehrere Tasks vom Standpunkt des Betriebssystems aus gleichrangig sind, richtet sich die Zuteilung nach einem in PEARL direkt zugänglichen Kriterium, der Priorität.

Prioritäten werden durch positive ganze Zahlen gekennzeichnet, wobei niedrigere Zahlen höhere Dringlichkeit bedeuten. Die Priorität einer Task wird durch einen Ausdruck vom Typ INTEGER hinter dem Schlüsselwort PRIORITY im Aktivierungsstatement angegeben:

ACTIVATE T PRIORITY N+3;

Sie kann danach mit einer Anweisung der Form

CONTINUE T PRIORITY N-2;

beliebig oft geändert werden.

In Bezug auf ihre Prioritäten stehen zunächst alle Tasks unabhängig von ihrer Einordnung in die Taskhierarchie parallel nebeneinander. Da dies aber in manchen Implementationen zu Schwierigkeiten führen könnte, gibt es in PEARL als Alternative sog. Relativprioritäten. Sie werden durch Einfügen eines Schlüsselwortes REL hinter dem Prioritätsausdruck gekennzeichnet, z.B.

ACTIVATE T PRIORITY 7 REL;

Bei Tasks, die auf Modulebene vereinbart sind, besteht zwischen der gewöhnlichen (System-) Priorität und der Relativpriorität kein Unterschied. Bei Subtasks jedoch sind Relativprioritäten praktisch Subprioritäten der Priorität der Mastertask, der selbst die Subpriorität 0 zuzuordnen ist.

Für den Zuteilungsalgorithmus bewirken Relativprioritäten eine Unterteilung der Dringlichkeitsreihenfolge analog zu der üblichen Kapiteleinteilung eines Buches. Hat z.B. eine Mastertask die Prioritätsziffer 12, so wirkt die Relativpriorität 7 wie eine Systempriorität 12.7.

Relativprioritäten bieten die Möglichkeit, einzelnen Tasks eines komplizierten Systems intern beliebige Struktur geben zu können, ohne deswegen undurchsichtige Komplikationen bei der Betriebsmittelverwaltung befürchten zu müssen.

5. Zusammenfassung

PEARL enthält so viele Möglichkeiten zur Organisation von Tasks, daß hier nur die wichtigsten Formen vorgestellt werden konnten. Ob die verfügbaren Sprachmittel jedoch wirklich für die Prozeßautomatisierung adäquat sind, kann letztlich nur die Praxis erweisen. Es ist durchaus wahrscheinlich, daß sich bei den derzeit beginnenden Implementationen und den nachfolgenden ersten Einsätzen noch Unzulänglichkeiten von PEARL herausstellen, die zu entsprechenden Anpassungen der Sprache führen.

Literatur

Brandes et al.: PEARL, The Concept of a Process- and Experiment-oriented Programming Language. edv 10, S. 429-442 (1970)

Eine weitere Arbeit mit der genauen Definition von PEARL einschließlich Syntax erscheint demnächst.

ADRESSEN DER AUTOREN

Abel, Manfred; AEG-Telefunken,
6453 Seligenstadt, Postfach 60

Bächle, A.; AEG-Telefunken,
7900 Ulm, Postfach 830

Barton, Robert S.; Burroughs Corp.,
La Jolla, Calif., 1120 Silverado, USA

Bautz, Jürgen; AEG-Telefunken,
6453 Seligenstadt, Postfach 60

Benz, C.; Siemens AG,
7500 Karlsruhe, Rheinbrückenstr.50

Casper, K.; Max-Planck-Institut f. Kohleforschung,
4330 Mühlheim/Ruhr, Kaiser-Wilhelm-Pl.1

Dathe, Gert; Software AG,
6100 Darmstadt, Schöfferstr.2

Dürre, Karl; Institut f. Informatik d. Univ. Karlsruhe,
7500 Karlsruhe, Zirkel 2

Ecker, Klaus; GMD,
5205 St. Augustin, Schloß Birlinghoven

Eggers, Bleicke; TU Berlin - FB 20,
1000 Berlin 10, Ernst-Reuter-Pl.8

Eichenauer, Bernd; Elektronik System GmbH,
8000 München 86, Postfach 86 03 05

Eickel, Jürgen; Mathematisches Institut der T.U.M.,
8000 München 2, Arcisstr.21

Enderle, G.; Gesellschaft f. Kernforschung
7500 Karlsruhe, Weberstr.5

Falkenberg, Eckhard; Institut f. Informatik d. Univ. Stuttgart,
7000 Stgt-Vaihingen, Pfaffenwaldr.64,
(beteiligt: Beck,P.; Christ,P.; Lindig,E.; Schneider,H.-J.;
Stübel,G.; Thomann,T.; Wender,K.)

Fenzl, W.; Max-Planck-Institut f. Kohleforschung,
4330 Mühlheim/Ruhr, Kaiser-Wilhelm-Pl.1

Fleck, Gerhard; GfK - Institut f. Datenverarbeitung i.d. Technik,
7501 Leopoldshafen

Gebhardt, Friedrich; GMD,
5205 St.Augustin, Schloß Birlinghoven

Göller, Reinhard, Institut f. Informatik d. Univ. Karlsruhe,
7500 Karlsruhe, Zirkel 2

Grotz, Klaus; Telefunken Computer GmbH,
7750 Konstanz, M.-Stromeyer-Str.116

Hartenstein, Reiner, Institut f. Informatik d. Univ. Karlsruhe,
7500 Karlsruhe, Zirkel 2

von Henke, Friedrich W., GMD,
5205 St.Augustin, Schloß Birlinghoven

Hilse, Dieter; GfK - Institut f. Datenverarbeitung i.d. Technik,
7501 Leopoldshafen

Holmberg, Donna L.; Telefunken Computer GmbH,
5300 Bonn-Bad Godesberg, Riemenschneiderstraße

Horn, Klaus; Telefunken Computer GmbH,
7750 Konstanz, M.-Stromeyer-Str.116

Indermark, Klaus; Institut f. Angew.Math. u. Informatik,
5300 Bonn, Wegeler Str.6

Jung, Dieter F.; IBM-Labor,
7030 Böblingen, Postfach 210

Kääb, H.; Telefunken Computer GmbH,
7750 Konstanz, M.-Stromeyer-Str.116

Kemp, Rainer; Universität des Saarlands,
6600 Saarbrücken, Im Stadtwald

Konrad, E; TU Berlin - FB Kybernetik,
1000 Berlin 10, Ernst-Reuter-Pl.8

Koster, C.H.A.; TU Berlin - FB 20,
1000 Berlin 10, Ernst-Reuter-Pl.8

Krüger, Burkhard; BBC,
6800 Mannheim, Neustadter Str.62

Kubosch, Sigurd; Norwegian Computing Center,
Oslo 3, Forskningsvn. 1B, Blindern, Norwegen

Kuck, Conrad; Telefunken Computer GmbH,
7750 Konstanz, Neuhauserstr.11

Kümmel, Peter; Universität Stuttgart,
7000 Stuttgart, Herdweg 51

Küspert, H.-J.; AEG-Telefunken,
7900 Ulm, Postfach 830

Lagally, Klaus; Rechenzentrum der T.U.M.,
8000 München 2, Arcisstr.21

Leinemann, K.; Gesellschaft f. Kernforschung,
7500 Karlsruhe, Weberstr.5

Lockemann, Peter C.; GMD - jetzt:
7500 Karlsruhe, Zirkel 2

Löhr, Klaus-Peter; TU Berlin - FB Kybernetik,
1000 Berlin 10, Ernst-Reuter-Pl.8

Martin, J.;
6520 Worms, Bachweg 19

Müller, Bernd S.; Telefunken Computer GmbH,
5300 Bonn-Bad Godesberg, Riemenschneiderstraße

Nehmer, Jürgen; GfK - Institut f. Datenverarbeitung i.d. Technik,
7500 Karlsruhe, Postfach 3640

Neuhold, E.J.; IBM - jetzt:
7000 Stuttgart, Herdweg 51

Nienaber, Bernd; Universität Karlsruhe - jetzt:
4904 Enger-Dreyen, Meller Str.199

Palmboom, Adrian; Philips Electrologica,
Apeldoorn, Postfach 245, Niederlande

Pantele, Erich; T.U.M. - Betriebssystemgruppe,
8000 München 2, Arcisstr.21

Paul, Wolfgang J.; Institut f. Angew. Mathematik d. Univ. d. Saarlands,
6600 Saarbrücken, Im Stadtwald

Pfeuffer, Klaus; Telefunken Computer GmbH,
7750 Konstanz, Postfach 142

Rieder, Peter; Siemens AG,
7500 Karlsruhe, Rheinbrückenstr.50

Rohlfing, Helmut; Institut f. Informatik d. Univ. Karlsruhe,
7500 Karlsruhe, Zirkel 2

Schecher, Heinz; Mathematisches Institut der T.U.M.,
8000 München 2, Arcisstr.21

Schindler, Sigram; TU Berlin - FB 20,
1000 Berlin 10, Ernst-Reuter-Pl.8

Schlechtendahl, Ernst G.; Gesellschaft f. Kernforschung,
7500 Karlsruhe, Weberstr.5

Schmid, Detlef; Institut f. Informatik d. Univ. Karlsruhe,
7500 Karlsruhe, Zirkel 2

Schmid, Hans-Albrecht; Institut f. Informatik d. Univ. Karlsruhe,
7500 Karlsruhe, Zirkel 2

Schnauder, H.; Gesellschaft f. Kernforschung,
7500 Karlsruhe, Weberstr.5

Schneeweiss, W.; Siemens AG,
7500 Karlsruhe, Rheinbrückenstr.50

Schneider, Hans-Jochen; Institut f. Informatik d. Univ. Stuttgart,
7000 Stgt-Vaihingen, Pfaffenwaldr.64,
(beteiligt: Fichtner,M.; Fritsch,H.; Messer-Bossler,B.)

Schneider Hans Jürgen; Lehrstuhl f. Informatik d. Univ.
8520 Erlangen, Egerlandstr.13

Schnupp, Peter; Software-Labor,
8000 München 80, Maria-Theresia-Str.12

Schulz, Klaus; IBM,
7030 Böblingen, Postfach 210

Schumann, U.; Gesellschaft f. Kernforschung,
7500 Karlsruhe, Weberstr.5

Schuster, Richard; Gesellschaft f. Kernforschung,
7500 Karlsruhe, Weberstr.5

Schwarzhuber, Manfred; COM-Service-Büro,
8000 München 19, Leonrodpl.1

Siewert, Gertrud; Institut f. Informatik d. Univ. Stuttgart,
7000 Stgt-Vaihingen, Pfaffenwaldr.64,
(beteiligt: siehe unter Schneider Hans-Jochen)

Sonnenberg, Walter; GfK - jetzt:
7500 Karlsruhe, Zirkel 2

Sumner, Frank H.; University of Manchester MB 9 PL,
Manchester, England

Wegner, Eberhard; TU Berlin,
1000 Berlin 10, Ernst-Reuter-Pl.8

Weihrauch, Klaus; GMD,
5205 St. Augustin, Schloß Birlinghoven

Weimann, Bruno; Max-Planck-Institut f. Kohleforschung,
4330 Mühlheim/Ruhr, Kaiser-Wilhelm-Pl.1

Weller, Thyge; Institut f. Informatik d. Univ. Stuttgart,
7000 Stuttgart, Herdweg 51,
(beteiligt: Krayl,H.; Siewert,H.J.; Stolz,O.; Unger,C.)

Wildpaner, Hubert; I.R.A.,
6000 Frankfurt 70, Böcklinstr.3

Will, H.J.; University of British Columbia
Vancouver 8, Kanada

Zeckendorf, Louis J.; Philips Electrologica,
Apeldoorn, Postfach 245, Niederlande

Lecture Notes in Economics and Mathematical Systems

(Vol. 1–15: Lecture Notes in Operations Research and Mathematical Economics, Vol. 16–59: Lecture Notes in Operations Research and Mathematical Systems)

Vol. 1: H. Bühlmann, H. Loeffel, E. Nievergelt, Einführung in die Theorie und Praxis der Entscheidung bei Unsicherheit. 2. Auflage, IV, 125 Seiten 4°. 1969. DM 16,–

Vol. 2: U. N. Bhat, A Study of the Queueing Systems M/G/1 and GI/M/1. VIII, 78 pages. 4°. 1968. DM 16,–

Vol. 3: A. Strauss, An Introduction to Optimal Control Theory. VI, 153 pages. 4°. 1968. DM 16,–

Vol. 4: Branch and Bound: Eine Einführung. 2., geänderte Auflage. Herausgegeben von F. Weinberg. VII, 174 Seiten. 4°. 1972. DM 18,–

Vol. 5: Hyvärinen, Information Theory for Systems Engineers. VIII, 205 pages. 4°. 1968. DM 16,–

Vol. 6: H. P. Künzi, O. Müller, E. Nievergelt, Einführungskursus in die dynamische Programmierung. IV, 103 Seiten. 4°. 1968. DM 16,–

Vol. 7: W. Popp, Einführung in die Theorie der Lagerhaltung. VI, 173 Seiten. 4°. 1968. DM 16,–

Vol. 8: J. Teghem, J. Loris-Teghem, J. P. Lambotte, Modèles d'Attente M/G/1 et GI/M/1 à Arrivées et Services en Groupes. IV, 53 pages. 4°. 1969. DM 16,–

Vol. 9: E. Schultze, Einführung in die mathematischen Grundlagen der Informationstheorie. VI, 116 Seiten. 4°. 1969. DM 16,–

Vol. 10: D. Hochstädter, Stochastische Lagerhaltungsmodelle. VI, 269 Seiten. 4°. 1969. DM 18,–

Vol. 11/12: Mathematical Systems Theory and Economics. Edited by H. W. Kuhn and G. P. Szegö. VIII, IV, 486 pages. 4°. 1969. DM 34,–

Vol. 13: Heuristische Planungsmethoden. Herausgegeben von F. Weinberg und C. A. Zehnder. II, 93 Seiten. 4°. 1969. DM 16,–

Vol. 14: Computing Methods in Optimization Problems. Edited by A. V. Balakrishnan. V, 191 pages. 4°. 1969. DM 16,–

Vol. 15: Economic Models, Estimation and Risk Programming: Essays in Honor of Gerhard Tintner. Edited by K. A. Fox, G. V. L. Narasimham and J. K. Sengupta. VIII, 461 pages. 4°. 1969. DM 24,–

Vol. 16: H. P. Künzi und W. Oettli, Nichtlineare Optimierung: Neuere Verfahren, Bibliographie. IV, 180 Seiten. 4°. 1969. DM 16,–

Vol. 17: H. Bauer und K. Neumann, Berechnung optimaler Steuerungen, Maximumprinzip und dynamische Optimierung. VIII, 188 Seiten. 4°. 1969. DM 16,–

Vol. 18: M. Wolff, Optimale Instandhaltungspolitiken in einfachen Systemen. V, 143 Seiten. 4°. 1970. DM 16,–

Vol. 19: L. Hyvärinen, Mathematical Modeling for Industrial Processes. VI, 122 pages. 4°. 1970. DM 16,–

Vol. 20: G. Uebe, Optimale Fahrpläne. IX, 161 Seiten. 4°. 1970. DM 16,–

Vol. 21: Th. Liebling, Graphentheorie in Planungs- und Tourenproblemen am Beispiel des städtischen Straßendienstes. IX, 118 Seiten. 4°. 1970. DM 16,–

Vol. 22: W. Eichhorn, Theorie der homogenen Produktionsfunktion. VIII, 119 Seiten. 4°. 1970. DM 16,–

Vol. 23: A. Ghosal, Some Aspects of Queueing and Storage Systems. IV, 93 pages. 4°. 1970. DM 16,–

Vol. 24: Feichtinger, Lernprozesse in stochastischen Automaten. V, 66 Seiten. 4°. 1970. DM 16,–

Vol. 25: R. Henn und O. Opitz, Konsum- und Produktionstheorie. I. II, 124 Seiten. 4°. 1970. DM 16,–

Vol. 26: D. Hochstädter und G. Uebe, Ökonometrische Methoden. XII, 250 Seiten. 4°. 1970. DM 18,–

Vol. 27: I. H. Mufti, Computational Methods in Optimal Control Problems. IV, 45 pages. 4°. 1970. DM 16,–

Vol. 28: Theoretical Approaches to Non-Numerical Problem Solving. Edited by R. B. Banerji and M. D. Mesarovic. VI, 466 pages. 4°. 1970. DM 24,–

Vol. 29: S. E. Elmaghraby, Some Network Models in Management Science. III, 177 pages. 4°. 1970. DM 16,–

Vol. 30: H. Noltemeier, Sensitivitätsanalyse bei diskreten linearen Optimierungsproblemen. VI, 102 Seiten. 4°. 1970. DM 16,–

Vol. 31: M. Kühlmeyer, Die nichtzentrale t-Verteilung. II, 106 Seiten. 4°. 1970. DM 16,–

Vol. 32: F. Bartholomes und G. Hotz, Homomorphismen und Reduktionen linearer Sprachen. XII, 143 Seiten. 4°. 1970. DM 16,–

Vol. 33: K. Hinderer, Foundations of Non-stationary Dynamic Programming with Discrete Time Parameter. VI, 160 pages. 4°. 1970. DM 16,–

Vol. 34: H. Störmer, Semi-Markoff-Prozesse mit endlich vielen Zuständen. Theorie und Anwendungen. VII, 128 Seiten. 4°. 1970. DM 16,–

Vol. 35: F. Ferschl, Markovketten. VI, 168 Seiten. 4°. 1970. DM 16,–

Vol. 36: M. P. J. Magill, On a General Economic Theory of Motion. VI, 95 pages. 4°. 1970. DM 16,–

Vol. 37: H. Müller-Merbach, On Round-Off Errors in Linear Programming. VI, 48 pages. 4°. 1970. DM 16,–

Vol. 38: Statistische Methoden I, herausgegeben von E. Walter. VIII, 338 Seiten. 4°. 1970. DM 22,–

Vol. 39: Statistische Methoden II, herausgegeben von E. Walter. IV, 155 Seiten. 4°. 1970. DM 16,–

Vol. 40: H. Drygas, The Coordinate-Free Approach to Gauss-Markov Estimation. VIII, 113 pages. 4°. 1970. DM 16,–

Vol. 41: U. Ueing, Zwei Lösungsmethoden für nichtkonvexe Programmierungsprobleme. VI, 92 Seiten. 4°. 1971. DM 16,–

Vol. 42: A. V. Balakrishnan, Introduction to Optimization Theory in a Hilbert Space. IV, 153 pages. 4°. 1971. DM 16,–

Vol. 43: J. A. Morales, Bayesian Full Information Structural Analysis. VI, 154 pages. 4°. 1971. DM 16,–

Vol. 44: G. Feichtinger, Stochastische Modelle demographischer Prozesse. XIII, 404 Seiten. 4°. 1971. DM 28,–

Vol. 45: K. Wendler, Hauptaustauschschritte (Principal Pivoting). II, 64 Seiten. 4°. 1971. DM 16,–

Vol. 46: C. Boucher, Leçons sur la théorie des automates mathématiques. VIII, 193 pages. 4°. 1971. DM 18,–

Vol. 47: H. A. Nour Eldin, Optimierung linearer Regelsysteme mit quadratischer Zielfunktion. VIII, 163 Seiten. 4°. 1971. DM 16,–

Vol. 48: M. Constam, Fortran für Anfänger. VI, 143 Seiten. 4°. 1971. DM 16,–

Vol. 49: Ch. Schneeweiß, Regelungstechnische stochastische Optimierungsverfahren. XI, 254 Seiten. 4°. 1971. DM 22,–

Vol. 50: Unternehmensforschung Heute – Übersichtsvorträge der Züricher Tagung von SVOR und DGU, September 1970. Herausgegeben von M. Beckmann. VI, 133 Seiten. 4°. 1971. DM 16,–

Vol. 51: Digitale Simulation. Herausgegeben von K. Bauknecht und W. Nef. IV, 207 Seiten. 4°. 1971. DM 18,–

Vol. 52: Invariant Imbedding. Proceedings of the Summer Workshop on Invariant Imbedding Held at the University of Southern California, June – August 1970. Edited by R. E. Bellman and E. D. Denman. IV, 148 pages. 4°. 1971. DM 16,–

Vol. 53: J. Rosenmüller, Kooperative Spiele und Märkte. IV, 152 Seiten. 4°. 1971. DM 16,–

Vol. 54: C. C. von Weizsäcker, Steady State Capital Theory. III, 102 pages. 4°. 1971. DM 16,–

Vol. 55: P. A. V. B. Swamy, Statistical Inference in Random Coefficient Regression Models. VIII, 209 pages. 4°. 1971. DM 20,–

Vol. 56: Mohamed A. El-Hodiri, Constrained Extrema. Introduction to the Differentiable Case with Economic Applications. III, 130 pages. 4°. 1971. DM 16,–

Vol. 57: E. Freund, Zeitvariable Mehrgrößensysteme. VII, 160 Seiten. 4°. 1971. DM 18,–

Vol. 58: P. B. Hagelschuer, Theorie der linearen Dekomposition. VII, 191 Seiten. 4°. 1971. DM 18,–

Vol. 59: J. A. Hanson, Growth in Open Economics. IV, 127 pages. 4°. 1971. DM 16,–

Vol. 60: H. Hauptmann, Schätz- und Kontrolltheorie in stetigen dynamischen Wirtschaftsmodellen. V, 104 Seiten. 4°. 1971. DM 16,–

Vol. 61: K. H. F. Meyer, Wartesysteme mit variabler Bearbeitungsrate. VII, 314 Seiten. 4°. 1971. DM 24,–

Vol. 62: W. Krelle u. G. Gabisch unter Mitarbeit von J. Burgermeister, Wachstumstheorie. VII, 223 Seiten. 4°. 1972. DM 20,–

Vol. 63: J. Kohlas, Monte Carlo Simulation im Operations Research. VI, 162 Seiten. 4°. 1972. DM 16,–

Vol. 64: P. Gessner u. K. Spremann, Optimierung in Funktionenräumen. IV, 120 Seiten. 4°. 1972. DM 16,–

Vol. 65: W. Everling, Exercises in Computer Systems Analysis. VIII, 184 pages. 4°. 1972. DM 18,–

Vol. 66: F. Bauer, P. Garabedian and D. Korn, Supercritical Wing Sections. V, 211 pages. 4°. 1972. DM 20,–

Vol. 67: I. V. Girsanov, Lectures on Mathematical Theory of Extremum Problems. V, 136 pages. 4°. 1972. DM 16,–

Vol. 68: J. Loeckx, Computability and Decidability. An Introduction for Students of Computer Science. VI, 76 pages. 4°. 1972. DM 16,–

Vol. 69: S. Ashour, Sequencing Theory. V, 133 pages. 4°. 1972. DM 16,–

Vol. 70: J. P. Brown, The Economic Effects of Floods. Investigations of a Stochastic Model of Rational Investment Behavior in the Face of Floods. V, 87 pages. 4°. 1972. DM 16,–

Vol. 71: R. Henn und O. Opitz, Konsum- und Produktionstheorie II. V, 134 Seiten. 4°. 1972. DM 16,–

Vol. 72: T. P. Bagchi and J. G. C. Templeton, Numerical Methods in Markov Chains and Bulk Queues. XI, 89 pages. 4°. 1972. DM 16,–

Vol. 73: H. Kiendl, Suboptimale Regler mit abschnittweise linearer Struktur. VI, 146 Seiten. 4°. 1972. DM 16,–

Vol. 74: F. Pokropp, Aggregation von Produktionsfunktionen. VI, 107 Seiten. 4°. 1972. DM 16,–

Vol. 75: GI-Gesellschaft für Informatik e.V. Bericht Nr. 3. 1. Fachtagung über Programmiersprachen · München, 9.–11. März 1971. Herausgegeben im Auftrag der Gesellschaft für Informatik von H. Langmaack und M. Paul. 1972. VII, 280 Seiten. 4°. DM 24,–

Vol. 76: G. Fandel, Optimale Entscheidung bei mehrfacher Zielsetzung. 121 Seiten. 4°. 1972. DM 16,–

Vol. 77: A. Auslender, Problemes de Minimax via l'Analyse Convexe et les Inégalités Variationnelles: Théorie et Algorithmes. VII, 132 Seiten. 4°. 1972. DM 16,–

Vol. 78 : GI-Gesellschaft für Informatik e.V. 2. Jahrestagung, Karlsruhe, 2.–4. Oktober 1972. Herausgegeben im Auftrag der Gesellschaft für Informatik von P. Deussen. XI, 576 Seiten. 4°. 1973. DM 36,–